IET PROFESSIONAL APPLICATIONS OF COMPUTING SERIES 10

SysML for Systems Engineering

Other volumes in this series:

SysML for Systems Engineering

2nd Edition: A model-based approach

Jon Holt and Simon Perry

The Institution of Engineering and Technology

Published by The Institution of Engineering and Technology, London, United Kingdom

The Institution of Engineering and Technology is registered as a Charity in England & Wales (no. 211014) and Scotland (no. SC038698).

© The Institution of Engineering and Technology 2008, 2014

First published 2008 (0 86341 825 9)
Second edition 2013

The Institution of Engineering and Technology
Michael Faraday House
Six Hills Way, Stevenage
Herts, SG1 2AY, United Kingdom

www.theiet.org

British Library Cataloguing in Publication Data
A catalogue record for this product is available from the British Library

ISBN 978-1-84919-651-2 (hardback)
ISBN 978-1-84919-652-9 (PDF)

Typeset in India by MPS Limited
Printed in the UK by CPI Group (UK) Ltd, Croydon

This book is still dedicated to the memory of Martha
JDH

To John Geoffrey Shingler 1945–2012
See you later, old pal!
SAP

Contents

Acknowledgements

'You're gonna need a bigger boat'

Chief Martin Brody

This book represents much of what I learned about MBSE in this and the previous millennium. The book started off as an update to our previous SysML book and has since evolved into the monster that you now hold in your hands.

It would be impossible to thank everybody, so I shan't, but there are a few notable people who should be mentioned. Simon who needs no thanks but will get them anyway, Mikey B who will return hopefully in future books, Mike and Sue (without whom, etc, etc.), the staff at the IET who never learn and keep inviting us back, and all of my co-workers, clients and many others.

Finally, to my beautiful wife Rebecca, my children: Jude, Eliza, Roo, and, of course, to Betty and Olive.

Jon Holt, September 2013

This book is the culmination of over a decade of working on the various topics covered with Jon, first as a client of his, then as a colleague and now as a friend. Thanks Jon for helping me to see the light all those years ago.

Thanks also to all those clients and colleagues, past and present, whose questions, ideas and comments have made me a better engineer. While far too many to name, you know who you are. This book wouldn't exist without you.

Since my last book was written Motley the Cat, our feline alarm clock, is sadly no longer with us; old age finally caught up with her. She is not forgotten but the cat-shaped hole she left behind has, for now, been filled by Walter and Dolly who daily prove that people don't own cats.

Finally, I must, as ever, thank my wife Sally for her patience, love, friendship and wisdom. Without her I would be a lesser person.

S. A. Perry, August 2013

Part 1

Introduction

P1.1 Overview

This part of the book is structured according to the diagram in Figure P1.1.

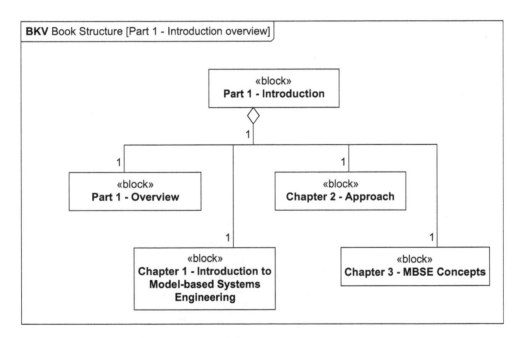

Figure P1.1   Structure of 'Part 1 – Introduction'

Part 1 introduces and describes all of the basic concepts that will be used in this book, and comprises three main chapters.

- 'Chapter 1 – Introduction to Model-based Systems Engineering'. This chapter provides a high-level general introduction to the field of systems engineering, with a particular emphasis on model-based systems engineering.
- 'Chapter 2 – Approach'. This chapter introduces the standard approach that will be adopted in the rest of the book by introducing and discussing the

concepts of 'Ontology, Framework and Views'. This chapter also covers the writing conventions that will be used throughout the book.

- 'Chapter 3 – MBSE Concepts'. This chapter identifies all of the key concepts that are relevant for model-based systems engineering and that will form the backbone of everything in this book. Each concept is identified, based on a number of source references, and then defined in terms of the terminology and the meaning of the concept. All of these concepts are then brought together into the so-called MBSE Ontology.

It is essential to obtain a good understanding of the concepts introduced in Part 1 before moving on to the rest of the book. It is impossible to implement the approaches and techniques taught in this book without understanding the chapters in this part.

Chapter 1

Introduction to model-based systems engineering

You will never find a more wretched hive of scum and villainy. We must
be cautious.

Obi Wan Kenobi

1.1 Introduction

The world of systems engineering is changing. In recent years, the whole field of
systems engineering has been seen as no longer an emerging discipline but as a
valid approach to realising successful systems. Systems engineering is a broad field
that encompasses many disciplines, can be utilised in many industries and can be
applied across many and varied life cycles.

If you have read this far into this book (the first two sentences) and find
yourself agreeing with the basic, common-sense statements in the previous paragraph, then consider the following:

- What do we mean by systems? For example: technical systems, social systems
  and economic systems.
- What disciplines do we include when we refer to 'many disciplines'? For
  example: engineering, management, acquisition and quality assurance.
- What life cycles do we refer to? For example: the product life cycle, the project
  life cycle and the programme life cycle.

There are only three questions here, but they are certainly significant ones. Before
progressing any further and trying to define some of these terms more fully consider that
even with the simple statements in the first paragraph and subsequent three questions,
there are three properties that can be applied to everything stated so far, which are:

- Complexity. There is clearly much complexity here with regard to the number
  of questions that may be asked.
- A need for understanding. What exactly do we mean by these terms?
- A need for effective communication. Can we convey this information to
  interested parties?

The main aim of this book is to address these three properties of systems
engineering by the application of effective modelling. In fact, this will be

just the starting point as we will then use the same modelling techniques to drive every aspect of systems engineering that falls within the scope of this book.

We will be using modelling to:

- Understand the concepts and terms that will be used throughout the book
- Understand why we do what we do and define an approach
- Understand the common notation that we will be adopting throughout the book
- Understand how to apply the approach for specific areas of systems engineering
- Understand how to implement such an approach in real organisations

When we use the model to drive the whole approach of systems engineering, we will term this Model-based Systems Engineering, or MBSE. The aim of this book is therefore to help people implement MBSE effectively and efficiently.

1.2   Understand the concepts and terms that will be used throughout the book

It is crucial for the success of any systems engineering endeavour that we can communicate and understand one another at a basic level. One aspect of this is having a clear and concise definition of all the key concepts and terms that will be used. This is a book that is concerned with model-based systems engineering, so it would seem appropriate that before we go any further we define a few basic concepts. As with many key concepts in life, there is no single definition; therefore, we shall look at a few of the main definitions and then abstract our own working definition for the purposes of this book.

1.2.1   Systems engineering

In order to understand model-based systems engineering, it is important to have a good definition of the meaning of systems engineering.

There are many definitions of systems engineering, all of which tend to differ depending on the context of the systems and the point of view or background of the author. This section presents a few of the more widely recognised definitions and then discusses each in turn.

The first definition comes from the legendary Simon Ramo as part of the *Aviation Authority Systems Engineering Manual*:

> '*Systems engineering is a discipline that concentrates on the design and application of the whole (system) as distinct from the parts. It involves looking at a problem in its entirety, taking into account all the facets and all the variables relating the social to the technical aspect.*' [1]

Notice that in this definition there is an emphasis on looking at the bigger picture and this is brought up several times: 'whole system', 'problem in its entirety' and 'all the facets'. This is a key concept in systems engineering, where a system is looked at across its whole life cycle and not just at one small part. Also notice here that non-technical facets of the system are mentioned as having an influence on the system.

The next definition comes from Howard Eisner:

'Systems engineering is an iterative process of top-down synthesis, development and operation of a real-world system that satisfies, in a near optimal manner, the full range of requirements for the system.' [2]

There are a few concepts introduced here that are not seen in the previous definitions. The first is the concept of an iterative process. Real-life systems are rarely developed in a linear fashion as, even with what may be perceived as a linear life cycle model, for example, there will be much iteration involved inside each stage. The second interesting point here is that requirements have been mentioned for the first time in any of the definitions. Indeed, this definition talks about satisfying requirements, which must be one of the basic goals of any systems engineer. This is also qualified, however, by stating that this should be in a near-optimal manner. Obviously, in an ideal scenario, all requirements should be met in an optimum fashion but, in the real world, it is often the best that can be achieved given the resources and technology at one's disposal. This definition also includes a rather contentious statement in that the development is said to be 'top-down', which could be interpreted as being rather limited.

Perhaps the most widely acknowledged authority on systems engineering is the International Council on Systems Engineering (INCOSE), which has a very pragmatic definition.

'Systems engineering is an inter-disciplinary approach and means to enable the realisation of successful systems.' [3]

The INCOSE definition of systems engineering is rather more terse than the previous two, yet no less accurate. This statement simply states what must be the highest level need for any systems engineer, which is to realise successful systems by using any appropriate means necessary.

The final definition is an early definition from the pre-SysML days of modelling from one of the authors.

'Systems engineering is the implementation of common sense.' [4]

The final definition that is looked at here is definitely from the 'less is more' camp and makes a rather bold statement about systems engineering generally, in that it is mostly good common sense. But, of course, as any school child will tell you, the strange thing about common sense is that it is not at all that common!

So, there have been four definitions presented here, each of which is correct, yet each of which is very different. This is, perhaps, symptomatic of a discipline that includes all other disciplines, which cannot be bounded and which can be applied to any system in any domain!

The definition that will be used for the purposes of this book is:

'Systems engineering is a multi-disciplinary, common-sense approach that enables the realisation of successful systems.'

Having established this definition, let us see how modelling fits in with systems engineering.

1.2.2   Model-based systems engineering

Similar to the term 'systems engineering' there are also several definitions of the term 'model-based systems engineering'. The first definition is taken from INCOSE and is arguably the most widely accepted of all the definitions in the world today:

'Model-based systems engineering (MBSE) is the formalized application of modeling to support system requirements, design, analysis, verification and validation activities beginning in the conceptual design phase and continuing throughout development and later life cycle phases.' [5]

The definition here states that modelling is used in a supporting role for what basically amounts to engineering activities within the development life cycle. This statement is not wrong but it is far too narrow definition for the purposes of this book. First, the statement that modelling is a support role plays down the potential impact that modelling can have on systems engineering. The modelling should drive the systems engineering activities, rather than merely support them. The second point that the definition here states is that the activities cover the whole of the development life cycle. Again, this is true but not nearly comprehensive enough. Many types of life cycle exist, such as development life cycle, project life cycle, acquisition life cycle, etc., and we can apply our modelling approach to all of these.

The next definition is taken from Joe Jenney's recent book on systems engineering methods:

'Traditional systems engineering is a mix of prose based material, typically requirements and plans, and models such as functional diagrams, physical diagrams and mode diagrams. Eventually design documentation ends in drawings, which are models. MBSE can be thought of as replacing the prose documents that define or describe a system, such as requirements documents, with models. We are not concerned as much with plans although plans like test plans are greatly improved by including many diagrams, photos and other models with a minimum of prose.' [6]

The definition here raises a few important points but, once more, does not go far enough. One point is that prose may be replaced by models, which is true, but there seems to be a fundamental misunderstanding of what a model is here. There is a suspicion here that when this definition talks about models, it really refers to diagrams. This is then confirmed with the second half of the definition that states that things can be greatly improved by the introduction of 'diagrams, photos and other models'. Diagrams do not equate to a true model. One of the main points that will be made throughout this book is that using diagrams, even with a standard notation such as SysML, does not necessarily result in a model.

For the next definition, we return to INCOSE, but this time to their long-term vision for the future of systems engineering:

> '*MBSE is part of a long-term trend toward model-centric approaches adopted by other engineering disciplines, including mechanical, electrical and software.*
>
> *In particular, MBSE is expected to replace the document-centric approach that has been practiced by systems engineers in the past and influence the future practice of systems engineering by being fully integrated into the definition of systems engineering processes.*' [5]

This statement, although not strictly speaking a definition for MBSE, makes a very important point in much stronger terms – mainly, the use of the terms 'model-centric' and 'fully integrated'. This really goes to reinforce the importance of MBSE and is far closer to what we propose in this book, rather than that in the original INCOSE definition.

The definition of model-based systems engineering that will be used for the purposes of this book is:

> '*Model-based systems engineering is an approach to realising successful systems that is driven by a model that comprises a coherent and consistent set of views that reflect multiple viewpoints of the system.*'

These definitions will be used throughout the book and will provide the drive behind everything that is presented and discussed.

1.3   Understand why we do what we do and define an approach

It has been established that it is difficult to pin down an exact definition for systems engineering. However, it is not so difficult to pin down why we need systems engineering. To put it as simply as possible, many systems end in failure or disaster. The term failure here refers to a system where the project never reached delivery and where time and money were wasted because time or cost overran. The term disaster here refers to a system where people were hurt or the environment was damaged as a result of the system failure.

> '*The fundamental reason, therefore, why we need systems engineering is that it is very easy for things to go wrong, resulting in disasters or failures.*'

We need to understand how likely it is that something will go wrong and the severity of the consequences of it going wrong. To put this into other words – we need to understand the risk.

In order to understand how likely it is that something will go wrong, we need to understand why things go wrong. Luckily for us, this has been done many times before, and almost all disasters and failures can be attributed to the three evils of engineering, which are complexity, lack of understanding and poor communications.

Traditional systems engineering provides an approach that can be applied to minimise the risk, such as understanding requirements, analysis, design, testing, etc., but this approach itself is complex and requires understanding and good communications.

The main aim of modelling, as will be discussed in more detail throughout this book, is to address these three evils. We can apply modelling to the projects and systems, of course, but we can also apply the modelling to the fundamental approach itself, and this forms the heart of the philosophy of this book and of model-based systems engineering.

The approach described in this book forms part of an overall model-based systems engineering (MBSE) approach. There are many benefits associated with the application of effective MBSE (note the use of the word 'effective' here), which are:

- *Automatic generation and maintenance of system documents.* All system documents may be generated automatically from the model, resulting in simpler document maintenance, more consistent document content and drastically reduced documentation effort and time.
- *Complexity control and management.* Models may be measured and, therefore, controlled. This measurement may be automated and the results may be used to control and manage the complexity of the model, hence the project or system.
- *Consistency of information.* A true model results in consistent and coherent views across the whole system architecture.
- *Inherent traceability.* When the model is correct, then traceability between all the system artefacts, across all life cycle stages, is contained within the model.
- *Simpler access to information.* The model represents the knowledge of the project or system and, as the previous point mentioned, traceability exists to all project or system information. Without a coherent model knowledge of the system is potentially spread across multiple sources, such as heterogeneous models, spread sheets and documents.
- *Improved communication* – language. When a model is in place and it has been defined using an established modelling notation, then it is possible to use this notation as a common language.
- *Improved communication* – concepts and terminology. A consistent and coherent model will have an underlying definition of all the relevant concepts and terms, referred to later in this book as an ontology, which is used as basis for the views that make up the model.
- *Increased understanding.* The very act of modelling, particularly with small teams of people, provides an excellent way to achieve a common understanding and obtain consensus.

When trying to sell the idea of MBSE to other people in an organisation, it is essential that the above benefits are related directly back to saving cost, time or resources. Each of these points should be tailored to reflect the way that you work in your organisation to achieve the full impact of the benefits.

1.4 Understand the common notation that we will be adopting throughout the book

An essential part of realising successful MBSE is having a common language in the form of an established modelling notation. Any suitable notation may be used but the one adopted in this book is the systems modelling language, or the SysML, as it is commonly known.

The justification for the choice of SysML is fully discussed in Part 2, so it will not be dwelt on here. In summary, SysML is an excellent general-purpose modelling language that may be used, through the use of a defined set of diagrams, to visualise the views that make up the model. The SysML also provides mechanisms to integrate with other modelling techniques and notations, for example mathematics and formal methods. This means that the SysML notation does not preclude the use of any other notations.

1.5 Understand how to apply the approach for specific areas of systems engineering

Systems engineering covers a multitude of areas of work and activities. It would be impossible to address every area of application of systems engineering, even given a life time of work. There are a number of specific areas of application that fall within the scope of this book, which are intended to reflect areas that most practising systems engineers will be familiar with. These areas are processes (including standards), competence, needs, systems, life cycle, architectures, architecture frameworks and projects.

These broad areas cover many aspects of systems engineering and the use of modelling will be demonstrated for each.

1.6 Understand how to implement such an approach in real organisations

One of the biggest problems that face most people in the real world is that of how to implement MBSE in a real organisation. There are three fundamental aspects of the business that need to be addressed for implementing MBSE, which are:

- People, by which we mean competent people with the right skills
- Process, by which we mean having an effective approach
- Tools, by which we mean enablers to achieve the people and processes

This book will cover how to understand, define and implement each of these in order to start to realise the benefits of MBSE in your organisation.

1.7   Using this book

This book is intended to be both educational and practical at the same time. It is intended that the readers can use the book as both a source for learning new techniques and a reference for remembering existing knowledge.

It should come as no surprise to the readers that the content of the book itself has been modelled to satisfy a set of needs that were identified by the authors. The full model of the book would test the patience of any sensible systems engineer, so only a single view from the model will be used as an overview and guide to the structure and content of the book.

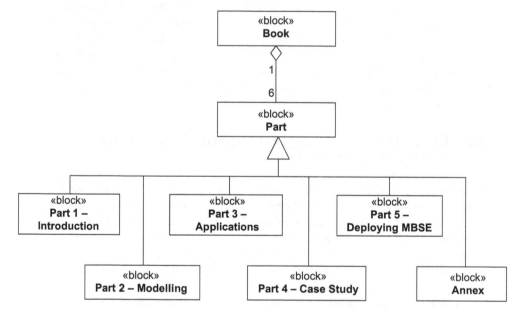

Figure 1.1   Overview of the structure and content of the book

The diagram in Figure 1.1 not only shows the content and structure of the book but is also the first SysML diagram of the book! Don't worry if you are not yet familiar with the notation, as this will be explained as we progress through the book.

The diagram shows that the 'Book' is made up of six 'Part', which are:

- 'Part 1 – Introduction', where we introduce the book (this bit!), define the approach and define the concepts and terms that will be used throughout the book and that will form the basis for all the modelling.
- 'Part 2 – Modelling', where we introduce the concept of modelling, why we need to model, the needs for modelling and then provide a description of the SysML and how it should be used to maximise its effectiveness.
- 'Part 3 – Applications', where we discuss a number of specific uses of SysML for specific applications, including process modelling, advanced process

modelling (standards, competencies and life cycles), requirements, systems of systems requirements, architectures and architectural frameworks.

- 'Part 4 – Case study', where we apply the techniques discussed so far in the book to a somewhat bizarre and terrifying case study.
- 'Part 5 – Deploying MBSE', where we discuss how to implement MBSE in your business, by considering people, process and tools.
- 'Annex', where we provide a summary of the notation including crib-sheets and a glossary, present models that can be used in practice (standards, example processes, competency scopes, etc.) and even a memory palace to help you to remember all of the key concepts and terms used in the book.

This book represents the combined knowledge of our work and experience in the field of MBSE over the course of both our careers. These experiences have more often than not been good but have also been egregious in many ways. One of the hopes that we have for this book is to enable people to make the right decisions, shorten their learning curves and help them to avoid some of the many mistakes, disasters and farces that we have seen (and occasionally been involved in) over the last two decades.

References

1. Jenney J. *Modern Methods of Systems Engineering: With an Introduction to Pattern and Model Based Methods.* CreateSpace Independent Publishing Platform; 2011
2. INCOSE. *INCOSE Systems Engineering Handbook – a Guide for System Life Cycle Processes and Activities, Version 3.0.* International Council on Systems Engineering (INCOSE); 2006
3. FAA. *Federal Aviation Agency (USA FAA) Systems Engineering Manual* [definition contributed by Simon Ramo]; 2004
4. Eisner H. *Essentials of Project and Systems Engineering Management.* 3rd edn. Chichester, UK: Wiley; 2008
5. Holt J. *UML for Systems Engineering – Watching the Wheels.* 2nd edn. Stevenage, UK: IEE; 2003 [reprinted by IET; 2007]
6. INCOSE. *International Council on Systems Engineering, Systems Engineering Vision 2020.* INCOSE-TP-2004-004-02, Version/Revision: 2.03; September 2007

Chapter 2

Approach

It's not the size mate, it's how you use it.

Nigel Powers

2.1 Introduction

This short chapter introduces the basic approach that will be taken in all of the following chapters that discuss specific applications of model-based systems engineering (MBSE) using SysML.

The approach itself promotes the use of three concepts: 'Ontology, Framework and Views', which is an established approach to MBSE – see References 1–3 for examples. Each of these will be discussed in the following sections.

2.1.1 The fundamental approach – I know an old lady

One of the main themes presented in this book for the successful implementation of MBSE is undoubtedly the need to know "why". This comes down to understanding the fundamental needs for each aspect of MBSE. In order to deliver any system successfully, it is essential to understand the initial needs. Likewise, in order to know whether one has achieved what one has set out to achieve, it is essential to understand those needs.

Unfortunately, too many attempts at MBSE either fail or deliver no benefits (fail) as the original needs for the exercise are not known in the first place. This is somewhat akin to the children's poem "I know an old lady".

"I know an old lady who swallowed a fly". MBSE can be an excellent way to deliver successful systems and this book will emphasise the importance of having the right people, process and tools. However, in order for the people, processes and tools to be put into place, it is essential to understand the "why". This is rather like the old lady from the old nursery rhyme who swallowed a fly.

"I don't know why she swallowed a fly". Why did the old lady swallow a fly? What was she trying to achieve? Unfortunately, we never find out. The old lady goes further and further through an ever-increasing array of solutions to a problem that is never defined. By not understanding why she swallowed the fly in the first place, all subsequent actions are doomed to failure. When we want to understand the "why", we need to consider a few points, for example why do you want an

MBSE, what will it be used for, and who will be using it? It is essential that the "why" of MBSE is considered and by this we really mean carrying out a proper needs capture and analysis exercise, rather than just generating a wish list. When engineering any type of system, the first step is always to get a good idea of exactly what the needs are for that system. Implementing MBSE should be treated like implementing any other system. Bear in mind that there will be many stakeholder roles interested in MBSE and each of them, potentially, has a different point of view on what benefits they want to realise from the MBSE activities and how they can be used. These different points of view will result in conflicts, common interest and overlapping needs, all of which must be resolved. It is essential that all pertinent stakeholder roles are identified and that an understanding of the "why" for each stakeholder is arrived at.

"I know an old lady who swallowed a spider (that wriggled and jiggled about inside her)". When confronted with a fly in the stomach, the temptation is to look for tried and tested approaches to fly removal, such as spiders, but is this suitable? When implementing MBSE, the temptation is to look for best practice approaches that people have followed before and that have a number of success stories associated with them. Indeed, there are many best practice models and standards (this will be discussed in Chapter 3) that are readily available. However, each of these must be tailored for any business and their suitability assessed. Just because a particular approach to MBSE works for one organisation does not necessarily mean that it will work for another – only when the context is the same will this be the case; therefore, the needs for MBSE must be considered in an appropriate context before they can be assessed.

"I know an old lady who swallowed a bird/cat/dog". Spiders in the stomach bring their own problems. There may be a clearly understood and logical progression of eating slightly larger animals to solve the problem, but does the old lady actually understand the nature of her problem or, for that matter, her own physiology? Alongside the "why" of MBSE, it is essential to be able to relate this to the system being developed. Key to this understanding is having a common understanding of the key terms and concepts that relate to the domain for which the architecture is being developed. Before we can realise people, process and tools, we need to talk a common language.

"I know an old lady who swallowed a goat/cow". Goats are renowned for eating anything – but would a goat eat a dog? Cows are herbivores, so the eating of goats is simply not consistent with a cow's normal behaviour. By focusing too much on identifying larger and larger mammals, is the old lady losing sight of her goals and losing touch with reality?

The visual manifestation of MBSE is through describing a number of viewpoints and realising these as views that make up the model. Views are actually very easy to generate, but there must be a reason why the views are needed. It is all too easy to generate a set of random views that are not contributing to meeting the underlying needs. Also, all these views must be consistent with one another or the result is a set of pictures rather than a true model.

"I know an old lady who swallowed a horse – She's dead of course!" There are a few key points that emerge from the points presented in this section:

- Understanding why – understand the fundamental needs for MBSE from different points of view by considering contexts.
- Speak a common language – understanding the terms and concepts is essential – generate an ontology.
- Views must have a purpose – do you understand which of the needs are satisfying?
- Views must be consistent – they must form part of a model and not be just a set of pictures.

People, process and tools are essential for realising MBSE, but bear in mind that each of these may bring its own problems. Simply applying more, or bigger, people, process and tools at a problem (fly, spider, bird, cat, dog, goat, cow and horse) is not the best approach.

It is all too easy to end up with a house full of dead bodies, hay and horse dung.

2.1.2 *Writing conventions adopted in the book*

When thinking about MBSE and describing and discussing the different aspects of MBSE, there is a lot of potential for confusion. Some terms that are used in the SysML notation, for example, are also widely accepted MBSE terms and are also everyday words. Therefore, when using a specific term, we want to differentiate between the MBSE term, the SysML term, specific elements from diagrams and everyday usage of such terms. In order to minimise this confusion, the following writing conventions are adopted in this book.

- All terms from the SysML notation, which form part of the standard, are written in italics. Therefore, the use of *block* refers to the SysML construct, whereas the same word without italics – block – refers to an impediment (or piece of cheese).
- All terms that are defined as part of the overall model presented in this book, such as the MBSE Ontology and MBSE Framework, are presented with capitalised words. Therefore, the use of Project refers to the Ontology Element, whereas the same word without capitals – project – refers to a non-specific usage of the term as a noun or verb.
- All words that are being referenced from a specific diagram are shown in quotes. Therefore, the use of 'Ontology Element' is referring to a specific element in a specific diagram.
- All View names are shown as singular. Therefore, the term Process Behaviour View may be referring to any number of diagrams, rather than a single one.
- Any word that requires emphasis is shown in "double quotes".

Some examples of this are shown in Table 2.1.

Table 2.1 shows some example sentences, the convention adopted and how they should be read. In summary, look out for 'Quotes', Capitalisation and *italics* as these have specific meaning. Finally, remember that the use of "double quotes" simply represents emphasis.

Table 2.1   Example sentencing to illustrate the convention

Example sentence	Meaning
A Use Case may be visualised as a *use case*	Use Case – term from the MBSE Ontology *use case* – the term from SysML notation
Engineering activity can be shown as an Activity on a Process and may be visualised as an *activity*	activity – the everyday usage of the word Activity – the term from the MBSE Ontology *activity* – the term from the SysML notation
The diagram here shows the 'MBSE Process Framework' is made up of one or more 'Process Behaviour View'	'MBSE Process Framework' – a specific term from a specific diagram that is being described 'Process Behaviour View' – a specific term from a specific diagram that is being described
When defining Processes it is typical to create a number of *activity diagrams* that will visualise the Process Behaviour View	Processes – the term from the MBSE Ontology *activity diagram* – the term from SysML notation Process Behaviour View – the term from the MBSE Framework
It is important to understand the "why" of MBSE	"why" – emphasis of the word

There are very many diagrams presented in this book, and they are used for two different purposes that may be easily differentiated between:

- Diagrams used by way of an explanation, such as all of those found in this chapter, are presented without *frame* and represented visually by a named box around the border of the diagram.
- Diagrams used as specific examples, such as those found in Part 4 that presents a case study, will each have a *frame* around them.

The concept of a *frame* is discussed in more detail in Chapter 5.

2.2   The approach

This basic approach is summarised in the diagram in Figure 2.1.

The diagram shows that the basic approach is made up of three main elements: the 'Ontology', the 'MBSE Framework' and the 'Viewpoint', which may be described briefly as:

- 'Ontology' – that identifies and defines the concepts and terms to be used for the entire book.
- 'MBSE Framework' – that describes a specific use of the 'Ontology', such as model-based processes and model-based requirements.

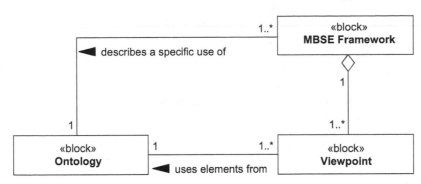

Figure 2.1   Summary of the approach taken in this book

- 'Viewpoint' – that focuses on a subset of the 'Ontology' and that has a specific purpose. Each 'Viewpoint' is made up of one or more 'Viewpoint Element', one or more of which visualises an 'Ontology Element'. It is this 'Viewpoint' that is used to define Views that are used throughout this book.

Each of these main elements is discussed in detail in the following sections.

2.2.1   The 'MBSE Ontology'

The MBSE Ontology forms the heart of the MBSE endeavour. It is the approach that both is advocated by this book and has been used to drive all of the content of this book. In this book the so-called MBSE Ontology is used for the following activities:

- Defining concepts and terms. The MBSE Ontology provides a visualisation of all the key concepts, the terminology used to describe them and the inter-relationships between said concepts. The MBSE Ontology, however, plays a pivotal role in the definition and use of any rigorous MBSE Framework.
- Defining frameworks that can be used for different aspects of MBSE. Examples of these frameworks in this book include Processes, Needs, Architectures, etc. Whenever any Framework is defined in terms of a set of Viewpoints, then an Ontology is essential. It is the MBSE Ontology in this book that enforces the consistency and rigour demanded by such Frameworks. See Part 3 for several examples.
- Defining MBSE Competencies. When defining Competencies for MBSE activities, there needs to be a core knowledge base that underpins the Competencies, and this is realised by the MBSE Ontology. See Chapter 14 for a full discussion on how the MBSE Ontology may be used to define Competencies.
- Course content generation. The MBSE Ontology may be thought of as the heart of the body of knowledge for MBSE and, therefore, is an ideal basis for any course content that must be developed. See Chapter 14 for a full discussion on how the MBSE Ontology may be used to define course content.

- Process implementation. Many aspects of the Process, such as the Process model, the Artefacts and the execution in Life Cycles, will be based directly on the MBSE Ontology. See Chapters 7 and 8 for examples of how the MBSE Ontology may be used as a basis for Process modelling and advanced Process modelling, and Chapter 15 for examples of Process deployment.
- Tool implementation. In order to optimise the use and therefore benefits of tool implementation of MBSE, a full understanding of the MBSE Ontology is essential. This is described in more detail in Chapter 16.
- Applications. This basic approach of 'Ontology, Framework and Views' is used in all the example applications in this book in Chapters 7 through to 11 and Chapters 14 through to 16.

The structure of the MBSE Ontology is introduced in the diagram in Figure 2.2.

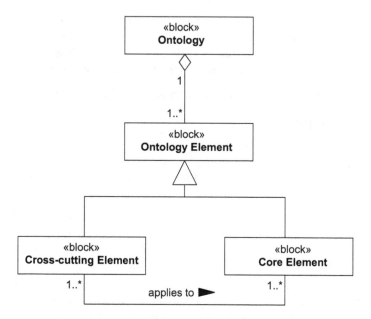

Figure 2.2   Breakdown of the MBSE Ontology

The 'Ontology' is made up of one or more 'Ontology Element', each of which may be classified as one of two types: a 'Cross-cutting Element' or a 'Core Element'.

- A 'Core Element' represents a specific MBSE concept and has its relationships to other Ontology Elements shown on the MBSE Ontology.
- A 'Cross-cutting Element', however, has more complex relationships and may be applied to several basic elements.

Examples of these special types of 'Cross-cutting Element' are shown in the diagram in Figure 2.3 and are elaborated upon in the subsequent detailed descriptions.

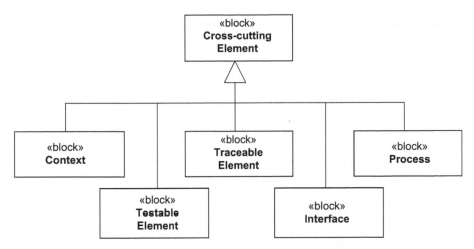

Figure 2.3   Examples of 'Cross-cutting Element'

Some of the concepts that are used in this book have applications across the whole of the MBSE Ontology. Due to the fact that they apply to multiple elements from the MBSE Ontology, they either are not explicitly shown on the MBSE Ontology or do not have all of their relationships shown, simply because the full MBSE Ontology would become totally unreadable.

- 'Testable Element'. Any Ontology Element in the MBSE Ontology may be tested and, therefore, may be thought of as a Testable Element.
- 'Traceable Element'. Any Ontology Element in the MBSE Ontology may be traced to another Ontology Element in the model and, therefore, may be thought of as a Traceable Element.
- 'Interface Element'. Many Ontology Elements in the MBSE Ontology may have interfaces, such as Process, Stage and View, and, therefore, may be thought of as an Interface Element.
- 'Context'. Many Ontology Elements in the MBSE Ontology may have their own Context, such as Need, Project, Product, Life Cycle, Process, Stakeholder and Programme and, therefore, may be thought of as a Context element.
- 'Process'. Many Ontology Elements in the MBSE Ontology have Processes associated with them, such as Need, Life Cycle and Architecture, and, therefore, may be thought of as a Process element.

It should be noted that it is possible for an Ontology Element to be both a Cross-cutting Element and a Core Element, such as Context and Process, whereas others will be one or the other, such as Traceability Element.

It should be clear now that if all of these relationships were shown on the MBSE Ontology, then the diagram would be completely unreadable.

2.2.2   The 'MBSE Framework'

There are some very pragmatic reasons why the definition of the MBSE Framework is important:

- Coverage. It is important that the whole of the MBSE Ontology is realised. Each Viewpoint considers a small set of the MBSE Ontology and the totality of the Viewpoints covers the whole MBSE Ontology.
- Rigour. By generating all the Views (see the description in the next section), based on the defined Viewpoints, applying the appropriate Rules for each Viewpoint and ensuring consistency, we produce a true model. This true model provides the rigour for underlying approach: realising all the Views provides the highest level of rigour, whereas realising only some of the Views provides less rigour. This means that the approach is flexible for projects of different levels of rigour.
- Approach. The approach defines how we do things, or to put it another way, the Process that we follow to realise the MBSE Framework by creating Views based on the Viewpoints.
- Flexibility of scale. The MBSE Framework defines a number of Viewpoints but, depending on the type of Project being undertaken, not all of these Viewpoints need to realised as Views. This ability to realise some or all Views makes the MBSE approach very flexible in terms of the size of the Project.
- Flexibility of realisation. The Viewpoints defined by MBSE approach may be realised as Views, each of which may be visualised in any number of different ways. The approach promoted in this book is primarily through using the SysML notation, but any suitable notation may be used to realise the Views. In the same way, any suitable tool may also be used.
- Integration with other processes. The MBSE Framework allows integration with any other systems engineering Processes providing that the Information Views for the Processes are known. This allows the MBSE approach to be used with many other methodologies and systems engineering approaches.
- Automation. The MBSE Framework provides the basis for automating MBSE approach using sophisticated systems engineering tools. One of the main benefits of an MBSE approach is that it saves a lot of time and effort as many of the Process Artefacts may be automatically generated.

All of these points will be covered in greater detail in Part 5, where implementing an MBSE approach on real Projects is discussed.

2.2.3   The 'View'

The third of the main concepts is that of the 'View'. The concepts and terminology used here are very important because of the similarity and, therefore, potential confusion between the terms 'View' and 'Viewpoint'. The relationship and differences between them is shown in the diagram in Figure 2.4.

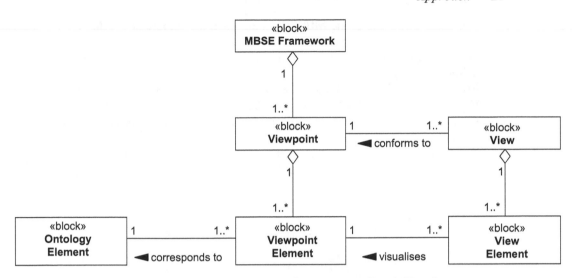

Figure 2.4   The concepts of a 'Viewpoint' and 'View'

The diagram here shows that the 'MBSE Framework' is made up of one or more 'Viewpoint' and that each of these, in turn, is made up of one or more 'Viewpoint Element'. The following definitions apply to this diagram:

- A 'Viewpoint' defines the template of one or more 'View' and, therefore, each 'View' must conform to its associated 'Viewpoint'. The 'Viewpoint', therefore, is defined as part of the 'MBSE Framework'.
- A 'Viewpoint Element' is the basic unit of the 'Viewpoint' and corresponds directly back to an 'Ontology Element', which ensures consistency.
- A 'View' represents an actual artefact, usually visualised by a diagram, which is produced as part of a project. Each 'View' must conform to its associated 'Viewpoint' that defines its template.
- A 'View Element' represents a visualisation of a 'Viewpoint Element', usually realised by an element on a diagram.

Therefore, to summarise, each 'Viewpoint' is defined as part of the 'MBSE Framework' and provides the template for one or more 'View', which are created as part of the MBSE activities on a Project. A Viewpoint is a definition and a View is the realisation of its defining Viewpoint.

2.2.3.1   Defining Viewpoints and creating Views

In order to create Views effectively it is important that the Viewpoint is well understood and well defined. Therefore, throughout this book, each Viewpoint will be defined in the following manner:

- *Rationale*. The rationale of why the View is needed, which will drive the definition of the Viewpoint, will be described.

- *Ontology.* The areas of the MBSE Ontology that are important for the View and therefore that appear on the Viewpoint will be identified.
- *Relationships with other Views.* The relationships to other Views will be defined.
- *Visualising the View.* How each Viewpoint may be visualised as one or more View showing examples of graphical notations, text, mathematics, etc.
- *Rules.* The rules that must be enforced on the view to ensure correctness and consistency.
- *Discussion.* Any point of consideration associated with the View, such as usage, pitfalls and general advice will be discussed here.

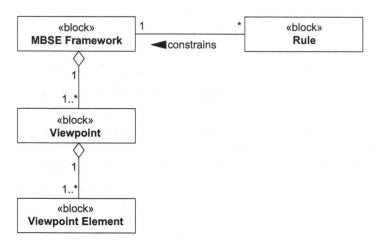

Figure 2.5   The concept of a 'Rule'

Chapter 10 defines a number of Viewpoints that can be used to capture the above information when defining a Framework.

An important aspect of getting the MBSE Framework right is the application of Rules to the MBSE Framework that enforce the points raised above.

The diagram in Figure 2.5 shows that 'Rule' constrains the 'MBSE Framework'. It should also be noted that because of the structure that sits below the 'MBSE Framework' that the 'Rule' may apply at the 'Viewpoint' or 'Viewpoint Element' level.

2.3   Summary

All of the concepts discussed so far in this chapter have been brought together in the diagram in Figure 2.6.

The diagram here brings together all of these concepts and will be referred to, from this point on, as the MBSE Meta-model. A meta-model may be thought of as a model of a model, and everything from this point onwards

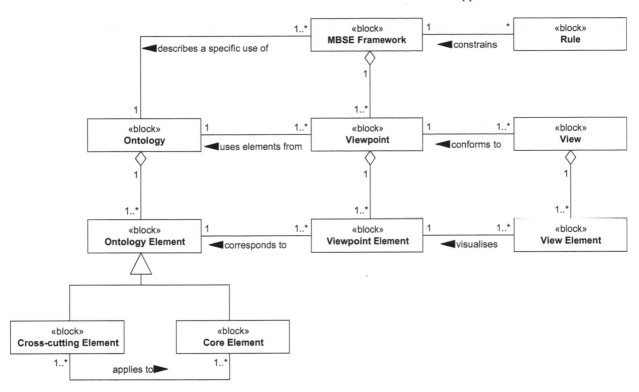

Figure 2.6   The MBSE Meta-model

in the book will correspond to, and therefore be consistent with, the MBSE Meta-model.

All of the information in this book has been defined according to an MBSE approach. This chapter has introduced the three main concepts of Ontology, Framework and Views that dictate the MBSE approach. Each concept has been expanded and discussed before being brought back together in the form of the MBSE Meta-model.

All subsequent information in this book is consistent with this meta-model.

References

1.   Holt J. *A Pragmatic Guide to Business Process Modelling*. 2nd edn. Swindon, UK: BCS Publishing; 2009
2.   Holt J., Perry S. *Modelling Enterprise Architectures*. Stevenage, UK: IET; 2010
3.   Dickerson C.E., Mavris D.N. *Architecture and Principles of Systems Engineering*. Florida, USA: CRC Press; 2009

Chapter 3

MBSE concepts

Death by Mau-Mau!

Traditional joke

3.1 Introduction

This chapter discusses the main systems engineering concepts that were introduced briefly in Chapter 1.

Understanding the concepts is essential for a number of different reasons, some of which are obvious and some of which are more subtle:

- Clearly, by not understanding the basic concepts, actually performing any work in the world of systems engineering is going to be very difficult, to the point of impossibility. The only way to succeed while not understanding the concepts is through pure chance. This is not a good approach!
- In order to address the "three evils" of systems engineering, understanding is crucial. It is one of the basic evils, as was discussed previously, that drives the other two evils.
- The basic approach that is advocated in this book for model-based systems engineering (MBSE) is that of 'Ontology, Framework and Views'. The concepts needed for MBSE are defined in the so-called MBSE Ontology, which forms the cornerstone of any MBSE exercise.

Understanding the concepts is, therefore, essential, and these concepts will be defined using the MBSE Ontology. This Ontology will then be used throughout the rest of this book for all of the examples, approaches and applications of MBSE.

3.1.1 Provenance of the MBSE Ontology

The MBSE Ontology itself is based on a number of best-practice sources that are used throughout the world of systems engineering. The problem with trying to define the MBSE Ontology is that there is no single definitive set of terms for MBSE; therefore, a number of sources were considered. The list of information sources is not intended to be exhaustive but is intended to represent a good cross-section of current thought on MBSE. Each of the information sources has its own strengths and weaknesses and, therefore, the approach was to take a consensus of terms wherever possible and where not possible to give priority to information sources that specialise in a specific area of MBSE. Examples of these information sources include:

- 'ISO 15288 – systems and software engineering life cycle processes' [1]. This standard is the most widely used systems engineering standard in the world. The standard itself is now considered to be quite mature as its first version was published in 2002 and its current version was published in 2008. The standard considers four main areas of processes that ISO suggests should exist in any organisation: technical, project, organisational and agreement. The emphasis of the standard focuses on the technical and project process areas, rather than the organisational and agreement process areas. Indeed, this standard is considered to be particularly weak in depth for both of these areas. Having said that, however, ISO 15288 is an excellent start point for any systems engineering endeavour and should always be considered when looking for good systems engineering source information.
- 'INCOSE systems engineering handbook' [2]. The International Council on Systems Engineering (INCOSE) produces a best-practice guide for systems engineering in the form of a handbook. The handbook itself is based directly on ISO 15288 and, therefore, uses many of the same concepts and terminology. The INCOSE handbook expands greatly on all of the processes in ISO 15288 and also discusses different techniques and approaches to systems engineering. The handbook also has a rich appendix with many examples and case studies of applying systems engineering best practice.
- 'CMMI – Capability Maturity Model Integration' [3]. The CMMI comprises a suite of documents that allow any given set of processes to be assessed in terms of its capability and maturity. The CMMI has an excellent pedigree and is the result of a colossal volume of work. The CMMI is particularly strong when concerned with processes, but rather weaker in other areas, such as architecture.
- 'DoD – systems engineering guide for systems-of-systems' [4]. This set of guidelines represents current best practice in the US Department of Defense (*sp*). This is a particularly valuable source of information as there is a dearth of good, accepted knowledge concerning systems of systems since it is a relatively new area.
- 'ISO/IEC/IEEE 42010 Systems and software engineering – Architecture description' [5]. This is an evolution of 'IEEE 1471 – Architectures for software-intensive systems' [6] and, bearing in mind the history of IEEE 1471, this is now a mature standard. This is an excellent information source for architectures, architecture descriptions and architecture frameworks.
- Various architectural frameworks, including Zachman [7,8], MODAF [9], DoDAF [10], NAF [11] and TRAK [12]. Architectural frameworks are widely used in today's industry and provide a good source of information for architectures, architecture descriptions and architectural frameworks. Also, other useful knowledge sources include common notations for frameworks, such as the Unified Profile for DoDAF and MODAF (UPDM) [13] and development processes, such as The Open Group Architectural Framework (TOGAF) [14].

- Various competency frameworks, including UKSPEC [15], the INCOSE systems engineering competencies framework [16], SFIA [17] and APM [18,19]. Competency frameworks are widely used in today's industry in order to demonstrate the ability of people in an organisation.
- Various modelling notations, including SysML [20,21], UML [22,23], SOAML [24] and BPMN [25]. There are a number of different modelling notations that may be used for MBSE. This book is concerned with the use of SysML. However, there are some concepts and definitions that are used in other notations that may be of value to the MBSE Ontology.
- Various best-practice books. In terms of methodologies and approaches, there are a number of books that contain valuable knowledge concerning performing MBSE [23,26–28].
- Various papers and other publications such as References 29 and 30.

For each of the main concepts that will be used in the MBSE Ontology, a number of source references will be discussed. The references chosen will vary, depending on the nature of the key concept. For example, CMMI focuses mainly on processes and is therefore an excellent source reference for the Process concept, whereas it does not even mention Systems of Systems and is therefore not a good reference for that concept.

3.1.2   The Systems Engineering Body of Knowledge (SEBoK)

There is an excellent project that is concerned with creating a body of knowledge for systems engineering, known as SEBoK [31]. This project began in 2009 as part of the larger Body of Knowledge to Advance Systems Engineering (BKCASE) project [32] with the goal of creating a systems engineering body of knowledge (SEBoK).

There were 70 contributors to the project and one of the goals was to provide a comprehensive set of key references and resources that are relevant to systems engineering and systems engineers.

Released as version 1.0 in 2012, the SEBoK brings together a set of definitions and terms and provides discussion points around them. The goal of SEBoK was not to develop a definite set of terms, but to highlight best practice and to point out differences between them.

It can be plainly seen that there are obvious parallels with this chapter, but with a few notable differences:

- The main focus of this book is specifically MBSE rather than systems engineering.
- The aim of the MBSE Ontology presented in this chapter is, just like SEBoK, to identify any differences of opinion between source references. Unlike SEBoK, however, the MBSE Ontology resolves these discrepancies by making a judgement call and going as far as providing a single definition for each concept, while maintaining a mapping back to the source references.
- All of the analysis of source concepts and terms in this book were performed using modelling techniques.

Both the SEBoK and this chapter use many of the same references and, therefore, there is not a graphical representation of SEBoK shown for each of the concepts, as the SEBoK definitions are based directly on source references. Thus, to avoid repetition, the reference to SEBoK is provided once here and not in each section. The SEBoK contains an excellent glossary where the source references for each term can be found.

3.1.3   Disagreements with the MBSE Ontology

This chapter is intended to define the set of concepts and terms that will be used in this book. They are all based on best-practice definitions but, inevitably, different people in different organisations will disagree with some of the concepts and terms here. The idea of a single Ontology that will be directly and exactly applicable to every organisation can only exist in a utopian world and is simply not realistic in real life. It should be remembered, however, that disagreeing with what is presented here is fine, bearing in mind the following points:

- Disagreeing with terms. It is perfectly natural to disagree with the actual terms that are being used. People working in different organisations, in different industries and even in the same organisation will often use different words to describe the same concept. This is not a problem as long as people are aware of the different terms being used. This is the same as two people speaking two different languages – it does not mean that they cannot communicate, but does mean that there is a requirement for translation between them. The use of an Ontology is an excellent mechanism to achieve this translation.
- Disagreeing with concepts – wrong definition. In some cases there may a concept that is used in the MBSE Ontology, which is considered to be completely wrong. Again, this is not necessarily a problem but it does mean that the concept will need to be redefined. This is achieved by modifying the MBSE Ontology and ensuring that the meaning is still consistent with the rest of the MBSE Ontology.
- Disagreeing with concepts – irrelevant concepts. In some cases there may be concepts on the MBSE Ontology that are considered irrelevant or superfluous to the need of your business. In this case, simply remove them. For example, if your business does not consider Systems of Systems, then there is no value in having that concept on the MBSE Ontology.
- Disagreeing with concepts – missing concepts. In some cases there may be organisation-specific or industry-specific concepts that do not exist on this generic MBSE Ontology. In this case the new concepts need to be added to the MBSE Ontology. Obviously, care must be taken to ensure that the new concepts are consistent with the original MBSE Ontology.

Remember, the MBSE Ontology provided here is not intended to be definitive for every organisation or industry but, rather, is intended to be a good starting point for creating and tailoring an ontology for your own MBSE activities.

3.2   The MBSE Ontology

This section provides the main definition for the MBSE Ontology along with a discussion of each of the concepts, including the provenance of each.

The basic MBSE Ontology was introduced and described briefly in Chapter 1. The same high-level overview is presented again here for reference.

The diagram in Figure 3.1 shows the high-level overview of the MBSE Ontology that was introduced in Chapter 1. This chapter will take each of the high-level concepts and consider them in more detail. Each concept is grouped with similar and related concepts and presented, described and discussed in its own section. These major groupings are:

- System concepts, which cover the basic concepts associated with System, Systems of Systems, Constituent Systems, etc.
- Need concepts, which cover all concepts associated with System Needs, such as Requirements, Capabilities and Goals.
- Architecture concepts, where the description and structure of Architectures using Architectural Frameworks are discussed.
- Life Cycle concepts, where different Life Cycles and Life Cycle Models are discussed, along with the interactions between Life Cycles.
- Process concepts, where the structure, execution and responsibility of Processes are discussed.
- Competence concepts, where the ability of people associated with Stakeholder Roles is defined.
- Project concepts, where Project and Programme-related concepts are defined.

It is the combination of all these detailed views that will make up the MBSE Ontology in its entirety and which will be presented as a single diagram, showing these major groupings, at the end of this chapter. The MBSE Ontology shown in this chapter is a simplified version of the full MBSE Ontology, which itself is shown in Appendix A.

Each of the major groupings focuses on a number of key concepts that are abstracted from a variety of the source references. These source references are described, discussed and where necessary a model is shown. The concepts are then compared and contrasted, and a fully traceable description is defined that will be used throughout the rest of this book.

3.2.1   The System concept

One of the most fundamental terms that are used in MBSE is that of the System. This forms the core definition at the heart of systems engineering and around which the whole MBSE Ontology is based.

3.2.1.1   System-related concepts as described by the International Standards Organisation (ISO)

'ISO 15288 – systems and software engineering life cycle processes' [1] defines a system as a:

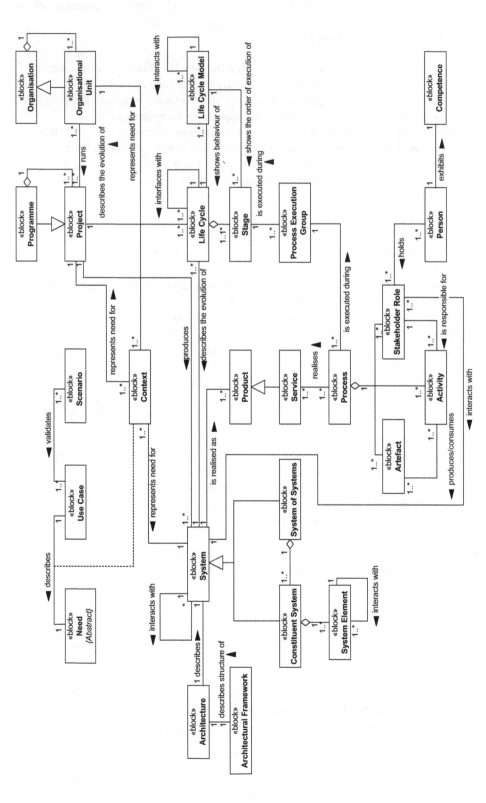

Figure 3.1 The high-level MBSE Ontology used throughout this book

'*combination of interacting elements organised to achieve one or more stated purposes*'.

And then goes on to qualify this with an additional note that states:

'*a system may be considered as a product or as the services that it provides*'.

The standard then continues with a definition of system element as follows:

'*member of a set of elements that constitutes a system*'.

With a qualifying note that states:

'*... a system element can be hardware, software, data, humans, processes ... procedures ... facilities, materials and naturally-occurring entities ... or any combination*'.

In terms of thinking about the System at a conceptual level, ISO defines that a System may be considered as one of two types: a System of Interest or an Enabling System, which are defined as:

'*system of interest (is a) system whose life cycle is under consideration in the context of this International Standard*'.
    '*enabling system (is a) system that supports a system of interest during its life cycle stages but does not necessarily contribute to its function during operation*'.

This standard is particularly weak when it comes to defining a System of Systems, but does hint at one by stating:

'*for a more complex system of interest, a prospective system element may itself need to be considered as a system (that is in turn comprised of system elements) before a complete set of system elements can be defined with confidence*'.

Therefore, in summary, the ISO 15288 System-related concepts may be visualised by the diagram in Figure 3.2.

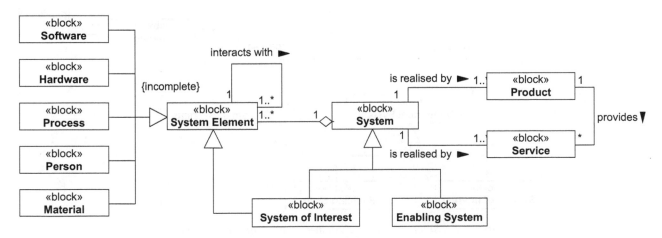

Figure 3.2   Summary of System-related concepts for ISO 15288

The concepts shown in this diagram will be used as a basis for the definitions of the concepts in the MBSE Ontology that will be used for the remainder of this book.

3.2.1.2   System-related concepts as described by the International Council on Systems Engineering (INCOSE)

The 'INCOSE systems engineering handbook' [2] is based directly on ISO 15288 but expands on all of the points made in it, including definitions, processes and life cycles. As a result of this, the definitions for System, Enabling System, System of Interest and System Element are exactly the same as the definitions provided in ISO 15288. INCOSE does not explicitly define the terms Products or Services, but does allude to the fact that systems engineering is intended to '*establish agreement for the creation of products and services*', which may be interpreted as a similar definition to that provided in ISO 15288.

INCOSE, however, does enter into more detail when defining a System of Systems, using the definition:

> '*systems of systems (SoS) are defined as an interoperating collection of component systems that produce results unachievable by the individual systems alone*'.

This provides a difference from the loose definition provided in ISO 15288 and introduces the idea that a System of Systems has its own 'results' – this is not explicit in the ISO 15288 definition.

Therefore, in summary, the INCOSE System-related concepts may be visualised by the diagram in Figure 3.3.

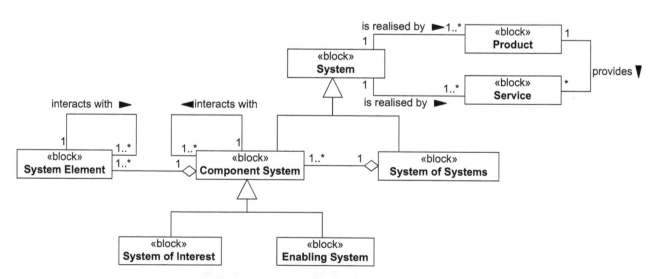

Figure 3.3   Summary of the System-related concepts for INCOSE

The concepts shown in this diagram will be used as a basis for the definitions of the concepts in the MBSE Ontology that will be used for the remainder of this book.

3.2.1.3 System-related concepts as described by the US Department of Defense

The US Department of Defense (DoD) has issued a set of systems engineering guidelines that are aimed specifically at Systems of Systems [4]. The guidelines define a System as:

> '*a functionally, physically and/or behaviourally related group of regularly interacting or interdependent elements; that group of elements forming a unified whole*'.

This definition, while using different terms, is very similar to that used in both ISO 15288 and the INCOSE handbook. The emphasis of these guidelines is on the concept of Systems of Systems; therefore, the definition used should be particularly interesting.

> '*An SoS is defined as a set or arrangement of systems that results when independent and useful systems are integrated into a larger system that delivers unique capabilities.*'

The relationship between the concepts of System and System of Systems is further elaborated on by the statement:

> '... *although an SoS is a system, not all systems are SoS*'.

This definition really states that there is a generalisation relationship between System and System of Systems.

The guidelines then continue by identifying four main types of System of Systems, as defined by Maier [30], which are:

- Virtual – '*Virtual SoS lack a central management authority and a centrally agreed upon purpose for the system of systems. Large-scale behavior emerges – and may be desirable – but this type of SoS must rely upon relatively invisible mechanisms to maintain it.*'
- Collaborative – '*In collaborative SoS the component systems interact more or less voluntarily to fulfill agreed upon central purposes. The Internet is a collaborative system. The Internet Engineering Task Force works out standards but has no power to enforce them. The central players collectively decide how to provide or deny service, thereby providing some means of enforcing and maintaining standards.*'
- Acknowledged – '*Acknowledged SoS have recognized objectives, a designated manager, and resources for the SoS; however, the constituent systems retain their independent ownership, objectives, funding, and development and sustainment approaches. Changes in the systems are based on collaboration between the SoS and the system.*'

- Directed – '*Directed SoS are those in which the integrated system of systems is built and managed to fulfill specific purposes. It is centrally managed during long-term operation to continue to fulfill those purposes as well as any new ones the system owners might wish to address. The component systems maintain an ability to operate independently, but their normal operational mode is subordinated to the central managed purpose.*'

Therefore, in summary, the US DoD System-related concepts may be visualised by the diagram in Figure 3.4.

The concepts shown in this diagram will be used as a basis for the definitions of the concepts in the MBSE Ontology that will be used for the remainder of this book.

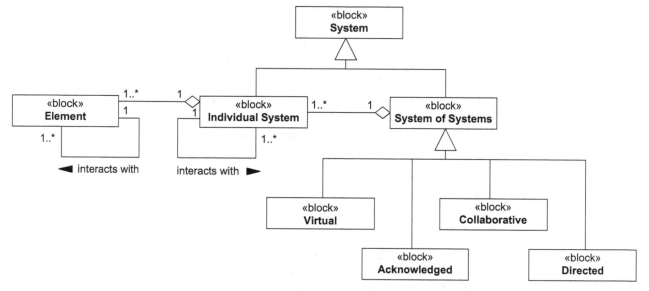

Figure 3.4   Summary of System-related concepts for the DoD

3.2.1.4   The MBSE Ontology definition for System-related concepts

The concepts and definitions that will be used in this book are shown in the diagram in Figure 3.5.

The diagram here shows the MBSE Ontology for the main concepts that are related to the System. The structure of the diagram is very similar to those of ISO 15288 and the DoD guide. The main structure of the 'System' is taken from ISO 15288, whereas the 'System of Systems' structure is taken mainly from the DoD guide.

These concepts are defined as follows:

- 'System' – set of interacting elements organised to satisfy one or more 'System Context'. Where the 'System' is a 'System of Systems', its elements will be one or more 'Constituent System', and where the 'System' is a 'Constituent System', its elements are one or more 'System Element'. A 'System' can interact with one or more other 'System'.

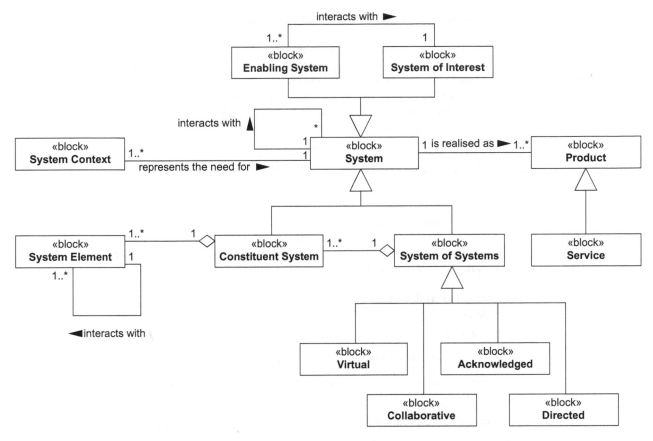

Figure 3.5 MBSE Ontology focused on System concepts

- 'Constituent System' – a special type of 'System' whose elements are one or more 'System Element'.
- 'System of Systems' – a special type of 'System' whose elements are one or more 'Constituent System' and which delivers unique functionality not deliverable by any single 'Constituent System'.
- 'System of Interest' – a special type of 'System' that describes the system being developed, enhanced, maintained or investigated.
- 'Enabling System' – a special type of 'System' that interacts with the 'System of Interest' yet sits outside its boundary.
- 'System Element' – a basic part of a 'Constituent System'.
- 'Product' – something that realises a 'System'. Typical products may include, but are not limited to software, hardware, Processes, data, humans, facilities, etc.
- 'Service' – an intangible 'Product' that realises a 'System'. A 'Service' is itself realised by one or more 'Process'.
- 'Virtual' – a special type of 'System of Systems' that lacks central management and resources, and no consensus of purpose.

- 'Collaborative' – a special type of 'System of Systems' that lacks central management and resources, but has consensus of purpose.
- 'Acknowledged' – a special type of 'System of Systems' that has designated management and resources, and a consensus of purpose. Each 'Constituent System' retains its own management and operation.
- 'Directed' – a special type of 'System of Systems' that has designated management and resources, and a consensus of purpose. Each 'Constituent System' retains its own operation but not management.

This subset of the MBSE Ontology has direct relationships to the 'Need', 'Life Cycle' and 'Process' subsets that are described in this chapter.

3.2.2   The Need concept

The concept of a Need that is used here is a generalisation of a number of terms, including the terms Requirement, Capability and Goal. This section will therefore look at several definitions of these terms and then define exactly what is meant by them for the purposes of this book.

3.2.2.1   Need-related concepts as described by the *Oxford English Dictionary*

The basic definition of a Requirement in the *Oxford English Dictionary* is:

'*(noun) a thing that is needed or wanted*' [33].

This definition, albeit a very high-level one, is very interesting for two main reasons:

- A Requirement is basically defined as a 'thing' – not the most unambiguous of definitions.
- This 'thing' is either 'needed' or 'wanted'. This is particularly interesting as there is often a big difference between what a Stakeholder Role wants and what stakeholders actually need. Indeed, part of any Requirements analysis activity should concern itself with the difference between these two terms.

This is a somewhat ambiguous definition of the term.

3.2.2.2   Need-related concepts as described by the International Council on Systems Engineering (INCOSE)

The next definition that will be considered is taken from the world of systems engineering. The whole area of systems engineering advocates that requirements must be understood so much so that the areas of Requirements engineering and systems engineering are often confused. The next definition, therefore, is taken from the INCOSE handbook [2].

'*A statement that identifies a system, product or process characteristic or constraint, which is unambiguous, clear, unique, consistent, stand-alone (not grouped), and verifiable, and is deemed necessary for stakeholder acceptability.*'

This definition is more complex than the previous one, but also shares some characteristics with it. Consider the following:

- For the first time, this definition states explicitly that a Requirement takes the form of a 'statement'.
- This definition then states that a Requirement is a 'system, product or process characteristic or constraint'. This is, essentially, putting a better definition to the term 'thing' that was used in the first definition.
- The definition then goes on to qualify this statement, by stating that it must be 'unambiguous, clear, unique, consistent, stand-alone (not grouped), and verifiable'. This set of basic characteristics will be discussed throughout this book but, suffice to say, there exists a set of desirable characteristics for any Requirement.
- The final part of the INCOSE definition states that the Requirement is 'deemed necessary for stakeholder acceptability'. This is very much in the 'needed' rather than 'wanted' camp when compared to the OED definition.

In conclusion, therefore, this is a fuller definition of the term that adds more detail when compared with the OED definition.

3.2.2.3 Need-related concepts as described by the Modelling Community

The next definition of the term Requirement is taken from the world of modelling. This is an important definition as modelling is core to the whole approach taken in this book. This definition is taken from the Unified Modelling Language definition:

> '*a desired feature, property or behaviour of a system*' [34].

This definition is certainly simpler that the INCOSE one and has a number of noteworthy aspects.

- The term 'desired' is used here, which really sits somewhere between 'wanted' and 'needed'.
- The term Requirement is defined in the Context of being a property of a System, rather than the Context of the Stakeholder.

In conclusion, therefore, this is another simple definition and, again, one that is very similar to both the INCOSE and OED definitions.

In the seminal book 'Model-based requirements engineering' [26] the idea of a Need is taken further by considering the Context and also how it will be validated. The key terms are shown in the diagram in Figure 3.6.

The concepts here consider the 'Requirement' as an abstract concept that has a 'Requirement Description' but that also has its 'Context' defined in terms or one or more 'Use Case'. Each 'Use Case' may then be validated by one or more 'Scenario'. This is the first definition where the concepts of a basic need (shown here as 'Requirement') are taken further and related to other established modelling concepts (the 'Use Case' and the 'Scenario'). This is further extended by considering traceability

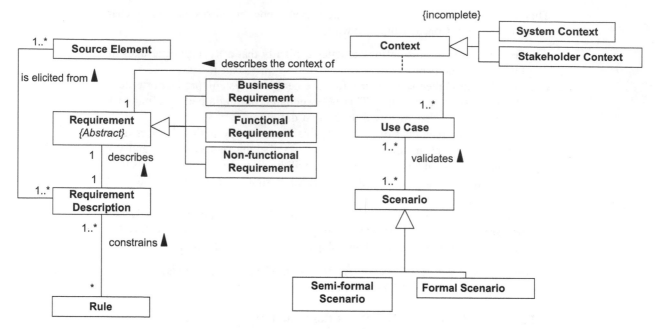

Figure 3.6   Summary of Need-related concepts as described in 'Model-based requirements engineering'

back to one or more 'Source Element' and the concept of a 'Rule' that may be defined in order to constrain one or more 'Requirement'.

3.2.2.4   Need-related concepts as described by the International Standards Organisation (ISO)

The next definition that will be considered is taken from the generic quality-based standard – ISO 9001 [35], which defines a Requirement as:

> '*need or expectation that is stated, generally implied or obligatory*'.

Again, this may appear to be a simple definition, but there are some interesting points to be made here.

- For the first time, the term 'expectation' is used here as an alternate to 'need'. The main difference between these two terms is that one is more specific than the other. A need must be stated, whereas an expectation may be viewed as more assumed than stated.
- Following directly on from the previous point, this definition provides three qualifiers on the term 'requirement'. It states that a Requirement may be 'stated' explicitly, 'generally implied' implicitly or 'obligatory' in that it is mandatory.

In conclusion, therefore, this definition has similarities with the previous definitions, but adds more detail with the nature of the Requirement.

3.2.2.5 The MBSE Ontology definition for Need-related concepts

Based on these information sources, the section of the MBSE Ontology shown in Figure 3.7 was defined.

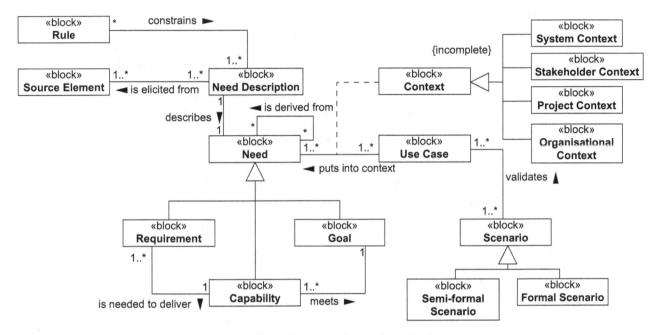

Figure 3.7 MBSE Ontology focused on Need concepts

The diagram here shows the MBSE Ontology for the main concepts that are related to need concepts. These are defined as follows:

- 'Need' – a generic abstract concept that, when put into a 'Context', represents something that is necessary or desirable for the subject of the Context.
- 'Need Description' – a tangible description of an abstract 'Need' that is defined according to a pre-defined set of attributes.
- 'Goal' – a special type of 'Need' whose 'Context' will typically represent one or more 'Organisational Unit' (as an 'Organisational Context'). Each 'Goal' will be met by one or more 'Capability'.
- 'Capability' – a special type of 'Need' whose 'Context' will typically represent one or more 'Project' (as a 'Project Context') or one or more 'Organisational Unit' (as an 'Organisational Context'). A 'Capability' will meet one or more 'Goal' and will represent the ability of an 'Organisation' or 'Organisational Unit'.
- 'Requirement' – a property of a System that is either needed or wanted by a 'Stakeholder Role' or other Context-defining element. Also, one or more 'Requirement' is needed to deliver each 'Capability'.
- 'Source Element' – the ultimate origin of a 'Need' that is elicited into one or more 'Need Description'. A 'Source Element' can be almost anything that inspires, affects or drives a 'Need', such as a Standard, a System, Project documentation, a phone call, an e-mail, a letter and a book.

- 'Rule' – a construct that constrains the attributes of a 'Need Description'. A 'Rule' may take several forms, such as equations, heuristics, reserved word lists and grammar restrictions.
- 'Use Case' – a 'Need' that is considered in a specific 'Context' and that is validated by one or more 'Scenario'.
- 'Context' – a specific point of view based on, for example, Stakeholder Roles, System hierarchy level, Life Cycle Stage, etc.
- 'Scenario' – an ordered set of interactions between one or more 'Stakeholder Role', 'System' or 'System Element' that represents a specific chain of events with a specific outcome. One or more 'Scenario' validates each 'Use Case'.
- 'Formal Scenario' – a 'Scenario' that is mathematically provable using, for example, formal methods.
- 'Semi-formal Scenario' – a 'Scenario' that is demonstrable using, for example, visual notations such as SysML, tables and text.

The 'Need' subset of the MBSE Ontology has relationships with the 'Project' and 'System' subsets.

3.2.3   The Architecture concept

The concept of an architecture is fundamental to any systems engineering undertaking. There is much confusion, however, due to the plethora of very similar terms involving the word architecture. The use of architecture has also changed significantly over the years as the definitions that apply to the world of software engineering have a significantly simpler scope than the world of systems engineering.

3.2.3.1   Architecture-related concepts as described by the International Standards Organisation (ISO)

There are two main ISO standards that will be considered for the source knowledge for defining architecture, which are:

- ISO 15288 – Systems and software engineering – System life cycle processes. This standard is used many times in this book, but has surprisingly little information concerning architecture [1].
- ISO 42010 – Systems and software engineering – Architecture description. This standard is more recent than ISO 15288 and is concerned solely with architectures. The terminology provided in this standard, therefore, is very well defined and has far more detail than in ISO 15288 [5].

In ISO 15288, the definition of an architecture is given as:

'fundamental organisation of a system embodied in its components, their relationships to each other, and to the environment, and the principles guiding its design and evolution'.

ISO/IEC 42010 defines a number of terms:

- *'architecting: process of conceiving, defining, expressing, documenting, communicating, certifying proper implementation of, maintaining and improving an architecture throughout a system's life cycle'.*

- '*architecture: fundamental concepts or properties of a system in its environment embodied in its elements, relationships, and in the principles of its design and evolution*'.
- '*architecture description (abbreviation 'AD'): work product used to express an architecture*'.
- '*architecture description language (abbreviation 'ADL'): any form of expression for use in architecture descriptions*'.
- '*architecture framework: conventions, principles and practices for the description of architectures established within a specific domain of application and/or community of stakeholders*'.
- '*architecture viewpoint: work product establishing the conventions for the construction, interpretation and use of architecture views to frame specific system concerns*'.
- '*architecture view: work product expressing the architecture of a system from the perspective of specific system concerns*'.
- '*concern: interest in a system relevant to one or more of its stakeholders. A concern pertains to any influence on a system in its environment, including developmental, technological, business, operational, organizational, political, economic, legal, regulatory, ecological and social influences*'.
- '*environment: context determining the setting and circumstances of all influences upon a system. The environment of a system includes developmental, technological, business, operational, organizational, political, economic, legal, regulatory, ecological and social influences*'.
- '*stakeholder: individual, team, organization, or classes thereof, having an interest in a system*'.

The fundamental definition of the term 'architecture' is almost identical between the two standards, but ISO 42010 provides far more definitions than ISO 15288 and will be used as the main knowledge source for this section.

The diagram in Figure 3.8 shows a summary of the architecture-related terms for ISO 42010. As the definition of 'architecture' in ISO 15288 is almost identical, this diagram can be seen to represent both standards accurately.

3.2.3.2 Architecture-related concepts as described by the International Council on Systems Engineering (INCOSE)

The INCOSE handbook does not provide an explicit definition of an architecture, yet does refer to several different types of architecture, such as system architecture, logical architecture, functional architecture and enterprise architecture.

> '*there may be several required operational views of the system driven by architectural frameworks*'.

As has been mentioned previously, the INCOSE handbook is, in many ways, an expansion of ISO 15288, which itself is weak where architectures are concerned.

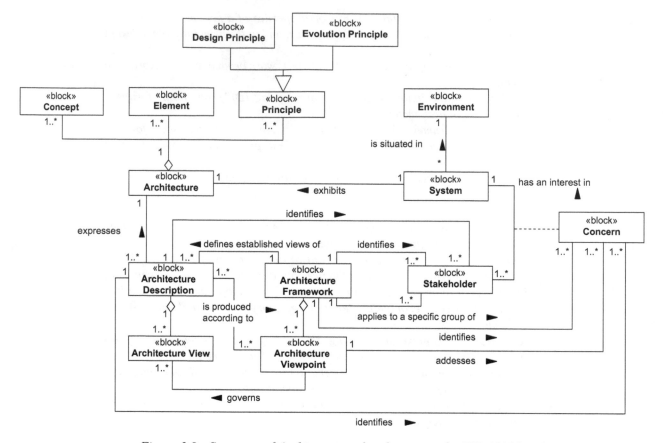

Figure 3.8   Summary of Architecture-related concepts for ISO 42010

3.2.3.3   Architecture-related concepts as described by the Architecture Framework community

When architectures are used for a specific industry, or a specific stakeholder group, it is quite common for an Architecture Framework to be defined. An Architecture Framework is not, in itself, an Architecture, but defines a set of Views that are required to describe an Architecture.

A number of Architecture Frameworks will be considered at a very high level. For a more in-depth description see Reference 27.

3.2.3.4   The Zachman Framework

The Zachman Framework is a framework for Enterprise Architecture. The Zachman Framework is one of the oldest and most mature frameworks and is certainly one of the most widely used frameworks in industry today [7,8].

Zachman derived the framework from the world of classical (building) architecture and, hence, the names of the views and the perspectives relate to the terminology of architecture.

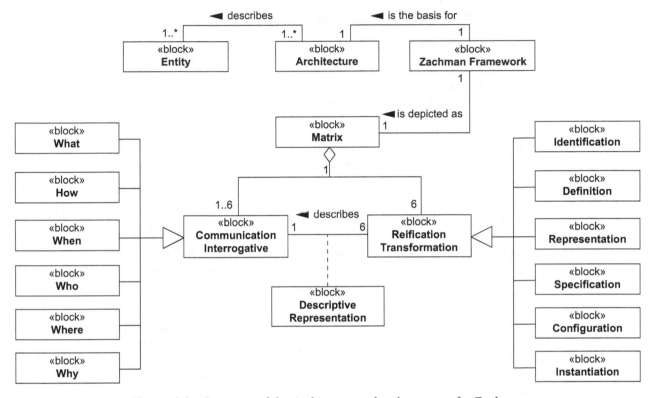

Figure 3.9   Summary of the Architecture-related concepts for Zachman

The diagram in Figure 3.9 shows a high-level view of the Zachman Framework.

The framework itself takes the form of a simple 'Matrix' comprising rows and columns with intersecting cells that describe aspects of an entity. Usually there are 36 cells as the matrix usually has 6 rows and always has 6 columns.

Each row represents between one and six 'Communication Interrogative', each of which asks a basic question regarding the 'Entity' that is under consideration. These questions take the basic form of 'What', 'How', 'When', 'Who', 'Where' and 'Why'. Each column represents a 'Reification Transformation' that covers the broad transformation of information from a vague abstraction into a solid instantiation. These are:

- 'Identification', which is often represented on the matrix as scope contexts and which is mainly applicable to strategists as theorists.
- 'Definition', which is often represented on the matrix as business contexts and which is mainly applicable to executive leaders as owners.
- 'Representation', which is often represented on the matrix as system logics and which is mainly applicable to architects as designers.
- 'Specification', which is often represented on the matrix as technology physics and which is mainly applicable to engineers as builders.

- 'Configuration', which is often represented on the matrix as component assemblies and which is mainly applicable to technicians as implementers.
- 'Instantiation', which is often represented on the matrix as operations and instance classes and which is mainly applicable to workers as participants.

The Zachman Framework has been used as a major reference for most architectural frameworks, including the ones described in this section.

3.2.3.5 Defence-based Architecture frameworks

The defence industry has a number of architectural frameworks that originate in and are used by particular countries. These include:

- MODAF – Ministry of Defence Architecture Framework [9], which originated and is used in the UK.
- DoDAF – Department of Defense Architecture Framework [10], which originated and is used in the USA.
- NAF – NATO Architecture Framework [11], which is used in NATO countries.
- DNDAF – DND/CF Architecture Framework [36], which originated and is used in Canada.

The list goes on with many countries having their own specific framework, but most of them are closely related and, therefore, have very similar constructs and concepts. For the sake of brevity and the reader's sanity, a single one will be considered as a knowledge source – for a more in-depth comparison see Reference 37. In addition, to learn more about common notation for defence frameworks, see Reference 13.

The UK Ministry of Defence Architectural Framework (MODAF) defines an architectural framework as:

> '*An Architectural Framework (AF) is a specification of how to organise and present architectural models. . . . an AF defines a standard set of model categories (called 'Views') which each have a specific purpose. These views are often categorised by the domain they cover – e.g. operational/ business, technical, etc. – which are known in MODAF as Viewpoints.*'

In terms of the application of MODAF, its scope includes:

> '*MODAF provides a rigorous method for understanding, analysing, and specifying: Capabilities, Systems, Systems of Systems (SoS), Organisational Structures and Business Processes.*'

The MODAF specification identifies seven viewpoints that are required to make up the full architectural framework. Note that this is a different definition of the term 'Viewpoint' from the one used in ISO 42010 (Figure 3.10).

The MODAF is made up of seven 'Viewpoint' each of which is made up of one or more 'View'. These viewpoints are simply collections of views and serve to group views that are used for similar purposes. The viewpoints are 'All Views' that describe information that applies to all viewpoints, the 'Strategic' viewpoint that describes capabilities, the 'Operational' viewpoint that describes concepts, the 'System' viewpoint that describes the actual systems, the 'Service-oriented' viewpoint that describes the actual services, the 'Acquisition' viewpoint that describes

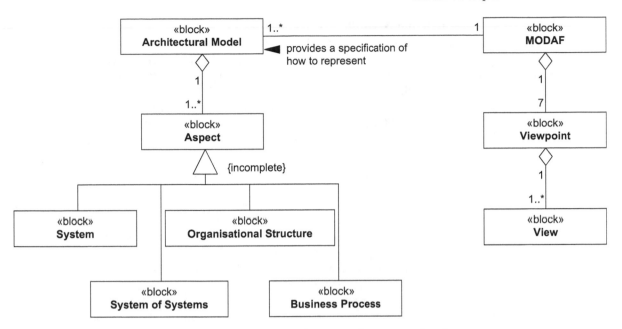

Figure 3.10   Summary of the MODAF architecture-related concepts

Table 3.1   Comparison of terms in defence-based architectural frameworks

MODAF	DoDAF	NAF
Viewpoint	View	View
View	Product	Subview
All Viewpoint	All View	NATO All View
Acquisition Viewpoint	–	NATO Programme View
Strategic Viewpoint	–	NATO Capability View
Operational Viewpoint	Operational View	NATO Operational View
Systems Viewpoint	Systems and Services View	NATO Systems View
Service-oriented Viewpoint	Systems and Services View	NATO Service-oriented View
Technical Viewpoint	Technical Standards View	NATO Technical view

acquisition programme views and the 'Technical' viewpoint that identifies relevant standards.

The various defence-based frameworks are related to each other and so, unsurprisingly, have a number of similarities. In order to illustrate these similarities Table 3.1 provides a high-level mapping between the terms that are used in several frameworks.

Table 3.1 is not intended to be an exhaustive comparison but is intended to make the point that there are many similarities between the various defence-based architectural frameworks. For a full discussion on the similarities and differences between these frameworks, including models of the different structures, see Reference 27.

3.2.3.6   Non-defence Architecture frameworks

Alongside the defence-based architectural frameworks, there are a number of non-defence architecture frameworks (note the difference in terms here, where the term 'architectural framework' was used in defence, the term 'architecture framework' is used here; both mean the same thing).

Perhaps the most widely known architecture framework is The Open Group Architecture Framework (TOGAF) [14], which is not actually an architecture framework but, rather, a set of phases and associated processes in the form of an architecture development method (ADM) that will enable an enterprise architecture to be created for an organisation.

TOGAF does not define any particular views (although it does hint strongly at some) but focuses on how to manage the development and delivery of the architecture. This is an important point as the TOGAF is effectively a management-based approach and, hence, focuses largely on management and planning, rather than the actual development of the architecture and its views.

Another example of a non-defence architecture framework is TRAK, which was originally commissioned by London Underground Limited in the UK but has since been adopted by a number of organisations [12]. TRAK cites both ISO 15288 and ISO 42010 as major references, was developed using many of the concepts from MODAF and has a strong systems engineering flavour. The diagram in Figure 3.11 shows an overview of TRAK.

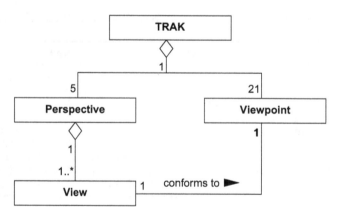

Figure 3.11   Summary of the TRAK architecture-related concepts

The diagram here shows that 'TRAK' is made up of five 'Perspective' that groups one or more related 'View' and 21 'Viewpoint'. Each 'View' is defined according to one 'Viewpoint'.

3.2.3.7   The MBSE Ontology definition for Architecture

Based on these knowledge sources, the Ontology shown in Figure 3.12 was defined. The concepts shown in Figure 3.12 are defined as follows:

- 'Architectural Framework' – a defined set of one or more 'Viewpoint' and an 'Ontology'. The 'Architectural Framework' is used to structure an 'Architecture' from the point of view of a specific industry, Stakeholder Role set, or

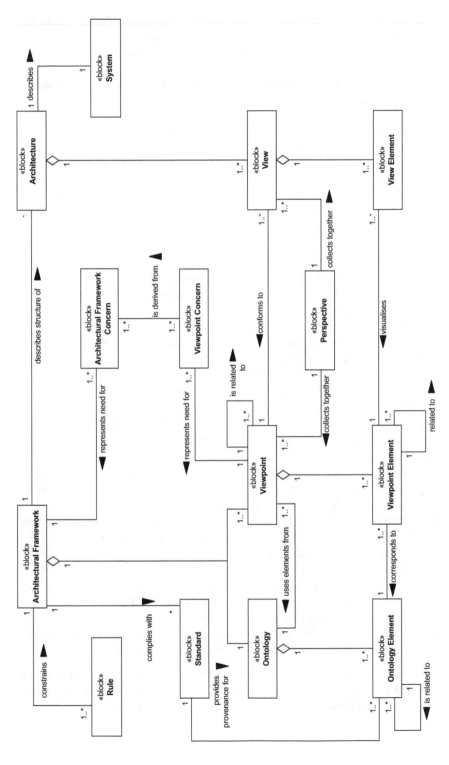

Figure 3.12 *MBSE Ontology for Architectures and Architectural Frameworks*

Organisation. The 'Architectural Framework' is defined so that it meets the Needs defined by one or more 'Architectural Framework Concern'. An 'Architectural Framework' is created such that it complies with zero or more 'Standard'.

- 'Architectural Framework Concern' – defines a Need that an 'Architectural Framework' has to address.
- 'Ontology' – an element of an 'Architectural Framework' that defines all the concepts and terms (one or more 'Ontology Element') that relate to any 'Architecture' structured according to the 'Architectural Framework'.
- 'Ontology Element' – the concepts that make up an 'Ontology'. Each 'Ontology Element' can be related to each other and is used in the definition of each 'Viewpoint' (through the corresponding 'Viewpoint Element' that makes up a 'Viewpoint'). The provenance for each 'Ontology Element' is provided by one or more 'Standard'.
- 'Viewpoint' – a definition of the structure and content of a 'View'. The content and structure of a 'Viewpoint' use the concepts and terms from the 'Ontology' via one or more 'Viewpoint Element' that make up the 'Viewpoint'. Each 'Viewpoint' is defined so that it meets the needs defined by one or more 'Viewpoint Concern'.
- 'Viewpoint Concern' – defines a Need that a 'Viewpoint' has to address.
- 'Viewpoint Element' – the elements that make up a 'Viewpoint'. Each 'Viewpoint Element' must correspond to an 'Ontology Element' from the 'Ontology' that is part of the 'Architectural Framework'.
- 'Architecture' – a description of a 'System', made up of one or more 'View'. One or more related 'View' can be collected together into a 'Perspective'.
- 'View' – the visualisation of part of the 'Architecture' of a 'System' that conforms to the structure and content defined in a 'Viewpoint'. A 'View' is made up of one or more 'View Element'.
- 'View Element' – the elements that make up a 'View'. Each 'View Element' visualises a 'Viewpoint Element' that makes up the 'Viewpoint' to which the 'View', on which the 'View Element' appears, conforms.
- 'Perspective' – a collection of one or more 'View' (and hence also one or more defining 'Viewpoint') that are related by their purpose. That is, one or more 'View' that address the same architectural needs, rather than being related in some other way, such as by mode of visualisation.
- 'Rule' – a construct that constrains the 'Architectural Framework' (and hence the resulting 'Architecture') in some way, for example by defining one or more 'Viewpoint' that are required as a minimum.
- 'System' – set of interacting elements organised to satisfy one or more Needs. The artefact being engineered that the 'Architecture' describes.

It is important to note here that an Architecture is simply considered to be a description of a System, represented by a number of Views that are created according to a number of predefined Viewpoints from a given Architectural Framework.

There are a number of terms from the Ontology in Figure 3.12 that perhaps need some clarification, namely Architectural Framework, Architecture, Viewpoint and View. The following clarification should help:

- An Architectural Framework is made up of a number of Viewpoints that define the information that can be presented.
- An Architecture is based on an Architectural Framework. It is made up of Views, with each View being a realisation of a Viewpoint.
- Viewpoint defines the information that can be presented; it is a definition of what can be produced when an Architecture is based on an Architectural Framework.
- A View is an artefact, produced as part of an Architecture. It describes an aspect of that Architecture. If the Architecture is created using an Architectural Framework, then every View will conform to a Viewpoint in the Architectural Framework.

Not all Architectural Frameworks make this distinction. For example MODAF makes no such distinction. It defines a number of Views but does not differentiate between the definition and realisation in terms of the language and terms used. Even more confusingly MODAF does use the term "viewpoint", but in MODAF a "viewpoint" is the same as Perspective in Figure, simply a collection of related Views.

The 'Architecture' subset has relationships with the 'System' and the 'Need' subsets.

3.2.4   The 'Life Cycle' concept

The concept of a Life Cycle may seem to be quite a simple one. However, complexity creeps in when the following are considered:

- The application of the Life Cycle. For example, does the Life Cycle apply to development, acquisition, a Product, a Project, an Organisation, etc.?
- The relationships and interactions between different Life Cycles. For example, how do acquisition and development Life Cycles interact with one another?

Life Cycles also feature heavily in the world of Processes, so some additional knowledge sources start to become relevant here, such as CMMI.

3.2.4.1   Life Cycle-related concepts as described by the International Standards Organisation (ISO)

The concept of a Life Cycle is fundamental to ISO 15288 and, indeed, features in the title of the standard [1]. ISO 15288 describes a life cycle as the:

'evolution of a system, product, service, project or other human-made entity from conception through retirement'.

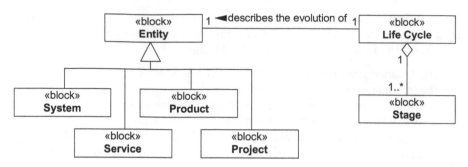

Figure 3.13   Summary of the Life Cycle-related concepts for ISO 15288

The standard then continues to describe a stage as:

> '*period within the life cycle of an entity that relates to the state of its description or realization*'.

The standard also describes a number of typical stages that are not covered here but will be discussed in more detail in Chapter 8.

The diagram in Figure 3.13 shows that a 'Life Cycle' is made up of one or more 'Stage' and that it describes the evolution of an 'Entity' that can have many types.

Again, the diagram here appears to be quite simple with a straightforward structure, but more complexities will be discussed in Chapter 8 where life cycles and processes will be considered in greater detail.

3.2.4.2   Life Cycle-related concepts as described by the Capability Maturity Model Integration (CMMI)

The Capability Maturity Model Integration (CMMI) is mainly concerned with processes but also covers life cycles in some detail [3]. CMMI uses the term 'life cycle model', which is defined as:

> '*A partitioning of the life of a product or project into phases*'.

CMMI also uses the term 'product life cycle' which is defined as:

> '*The period of time, consisting of phases, which begins when a product is conceived and ends when the product is no longer available for use. Since an organization may be producing multiple products for multiple customers, one description of a product lifecycle may not be adequate. Therefore, the organization may define a set of approved product lifecycle models. These models are typically found in published literature and are likely to be tailored for use in an organization. A product lifecycle could consist of the following phases: (1) concept/vision, (2) feasibility, (3) design/development, (4) production, and (5) phase out.*'

These concepts are summarised in the diagram in Figure 3.14.

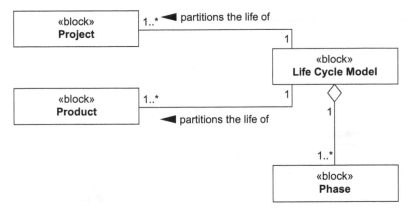

Figure 3.14   Summary of Life Cycle-related concepts for CMMI

The diagram here shows that a 'Life Cycle Model' is made up of one or more 'Phase' and partitions the life of one or more 'Project' or 'Product'. Note that there is an ambiguity in the terms that are used in CMMI between 'Product Life Cycle', 'Life Cycle Model' and 'Product Life Cycle Model', which all seem to be used interchangeably.

3.2.4.3   The MBSE Ontology definition

Based on these knowledge sources, the MBSE Ontology shown in Figure 3.15 was defined.

The diagram in Figure 3.15 shows the MBSE Ontology for the main concepts that are related to life cycles. These are defined as follows:

- 'Life Cycle' – a set of one or more 'Stage' that can be used to describe the evolution of 'System', 'Project', etc., over time.
- 'Life Cycle Model' – the execution of a set of one or more 'Stage' that shows the behaviour of a 'Life Cycle'.
- 'Stage' – a period within a 'Life Cycle' that relates to its realisation through one or more 'Process Execution Group'. The success of a 'Stage' is assessed by a 'Gate'.
- 'Gate' – a mechanism for assessing the success or failure of the execution of a 'Stage'.
- 'Life Cycle Interface Point – the point in a 'Life Cycle' where one or more 'Life Cycle Interaction' will occur.
- 'Life Cycle Interaction' – the point during a 'Life Cycle Model' at which one or more 'Stage' interact with each other.
- 'Process Execution Group' – an ordered execution of one or more 'Process' that is performed as part of a 'Stage'.

The 'Life Cycle' subset of the ontology has relationships with the 'System', 'Project' and 'Process' subsets.

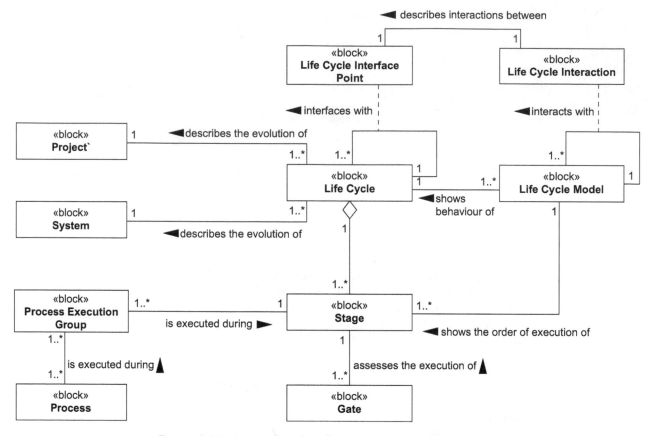

Figure 3.15   MBSE Ontology focused on Life Cycle concepts

3.2.5   The Process concept

The concept of a Process is particularly important when considering systems engineering, as systems engineering has been previously defined as being an approach. Also, as has been discussed many times in this book, there are three important aspects to realise for successful MBSE, which are 'People, Process and Tools'. Clearly, then processes are very important.

3.2.5.1   Process-based concepts as described by the International Standards Organisation (ISO)

The starting point for looking at process definition is ISO 15288, which is very strong on process, as would be expected with a standard whose scope and title include the idea of a 'process' [1].

ISO 15288 describes a process as:

> *'a set of interrelated or interacting activities which transforms inputs into outputs'.*

The standard then continues to talk about the rationale behind the process in the form of a process purpose, which is described as:

> '*high level objective of performing the process and the likely outcomes of effective implementation of the process*'.

The new term 'outcomes' is introduced as part of this definition, which is defined as:

> '*observable result of the successful achievement of the process purpose*'.

Another important concept that is defined by ISO 15288 and is strongly related to process is that of a 'stakeholder' that is defined as:

> '*individual or organisation having a right, share, claim or interest in a system or in its possession characteristics that meet their needs and expectations*'.

Finally, the concept of a 'resource' is considered that is defined in ISO 15288 as:

> '*asset that is utilised or consumed during the execution of a process*'.

All of these definitions were then brought together and are summarised in the diagram in Figure 3.16.

The diagram here shows the summary of the ISO 15288 concepts and terminology.

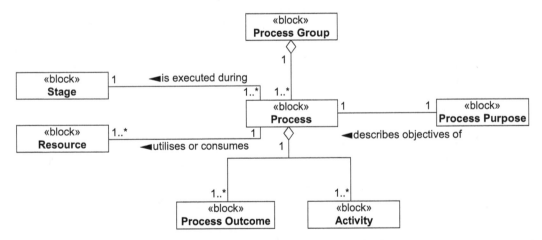

Figure 3.16   Summary of Process-related concepts for ISO 15288

3.2.5.2   Process-based concepts as described by the Capability Maturity Model Integration (CMMI)

The CMMI is very strong on the area of process; therefore, it is no surprise that there are some very in-depth definitions of process-related terms in this standard [3]. CMMI defines a process as:

> '. . . *activities that can be recognized as implementations of practices in a CMMI model. These activities can be mapped to one or more practices in*

CMMI process areas to allow a model to be useful for process improvement and process appraisal.'

In CMMI, the 'process' is an abstract concept that must be described in the form of a 'process description' that is defined by the standard as:

'A documented expression of a set of activities performed to achieve a given purpose. A process description provides an operational definition of the major components of a process. The description specifies, in a complete, precise, and verifiable manner, the requirements, design, behavior, or other characteristics of a process. It also may include procedures for determining whether these provisions have been satisfied. Process descriptions can be found at the activity, project, or organizational level.'

Despite the fact that the term 'process component' is used here to define a generic element in a process, the standard formally uses the term 'process element' in its glossary, which is defined as:

'The fundamental unit of a process. A process can be defined in terms of subprocesses or process elements. A subprocess can be further decomposed into subprocesses or process elements; a process element cannot.... Each process element covers a closely related set of activities (e.g., estimating element and peer review element). Process elements can be portrayed using templates to be completed, abstractions to be refined, or descriptions to be modified or used. A process element can be an activity or task.'

All of this information was then brought together and is summarised in the diagram in Figure 3.17.

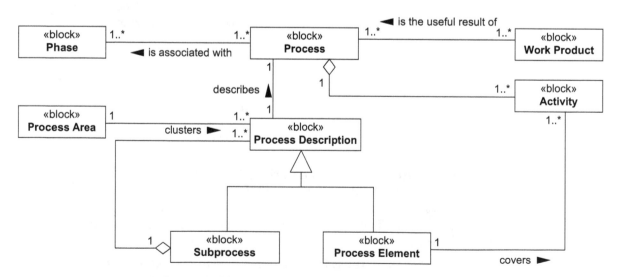

Figure 3.17   Summary of the CMMI process-related concepts

The diagram here shows a summary of the process-related terms used in the CMMI.

3.2.5.3   The MBSE Ontology definition for Process-related concepts

Based on these knowledge sources, the MBSE Ontology shown in Figure 3.18 was defined.

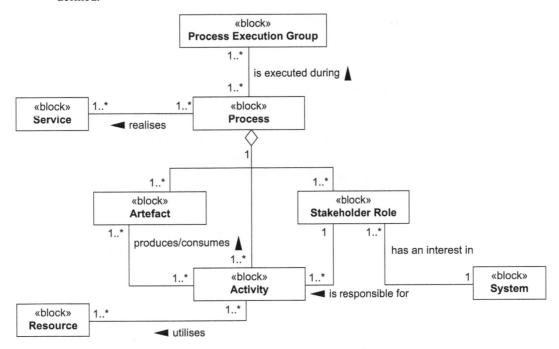

Figure 3.18   MBSE Ontology focused on Process-related concepts

The diagram in Figure 3.18 shows the MBSE Ontology for the main concepts that are related to the process. These are defined as follows:

- 'Process' – a description of an approach that is defined by one or more 'Activity', one or more 'Artefact' and one or more 'Stakeholder Role'. One or more 'Process' also defines a 'Service'.
- 'Artefact' – something that is produced or consumed by an 'Activity' in a 'Process'. Examples of an 'Artefact' include documentation, software, hardware and systems.
- 'Activity' – a set of actions that need to be performed in order to successfully execute a 'Process'. Each 'Activity' must have a responsible 'Stakeholder Role' associated with it and utilises one or more 'Resource'.
- 'Stakeholder Role' – the role of anything that has an interest in a 'System'. Examples of a 'Stakeholder Role' include the roles of a 'Person', an 'Organisational Unit', a 'Project', a 'Source Element' and an 'Enabling System'. Each 'Stakeholder Role' requires its own 'Competency Scope' and will be responsible for one or more 'Activity'.

- 'Resource' – anything that is used or consumed by an 'Activity' within a 'Process'. Examples of a 'Resource' include money, locations, fuel, raw material, data and people.
- 'Process Execution Group' – a set of one or more 'Process' that are executed for a specific purpose. For example, a 'Process Execution Group' may be defined based on a team, function, etc.

The term 'System' has been defined previously and the link between processes and life cycles is realised by the concept of the 'Process Execution Group'.

3.2.6   The Competence concept

One of the themes of this book is the importance of 'People, Process and Tools', so it should be no surprise that the area of Competence is so essential.

3.2.6.1   The competence-related concepts as described by the International Standards Organisation (ISO)

One area that is not very strong on ISO 15288 is that of competence or competency [1]. Indeed, this whole area is only mentioned three times in the standard:

> '*to maintain their competencies, consistent with business needs*', '*assessment of the adequacy of team member competencies to perform project roles*', and '*confirm that the specified range and level of competence has been attained*'.

The concept of competence is important, but ISO 15288 is not a good place to look for definitions.

3.2.6.2   The Competence-related concepts as described by the Capability Maturity Model Integration (CMMI)

One area that the CMMI is surprisingly weak in is that of competence. The terms 'competence' and 'competency' are not explicitly defined in the standard, although each is mentioned several times. For example, the standard uses the phrases:

> '*competence and heroics of the people*', '*competence of the process group staff*', '*need to provide competency development for critical functional areas*', '*maintain the competencies and qualifications of personnel*', '*this approach includes integration of tools, methods, and procedures for competency development*', '*critical competencies and roles needed to perform the work*' and '*core competencies*'.

There is therefore a clear need to have a concept of competence although the CMMI is not the best place to look for its definition.

3.2.6.3   The Competence-related concepts as described by Competency Framework Community

The whole concept of Competence and Competency has been identified as a key term, but has not been defined sufficiently well in any of the knowledge sources looked at so far. In this case, there are a number of competency frameworks that are available to be used as knowledge sources, such as:

- UKSPEC – the UK Standard for Professional Engineering Competence. The UKSPEC is the cornerstone of all technical competences in the UK. The UKSPEC is used as the basis for professional accreditation, such as Chartered Engineer (CEng) and Chartered IT Professional (CITP), and all UK professional bodies use it as part of their professional assessment. The UKSPEC is owned and managed by the Engineering Council – see Reference 15 for more details.
- SFIA – Skills Framework for the Information Age. The acronymically challenged framework known as SFIA (pronounced 'Sophia') is a framework that is geared towards the skills required for the effective implementation and use of Information Systems (IS) making use of Information and Communications Technology (ICT). The SFIA framework maps directly back to UPSPEC and is owned and managed by the SFIA Foundation – see Reference 17 for more details.
- INCOSE Systems Engineering Competencies Framework. The International Council on Systems Engineering is an international body that is committed to furthering the discipline of systems engineering. They have produced a competency framework that maps back to the UKSPEC and covers various cross-cutting concepts associated with systems engineering. Please note that the term 'systems engineering' is the engineering definition of the term, rather than the IT definition of the term. The INCOSE framework is owned and managed by INCOSE – see Reference 16 for more details.
- APM – the Association for Project Management Body of Knowledge. The APM framework forms the heart of the APM assessment and accreditation and is aimed specifically at the discipline of project management for all industries. The APM Body of Knowledge is owned and managed by the APM – see Reference 18 for more details.
- APMP – the Association of Proposal Management Professionals framework. The APMP (not to be confused with APM) framework is aimed specifically at proposal and bid management within an organisation and identifies a number of skills required for such activities. The APMP framework is owned and managed by the APMP – see Reference 19 for more details.

For purposes of brevity, only two will be considered here, but for a full exploration of these different frameworks, see Reference 38.

3.2.6.4   UKSPEC

It was stated earlier that the UKSPEC is the cornerstone of all technical competences in the UK. The UKSPEC is used as the basis for professional accreditation, such as CEng and CITP, and all UK professional bodies use it as part of their professional assessment. It is essential therefore that the UKSPEC is understood before any other framework is looked at. To put matters bluntly, if a framework does not map onto the concepts in UKSPEC, then it will not be recognised at a professional level.

The UKSPEC has a simple ontology that is shown in the diagram in Figure 3.19.

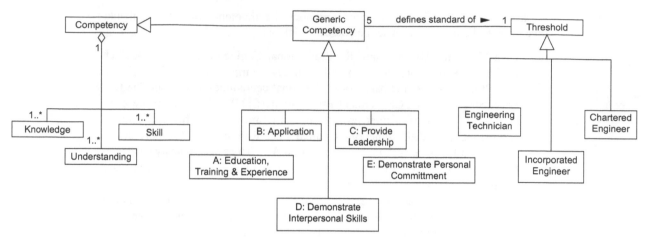

Figure 3.19   Summary of Competency-related concepts for UKSPEC

The diagram in Figure 3.19 shows the key concepts and terminology for the UKSPEC. It can be seen that 'Competency' is made up of the following concepts:

- 'Knowledge' that refers to having domain knowledge in a particular discipline or application area. For example, a university degree in engineering will provide a basic knowledge of engineering (the discipline) while experience in industry would also provide knowledge of the field (domain knowledge).
- 'Skill' that refers to the techniques, tools, methodologies and approaches that are employed in order to implement the knowledge. The skill depends upon having the knowledge in the first instance and really makes the knowledge useful, rather than knowledge for the sake of knowledge.
- 'Understanding' that refers to the ability to be able to apply the right knowledge and skills at the right time and to understand the implications for such use. This is the really difficult aspect of competence to get right. It involves understanding why the knowledge and skills have been employed and what benefits have been realised in doing so.

Competency may be thought of as existing in five 'Generic competency' categories, and these competencies are held at a particular level or 'Threshold' and, currently, there are three levels of recognition within the Engineering Council UK.

The high-level concepts contained within UKSPEC form a common pattern throughout many other frameworks.

3.2.6.5   INCOSE competencies framework

The focus of the framework is concerned with the concept of 'Systems Engineering Ability', which is described in the diagram in Figure 3.20.

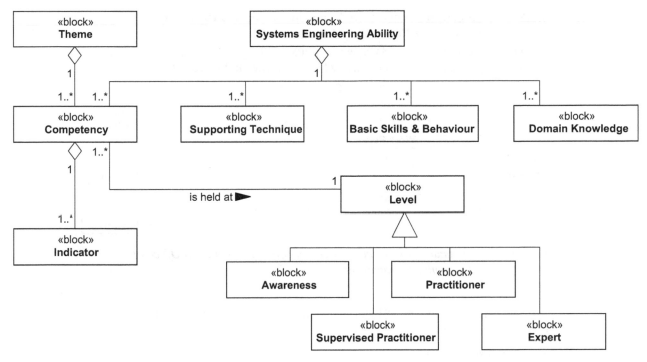

Figure 3.20   Summary of Competency-related concepts for INCOSE

The INCOSE competencies framework has a concept of 'Systems Engineering Ability', which may be broken down into four main areas:

- 'Supporting Technique'. A supporting technique is a specific technique that is used to support the main competencies.
- 'Basic Skills & Behaviour'. These represent the soft skills that are required in order to be a systems engineer.
- 'Domain Knowledge'. This knowledge is related directly to the domain in which the person is working.
- 'Competency'. The term, when used by INCOSE, refers to the core skills required for a systems engineer. Each 'Competency' is categorised by a 'Theme', of which there are three in total. Each 'Competency' is made up of one or more 'Indicator', which is measured to assess whether the 'Competency' has been achieved at the desired 'Level'.

When relating these concepts back to the UKSPEC, it should be noted that what INCOSE refers to as 'Systems Engineering Ability' the UKSPEC refers to as 'Competency'.

3.2.6.6 The Competence-related concepts as described by the US Office of Personnel Management

The US Office of Personnel Management (OPM) [39] identifies and defines a key set of concepts related to competence, which are shown in Figure 3.21.

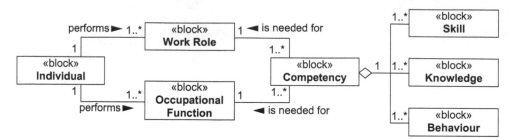

Figure 3.21   Summary of Competence-related concepts for the US Office of Personnel Management

The diagram in Figure 3.21 shows that the main key concept of 'Competency' is made up of three main elements:

- One or more 'Skill'
- One or more piece of 'Knowledge'
- One or more 'Behaviour'

This basic structure is very similar to that in many of the competency frameworks described in this section. Similarly, the 'Competency' itself is needed for both 'Work Role' and 'Occupational Function', a number of which are carried out by an 'Individual'.

3.2.6.7 The MBSE Ontology for Competence-related concepts

The diagram in Figure 3.22 summarises the Competence-related concepts that are defined as part of the MBSE Ontology.

The diagram here shows the MBSE Ontology for the main concepts that are related to Competence. These are defined as follows:

- 'Person' – a special type of 'Resource', an individual human, who exhibits 'Competence' that is represented by their 'Competency Profile'. A 'Person' also holds one or more 'Stakeholder Role'.
- 'Competence' – the ability exhibited by a 'Person' that is made up of a set of one or more individual 'Competency'.
- 'Competency' – the representation of a single skill that contributes towards making up a 'Competence'. Each 'Competency' is held at a 'Level' that describes the maturity of that 'Competency'. There are four 'Level' defined for the MBSE Ontology.
- 'Competency Profile' – a representation of the actual measured 'Competence' of a 'Person' and that is defined by one or more 'Competency'. An individual's

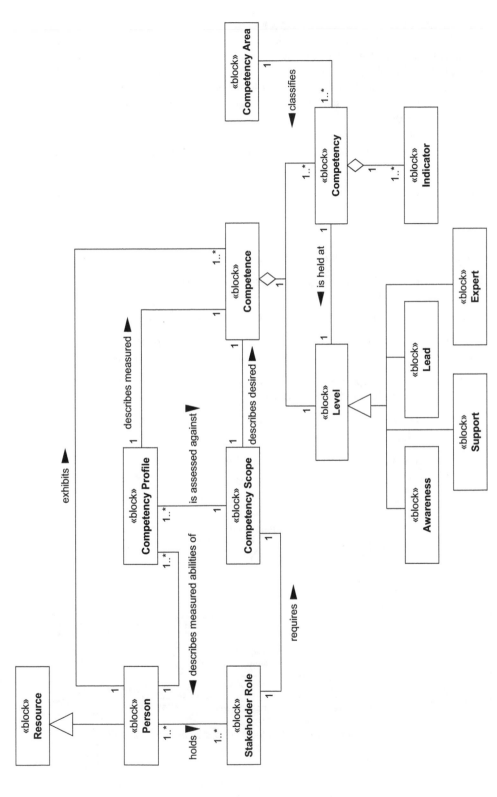

Figure 3.22 MBSE Ontology focused on Competence-related concepts

'competence' will usually be represented by one or more 'Competency Profile'. A 'Competency Profile' is the result of performing a competence assessment against a 'Competence Scope'.

- 'Competency Scope' – representation of the desired 'Competence' required for a specific 'Stakeholder Role' and that is defined by one or more 'Competency'.
- 'Stakeholder Role' – the role of a person, organisation or thing that has an interest in the system.
- 'Indicator' – a feature of a 'Competency' that describes knowledge, skill or attitude required to meet the 'Competency'. It is the 'Indicator' that is assessed as part of competency assessment.

The Competence-related concepts are strongly related to the Process-related concepts.

3.2.7   The Project concept

The concept of a Project is used in every organisation to describe the work that is actually done in order to develop and deliver Systems.

3.2.7.1   The Project-related concepts as described by the International Standards Organisation (ISO)

In ISO 15288 [1], the concept of a 'project' is well defined as:

'*(an) endeavour with defined start and finish criteria undertaken to create a product or service in accordance with specified resources and requirements*'.

There is also the concept of a higher-level, or collection of projects that is identified as a 'project portfolio' and is defined as:

'*(a) collection of projects that addresses the strategic objectives of the organization*'.

These concepts and terms were then collected together and are summarised in the diagram in Figure 3.23.

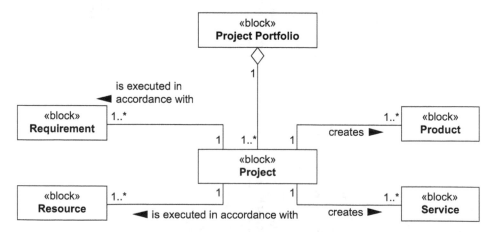

Figure 3.23   Summary of the Project-related concepts for ISO 15288

The diagram shows a summary of the ISO 15288 Project-related concepts. There is one ambiguous statement in this diagram: each 'Project' is executed in accordance with one or more 'Resource'. It is unclear from the standard exactly what is meant by the phrase 'in accordance with'.

3.2.7.2 The Project-related concepts as described by the Capability Maturity Model Integration (CMMI)

The CMMI also defines two basic terms associated with projects [3]. The basic concept of a project is defined as:

> '*a managed set of interrelated resources which delivers one or more products to a customer or end user. A project has a definite beginning (i.e., project start-up) and typically operates according to a plan. Such a plan is frequently documented and specifies what is to be delivered or implemented, the resources and funds to be used, the work to be done, and a schedule for doing the work. A project can be composed of projects.*'

Notice here that a 'project' itself can be made up of a number of projects, but there is also the concept of a 'program' that has a similar definition:

> '*(a) project (or) collection of related projects and the infrastructure that supports them, including objectives, methods, activities, plans, and success measures*'.

In terms of what a 'Project' can deliver, CMMI identifies two possibilities:

- 'Product' – '*a work product that is intended for delivery to a customer or end user*'
- 'Service' – '*a product that is intangible and non-storable*'

These concepts and terms were then collected together and are summarised in the diagram in Figure 3.24.

The diagram here shows the summary of the key concepts for CMMI and it can be seen that there is much in common with the other major sources here, in terms of the terms 'Project', 'Program', 'Resource', etc.

3.2.7.3 The Project-related concepts as described by the US Project Management Institute (PMI)

The Project Management Institute (PMI) is the world's largest organisation for project management, with chapters across the world. The PMI has its own body of knowledge, known as the Project Management Body of Knowledge (PMBOK) [40].

The concept of a project in the PMBOK is defined as:

> '*A temporary endeavour undertaken to create a unique product, service, or result*'.

And then defines a program as:

> '*A group of related projects managed in a coordinated way to obtain benefits and control not available from managing them individually.*

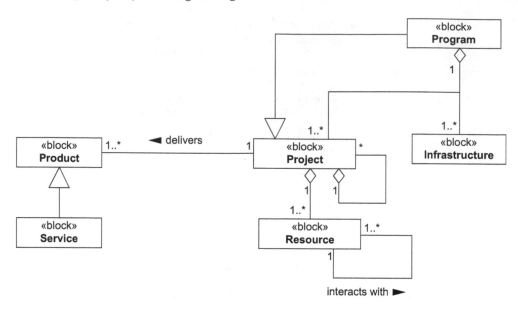

Figure 3.24   Summary of Project-related concepts for CMMI

> *Programs may include elements of related work outside of the scope of the discrete projects in the program.'*

There is a strong relationship between the terms Project and Program here, as can be expected, and this can be summarised in the diagram in Figure 3.25.

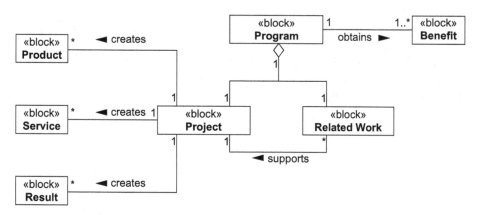

Figure 3.25   Summary of Project-related concepts for the US Project Management Institute

The diagram shows the summary of the main concepts in the PMI PMBOK and it can be seen that there are many similarities with the other source references used in this section.

3.2.7.4 The Project-related concepts as described by the Association for Project Management (APM) Institute

The Association for Project Management (APM) is a UK-based professional body that is dedicated to promoting and furthering project and programme management to its members [18]. The APM has its own body of knowledge that forms the basis for its own qualification and accreditation scheme.

The APM body of knowledge defines a 'project' as:

'A unique, transient endeavour undertaken to achieve planned objectives'.

The concept of a 'programme' is defined as:

'A group of related projects and change management activities that together achieve beneficial change for an organisation'.

Based on these definitions, the diagram in Figure 3.26 was generated.

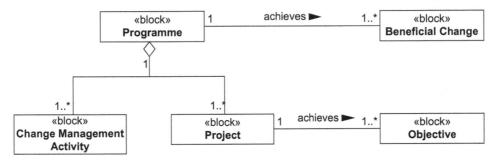

Figure 3.26 Summary of Project-related concepts for the Association for Project Management (APM) Institute

The diagram shows that, once again, there is very strong consensus between many of the previous sources and the definitions in the APM body of knowledge.

3.2.7.5 MBSE Ontology definition for Project-related concepts

Based on these knowledge sources, the area of MBSE Ontology shown in Figure 3.27 was defined.

The diagram in Figure 3.27 shows the MBSE Ontology for the main concepts that are related to the Process. These are defined as follows:

- 'Project' – One or more 'Project' is run by an 'Organisational Unit' in order to produce one or more 'System'.
- 'Programme' – a special type of 'Project' that is itself made up of one or more 'Project'.
- 'Organisational Unit' – a special type of 'Organisation' that itself can make up part of an 'Organisation'. An 'Organisational Unit' also runs one or more 'Project' and will have its own 'Organisational Context'.
- 'Organisation' – a collection of one or more 'Organisational Unit'. It runs one or more 'Project' and will have its own 'Organisational Context'.

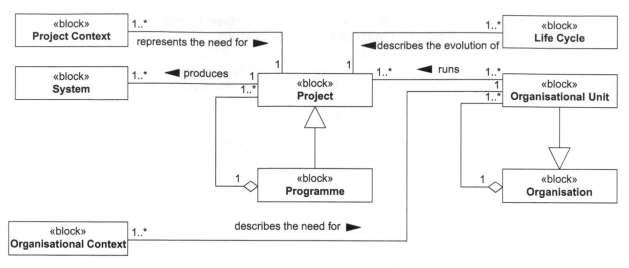

Figure 3.27   MBSE Ontology focused on Project-related concepts

This subset of the MBSE Ontology also has relationships with the 'Need', 'System' and 'Life Cycle' subsets.

3.3   Summary

All of the key concepts associated with MBSE that have been identified for the purposes of this book have been:

- Identified, by the very fact that they exist on the MBSE Ontology.
- Defined, by providing a single text-based definition that uses terms from the MBSE Ontology.
- Related together, to ensure consistency of definition between the terms.
- Mapped, to ensure that all definitions have good provenance and can be traced back to best-practice sources.

The MBSE Ontology covers seven main areas of:

- System-related concepts, which cover the basic concepts associated with System, Systems of Systems, Constituent Systems, etc.
- Need-related concepts, which cover all concepts associated with System Needs, such as Requirements, Capabilities and Goals.
- Architecture-related concepts, where the description and structure of Architectures using Architectural Frameworks are discussed.
- Life Cycle-related concepts, where different Life Cycles and Life Cycle Models are discussed, along with the interactions between Life Cycles.
- Process-related concepts, where the structure, execution and responsibility of Processes are discussed.

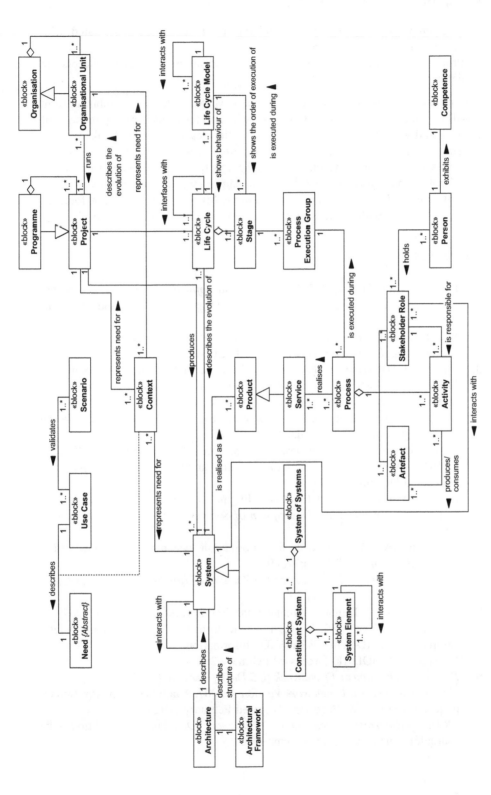

Figure 3.28   The complete MBSE Ontology – simplified

- Competence-related concepts, where the ability of people associated with Stakeholder Roles is defined.
- Project-related concepts, where Project and Programme-related concepts are defined.

Each of these areas focuses on a specific area of MBSE that, when combined, form the MBSE Ontology. The MBSE Ontology will form the basis for the remainder of this book and will drive all of the MBSE activities described in the book.

The diagram in Figure 3.28 shows a simplified version of the MBSE Ontology that consists of all of the smaller, focused diagrams that have been described so far in this book. Some information has been omitted from this diagram for the purposes of brevity and readability, but a full version of the MBSE Ontology can be found in Appendix A, along with a definition for each term in the form of a tabular glossary.

References

1. ISO/IEC. *ISO/IEC 15288:2008 Systems and Software Engineering – System Life Cycle Processes*. 2nd edn. International Organisation for Standardisation; 2008
2. INCOSE. *Systems Engineering Handbook – A Guide for System Life Cycle Processes and Activities. Version 3.2.2*. INCOSE; 2011
3. *CMMI for Development, Version 1.3*. Carnegie Mellon University Software Engineering Institute; November 2010. http://www.sei.cmu.edu/library/abstracts/reports/10tr033.cfm [Accessed 16 February 2011]
4. Office of the Under Secretary of Defense. *Systems Engineering Guide for Systems of Systems*. USA DoD; August 2008
5. *Systems and Software Engineering – Architecture Description ISO/IEC/IEEE 42010*. Available from http://www.iso-architecture.org/ieee-1471/cm/ [Accessed November 2011]
6. Institute of Electrical and Electronic Engineers. *IEEE 1471, Recommended Practice for Architectural Description of Software-Intensive Systems*. IEEE; 2000
7. Zachman J.A. 'A framework for information systems architecture'. *IBM Systems Journal*. 1987;**26**(3):276–92
8. Zachman J. *Concise Definition of the Zachman Framework*. Zachman International; 2008
9. The Ministry of Defence Architectural Framework. *Ministry of Defence Architectural framework*. 2010. Available from http://www.mod.uk/DefenceInternet/AboutDefence/WhatWeDo/Information Management/MODAF/ [Accessed February 2012]
10. *DoDAF Architectural Framework (US DoD), Version 1.5*; 2007
11. *NATO Architectural Framework Version 3*. 2007. Available from http://www.nhqc3s.nato.int/HomePage.asp [Accessed February 2012]
12. *TRAK – Enterprise Architecture Framework*. Available from http://trak.sourceforge.net/ (accessed November 2012)

13. Unified profile for the Department of Defense Architectural Framework (DoDAF), Ministry of Defence Architectural Framework (MODAF). *OMG Standard*; 2011. Available from http://www.omg.org/spec/UPDM/ [Accessed February 2012]

14. *The Open Group Architectural Framework (TOGAF), Version 9*. Available from http://www.opengroup.org/architecture/togaf9-doc/arch/ [Accessed February 2012]

15. The UK Standard for Professional Engineering Competence (UK-SPEC). Available from http://www.engc.org.uk/professional-qualifications/standards/uk-spec [Accessed March 2012]

16. INCOSE Competencies Framework. Available from http://www.incoseon-line.org.uk/Groups/SE_Competencies/Main.aspx?CatID=Groups [Accessed March 2012]

17. Skills Framework for the Information Age. Available from http://www.sfia.org.uk/ [Accessed March 2012]

18. APM Competence Framework. Available from http://www.apm.org.uk/ [Accessed March 2012]

19. APMP Competency Framework. Available from http://www.apmp.org/ [accessed March 2012]

20. *OMG Systems Modeling Language (OMG SysML™) Version 1.2*. Object Management Group; 2010. Available from http://www.omg.org/spec/SysML/1.2 [Accessed March 2012]

21. Holt J., Perry S. *SysML for Systems Engineering*. Stevenage, UK: IET; 2008

22. Unified Modelling Language. Available from http://www.uml.org [Accessed February 2012]

23. Holt J. *UML for Systems Engineering*. 2nd edn. Stevenage, UK: IET; 2005

24. Service-oriented Architecture Modelling Language. Available from http://www.omg.org/spec/SoaML [Accessed February 2012]

25. *Business Process Model and Notation*. Available from http://www.omg.org/cgi-bin/doc?bmi/2007-6-5 [Accessed February 2012]

26. Holt J., Perry S., Brownsword M. *Model-Based Requirements Engineering*. Stevenage, UK: IET; 2011

27. Holt J., Perry S. *Modelling Enterprise Architectures*. Stevenage, UK: IET; 2010

28. Dickerson C.E., Mavris D.N. *Architecture and Principles of Systems Engineering*. Florida, USA: CRC Press; 2009

29. Lewis G.A., Morris E., Place P., Simanta S., Smith D.B. 'Requirements engineering for systems of systems'. *IEEE SySCon 2009 – 3rd Annual IEEE International Systems Conference*. Vancouver, Canada: IEEE; March 2009

30. Maier M.W. 'Architecting principles for systems-of-systems'. *Systems Engineering*. 1998; 1(4):325–45

31. Pyster A., Olwell D., Hutchison N., Enck S., Anthony J., Henry D., *et al.* (eds.). 2012. *Guide to the Systems Engineering Body of Knowledge (SEBoK) Version 1.0.1*. Hoboken, NJ: The Trustees of the Stevens Institute of Technology; 2012. Available from http://www.sebokwiki.org [Accessed December 2012]

32. Body of Knowledge and Curriculum for Advanced Systems Engineering. Available from http://www.bkcase.org/ [Accessed December 2012]

33. *OED Online.* Available from http://oxforddictionaries.com/definition/requirement [Accessed March 2012]

34. Rumbaugh J., Jacobson I., Booch G. *The Unified Modelling Language Reference Manual.* 2nd edn. Boston, USA: Addison Wesley; 2004

35. *ISO 9001:2008 Quality management systems – Requirements.* International Standards Organisation; 2008

36. *DND/CF Architecture Framework (DNDAF).* Available from http://www.img-ggi.forces.gc.ca/pub/af-ca/index-eng.asp [Accessed September 2012]

37. *Survey of Architecture Framework.* Available from http://www.iso-architecture.org/ieee-1471/afs/frameworks-table.html [Accessed September 2012]

38. Holt J., Perry S. *A Pragmatic Guide to Competency.* Swindon, UK: BCS; 2011

39. *Human Capital Assessment and Accountability Framework (HCAAF) Resource Center – Glossary.* U.S. Office of Personnel Management (OPM). Available from http://www.opm.gov/hcaaf_resource_center/glossary.asp [Accessed December 2012]

40. *A Guide to the Project Management Body of Knowledge (PMBOK® Guide),* 4th edn. Newtown Square, PA: Project Management Institute (PMI); 2008

Part 2

Modelling

P2.1 Overview

This part of the book is structured according to the diagram in Figure P2.1.

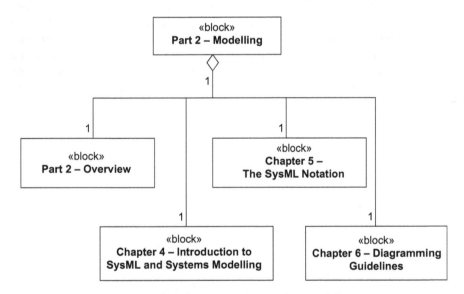

Figure P2.1 Structure of 'Part 2 – Modelling'

Part 2 introduces the fundamentals of modelling, the notation that will be used throughout the book and then a guide on the style of modelling adopted throughout. It comprises three main chapters.

- 'Chapter 4 – Introduction to SysML and systems modelling'. This chapter provides a high-level introduction to the whole field of systems modelling by introducing and describing the key concepts involved with modelling any kind of system using any notation. Once this has been established, the modelling notation that will be used throughout the rest of the book, the systems modelling language, SysML, is introduced. The main aspects of a SysML model, the structure and behaviour, are then introduced and discussed using two of the nine diagrams that make up the SysML.

- 'Chapter 5 – The SysML Notation'. This chapter takes an in-depth look at the SysML notation including its structure, its diagrams and how to use them on an example system. This chapter also discusses the underlying meta-model that gives the SysML its rigour and that is itself modelled.
- 'Chapter 6 – Diagramming Guidelines'. This chapter defines how the SysML will be used throughout the book by defining a number of styles that will be adopted. This will include the use of sentence cases and font styles for different aspects of the SysML that allow all of the models presented in this book to have the same look and feel.

A good understanding of the basics of modelling and the SysML notation is essential for implementing the approach in this book. Any readers new to systems modelling should treat this part of the book as essential reading.

Experienced modellers may be tempted to miss out this part of the book, particularly if they have read some of our other books, but there are a few points to bear in mind. This part of the book describes the latest version of SysML, version 1.3, which contains many changes from the versions described in previous books. Also, the style guide is completely new to this book and is something that even experienced modellers may use to enhance the way that they model. Even when you are comfortable with modelling and the SysML, this part forms an excellent reference for future modelling.

Chapter 4

Introduction to SysML and systems modelling

I'm no model lady. A model's just an imitation of the real thing.

Mac West (1893–1980)

4.1   Introduction

This is a book concerned with model-based systems engineering (MBSE), and thus modelling is fundamental to everything that is presented in it. It makes sense, therefore, before we consider MBSE in detail in Parts 3–5, to first consider the modelling aspects.

This chapter discusses why modelling is so important in the context of the "three evils" of engineering, briefly discusses the history of the systems engineering modelling language (SysML), establishes the basic requirements for modelling, introduces the concept of modelling and introduces to the SysML that is used as the modelling language throughout the rest of the book. Only the briefest of syntax will be looked at in this chapter – for a more full description of the SysML syntax see Chapter 5.

4.2   Why we model?

It is vital to understand the reasons why we must model things. In order to justify the need for models, three simple examples will be considered. These examples aim to justify modelling in general terms and not simply with regard to systems engineering, which demonstrates the need for flexibility when modelling – indeed, the three examples used here are not directly related to systems engineering. The examples are taken from Reference 1 and were created by the master of modelling and co-developer of the Unified Modelling Language (UML) on which the SysML is based, Grady Booch. They are based on Booch's doghouse, house and office block.

4.2.1   The kennel (doghouse)

For the first example of modelling, consider the example of building a kennel, a small house where dogs can spend some time outside without being exposed to the elements. The basic Requirement for a kennel is to keep the dog happy. This will include building a structure that is waterproof and large enough to fit the dog inside. In order to fit inside, there must be an entrance in the kennel that is larger than the dog itself. The inside should also be large enough for the dog to be able to turn around in order to leave. Dogs are particularly bad at walking backwards, which makes this last point crucial. Finally, the dog should be comfortable enough to sleep in the kennel and thus some bedding or cushions may be in order.

Figure 4.1   The kennel (doghouse)

If you were about to build the kennel shown in Figure 4.1, then consider for a moment the basic skills and resources that you would require. You would be wise to have:

- Basic materials such as timber and nails. The quality is not really that important as it is only for a dog. This might involve looking for any old pieces of wood around the house or even making a trip to a hardware store.
- The money needed to pay for the kennel would be your own, but is unlikely to be a large outlay. In terms of your personal income, it would be a fraction of a week's salary – perhaps the cost of a social evening out.
- Some basic tools, such as a hammer, a saw and a tape measure. Again, the quality of the tools need not be wonderful, providing they get the job done.
- Some basic building skills. You need not be a skilled craftsman, but basic hand-to-eye co-ordination would be an advantage.

These relate directly to the concepts of Person, Process and Tool discussed throughout this book. The Person who builds the kennel must have the necessary skills and basic carpentry knowledge (Competence) along with material and equipment (the Tools) to carry out the job (execute the Process). If you have this, then at the end of the day (or weekend), you will probably end up with a kennel that is functional and in which the dog would be happy to shelter from the rain.

If the kennel was somewhat less than functional and the dog was not very happy with its new accommodation, you could always start again (after destroying the first attempt) and try a bit harder, learning from past mistakes. It would also be possible to destroy the kennel and then to deny all knowledge of ever having built one in the first place, thus avoiding embarrassment later. Alternatively, you could get rid of the dog and buy a less demanding pet such as a tortoise, as there is no need to build a kennel for an animal that carries its own accommodation on its back. After all, the dog is in no position to argue or complain.

This is Booch's first example of modelling: the kennel or, for our trans-Atlantic readers, the doghouse.

4.2.2   The house

Consider now, maybe based on the resounding success of your kennel, that you were planning to build a house for your family. This time the Requirements would be somewhat different. There would need to be adequate space for the whole family in which to sit and relax. In addition, there would have to be adequate sleeping arrangements in the number of bedrooms that are chosen. There would need to be a kitchen, maybe a dining room and one or more bathrooms and toilets. As there will be more than one room, some thought should be given to the layout of the rooms in terms of where they are in the house and where they are in relation to one another.

Figure 4.2   The house

If you were to build a house (Figure 4.2) for your family, you would (hopefully) approach the whole exercise differently from that of the kennel:

- You would have to start with some basic materials and tools, but the quality of these resources would no doubt be of a higher concern than those used for the kennel. It would not be good enough to simply drive down to a local hardware store and pick up some materials as the quantity would need to be far greater and it would not be possible to guess, with any degree of accuracy, the amount of materials required.
- Your family would also be far more demanding and vocal than the dog. Rather than simply guessing your family's Requirements, it would be more appropriate to ask them their opinions and perhaps get a professional architect in to listen to and discuss their needs.
- Unless you have built many houses before, it would be a good idea to draw up some plans. If you were hiring skilled craftsmen to do the job, you would certainly have to draw up plans in order to communicate your requirements to the builders. These plans may require some input from an architect in order that they achieve a standard that may be used effectively by the people who will be building the house.
- The house would also have to meet building regulations and require planning permission. This may involve contacting the local council or government representative and possibly applying for permission to build. This in turn would almost certainly involve submitting plans for approval before any work could be started.
- The money for the house would probably be yours, and thus you would have to monitor the work and ensure that people stick to the plans in order to get the job done in time, within budget and to meet your family's original requirements. The scale of the financial outlay is likely to be in the order of several years' salary and would probably be borrowed from a bank or building society and would thus have to be paid back, regardless of the outcome of the project.

Again, we can relate these to the Person, Process and Tool concepts discussed throughout this book. A number of people are involved, such as builders, architects and electricians, who must have the necessary skills and knowledge (the Competence) along with material and equipment (the Tools) to carry out the job (i.e. to execute the various Processes). However, their skills don't just relate to building or wiring a house but must include those needed to work with and communicate with other people, both the other craftsmen involved and the customer so that they can understand all the different requirements governing what they do on the job. The Processes they follow are necessarily more complex, since legislation, such as building and wiring regulations, now has to be followed that governs how they do their job.

If the house turns out not to suit the Requirements, the consequences would be more serious than in the case of the kennel. The house cannot be knocked down and started again as the kennel could, because considerably more time and money would have gone into the house building. Similarly, you cannot simply get a less demanding family (in most cases) and living with the consequences of failure is not worth thinking about!

This is Booch's second example: the house.

4.2.3   The office block

Taking the two building projects that have been discussed so far even further, imagine that your ambition knows no bounds and that you decide to build an entire office block (Figure 4.3).

Figure 4.3   The office block

Consider once more the resources that would be required for this, the third and final building project:

- It would be infinitely stupid to attempt to build an office block by yourself.
- The materials required for building an office block would be in significantly larger quantities than the house. The materials would be bought direct from source and may even need to be brought in from specialist suppliers, perhaps even in different counties or countries.
- You will probably be using other people's money and thus the requirements for the building will probably be their requirements. In addition, their requirements will no doubt change once you have started building the office block.
- More permissions are required to build an office block than a house and many more regulations must be considered. Consider, for example, environmental conditions that the office building may have to meet – the building must not

block anyone's light, it may be required to blend in with its surroundings, or it may have to conform to so-called 'carbon footprint' legislation.

- You will have to carry out extensive planning and be part of a larger group who are responsible for the building. Many teams will be involved from different areas of work (builders, plumbers, electricians, architects, etc.), all of whom must intercommunicate.

Unsurprisingly, these points again relate to the Person, Process and Tool concepts. On a project of this size there are many more different kinds of Person involved carrying out much more complex Processes using far more (and more specialised) Tools and material than is the case when building a house. If you get the right teams involved and enjoy a degree of luck, you will produce the desired building.

If the project does not meet the investor's Requirements, you would face severe repercussions, including the potential of no further work and the loss of reputation.

This is Booch's third example: the office block.

4.2.4   The point

These three examples from Booch may seem a little strange and somewhat trivial at first glance; however, there is a very serious and fundamental point behind all of this.

Nobody in their right mind would attempt to build an office block with basic Do It Yourself (DIY) skills. In addition, there is the question of resources, and not only in terms of the materials needed. In order to build an office block, you would need the knowledge to access the necessary human resources (including people such as architects, builders and crane operators), plenty of time and plenty of money.

The strange and worrying thing is that many people will approach building a complex system with the skills and resources of a kennel-builder, without actually knowing if it is a kennel, house or office block that is required. When contemplating any complex system, you should assume that it will be, or has the potential to turn into, an office block building. Do not approach any project with a "kennel" mentality. If you approach a project as if it were an office block and it turns out to be a kennel, you will end up with a very well made kennel that is the envy of all canines. If, however, you approach a project as if it were a kennel and it turns out to be an office block, the result will be pure disaster!

One of the reasons why it is so easy to misjudge the size and complexity of a project is that, in many cases, many elements of the System will not be tangible or comprehensible. Consider, for example, a smartphone. Who can tell, simply by looking at these increasingly ubiquitous devices, what components it is made of? And even if the device is dismantled in order to understand the hardware used in its construction, what about its functionality? Yes, you will expect it to function as a phone and a camera, a web browser and music player. But what else? With the tens of thousands of applications available for the more popular models, it is impossible to know, without powering-up the device and looking to see what is installed and trying the applications out to understand what they do, just what else the smartphone is capable of. Also, what about the infrastructure needed to support the creation and delivery of such applications, let alone that needed to allow the phone to be used for its most fundamental purpose of making phone calls? How complicated is the infrastructure? Who runs it? How is it paid for? The fact is that all projects that involve complex systems will have an intangible element about them, whether it is a control system, a process or whatever.

The important term that is used here is "complexity" rather than size, as size is not necessarily a reflection of the complexity of a system. The next section discusses complexity in more detail.

4.3 The three evils

Projects fail and disasters occur for many reasons. However, there are three underlying reasons why things go wrong, the "three evils" of complexity, a lack of understanding and communication issues.

4.3.1 Complexity

The concept of complexity will be illustrated in two ways – one that emphasises the importance of relationships and one that uses a brontosaurus to visualise the nature of the evolution of complexity.

For the first example, consider five boxes that may represent five elements within a System, as shown in Figure 4.4(a). Each element may represent almost anything, ranging from a text sentence that represents a Requirement, to an assembly that makes up a System, to users that relate to a System. Each of these elements may very well be understood by whoever is reading the diagram, but this does not necessarily mean that the System itself is understood.

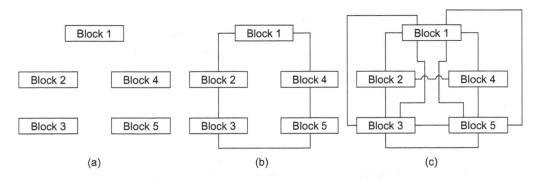

Figure 4.4 Complexity manifesting through relationships

Consider now Figure 4.4(b) and it is quite clear that this diagram is more complex than the previous one, although nothing has changed in the elements themselves, only the relationships between them.

Consider now Figure 4.4(c) where it is, again, obvious that this diagram is more complex than its predecessor and far more complex than the first.

In fact, the more relationships are added between the System Elements, the higher the complexity of the overall System. More and more lines could be drawn onto this diagram and the complexity will increase dramatically, despite the fact that the complexity of each of the five elements has not actually increased.

The point that is being communicated here is that just because someone understands each element within a System, this does not mean that the System itself is understood. The complexity of a System manifests itself by relationships between things – in this case the System Elements. It should be borne in mind, however, that these elements may exist at any level of abstraction of the System, depending on what they represent; therefore, the complexity may manifest itself at any point in the System. The complexity of the whole of the System is certainly higher than the complexity of the sum of its parts.

This may be thought of as being able to see both the woods and the trees.

The second way that complexity is illustrated is through the concept of the "Brontosaurus of Complexity". In this slightly bizarre analogy, the magnitude of the complexity is analogous to the thickness of the brontosaurus, in that the complexity of a System at the outset is represented by the dinosaur's head and, as the Project Life Cycle progresses, this complexity increases (travelling down the neck), increases even further (through the belly) before reducing and finally ending up at the tail of the brontosaurus.

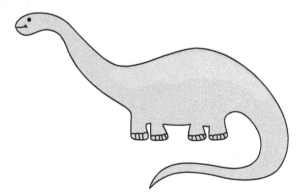

Figure 4.5   A brontosaurus

This fits with the shape of the brontosaurus, which is "*thin at one end, much much thicker in the middle, and then thin again at the far end*" [2]. The perceived complexity of a Project is almost always low to begin with, but balloons during the analysis of a Project, as the understanding of the full impact of the Requirements and the constraints is fully understood. By the time the problem is fully understood, a Project is well and truly in the "belly of the brontosaurus", whereas when the design begins and becomes optimised, then the Project should be heading towards the "tail of the brontosaurus". By applying the brontosaurus of complexity analogy, it is shown that one must go from the head (initial ideas and Requirements) to the tail (System) but that it is impossible to do this without going through the belly of the brontosaurus.

Consider the situation when a Project is at the head of the brontosaurus, then this may be visualised as the illustration in Figure 4.4(a). As the complexity of the Project increases and we move down the neck of the brontosaurus, the complexity increases, as shown in Figure 4.4(b). In fact, the more relationships are added between the System Elements (and, hence, the more interactions between them), the closer to the belly of the brontosaurus we actually get.

Many Projects will fail because the Project never left the belly or, in some cases, was left even higher up in the neck. If a Project stays in the head or neck, then there is a great danger of the System being oversimplified and the complexity inherent in the System is never uncovered until it is too late. If the Project remains in the belly, however, then the complexity has been realised, but it has not been managed effectively.

Unfortunately, when a Project is in the belly of the brontosaurus, then it may seem to the Project personnel that the world is at an end and that there is no understanding of the Project as a whole. Successfully developing a System is about being able to see the brontosaurus as a whole and that there is life after the belly.

In a final twist to this analogy, there is major difference between complexity and the brontosaurus. Complexity is difficult to visualise, but definitely exists in any System. A brontosaurus, on the other hand, is easy to visualise (see Figure 4.5) but never actually existed (it was demonstrated in 1974 that the brontosaurus was actually the body of the Apatosaurus and the head of the Camarasaurus).

4.3.2   Lack of understanding

A lack of understanding may occur at any Stage of the System Life Cycle and also may occur during any Process. Consider the following examples of a lack of understating affecting a Project.

- A lack of understating may occur during the conception Stage of a Project, during a Requirement-related Process. If the Requirements are not stated in a concise and unambiguous fashion (or, in reality, as unambiguous possible), then this lack of understanding will cascade throughout the whole Project. It is widely accepted that mistakes made during early Stages of the Life Cycle cost many times more to fix during later Stages of the Life Cycle, so it makes sense to get things right as early as possible [3].
- A lack of understanding may occur during the development Stage of a Project, during an analysis-related Process. For example, there may be a lack of domain

knowledge during analysis that may lead someone to state false assumptions, or to actually get something completely wrong due to insufficient knowledge. Again, uncorrected mistakes here will lead to larger problems further down the development Life Cycle.

- A lack of understanding may occur during the operational Stage of a Project, during an operation-related Process. Incorrect usage of a System may lead to a System failure or disaster. For example, people not following safety procedures and people not using the correct tools.

Of course, these examples are a merely a representation of some ways that a lack of understanding can manifest itself in a System – there are many other places in the Life Cycle where problems may occur.

4.3.3   Communication

The third of the three evils is the problem of communication or, more correctly, ineffective communication. The richness and complexity of human communication is what separates humans from other species. One of the earliest recorded examples of Project failure is that of the Tower of Babel, as described wonderfully by Fred Brookes [4]. The Tower of Babel started life as a very successful Project and the first few Stages of the Project went off without a hitch and the Project was running on schedule, within budget and was meeting all the Project Requirements. However, one of the key stakeholder's Requirements was not considered properly, which was to cause the downfall of the Project. When the stakeholder intervened in a divine fashion, the communication between Project personnel was effectively destroyed.

Communication problems may occur at any level of an Organisation or Project, for example:

- Person-to-person level. If individuals cannot communicate on a personal level, then there is little hope for Project success. This may be because people have different spoken languages, technical backgrounds or even a clash of personalities.
- Group-to-group level. Groups, or Organisational Units within an Organisation, must be able to communicate effectively with one another. These groups may be from different technical areas, such as hardware and software groups, or the groups may span boundaries, such as management and technical groups, or marketing and engineering. Such groups often use language specific to themselves, making inter-group communication difficult.
- Organisation-to-organisation level. Different Organisations speak different languages – each will have their own specific terms for different concepts, as well as having an industry-specific terminology. When two Organisations are working in a customer–supplier relationship, the onus is often on the supplier to speak the customer's language so that communication can be effective, rather than the customer having to speak the supplier's language. After all, if the supplier won't make an effort to speak the customer's language, it is quite likely that they will not retain customers for very long.

- System-to-system level. Even non-human Systems must be able to communicate with one another. Technical Systems must be able to communicate with technical Systems, but also with financial Systems, accountancy Systems, environmental Systems, etc.
- Any combination of the above. Just to make matters even more confusing, just about any combination of the above communication types is also possible.

These problems, therefore, lead to ambiguities in interpreting any sort of communication, whether it is a spoken language or an application-specific or technical language.

4.3.4 The vicious triangle

Having established that these three evils exist, matters become even worse. Each of these three evils does not exist in isolation, but will feed into one another. Therefore, unmanaged complexity will lead to a lack of understanding and communication problems. Communication problems will lead to unidentified complexity and a lack of understanding. Finally, a lack of understanding will lead to communication problems and complexity.

The three evils, therefore, form a triangle of evil that is impossible to eliminate. In fact, the best that one may hope for is to address each of these evils individually when looking at any view of a system.

4.4 What is SysML?

SysML is defined on the website of the OMG (the Object Management Group – the industry standards body which manages and configures the SysML) as '*a general-purpose graphical modeling language for specifying, analyzing, designing, and verifying complex systems that may include hardware, software, information, personnel, procedures, and facilities. In particular, the language provides graphical representations with a semantic foundation for modeling system requirements, behavior, structure, and parametrics*' [5].

The language originated from an initiative between the OMG and the International Council on Systems Engineering (INCOSE) in 2003 to adapt the UML for systems engineering applications. For more on the history of SysML, see Section 4.4.2. The primary audience for SysML is systems engineers and the SysML is intended to provide a general-purpose systems engineering modelling language.

4.4.1 SysML's Relationship with UML

The SysML is based on the UML, a general-purpose graphical modelling language aimed at software engineers and which, on its appearance in 1997, represented a major unification of the large number of such languages that sprang up in the late 1980s and early 1990s.

The UML defines 13 types of diagram that allow the requirements, behaviour and structure of a software system to be defined. Because of its appearance the

UML has been increasingly adopted for use outside the software field, and is now widely used for such things as systems engineering and process modelling.

Despite this growing use of UML for systems engineering there was still a perceived need for a tailored version of UML that was aimed specifically at systems engineers, with some of the elements and diagrams of UML considered to be aimed more at software systems removed. The result of this perceived need is the SysML, which has 9 diagrams compared to the 13 of UML.

So what is the relationship between SysML and UML? Figure 4.6 illustrates the overlap between the two languages.

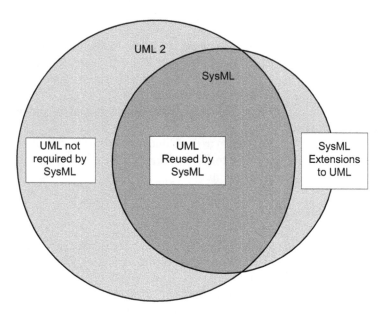

Figure 4.6   The relationship between SysML and UML

As can be seen in Figure 4.6, SysML makes use of much of the UML. However, some parts of the UML were considered to be not required by SysML. In particular the following diagrams are not used: *object diagram, deployment diagram, component diagram, communication diagram, timing diagram* and *interaction overview diagram.*

In addition, SysML adds some new diagrams and constructs not found in UML: the *parametric diagram,* the *requirement diagram, required* and *provided features* and *flow properties.* Those parts of the UML that are reused by UML are also subject to some changes to make the notation more suitable for systems engineering, for example replacing the concept of the *class* with that of the *block.*

Although the *object diagram* does not exist in SysML, *instance specifications* (the SysML term for UML *objects*) can be shown on a *block definition diagram.* Also, although *component diagrams* and *components* do not exist in SysML, the SysML *block* has aspects of both the *class* and the *component*, and the *block definition diagram* can be considered a combination of the *class diagram* and *component diagrams*.

Given the close connection between UML and SysML, the reader should not be surprised to learn that it is possible to use the SysML concepts in UML. Appendix D gives information on how to do this.

4.4.2 A brief history of SysML

SysML has undergone a long and tedious evolution, with a history extending back to 2003 when the OMG issued the "UML for Systems Engineering Request for Proposal" following a decision by INCOSE to customise UML for systems engineering applications.

In response to this request for proposal (RFP) there were several major drafts of SysML, which differed in terms of the content and concepts. At one point, the SysML team split into two groups, each led by a different CASE (Computer-Aided Systems/Software Engineering) tool vendor, which both produced separate specifications for the standard. For a time, in late 2005 and early 2006 both of these versions of SysML were in use by different early adopters of the language. In February 2006 one of these specifications was chosen as the basis for the official SysML by the OMG. Version 1.0 of the language was published in September 2007, since then three further versions have been released. A (very) brief summary of the various versions of SysML is given in Table 4.1. For a full discussion of the history of SysML leading up to version 1.0, see Reference 7.

As can be seen from Table 4.1, the most significant changes to the language took place in version 1.2, with the addition of the hitherto nonsensically missing ability to model *instance specifications*, and in the latest edition of the language, version 1.3, with a major change to the way SysML supports the definition and modelling of *ports*. In the opinion of the authors, the change in version 1.2 was long overdue, but most of the changes in version 1.3 smack somewhat of change for change sake.

Having discussed the relationship between SysML and UML and considered some aspects of its history it is now time to look at modelling in more detail.

Table 4.1 Summary of major differences between SysML versions

Version	Publication date	Major differences from previous version
1.3	June 2012	Major change to *ports*: removal of *standard ports* and *flow ports* and *flow specifications* and replacement with *full ports* and *proxy ports* and *flow properties*; support for *nested ports*; support for *provided* and *required features*
1.2	June 2010	Addition of *instance specifications*; change to *conjugated flow port* notation
1.1	December 2008	No significant changes
1.0	September 2007	Initial version

4.5   Modelling

This section introduces a definition of modelling and some of the principles associated with it that form the foundations for the rest of the book. Modelling allows us to identify complexity, aid understanding and improve communication – the core abilities needed when adopting a model-based approach to systems engineering.

4.5.1   Defining modelling

In order to understand modelling, it is important to define it. We define a model as a simplification of reality [1]. It is important to simplify reality in order to understand the System. This is because, as human beings, we cannot comprehend complexity [6].

If a model is a simplification of reality, there are many things then that may be thought of as a model:

- Mathematical models, which allow reasoning about the System to be performed. A mathematical model can range from equations that represent different aspects of a System to formal specifications, using specialised formal methods, that may be used as part of a formal analysis or proof.
- Physical models, such as mock-ups, which may be used to provide a picture of what the final System will look like or may be used as part of a physical simulation or analysis.
- Visual models, such as drawings and plans, which may be used as a template for creation or the basis of analysis.
- Text models, such as written specifications, which are perhaps the most widely used of the Tools at our disposal. Regarding text as a model can be initially quite surprising but the second that we start to describe something in words, we are simplifying it in order to understand it.

This is by no means an exhaustive list, but it conveys the general message.

It is important to model so that we can identify complexity, increase our understanding and communicate in an unambiguous (or as unambiguous-as-possible) manner.

In order to model effectively, it is essential to have a common language that may be used to carry out the modelling. There are many modelling approaches that exist, including graphical, mathematical and textual, but, regardless of the approach taken, there are a number of Requirements for any modelling language:

- The choice of model
- The level of abstraction
- Connection to reality
- Independent views of the same system

Each of these is considered below.

4.5.2 The choice of model

The choice of model refers to the fact that there are many ways to solve the same problem. Some of these will be totally incorrect but there is always more than one correct way to solve the problem at hand. Although all these approaches may be correct, some will be more appropriate and, hence, more correct for the application. For example, if you want to know the answer to a mathematical equation, there are several approaches open: you may simply ask someone else what the answer is, you may guess the answer, you may apply formal mathematical analysis and formulae or you may enter the equation into a mathematical software application. All may yield a correct answer, but the most appropriate approach will be dependent on the reason why you are asking the question. If you are merely curious to answer to the equation, then guessing or asking someone else may be entirely appropriate. If, on the other hand, the equation is an integral part of the control algorithm for an aeroplane, then something more formal would be more appropriate.

It is important that we have a number of different tools available in order to choose the most appropriate solution to a problem, rather than just relying on the same approach every time.

Therefore, one Requirement for any modelling language is that it must be flexible enough to allow different representations of the same information to allow the optimum solution to be chosen. That is, a modelling language should be flexible enough to allow different Views of the information to be produced. The concept of Views is central to the approach in this book as discussed in Chapter 2.

4.5.3 The level of abstraction

Any System may be considered at many different levels of abstraction. For example, an office block may be viewed as a single entity from an outside point of view. This is known as a high level of abstraction. It is also possible to view a tiny part of the office block, for example the circuit diagram associated with a dimmer light switch in one of the offices. This is what is known as a low level of abstraction.

As well as the high and low levels of abstraction, it is also necessary to look at many intermediate levels of abstraction, such as each floor layout on each level, each room layout, the lifts (or elevators) and the staircases. Only by looking at something at high, low and in-between levels of abstraction it is possible to gain a full understanding of a System.

Therefore, the second Requirement for any modelling language is that any System must be able to be represented at different levels of abstraction.

4.5.4 Connection to reality

It has been already stated that, by the very nature of modelling, we are simplifying reality and there is a very real danger that we may oversimplify to such a degree that the model loses all connection to reality and, hence, all relevant meaning.

One type of modelling in which it is very easy to lose the connection to reality is that of mathematical modelling. Mathematical modelling is an essential part of any engineering endeavour, but it can often be seen as some sort of dark art as very few people possess sufficient knowledge as to make it usable and, indeed, many people are petrified of maths! Consider the example of the mathematical operation of differentiation that is used to solve differential equations. As every school child knows, differentiation can be applied in a quite straightforward manner to achieve a result. What this actually means in real life, however, is another matter for discussion entirely. Differentiation allows us to find the slope of a line that, when taken at face value, and particularly when at school, can be viewed as being utterly meaningless. To take this example a little further, we are then told that integration is the *opposite* of differentiation (what is the opposite of finding the slope of a line?), which turns out to be measuring the area underneath a line. Again, when first encountered, this can be viewed as being meaningless. In fact, it is not until later in the educational process when studying subjects like physics or electronics that one realises that finding the slope of a line can be useful for calculating rate of change, velocity, acceleration, etc. It is this application, in this example, that provides the connection to reality and hence helps communicate "why".

The third Requirement for any modelling language, therefore, is that it must be able to have a strong connection to reality and, hence, be meaningful to observers who, in many cases, should require no specialist knowledge, other than an explanation, to understand the meaning of any model.

4.5.5 Independent views of the same system

Different people require different pieces of information, depending on who they are and what their role is in the System. It is essential that the right people get the right information at the right time. Also, for the purpose of analysing a System, it is important to be able to observe a System from many different points of view. For example, consider the office block again where there would be all different types of people who require different information. The electricians require wiring diagrams – not colour charts, nor plumbing data; the decorators require colour charts and not wiring diagrams; and so on.

There is a potentially very large problem when considering things from different points of view and this is consistency. Consistency is the key to creating a correct and consistent model and, without any consistency, it is not possible to have or demonstrate any confidence in the system.

The fourth Requirement, therefore, for any modelling language, is that it must allow any system to be looked at from different points of view and that these Views must be consistent. The MBSE approach taken in this book is based around this concept of a number of different, yet consistent, Views of a System. None of these Views taken alone is sufficient to describe the System; it is the information captured in the set of Views that gives a full and consistent model.

4.6 The SysML diagrams

Any SysML model has two aspects, the structural and the behavioural. Both aspects must exist and must be consistent. There are nine SysML diagrams available to realise the model, five diagrams that can be used to realise the structural aspect (see Figure 4.7) and four diagrams that can be used to realise the behavioural aspect (see Figure 4.8).

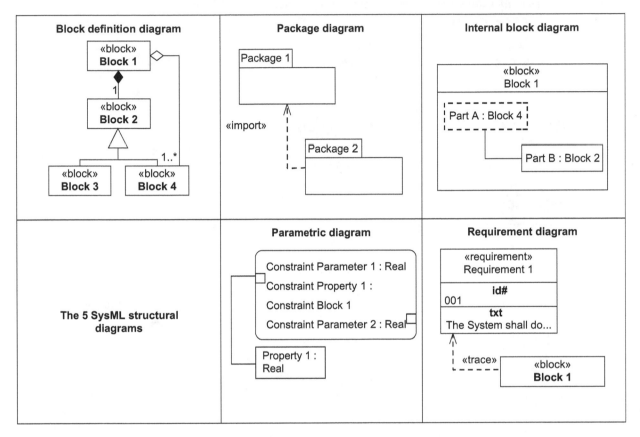

Figure 4.7 SysML structural diagrams

In brief, the five SysML *structural diagrams* are used as follows:

- A *block definition diagram* describes the System hierarchy and System/component classifications. It allows *properties* and behaviour of System Elements to be modelled.
- The *package diagram* is used to organise the model.
- The *internal block diagram* describes the internal structure of a System in terms of its *parts, ports* and *connectors*.
- The *parametric diagram* represents *constraints* on System *property values*, allowing engineering analysis models to be produced as well as defining complex constraint relationships that can be used in verification and validation of activities.

- The *requirements diagram* captures *requirements* hierarchies and *requirements* derivation. It allows a *requirement* to be related to model elements that satisfy or verify the *requirement*.

The *block definition diagram* is introduced in Section 4.7. The other diagrams are discussed in Chapter 5.

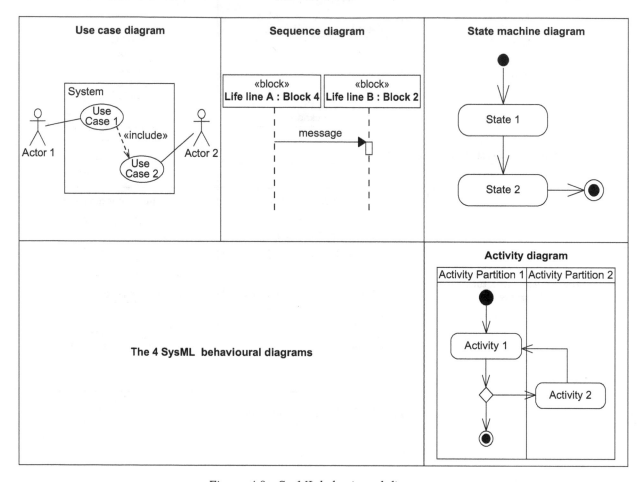

Figure 4.8   SysML behavioural diagrams

The four SysML *behavioural diagrams* are used as follows:

- The *use case diagram* provides a high-level description of functionality that is achieved through interaction among Systems or System Elements. It shows *requirements* in context.
- The *sequence diagram* represents *interactions* between collaborating parts of a System, allowing the *messages* between System Elements to be modelled in order to capture behavioural scenarios.

- The *state machine diagram* describes the *state transitions* and *actions* that a System or its elements perform in response to *events*.
- The *activity diagram* represents the flow of data and control between *activities* and is often used to model the internal behaviour of the *operations* of System Elements.

The *state machine diagram* is introduced in Section 4.8. The other diagrams are discussed in Chapter 5.

4.7   Structural modelling

The structural aspect of a model shows the "what" of the System. It identifies and defines System Elements, defines their *properties*, identifies their behaviours and identifies the *relationships* between the System Elements.

There are five *structural diagrams* in SysML, as can be seen in Figure 4.7. Similar concepts apply to all five of these diagrams, and in order to illustrate the concepts behind structural modelling, one of the five *structural diagrams* will be used to show some simple examples. The diagram chosen is the *block definition diagram* as this forms the backbone of the SysML.

There are two basic elements that make up a *block definition diagram*: the *block* and the *relationship*. A *block* represents a type of "thing" that exists in the System being modelled. A *relationship* relates together one or more *block*. *Blocks* should be named using nouns or noun phrases and *relationships* should have names that form sentences when read together with their associated *blocks*.

Figure 4.9   Example blocks

Figure 4.9 is a *block definition diagram* showing two *blocks*, 'Block 1' and 'Block 2'. *Blocks* are represented by rectangles and each must have a name, which is written inside the rectangle. The rectangles also contain the *stereotype* «block». *Stereotypes* are discussed in Chapter 5.

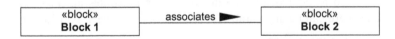

Figure 4.10   Representing relationships

Figure 4.10 shows how to represent a *relationship* between two *blocks*. The type of *relationship* shown is known as an *association* and is a general type of *relationship* that relates together one or more *block*. The *association* is represented by a line that joins two *blocks*, with the *association name* written on the line and a direction marker showing which way the *relationship* should be read. This diagram reads: 'Block 1' associates 'Block 2'.

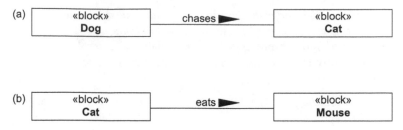

Figure 4.11   Examples of blocks and associations

Figure 4.11 shows two more examples. Figure 4.11(a) reads: there are two *blocks*: 'Dog' and 'Cat' where 'Dog' chases 'Cat'. Likewise, Figure 4.11(b) reads: there are two *blocks*: 'Cat' and 'Mouse' where 'Cat' eats 'Mouse'.

An important point concerning *blocks* is that *blocks* are conceptual and do not actually exist in the real world. There is no such thing as 'Cat', but there do exist many examples of 'Cat'. A *block* represents a grouping of things that look and behave in the same way as, at one level, all examples of 'Cat' will have a common set of features and behaviours that may be represented by the *block* 'Cat'. What this *block* is really representing is the blueprint of 'Cat', or the essence of 'Cat'.

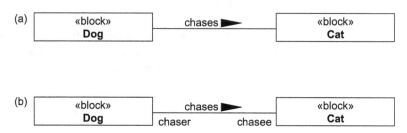

Figure 4.12   Showing direction with role names

The *direction* of an *association* is shown by a small filled-in triangle, as seen in the examples shown in Figures 4.10–4.12(a). The diagram reads 'Dog' chases 'Cat' and definitely not 'Cat' chases 'Dog'. If, in the System being modelled, dogs chase cats and cats chase dogs, then a second *association* running in the opposite direction would need to be added to the diagram. This illustrates an important point, namely that there can be any number of *relationships* between two *blocks*.

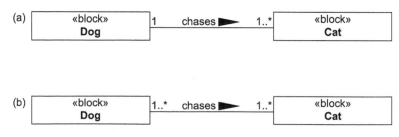

Figure 4.13   Showing multiplicity

The directionality of an *association* can be augmented through the use of *role names* on each end of the *association*, as shown in Figure 4.12(b). In this case, the two *role names* that have been defined are 'chaser' and 'chasee'. The diagram can now be read as: 'Dog', in the *role* 'chaser', chases 'Cat', in the *role* 'chasee'. The choice of *association* and *role names* should be chosen such that they make the diagrams as unambiguous as possible.

As well as showing the *direction* of an *association* between *blocks*, SysML allows the *multiplicity* of the *blocks* involved in the *association* to be shown. Figure 4.13(a) shows that each 'Dog' chases one or more 'Cat'. Although the number is 1, it does not necessarily indicate that there is only one dog, but rather that each 'Dog' in the system chases one or more 'Cat'. The *multiplicity* at the other end of the 'chases' *association* states '1..*', which means 'one or more' or somewhere between one and many. Therefore, the *association* shows that each 'Dog' chases one or more 'Cat', and that each 'Cat' is chased by only one 'Dog'.

Figure 4.13(b) shows a case where the *multiplicity* has been changed, which changes the entire meaning of the model. In this case, the diagram is read as: one or more 'Dog' chases one or more 'Cat'. This could mean that a single dog chases a single cat, a single dog chases any number or a herd of cats, or that an entire pack of dogs is chasing a herd of cats.

The appropriate *multiplicity* depends, of course, on the System being modelled. As the model evolves, the *multiplicities* may require changing. Common *multiplicities* are:

0..1 – Which indicates an optional value
1 – Which indicates exactly one
0..* – Which indicates any number, including zero
– Same as 0..*
1..* – Which indicates one or more

In fact, any subset of the non-negative integers can be used to specify a *multiplicity*. If, for example, a dog can chase between 1 and 3 cats, then the *multiplicity* at the 'Cat' end of the *association* in Figure 4.13(a) and (b) would be changed to '1..3'.

Modelling *blocks* and the *relationships* between them is an essential part of structural modelling, but the amount of detailed information for each *block* is very low. If the *block* 'Cat' represents all cats that look and behave in the same way, it is important to be able to show how a cat looks or behaves. This information is added to a *block* by using *properties* and *operations*.

The common *properties* of a 'Cat' are represented using SysML *properties*. It is very important to limit the number of general *properties* that are identified to only those that are relevant, as it is very easy to get carried away and over-define the amount of detail for a *block*. For this example, suppose that we wish to represent the features 'age', 'colour', 'favourite food' and 'weight' on the *block* 'Cat'.

These features are represented on the *block* as *properties*, one for each feature as shown in Figure 4.14.

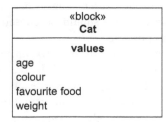

Figure 4.14   Properties of the 'Cat' block

When modelling, it is possible to add more detail at this point, such as the *type* and *default value*. As *properties* represent features of a *block*, they are usually represented by nouns and they must also be able to take on different values. For example, 'colour' is a valid *property*, whereas 'red' would not usually be, as 'red' would represent an actual value of a *property* rather than a *property* itself. It is possible for 'red' to be a *property*, but this would mean that the property would have a Boolean type (true or false) to describe a situation where we would only be interested in red cats and not any other type. SysML allows three different kinds of *property* to be defined: *value, part* and *reference properties*. As can be seen from the **values** heading in the compartment in Figure 4.14, the four *properties* shown for the 'Cat' block are all *value properties*. The differences between these three kinds of *property* are discussed in detail in Chapter 5 and are summarised briefly below:

- *Part properties* are owned by the *block*. That is, they are *properties* that are intrinsic to the *block* but which may have their own identity. A *composition* or *aggregation relationship* (see Section 4.7.1) creates *part properties* between the owning *block* and the *blocks* that it is composed of.
- *Reference properties* are referenced by a *block*, but not owned by it. An *association* between two *blocks* creates a *reference property* in the 'from' *block* to the *block* at the other end of the *association*. For example, the *association* between 'Dog' and 'Cat' in Figure 4.13 creates a *reference property* to 'Cat' within the 'Dog' *block*.
- *Value properties* represent properties that cannot be identified except by the value itself, e.g. age and colour, in Figure 4.14.

Properties provide a mechanism to represent features of a *block* – to show what it looks like – but they do not describe what the *block* does. This is shown using *operations*. *Operations* show what a *block* does, rather than what it looks like, and are thus named using verbs or verb phrases. An example is shown in Figure 4.15.

In the case of the *block* 'Cat' we have identified three things that the cat does, which are 'eat', 'sleep' and 'run'. *Operations* are represented in the SysML by

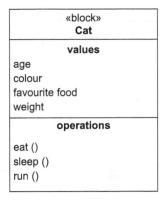

Figure 4.15   Operations of the 'Cat' block

adding an **operations** rectangle to the *block* and writing the *operation* names within it. The name of an *operation* is followed by two brackets. These are not optional and form part of the name of the *operation*. Thus in Figure 4.15 the *operation* name is 'eat()' and not 'eat'. Extra detail can be added to *operations* as necessary, such as *parameters* and *return values*. For example, an *operation* that takes two integers adds them and returns the result as an integer, which might be named as:

add(a : Integer, b : Integer): Integer

This illustrates the full form of an *operation* in SysML, namely:

operation name(parameter name : parameter type, . . .) : return type

An *operation* can have any number of *parameters*, as shown by the ', . . . ' in the general form above.

Although a number of *properties* and *operations* have been defined for the 'Cat' *block* in Figure 4.15, this does not mean that these *properties* and *operations* have to be shown in every diagram. Most SysML tools will allow the *property* and *operation compartments* to be turned on or off for a *block*, allowing a *block* to be shown in different levels of detail in different diagrams such as has been done in Figures 4.13(a) and (b) and 4.15. As with everything in the SysML, only use as much detail as is necessary, rather than as much as is possible.

4.7.1   Adding more detail to relationships

While *properties* and *operations* allow more detail to be added to *blocks*, SysML allows the modeller to add more detail to *relationships*, by defining some special types that are commonly encountered in modelling. One of these types of *relationship*, the *association*, has already been discussed in Section 4.7. This section will cover the other two main *relationship* types that exist, namely the *composition* and the *specialisation/generalisation*.

Composition allows emphasis to be placed on the "whole/part" relationships between System Elements. An example of *composition* is shown in Figure 4.16.

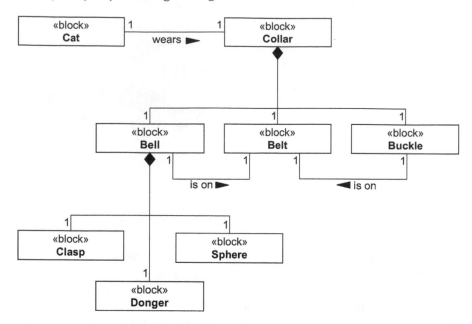

Figure 4.16   An example of composition

The diagram in Figure 4.16 makes use of *composition* to show the structure of the 'Collar' worn by a 'Cat'. The *composition* is shown by the use of a solid diamond at the "whole" end of the relationship. The diagram could be read as follows: A 'Cat' wears a 'Collar', which is composed of a 'Bell', a 'Belt' and a 'Buckle'. The 'Bell' is on the 'Belt' and the 'Buckle' is on the 'Belt'. The 'Bell' is composed of a 'Clasp', a 'Donger' and a 'Sphere'. Like *associations*, the *composition* can also take *multiplicities* and *role names*. *Composition* can also be named like an *association*, although this is rare.

A variant on *composition* exists in SysML. This is known as *aggregation* and looks the same but with a hollow diamond. The difference between them is concerned with uniqueness of ownership and is discussed further in Chapter 5. Essentially, *composition* shows that the *block* representing the part can only be part of one owning *block* at a time. In Figure 4.16, for example, a 'Bell' can only ever be a part of one 'Collar' at a time. *Aggregation* allows the *block* representing the *part* to be *part* of more than one owning *block* at the same time. For example, if the 'Bell' in Figure 4.16 was attached to two 'Collar' at the same time, then an *aggregation*, with multiplicity 2 at the 'Collar' end would be needed between 'Collar' and 'Bell' rather than a *composition*.

As well as showing structural hierarchies using *composition* or *aggregation*, it is often necessary to model type hierarchies or taxonomies. SysML allows this through the use of the *specialisation/generalisation* relationship. An example of its use is shown in Figure 4.17.

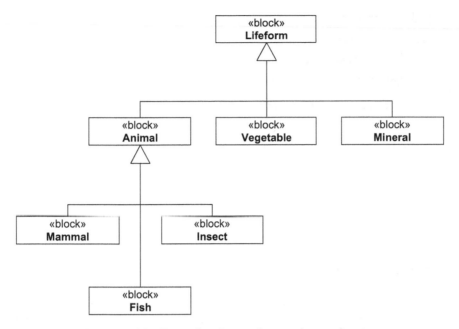

Figure 4.17   Example of specialisation/generalisation

Specialisation/generalisation is shown by a line with an unfilled triangular arrowhead at one end. *Specialisation* refers to the case when a *block* is being made more special or is being refined in some way. *Specialisation* may be read as "has types". In the somewhat science fiction inspired types of lifeform, shown in Figure 4.17, 'Lifeform' has types 'Animal', 'Vegetable' and 'Mineral'.

If the relationship is read the other way around, then the triangle symbol is read as 'is a type of', which is a *generalisation*. Thus, in Figure 4.17, 'Mammal', 'Fish' and 'Insect' are types of 'Animal'. Therefore, read one way the *block* becomes more special (*specialisation*), and read the other way the *block* becomes more general (*generalisation*).

Specialisation is used to show *child blocks* of a *parent block*. An important property of the *specialisation/generalisation* relationship is that of inheritance: *child blocks* inherit their *properties* and *operations* from their *parent blocks*, but will be different in some way in order to make them special. In SysML terms, this means that a *child block* will inherit any *properties* and *operations* that its *parent block* has, but may have additional *properties* or *operations* that make the *child block* special.

Consider Figure 4.18(a). This shows that 'Cat' is a type of 'Mammal'. Taken together with Figure 4.17, a 'Cat' is therefore also a type of 'Animal' and a type of 'Lifeform'. A 'Cat', therefore, inherits all the *properties* and *operations* of all its *parent blocks*. Given the information in Figures 4.17 and 4.18, a 'Cat' also has two *operations*, namely 'suckle young()' and 'breathe air()'.

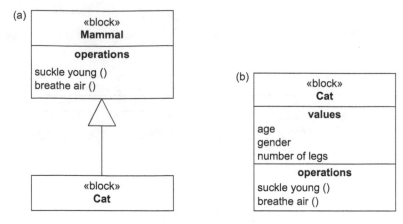

Figure 4.18   Inheritance

A *block* can have additional *properties* and *operations* not found in any of its ancestor *blocks* (*parent block, parent block* of *parent block,* etc.), and in Figure 4.18(b) the 'Cat' *block* is shown with some additional *properties* that have been defined for 'Cat'. The inherited *operations* from 'Mammal' are also shown for completeness. Remember that inheritance only runs from *parent blocks* to *child blocks.* Thus, defining the 'age' *property* in 'Cat' does not mean that it is inherited by its parent 'Mammal'. If, when modelling this lifeform-type hierarchy, it was found that 'age' was being added into all types of 'Mammal', types of 'Fish', etc., then this is a sign that the *property* should be moved up the hierarchy to 'Animal' or perhaps even 'Lifeform', so that it is defined in one place and inherited by all the descendant *blocks.*

4.8   Behavioural modelling

The behavioural aspect of a model shows the "how" of the system. It identifies the behaviour of the System at the System level, between System Elements, within System Elements and within *operations* of System Elements.

There are four *behavioural diagrams* in SysML, as can be seen in Figure 4.8. Similar concepts apply to all four of these diagrams, and in order to illustrate the concepts behind behavioural modelling, one of the four *behavioural diagrams* will be used to show some simple examples. The diagram chosen is the *state machine diagram. State machine diagrams* have a very strong relationship with *block definition diagrams* and the concept of modelling the *states* that Systems and their elements operate in is commonly encountered in systems engineering. For more in-depth discussion concerning *state machine diagrams* and behavioural modelling, see Reference 8.

State machine diagrams are used to model the behaviour of *blocks* throughout the lifetime of a *block.* That is, they describe the behaviour of instances of *blocks,* known in SysML as *instance specifications* (see Chapter 5 for a discussion of *instance specifications*). *State machine diagrams* are used when the element represented by the *block* exhibits behaviour (i.e. has *operations*) and, more fundamentally, when such behaviour is related to the element being in a defined *state*. Such elements are said to exhibit stateful behaviour. An example of an everyday system that exhibits stateful behaviour and hence which could be modelled using a *state machine diagram* is a Blu-ray player; such a device can be playing, fast-forwarding, etc. Each of these is a *state* that the player is in during which it exhibits behaviour. So, let us now consider the basic modelling elements in a *state machine diagram*.

The basic modelling elements in a *state machine diagram* are *states*, *transitions* and *events*. *States* describe what is happening within a System at any given point in time, *transitions* show the possible paths between such *states* and *events* govern when a *transition* can occur. Each of these elements will now be looked at in more detail, starting with the *state*, an example of which is shown in Figure 4.19.

Figure 4.19   Representation of a state

Figure 4.19 shows a very simple *state*, which is shown in the SysML by a box with rounded corners. This particular *state* has the name 'state 1' and this diagram should be read as 'there is a single state, called 'state 1''. This shows what a *state* looks like, but what exactly is a *state*? The following three points discuss the basics of a *state*:

- A *state* may describe a situation in which the System is doing something. *States* are assumed to take a finite amount of time, whereas *transitions* are assumed to take no time. There are two things that can be happening during such a *state*: an *activity* and/or one or more *actions*. An *activity* is a unit of behaviour that is *non-atomic* and, as such, can be interrupted. *Actions* are units of behaviour that are *atomic* and cannot be interrupted. *Activities* can only appear inside a *state*, whereas an *action* can exist either within a *state* or on a *transition*. *Activities* can be differentiated from *actions* inside *states* by the presence of the keyword *do*, whereas *actions* will have other keywords, including *Entry* and *Exit*.
- A *state* may describe situations in which the System satisfies a particular condition, in terms of its *property values* or *events* that have occurred. This may, for example, be "loaded" or "saved", so that it gives an indication as to something that has already happened.
- A *state* may also describe a situation in which a System does nothing or is waiting for an *event* to occur. This is often the case with event-driven Systems, such as windows-style software where, in fact, most of the time the System sits idle and is waiting for an *event* to occur.

In order for the *instance specification* that owns the *state machine* diagram to move from one *state* to another, a *transition* must be crossed. In order to cross a *transition*, some sort of *event* must occur. Figure 4.20 shows a simple example of how *states* and *transitions* are represented using the SysML.

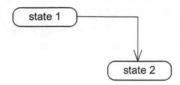

Figure 4.20   States and transitions

From the diagram in Figure 4.20 it can be seen that two *states* exist: 'state 1' and 'state 2', represented by rounded boxes. There is a single *transition* that goes from 'state 1' to 'state 2', which is represented by a directed line that shows the direction of the *transition*. These *transitions* are unidirectional and, in the event of another *transition* being required going in the other direction, an entirely new *transition* is required – the original *transition* cannot be made bi-directional.

In order to cross a *transition*, which will make the *instance specification* exit one *state* and enter another, an *event* must occur. This *event* may be something simple, such as the termination of an *activity* in a *state* (the *state* has finished what it is doing) or may be more complex and involve receiving *messages* from another element in another part of the System. *Event names* are written on the *transition* lines using a notation that is described in the following sub-section, where the concepts and notation are explored through a simple example.

4.8.1   Behavioural modelling – a simple example

In order to illustrate the use of *state machine diagrams*, a simple example will be used; that of a game of chess, a game with which most people are at least vaguely familiar. While chess is a very complex game to master, its rules are relatively simple, as will be our model where we will focus on the behaviour of the players.

Figure 4.21 shows a *block definition diagram* that represents, at a very simple level, a game of chess. From the diagram a 'Chess Match' is made up of two 'Player'. Each 'Player' has *properties* – 'Status', 'Result' and 'Initiator' – and a single *operation* 'move'. The *property* 'Result' reflects the result of the game and may have values: 'Player 1 win', 'Player 2 win', 'Draw' or 'Undecided'. The *property* 'Status' reflects the current status of the game and may take the values 'Checkmate', 'Stalemate' and 'Game in Progress'. Finally, the *property* 'Initiator' represents the player who goes first and can take values 'Player 1' or 'Player 2'. Note that the definition and display of the *types* associated with these *properties* have been omitted for clarity.

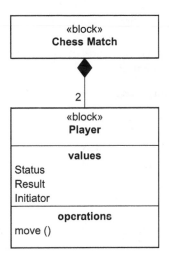

Figure 4.21   A simple block definition diagram for a game of chess

4.8.1.1   Simple behaviour

A very simple *state machine diagram* for a game of chess is shown in Figure 4.22, by defining the behaviour of the *block* 'Player'.

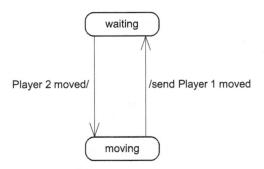

Figure 4.22   A simple state machine diagram for a game of chess

From the diagram, the *instance specification* of 'Player' may be in one of two *states*: 'waiting' or 'moving'. In order to cross from 'waiting' to 'moving', the *event* 'Player 2 moved' must have occurred. In order to cross from 'moving' to 'waiting', the *event* 'Player 1 moved' must be sent.

The two *transitions* illustrate *receipt events* and *send events*. The *event* 'Player 2 moved' is an example of a *receipt event*, an *event* that is received from outside the boundary of the *state machine diagram*. *Receipt events* trigger *transitions*. The *event* 'Player 1 moved' is an example of a *send event* (as indicated by the *send* keyword), an *event* that is broadcast outside the boundary of the *state machine* to other *instance specifications*. A *send event* is an example of an *action* taking place on the *transition* (see the discussion earlier in this section on *activities* and *actions*); it is atomic and cannot be interrupted.

These two events illustrate two parts of the notation that is applied to a *transition*. The three parts of the notation are:

event [guard condition] / action

The square brackets and slash are part of the notation and each of the three parts is optional. *Guard conditions* will be introduced in the next sub-section 4.8.1.2. The text-based notation used here is only one presentation option and reflects the modelling preferences of one of the authors. There is also a graphical notation, which is discussed in Chapter 5.

Thus it can be seen that the *transition* from 'waiting' to 'moving' only has an *event* and the *transition* from 'moving' to 'waiting' only has an *action*. When a *transition* exists that does not have an *event*, then the *transition* occurs (we say the *transition* fires) after all the behaviour (*activity* and *actions*) within the originating *state* is completed.

At a very simple level Figure 4.22 shows how a game of chess is played, by modelling the behaviour of each player. However, the model is by no means complete as the chess game described here has no beginning or end and will thus go on forever. This is modelled in the SysML by introducing *initial states* and *final states*.

The next step, therefore, is to add more detail to this *state machine diagram*. It is interesting to note that this is actually how a *state machine diagram* (or any other SysML diagram, for that matter) is created. The diagram almost always starts off as a simple collection of *states* and then evolves over time. As more detail is added, the model starts to get closer and closer to the reality that it is intended to represent.

4.8.1.2   Adding more detail

The next step is to add a beginning and an end for the *state machine diagram*, using *initial states* and *final states*. An *initial state* describes what has happened before the *instance specification* is created and is shown visually by a filled-in circle. A *final state*, by comparison, shows the *state* of the *instance specification* once the *instance specification* has been destroyed and is represented visually by a bull's eye symbol.

Initial states and *final states* are treated just like other *states* in that they require *transitions* to take the *instance specification* into another *state*. Whereas *transitions* to *final states* can be triggered by any kind of *event*, *initial states* behave somewhat differently. In general, the *transition* from an *initial state* may not have an *event* that triggers the *transition* (technically, the *initial state* is known as a *pseudostate*). This is shown in Figure 4.23, an expanded *state machine diagram* that has *initial states* and *final states* along with appropriate *events*. Note that the *transition* from the *initial state* has no *event*; when the *instance specification* of 'Player' is created, the *transition* immediately fires and the *state machine* moves into the 'starting' *state*.

From the 'starting' *state* two *transitions* can fire that can move the *state machine diagram* into either the 'waiting' or the 'moving' *state*. Both of these

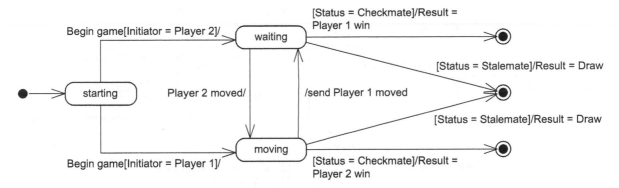

Figure 4.23 Expanded state machine diagram showing initial and final states

transitions are triggered by receipt of the 'Begin game' *event*. Which of these *transitions* that fires is governed by the *guard conditions* on the *transitions*, depending on which player goes first. There are three different *final states*, depending on which player, if either, wins, or whether the game is a draw. The model is now becoming more realistic; its connection to reality is getting closer, but there is still room for ambiguity. Notice in this diagram that the *guard conditions* relate directly back to the *properties* from their *parent block*, providing some basic consistency between a *block* and its associated *state machine diagram*.

We know from the *block definition diagram* that the *block* 'Player' does one thing, 'move', but we do not know in which *state* of the *state machine diagram* that this *operation* is executed. As it happens, it is fairly obvious that the *state* in which the *operation* occurs is 'moving'. *Operations* on a *state machine diagram* may appear as either *activities* in a *state* or *actions* in a *state* or on a *transition*, but remember that *actions* are atomic whereas *activities* are not.

The 'move' *operation* must be non-atomic (otherwise it would be impossible to interrupt a game of chess until a player had moved) and so an *activity* within a *state* must be used. This may now be shown by adding the *activity* to its appropriate *state* by writing 'do': in the *state* box and then adding the *activity* name (the *operation* from the *block definition diagram*), which is shown in Figure 4.24.

The model is now getting even closer to reality; the model is evolving. It is almost impossible to get a model right the first time, a good model will continue to evolve for as long as it exists. However, there is yet another problem with the *state machine diagram*, as, although it seems to work well for any situation in a chess game, it is impossible for the game to run. To illustrate this, consider what happens when we begin a game of chess.

4.8.1.3 Ensuring consistency

The first thing that will happen is that two *instance specifications* of 'Player' need to be created so that we have the correct number of players. The behaviour of each player is described by the *state machine diagram* for the *block* 'Player'.

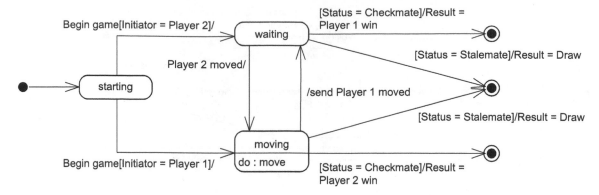

Figure 4.24   Expanded state machine diagram showing activity

For arguments' sake, we shall name the two players 'Player 1' and 'Player 2' and see if the *state machine diagram* will hold up to the full game of chess. Figure 4.25 shows two, identical *state machine diagrams*, one for each *instance specification*, that are positioned above one another to make comparisons easier.

In order to begin a game of chess, an *instance specification* 'Chess Match' would be created, which would in turn create two *instance specifications* of 'Player'. In this example, the *instance specification* names 'Player 1' and 'Player 2' have been chosen. Let us now imagine that a game of chess has been started and that 'Player 1' is to begin. The *event* that will occur is 'Begin game', which is present on both *state machine diagrams*. The 'Initiator' *property* is set to 'Player 1'. However, this will put both players straight into the 'moving' *state*, which will make the game of chess impossible to play. This is because the *events* were named specific to one player, rather than being generic so that they are applicable to any player. In order to make the game work, it is necessary to rename the *events* so that they are player-independent.

It is important to run through a *state machine diagram* (by simulation or animation, if a suitable Tool is available) to check for consistency. In this case, the error was a simple, almost trivial, misnaming of an *event*. However, this trivial mistake will lead to the System failing.

4.8.1.4   Solving the inconsistency

There are many ways to solve the inconsistency problems that were highlighted in the previous section, two of which are presented here. The first solution is to make the generic *state machine diagram* correct, while the second is to change the *block definition diagram* to make the *state machine diagrams* correct.

Changing the state machine diagram

The first solution to the inconsistency problem that is presented here is to make the *state machine diagram* more generic, so that the *properties* checked in *guard conditions* and *events* now match up. The *state machine diagram* for this solution is shown in Figure 4.26.

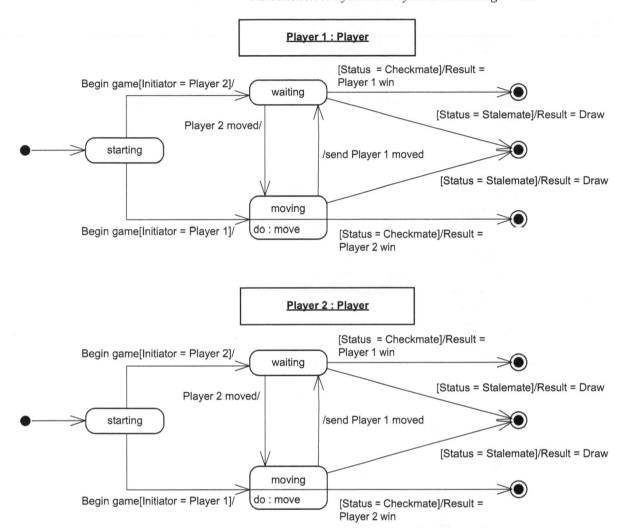

Figure 4.25   Comparison of two state machine diagrams

Figure 4.26 represents a correct solution to the chess model. In this diagram the values that are assigned to the 'Initiator' *property* of each 'Player' block are now relative to each *instance specification*, rather than specific, so the allowed values are changed from 'Player 1' to 'This' and from 'Player 2' to 'Other'. The *receipt events* and *send events* on the *transitions* between the 'waiting' and 'moving' *events* have also been changed. Previously, the names were instance-specific, being as they were, 'Player 1 moved' and 'Player 2 moved'. These names have now changed to a more-generic 'moved' *event*, which will apply equally to both *instance specifications*.

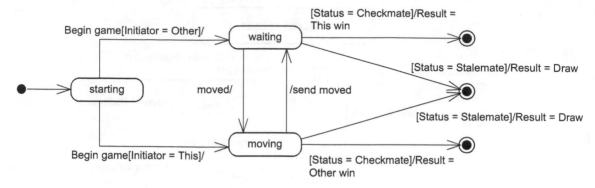

Figure 4.26   New state machine diagram with correct event names

This is by no means the only solution to the problem and another possible solution is presented in the next section, where the *block definition diagram* is changed to make the *state machine diagram* correct, rather than changing the *state machine diagram*.

Changing the block definition diagram

The second solution to the consistency problem is to change the *block definition diagram* rather than the *state machine diagram*, as shown in Figure 4.27.

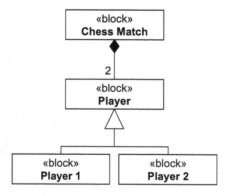

Figure 4.27   A modified block definition diagram for the chess match

Figure 4.27 shows a modified *block definition diagram* in which two new *sub-blocks* of 'Player' have been added. This would mean that, rather than the *block* 'Player' being instantiated, one instance of each *block* 'Player 1' and 'Player 2' would be created. This has implications on the *state machine diagrams* as the *block definition diagram* shown here would require a *state machine diagram* for both 'Player 1' and 'Player 2', rather than single *state machine diagram* for 'Player'. This would also mean that the initial *state machine diagram* shown in Figure 4.24

would now be correct for 'Player 1', but that a new *state machine diagram* would have to be created for the block 'Player 2'.

Taking this idea a step further, it is also possible to make the two *sub-blocks* more specific as, in the game of chess, one player always controls white pieces and the other player only controls black pieces. This would have an impact on the *block definition diagram* again, as each *sub-block* could now be named according to its colour. This is shown in Figure 4.28.

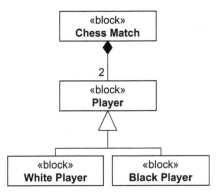

Figure 4.28   Further modification of the chess block definition diagram

Figure 4.28 shows a *block definition diagram* where the *blocks* have been named according to colour, rather than simply 'Player 1' and 'Player 2'. This has even more impact on the *state machine diagram* as, in the standard rules of chess, the white player always moves first.

The problem encountered with the *state machine diagram* serves to illustrate a very important point that relates to the different levels of abstraction of the same model. The chess game was modelled only at the instance level in terms of its behaviour, which, it is entirely possible, would have resulted in the *block* being implemented and even tested successfully if treated in isolation and under test conditions. It would only be at the final System test level that this error would have come to light. Issues around modelling at different levels of abstraction are considered in Section 4.10.

4.9   The relationships between behavioural diagrams and structural level

Having introduced structural and behavioural modelling, this section discusses the relationships between the two aspects of a SysML model. Whereas the SysML *structural diagrams* can be used to model any level of a System's structure, from high-level Systems through to low-level components, different SysML *behavioural diagrams* are typically used to model the behaviour of the System at the levels identified in Section 4.8. This section discusses the relationship between *behavioural diagrams* and System structural level, considering consistency and looking how the various SysML behavioural models relate to typical engineering activities.

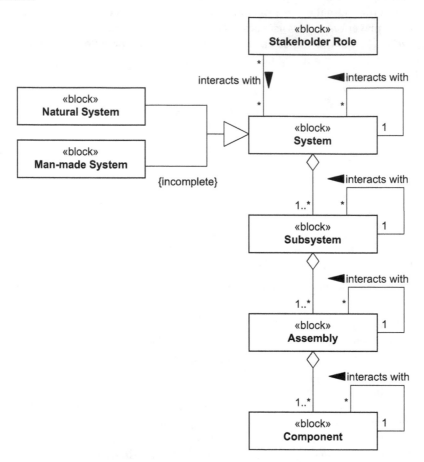

Figure 4.29   Typical structural hierarchy

Figure 4.29 shows a typical and generic structural hierarchy for a System. There are many different types of 'System' that exist, 'Natural System' and 'Man-made System' being just two examples. A 'System' is typically made up of one or more 'Subsystem'. These can themselves be further broken down into one or more 'Assembly' and then down into one or more 'Component'. There is typically interaction between elements at each of these levels: a 'System' interacts with zero or more 'System', a 'Subsystem' interacts with zero or more 'Subsystem', and so on.

The System hierarchy from Figure 4.29 is reproduced in Figure 4.30, which also shows the typical SysML *behavioural diagrams* that are used at each level.

• At the System level it is highest level of behaviour that needs to be modelled, that of the System itself and the interactions between the System and

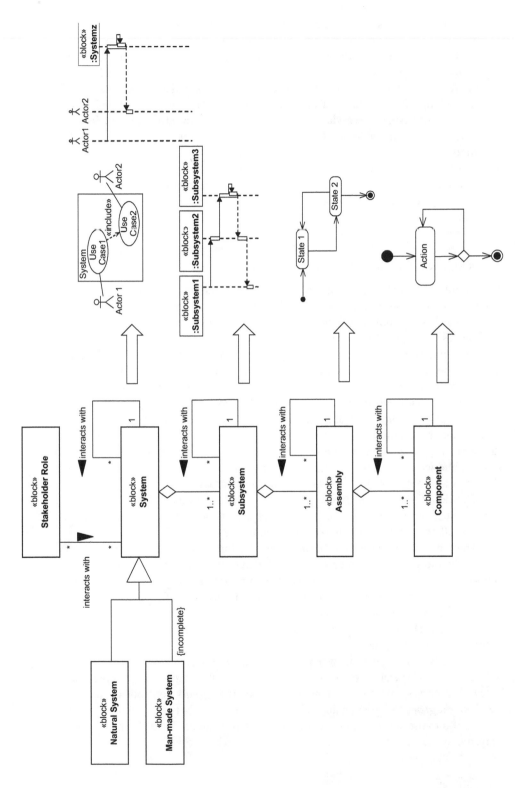

Figure 4.30 Relating behavioural diagrams to structural level

Stakeholder Roles (which may, of course, themselves be other systems). Such behaviour is usually modelled using *use case diagrams* and *sequence diagrams*. *Use case diagrams* allow Requirements in Context to be modelled and *sequence diagrams* allow Scenarios for the *use cases* to be developed.

- At the subsystem level it is the behaviour *between* System Elements that is modelled, allowing the interfaces between subsystems to be explored from a behavioural perspective via typical Scenarios showing how subsystems work together to achieve some goal. The *sequence diagram* is most often used to model behaviour at this level.

- At the assembly level the behaviour within an assembly is often of most interest, allowing exploration of how assemblies respond to events and under what circumstances they carry out their operations to be made. The *state machine diagram* is typically used at this level.

- At the component level it is the low-level internals of a component that is of interest. This usually equates to modelling the behaviour of the *operations* of a component for which an *activity diagram* is used.

It is essential to remember about System hierarchies and behavioural modelling that one person's subsystem is another's System (and similarly for the other levels). This means that behavioural modelling is never as simple and clear cut as described in Section 4.8. While the System developer may well model subsystem behaviour using *sequence diagrams*, those subsystems may be developed by other suppliers. For them, they will be considered as Systems and therefore modelled using *use case diagrams* and *sequence diagrams*. Similar considerations apply across the whole hierarchy, which means that the *behavioural diagrams* used depend entirely on context.

The various *structural* and *behavioural diagrams* produced as part of a System model must be consistent with one another. Consider Figure 4.31, which contains the same *structural* and *behavioural diagrams* as shown in Figure 4.30, but which has double-headed arrows at each level between the *structural* and *behavioural diagrams* and between the *behavioural diagrams* across each level.

The double-headed arrows in Figure 4.31 show the kinds of consistency that must exist if the various SysML diagrams of a System are to give a *model* of the System rather than simply being a collection of pictures.

There has to be consistency between the structural and behavioural aspects of a System at the same level. For example, the Systems appearing as *lifelines* on a *sequence diagram* must exist as elements on a *structural diagram* such as a *block definition diagram*. At the component level, each operation of a component, modelled as a *block*, should have its behaviour modelled using an *activity diagram*; conversely, each *activity diagram* should correspond to the *operation* on a *block* representing a component.

Similarly, consistency between *behavioural diagrams* across System levels is also essential. For example, the *messages* between subsystems on a *sequence diagram* may correspond to *events* received by or the *signals* sent out by the *state machine diagram* for an assembly. These same messages between subsystems may correspond to the *self-messages* sent from a system's *lifeline* to itself on a *sequence diagram* at the system level.

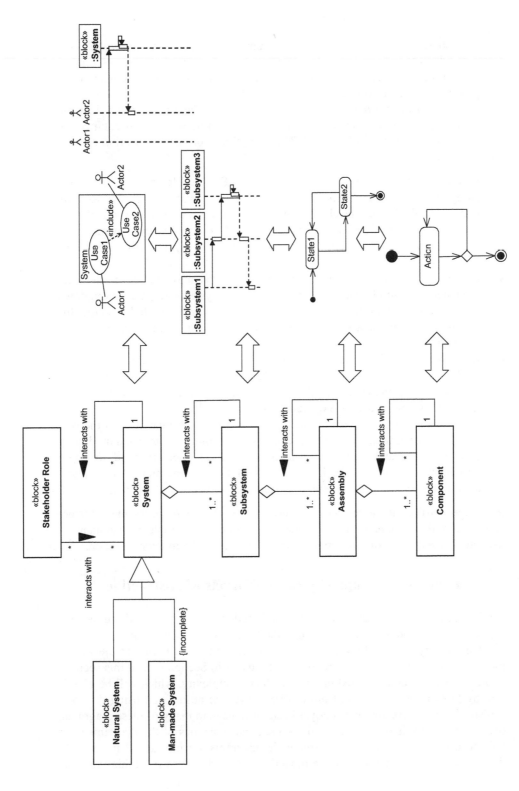

Figure 4.31 Structural and behavioural consistency

As well as considering behavioural diagrams with respect to the typical System levels at which they are used and in terms of the consistency that is essential to ensure the diagrams give a model of the System, it is also possible to consider them in terms of engineering activity. See Figure 4.32.

The *structural* and *behavioural diagrams* seen in Figures 4.30 and 4.31 are shown in Figure 4.32 but this time with boxes indicating the type of engineering activity in which they are often used. There are four types of engineering activity shown in the diagram:

- Requirements engineering, in which the main System Elements are identified along with their Requirements and validating Scenarios. In order to fully understand the System-level Requirements, it may be necessary to consider the structural aspects of the System at the next level of decomposition, namely that of the subsystem. The behavioural aspects at the subsystem level would also be investigated.
- System design, in which the main subsystems that make up the System are modelled structurally and behaviourally. The subsystems may be broken down into assemblies, with the behaviour within each assembly modelled so that the events that govern an assembly's behaviour and its response to such events can be explored.
- Implementation, in which the low-level assemblies and components are modelled. The internal behaviour of assemblies is captured as is the low-level behaviour of component operations, allowing the flow and manipulation of information and data within operations to be modelled.
- Reverse engineering, in which the System is often investigated from the bottom up, starting with the lowest level components of the System and modelling their structure and low-level behaviour. This can then be used to begin abstracting up through the higher levels of the System hierarchy to allow assemblies, subsystems and entire Systems to be reverse engineered.

As well as considering the relationships between *behavioural diagrams* and the structural level of the System, it is also important to consider how complexity can manifest itself at different levels of abstraction. This is discussed in the following section.

4.10   Identifying complexity through levels of abstraction

Having introduced structural and behavioural modelling, this section discusses one of the important themes that run through the book, namely complexity.

Complexity is one of the three evils of engineering and is one of the fundamental reasons why we need to model, as discussed in Section 4.3. In this section, two Systems will be compared in terms of their complexity, which will be identified by looking at the System from different levels of abstraction using different SysML diagrams. As you have not yet been introduced to many of these diagrams, the intention here is not to discuss the syntax and semantics of the diagrams (that will be discussed in Chapter 5). Rather the diagrams are introduced in order to discuss levels of abstraction and the modelling issues that arise from this example.

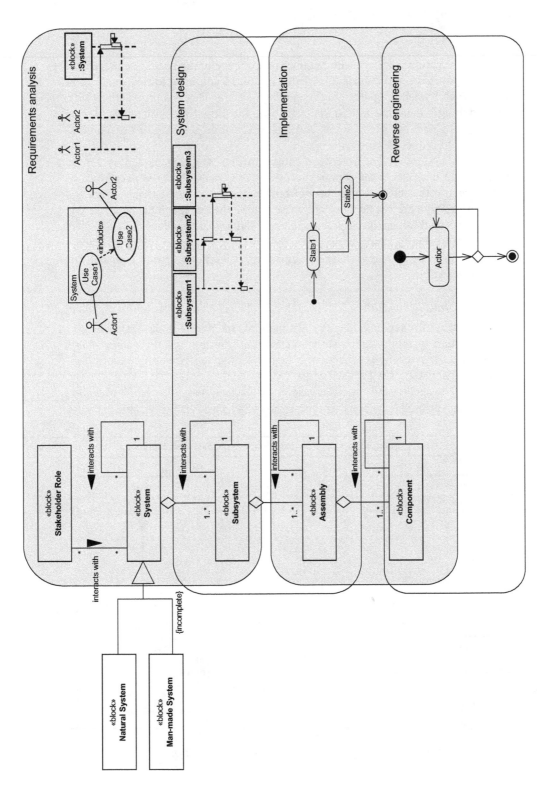

Figure 4.32   Typical behavioural diagram usage by engineering activity

4.10.1   The Systems

Imagine a situation where you are put in charge of developing two Systems, neither of which you have any domain knowledge of and so you have to rely on descriptions of each System to gain an understanding of them. This is a prime application for modelling – there is a lack of understanding about the two Systems, there is no indication of how complex each is and this information will need to be communicated to the Project teams.

The two Systems that have been chosen to illustrate how modelling can be used to help understand the complexity of Systems and to show where the complexity manifests itself have been taken from the domain of board games: chess and Monopoly. If you are *not* familiar with these games, then so much the better. If you are, then try to think about them as completely unfamiliar Systems.

Before beginning to model these two Systems, ask yourself a simple question – which is the more complex, chess or Monopoly? Take a moment to consider this before reading on.

4.10.2   Structural view

Often when confronted with new systems the first, and normally the easiest, aspect of the System to model is the structural aspect. This is often done using *block definition diagrams*, and the diagram in Figure 4.33 shows two simple *block definition diagrams* representing each of the two Systems.

Having modelled the structural aspect of each system, the *block definition diagrams* can be used to help answer the question of which of the two is more complex.

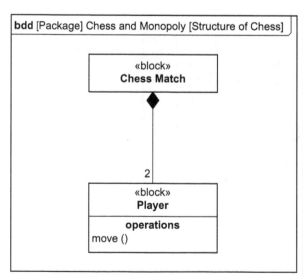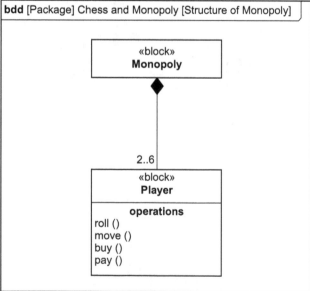

Figure 4.33   Comparing complexity – block definition diagrams

The two Systems have a lot in common, as can be shown by the identical pattern in each System's *block definition diagram* – each game is made up of a number of 'Player'. In terms of complexity, at least as far as can be identified from this structural model, there is really not much to choose between the two. If forced to choose one, then 'Monopoly' could be considered more complex than 'Chess', as it has a higher *multiplicity* on the *block* 'Player' (more players in the game) and it has four *operations* compared to one in 'Chess' (more things that can be done in the game).

Is it sufficient to conclude that 'Monopoly' is more complex than 'Chess'? Since we have only considered the structural aspect of each system the answer has to be no. Further modelling of each system is needed, but this time the behavioural aspects of the systems need to be captured. As each of the 'Player' *blocks* has at least one *operation*, a *state machine diagram* could be used to start the behavioural modelling.

4.10.3 Behavioural views

Simple *state machine diagrams* for 'Chess' and 'Monopoly' have been created and are shown in Figure 3.34. The complexity of the two Systems will now be considered by comparing these two *state machine diagrams*.

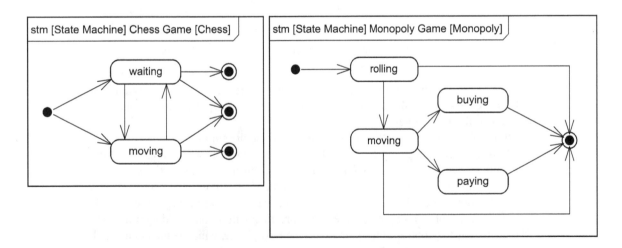

Figure 4.34 Comparing complexity – state machine diagrams

A direct comparison of the two *state machine diagrams* in Figure 4.34 again seems to suggest that 'Monopoly' is more complex than 'Chess' as there are more *states* in the *state machine diagram* for 'Monopoly', reflecting the number of different things that a player can do in a game of 'Monopoly' (rolling, moving, buying and paying).

However, 'Monopoly' only has two more *states* than 'Chess' and both diagrams have the same number of *transitions* between *states*. So, once more, deciding which game is the more complex is not an easy decision to make.

Further behavioural modelling is needed. This time the behaviour will be modelled at a higher level of abstraction than the *state machine diagram* using the *sequence diagram*.

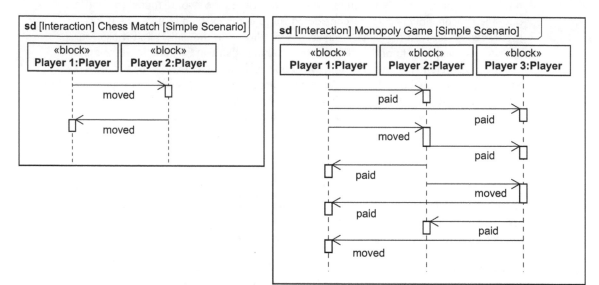

Figure 4.35   Comparing complexity – sequence diagrams

The *sequence diagram* in Figure 4.35 shows a higher level of behaviour for both the 'Chess' and 'Monopoly' examples and shows a typical playing Scenario for each of the two games.

In the Scenario shown, 'Chess' still appears to be the simpler of the two – there is only one interaction going each way between the two 'Player' *lifelines*, resulting in a total of two interactions. A *lifeline* represents an individual participant in an interaction and will be discussed further in Chapter 5. For now, you can think of a *lifeline* as showing the behaviour of an *instance specification* through time.

In the case of 'Monopoly', there are more interactions on the diagram. Each 'Player' passes the control of the game onto the next player, which results in a single *interaction* between each subsequent *lifeline*. Also, any 'Player' can pay money to any other 'Player', which results in an extra six interactions for this Scenario with three players, and an extra 30 interactions in the Scenario with 6 players!

When comparing these two diagrams, it is clear that the 'Monopoly' diagram is the more complex of the two and it would be reasonable to assume that 'Monopoly' is a more complex game than 'Chess'. However, there is one final diagram that we can use to model the games at their lowest level of abstraction, the *activity diagram*.

The diagrams in Figure 4.36 show the lowest level of abstraction for both examples using *activity diagrams*.

In the case of 'Chess', a single *activity diagram* is used to describe the behaviour of the single *operation* from the *block definition diagram*, that of 'move'.

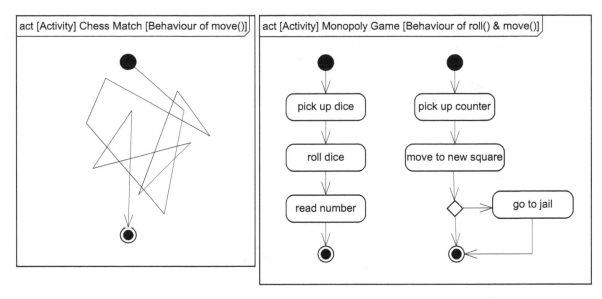

Figure 4.36   Comparing complexity – activity diagrams

Bearing in mind that the 'move' *activity* describes all the planning, strategies and movement of the chess pieces, this would result in a very complex diagram indeed – represented in the diagram by a tangled mess.

In the case of 'Monopoly', there are more *activity diagrams* needed (four in total, one for each *operation* – only two are shown here), but each *activity diagram* is so simple as to be almost trivial.

The diagram in Figure 4.37 shows each of the three *behavioural diagrams* for each example alongside one another so that they can be compared directly.

The diagram in Figure 4.37 shows all the *behavioural diagrams* that have been produced for the two games. In summary, the following conclusions were drawn:

- When comparing the original *block definition diagrams*, there was not much to choose between the two, but 'Monopoly' was slightly more complex than 'Chess'.
- When comparing the *state machine diagrams*, again there was not much to choose between the two, but once again the *state machine diagram* for 'Monopoly' was deemed to be more complex than the one for 'Chess'.

At this stage, there is nothing to really distinguish between the two games. In each diagram 'Monopoly' was deemed slightly more complex than 'Chess', but only marginally so. It is interesting to see how things change quite dramatically when the Systems are looked at from higher and lower levels of abstraction.

- When looking at the higher level of abstraction, using the *sequence diagram*, it was very clear that 'Monopoly' was far more complex than 'Chess'.

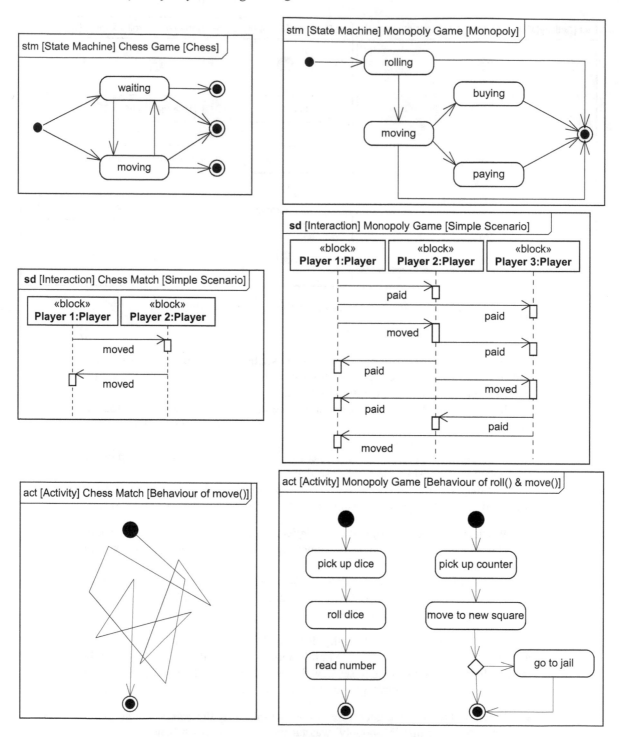

Figure 4.37   Summary of diagrams to assess complexity

- When looking at the lowest level of abstraction using the *activity diagram*, it was very clear that 'Chess' was far more complex than 'Monopoly'. Indeed, the *activity diagram* for the 'move' operation for 'Chess' was so complex that it couldn't be drawn easily.

There are a number of conclusions that may be drawn at this point concerning not just complexity, but also general modelling:

- The complexity of the Systems manifested itself at different levels of abstraction. In the case of 'Chess', the complexity manifested itself at the lower levels of abstraction, whereas in the 'Monopoly' System, complexity abounded at the higher levels. This actually makes nonsense of the question of which is the more complex System. Neither is "more" complex as such, but in each System the complexity manifested itself at different levels of abstraction.
- If any of these views was taken individually and compared, there is no way whatsoever that any realistic comparison could be made between the two Systems. For example, just comparing *block definition diagrams* gives no real insight into each System. This may seem obvious, but many people will construct a *block definition diagram* and then state that this is the model of their System. To understand any System and to create a useful model, both the structural and behavioural aspects of the model must be looked at.
- Even when both the structural and behavioural aspects of the model are realised, it is essential to look at the model at different levels of abstraction for the System to be understood, since the complexity may manifest itself at any level and by not looking at a System at all levels of abstraction the complexity may be missed.
- It is also possible that the complexity of the System changes depending on the point of view of the stakeholder. For example, imagine a passenger train System, and imagine it now from two different stakeholders' points of view – the engineers involved in train development and the signalling engineers. The train development engineers may view the System in a similar way to the chess System, in that the complexity occurs at a low level of abstraction, as individual trains are very complex machines but, at a higher level, they simply drive along a set of rails. The signalling engineers may view the same System in a similar way to the Monopoly system, in that each train is viewed as a simple System as a train is a machine that goes backwards or forwards along the rails. However, stopping these simple machines from colliding and making them run on time is a very complex undertaking.

It is essential when modelling, therefore, to look at both the structural and behavioural aspects of the System and to look at the System at different levels of abstraction. In this way, areas of complexity may be identified and hence managed. It is also important to look at the System in different ways and from different stakeholders' points of view, which helps to keep the connection to reality for all stakeholders.

4.11　Summary

This chapter has discussed the important question of why we model, considering the question in light of the three evils of engineering: complexity, lack of understanding and communication. We model, that is we build a simplification of reality, in order to help us address these evils and the SysML gives us a general-purpose modelling language that allows us to do so in a way that addresses the key Requirements for any modelling language:

- The choice of model
- The level of abstraction
- Connection to reality
- Independent views of the same System

These Requirements have been discussed in this chapter, enabling the key issues of modelling to be considered before introducing the SysML language. Some of its history and the motivation behind the language have been given, along with a brief overview of the diagrams that make up the SysML. The two key aspects of any SysML model, namely that of structure and behaviour, have been discussed in some detail through a discussion of two of the SysML diagrams, the *block definition diagram* and the *state machine diagram*. The relationships between the *behavioural diagrams* and their use at different levels of System hierarchy were discussed. Finally, the chapter considered the identification of System complexity as it relates to levels of abstraction of a System's behaviour.

In Chapter 5 each of the nine SysML diagrams will be described in detail. Following this, Chapter 6 presents a number of diagramming guidelines that are intended to aid in the production of SysML models that have a consistent presentation style.

References

1. Booch G., Rumbaugh J., Jacobson I. *The Unified Modeling Language User Guide*. 2nd edn. Boston, MA: Addison-Wesley; 2005
2. Elk A. *The Brontosaurus Sketch*. Monty Python's Flying Circus. BBC TV; 1974
3. Pressman R. *Software Engineering: A Practitioner's Approach: European Adaptation*. Maidenhead: McGraw-Hill; 2000
4. Brookes F.P. *The Mythical Man-Month*. Boston, MA: Addison-Wesley; 1995
5. Object Management Group. *What Is OMG SysML?* [Online]. 2012. Available from http://www.omgsysml.org [Accessed April 2013]
6. Miller G.A. 'The magical number seven, plus or minus two: Some limits on our capacity for processing information'. *Psychological Review*. 1956; 63:81–97
7. Holt J., Perry S. *SysML for Systems Engineering*. Stevenage, UK: IET; 2008
8. Holt J. *UML for Systems Engineering – Watching the Wheels*. 2nd edn. Stevenage, UK: IET; 2004

Chapter 5

The SysML notation

Words are but symbols for the relations
of things to one another and to us;
nowhere do they touch upon absolute truth.

Friedrich Nietzsche (1844–1900)

5.1 Introduction

This chapter describes the nine SysML diagrams. Following this introduction, the terminology used throughout the chapter is explained and the structure of SysML diagrams is discussed. This is followed by a discussion of *stereotypes* and then of the SysML meta-model, which forms the basis of this chapter. Following this, each of the nine diagrams is described in turn. For each diagram type there is a brief introduction, a discussion of the diagram elements through its meta-model and notation, examples of how to use the diagram and a summary.

5.1.1 Diagram ordering

So far, we have looked at two of the diagrams in some detail when *block definition diagrams* and *state machine diagrams* were used to illustrate structural and behavioural modelling in Chapter 4; these diagrams are shown again in this chapter for the sake of completeness and also to introduce the meta-model using diagrams that are already well known.

The chapter first covers the *structural diagrams* and then the *behavioural diagrams*. Within these groupings there is no significance in the ordering of the diagrams. They are simply presented in, what is from the author's point of view, a logical order. Therefore, the various parts of this chapter may be read in any order.

5.1.2 The worked example

When discussing each of the SysML diagrams in the sections that follow, they will be discussed using an example System taken from the world of escapology. The System consists of an escapologist who is placed in a rectangular coffin, which is then placed into a hole. Concrete is pumped into the hole, under computer control, until the hole is full. The escapologist has to escape from the coffin and the concrete-filled hole before his breath runs out. Figure 5.1 shows the set-up for the escape.

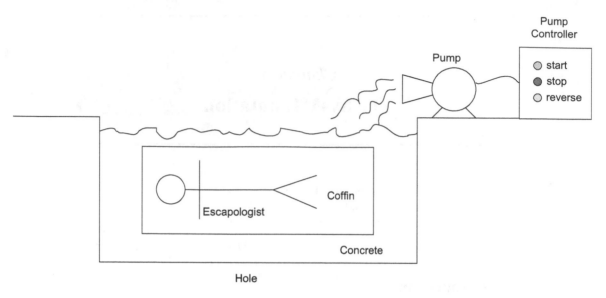

Figure 5.1   The coffin escape stunt

This is a classic escapology stunt that has been performed by many people. It is also a dangerous one, and escapologists have lost their lives performing it because the System Requirements and constraints were not properly understood or evaluated. One such performer was Joe Burrus who died 30 October 1990 when the weight of the concrete crushed the coffin he was in. This example is a socio-technical System that includes hardware, software, People and Process. It lends itself readily to the use of all of the SysML diagrams. What is more, it is not an example based around a library, an ATM or a petrol pump. The literature is already too full of such examples.

5.2   The structure of SysML diagrams

Each diagram in the SysML has the same underlying structure, which is intended to provide a similar appearance for each, as well as making cross-referencing between diagrams simpler. The structure of each diagram is shown in Figure 5.2.

The diagram in Figure 5.2 shows that each 'diagram' is made up of one or more 'graphic node' and one or more 'graphic path'. Each 'graphic path' relates together one or two 'graphic node'. Examples of graphic nodes include *blocks* on *block definition diagrams* and *states* on *state machine diagrams*. Examples of graphic paths include: *relationships* on *block definition diagrams* and *control flows* on *activity diagrams*.

The text '«stereotype»' on the *blocks* is an example of ... a *stereotype*. *Stereotypes* are a mechanism by which the SysML can be extended. Indeed, the

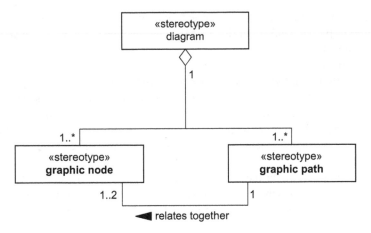

Figure 5.2   Structure of each SysML diagram

SysML itself is defined using *stereotypes* on the underlying unified modelling language (UML). *Stereotypes* are discussed in Section 5.3.

5.2.1   Frames

Any SysML diagram must have a graphic node known as a *frame* that encapsulates the diagram in order to make identification of, and navigation between, diagrams simpler. *Frames* have a defined format. This format, along with other guidelines for the use of *frames*, is described in detail in Chapter 6. Examples of *frames* will be seen around all the diagrams in the Examples subsections for each of the SysML diagrams in the following sections.

5.3   Stereotypes

Stereotypes provide a way to extend the SysML. They represent a powerful way to define new SysML elements by tailoring the SysML to your needs.

In order to use *stereotypes* effectively, it is first necessary to be able to spot one within a model. Visually, this is very simple, as *stereotypes* are indicated by enclosing the name of the *stereotype* within a set of double chevrons. Indeed, the SysML block itself contains the «block» *stereotype*.

Figure 5.3 shows two example *stereotypes*: «testCase» applied to a *block* (here representing a Scenario) and «validate» applied to a *dependency*.

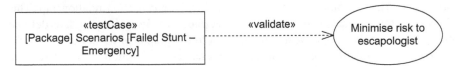

Figure 5.3   Example stereotypes

A *dependency*, represented by a dashed line with an open arrowhead, can be considered to be the weakest of the SysML relationships since it simply shows that there is some kind of (usually) unspecified relationship between the connected diagram elements. *Dependencies* are not named and cannot have any *multiplicities* associated with them. SysML makes use of a number of stereotyped *dependencies*, particularly in the *requirement diagram* and *use case diagram*, as described in Sections 5.5.5 and 5.5.9. In Figure 5.3, a new *stereotype* is used, one not found in the standard SysML, in order to show that a *test case* validates a *use case*. Note that «testCase» is a SysML stereotype and that the camel case naming is part of the SysML.

Stereotypes can be defined for any of the standard SysML elements. Unfortunately, the method by which *stereotypes* are defined varies from SysML tool to tool. However, a common diagrammatic method of defining a *stereotype*, found in many tools, is shown in Figure 5.4.

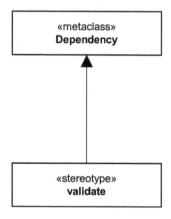

Figure 5.4   Defining a stereotype

The diagram in Figure 5.4 shows the definition of the «validate» *stereotype*. The diagram shows two *blocks*, 'Dependency' and 'validate', which are related together by a special type of *specialization/generalization* known as an *extension*. An *extension* is used specifically when defining *stereotypes*. An *extension* is represented graphically by a filled-in triangle – very similar to the *specialisation/generalisation* symbol.

The new *stereotype* to be defined, in this case 'validate', is shown in a *block*, which is itself stereotyped «stereotype». The SysML element that is being stereotyped, in this case a *dependency*, is shown in a *block* containing the «metaclass» *stereotype*. The two *blocks* are then connected with an *extension* relationship. This shows that the «validate» *stereotype* can be applied to a *dependency* and, as defined in Figure 5.4, only a *dependency*. In addition to the graphical definition, it is considered good modelling practice to provide a textual description of the *stereotype* that describes its intended use.

The diagram in Figure 5.4 can be generalised to give a rubber stamp version that forms the basis of the definition of any *stereotype*. Such a diagram is given in Figure 5.5.

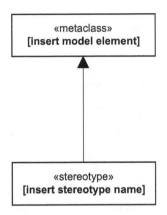

Figure 5.5   "Rubber stamp" diagram for stereotype definition

To use this diagram simply replace indicated text. For example, if it a modeller wanted to be able to apply the *stereotype* «ethernet» to an *association* on a *block definition diagram*, then start with Figure 5.5 and simply replace '[insert stereotype name]' with 'ethernet and '[insert model element]' with 'Association', giving the diagram as shown in Figure 5.6.

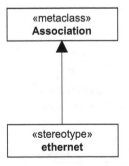

Figure 5.6   Another example of stereotype definition

When defining *stereotypes*, SysML also allows information to be associated with the *stereotype*. These *properties* are known as *tags* and they are defined as *properties* of the *stereotype block*. An example is given in Figure 5.7.

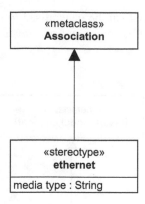

Figure 5.7   Stereotype with tag definition

The «ethernet» *stereotype* in Figure 5.7 has been extended through the definition of the 'media type' *tag*, intended to be used to show the type of ethernet being used. When the «ethernet» *stereotype* is applied to an *association* then a value can be given to any *tags* defined for that *stereotype*. These *tags* are then shown in a comment, as in the example in Figure 5.8.

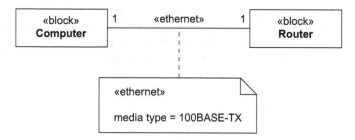

Figure 5.8   Example of stereotype usage with tags shown in comment

Note that not all SysML tools show *tags* in this way. For example, some tools show *tags* along with the stereotype as in Figure 5.9.

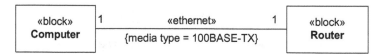

Figure 5.9   Example of stereotype usage with tags shown as part of stereotype

Each *tag* is shown with its value on a separate line underneath the *stereotype*. It is enclosed in curly braces. If a *stereotype* has multiple *tags*, then each will be displayed on a separate line.

5.4 The SysML meta-model

The SysML specification defines SysML in terms of the underlying UML on which SysML is based, and is done so using UML via the SysML meta-model. This is a model, in UML, of the SysML.

This chapter presents a partial meta-model for each of the nine SysML diagrams. In keeping with the use of UML in the SysML specification, UML *class diagrams* have been used to produce the SysML meta-model diagram throughout this chapter. These diagrams are the same as would be produced if using SysML *block definition diagrams*, and therefore can be read as SysML *block definition diagrams*. Thus, it *would* be possible to model the SysML using the SysML if desired.

The SysML meta-model itself is concerned with the modelling elements within the SysML, how they are constructed and how they relate to one another. The full UML meta-model on which SysML is based is highly complex and, to someone without much SysML (or UML) experience, can be quite impenetrable. The meta-models presented in this book show highly simplified versions of the actual meta-model in order to aid communication and to group different aspects of the model according to each diagram – something that is not done in the actual meta-model.

5.5 The SysML diagrams

This section describes each of the nine SysML diagrams, beginning with the five *structural diagrams* and concluding with the four *behavioural diagrams*.

5.5.1 Block definition diagrams

This section introduces what is perhaps the most widely used of the nine SysML diagrams: the *block definition diagram*. The *block definition diagram* was introduced in Chapter 4 in order to illustrate structural modelling and this section expands upon that information, covering more of the syntax and showing a wider range of examples, which are all taken from the escapology example that runs throughout this chapter.

Block definition diagrams realise a structural aspect of the model of a System and show what conceptual things exist in a System and what relationships exist between them. The things in a System are represented by *blocks* and their relationships are represented, unsurprisingly, by *relationships*.

5.5.1.1 Diagram elements

Block definition diagrams are made up of two basic elements: *blocks* and *relationships*. Both *blocks* and *relationships* may have various types and have more detailed syntax that may be used to add more information about them. However, at the highest level of abstraction, there are just the two very simple elements that must exist in the diagram. A *block definition diagram* may also contain different kinds of *ports* and *interfaces*, together with *item flows*, but at their simplest will just contain *blocks* and *relationships*.

Blocks describe the types of things that exist in a System, whereas *relationships* describe what the relationships are between various *blocks*.

Figure 5.10 shows a high-level meta-model of *block definition diagrams*.

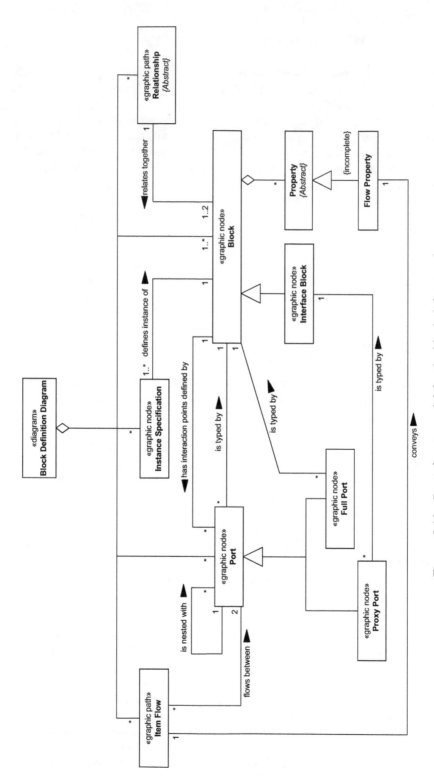

Figure 5.10 Partial meta-model for the block definition diagram

From Figure 5.10 we can see that a 'Block Definition Diagram' is made up of one or more 'Block', zero or more 'Relationship', zero or more 'Port', zero or more 'Item Flow' and zero or more 'Interface Specification'.

Each 'Relationship' relates together one or two 'Block'. Note that the multiplicity on the 'Block' side of the *association* is one or two, as it is possible for a 'Relationship' to relate together one 'Block' – that is to say that a 'Block' may be related to itself. A special kind of *block* is the 'Interface Block', used specifically to define Interfaces. An 'Instance Specification' defines an *instance* (real-world examples) of a 'Block'. Many such *instance specifications* may be defined for a 'Block'.

A 'Block' has interaction points defined by zero or more 'Port'. Each 'Port' is typed by a 'Block' and can be nested with zero or more other 'Port'. A 'Port' can be specialised further through two main sub-types:

- 'Full Port', used to represent an interaction point that is a separate element of the model. That is, a *full port* can have its own internal *parts* and behaviour.
- 'Proxy Port', used to represent an interaction point that identifies features of its owning *block* that are available to other, external *blocks*. They are not a separate element of the model and therefore do not specify their own internal *parts* and behaviour. Any such features and behaviour that they make available are actually those of its owning *block*. A 'Proxy Port' only be typed by an 'Interface Block'.

Neither *full ports* nor *proxy ports* have to be used. If it is unclear, when modelling, whether a *port* needs to be a *full port* or a *proxy port*, then leave it as a plain *port*. The decision whether to change to a *full* or *proxy port* can be made later as the model evolves.

Used in conjunction with the 'Port' is the 'Item Flow', which flows between two 'Port' and which conveys a 'Flow Property', a type of 'Property' of a 'Block' that is described below.

Each 'Block' is made up of zero or more 'Property', zero or more 'Operation' and zero or more 'Constraint' as shown in Figure 5.11.

The diagram in Figure 5.11 shows the partial meta-model for *block definition diagrams* showing the elements of a *block*. There are four types of 'Property':

- 'Part Property', which is owned by the 'Block'. That is, a *property* that is intrinsic to the *block* but which will have its own identity. A *part property* can be wholly owned by its parent *block* or may be shared between multiple parent *blocks*.
- 'Reference Property', which is referenced by the 'Block', but not owned by it.
- 'Value Property', which represents a 'Property' that cannot be identified except by the value itself, for example numbers or colours.
- 'Flow Property', which defines elements that that can flow to or from (or both) a *block*. They are mainly used to define the elements that can flow in and out of *ports* and all *item flows* that flow between *ports* are typed by *flow properties*.

Both an 'Operation' and a 'Property' (with the exception of a 'Flow Property') can be marked as being a 'Feature'. A *feature* is a *property* or *operation* that a *block* supports for other *blocks* to use (a 'Provided Feature') or which it requires other

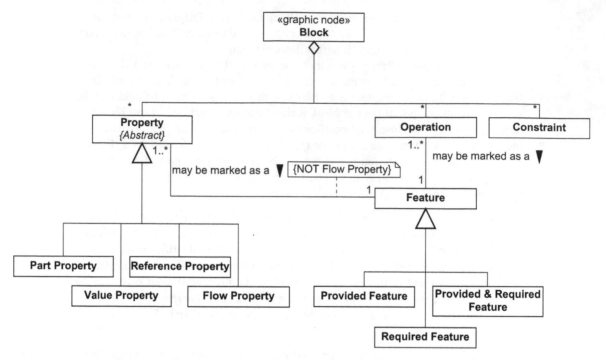

*Figure 5.11   Partial meta-model for the block definition diagram showing block
elements*

blocks to support for its own use (a 'Required Feature'), or both (a 'Provide &
Required Feature').

The differences between the first three types of *property* can be confusing. An
example will help and is illustrated in Figure 5.12.

The *block definition diagram* in Figure 5.12(a) models the structure of the
Coffin Escape stunt and the reader is directed to Figure 5.14 for a description of the
notation. The diagram shows that the 'Coffin Stunt' is composed of a 'Reservoir', a
'Coffin', a 'Pump', a 'Hole', a Pump Controller', a 'Fluid' and an 'Escapologist'.
The 'Fluid' has a 'Density', which will be represented as 'kg/m^3' (representing
kilograms per cubic metre). The 'Fluid' is pumped into the 'Hole' via the 'Pump'
and is supplied from the 'Reservoir'. Note the use of *role names* at the ends of the
composition and *association relationships*.

The 'Density' is simply a number – it does not have any individual identity –
and is therefore treated as a *value* property.

The 'Reservoir', 'Coffin', 'Pump', etc., are all intrinsic parts of the 'Coffin
Escape'. That is, they can be thought of as having their own identity but form elements of the 'Coffin Escape'. Therefore, they are modelled as *part properties*, which
is shown using *composition*. If a *part* can be an element of more than one owning
block at the same time, then *aggregation* would be used rather than *composition*.

The 'Fluid' is not part of the 'Hole' or the 'Reservoir'. It is pumped into the
former and supplied by the latter. It has its own identity. For this reason, it is related

(a)
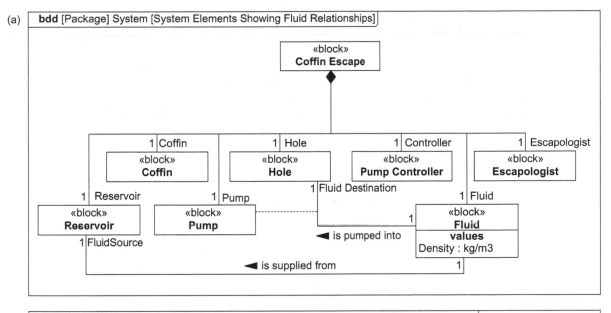

(b)
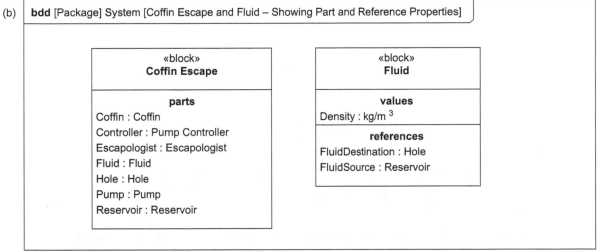

Figure 5.12   Types of property – alternative representations

to 'Hole' and to 'Reservoir' through *associations*. Any *block* related to another through an *association* can be considered to be a *reference* property of the *block* it is related to.

The nature of such *relationships* and the types of *property* they represent can be seen clearly in the *block definition diagram* in Figure 5.12(b). This shows exactly the same information but in a different format that uses named *property compartments* rather than via graphical paths and nodes. This shows how the various graphical representations can be rendered into a textual format. There are two things to note. First, the *role names* on the *relationships* are used to name the *properties* when displayed in *property compartments*. Second, in the case of *reference properties*, the *association name* ('is supplied from' or 'is pumped into' in the example above) does not form part of the information in the *property compartment*, which is a loss of information. The *property* compartment notation is more compact than the full *composition* and *association* notation, although perhaps not as clear; useful perhaps when producing summary diagrams.

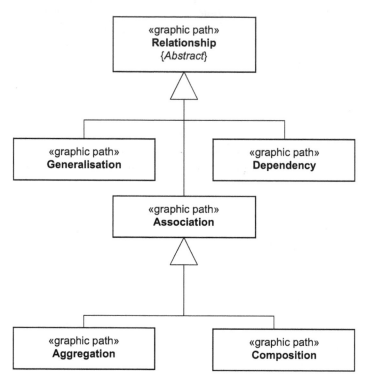

Figure 5.13   Partial meta-model for the block definition diagram showing types of relationship

Continuing our breakdown of the meta-model for the block definition diagram, there are three main types of 'Relationship' as shown in Figure 5.13:

- 'Association', which defines a simple *relationship* between one or more *blocks*. There are also two *specialisations* of 'Association' known as 'Aggregation' and 'Composition', which show *shared parts* and *owned parts* respectively, as discussed earlier in this section.
- 'Generalisation', which shows a 'has types' *relationship* that is used to show parent and child *blocks*.

- 'Dependency', which is used to show that one *block* (often referred to as the client) somehow depends on another *block* (often referred to as the supplier) such that a change to the supplier may impact the client. 'Dependency' can be considered to be the weakest of the *relationships* since it simply shows that there is some kind of (usually) unspecified *relationship* between the connected *blocks*.

A summary of the notation used in the *block definition diagram* is shown in Figure 5.14.

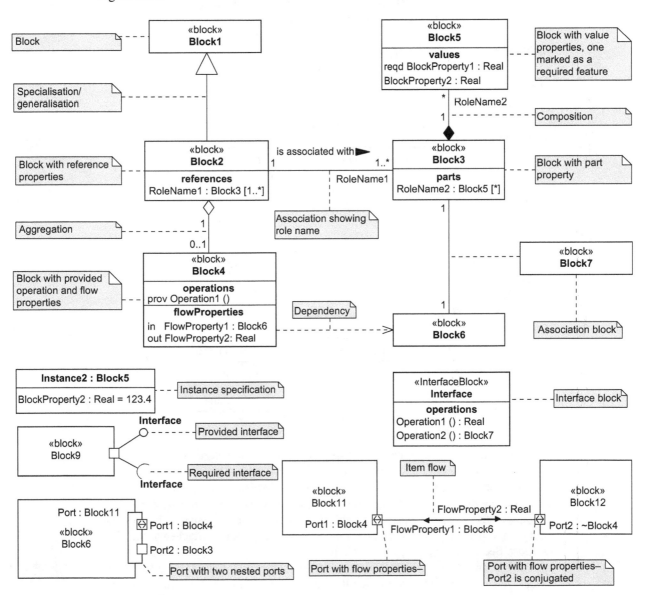

Figure 5.14   Summary of block definition diagram notation

The diagram in Figure 5.14 shows the graphical symbols used to represent elements in a *block definition diagram*. The basic symbol is the *block*, which is represented by a rectangle. Rectangles are also used to show other types of element in the SysML, so it is important to be able to differentiate between a *block* rectangle and any other sort of rectangle. A *block* rectangle will simply contain a single name, with no colons. It will also contain the *stereotype* «block».

When *properties*, *operations* and *constraints* are present, these are shown in *compartments* drawn underneath the block name, with the *properties*, *operations* and *constraints* contained within. Each of these *compartments* will be labelled to show what they contain, and the *property compartments* will be further sub-divided to show *part*, *reference*, *value* and *flow properties*.

Any *properties* or *operations* that are *features* are prefixed as shown in Table 5.1.

Table 5.1   Prefixes used with features

Type of feature	Prefix
Required	reqd
Provided	prov
Provided & Required	provreqd

Flow properties have their direction indicated with prefixes as shown in Table 5.2.

Table 5.2   Prefixes used with flow properties

Direction of flow property	Prefix
In	in
Out	out
In & out	inout

The *interfaces* are defined using special *blocks* that are *stereotyped* «interface» and which usually only have *operations*, but no *properties*. The *operations* represent the services provided by a *block* (or *port*) that has that *interface* as a *provided interface*, or the services required by a *block* (or *port*) that has it as a *required interface*. *Provided* and *required interfaces* can be shown graphically using a ball or cup notation respectively, labelled with the name of the *interface* and attached to the *block* or *port*. See for example 'Block9' in Figure 5.14.

Ports are shown as small squares (or rectangles) straddling the edge of the *block*. They can be labelled to give the *port* a name and to identify the *block* that types the *port*. For example, in Figure 5.14 'Block11' has a *port* with the name

'Port1', which is typed by 'Block4'. *Full* and *proxy ports* are indicated by placing the «full» or «proxy» *stereotype* next to the *port*.

Ports that have *flow properties* contain a small arrow showing the direction of the flow (whether into the *port*, out of the *port*, or both). See 'Port1' on 'Block11' in Figure 5.14 for an example of a *port* with *flow properties* that go both into and out of the *port*.

If a *port* has some *flow properties* that flow in and some that flow out, then when connected to another *port* it is necessary to show that these flows need to be shown in the opposite direction. For example, look again at 'Port1' on 'Block11'. This *port* is typed by 'Block4', which has two *flow properties*: 'FlowProperty1' flows in and 'FlowProperty2' flows out. This means that 'Port1' has the same *flow properties*, since it is typed by 'Block4'. However, now consider 'Port2' on 'Block12'. This is connected to 'Port1' on 'Block11' and, therefore, will have 'FlowProperty1' flowing out and 'FlowProperty2' flowing in; the opposite way round to how they have been specified in 'Block4'.

How do we resolve this? The answer is to make 'Port2' on 'Bock12' a *conjugated port*. This is indicated by the tilde "~" prefixing the name of the *block* typing the *port*: 'Port2: ~Block4'. The tilde reverses all the ins and outs prefixing the *flow properties* in the *block* that it prefixes. So, as far as 'Port2' is concerned, it has two *flow properties*: 'FlowProperty1', which flows out and 'FlowProperty2', which flows in. As the directions on the two ends now match up correctly, the *ports* can be connected and the flows shown using *items flows*.

Item flows are represented by a labelled triangle or a solid arrow attached to an *association*. The *item flow* can have a name by which it can be identified and is also labelled with the *property* that is transferred. This latter may appear at first to be redundant, as *item flows* connect *ports* that themselves are typed. However, SysML allows the modeller to differentiate between what may be transferred and what is transferred. The *type* of a *port* shows what may be transferred, with the *type* of an *item flow* showing what is transferred. However, the type of the *item flow* must be related to the type of the *port* by a specialisation–generalisation relationship. An example of this is given in the following section.

Instance specifications have a compartment that shows the *name* of the *instance specification* (so that multiple *instance specifications* of the same type can be differentiated) and the *block* that it is an instance of. This is underlined. For example, in Figure 5.14 there is an *instance specification* labelled 'Instance2 : Block5'. This *instance specification* has a name, 'Instance2' and is an instance of 'Block5'. An additional *compartment* can be shown, in which *properties* of the typing *block* may be given values for this instance. In this example, the *property* 'BlockProperty2' is given the value '123.4'.

5.5.1.2 Examples

This section presents some examples of *block definition diagrams* and related diagramming elements. Further examples will be found in the case study in Chapter 13.

Figure 5.15 shows the main structural elements for the Coffin Escape Stunt. It shows that there is a 'Coffin Escape' that is composed of a 'Reservoir', a 'Coffin',

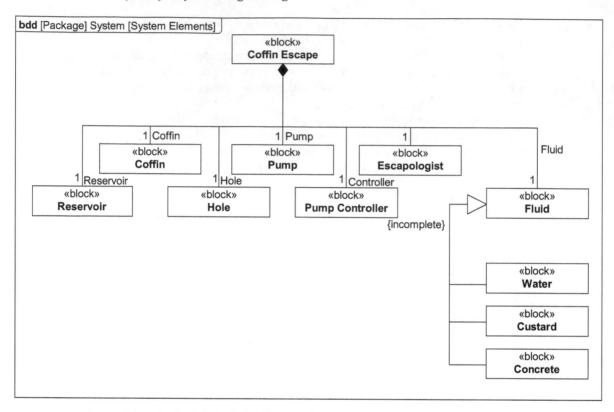

Figure 5.15   Example block definition diagram showing main structural elements of the Coffin Escape Stunt

a 'Hole', a 'Pump', an 'Escapologist' and a 'Fluid'. Three types of 'Fluid' are defined: 'Water', 'Custard' and 'Concrete'. The use of the {incomplete} *constraint* indicates that there may be additional types of 'Fluid' that are not shown in this diagram.

Note that there are no *properties* or *operations* defined for any of the *blocks* on the diagram, nor any *relationships*. This has been done deliberately in order to keep the diagram simple. This information is shown on additional *block definition diagrams*, starting with the one shown in Figure 5.16, which expands on the definition of 'Fluid'.

In Figure 5.16 the definition of 'Fluid' and its *sub-types* is expanded in order to show that 'Fluid' has a *value property* named 'Density'. Since 'Water', 'Custard' and 'Concrete' are all *sub-types* of 'Fluid' they inherit this *property*. SysML allows *value properties* to be given default values, as shown here.

Properties and *operations* of some of the other *blocks*, along with the *relationships* between them, are shown in Figure 5.17.

Figure 5.17 shows a lot more information about the various System Elements that make up the Coffin Escape System. We can see that an 'Escapologist' escapes

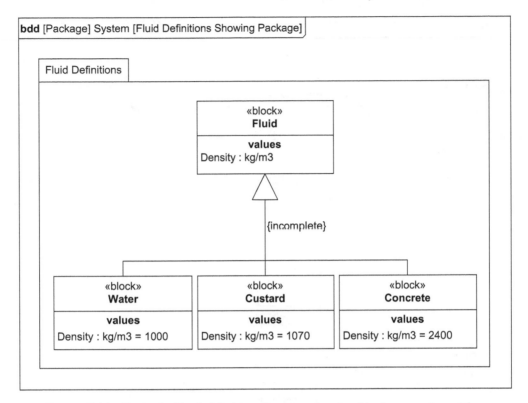

Figure 5.16   Example block definition diagram showing block properties with default values

from a 'Coffin' that is placed in the bottom of a 'Hole'. A 'Pump Controller' controls a 'Pump'. 'Fluid' is pumped into the 'Hole' via the 'Pump'. This latter aspect of the model is captured through the use of an *association block*: the 'Pump' *block* is connected to the *association* between 'Fluid' and 'Hole' with a dashed line, making 'Pump' an *association block*. It is a *block* in its own right, but adds information to the *association*. A maximum of one *block* can act as an *association block* on any given *association*.

Many of the *blocks* have *value properties* that help to define them further and 'Pump' has a number of *operations* that show the behaviour that it can carry out. Both 'Hole' and 'Pump' have two *ports* defined. These *ports* have been shown using a *port compartment* and shown textually rather than graphically. This has been done simply to reduce visual clutter on the diagram.

It is worth considering these *ports* in a little more detail. 'Pump' has a *port*, 'pOut', that is typed by the *block* 'FluidFlow' (see Figure 5.18).

This 'FluidFlow' *block* defines a single *flow property*: 'out fluid : Fluid'. This says that elements typed by 'FluidFlow' will have a single *flow property*, of type 'Fluid', flowing out of them. This agrees with the definition of the *port* 'pOut', since this *port* has the *out flow direction* prefixed. 'Pump' has another *port* defined, 'pIn'.

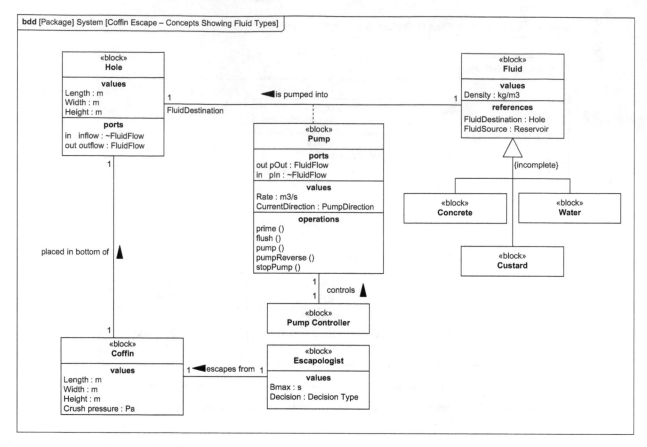

Figure 5.17   Example block definition diagram showing properties, operations and relationships

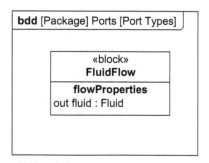

Figure 5.18   Example block definition diagram defining type of ports through use of flow properties

The intention is that this *port* takes in whatever *flow properties* are defined by 'FluidFlow'. However, if it was defined as 'in pIn : FluidFlow' then we would have a consistency issue. The *port* is marked with an *in flow direction* but the *flow property* in its *type* has an *out flow direction*. The solution is to make 'pIn' a *conjugated port*. This has been done through the use of a tilde in the definition: 'in pIn : ~FluidFlow'. The directions of the *flow properties* defined in 'FluidFluid' are now reversed as far as 'pIn' is concerned. A similar discussion holds for the *ports* of 'Hole'. The notation and use of *conjugated ports* perhaps makes more sense when they are shown connected together. An example will be shown in Section 5.5.2.

A final point to make about Figure 5.17 concerns the *reference compartment* in the 'Fluid' *block*. This shows two *reference properties*. Remember that these correspond to *associations* that the *block* is involved in. One of these is shown on the diagram, as can be deduced via the *role name* 'FluidDestination' on the *association* between 'Fluid' and 'Hole'. The other *reference property* corresponds to an *association* that is not shown. We can deduce from the *reference property* that 'Fluid' has an *association* with a *block* called 'Reservoir' and that the *role* that 'Reservoir' plays in the *association* is that of 'FluidSource'. For completeness, this association is shown explicitly in Figure 5.19.

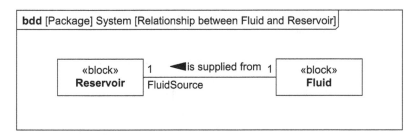

Figure 5.19   Example block definition diagram showing a reference property explicitly as an association

Figure 5.19 illustrates an important point when modelling: don't be afraid to limit what you show on a diagram. SysML tools make the consistent creation of diagrams quick and easy, provided of course that they are a robust and sharp tool (see Chapter 16 for a discussion of tools). If information is best omitted from one diagram, then do so. You can always create another diagram that does show the information.

As two final examples of a *block definition diagram* in this section, consider Figures 5.20 and 5.21.

The *blocks* in Figure 5.20 do not represent items of hardware or software or material, etc., but rather they represent Source Elements for Need Descriptions, produced as part of a requirements engineering activity. The diagram *frame* uses the *frame tag* 'SEV' to show that this *block definition diagram* is being used as a Source Element View. For a discussion of model-based requirements engineering and the ACRE Framework from which the concept of a Source Element View is taken, see Chapter 9.

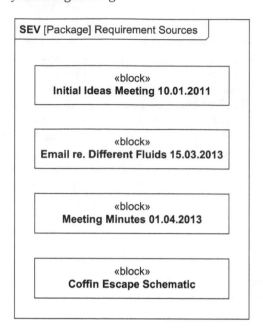

Figure 5.20   Example block definition diagram used to model Source Elements of Requirements

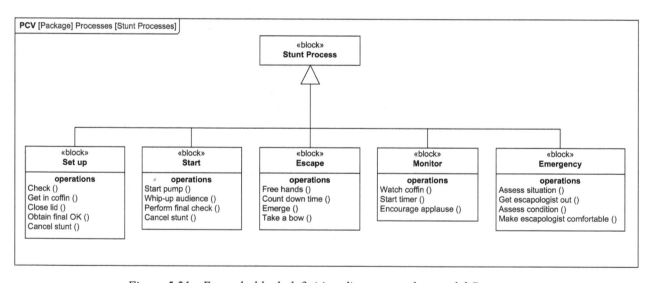

Figure 5.21   Example block definition diagram used to model Processes

The *blocks* in Figure 21 also do not represent items of hardware or software or material, etc., but rather they represent Processes, produced as part of a Process modelling activity. The diagram *frame* uses the *frame tag* 'PCV' to show that this *block definition diagram* is being used as a Process Content View. For a discussion of a model-based approach to Process modelling and the "seven views" Framework from which the concept of a Process Content View is taken, see Chapter 7.

5.5.1.3   Summary

Block definition diagrams can be used to model just about anything and form the backbone of any SysML model. *Block definition diagrams* are perhaps the richest in terms of the amount of syntax available and, as with all the meta-models in this chapter, the one given for *block definition diagrams* is incomplete. For example, it could be extended to include extra detail that can be added to relationships, such as *role names* and *qualifiers*.

The main aim of the *block definition diagram*, as with all SysML diagrams, is clarity and simplicity. *Block definition diagrams* should be able to be read easily and they should make sense. A diagram that is difficult to read may simply indicate that there is too much on it and that it needs to be broken down into a number of other diagrams. It may also be an indication that the modelling is not correct and that it needs to be revisited. Another possibility is that the diagram is revealing fundamental complexity inherent in the System, from which lessons may be learned.

Another fundamental point that must be stressed here is that *block definition diagrams* are not used in isolation. They will form the main structural aspect of a System but must be used in conjunction with the other eight SysML diagrams to provide structural and behavioural views of a System. These diagrams are described in the rest of this chapter.

5.5.2   *Internal block diagrams*

Internal block diagrams are used to model the internal structure of a *block* (hence the name). By using an *internal block diagram*, in which *compositions* and *aggregations* are implicitly represented by the containment of *parts* within the owning *block* or within other *parts*, an emphasis may be put on the logical relationships between elements of the *composition*, rather than the structural breakdown itself. This adds a great deal of value, as it forces the modeller to think about the logical relationship between elements, rather than simply which *blocks* are part of which other *blocks*.

5.5.2.1   Diagram elements

The basic element within *an internal block diagram* is the *part* that describes *blocks* in the context of an owning *block*. An *internal block diagram* identifies *parts* and their internal structures, showing how they are connected together through *ports* and showing the *item flows* that flow between *parts*.

The diagram in Figure 5.22 shows the partial meta-model for the *internal block diagram*. It can be seen that a 'Internal block diagram' is made up of one or more 'Part', zero or more 'Port' and zero or more 'Binding Connector' and zero or more 'Item Flow'.

A 'Port' defines an interaction point for a 'Part', just as they do for *blocks* (see Section 5.5.1.1) and again come in two types: 'Full Port' and 'Proxy Port'. A 'Part'

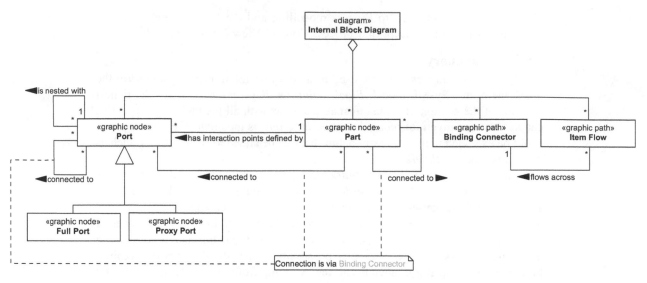

Figure 5.22   Partial meta-model for the internal block diagram

can be directly connected to zero or more 'Part' via a 'Binding Connector'. This connection may also be from a 'Part' to the 'Port' on another 'Part'. A 'Port' may also be connected to zero or more 'Port'. An 'Item Flow' can flow across a 'Binding Connector'.

The intention in the SysML specification seems to be that these connections should be shown only on an *internal block diagram*, with a *block definition diagram* showing the *ports* on a block, but not the connections between them. For this reason the *block definition diagram* meta-model in Section 5.5.1.1 omits such connection possibilities, but the authors see no reason why the same types of connection should not be shown on a *block definition diagram*.

The diagram in Figure 5.23 shows the notation used on an *internal block diagram*. Much of the notation is the same as can be found on a *block definition diagram* and will not be discussed further. However, some notational and usage points do need discussion, namely:

- The relationship between *internal block diagrams* and *block definition diagrams*, and hence that of *parts* and *blocks*
- The notation for *parts*
- *Shared parts*

Before looking at the notation for *parts*, let us first consider the relationship between *internal block diagrams* and *block definition diagrams*, and hence that of *parts* and *blocks*. The first thing to say is that an *internal block diagram* is owned by a *block*. It is used, when a *block* is composed of other *blocks*, to represent that composition in an alternative fashion and to allow the modeller to concentrate on

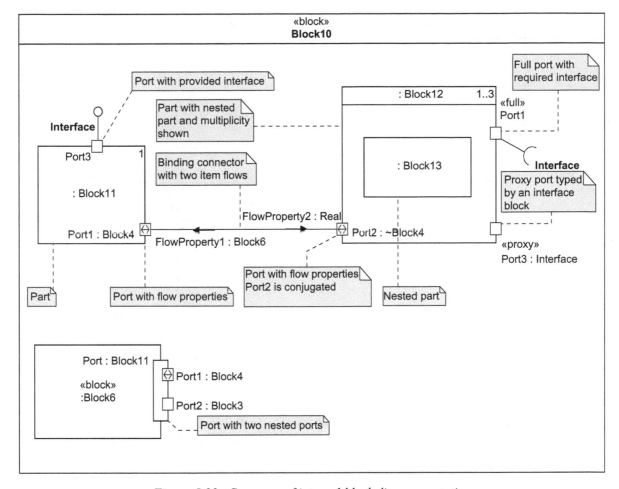

Figure 5.23   Summary of internal block diagram notation

the connections between the *blocks* rather than on the composition. From a *block* that is decomposed into sub-blocks it is possible to automatically create an *internal block diagram* for that *block* and, indeed, many SysML tools will do this for you. The *internal block diagram* in Figure 5.23 has been created for 'Block10', based on the *block definition diagram* in Figure 5.24.

The *internal block diagram* in Figure 5.23 is owned by 'Block10' and can be thought of as being inside, or internal to (hence the name) 'Block10'. 'Block10' is shown as containing *block* with the *blocks* that it is composed of shown as *parts*. (Note that the *ports* in Figure 5.23 could have also been shown in Figure 5.24 but have been omitted for clarity). So, a *block* that is composed of *sub-blocks*, as detailed on a *block definition diagram*, can have its internal structure modelled on an *internal block diagram* owned by the *block*. The *blocks* that it is composed of are shown as *parts* on the *internal block diagram*.

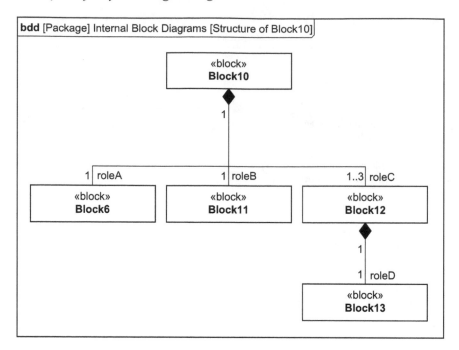

Figure 5.24   Example block definition diagram used to show its relationship to internal block diagram

This brings us on to the second point, namely the notation used for *parts*. *Parts* are represented using a rectangle that contains the name of the *part*. The name has the form:

Part name : Type Name

The *part name* serves as an identifier for the *part* and the *type name* shows the *block* that the *part* is a type of. The *part name* can be omitted if distinction between different *parts* of the same type is not necessary. The *type name* can also be omitted, but this is less common. In Figure 5.23 each *part* has its *part name* omitted and its *type name* shown. Where the *block* involved in a composition has a *role name* associated with it, then the *part name* is usually directly related to the *role name*. See Figure 5.25.

Figure 5.25 is another *internal block diagram* for 'Block10' from Figure 24, but this time with all *ports*, *interfaces* and *connectors* omitted. Also, on this diagram *part names* are shown and their relationship to the *role names* in Figure 5.24 can also be seen.

Two other points can also be seen in both Figures 5.23 and 4.24. First, if a *part* has a *multiplicity* greater than one, this is shown in the top right corner of the *part*. This can be seen for the *part* typed by 'Block12' in both diagrams, where the *multiplicity* '1..3' is shown in the top right corner of the *part*. Second, *parts* can also

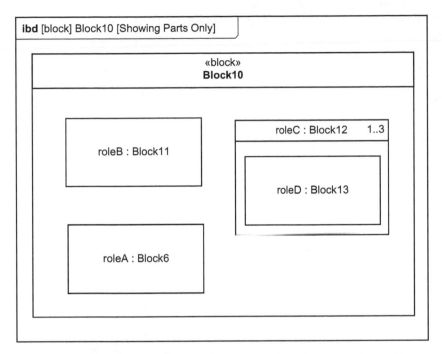

Figure 5.25   Example internal block diagram used to show its relationship to block definition diagram

be nested and this can be seen for the *part* 'roleD : Block13', which is shown inside the *part* 'roleC : Block12'. This corresponds to the *composition relationship* between 'Block12' and 'Block13'. This *composition relationship* also means that 'Block12' could have its own *internal block diagram*, which would have a single *part*, 'roleD : Block13'. For completeness, refer Figure 5.26.

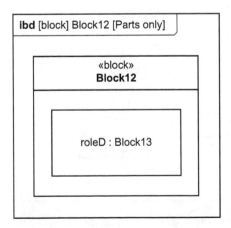

Figure 5.26   Example internal block diagram for Block12

Finally, let us consider *shared parts*. As was discussed briefly in Section 5.5.1.1, the decomposition of a *block* can be shown on a *block definition diagram* using a *composition* or an *aggregation*. A *block* may be wholly owned by its parent *block* (shown using *composition*) or may be shared between multiple parent *blocks* (shown using *aggregation*). The use of *composition* or *aggregation* has an effect on the way that *parts* are shown. An example will help.

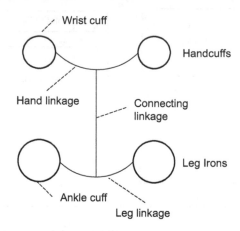

Figure 5.27   Example system schematic showing owned and shared parts

The non-SysML diagram in Figure 5.27 shows the restraints worn by the escapologist as part of the Coffin Escape Stunt: a set of handcuffs and a set of leg irons joined by a connecting linkage. The structure can be modelled using a *block definition diagram* as shown in Figure 5.28.

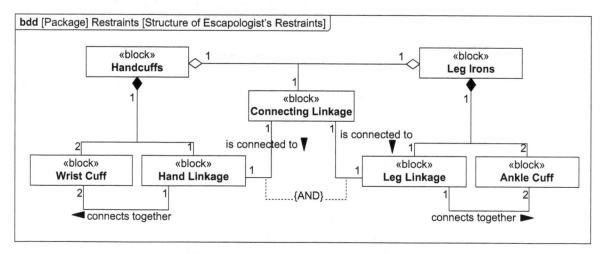

Figure 5.28   Example block definition diagram showing modelling of owned and shared parts

The restraints consist of a set of 'Handcuffs' composed of two 'Wrist Cuff' connected together by a 'Hand Linkage' and a set of 'Leg Irons' composed of two 'Ankle Cuff' connected together by a 'Leg Linkage'. The 'Hand Linkage' and the 'Leg Linkage' are connected together by a 'Connecting Linkage'. Since the 'Wrist Cuff' and 'Hand Linkage' are only part of the 'Handcuffs', *composition* is used. Similarly for the 'Ankle Cuff' and 'Leg Linkage'. However, the 'Connecting Linkage' is shared between both the 'Handcuffs' and the 'Leg Irons'. For this reason, *aggregation* is used. This has a direct effect on the notation used in the *internal block diagrams* for the 'Handcuffs' and the 'Leg Irons'. The *internal block diagram* for the 'Handcuffs' is shown in Figure 5.29. That of the 'Leg Irons' would be similar.

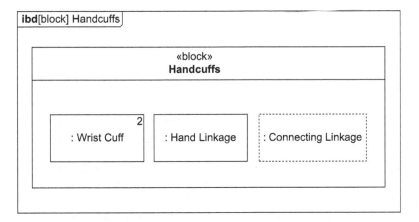

Figure 5.29   Example internal block diagrams showing owned and shared parts

The difference in notation for *shared parts* can be seen in the *internal block diagram* in Figure 5.29. A *shared part* is shown with a dashed outline. Note also the *multiplicity* in the top right of the 'Wrist Cuff' *part*. Also, note that it is not possible to tell from this diagram what else the 'Connecting Linkage' is shared with. The *block definition diagram* in Figure 5.28 is needed for this.

5.5.2.2   Examples

This section presents some examples of *internal block diagrams* and related diagramming elements. Further examples will be found in the case study in Chapter 13.

Having defined the structure of the 'Coffin Escape' stunt in section 5.5.1 on *block definition diagrams* (see Figures 5.15 and 5.17), an *internal block diagram* can be used to explore the interfaces between the System Elements of the 'Coffin Escape'. This has been done in Figure 5.30.

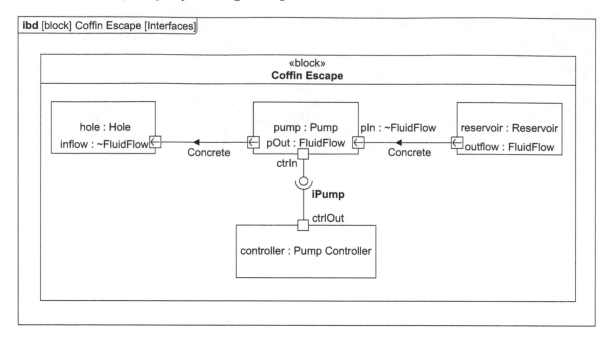

Figure 5.30   Example internal block diagram showing main Interfaces of the
Coffin Escape Stunt

Figure 5.30 shows an *internal block diagram* for the 'Coffin Escape' *block*. The *parts* shown on this diagram can be populated automatically from the structural information, shown using *composition*, in Figure 5.15. Note, however, that the 'Escapologist', 'Coffin' and 'Fluid' *blocks* have not been shown in Figure 5.30. This is because, as indicated in the *diagram frame*, this *internal block diagram* has been produced to show interfaces between the main system elements. This again reinforces the point that in SysML you should be producing diagrams for a specific purpose. You do not have to try to show everything on a single diagram, nor should you try to.

Whereas Figure 5.17 implicitly indicated the various *ports* and their connections, through the use of *port compartments* on the *blocks*, these connections have been made explicit in Figure 5.30. This is a very common use of the *internal block diagram*.

There are two points worth discussing further on this diagram. The first concerns the nature of the two *item flows* on the diagram and the second that of the interface between the 'Pump Controller' and the 'Pump'.

In Figure 5.17 there are a number of *ports* defined on the 'Pump' and 'Hole' blocks. Each of these is typed by the 'FluidFlow' *block* that has a single *flow property* typed by the 'Fluid' *block*. 'Reservoir' has a similar *port* but it is not shown in Figure 5.17. In Figure 5.30 these *ports* have been connected together with *binding connectors* carrying *item flows*. The 'outflow' *port* of 'Reservoir' sends an *item flow* to the 'pIn' *port* of 'Pump', which in turn sends and *item flow* from its 'pOut' *port* to the 'inFlow' *port* of 'Hole'. The direction of each of the *item flows* honours the direction of each *port* and of the *flow property* defined by 'FluidFlow'.

However, whereas 'FluidFlow' defines a *flow property* of type 'Fluid', the *item flow* shows 'Concrete' flowing between the *ports*. Do we have an inconsistency here? The answer is no, because 'Concrete' is a type of 'Fluid', as can be seen in Figure 5.15. This is an important point, and one that makes *item flows* and *flow properties* useful. It is possible, through *flow properties*, to define the type of things that can flow between *ports* and keep this at a rather general level of abstraction (e.g. 'Fluid'). Then, through *item flows*, it is possible to show what actually does flow in a particular usage of the various *blocks*. Although the 'Pump' modelled in Figures 5.15 and 5.17 can pump a number of types of 'Fluid', when it is being used in the 'Coffin Escape', as shown in Figure 5.30, it will be used to pump 'Concrete'. The *type* of the *item flow* has to be the same as, or a *sub-type* of, the *type* of its defining *flow property*. The *flow property* is of *type* 'Fluid' and the *item flow* is of *type* 'Concrete', which is a *sub-type* of 'Fluid', so this is allowed.

The second point to discuss is the interface between the 'Pump Controller' and the 'Pump'. This connection is explicitly shown in Figure 5.30, where the 'Pump' has a *provided interface* of *type* 'iPump' and where the 'Pump Controller' has a *required interface* of the same *type*. These are shown connected together and the *type* of the *interface*, 'iPump', is also shown. This *interface* has not yet been defined. Its definition is made on a *block definition diagram* using an *interface block*, as shown in Figure 5.31.

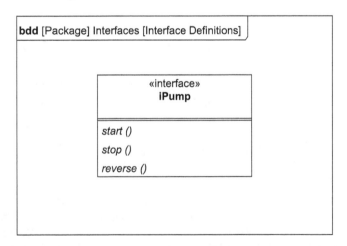

Figure 5.31   Example block definition diagram defining the iPump interface

Figure 5.31 defines a single *interface*, 'iPump', which has three *operations* 'start()', 'stop()' and 'reverse()'. In the SysML model from which this diagram is taken, each of these three *operations* would have a full description of their expected behaviour, both in text, as part of their definition in the 'iPump' *interface block*, and possibly also in SysML using an *activity diagram*. Although Figure 5.31 only defines a single *interface block*, there is no reason why other *interface blocks* could not be defined on the same diagram; the SysML does not require them to be defined on separate diagrams.

When connecting a *required interface* to a *provided interface* it is important that the *types* of the *interfaces* match (i.e. that they are defined by the same *interface block*). Actually, there is a little more flexibility allowed: the *type* of the *provided* interface must be the same as, or a *sub-type* of, the *type* of the *required interface*. This works because when a *sub-type* is defined, the *sub-type* can add additional *operations* but cannot remove any. Consider Figure 5.32.

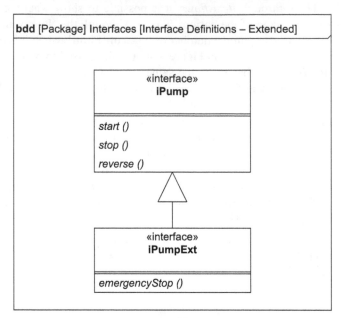

Figure 5.32   Example block definition diagram showing extended iPump interfaces

A new *interface,* 'iPumpExt', is defined in Figure 5.32. This defines a new *operation,* 'emergencyStop()'. Since 'iPumpExt' is a *sub-type* of 'iPump' it also inherits all three *operations* that are defined for 'iPump'.

Now imagine that 'Pump' in Figure 5.30 has a *provided interface* that is of *type* 'iPumpExt' rather than 'iPump'. The *required interface* on 'Pump Controller' can still be connected to this *provided interface* because 'iPumpExt' provides all the *operations* that 'iPump' did (and that are required by the 'Pump Controller'), plus one more. It happens that 'Pump Controller' will never require the use of this additional *operation*, which is okay.

However, if the *required interface* on 'Pump Controller' was of *type* 'iPumpExt' and the *provided interface* on 'Pump' was of *type* 'iPump', then the connection could not be made. This is because 'Pump Controller' requires the use of the 'emergencyStop()' *operation* defined on 'iPumpExt'. However, this is not present in the 'iPump' *interface* provided by 'Pump'.

Internal block diagrams can also be used with *association blocks*, since an *association block* is, in effect, simply a *block* connected to an *association*. This is useful when the *association block* is being used to model a connector between two physical System Elements, as shown in Figure 5.33.

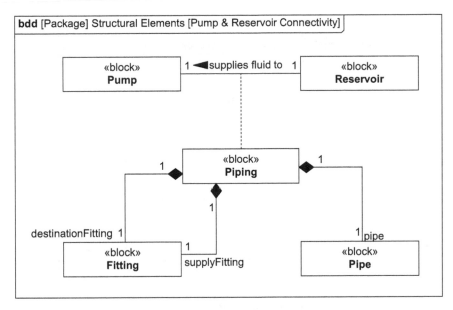

Figure 5.33   Example block definition diagram showing connectivity using an association block

In Figure 5.33, the connectivity between the 'Reservoir' and the 'Pump' is modelled using an *association block*, 'Piping', which is composed of a length of 'Pipe' and two 'Fitting', one for each end. The way that the 'Piping' is assembled is modelled using an *internal block diagram*, shown in Figure 5.34.

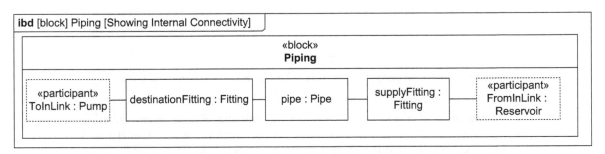

Figure 5.34   Example internal block diagram showing structure of Piping

In Figure 5.34 the *parts* from which 'Piping' is composed are shown connected using *binding connectors*. The diagram also shows two *shared parts*: 'FromInLink : Reservoir' and 'ToInLink : Pump'. These *shared parts* actually represent the ends of the *association* between 'Reservoir' and 'Pump' for which 'Piping' acts as an *association block*.

As a final example, consider Figure 5.35 that shows two *internal block diagrams* that concentrate on the 'Power Supply Unit' used in the Coffin Escape Stunt to power the 'Pump'.

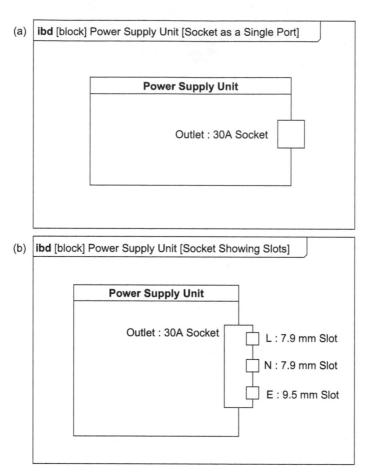

Figure 5.35   Example internal block diagram showing nested ports

In the *internal block diagram* (Figure 5.35(a)) the 'Power Supply Unit' is shown as having a 30A outlet, modelled as a *port* with the name 'Outlet : 30A Socket'. Nothing of the structure of the socket is shown here. This is fine, as long as this is the level of abstraction that is needed in the model. The *port* can be connected to another *port* representing a 30 A plug, for example, and a single *item flow* defined that connects them representing the transfer of AC current at 30 A.

However, it might be the case that the socket (and any associated plug) needs to be modelled at a lower level of abstraction. This is done in the *internal block diagram* in Figure 5.35(b), where the three slots making up the socket are shown explicitly using three *nested ports*. The 30A plug could be modelled in the same way, showing each pin using a *nested port*. Each pin and slot could then be connected individually, with the high-level *item flow* decomposed into three separate *item flows*, one connecting each pin and slot pair. This is left as an exercise for the reader.

5.5.2.3 Summary

The *internal block diagram* is very strongly related to the *block definition diagram*, using *parts* to show the structure of a complex *block*. This allows the emphasis of the diagram to be placed more on the logical relationships between elements of the *block*, rather than identifying that they are actually elements of a particular *block* (using relationships such as *aggregation* and *composition*). The way that the various *parts* are connected, through the use of *ports*, *interfaces* and *binding connectors*, and the items that flow between *parts*, through the use of *item flows*, can also be shown. The diagram also allows a distinction to be made between *parts* that are wholly owned by a parent *block*, and those that are *shared parts*, which are shared among multiple *blocks*.

5.5.3 Package diagrams

The *package diagram*, as the name implies, identifies and relates together *packages*. *Packages* can be used on other diagrams as well as on the *package diagram*; in both cases the concept of the *package* is the same – each *package* shows a collection of *diagram elements* and implies some sort of ownership. *Packages* can be related to each other using a number of different *dependency relationships*.

5.5.3.1 Diagram elements

The syntax for the *package diagram* is very simple and can be seen in Figure 5.36.

The diagram in Figure 5.36 shows the partial meta-model for the 'Package Diagram'. It can be seen that there are two main elements in the diagram – the 'Package' and the 'Dependency'. There is one type of 'Dependency' defined – the 'Package Import'. The 'Package Import' has two types, the 'Public Package Import' and the 'Private Package Import'.

The graphical notation for the *package diagram* is shown in Figure 5.37.

The diagram in Figure 5.37 shows that there are really only two symbols on the diagram: the graphical node representing a *package* and the graphical path representing a *dependency*.

A *package* is represented by a rectangle with a smaller tag rectangle on the top left-hand edge. This is similar to the folder icon that can be seen in Windows systems and, indeed, has a very similar conceptual meaning. The name of the *package* can either be shown in the tag (as seen here) or, in the case of long names, will often be shown inside the main rectangle.

The *dependency* may appear as an unadorned, regular *dependency*, or may appear with one of two *stereotypes* – «import» or «access» – representing a *public package import* or *private package import* respectively.

A *package import* (of either type) means that the *package* being pointed to (target) is imported into the other *package* (source) as part of the *source package*,

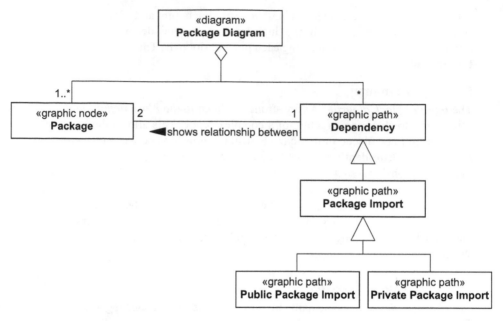

Figure 5.36   Partial meta-model for the package diagram

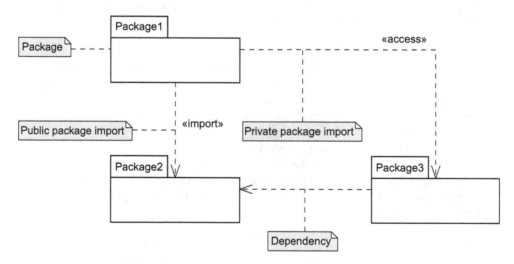

Figure 5.37   Summary of package diagram notation

but with the *target package* remaining its own *package*. Any name clashes are resolved with the *source package* taking precedence over the *target package*.

Public package import and *private package import* differ in the *visibility* of the information that is imported. What does this mean? Consider the two examples in Figure 5.38.

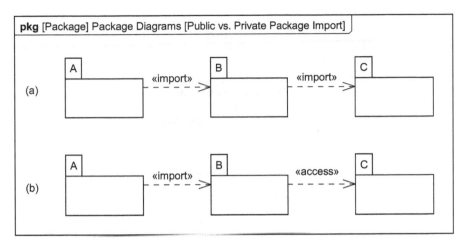

Figure 5.38   Importing packages using «import» and «access»

In example (a) *package* 'B' imports the contents of *package* 'C' using a *public package import*. *Package* 'A' then imports the contents of *package* 'B' using a *public package import*. Since 'A' has imported 'B' and 'B' has publicly imported 'C', *package* 'A' can also see the contents of *package* 'C'.

In example (b) *package* 'B' imports the contents of *package* 'C' using a *private package import*. *Package* 'A' then imports the contents of *package* 'B' using a *public package import*. Since 'A' has imported 'B' and 'B' has *privately* imported 'C', *package* 'A' cannot see the contents of *package* 'C', although it can see the contents of *package* 'B'.

Packages are used to structure a model in exactly the same way the folders (directories) organise files on a computer. Figure 5.39 helps to show how this is achieved.

The diagram in Figure 5.39 shows that a 'Package' is made up of a number of 'Packageable Element'. In the SysML, almost anything can be enclosed within a *package*, so only a few examples are shown here (indicated by the *{incomplete} constraint*). Note that a 'Package' is itself a 'Packageable Element' and thus a *package* can contain other *packages*.

5.5.3.2   Examples

Package diagrams are typically used to show model structure and *relationships* within a model at a very high level. *Packages* are often also shown on other SysML diagrams to provide information on where in a model the diagram elements can be found. Some examples are given in Figure 5.40.

The diagram in Figure 5.40 shows three *packages* from the escapology stunt. Part of the model for this stunt represents the Life Cycle Model for the Project. This is contained in the 'Life Cycle Model' *package*. This *package* makes use of the Students Managing Projects Intelligently (STUMPI) Processes, contained in the

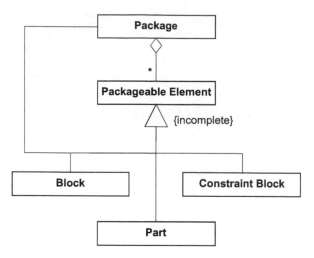

Figure 5.39　Relationships between package diagram elements and the rest of the SysML

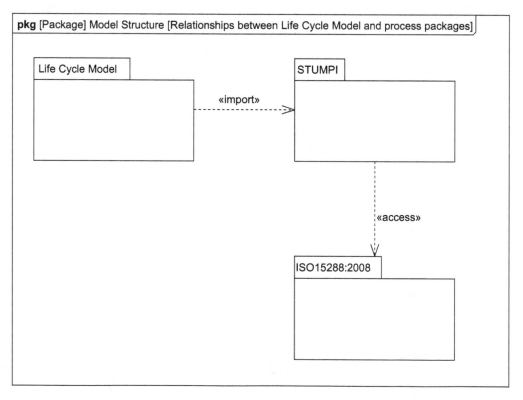

Figure 5.40　Example package diagram showing relationships between model packages

'STUMPI' *package*. Information in this *package* is visible inside the 'Life Cycle Model' *package*, as indicated by the *public package import dependency*. The STUMPI Processes themselves make use of the ISO15288:2008 process model, contained in the 'ISO15288:2008' *package* and imported using a *private package import dependency*. This means that the contents of 'ISO15288:2008' are visible within 'STUMPI' but not visible within 'Life Cycle Model'.

Packages are often shown on other diagrams. An example of this is shown in Figure 5.41.

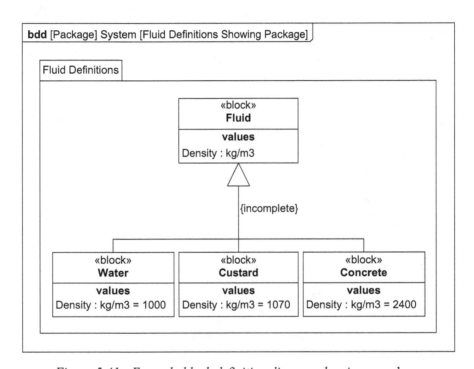

Figure 5.41   Example block definition diagram showing a package

Figure 5.41 shows a *block definition diagram* that is displaying a number of different types of 'Fluid'. From the *diagram frame* it can be seen that the *block definition diagram* is located in a *package* named 'System'. The diagram also shows a *package* named 'Fluid Definitions' surrounding the 'Fluid' *block* and its three *sub-types*. This has been done to make it explicit to the reader of this diagram that the 'Fluid', 'Water', 'Custard' and 'Concrete' *blocks* are not contained directly in the 'System' *package* but rather can be found in the 'Fluid Definitions' *package* within the 'System' *package*.

In practice, *package diagrams* are not that widely used. The use of *packages* on other diagrams is more common where it is useful for the modeller to be able to make explicit the location within a model of the diagram elements appearing on a diagram.

5.5.3.3   Summary

Package diagrams are useful for showing aspects of a model's structure where it is necessary to make clear how one *package* uses information from another (essentially how one *package* depends on another).

Packages are used within a SysML tool to structure a model. They can also be shown on any SysML diagram to indicate where particular diagram elements can be found in the model. However, such use must be tempered with the need to maintain readability of a diagram. *Packages* should be used in this way when necessary, but not as a matter of course lest the diagrams become too cluttered to be readable.

5.5.4   Parametric diagrams

The SysML *constraint block* and associated *parametric diagram* allow for the definition and use of networks of constraints that represent Rules that constrain the properties of a System or that define rules that the System must conform to.

5.5.4.1   Diagram elements

Parametric diagrams are made up of three main elements, *constraint blocks, parts* and *connectors* as shown in Figure 5.42.

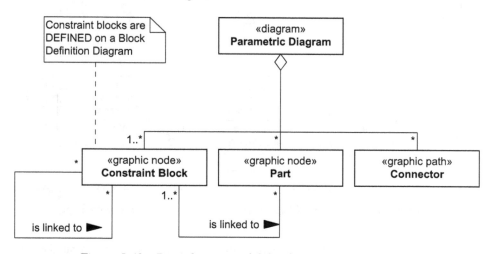

Figure 5.42   Partial meta-model for the parametric diagram

Figure 5.42 shows the partial meta-model for *parametric diagrams*. From the model it can be seen that a 'Parametric Diagram' is made up of one or more 'Constraint Block', zero or more 'Part' and zero or more 'Connector'. Zero or more 'Constraint Block' can be connected to zero or more 'Constraint Block' and one or more 'Constraint Block' can be connected to zero or more 'Part'. Although used on a 'Parametric Diagram', a 'Constraint Block' is defined on a 'Block Definition Diagram'.

There are two aspects to parametric constraints in SysML: their definition and their usage. The notations for both aspects are show in Figures 5.43 and 5.45 respectively.

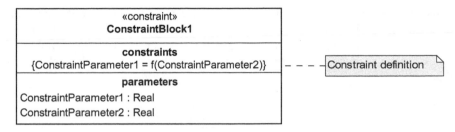

Figure 5.43 Summary of parametric diagram notation – definition of constraint block

A *constraint block* is defined using a *block* with the «constraint» *stereotype* and is given a name by which the constraint can be identified. The *constraint block* has two compartments labelled 'constraints' and 'parameters'. The *constraints compartment* contains an equation, expression or rule that relates together the *parameters* given in the *parameters compartment*. Figure 5.43 defines a *constraint block* called 'ConstraintBlock1' with two *parameters* 'ConstraintParameter1' and 'ConstraintParameter2', both of which are defined to be of type 'Real'. These *parameters* are related together by the expression 'ConstraintParameter1 = f(ConstraintParameter2)', with 'f' representing a function taking 'Constraint-Parameter2' as a *parameter*.

Such *constraint blocks* are defined on a *block definition diagram*. A concrete example of a *constraint block* can be seen in Figure 5.44.

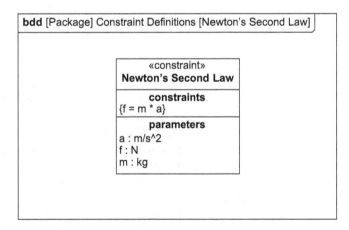

Figure 5.44 Example block definition diagram showing constraint block definition

The example in Figure 5.44 defines a *constraint block* called 'Newton's Second Law' that relates the three *parameters* 'f', 'm' and 'a' given in the *parameters compartment* by the equation 'f = m * a', as shown in the *constraints compartment*.

Although *constraint blocks* are defined on *block definition diagrams*, it is convention that such definitions are not mixed with regular *blocks* on the same diagram.

Once *constraint blocks* have been defined they can be used any number of times on one or more *parametric diagrams*, the notation for which is shown in Figure 5.45.

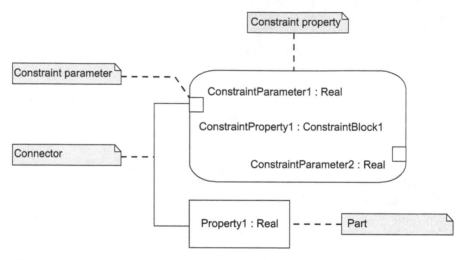

Figure 5.45   Summary of parametric diagram notation – use of constraint block

Each *constraint block* can be used multiple times on a *parametric diagram*. The use of a *constraint block* is shown as a round-cornered rectangle known as a *constraint property*. Each *constraint property* is to be named thus:

Name : Constraint Name

This allows each use of a *constraint block* to be distinguished from other uses of the same *constraint block*. In Figure 5.45 a single *constraint block*, 'ConstraintBlock1', is being used and it has been given the name 'ConstraintProperty1'.

Small rectangles attached to the inside edge of the *constraint property* represent each *constraint parameter*. These are named and their names correspond to the *parameters* defined for the *constraint block* in its definition.

These *constraint parameters* provide connection points that can be connected, via *connectors*, to other *constraint parameters* on the same or other *constraint properties* or to *block properties*. When connecting a *constraint parameter* to a *block property*, this *block property* is represented on the diagram by a rectangle known as a *part*. In Figure 5.45 a single *part* is shown, with the name 'Parametric Constraints Diagram.Block1.Property1'. This shows that this is the 'Property1' *property* of the *block* 'Block1' in the *package* 'Parametric Constraints Diagram'. *Packages* are used to structure SysML models as discussed in the previous section.

In Figure 5.45, the *part* 'Parametric Constraints Diagram.Block1.Property1' is connected to 'ConstraintParameter1'. There is nothing connected to 'ConstraintParameter2' and therefore the diagram is incomplete.

5.5.4.2 Examples

This section presents some examples of *parametric diagrams* and related diagramming elements.

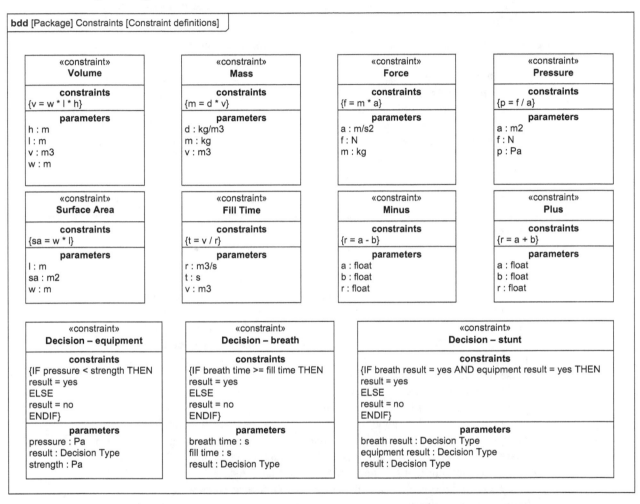

Figure 5.46 Example block definition diagram showing definition of parametric constraints

Figure 5.46 shows a number of definitions of *constraint blocks* that are defined for the Coffin Escape Stunt used as the source of examples for this chapter. As noted previously such *constraint blocks* are actually defined on a *block definition diagram*, and also as noted previously, good modelling practice has been followed with *constraint blocks* being kept separate from normal SysML *blocks*.

It can also be observed that the eight *constraint blocks* on the top two rows of the diagram are all general constraints that could be used on a number of projects, whereas the three *constraint blocks* on the bottom row are all specific to the particular System being considered (in this case the Concrete Coffin Escape). For this reason, a better way to organise them would be to split them out onto two separate diagrams and perhaps even two separate *packages* within the model in order to maximise reuse and decouple generic constraints from solution specific ones.

Another observation that can be made is that there are three different types of constraint defined:

- Constraints representing physical laws or other formulae, such as the definitions of 'Force' or 'Pressure'.
- Constraints representing mathematical and logical operators that make it easier for other constraints to be connected together in a constraint usage network, such as the definitions of 'Plus' and 'Minus'.
- Constraints representing decisions (heuristics) rather than calculation-type constraints, evaluating input parameters against some criteria and returning a result, which could be, for example, a 'yes/no', 'true/false' or 'go/no-go'. The three 'Decision' *constraint blocks* in Figure 5.46 are examples.

If so desired, the SysML stereotyping mechanism could be used to explicitly mark the *constraint blocks* as one of these three types, as shown in Figure 5.47. This can be done in order to convey extra information about the constraints, perhaps useful if *constraint blocks* and *parametric diagrams* are to be implemented in a tool such as Simulink.

From the point of view of modelling best practice, it would probably be better to split Figures 5.46 and 5.47 into two diagrams, with the top two rows of *constraint blocks* on one diagram and the bottom row on another. From a SysML point of view there is nothing wrong with the diagrams. However, the bottom row differs from the others in that all the *constraint blocks* defined in that row happen to be specific to the Coffin Escape Stunt System, whereas those on the top two rows are general-purpose definitions that could be reused for other Systems.

An example *parametric diagram* showing the *constraint blocks* defined in Figure 5.46 being used is shown in Figure 5.48. This diagram shows the *constraint blocks* being used to determine a go/no-go decision for the escapologist based on various system properties. That is, the *parametric diagram* is being used to help validate a *use case*, namely 'Minimise risk to escapologist'. This can be seen in the *callout note* showing that the diagram *traces* to that *use case*.

A better relationship from this diagram to the *use case* would be a *verify relationship*, with the *parametric diagram* marked as a *test case*, since that is essentially the role that it is playing here: the *parametric diagram* determines a go/no-go decision based on the other system parameters that test whether the *use case* can be met or not. However, SysML does not allow *parametric* diagrams to be marked as *test cases*, and so a simple *trace relationship* has been used. For a discussion of the various types of *traceability relationships* and the concept of a *test case*, see the following section on the *requirement diagram*.

A convention adopted by the authors, but not part of SysML, is to draw such *parametric diagrams* with an implied left to right direction. In Figure 5.48 the *parametric diagram* is drawn as though the 'result' *constraint parameter*, connected to the 'Decision' *property* of the 'Escapologist' *block*, is the output of

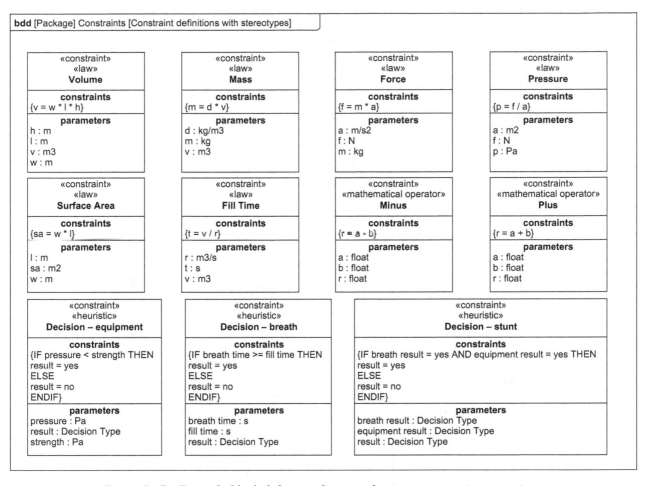

*Figure 5.47   Example block definition diagram showing parametric constraints
with stereotypes showing type*

the diagram. Similarly, the *constraint parameters* are arranged around each *constraint property* with 'inputs' on the left and 'outputs' on the right. This is done as an aid in thinking about and constructing the diagram and, indeed, reflects the purpose of the diagram.

However, one could think about going 'backwards' through Figure 5.48: we could use 'Escapologist.Bmax' and 'Pump.Rate' to determine the maximum volume of concrete that can be pumped before the escapologist runs out of breath, and hence the maximum volume of the hole. If the hole is just a little longer and wider than coffin (i.e. we can set values on 'Hole.Length' and 'Hole.Width') then knowing the maximum volume of the hole would allow the height of the hole to be determined. Perhaps this usage would be used by the safety officer to calculate the hole size. If so then it could be redrawn and linked to the appropriate *use case* as shown in Figure 5.49.

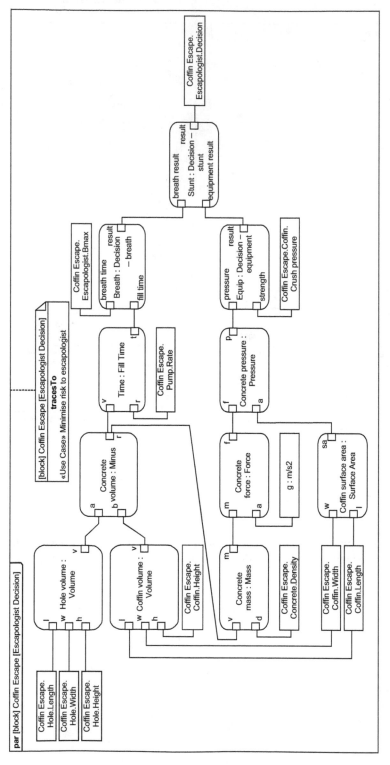

Figure 5.48   Example parametric diagram for determining go/no-go decision

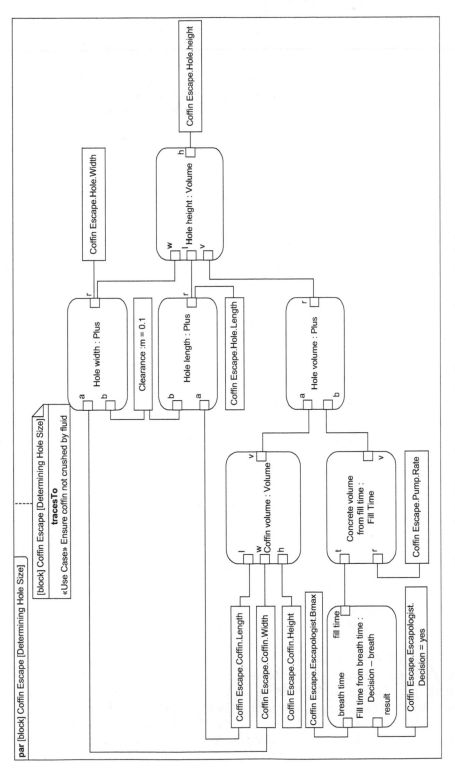

Figure 5.49 Example parametric diagram to determine hole size

Parametric constraints can also be nested, that is they can be grouped into higher level *constraint blocks* that make use of existing *constraint blocks*. Consider the three *parametric constraints* in the top left of Figure 5.48 that are used to calculate the amount of concrete needed to fill the space in the hole above the coffin. These three constraints can be grouped into a 'HoleFillVolume' *constraint block*. First we define the new *constraint block* as shown in Figure 5.50.

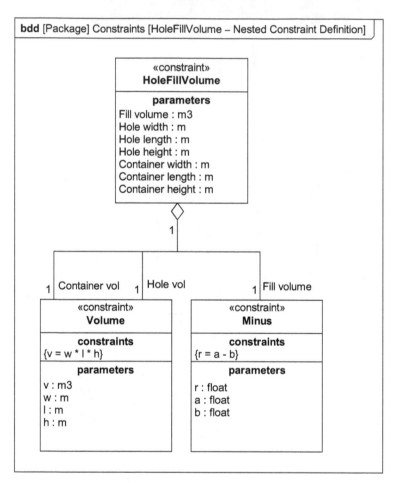

Figure 5.50   Example block definition diagram showing how higher level constraints can be constructed for the Coffin Escape Stunt

'HoleFillVolume' is defined as being made up of two 'Volume' *constraint blocks* and one 'Minus' *constraint block* and has a number of *parameters* defined. Note the use of *role names* to distinguish the role that each *constraint block* plays. Also note the use of *aggregation* rather than *composition* in the definition of 'HoleFillVolume'. This was chosen since the 'Volume' and 'Minus' *constraint blocks* are not restricted to being only *parts* of the 'HoleFillVolume' *constraint block*, but can also form *parts* of other *constraint blocks*, that is they can be *shared parts* and hence the use of *aggregation.*

It can also be seen that the actual *constraint expression* is not defined on this diagram. For this we need a special *parametric diagram* that shows how the component *constraint blocks* are used. This is shown in Figure 5.51; this *parametric diagram* is needed to fully define this nested constraint and must be considered as part of the definition.

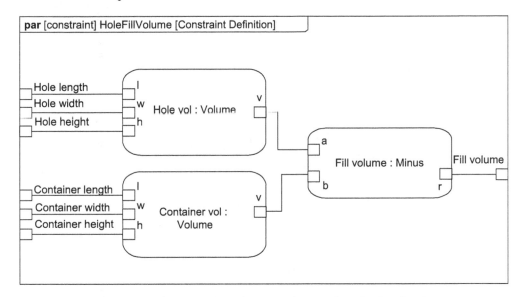

Figure 5.51   *Example parametric diagram showing how higher level constraints can be constructed for the Coffin Escape Stunt*

Note how, in Figure 5.51, the *parameters* of the high-level *constraint block* are attached to the *diagram frame* with *binding connectors* used to connect these to the *constraint parameters* of the internal *constraint properties.*

Having defined this high-level 'HoleFillVolume' constraint Figure 5.48 can now be redrawn to show how it can be used. This is shown in Figure 5.52.

The same approach could be taken for other groups of *constraints blocks*, resulting in a high-level *parametric diagram* that uses perhaps three or four high-level *constraint blocks*. This is left as an exercise for the reader.

It would be expected that, over time, an organisation would develop a library of constraint definitions, with lower level constraints being grouped into higher level ones for particular application usages.

5.5.4.3   Summary

SysML *parametric diagrams* show how constraints are related to each other and to properties of System Elements. They use *constraint blocks*, defined on *block definition diagrams*, which contain a *constraint expression* that relates together a number of *constraint parameters*. Each *constraint block* can be used multiple times

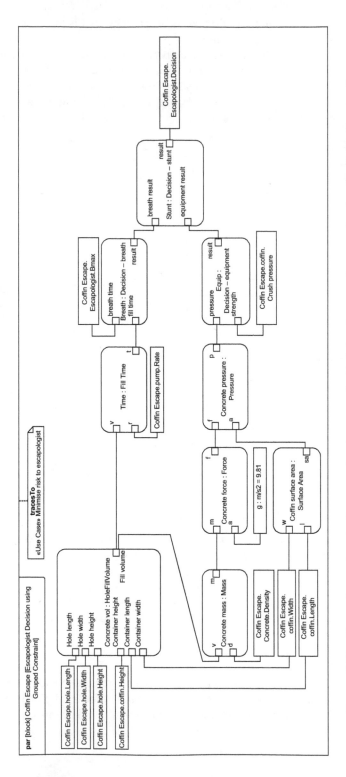

Figure 5.52   Example parametric diagram showing use of a high-level grouped constraint for the Coffin Escape Stunt

on multiple *parametric diagrams*, which relate the defined constraints to each other and to System Elements.

Parametric diagrams allow properties and behaviour of a System to be constrained and can provide an invaluable aid in understanding the often complex relationships between System properties. Modelling such inter-relationships allows analysis and design decisions to be made and also can be used to test whether Requirements have been or indeed can be satisfied. The use of *parametric diagrams* as Scenarios is discussed further in Chapter 9.

5.5.5 Requirement diagrams

The SysML has a dedicated *requirement diagram* that is used to represent Requirements and their relationships. This diagram is, in essence, a tailored *block definition diagram* consisting of a stereotyped *block* with predefined *properties* and a number of stereotyped *dependencies* and fixed-format *notes*. The various relationships provided by the *requirement diagram* also form an essential and central part of the Traceability Views that are a fundamental aspect of a model-based approach to systems engineering.

5.5.5.1 Diagram elements

Requirement diagrams are made up of three basic elements: *requirements*, *relationships* and *test cases*. *Requirements* are used, unsurprisingly, to represent Requirements, which can be related to each other and to other elements via the *relationships*. *Test cases* can be linked to *requirements* to show how the *requirements* are verified.

Figure 5.53 shows the partial meta-model for *requirement diagrams*. From the model it can be seen that a 'Requirement diagram' is made up of one or more 'Requirement', zero or more 'Relationship' and zero or more 'Test Case'. There are six types of 'Relationship': the 'Derive', 'Nesting', 'Satisfy', 'Trace', 'Refine' and 'Verify' relationships.

The notation used in SysML *requirement diagrams* is shown in Figure 5.54. This is followed by a description of the how the notation is used.

Central to the *requirement diagram* is the *requirement*. This is shown in SysML as a rectangle with the *stereotype* «requirement». The rectangle also contains a human-readable name for the *requirement*. In addition, all *requirements* have two *properties* predefined by SysML: the *id#* and *txt properties*. The *id# property* is there to hold a unique identifier for the *requirement*. The *txt property* holds descriptive text for the *requirement*. The display of *id#* and *txt* is optional and Figure 5.54 shows these compartments for 'Requirement1' and omits them for 'Requirement2', 'Requirement3' and 'Requirement4'.

A Requirement may be decomposed into one or more sub-Requirements, for example when the Requirement is not atomic in nature and it is desired to decompose it into a number of related atomic sub-Requirements. In SysML this decomposition is known as *nesting* and is indicated with a *nesting relationship* such as that shown between 'Requirement1' and 'Requirement2'.

When carrying out Requirements analysis it is often necessary to derive additional Requirements. A derived Requirement is one that is not explicitly stated by a

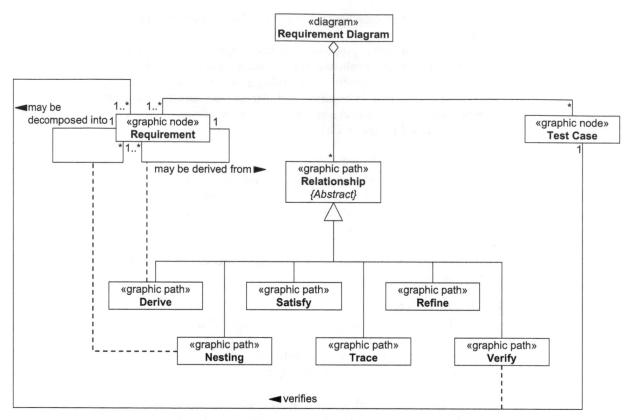

Figure 5.53   Partial meta-model for the requirement diagram

Stakeholder Role but one that has been derived by systems engineers from an explicit, stated Requirement as part of the requirements analysis process. Such derived Requirements can be linked back to their source Requirements in SysML by using a *derive relationship*, an example of which is shown in Figure 5.54 showing that 'Requirement3' is derived from 'Requirement1'.

The SysML *requirement diagram* also supports four other types of *relationships* that are used in the following ways:

- *Satisfy relationship*. This is used to show that a *model element* satisfies a *requirement*. It is used to relate elements of a design or implementation model to the Requirements that those elements are intended to satisfy. Although Figure 5.54 shows a *satisfy relationship* between a *block* and a *requirement*, it can be used between any SysML *model element* and a *requirement*.
- *Trace relationship*. This is used to show that a *model element* can be traced to a *requirement* or vice versa. This provides a general-purpose relationship that allows *model elements* and *requirements* to be related to each other.

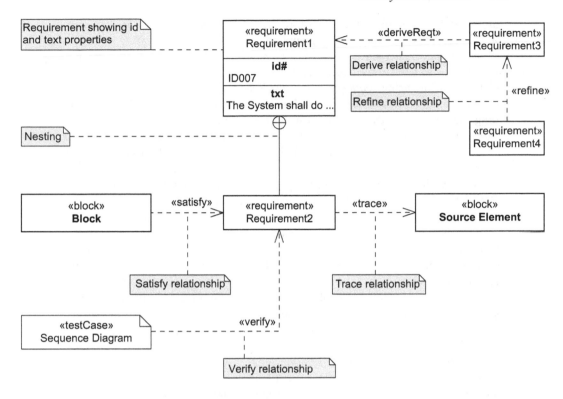

Figure 5.54   Summary of requirement diagram notation

An example of this is shown by the *trace relationship* between 'Requirement2' and 'Source Element' in Figure 5.54.

- *Refine relationship.* This is used to show how *model elements* and *requirements* can be used to further refine other *model elements* or *requirements*. This could be, for example, one *requirement* refining another as shown in Figure 5.54 where 'Requirement4' *refines* 'Requirement3'.

- *Verify relationship.* This is used to show that a particular *test case* verifies a given *requirement* and so can only be used to relate a *test case* and a *requirement*. However, a *test case* is not a specific type of SysML element. Rather it is a *stereotype*, «testCase», which can be applied to any SysML *operation* or *behavioural diagram* to show that the stereotyped element is a *test case* intended to verify a *requirement*. This stereotyped element – the *test case* – can then be related to the *requirement* it is verifying via the *verify relationship*. The *test case* is shown on a *requirement diagram* as a SysML *note* containing the name of the SysML element or diagram that is acting as a *test case* along with the *stereotype* «testCase». This is shown in Figure 5.54 by the *verify relationship* between the *test case* called 'Sequence Diagram' and 'Requirement2'.

Unfortunately, the definition of the «testCase» *stereotype* in the SysML specification [1] prevents the *stereotype* being applied to SysML *parametric diagrams*. This is a missed opportunity since *parametric diagrams*, discussed earlier in this section, are an ideal mechanism by which Formal Scenarios (*test cases*) can be modelled, which is possible using *sequence diagrams*. Readers who are adopting the techniques and approaches described in this book are urged to use the SysML's stereotyping mechanisms to define their own *test case stereotype* that can be applied to *parametric diagrams*. Similarly, a verify *stereotype* could be defined that can take a *use case* as a target given the issues with the verify relationship discussed earlier in this section.

These various types of *relationship* allow the modeller to explicitly relate different parts of a model to the *requirements* as a way of ensuring the consistency of the model. However, where possible one of the specific types of *relationship*, such as *satisfy*, should be used in preference to the more generic *trace relationship*, which has weakly defined semantics since it says nothing about the nature of the *relationship* other than that the two elements can be traced in some general and unspecified manner.

It should also be noted that, although shown in Figure 5.54 using stereotyped *dependencies*, these relationships can also be shown in SysML using special versions of the *note*. These *callout notes* can be useful when relating elements in widely different parts of a model since it avoids the need to produce additional diagrams specifically to show the *relationships*. However, they can lead to inconsistency, particularly when modelling is not being carried out using a tool (or using a tool that does not enforce consistency). Using the stereotyped *dependencies* gives an immediate and direct indication of the *relationship* since the two elements are explicitly connected by the *dependency*. Using *callout notes* hides the immediacy of the *relationship* inside the text of the note and also requires that two *notes* are added to the model: one to the source of the *relationship* and one to the target. If one of these notes is omitted the model will be inconsistent. An example of the use of *callout notes* is given in Section 5.5.5.2.

5.5.5.2   Examples

This section presents some examples of *requirement diagrams* and related diagramming elements. Further examples will be found in the case study in Chapter 13.

Figure 5.55 shows a number of SysML *requirements* for the Coffin Escape Stunt, each of which has its *id#* and *txt property* shown. Some of these *requirements* are broken down further into sub-requirements via *nesting*. At least two of these *requirements*, ES004 and ES005, have descriptive text in their *txt property* that could be considered to be untestable. In the case of ES005, the sub-requirements further describe what is meant by '...the risk to the escapologist is minimised'. However, in the case of ES004 further analysis is required. This might result in a number of *derived requirements* being created as shown in Figure 5.56.

The three *requirements* ES004-D001, ES004-D002 and ES004-D003 shown in Figure 5.56 are each derived from ES004 and show how the vague and

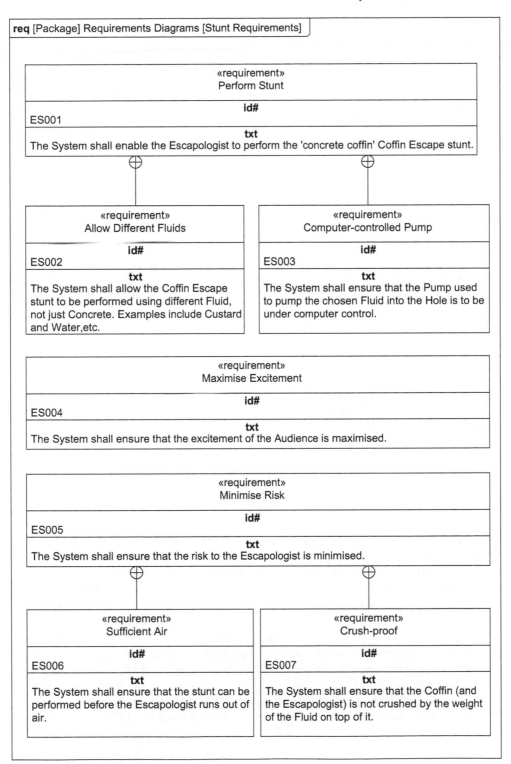

Figure 5.55 Example requirement diagram showing Requirements for the Coffin Escape Stunt

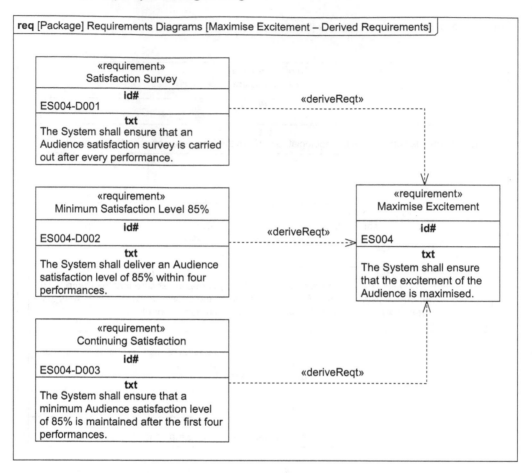

Figure 5.56   Example requirement diagram showing derived Requirements

untestable *requirement* that 'The System shall ensure that the excitement of the audience is maximised' may be further specified in a way that *is* testable.

Sometimes turning off the *id#* and *txt properties* of a *requirement* can make a diagram easier to read, particularly when additional information such as *trace relationships* are shown. This has been done in Figure 5.57, which shows the same *requirements* as are shown in Figure 5.55, but with the *id#* and *txt compartments* hidden and *trace relationships* added linking the *requirements* to *blocks* representing the source of the *requirements*. There is no significance in the sizing of the various *requirement*s, it has been done simply to ease the layout of the diagram.

A similar diagram is given in Figure 5.58, which concentrates on a single *requirement*, showing how it *traces* to source elements and in addition, showing a *use case* that *refines* the *requirement*. A seemingly obvious, but often overlooked,

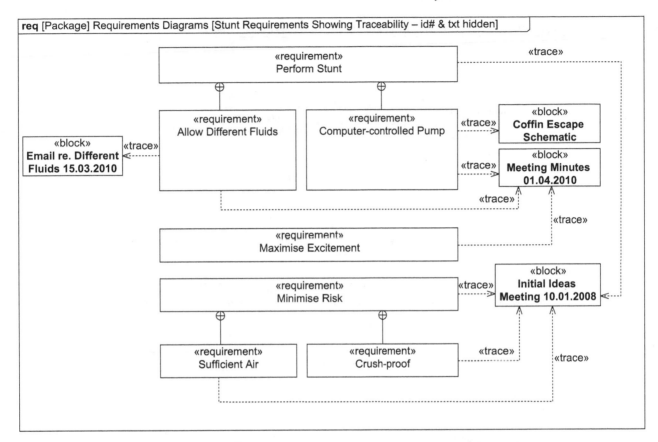

Figure 5.57 Example requirement diagram showing «trace» relationships

aspect of modelling is highlighted in Figure 5.58, namely that of keeping diagrams as simple as possible. There is often a temptation to overload diagrams with too many elements so that they add to the complexity and lack of understanding of the system rather than helping. The information shown on the four example diagrams earlier in this section could have been shown on a single diagram, but this would have made the communication of the understanding of the *requirements* and their *relationships* to other *model element* harder to achieve. Any sensible modelling tool will allow *model elements* to be reused on a number of different diagrams and this is to be encouraged, not only for *requirements diagrams* but for *any* of the SysML diagrams. If you find a diagram is becoming too complex (more than around 9 or 10 elements, as a crude heuristic), break it down into a number of simpler diagrams. Miller's comments on the limits on our capacity to process information are as valid today as when they were first written and apply just as much to SysML models. See Reference 2.

The final example of a *requirement diagram* is shown in Figure 5.59. This diagram shows exactly the same information as that shown in Figure 5.58 but uses

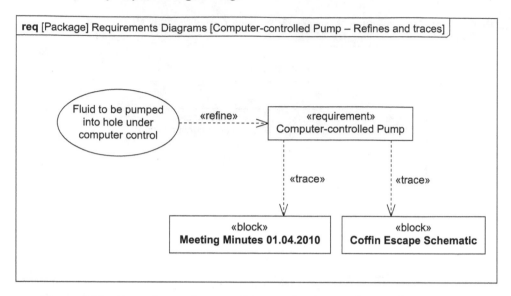

Figure 5.58   Example requirement diagram showing «refine» and «trace» relationships

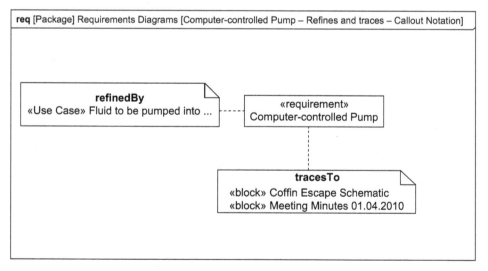

Figure 5.59   Example requirement diagram showing «refine» and «trace» relationships using callout notes

the *callout* notation rather than explicit *refine* and *trace relationships*. Some of the immediacy of information is lost using the *callout* notation since the symbols used do not, in this example, show graphically that the other model elements involved are a *use case* and two *blocks*. One has to read the content of the *callout notes* to understand the types of *model elements* involved. For this reason the authors recommend, where possible and appropriate, the explicit *relationships* as in Figure 5.58.

5.5.5.3   Summary

SysML *requirement diagrams* are used to show *requirements* and their *relationships* to each other and how they trace to, are satisfied by, are refined by and are verified by other *model element*. Wherever possible, use of the more specific types of *relationship* (such as *satisfy*) is preferred over the more generic *trace*. Each *requirement* has a name, unique identifier and a description. Most SysML tools allow the identifier and description to be hidden if desired, in order to simplify diagrams. Additional *properties* such as 'priority' may be defined if needed and examples are given in the SysML specification [1].

It should also be noticed that the scope of the requirement diagram may, and should, be extended to include other types of Need from the MBSE Ontology, rather than being restricted to Requirements only. The MBSE Ontology states that there are four types of Need: Requirement, Capability, Goal and Concern, each of which may be visualised using the SysML *requirement* concept.

5.5.6   State machine diagrams

So far we have been considering the SysML structural diagrams. In this section we now start looking at the SysML behavioural diagrams, beginning with the *state machine diagram*. *State machine diagrams* have been discussed in some detail in Chapter 4 and thus some of this section will serve as a recap. The focus here, however, will be the actual *state machine diagram*, whereas the emphasis previously has been on general behavioural modelling.

State machine diagrams realise a behavioural aspect of the model. They model the order in which things occur and the logical conditions under which they occur for instances of *blocks*, known in SysML as *instance specifications*. They show such behaviour by relating it to meaningful *states* that the System Element, modelled by a *block*, can be in at any particular time, concentrating on the *events* that can cause a change of *state* (known as a *transition*) and the behaviour that occurs during such a *transition* or that occurs inside a *state*.

5.5.6.1   Diagram elements

State machine diagrams are made up of two basic elements: *states* and *transitions*. These *states* and *transitions* describe the behaviour of a *block* over logical time. *States* show what is happening at any particular point in time when an *instance specification* typed by the *block* is active. *States* may show when an *activity* is being carried out or when the *properties* of an *instance specification* are equal to a particular set of values. They may even show that nothing is happening at all – that is to say that the *instance specification* is waiting for something to happen. The elements that make up a *state machine diagram* are shown in Figure 5.60.

Figure 5.60 shows the partial meta-model for *state machine diagrams*. *State machine diagrams* have a very rich syntax and thus the meta-model shown here

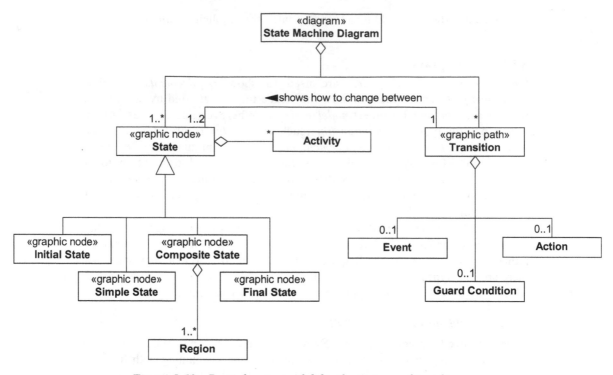

Figure 5.60   Partial meta-model for the state machine diagram

omits some detail – for example, there are different types of *action* that are not shown. See References 1 and 4 for more details.

From the model, it can be seen that a 'State Machine Diagram' is made up of one or more 'State' and zero or more 'Transition'. A 'Transition' shows how to change between one or two 'State'. Remember that it is possible for a *transition* to exit a *state* and then enter the same *state*, which makes the *multiplicity* one or two rather than two, as would seem more logical.

There are four types of 'State': 'Initial State', 'Simple State', 'Composite State' and 'Final state'. Each 'State' is made up of zero or more 'Activity'. An 'Activity' describes an on-going, non-atomic unit of behaviour and is directly related to the *operations* on a *block*. A 'Composite State' is divided into one or 'Region'. When there are more than one 'Region', each 'Region' is used to model concurrent (i.e. parallel) behaviour.

Each 'Transition' may have zero or one 'Guard Condition', a Boolean condition that will usually relate to the value of a *block* property. The 'Guard Condition' must evaluate to true for the 'Transition' to be valid and hence capable of being crossed.

A 'Transition' may also have zero or one 'Action'. An 'Action' is defined as an activity whose behaviour is *atomic*. That is, once started it cannot be interrupted and will always complete. An 'Activity', on the other hand, is *non-atomic* and can be interrupted. An 'Action' should be used for short-running behaviour.

Finally, a 'Transition' may have zero or one 'Event' representing an occurrence of something happening that can cause a 'Transition' to fire. Such an 'Event' can be thought of as the receipt of a *message* by the *state machine*.

If an 'Event' models the receipt of a *message*, often sent from one *state machine* to another, then how does one model the sending of such a *message* from a *state machine*? The answer is that there are actually two types of *event*: *receipt events* and *send events*.

The type of *event* described earlier in this section, which corresponds to the receipt of a *message* and which can trigger a *transition*, is actually an example of a *receive event*. A *send event* represents the origin of a *message* being sent from one *state machine* to another. It is generally assumed that a *send event* is broadcast to all elements in the System and thus each of the other elements has the potential to receive and react upon receiving the *event*. Obviously, for each *send event* there must be at least one corresponding *receipt event* in another *state machine*. This is one of the basic consistency checks that may be applied to different *state machine diagrams* to ensure that they are consistent. A *send event* is usually modelled as the *action* on a *transition*.

The notation for the *state machine diagram* is shown Figure 5.61.

The basic modelling elements in a *state machine diagram* are *states*, *transitions* and *events*. *States* describe what is happening within a system at any given point in time, *transitions* show the possible paths between such *states* and *events* govern when a *transition* can occur. These elements were discussed in detail in Chapter 4 and the reader is referred to that chapter. However, there are a number of elements in Figure 5.61 that weren't discussed in Chapter 5 and which need discussion here, namely:

- *Composite states*
- *Entry activities*
- *Exit activities*

Figure 5.61 shows two *composite states*: 'Composite State (Concurrent)' and 'Composite State (Sequential)'. *Composite states* allow *states* to be modelled that have internal behaviour that is further decomposed into *states*. They can be thought of as *states* that have their own *state machine diagrams* inside.

Let us consider 'Composite State (Sequential)' first. This *composite state* has a single *region* (the part of the *state* beneath the box containing the name). Since there is only one *region* the behaviour takes place sequentially within the *state* and hence this is a *sequential composite* state. In this example, 'Simple State 1' is entered first. This then leads on to 'Simple State 2' and when this *state* is left the *final state* is entered.

Now consider 'Composite State (Concurrent)'. This has two *regions* separated by a dashed line. Each *region* represents concurrent (i.e. parallel) behaviour and hence this is a *concurrent composite state*. The *transition* to 'Composite State (Concurrent)' causes both *regions* to become active and therefore the two small *state machine diagrams* in the *regions* become active. When both have completed, then the *transition* from 'Composite State (Concurrent)' to the *final state* can fire.

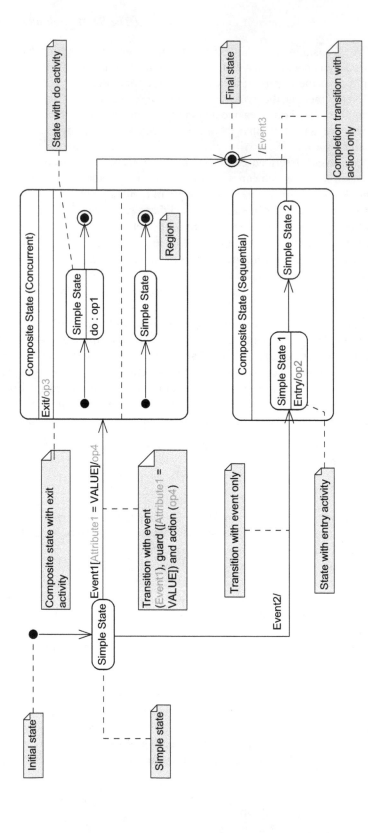

Figure 5.61   Summary of state machine diagram notation

Examples of *composite states*, along with a discussion of when *sequential composite states* are used, can be found in Section 5.5.6.2.

Entry and *exit activities* can be seen in 'Simple State 1', shown as 'Entry/op2' (an *entry activity)*, and in 'Composite State (Concurrent)' shown as 'Exit/op3' (an *exit activity*).

An *entry activity* represents an *activity* that takes place every time a *state* is entered. The notation is the keyword 'Entry/' followed by the behaviour to take place (in the example here, the invocation of an *operation* 'op2').

An *exit activity* represents an *activity* that takes place every time a *state* is exited. The notation is the keyword 'Exit/' followed by the behaviour to take place (in the example here, the invocation of an *operation* 'op3').

Unlike normal *activities* both the *entry activity* and the *exit activity* cannot be interrupted; they behave more like *actions* as they are guaranteed to run to completion. Section 5.5.6.2 gives examples.

Before moving on to consider some examples of *state machine diagrams* it is worth discussing some alternative notation that can be used for *events* (both *receipt events* and *send events*) and for modelling decision points (known as *junction states*).

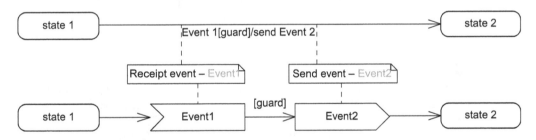

Figure 5.62   Alternative notations for receipt and send events

Figure 5.62 shows the two possible notations for modelling *receipt events* and *send events*. The top part of the diagram shows the textual notation. There is no keyword to indicate "receipt", an *event* preceding a *guard condition* represents a *receipt event*. The widely used notation for representing a *send event* is to place the word "send" in front of the *event name* as part of the *action* on the *transition*. Note, however, that this is a convention and is not specified by the SysML standard. Exactly the same transition is shown at the bottom of the diagram, but this time using graphical symbols that explicitly show which is a *receipt event* and which is a *send event*. This notation is also used on *activity diagrams* discussed in Section 5.5.8 below.

Figure 5.63 shows alternative notations that can be used when there are two or more *transitions* from a *state* that have the same *event* (or indeed no *event*) but different *guard conditions*. In the example, the same *event* 'Event1' will lead either to 'state 2' or 'state 3' depending on the value of the *guard condition*. This can be represented as two separate *transitions* from 'state 1' as in the upper part of the diagram, or as a single *transition* from 'state 1' to a *junction state* (the diamond) followed by two *transitions* from the *junction state*.

As to which notation to use? Well, use whatever you feel is best. Diagramming guidelines might specify (see Chapter 6 for a discussion of diagramming guidelines).

However, if they don't, you are advised to choose a style and use it consistently within a model. At least in that way your *state machine diagrams* will have a consistent look and feel.

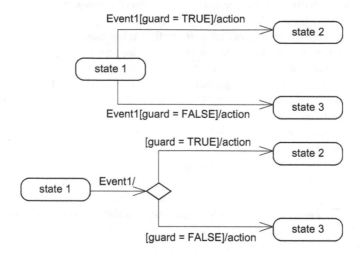

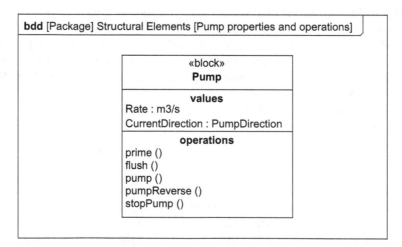

Figure 5.63   Alternative notations for decisions

5.5.6.2   Examples

This section presents some examples of *state machine diagrams* and related diagramming elements. Further examples will be found in the case study in Chapter 13.

The *block definition diagram* in Figure 5.64 shows a single *block* that models the 'Pump' used in the Coffin Escape Stunt. This was seen previously in Section 5.5.1.2

bdd [Package] Structural Elements [Pump properties and operations]

«block»
Pump

values
Rate : m3/s
CurrentDirection : PumpDirection

operations
prime ()
flush ()
pump ()
pumpReverse ()
stopPump ()

Figure 5.64   Example block definition diagram showing Pump properties and operations

when we looked at example *block definition diagrams*. The *block* has a number of *operations* and the 'Pump' that it models can be in a number of meaningful *states*, such as being powered down and pumping in either direction. It should, therefore, have its behaviour modelled using a *state machine diagram*. This has been done in Figure 5.65.

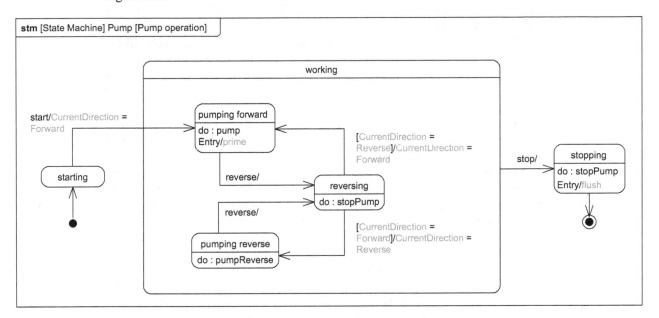

Figure 5.65   Example state machine diagram showing pump behaviour

The *state machine diagram* in Figure 5.65 has three main *states*, 'starting', 'working' and 'stopping', an *initial state* and a *final state*. The *state* 'working' is a *composite state*. It has one *region* and is therefore a *sequential composite state*. It contains three *states*: 'pumping forward', 'pumping reverse' and 'reversing'.

The *state machine* represented by this *state machine diagram* can be considered to come into existence when the 'Pump' is turned on. When this happens the *state machine diagram* begins in the *initial state* and then immediately transitions to the 'starting' *state*. It will stay in this *state* until the 'start' *event* is received. On receipt of this *event* the *transition* will fire and the *state machine* will move into the 'pumping forward' *state*. There are a number of points to discuss here. First, the *transition* has an *action* 'CurrentDirection = Forward'. As is common with many *actions* this is assigning a value to a *property* of the owning *block*. Is 'CurrentDirection' a *property* of the 'Pump' *block*? Yes, as it can be seen from Figure 5.64. So this *action* is consistent with the structural aspects of the model. Second, the *transition* crosses the boundary of the 'working' *composite state* and enters the 'pumping forward' *state* contained within 'working'. This is perfectly okay and is very common when working with *sequential composite states*. This initial *transition* and associated behaviour captures the fact that the 'Pump' in this example always starts pumping in the normal forward direction.

Once running, the 'Pump' can be switched to pump in a reverse direction. However, it has to stop pumping normally before it can make this change of direction. Similarly, if pumping in reverse, it can be switched back to pumping normally but, again, it has to stop pumping first. The operator does not have to explicitly tell the 'Pump' to stop before switching direction. The 'Pump' has to handle this itself. This is what the three *states* inside 'working', together with their associated *transitions*, do.

When the 'pumping forward' *state* is entered, the 'Pump' primes itself. This is achieved with an *entry activity* 'Entry/prime'. This invokes the 'prime' *operation* of the 'Pump'. This cannot be interrupted; the 'Pump' will always complete its 'prime' operation before it does anything else. Once the 'Pump' has finished priming itself, it then begins pumping via an *activity* 'do: pump'. This can be interrupted. If not interrupted, then the 'pump' *operation* will run to completion. If it is interrupted, then the 'pump' *operation* will cease and the 'pumping' state will be left along whichever *transition* fired causing the interruption.

So what *transitions* are possible from 'pumping' and what will cause them to happen? The most obvious is the *transition* from 'pumping' to 'reversing'. This *transition* has an *event* 'reverse' and no *guard condition* or *action*. If 'reverse' is received by the *state machine diagram* while in the 'pumping' *state* then this *transition* will fire and the 'reversing' *state* will be entered. Don't forget: the 'do: pump' *activity* can be interrupted, so this *event* can cause the 'pump' *operation* to cease prematurely. Another possibility, perhaps not so obvious, is the *transition* from the 'working' *sequential composite state* to the 'stopping' *state*. This *transition* is drawn from the boundary of 'working'. This means that it is a valid *transition* from all of the *states* contained within. Essentially all three *states* have a *transition* triggered by the 'stop' *event* to the 'stopping' *state*'. This illustrates the common use of *sequential composite states*; they are used to enclose *states* that all have the same *transitions* from them, allowing a cleaner diagram to be produced. Again, this *transition*, should it fire, will end the 'pump' *operation* prematurely.

If the *transition* to 'reversing' fires, then the *state machine* will move into the 'reversing' state where an *activity* will invoke the 'stopPump' *operation*. Again, this behaviour can be interrupted by the *transition* triggered by the 'stop' *event* from the 'working' *state*. However, it cannot be interrupted by either of the two *transitions*, which directly leave the 'reversing' *state*. Why? Because neither of the two *transitions* from 'reversing' has *events*. They only have *guard conditions* and *actions*. Only *transitions* with *events* can interrupt behaviour in a *state*. Those without *events* will be checked once any behaviour inside the state has completed. Thus, as soon as the 'stopPump' *operation* has finished (assuming the 'stop' *event* has not caused the *transition* to 'stopping' to fire), then the two *guard conditions* on the *transitions* are checked. Whichever is true determines which *transition* takes place. Both of these *guard conditions* check the value of the 'CurrentDirection' *property* to establish whether the 'Pump' is currently pumping in the normal direction or is pumping in reverse. In this case, the *guard condition* '[CurrentDirection = Forward]' will be true, since this is the direction that was set on entry to the 'pumping forward' *state*.

Therefore, the *transition* to the 'pumping reverse' *state* will fire, and the *action* 'CurrentDirection = Reverse' is executed to track that the 'Pump' is now in the 'pumping reverse' *state*.

The behaviour of the 'pumping reverse' *state* is now the opposite of the 'pumping forward' *state*. There is no need for the 'Pump' to prime itself as this was already done and the 'Pump' has just been pumping, so the 'pumpReverse' *operation* is immediately invoked. This will either run to completion or be interrupted in exactly the same way as for 'pump' in the 'pumping' *state*. A 'reverse' *event* will cause the *transition* to 'reversing' to fire or a 'stop' *event* will cause a *transition* to 'stopping' to fire. If the *transition* to 'reversing' happens, then the behaviour is described previously except that the other *guard condition* is now true and the *transition* back to 'pumping forward' will take place.

Thus, the 'start' *event* will start the 'Pump' pumping normally and each receipt of the 'reverse' *event* will cause it to toggle to pumping in reverse and then back to pumping normally, with the 'Pump' stopping automatically before changing direction.

When in any of the 'pumping forward', 'reversing' or 'pumping reverse' then receipt of the 'stop' *event* will cause the *transition* to the 'stopping' *state* to fire. On entry to this *state* the 'Pump' is flushed ('Entry/flush') before the 'stopPump' *operation* is invoked.

If all of the preceding explanation of the behaviour of the *state machine diagram* in Figure 5.65 seems convoluted, perhaps it will help to reinforce the benefits of modelling with a language such as SysML. An experienced modeller would have understood all of the above description simply by looking at the diagram in Figure 5.65.

Finally, an important consideration when constructing *state machine diagrams* is that of determinism. When leaving a *state* it is important that only one of the *transitions* can be followed. This means that the *events* and *guard conditions* on all the *transitions* from a *state* must be mutually exclusive; in this way only one *transition*, at most, will ever occur. If more than one *transition* could occur, then the *state machine diagram* is said to be non-deterministic and the exact behaviour is impossible to determine. There is a place for non-deterministic *state machine diagram* but their discussion is outside the scope of this book.

5.5.6.3 Summary

State machine diagrams realise a behavioural aspect of the model. They model the order in which things occur and the logical conditions under which they occur for instances of *blocks*, known in SysML as *instance specifications*. They show such behaviour by relating it to meaningful *states* that the System Element, modelled by a *block*, can be in at any particular time, concentrating on the *events* that can cause a change of *state* (known as a *transition*) and the behaviour that occurs during such a *transition* or that occurs inside a *state*.

There are a few rules of thumb to apply when creating *state machine diagrams*:

- All *blocks* that exhibit behaviour (have *operations*) must have their behaviour specified. If the System Element modelled by the *block* can be in a number of *states* then this behaviour should be modelled using a *state machine diagram*.

If it does not exhibit such stateful behaviour, then consider using *activity diagrams*. Whichever is chosen, the behavioural aspect of the *block* must be modelled.

- All *operations* in a particular *block* that has its behaviour modelled using a *state machine diagram* must appear on its associated *state machine diagram*. *States* may be empty and have no *activities*, which may represent, for example, an idle *state* where the System is waiting for an *event* to occur. *Messages* are sent to and received from other *state machine diagrams* as *send events* and *receipt events*.

Also, remember that there is a difference between behaviour modelled using *actions* on a *transition* and behaviour modelled using *activities* within a *state*. *Actions* are *atomic*. They are considered to take zero logical time and once started cannot be interrupted. *Activities*, on the other hand, do take time to run and can be interrupted (but remember that *entry activities* and *exit activities* are guaranteed to complete). It is important to differentiate between *activities* and *actions* as they can have a large impact on the way in which the model of a System will evolve and an even bigger impact on how it is implemented.

5.5.7   *Sequence diagrams*

This section introduces and discusses *sequence diagrams*, which realise a behavioural aspect of the model. The main aim of the *sequence diagram* is to show a particular example of operation of a System, in the same way as movie-makers may draw up a storyboard. A storyboard shows the sequence of events in a film before it is made. Such storyboards in MBSE are known as Scenarios. Scenarios highlight pertinent aspects of a particular situation and ignore all others. Each of these aspects is represented as an element known as a *life line*. A *life line* in SysML represents an individual participant in an interaction and will refer to an element from another aspect of the model, such as a *block*, a *part* or an *actor*. *Sequence diagrams* model interactions between *life lines*, showing the *messages* passed between them with an emphasis on logical time or the sequence of *messages* (hence the name).

5.5.7.1   Diagram elements

Sequence diagrams are made up of two main elements, *life lines* and *messages*, along with additional elements that allow other diagrams to be referenced, *interaction uses*, and constructions such as looping and parallel behaviour to be represented, represented using *combined fragments*. These elements are shown in Figure 5.66.

Figure 5.66 shows the partial meta-model for *sequence diagrams*. From the model it can be seen that a 'Sequence Diagram' is made up of one or more 'Life Line', one or more 'Message', zero or more 'Interaction Uses' and zero or more 'Combined Fragment', which has types 'Loop Combined Fragment', 'Parallel Combined Fragment' and 'Alternative Combined Fragment'. An 'Interaction Use' references a 'Sequence Diagram' and each 'Combined Fragment' spans one or more 'Life Line'. A 'Message' connects two 'Occurrence Specification', each of which occurs on a 'Life Line'. Each 'Life Line' is made up of zero or more 'Execution Specification'.

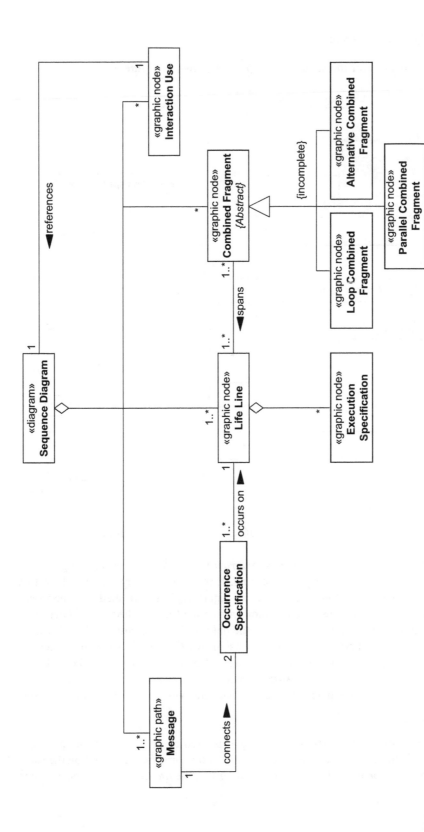

Figure 5.66   Partial meta-model for the sequence diagram

The notation for the *sequence diagram* is shown in Figure 5.67.

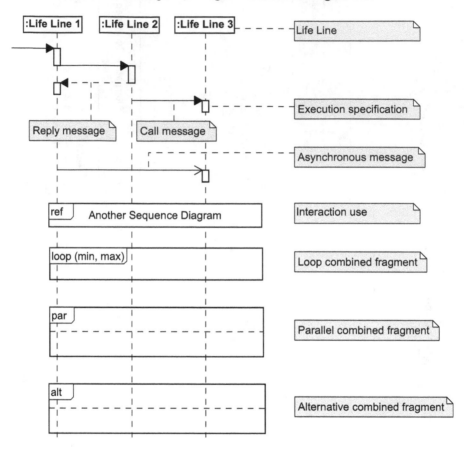

Figure 5.67   Summary of sequence diagram notation

The main element of a *sequence diagram* is the *life line*, representing a participant in a Scenario over a period of time. It is represented by a rectangle with a dashed line hanging below it, as shown in Figure 5.67. The dashed line represents logical time extending down the diagram, with earlier times at the top and later times at the bottom. The *sequence diagram* is the only SysML diagram in which layout is important, as indicated by this time dimension. A *life line* will refer to an element from another aspect of the model, such as a *block* or an *actor*; it can be thought of as an instance of that element that is taking part in the Scenario. This is reflected in the labelling of the *life line*, placed inside the rectangle, which takes the following form:

name : type

The *name* part of the label is optional and is used to give the *life line* a unique identifier in the case where multiple *life lines* of the same *type* are used on the same diagram. The *type* indicates the *block* or *actor* that the *life line* is an instance of and the rectangle can be adorned with the *stereotype* «block» or the stick man symbol to emphasise that the *life line* is typed by a *block* or an *actor* (see, for example, Figure 5.73).

The sequence of interaction between *life lines* is shown by *messages* drawn between the sending and receiving *life lines*. These *messages* can be annotated with text describing the nature of the interaction and show the sequence of interactions through time. The portion of time during which a *life line* is active is shown by the small rectangles on the dashed line, known as *execution specifications*. A *life line* can send a *message* to itself, to show that some internal behaviour is taking place. See, for example, Figure 5.73. The two *occurrence specifications* connected by a *message* are not explicitly shown, but are the points on the *life line* where a *message* leaves and joins a *life line*.

Complex Scenarios can be represented containing looping, parallel and alternative behaviour, shown using various types of *combined fragment*. In addition, a *sequence diagram* can refer to another via the *interaction use* notation, allowing more and more complicated Scenarios to be developed. Examples of the *combined fragment* and *interaction use* notation are shown in Figure 5.67. They are described further in the following subsections. However, it is worth sounding a note of caution here. The various *combined fragment* notations can be nested, allowing very complicated Scenarios to be modelled. In particular, the use of the *alternative combined fragment* notation allows alternative paths through a Scenario to be shown. What this means is that the *sequence diagram* is showing more than one Scenario. From a SysML perspective, there is nothing wrong with doing this. However, from a modelling perspective such an approach can, in all but the simplest of cases, lead to confusing diagrams. Apart from showing very simple alternatives on a single diagram the authors would recommend a one diagram, one scenario approach.

Showing parallel processing

Parallel paths through a Scenario can be shown in *sequence diagrams* using a *parallel combined fragment*. Each parallel path appears in a separate compartment within the *combined fragment frame*. The parallel compartments are divided by a dashed line, and the combined fragment uses the keyword *par*.

Figure 5.68 shows a *sequence diagram* with two *parallel combined fragments*, each of which has two parallel regions. The first *parallel combined fragment* shows the 'Begin stunt' *message* being sent from the 'Set up' *life line* to the 'Start' *life line* at the same time as the 'Set up' *life line* sends the 'Begin stunt' *message* to the 'Escape' *life line*. Similarly, the second *parallel combined fragment* shows the 'Start escape' *message* being sent between the 'Start' and 'Escape' *life lines* at the same time that it is sent between the 'Escape' and 'Monitor' *life lines*.

Referencing other diagrams

Often, when modelling Scenarios, common behaviour is observed. Rather than having to repeat this behaviour on every *sequence diagram* that needs it, SysML allows other *sequence diagrams* to be referenced to allow reuse of Scenarios.

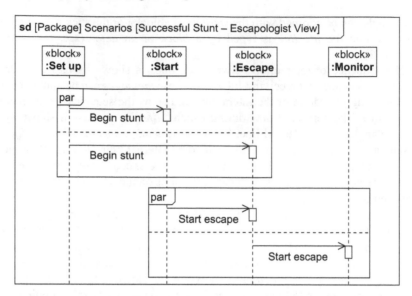

Figure 5.68   Example sequence diagram showing a parallel combined fragment

For example, say that we have some common functionality that we want to show on multiple Scenarios. First, we model this using a *sequence diagram*. An example is shown in Figure 5.69.

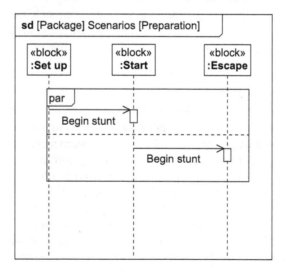

Figure 5.69   Example sequence diagram defining common functionality to be referenced

This functionality can then be reused on another *sequence diagram* using an *interaction use*. Each referenced Scenario appears in a separate frame with the keyword *ref*, as shown in Figure 5.70.

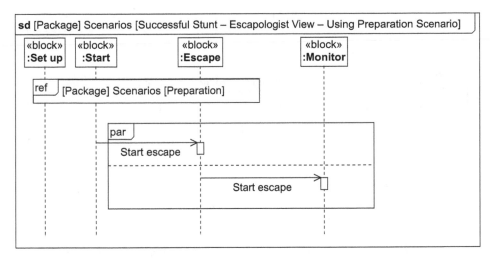

Figure 5.70   *Example sequence diagram showing the use of a reference combined fragment*

The *life lines* that appear in the *sequence diagram* referenced must appear on the referencing diagram and the *interaction use* must be placed over those *life lines* as in Figure 5.70.

Showing alternatives

Sometimes two or more Scenarios are so similar that showing alternative paths on a single diagram rather than one per diagram is desirable. SysML allows Scenarios to be modelled in this way using *alternative combined fragments*.

This consists of a *frame* with the keyword *alt* that is divided into separate compartments, one for each alternative, by dashed lines. Each compartment should have a *guard condition* that indicates the conditions under which that alternative is executed. The absence of a *guard condition* implies a true condition. The *guard condition else* can be used to indicate a condition that is true if no other *guard conditions* are true. Although there is nothing in SysML to prevent the use of *guard conditions* where more than one can evaluate to true, this leads to a non-deterministic *sequence diagram* and is to be avoided. An example of a *sequence diagram* showing two alternatives is shown in Figure 5.71.

The diagram in Figure 5.71 shows two Scenarios, since the *alternative combined fragment* has two compartments. Both Scenarios begin with the 'Assistant' sending a 'start' *message* to the 'Pump Controller', which itself sends a 'start' *message* to the 'Pump'. The 'Pump' then sends itself two *messages*, 'prime' followed by 'pump'.

In the first Scenario, when the *guard* 'Emergency = FALSE' holds, the first alternative takes place. The 'Assistant' sends a 'stop' *message* to the 'Pump Controller', which itself sends a 'stop' *message* to the 'Pump'. The 'Pump' then sends itself two *messages*, 'flush' followed by 'stopPump'.

In the second Scenario, when the *guard* 'Emergency = TRUE' holds, the second alternative takes place. The 'Assistant' sends a 'reverse' *message* to the 'Pump

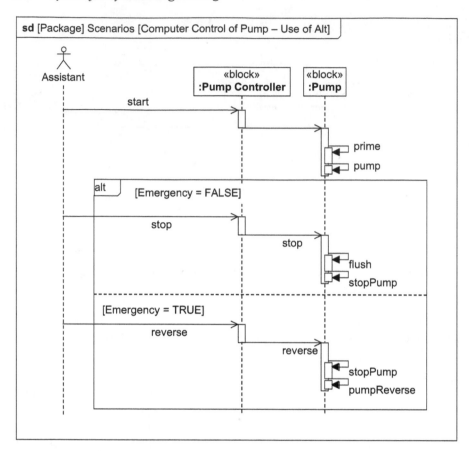

*Figure 5.71   Example sequence diagram showing the use of the alternative
combined fragment*

Controller', which itself sends a 'reverse' *message* to the 'Pump'. The 'Pump' then
sends itself two *messages*, 'stopPump' followed by 'pumpReverse'.

Showing loops

The final *combined fragment* to be considered allows looping behaviour to be
shown. The *looping combined fragment* is shown using a *frame* with the keyword
loop. The keyword may be accompanied by a *repetition count* specifying a
minimum and *maximum* count as well as a *guard condition*. The loop is executed
while the *guard condition* is true but *at least* the minimum count, irrespective of the
guard condition and *never* more than the maximum count.

The syntax for loop counts is

- loop   minimum = 0, unlimited maximum
- loop(repeat)   minimum = maximum = repeat
- loop(min, max)   minimum & maximum specified, min <= max

An example *sequence diagram* showing a loop combined fragment is shown in Figure 5.72.

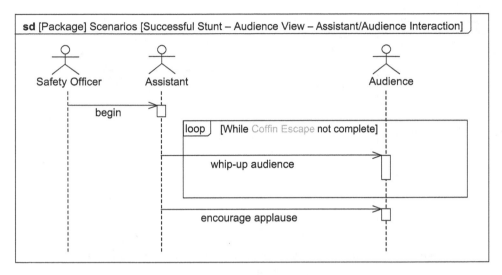

Figure 5.72   Example sequence diagram showing the use of a loop combined fragment

The diagram shows a *loop* with no *repetition count* (which is the same as a loop forever) and a *guard condition* that indicates that the *loop* is to continue while the Coffin Escape Stunt is not complete.

There are many other types of *combined fragment* defined, but the four discussed here are the most often used. For details of the other types of *combined fragment*, such as the *break* or *opt combined fragments*, see Reference 5.

In addition, there is nothing to prevent the nesting of *combined fragments*. For example, a loop may have a *parallel combined fragment* inside it, with *instance uses* and perhaps even *alternative combined fragments* in each parallel region. Remember, though, that one of the key aims of modelling is to improve the communication of complex ideas and such diagrams, while valid SysML should be used with caution as diagrams can rapidly become very difficult to understand and make the communication worse rather than better.

There is much more notation available for use on *sequence diagrams*, including the modelling of *timing constraints* between *messages* and the distinction between *synchronous* and *asynchronous* messages. See References 1, 3, 5 and 6 for further information.

5.5.7.2   Examples

This section presents some examples of *sequence diagrams*. Further examples of sequence diagrams can be found in the case study in Chapter 13.

Figure 5.73 is an example of a *sequence diagram* that treats the System (in this case the 'Coffin Escape') as a black box; that is, it concentrates on the interactions between Stakeholder Roles and the System, modelling the System as a single *life*

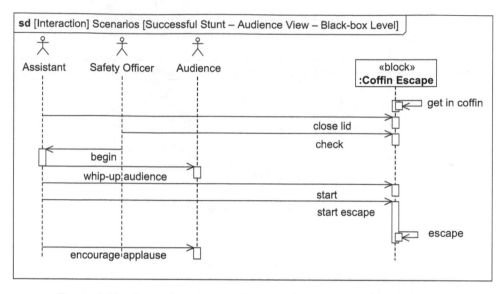

Figure 5.73   Example sequence diagram showing actors as life lines and System as a single block

line. As well as showing these interactions, it also shows some interactions that are internal to the System, namely the 'get in' and 'escape' *messages*.

Three other interactions are also worthy of comment, namely the 'begin', 'whip-up audience' and 'encourage applause' *messages*. These are of interest because they are between Stakeholder Roles rather than between Stakeholder Roles and the System. Some people (and indeed some SysML tools) would consider such interactions as illegal.

Nevertheless, these are essential interactions that are needed to fully describe the Scenario (in this case, that of a successful stunt) as it is impossible to model this Scenario fully without showing them. When considering the System to be the 'Coffin Escape' consisting of equipment, Processes and the Escapologist, then the Stakeholder Roles shown in Figure 5.73 as *actor life lines are* outside the System. But this is a question of context. In the wider context of the stunt being performed that includes all the necessary supporting roles and the audience, then these Stakeholder Roles are part of the System and therefore these interactions become interactions between System Elements.

Figure 5.74 shows a simple Scenario, that of the assistant starting and stopping the pump used in the stunt. However, unlike in Figure 5.73, the System is no longer treated as a black box. In this diagram, the individual elements of the System are shown along with the relevant Stakeholder Role who is shown interacting with one of the System Elements (the 'Pump Controller'). The internal interactions between the 'Pump Controller' and the 'Pump' are also shown, as is the behaviour that takes place inside the 'Pump'. Thus, it can be seen that when the 'Pump' receives a 'start' *message* it primes itself and then begins pumping. Similarly, on receipt of a 'stop' *message* it first flushes itself before stopping. Such white box Scenarios are

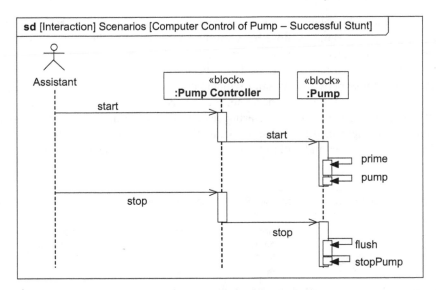

Figure 5.74   Example sequence diagram showing interactions between System Elements

typically developed from black box Scenarios, which may have been developed earlier during the requirements engineering process. An equivalent black box Scenario for Figure 5.74 is shown in Figure 5.75.

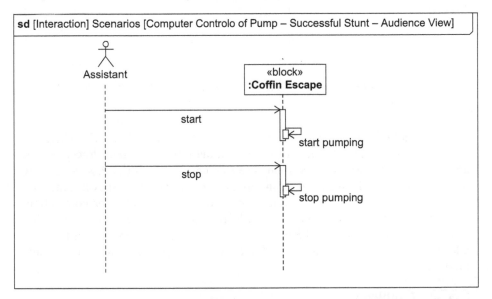

Figure 5.75   Example sequence diagram showing equivalent black box Scenario

As Figure 5.75 is intended to be the black box Scenario from which Figure 5.74 is developed, the diagrams should be consistent. One would expect the interactions between the 'Assistant' and the 'Coffin Escape' System in Figure 5.75 to be the same as those between the 'Assistant' and the relevant System Element (in this case the 'Pump Controller') in Figure 5.74, as indeed they are. Similarly the interactions of the System with itself in Figure 5.75 should be consistent with those between System Elements in Figure 5.74. In this case, although the *messages* are not labelled the same, they are consistent with one another. The difference here is due to the differing levels of abstraction shown on the two diagrams. A single *message* at the black box System level is refined into a number of *messages* between and within System Elements when the Scenario is modelled in more detail.

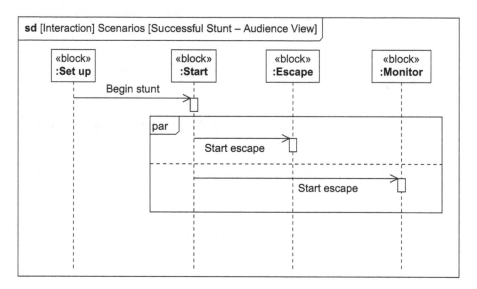

Figure 5.76   Example sequence diagram showing use of parallel combined fragment

The final example in this section, Figure 5.76, shows a Scenario where the System Elements are not pieces of equipment but rather represent Processes that are carried out as part of the System. The *messages* between the Processes show how one Process initiates another, in this case for the Scenario showing the successful execution of the stunt. In this Scenario the 'Start' Process, on completion, has to trigger the 'Escape' and 'Monitor' Processes that have to run in parallel. This is shown by the use of the *parallel combined fragment*, containing two parallel regions, surrounding the two 'Start Escape' *messages* sent by the 'Start' Process.

5.5.7.3   Summary

Sequence diagrams are used to model Scenarios. They show behaviour through time, through the passage of *messages* between *life lines* that represent the participants in the Scenario. When modelling Scenarios, this can be done as black box Scenarios, modelling the System as a single *life line*, or as white box Scenarios that show System Elements:

- Black box Scenarios are often generated when the Scenario is placing the emphasis on the interactions from the point of view of one or more Stakeholder Roles. An example of such a diagram is the Stakeholder Scenario View in ACRE (see Chapter 9).
- White box Scenarios are often generated when the emphasis is on the interactions between System Elements. An example of such a diagram is the System Scenario View in ACRE (see Chapter 9).

In practice, Stakeholder Roles often have to be shown interacting with System Elements, so the distinction is often blurred.

5.5.8 Activity diagrams

This section looks at another behavioural diagram, the *activity diagram*. *Activity diagrams*, generally, allow very low-level modelling to be performed compared to the behavioural models seen so far. Where *sequence diagrams* show the behaviour between elements and *state machine diagrams* show the behaviour within elements, *activity diagrams* may be used to model the behaviour within an *operation*. The other main use for *activity diagrams* is for modelling Processes. For a detailed discussion of Process modelling with SysML see Chapters 7 and 8.

5.5.8.1 Diagram elements

The main elements that make up *activity diagrams* are shown in Figure 5.77.

Figure 5.77 shows a partial meta-model for *activity diagrams*. It shows that an 'Activity Diagram' is made up of three basic elements: one or more 'Activity Node', one or more 'Activity Edge' and zero or more 'Region'. There are three main types of 'Activity Node', which are the 'Action', the 'Object' and the 'Control Node' all of which will be discussed in more detail later in this section. The 'Action' is where the main emphasis lies in these diagrams and represents a unit of behaviour on the 'Activity Diagram'. There are many different types of 'Action' available, the discussion of which is beyond the scope of this book. We will treat them all the same, but for a full discussion see Reference 4. An 'Action' can also have zero or more 'Pin', which can be used to show an 'Object Flow' that carries an 'Object'. This is discussed further.

An 'Activity Edge' connects one or two 'Activity Node'; it can connect an 'Activity Node' to itself, hence the multiplicity of one or two, rather than just two. The 'Activity Edge' element has two main types – 'Control Flow' and 'Object Flow'. A 'Control Flow' is used to show the main routes through the 'Activity Diagram' and connects together one or two 'Activity Node'. An 'Object Flow' is used to show the flow of information between one or more 'Activity Node' and does so by carrying the 'Object' type of 'Activity Node'.

The other major element in an *activity diagram* in the 'Region' has two main types: 'Interruptible Region' and 'Activity Partition'. An 'Interruptible Region' allows a boundary to be put into an *activity diagram* that encloses any *actions* that

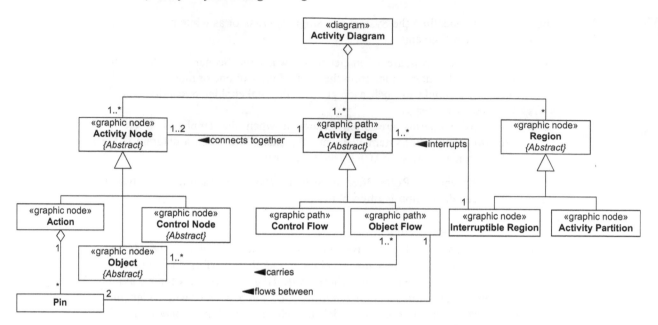

Figure 5.77   Partial meta-model for the activity diagram

may be interrupted. This is particularly powerful for Systems where behaviour may be interrupted by atypical conditions, such as software interrupts and emergency situations. For example, by a direct user interaction or some sort of emergency event. The 'Activity Partition' is the mechanism that is used to visualise swim lanes that allow different *actions* to be grouped together for some reason, usually to show responsibility for the *actions*.

The diagram in Figure 5.78 shows an expanded view of the types of 'Control Node' that exist in SysML. Most of these go together in twos or threes, so will be discussed together.

- The 'Initial Node' shows where the *activity diagram* starts. Conversely, the end of the *activity diagram* is indicated by the 'Activity Final Node'. The 'Flow Final Node' allows a particular *flow* to be terminated without actually finishing the diagram. For example, imagine a situation where there are two parallel control flows in a diagram and one needs to be halted whereas the other continues. In this case, a *final flow node* would be used as it terminates a single *flow* but allows the rest of the diagram to continue.

- The 'Fork Node' and 'Join Node' allow the *flow* in an *activity diagram* to be split into several parallel paths and then re-joined at a later point in the diagram. *Fork nodes* and *join nodes* (or *forks* and *joins* as they are usually known) use a concept of token passing, which basically means that whenever a *flow* is split into parallel *flows* by a *fork*, then imagine that each *flow* has been given a *token*. These *flows* can only be joined back together again when all *tokens* are present on the *join flow*. It is also possible to specify a Boolean condition on the *join* to create more complex rules for re-joining the *flows*.

- The 'Decision Node' and 'Merge Node' also complement one another. A 'Decision Node' allows a *flow* to branch off down a particular route according to a *guard condition*, whereas a 'Merge Node' allows several *flows* to be merged back into a single *flow*.

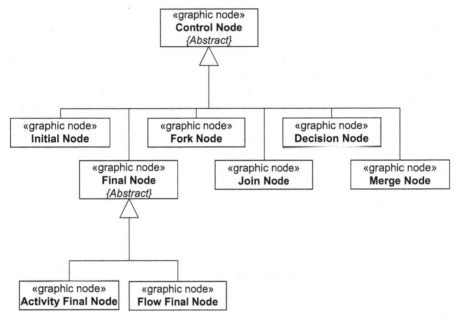

Figure 5.78 Expanded partial meta-model of the activity diagram, focusing on 'Control Node'

There are three types of symbol that can be used on an *activity diagram* to show the flow of information carried by an 'Object Flow': the 'Object Node', the 'Signal'

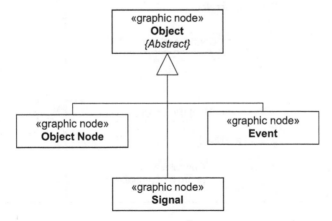

Figure 5.79 Expanded partial meta-model for the activity diagram, focusing on 'Object Node'

and the 'Event'. See Figure 5.79. The 'Object Node' is used to represent information that has been represented elsewhere in the model by a *block* and which is
forming an input to or an output from an *action*. It can be thought of a representing
an *instance specification*. The 'Event' symbol is used to show an *event* coming into
an *activity diagram*, whereas a 'Signal' is used to show an *event* leaving an *activity
diagram*. They correspond to *receipt events* and *send events* of a *state machine
diagram*. There is a special type of 'Event', known as a 'Time Event' that allows
the visualisation of explicit timing events.

Each of these diagram elements may be realised by either graphical nodes or
graphical paths, as indicated by their *stereotypes*, and is illustrated in Figure 5.80.

In addition to the elements mentioned so far, SysML has notation that can be
applied to an 'Activity Edge' and an 'Object Node'. This notation makes use of the

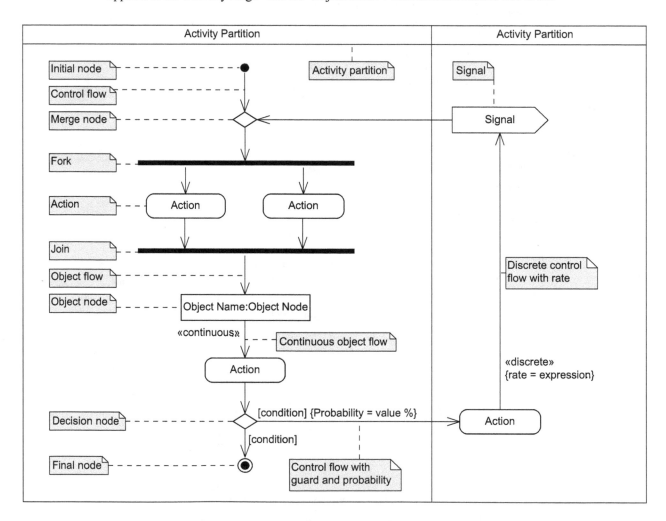

Figure 5.80 Summary of activity diagram notation

existing *constraint* and *stereotype* notation that is already present in SysML and simply defines some standard *constraints* and *stereotypes* for use on *activity diagrams*.

The first of these notations allows a *rate* to be applied to an 'Activity Edge' (and, more specifically, normally to an 'Object Flow') in order to give an indication of how often information flows along the edge. *Flows* can be shown to be *discrete* or *continuous*. This is shown by use of the «discrete» or «continuous» *stereotypes* placed on the *flow*. Alternatively the actual rate can be shown using a *constraint* of the form: {rate = expression}. For example, if data or material passed along a *flow* every minute, then this could be shown by placing the *constraint* {rate = per 1 minute} on the *flow*.

The second notation allows for a probability to be applied to an 'Activity Edge' (typically on 'Control Flow' edges leaving a 'Decision Node') and indicates the probability that the *edge* will be traversed. It can be represented as a number between 0 and 1 or as a percentage. All the probabilities on edges with the same source must add up to 1 (or 100%). It is important to note that the actual *edge* traversed is governed by the *guard conditions* on the 'Decision Node' and not by the probability. The probability is nothing more than an additional piece of information that can be added to the diagram.

The other notation modifies the behaviour of an 'Object Node' and is indicated by the use of the *stereotypes* «nobuffer» and «overwrite». If an *object node* is issued by an *action* and is not immediately consumed by its receiving *action*, then that *object node* can block the operation of the originating *action* until it is consumed by the receiving *action*. «nobuffer» and «overwrite» modify this behaviour:

- «nobuffer» means that the marked *object node* is immediately discarded if the receiving *action* is not ready to receive it. The originating *action* will not be blocked and can continue to generate *object nodes*, which will be discarded if not yet needed.

- «overwrite» means that the marked *object node* is overwritten if the receiving *action* is not ready to receive it. The originating *action* will not be blocked and can continue to generate *object nodes*. The latest generated will overwrite the previous one if not yet needed.

Figure 5.81 shows some additional notation that covers *interruptible regions* and the use of *pins* rather than *object nodes*.

Interruptible regions are shown by a dashed soft box surrounding the region to be interrupted. There must always be a normal flow of control through the *interruptible region*. In this example, the *flow* is into 'Action3' then to 'Action4' and then out of the *region*. There must also be an *event* that causes the interruption: 'Event1' in the example. The *event* is connected by a *control flow* to an *action* outside the *interruptible region*, which acts as an interrupt handler: 'Action7' in the example. The *control flow* is either annotated with a lightning bolt symbol, as here, or may be drawn as such a lightning bolt. In the example above the *interruptible region* shows that while 'Action3' or 'Action4' are taking place, they may be interrupted by 'Event1', which will cause control to transfer to 'Action7'.

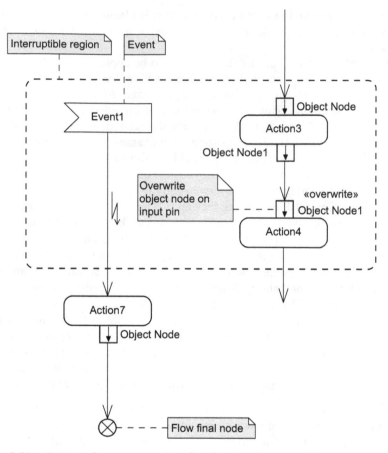

Figure 5.81   Activity diagram notation for showing interruptible regions and use of pins rather than object nodes

The diagram also shows the notation for a *flow final node* and shows how *pins* may be used instead of explicit *object nodes*. The part of the diagram involving 'Action3' and 'Action4' is equivalent to the one shown in Figure 5.82.

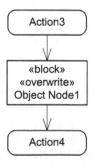

Figure 5.82   Object node notation equivalent to pin notation

Which notation is better, *pins* or *object nodes*, is a matter of personal preference (and perhaps organisational diagramming guidelines and options available in your SysML tool). The authors are firmly in favour of explicit *object nodes* rather than the version using *pins*.

5.5.8.2   Examples

The section will give a number of examples of *activity diagrams*. Additional examples can be found in Chapters 7, 8 and 13.

Figure 5.83 shows an example *activity diagram* containing a single *activity partition*. This is labelled with the model element (in this case 'Assistant') that is responsible for all the behaviour taking place inside that *activity partition*. It is

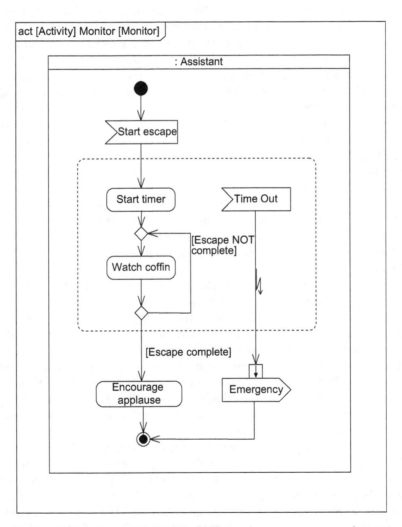

Figure 5.83   Example activity diagram showing decision, merge and interruptible region

possible to have multiple such *activity partitions* and an example is given later in this section. An *activity partition* is usually labelled with the name of a *block* or an *actor* that specifies the type of the model element responsible for the *activity partition*.

The behaviour in this *activity diagram* begins on receipt of a 'Start escape' event, after which control passes into an *interruptible region* where the *action* 'Start timer' takes place. Once this *action* is completed, control falls through a *merge node* and the 'Watch coffin' action takes place. When this *action* is completed a *decision node* is reached. If the *guard condition* '[Escape completed]' is true, then control passes to the 'Encourage applause' *action* and once this is finished the *activity final node* is reached and the *activity diagram* terminates. If, instead, the *guard condition* '[Escape NOT complete]' is true, then control passes back up to the *merge node* before re-entering the 'Watch coffin' *action*. The *merge node* is simply used to merge alternative *control flows* back into a single *control flow*.

However, the normal behaviour is not the only way in which this *activity diagram* can end. If the 'Time out' *event* is received at any time the 'Start timer' or 'Watch coffin' *actions* are executing, then the *interruptible region* is exited and the 'Emergency' *signal* is sent out of this diagram. Note the use of the *pin* on the *signal* in order to connect the *event* to the *signal*.

Another *activity diagram* is shown in Figure 5.84. This time all the behaviour is the responsibility of the 'Escapologist' and the *activity diagram* begins on receipt of the 'Begin stunt' *event*. When this is received, control enters a *fork node*, which leads to two parallel branches in which the 'Escapologist' is undertaking both the 'Free hands' *action* and the 'Count down time' *action*. Each of these leads into a *join node* and when both are completed, then control passes to the 'Emerge' *action*. If either of the two parallel *actions* failed to complete, then the 'Emerge' *action* would never be reached. After 'Emerge' is finished, the 'Escapologist' executes the 'Take a bow' *action* and then the *activity diagram* finished via the *activity final node*.

The final example we will consider here is shown in Figure 5.85. In this *activity diagram* there are two *activity partitions* and we can see from the diagram that the 'Assistant' is responsible for carrying out the 'Whip-up audience' and 'Start pump' actions and for issuing the 'Start escape' *signal*. The 'Safety Officer' is responsible for everything else in the diagram.

On receipt of the 'Begin stunt' event, the 'Safety Officer' will carry out the 'Perform final check' *action*. When this is complete control enters a *decision node* that has two branches leaving it. If the *guard condition* '[Problems found]' is true then the 'Safety Officer' carries out the 'Cancel stunt' *action* and *activity diagram* terminates via the *activity final node*.

If, however, the *guard condition* '[No problems]' is true, then responsibility passes to the 'Assistant' who carries out the 'Whip-up audience' and 'Start pump' *actions* in sequence and finally issues the 'Start escape' *signal*. The *activity diagram* then terminates via the *activity final node*.

However, this is not the end of the *actions* that the 'Assistant' has to carry out. How can this be, if there are no further *actions* in Figure 5.85? Look back at

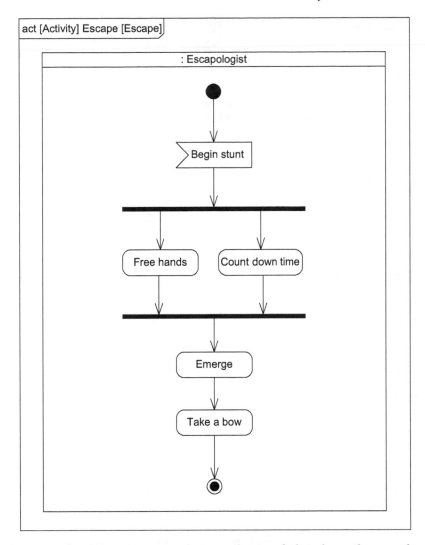

act [Activity] Escape [Escape]

: Escapologist

Begin stunt

Free hands   Count down time

Emerge

Take a bow

Figure 5.84   Example activity diagram showing fork nodes and join nodes

Figure 5.83. The *activity diagram* there is kicked off on receipt of a 'Start escape' *event*. This is the very event that the 'Assistant' has just issued as the 'Start escape' *signal* in Figure 5.85. The two *activity diagrams* are connected by this *event/signal* pair. This is an excellent example of the kinds of consistency between diagrams that you should be looking for when modelling. An *event* that comes into an *activity diagram* (or into a *state machine diagram* as a *receipt event*) must come from somewhere. There must be a corresponding *signal* on another *activity diagram* (or *send event* on a *state machine diagram*) that is the source of the *event*. This would,

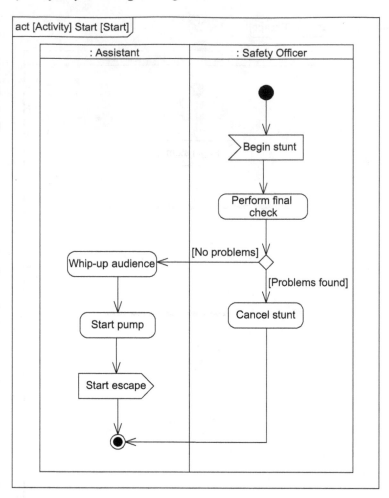

Figure 5.85   Activity diagram showing multiple activity partitions

perhaps, be less confusing if SysML used the same names across *activity diagrams* and *state machine diagrams*, but Table 5.3 may help you to remember.

Table 5.3   Equivalence of event terminology between activity *and* state machine diagrams

Activity diagram		State machine diagram
Event	is same as	*Receipt event*
Signal	is same as	*Send event*

Some of the nature of this communication and further consistency can be seen by looking at Figure 5.76. This shows the communication between a number of

System Elements (actually Processes). The internal behaviour of these processes is what has been modelled by the *activity diagrams* earlier in this section. Thus, the 'Start escape' *signal* in Figure 5.85 corresponds to the beginning of the 'Start escape' *message* in Figure 5.76 as it leaves the ':Start' *life line*. The Start escape' *event* in Figure 5.83 corresponds to the end of the 'Start escape' *message* in Figure 5.76 as it enters the ':Monitor' *life line*.

Thus, *activity diagrams* can communicate with other *activity diagrams* or with *state machine diagram* and vice versa. Furthermore, the *messages* corresponding to these *events* and *signals* can be modelled as *messages* on *sequence diagrams*. Isn't consistency great?

5.5.8.3   Summary

Activity diagrams are very powerful SysML *behavioural diagrams*, which can be used to show both low-level behaviour, such as *operations*, and high-level behaviour, such as Processes. They are very good for helping to ensure model consistency, relating to *state machine diagrams*, *sequence diagrams* and *block definition diagrams*.

Activity diagrams concentrate on *control* and *object flow*, showing behaviour defined using *actions* that use and produce *object nodes*. That is, they concentrate on behaviour that deals with information flow and transformation, rather than behaviour that concentrates on change of state (as in the *state machine diagram*) or that concentrates on the sequencing of messages (as in the *sequence diagram*). However, all of these diagrams can (and should) be used together to give a complete and consistent model of the interactions between System Elements.

5.5.9   Use case diagrams

The SysML *use case diagram* realises a behavioural aspect of a model, with an emphasis on functionality rather than the control and logical timing of the System. The *use case diagram* represents the highest level of behavioural abstraction that is available in the SysML. However, the *use case diagram* is arguably the easiest diagram to get wrong in the SysML. There are a number of reasons for this:

- The diagrams themselves look very simple, so simple in fact that they are often viewed as being a waste of time.
- It is very easy to go into too much detail on a *use case diagram* and to accidentally start analysis or design, rather than conducting context modelling.
- *Use case diagrams* are very easy to confuse with data flow diagrams as they are often perceived as being similar. This is because the symbols look the same as both *use cases* (in *use case diagrams*) and processes (in a data flow diagram) are represented by ellipses. In addition, both *use cases* and processes can be decomposed into lower level elements.
- *Use case diagrams* make use of perhaps the worst symbol in SysML, the stick person notation used to represent *actors*. This is discussed further in Section 5.5.9.1.

Nevertheless, *use case diagrams* are central to systems engineering, forming the basis of the model-based approach to requirements engineering as embodied by the ACRE approach described in Chapter 9, being used to model the Needs in Context for the System under development.

5.5.9.1   Diagram elements

Use case diagrams are made up of four main elements as shown in Figure 5.86.

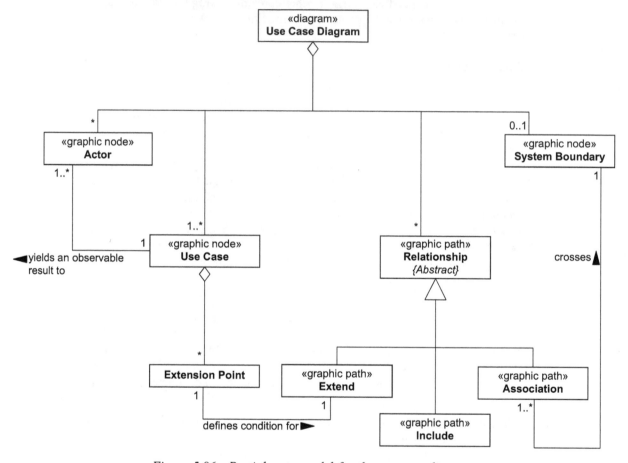

Figure 5.86   Partial meta-model for the use case diagram

Figure 5.86 shows a partial meta-model for *use case diagrams*. It shows that a 'Use Case Diagram' is made up of one or more 'Use Case', zero or more 'Actor', zero or one 'System Boundary' and zero or more 'Relationship'. Each 'Use Case' yields an observable result to one or more 'Actor'. There are three types of 'Relationship': the 'Extend', 'Include' and 'Association'. A 'Use Case' can be made up of zero or more 'Extension Point', each of which defines the condition for an 'Extend' *relationship*. Each 'Association' crosses the 'System Boundary'.

The notation that is used on *use case diagrams* is shown in Figure 5.87.

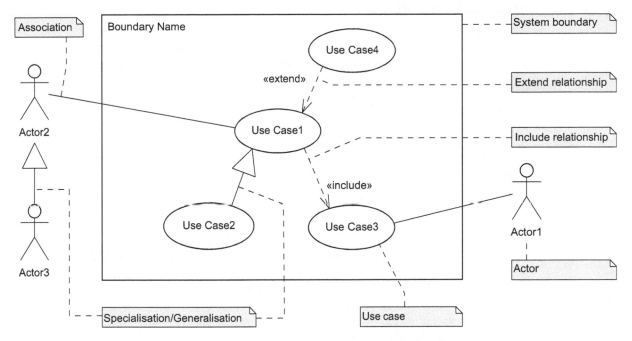

Figure 5.87   Summary of use case diagram notation

Use case diagrams are composed of four basic elements: *use cases*, *actors*, *relationships* and a *system boundary*. As a minimum a *use case diagram* must contain at least one *use case*; all other elements are optional.

Each *use case* describes behaviour of the system that yields an observable result to an *actor*. It is with the *actor* that the SysML notation is at its weakest, in terms of both the symbol and the name. The stick man symbol and the name *actor* suggest that this concept represents that of a person. This is not the case. An *actor* represents the role of a Person, place *or* thing that interacts with, is impacted by or has an interest in the System. So, while an *actor* can, indeed, represent a Person, it can also be used to represent an Organisation, other System or even a piece of legislation or a Standard. Furthermore, it is essential to understand that it is the role that is represented. This means that you should never see the names of People or Organisations or Standards, etc., on a *use case diagram*, but the role that they are playing. An *actor* named 'ISO15288' would be wrong, but one named 'Systems Engineering Standard' would be correct. It is also worth noting that a given role may be taken by more than one person, place or thing and that a given person, place or thing may take on more than one role.

In terms of the MBSE Ontology, the *actor* is directly analogous to the concept of the Stakeholder Role rather than the concept of the Person. The *use case* is directly analogous to the concept of the Use Case that represents a Need that has been put into Context.

Use cases are related to *actors* and to other *use cases* using a number of different types of *relationship*:

- *Association relationship*. This is used to relate *use cases* to *actors* and, unlike when used on a *block definition diagram*, is a simple unadorned line with neither *name* nor *multiplicity* as can been seen in the *association* between 'Actor2' and 'Use Case1' in Figure 5.87.
- *Include relationship*. This is used when a piece of functionality may be split from the main *use case*, for example to be used by another *use case*. A simple way to think about this is to consider the included *use case* as always being part of the parent *use case*. This is used to try to spot common functionality within a *use case*. It is highly possible that one or more of the decomposed *use cases* may be used by another part of the System. It is shown using a dashed line with an open arrow head, the line bearing the *stereotype* «include». The direction of the arrow should make sense when the model is read aloud. In Figure 5.87 'Use Case1' includes 'Use Case3'.
- *Extend relationship*. This is used when the functionality of the base *use case* is being extended in some way. This means that sometimes the functionality of a *use case* may change, depending on what happens when the System is running. A simple way to think about this is to consider the extending *use case* as sometimes being part of the parent *use case*. Extending *use cases* are often used to capture special, usually error-handling, behaviour. The *extend relationship* is also shown using a dashed line with an open arrow head, the line bearing the *stereotype* «extend». It is important to get the direction of the *relationship* correct, as it is different from the '«include»' direction. The direction of the arrow should make sense when the diagram is read aloud. In Figure 5.87 'Use Case4' extends 'Use Case1'. Every *use case* should be described (normally using text). Such a description must define the *extension points* where the behaviour of the *use case* is extended by the extending *use case*. An *extension point* has no specific graphical notation.
- *Specialisation/generalisation relationship*. This is exactly the same *relationship* as found on *block definition diagrams* and is used when one *use case* is a *specialisation* of another. Just like when used with *blocks*, *generalisation* between *use cases* allows for inheritance of behaviour and relationships. For example, consider the *use case diagram* shown in Figure 5.88. The general Use Case 'Allow stunt to be performed using different fluids' is specialised by the two Use Cases 'Perform using concrete' and 'Perform using custard', which inherit the behaviour described in 'Allow stunt to be performed using different fluids' as well as including the Use Case 'Ensure fluid chosen is suitable for venue', which is included by 'Allow stunt to be performed using different fluids'.

In a similar way, *generalisation* can be used between *actors*, as is shown in Figure 5.87, when one *actor* is a specialisation of another.

The final element that can appear on a *use case diagram* is the *system boundary*, used when describing the Context of a System. As its name suggests, the

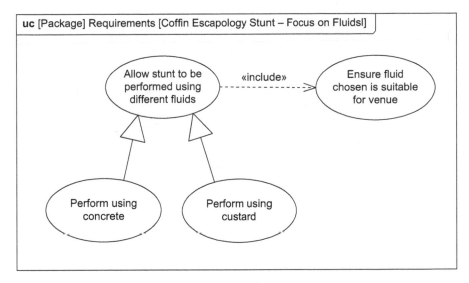

Figure 5.88   Example use case diagram showing generalisation

system boundary defines the boundary of the System from a particular point of view, that is Context. Everything inside the *system boundary* is part of the System, and everything outside the *system boundary* is external to the System. *Actors* are always outside the *system boundary*, and indeed, an *association* between an *actor* and a *use case* that crosses a *system boundary* indicates that there is an Interface between the *actor* and the System (which may be a sophisticated software and hardware Interface but equally could be an Interface in which a Person passes a note on a piece of paper to another Person).

System boundaries* are not mandatory on a *use case diagram*. They are used when *use cases* are being shown in a Context. Where a *use case diagram* is being drawn simply to expand on a *use case*, as shown in Figure 5.88, then no *system boundary* is needed.

5.5.9.2   Examples

This section presents some examples of *use case diagrams* and related diagramming elements. Further examples of use case diagrams can be found in Chapter 13 and throughout Chapters 7–11 and 14–16. In addition, this section concludes with some guidance notes on common patterns that are often seen in *use case diagrams* and that can guide the modeller in refinement of the *use case diagrams*.

Figure 5.89 shows a *use case diagram* identifying the high-level Use Cases for the Coffin Escape Stunt. The Context, as indicated by the presence and title of the *system boundary*, is for the stunt System rather than from the point of view of an individual Stakeholder Role. The relevant high-level Stakeholder Roles are shown as *actors*, with associations connecting them to the Use Cases in which they have an interest and the relationships between the Use Cases are shown. There are two

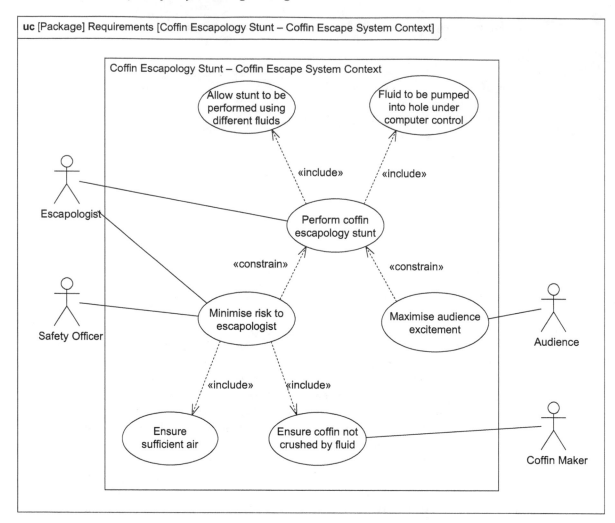

Figure 5.89   Example use case diagram showing System Context

points worth highlighting about this diagram: the number of Use Cases shown and the use of the «constrain» *dependency*.

The diagram shows only seven Use Cases, yet this is the top-level *use case diagram* showing the Use Cases for the whole coffin stunt System. Surely there must be more Use Cases than this? The answer to this is, of course, yes there are. However, this does not mean that all these Use Cases have to be shown on a single diagram. Other *use case diagrams* can be drawn that break these Use Cases down further and put them into the correct Context. Don't forget that these diagrams are produced to aid understanding and communication. A complicated diagram with tens of Use Cases on it may look impressive but is rarely of any practical use (other than for illustrating just how complicated the system is). Consider a System such as an aeroplane. There will be 1000s of Use Cases for the complete System, but how many high-level Use Cases are there? Probably not many more than 'Take off safely', Land safely', 'Have a fully-laden range of X km', 'Have a carrying capacity of X kg', etc.

The second point to discuss is that of the «constrain» *dependency*, such as the one between 'Minimise risk to escapologist' and 'Perform coffin escapology stunt'. The «constrain» *dependency* is not part of standard SysML, but is an extension used by the authors to show that one *use case* constrains another in some way. It is created using the SysML stereotyping mechanisms built into the language that allows existing language elements to be extended and is discussed in detail in Section 5.3.

Figure 5.90 shows another *use case diagram* showing Needs in Context. However, rather than showing the Use Cases for the entire System, this diagram shows them from point of view of a single Stakeholder Role, namely the

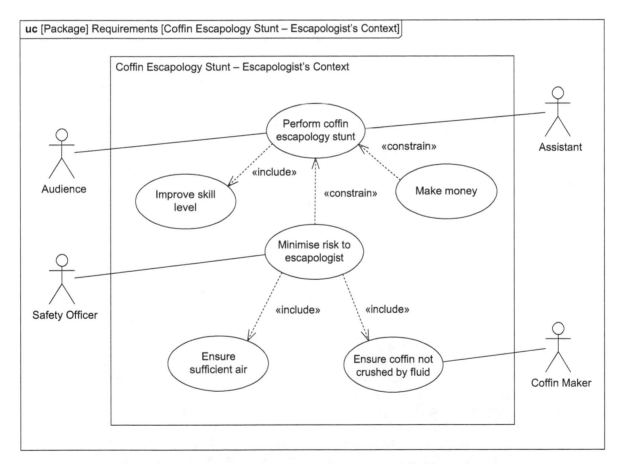

Figure 5.90   Example use case diagram showing a Stakeholder Role's Context

escapologist. Unsurprisingly some of the Use Cases are also shown in Figure 5.89, since the Escapologist is one of (if not *the*) main Stakeholder Roles in any escapology stunt. However, some of those in Figure 5.89 (such as 'Maximise audience excitement') are not of direct interest to the Escapologist and are therefore not shown in Figure 5.90. Conversely, there are Use Cases that are only relevant to the Escapologist (such as 'Improve skill level'), which are shown in Figure 5.90 but are not relevant from the System Context and are therefore not shown in Figure 5.89. This whole idea of Context is central to the ACRE approach to requirements engineering discussed in much more detail in Chapter 9. Note also the use of the «constrain» *dependency* in Figure 5.90.

As discussed in Section 5.5.9.1 a *use case diagram* does not have to show any *actors* or contain a *system boundary*. An example of such a *use case diagram* is shown in Figure 5.91.

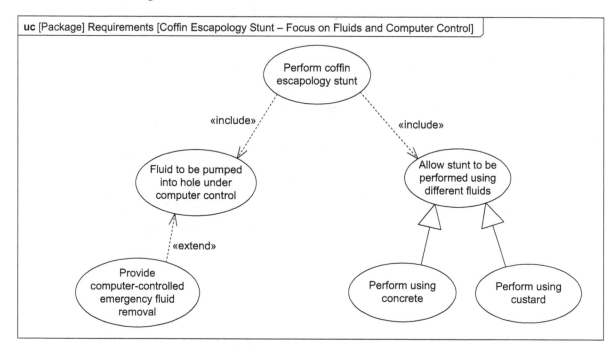

Figure 5.91   Example use case diagram without system boundary or actors

Figure 5.91 is focusing on Use Cases related to the use of different fluids in the stunt and to the computer control of the pump used in the stunt. Two specific types of fluids are identified and are shown via the use of the *generalisation relationship* between 'Allow stunt to be performed using different fluids' and 'Perform stunt using concrete' and 'Perform stunt using custard'. A Use Case representing special case behaviour 'Provide computer-controlled emergency fluid removal' *extends* the standard 'Fluid to be pumped into hole under computer control' Use Case.

When developing *use case diagrams* there are a number of common patterns that should be looked for as an aid towards the production of good *use case diagram*. This section concludes with a look at these patterns, which cover the following possible situations:

- *Use case* at too high a level
- *Actor* at too high a level
- Repeated *actors*
- Something missing

Each of these four patterns is discussed in the following sub-sections.

Use case too high-level

One common mistake is to model *use cases* at too high a level. Consider Figure 5.92.

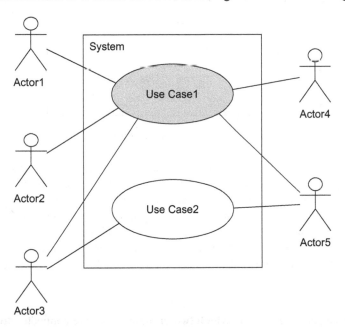

Figure 5.92   Use case too high level

Figure 5.92 shows a *use case*, 'Use Case1', that is linked to all *actors*. Such a pattern may indicate that the *use case* is at too high a level and that it should be decomposed further, making use of «include» and «extend» *dependencies* to link it to more detailed *use cases*. The *actors* would then be associated with the more detailed *use cases* rather than all being connected to the top-level *use case*.

Actor too high-level

Another common error is to model *actors* at too high a level. Consider Figure 5.93.

Figure 5.93 shows an *actor*, 'Actor2' (drawn with a surrounding box for emphasis), that is connected to every *use case*. Such a pattern may indicate that:

- The *actor* is at too high a level and that it should be decomposed further.
- The diagram has been drawn from the point of view of the Stakeholder Role represented by that *actor*.

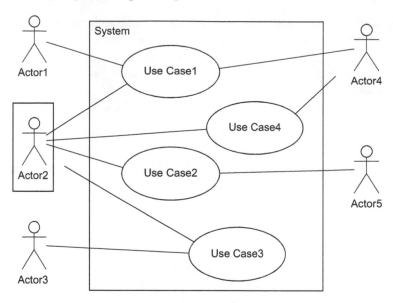

Figure 5.93   Actor too high level

If the *actor* is at too high a level, then it should be decomposed further and replaced on the diagram with the new *actors*. These *actors* will then be associated with the relevant *use cases* rather than being associated with all the *use cases*.

If the diagram has been drawn from the point of view of the Stakeholder Role represented by that *actor*, that is the *use case diagram* is drawn for that Stakeholder Role's Context, then the *actor* should be removed from the diagram. The *system boundary* should indicate that the diagram is drawn for that Stakeholder Role's Context.

Repeated actors

Sometimes a pattern is seen in which two or more *actors* are connected to the same *use cases*. Figure 5.94 shows this.

Here we see two *actors*, 'Actor1' and 'Actor 2' (drawn with a surrounding box for emphasis), that are both connected to the same three *use cases*. This pattern may indicate that the *actors* are repreisenting the same Stakeholder Role. Alternatively, it may indicate that instances of Stakeholder Roles have been used (check for names of specific people, organisations, standards, etc.). Instances should never be used. Remember that a Stakeholder Role represents the role of something that has an interest in the Project, not an actual instance involved. Any duplicate *actors* should be removed from the diagram.

Something missing – use cases without actors and actors without use cases

What does it mean if we have *use cases* or *actors* that are not related to anything? Consider Figure 5.95.

Figure 5.95 has a *use case*, 'Use Case5', and an *actor*, 'Actor5', that are not connected to anything else on the diagram.

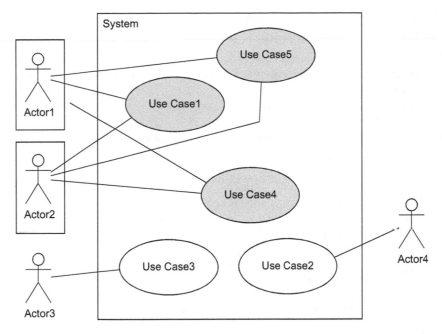

Figure 5.94 Repeated actors

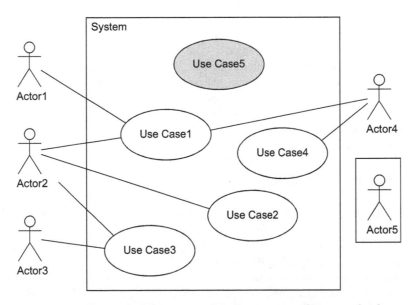

Figure 5.95 Something missing? Basic use case diagram checks

'Use Case5' has no *actors* associated with it. There are four possible reasons for this:

1. The *use case* is not needed and should be removed from the diagram.
2. There is an *actor* (or *actors*) missing that should be added to the diagram and linked to the *use case*.
3. There is an internal relationship missing; the *use case* should be linked to another *use case*.
4. There is an external relationship missing; the *use case* should be linked to an *existing actor*.

'Actor5' has no *use cases* associated with it. There are three possible reasons for this:

1. The *actor* is not needed and should be removed from the diagram.
2. There is a *use case* (or *use cases*) missing that should be added to the diagram and linked to the *actor*.
3. There is a *relationship* missing; the *actor* should be linked to an existing *use case*.

These two errors are very common, particularly when creating initial *use case diagrams*, and should be checked for on all *use case diagrams*.

5.5.9.3   Summary

Use case diagrams show the highest level behaviour of a system and are used to show Needs (Requirements, Concerns, Goals or Capabilities) in Context, along with the Stakeholder Roles involved and the relationships between them. This is the central theme of the ACRE approach described in Chapter 9, realised in its Requirement Context View.

Care is needed when producing *use case diagrams*. They should not be over-decomposed so that they start to look like data flow diagrams and become diagrams detailing the design of the System as they exist to show high-level behaviour as Needs in Context. There are a number of common patterns that should be looked for when producing *use case diagrams*, which can help you to spot when *use cases* or *actors* are at too high a level, where an *actor* has been repeated or where there is something missing from a *use case diagram*.

5.6   Auxiliary constructs

The SysML specification defines a number of *auxiliary constructs*, among which is included the *allocation*. The *allocation* will be described here. Some other examples of *auxiliary constructs* are given in Chapter 13. For full information on the other *auxiliary constructs*, see Reference 1.

An *allocation* is used to show how various model elements are allocated *to* and allocated from other elements. Such *allocations* may be used to show deployment or more generally to relate different parts of a model as the design progresses.

Figure 5.96 shows the partial meta-model for *allocations* and shows that an 'Allocation' can be represented in two ways: as an 'Allocation Compartment'

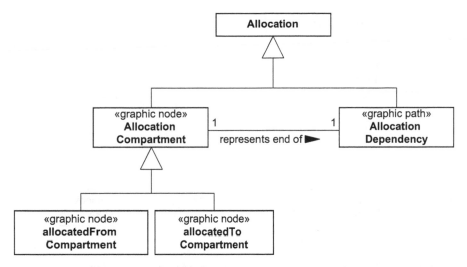

Figure 5.96   Partial meta-model for allocations

(either an 'allocatedFrom Compartment' or an 'allocatedTo Compartment') on an existing graphic node or as an 'Allocation Dependency' between model elements, with each end of such a *dependency* equivalent to one of the two types of 'Allocation Compartment'.

Rather than showing an 'Allocation Compartment' as a *compartment* of the relevant model element, it can also be shown using a *callout note* notation. This can be seen in Figure 5.97, where the notation used for *allocations* is shown.

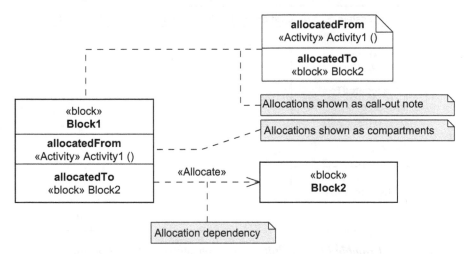

Figure 5.97   Summary of allocation notation on a block definition diagram

Allocations can be shown on diagrams other than the *block definition diagram* but the notation used is essentially the same. The following diagrams show examples of the notation in use.

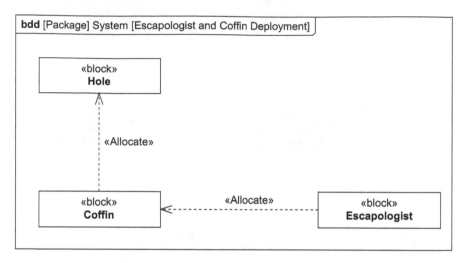

*Figure 5.98   Example block definition diagram showing allocation using a
        dependency*

Figure 5.98 shows *allocation* of the 'Escapologist' to the 'Coffin' and the
'Coffin' to the 'Hole' using the *allocation dependency* notation. The *block
definition diagram* here is essentially being used a kind of deployment diagram
(a diagram type present in UML but rather inexplicably, given the nature of systems
engineering, absent from the SysML).

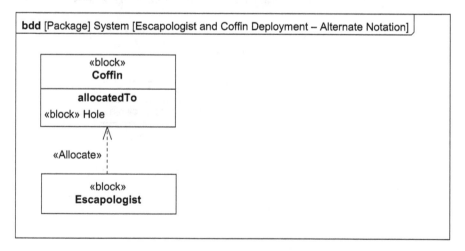

*Figure 5.99   Example block definition diagram showing allocation using
        compartments*

Figure 5.99 shows exactly the same information as is shown in Figure 5.98, but
makes use of both *allocation compartments* and an *allocation dependency*. Note

also that this diagram is lacking the 'Hole' *block* found in Figure 5.98. The *block* and the *relationship* to it can be deduced from the *allocatedTo compartment* in the 'Coffin' *block.*

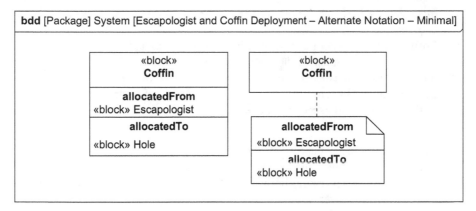

Figure 5.100   Example block definition diagram showing allocation – the minimalist approach

Finally, we can go very minimalist, as in Figure 5.100 where everything is done using *allocation compartments*. The diagram also shows how these *allocation compartments* would be shown using the *callout note* notation. In a "real" model, both notations would not be shown on the same diagram.

5.7   Summary

This chapter has described each of the nine SysML diagrams in turn, along with some of the auxiliary notation, and has provided examples of their use.

In order to conclude this chapter, there are a few pieces of practical advice that should be borne in mind when modelling using the SysML:

- Use whatever diagrams are appropriate. There is nothing to say that all nine diagrams should be used in order to have a fully defined System – just use whatever diagrams are the most appropriate.
- Use whatever syntax is appropriate. The syntax introduced in this book represents only a fraction of the very rich SysML language. It is possible to model most aspects of a system using the syntax introduced here. As you encounter situations that your known syntax cannot cope with, it is time to learn some more. There is a very good chance that there is a mechanism there, somewhere, that will.
- Ensure consistency between models. One of the most powerful aspects of the SysML is the ability to check the consistency between diagrams, which is often glossed over. Certainly, in order to give a good level of confidence in your models, these consistency checks are essential.

- Iterate. Nobody ever gets a model right the first time, so iterate! A model is an evolving entity that will change over time and, as the model becomes more refined, so the connection to reality will draw closer.
- Keep all models. Never throw away a model, even if it is deemed as incorrect, as it will help you to document decisions made as the design has evolved.
- Ensure that the system is modelled in both structural and behavioural aspects. In order to meet most of the above criteria, it is essential that the system is modelled in both aspects, otherwise the model is incomplete.
- Ensure that the system is modelled at several levels of abstraction. This is one of the fundamental aspects of modelling and will help to maintain consistency checks.

Finally, modelling using the SysML should not change the way that you work, but should aid communication and help to avoid ambiguities. Model as many things as possible, as often as possible, because the more you use the SysML, the more benefits you will discover.

References

1. Object Management Group. *SysML Specification* [Online]. 2012. Available from http://www.omgsysml.org [Accessed April 2013]
2. Miller G.A. 'The magical number seven, plus or minus two: some limits on our capacity for processing information'. *Psychological Review*. 1956;**63**:81–97
3. Holt J. *UML for Systems Engineering – Watching the Wheels*. 2nd edn. IET Publishing: Stevenage, UK; 2004
4. Rumbaugh J., Jacobson I., Booch G. *The Unified Modeling Language Reference Manual*. 2nd edn. Boston, MA: Addison-Wesley; 2005
5. Booch G., Rumbaugh J., Jacobson I. *The Unified Modeling Language User Guide*. 2nd edn. Boston, MA: Addison-Wesley; 2005
6. Holt J., Perry S. *SysML for Systems Engineering*. IET Publishing: Stevenage, UK; 2008

Chapter 6

Diagramming guidelines

Rules are just helpful guidelines for stupid people who can't make up their own minds.

House M.D. (2010)

6.1 Introduction

Producing consistent SysML (and UML) diagrams that have a common look and feel is crucial to efficient and effective modelling. One of the easiest ways of helping to ensure consistency within SysML models is to set and follow effective naming and diagramming conventions that ensure a common look and feel across diagrams and help to ensure that diagrams are easy to read. Such guidelines should also save time by limiting the number of stylistic choices faced, allowing focus to be directed to the modelling rather than the drawing. This chapter defines a set of rules and guidelines to be followed when producing SysML diagrams.

Following this introduction, the Naming Conventions section defines rules to be applied to elements on SysML *structural* and *behavioural diagrams* together with *stereotypes*. This is followed by the Diagram Frame Labels section which defines rules for naming SysML diagrams. The Additional Guidelines section defines rules for specific diagram types and gives some guidelines on producing diagrams using SysML CASE tools. Finally, the Model Structure section discusses ways in which SysML models can be structured.

The guidelines presented here are those used by the authors and are, in part, based on Reference 1. The guidelines form part of their SysML modelling Standard, i.e. the adoption by the authors is not optional. Of course, for the reader these are only guidelines and can therefore be followed, changed or ignored. Nevertheless, it is recommended that a defined SysML modelling standard be produced and enforced as part of the reader's systems engineering processes.

6.2 Naming conventions

This section defines general naming guidelines that should be followed when producing SysML diagrams.

When modelling Standards or producing models for customers, any naming conventions described in the Standard or used by the customer should be followed.

6.2.1 Structural diagrams

Figure 6.1 illustrates the naming conventions to be followed when producing SysML *structural diagrams*.

The case of the text used in all elements indicates the convention to be adopted for that element. For example, an *association* should be named all in lower case whereas a *property* should be named in sentence case (i.e. initial word starts with a capital letter, all others with a lower case letter).

The naming conventions shown in Figure 6.1 are summarised in Table 6.1.

Table 6.1   Structural diagram *naming conventions*

Diagram item	Naming conventions
Block	Name should have each word capitalised.
	Name should be singular.
	Compartments can be turned off to aid clarity. If necessary, add a *comment* to the diagram so that reader of the diagram knows that information has been omitted from the diagram.
	Compartments should be named.
Block property	*Property names* should be noun phrases.
	Property names should be in sentence case.
	Property types should have each word capitalised.
	The *direction* of *flow properties* must be stated.
Operation	*Operation names* are verb phrases; strong verbs should be used where possible.
	Operation names should be in lower case with spaces between words. NOTE: When modelling software, then *operation names* should be named in camel case, e.g. 'checkTime'.
	Parameter names should be in sentence case, but with underscores replacing spaces, e.g. 'Time_server'.
	Parameter types should have each word capitalised.
	Operation return types should have each word capitalised.
Interface	Name should have each word capitalised.
Association	Name *associations* using the active voice where possible.
	Name should be in lower case.
	Direction must be shown.
	Always show *multiplicity*, even when it is '1'.
	Role names should be in sentence case.
Requirement	Name should be in sentence case.
Package	*Package name* should have each word capitalised.
Constraint Block	Name should have each word capitalised.
	Parameter names should be in sentence case.
	Parameter types should have each word capitalised.
	If the constraint relationship is a Boolean test, then it should start with a lower-case letter, e.g. 'if...'
Note	A *note* can contain any style of content.

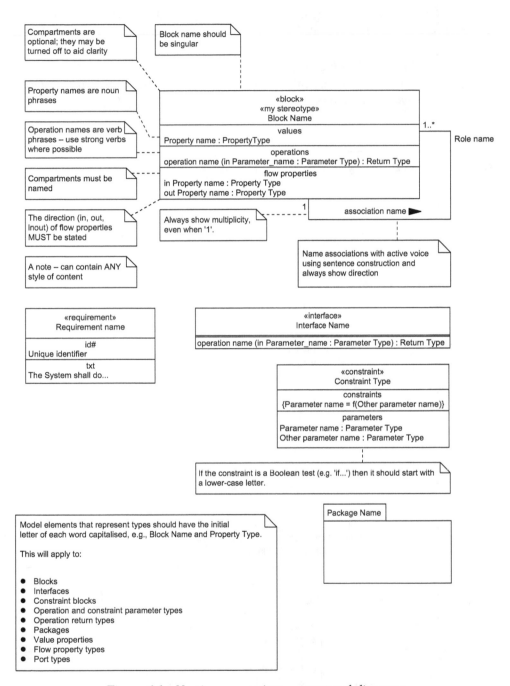

Figure 6.1   Naming conventions – structural diagrams

With the naming conventions for *structural diagrams* defined, the next section discusses the naming guidelines for *behavioural diagrams*.

6.2.2   Behavioural diagrams

Figure 6.2 illustrates the naming conventions to be followed when producing SysML *behavioural diagrams*.

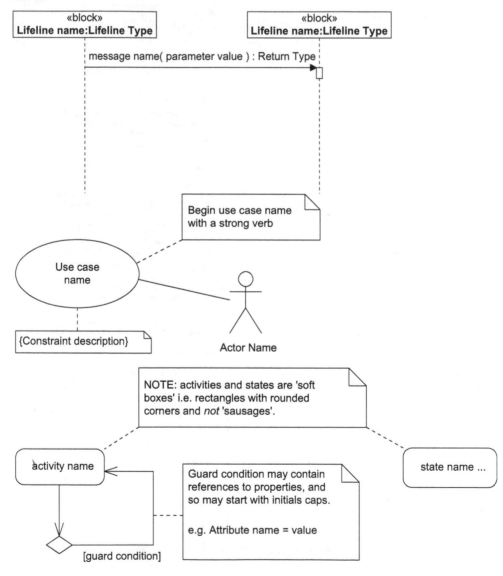

Figure 6.2   Naming conventions – behavioural diagrams

The case of the text used in all elements indicates the convention to be adopted for that element. For example, a *message* should be named all in lower case whereas a *use case* should be named in sentence case (i.e. initial word starts with a capital letter, all others with a lower case letter).

The naming conventions shown in Figure 6.2 are summarised in Table 6.2.

Table 6.2 Behavioural diagram *naming conventions*

Diagram item	Naming conventions
Lifeline	*Instance name* should be in sentence case.
	Type name should have each word capitalised.
Message	*Message name* should be in the same case as the *operation* or *event* that they correspond to (see Table 6.1).
	Parameter values should be in lower case.
	Return types should have each word capitalised.
Use case	Name should be in sentence case.
	Name should begin with a strong verb.
Actor	Name should have each word capitalised.
State	Names should be in lower case.
	Symbol is a rectangle with rounded corners (a "soft box") and not a sausage with semi-circular end.
Activity	Names should be in lower case.
	Symbol is a rectangle with rounded corners (a "soft box") and not a sausage with semi-circular end.
Guard condition	*Guard condition* may contain references to *properties* (see Figure 6.1 and Table 6.1) and so may start with initial capitals. Otherwise the condition should be in lower case.

With the naming conventions for *behavioural diagrams* defined, the next section discusses the naming guidelines for *stereotypes*.

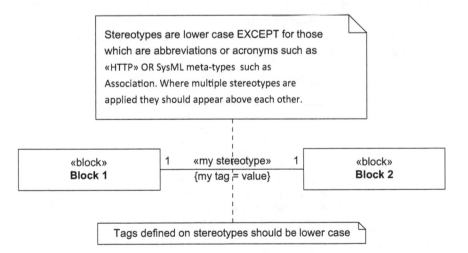

Stereotypes are lower case EXCEPT for those which are abbreviations or acronyms such as «HTTP» OR SysML meta-types such as Association. Where multiple stereotypes are applied they should appear above each other.

«block» **Block 1** — 1 — «my stereotype» {my tag = value} — 1 — «block» **Block 2**

Tags defined on stereotypes should be lower case

Figure 6.3 Naming conventions – stereotypes

6.2.3   *Stereotypes*

Figure 6.3 illustrates the naming conventions to be followed when using *stereotypes*.
The naming conventions shown in Figure 6.3 are summarised in Table 6.3.

Table 6.3   Stereotype *naming conventions*

Diagram item	Naming conventions
Stereotype	*Stereotypes* are lower case except for those which are abbreviations or acronyms such as «HTTP» or SysML *meta-types* such as Association. An exception to this rule is when a *stereotype* is defined that corresponds to an Ontology Element. For example, if defining a *stereotype* for the Project Ontology Element, the *stereotype* would be «Project». Multiple *stereotypes* applied to same item should appear above each other.
Tag	*Tags* defined on *stereotypes* are lower case.

With the naming conventions for *stereotypes* defined, the next section
discusses the naming of diagrams.

6.3   Diagram frame labels

This section defines guidelines to be followed when labelling diagrams.

All SysML diagrams must have a diagram frame that contains the name of the
diagram. Each diagram should be named in the following fashion:

<frame tag> [model element type] <model element name> [diagram name]

Each part is separated by a space and the *frame tag* is bolded. The *model element
type* and *diagram name* parts of the name are in brackets. The *frame tag* and *model
element name* are mandatory.

The abbreviations shown in Table 6.4 should be used to indicate the type of
diagram – known in SysML as the *frame tag*. If using a tool that automatically adds
a *diagram frame* and that does not allow the *frame tags* to be changed, then the tag
names used by the tool will be used.

Table 6.4   Diagram frame *labels*

Diagram type	Frame tag
Activity diagram	act
Block definition diagram	bdd
Internal block diagram	ibd
Package diagram	pkg
Parametric diagram	par
Requirement diagram	req
State machine diagram	stm
Sequence diagram	sd
Use case diagram	uc

The following shows the *model element type* associated with the different diagram kinds:

- Activity diagram – activity
- Block definition diagram – block, package, or constraint block
- Internal block diagram – block or constraint block
- Package diagram – package or model
- Parametric diagram – block or constraint block
- Requirement diagram – package or requirement
- Sequence diagram – interaction
- State machine diagram – state machine
- Use case diagram – package

The *model element type* indicates the *namespace* for the elements contained on the diagram.

The *model element name* identifies which model element type the diagram is describing.

The *diagram name* is used to give the diagram a unique name. This is particularly important when different diagrams of the same type are drawn for the same model element. The diagram name would differentiate between these diagrams since they would have the same diagram kind, model element type and model element name.

Some examples will help:

A *block definition diagram* is created inside a *package* named 'System Structure'. The diagram shows the structural hierarchy. The diagram might be named:

bdd [Package] System Structure [Structural Hierarchy]

The first three parts of the name are determined by its type and "owner".

A second *block definition diagram* is created in the same *package* and shows the *properties* and *operations* of the System Elements. It could be named:

bdd [Package] System Structure [Properties and Operations of System Elements]

Note that the first three parts of the name are the same, since the diagram type is the same as is its owner. The [diagram name] element of the full name differentiates between them.

A *parametric diagram* is created for a *block* named 'System'. The diagram shows power consumption. The diagram could be named:

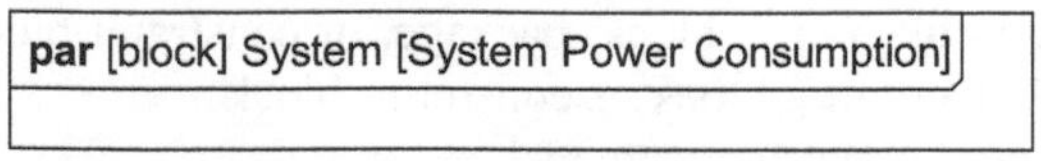

```
par [block] System [System Power Consumption]
```

The following capitalisation rules should be applied:

- The *frame tag* should be lower case and emboldened.
- The *model element type* should be lower case. (Note: the SysML specification is inconsistent on this, as are many SysML tools).
- The *model element name* will have the same capitalisation as the element it corresponds to in the model.
- The *diagram name* element should have each word capitalised.

When producing diagrams that are based on a Framework that defines a number of Views which have their own abbreviations, then:

- The View abbreviation should be in upper case. Lower-case letters are allowed in order to distinguish Views that would otherwise have the same abbreviation. For example, in a model-based requirement engineering Framework a Stakeholder Scenario View might have the abbreviation SSV, whereas a System Scenario View might have the abbreviation SysSV.
- The View abbreviation should replace the standard SysML *frame tag*. If the SysML tool being used does not allow replacement of *frame tags*, then the View abbreviation should be added to the *diagram name* element, separated by a hyphen.
- If *stereotypes* have been defined to indicate the diagram usage, then the *stereotype* should be shown in the *diagram frame*.

For example, an Ontology View has been defined as part of an Architectural Framework meta-model. It has been given the abbreviation ONT and has the *stereotype* «ontology view» associated with it. The diagram is a usage of a SysML *block definition diagram*. An Ontology View is created in a *package* called MBSE Ontology and is intended to show a simplified Ontology. The *diagram frame* for this diagram would look like Figure 6.4.

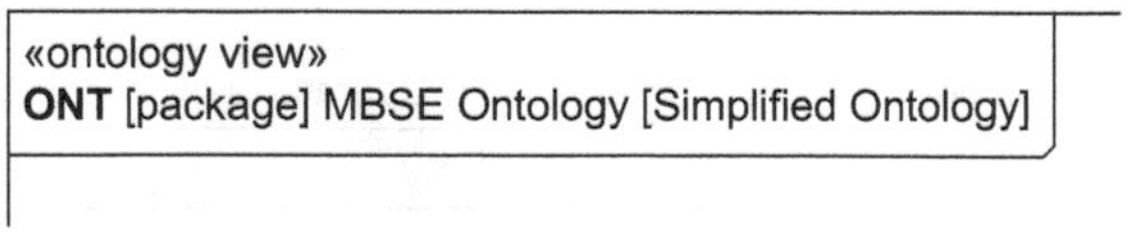

```
«ontology view»
ONT [package] MBSE Ontology [Simplified Ontology]
```

Figure 6.4   Example diagram frame showing user-defined view abbreviation replacing frame tag

In a tool that doesn't allow replacement of *frame tags*, the *diagram frame* would look like Figure 6.5.

«ontology view»
bdd [package] MBSE Ontology [ONT - Simplified Ontology]

Figure 6.5 Example diagram frame showing user-defined view abbreviation added to diagram name

6.4 Additional guidelines

This section contains additional guidelines that apply to particular diagram types.

6.4.1 *Block and internal block diagrams – showing interfaces*

This section defines guidelines to be followed when producing *block definition diagrams* and *internal block diagrams* that show *interfaces*.

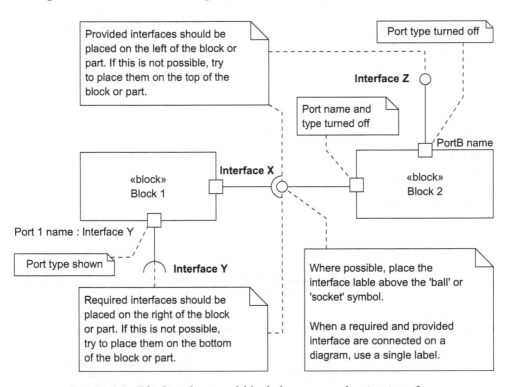

Figure 6.6 Block and internal block diagrams – showing interfaces

The guidelines shown in Figure 6.6 are summarised in Table 6.5.

With the guidelines for *interfaces* defined, the next section discusses the guidelines for the related subject of *item flows*.

Table 6.5   Interface *naming conventions*

Diagram item	Guidelines
Provided interface	Place on the *left* of the *block* or *part*. If this is not possible, try to place them on the *top* of the *block* or *part*. Where possible, place the *interface* label above the ball symbol. When a *required* and *provided interface* are connected on a diagram (as for Interface X in Figure 6.6), use a single label.
Required interface	Place on the *right* of the *block* or *part*. If this is not possible, try to place them on the *bottom* of the *block* or *part*. Where possible, place the *interface* label above the socket symbol. When a *required* and *provided interface* are connected on a diagram (as for Interface X in Figure 6.6), use a single label.
Port	*Port name* should be in sentence case *Port type* should have each word capitalised (corresponding to the model element that types the *port*). *Port names* and/or *types* can be omitted for clarity.

6.4.2   Block and internal block diagrams – showing item flows

This section defines guidelines to be followed when producing *block definition diagrams* and *internal block diagrams* that show *item flows*.

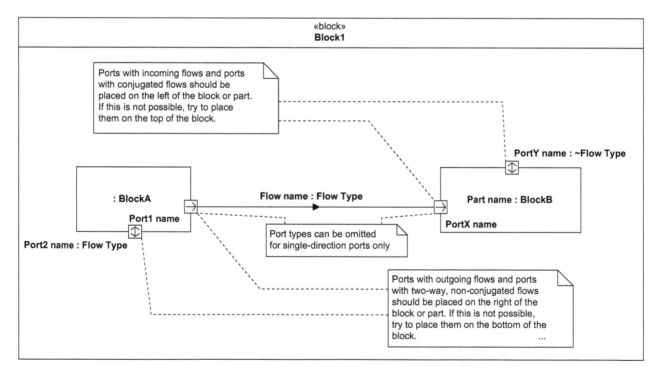

Figure 6.7   Block and internal block diagrams – showing item flows

The guidelines shown in Figure 6.7 are summarised in Table 6.6.

Table 6.6   Item flow *naming conventions*

Diagram item	Guidelines
Port with *incoming flows*	Place on the *left* of the *block* or *part*. If this is not possible, try to place them on the *top* of the *block* or *part*.
Port with *outgoing flows*	Place on the *right* of the *block* or *part*. If this is not possible, try to place them on the *bottom* of the *block* or *part*.
Port with conjugated flows	Place on the *left* of the *block* or *part*. If this is not possible, try to place them on the *top* of the *block* or *part*.
Port with *two-way, non-conjugated flows*	Place on the *right* of the *block* or *part*. If this is not possible, try to place them on the *bottom* of the *block* or *part*.
Port	*Port name* should be in sentence case.
	Port type should have each word capitalised (corresponding to the model element that types the *port*).
	Port types can be omitted **only** for single-direction *ports*.
Item flow	*Item flow name* should be in sentence case.
	Item flow type should be in upper case.
	Item flow name and *type* should be placed above the *connector* along which it flows.

With the guidelines for *item flows* defined, the next section discusses the guidelines for *activity diagrams*.

6.4.3   Activity diagrams

This section defines guidelines to be followed when producing *activity diagrams*.

The guidelines shown in Figure 6.8 are summarised in Table 6.7.

With the guidelines for activity diagrams defined, the next section discusses issues around tool settings.

6.4.4   Default tool settings

All SysML tools have default settings that control the appearance of diagrams in many ways, such as colour and navigability. This section discusses some of these issues.

6.4.4.1   *The use of colour*

The use of colour can be used to add extra information to a diagram or to make diagrams clearer. However, colour should not be used without careful consideration. As a general rule, all diagram elements should be drawn with black text on a white background. Where colour is used, the diagram must include a key that explains the colour scheme used.

In addition, some tools allow diagrams to be produced that have 3D effects, gradient fills, shadows and curved lines that can be applied to diagram elements.

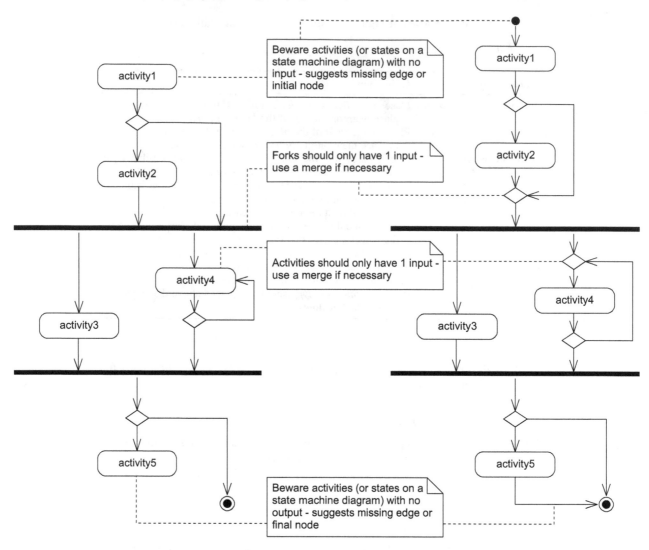

Figure 6.8   Activity diagrams

These should *not* be used, and should be turned off in the tools options. As an example, the following three diagrams are taken from a SysML tool.

Figure 6.9 shows the diagram as produced by the tool with the default graphical options turned on (but with the colour used for the *blocks* replaced with grey). Clearly this diagram is not fit for purpose. The use of curved connectors makes the diagram almost unreadable and the 3D effects and shadowing do nothing to add to either the clarity or meaning of the diagram.

The same diagram but without the use of curved lines, 3D effects and shadows is shown in Figure 6.10.

Table 6.7 Activity diagram *guidelines*

Diagram item	Guidelines
Activity Check that all *activities* (or *states* on a *state machine diagram*) have an output. Missing outputs suggest a missing edge or *final node*. *Activities* should have only one input. Use a *merge* if necessary.	Check that all *activities* (or *states* on a *state machine diagram*) have an input. Missing inputs suggest a missing edge or *initial node*.
Fork	*Forks* should have only one input. Use a *merge* if necessary.

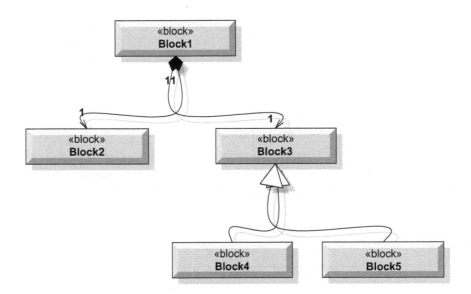

Figure 6.9   Example block definition diagram showing inappropriate use of shading and other graphical effects

The diagram, like the original in Figure 6.9, makes use of colour, with the blocks being filled with a pink background (here rendered as a grey background to the *blocks*). If colour is required, then thought should be given to its choice and purpose. For example:

- How well will the colour reproduce when printed in black and white or greyscale?
- Are any fonts or other symbols that lie on top of the colour readable?
- Will the chosen colours be problematic to those who are colour-blind?

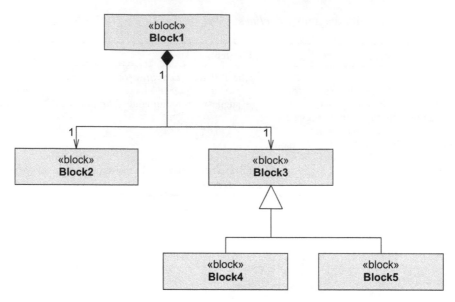

Figure 6.10   Example block definition diagram showing use of colour

- What meaning is attributed to the colours used?
- Have such meanings been made clear in a key?

Using colour is problematical at best. If it must be used, use it sparingly. The SysML specification does NOT define colours for SysML elements. The best approach is to use simple black and white, as shown in Figure 6.11.

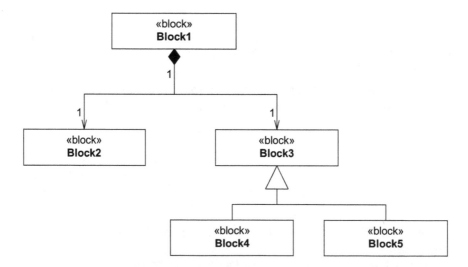

Figure 6.11   Example block definition diagram rendered in black and white

6.4.4.2   Navigability

In each of the figures in Section 6.4.4.1 the *compositions* from 'Block1' all have an open arrowhead at the part end of the *relationship*. These arrowheads are used to show the *navigability* of the *relationship*. However, this is a concept that is mainly needed when modelling software (the notation is part of SysML through its inheritance from the UML) and is used less often in more general systems modelling.

The arrowheads are shown on these diagrams because, in the tool used to produce these diagrams, the display of *navigability* is turned on by default. This requires the user to change this default setting, if the tool allows this, or if not permitted, requires the user to edit the setting for each *association* when added to the diagram.

6.4.4.3   *Other common settings*

Other common diagramming settings that need to be considered include the display of *role names* on *associations*, whether whole-part *relationships* should default to *composition* or *aggregation*, whether *association names* should be displayed by default, whether *compositions*, *aggregations* and *generalisation relationships* should be displayed in a tree layout, and what colours should be used for diagram elements such as *blocks*, *requirements*, and *use cases*.

A SysML tool should allow such settings to be changed once for a model and not force the modeller to change the settings for every diagram. Even more desirable is the ability to define these settings for all models created with the tool. This allows standard settings to be rolled out across an entire organisation. Unfortunately, not all tools allow changes to default settings to be made.

6.5   Model structure

When creating a SysML model it is important, in order to aid navigability and ease of use, that the model is well structured. However, it is impossible here to define a structure that is suitable for all projects; any structure adopted must be set up so as to meet the needs of the project for which the model is being created. The authors have created models that have been structured in many different ways. Some examples of structuring adopted by the authors on projects include:

- Life Cycle Stage
- Engineering process or activity
- System and sub-system
  - Structure
  - Behaviour
- Team
- Architecture framework
- Modelling framework

Sometimes model structure is a combination of these. For example, a model might first be structured by Life Cycle Stage, then within each Stage further structured by

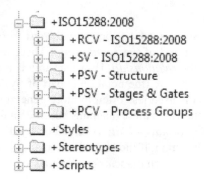

Figure 6.12   Example of a model structured by modelling Framework Views

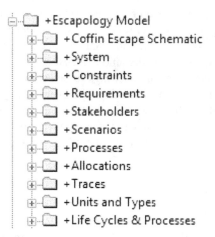

*Figure 6.13   Example of a model structured largely by engineering activity and
structural and behavioural split*

System. Figure 6.12 shows part of a model of a Standard (ISO 15288:2008 – see
ISO 15288:2008 and the Process model in Appendix E) that is structured according
to the seven views Process modelling Framework described in Chapter 7. Note the
use of additional *packages* to contain aspects of the model such as styles (symbol
colours etc.), *stereotypes* and scripts (the tool in which this model was produced
allows the user to enhance functionality through user-defined scripts).

   Another example is given in Figure 6.13. Here, the model is structured largely
into a structural and behavioural split influenced by engineering activity. For
example, the 'Coffin Escape Schematic', 'Requirements', 'Stakeholders' and
'Scenarios' *packages* contain the parts of the model concerned with Requirements,
whereas the 'System', 'Constraints', 'Processes' and 'Units and Types' packages

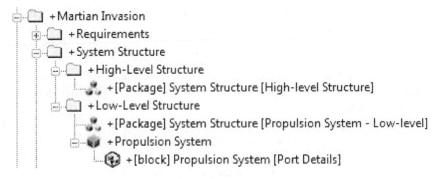

Figure 6.14   Model structure – viewed by package

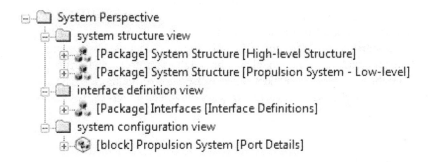

Figure 6.15   Model structure – viewed by Perspective and View

contain the parts of the model concerned with design, defining System structure and behaviour.

Some SysML tools have a very useful facility that allows the model to be navigated both by the *package* structure (as in Figures 6.12 and 6.13) and by model Perspective and View. The two diagrams in Figures 6.14 and 6.15 illustrate this. These examples are taken from the Martian invasion case study model, discussed in Chapter 13.

The model structure shown in Figure 6.14 is structured in a similar way to the model shown in Figure 6.13, showing a structure based on a structural and behavioural split influenced by engineering activity.

As discussed in Chapter 13, the model has been constructed using an Architectural Framework that defines a number of Perspectives and Viewpoints (see Chapter 10 for a discussion of Viewpoints, Views and Perspectives). The model consists of a number of Views that conform to the Viewpoints (which are simply the definition of Views). Irrespective of the model structure defined by the user, the tool allows the model to be navigated by the Perspectives and Views defined by the Framework. An example is shown in Figure 6.15, which shows the *packages* containing the Views that make up the System Perspective. The root package shows the Perspective and the sub-Packages correspond to each View in that Perspective (not all Views are shown). The View *packages* show all the model diagrams that conform to that View, no matter where in the *package* structure shown in Figure 6.14 they reside. The Perspective and View structure is defined by and enforced by the tool; the user is not allowed to change this structure in any way.

Note that the *package* names for the View *packages* are lower case, which contradicts the naming convention described in Section 6.2.1. This is because the tool used requires the use of *stereotypes* to name Views in a way that makes them browsable, as shown in Figure 6.15; so the *package* labelled system structure view is displaying the all diagrams stereotyped «system structure view» and similarly for the others. The naming convention can thus be seen to be consistent with the guidelines for naming *stereotypes* given in Section 6.2.3.

Finally, many SysML tools will suggest a predefined model structure when a new model is created in the tool. While such structures may be of use in suggesting a starting point for the way the model is organised, they are rarely of much use beyond that. The model will be much easier to navigate if time is taken to define the structure that makes sense to the users of the model. The structure is up to you, but should be covered in your engineering Processes or modelling style guides.

6.6   Summary

This chapter has presented a number of guidelines and conventions that should be followed to ensure that the diagrams in a SysML model have a common look and feel. These guidelines are a starting point only; feel free to use them, but remember that any such guidelines should be tailored to the needs of your Organisation. Producing a SysML modelling Standard that is incorporated into the reader's systems engineering Processes is to be encouraged as a way of enforcing the guidelines.

Wherever possible any SysML tool used should allow the modeller to organise a model as desired, perhaps providing multiple ways of viewing the model's contents. Avoid using the tool's default model structure, if it provides one; such a structure will rarely be suitable.

In addition, issues regarding the use of colour, shading, curved lines, default relationship settings etc. should be considered and guidelines produced. If possible the tool should be configured so that these defined settings are set as defaults.

Reference

1.   Ambler S.W. *The Elements of UML 2.0 Style*. NY, USA; Cambridge University Press; 2005

Part 3

Applications

P3.1   Overview

This part is structured according to the diagram in Figure P3.1.

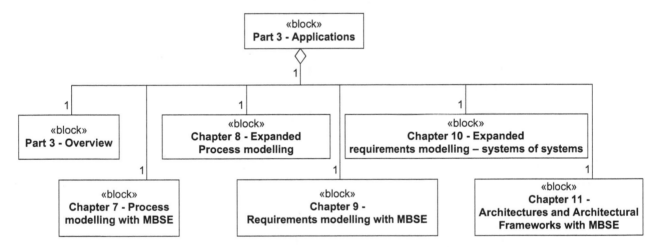

Figure P3.1   Structure of 'Part 3 – Applications'

Part 3 looks at how model-based systems engineering can be applied in a practical manner by considering a number of applications. This part comprises five main chapters.

–   'Chapter 7 – Process Modelling with MBSE'. This chapter introduces an established approach for modelling Processes using MBSE. This approach, known as the seven views, is fully described and then illustrated using an example Process model.

–   'Chapter 8 – Expanded Process Modelling'. This chapter builds upon the seven views approach that was described in the previous chapter by presenting a number of advanced applications of Process modelling including: modelling Standards, demonstrating compliance, modelling Competence, modelling Life Cycles and modelling Project management.

- 'Chapter 9 – Requirements Modelling with MBSE'. This chapter looks at an approach for modelling Requirements using MBSE. The approach describes a Context-based approach for modelling Requirements that may be used for Projects of differing degrees of size and rigour. The concept of a Requirement is described as being a special type of Need, alongside Goals, Capabilities and Concerns, all of which can be modelled using this approach.
- 'Chapter 10 – Expanded Requirements Modelling – Systems of systems'. This chapter builds on the basic approach introduced in the previous chapter by applying the same technique to Systems of Systems. Several new concepts are introduced and discussed that make the application of modelling to Systems of Systems different from its application Systems and, based on this, several new Views are described.
- 'Chapter 11 – Architectures and Architectural Frameworks with MBSE'. This chapter concentrates on the fundamental building blocks required for building Architectures and their underlying Architectural Frameworks. The approach to defining architecture Viewpoints and their associated Views is used throughout this book.

The approach taken for all of these application areas is the same as is used throughout the book, that of producing 'Ontology, Framework and Views'. All of this goes to show how important the modelling is to everything that we do in MBSE, including the approach itself.

Chapter 7
Process modelling with MBSE

'What the eyes see and the ears hear, the mind believes'

Ehrich Weiss

7.1 Introduction

This chapter looks at a model-based approach to Process modelling, which, although at first appearances, may seem quite simple; it will be shown that the application of modelling Processes has myriad uses in systems engineering.

The basic "seven views" approach that is described in this chapter may be applied to many other areas of systems engineering, such as modelling Standards, compliance, Life Cycle modelling, Competence modelling, and project management. These examples will be expanded upon in Chapter 8.

The definition of the "seven views" follows the basic 'Ontology, Framework and Views' approach, which is used throughout this book.

7.1.1 Background

In Chapter 15, we will be looking at some of the Needs behind providing a good Process, whereas this chapter looks at the specific Needs of Process modelling. The basic Needs behind these two areas, the provision of a Process and Process modelling, result in two different Contexts being produced. As we are concerned with Process modelling here, the following Context describes the Need for Process modelling.

The diagram in Figure 7.1 shows the overall Context that describes the *use cases* for Process modelling.

The main *use case* is concerned with defining an approach to Process modelling ('Define approach to process modelling') which has three main inclusions:

- There must be a mechanism for allowing the basic Needs of the Process to be defined ('Provide needs definition'). This is a fundamental Need for all aspects of the MBSE approach that is advocated in this book and the area of Process modelling is no exception.
- Obviously, there must be a mechanism to allow the Process itself to be defined ('Provide process definition'). This will have to meet the basic Needs of the Process that are defined in the previous point.

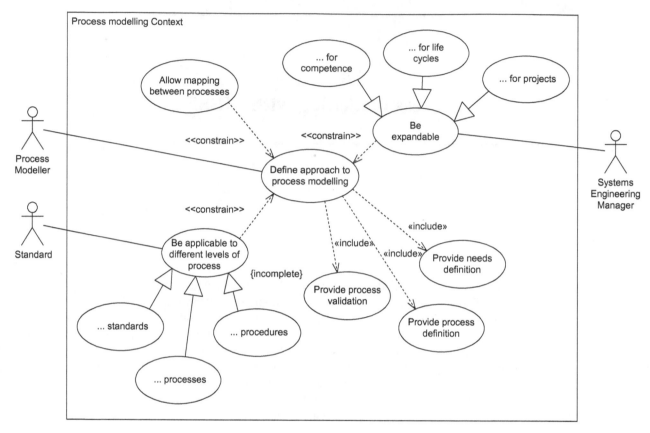

Figure 7.1   Process modelling Context

- If the Need and the Process have been defined, then there must be a mechanism in place to allow the Process definition to be validated against the Need ('Provide process validation').

There are three main constraints that are applied to defining the approach, which are:

- The approach must be able to be used with different types of Process that exist at different levels of abstraction ('Be applicable to different levels of process'), such as high-level Standards ('...standards'), medium levels of Process ('...processes') and low-level procedures ('...procedures'). The specific issue of modelling Standards is discussed in more detail in Chapter 8.
- The approach must be expandable for different applications ('Be expandable') – this is covered in more detail in Chapter 8, which discusses more applications of the approach described in this chapter.
- The approach must allow for various Processes to be mapped together ('Allow mapping between processes').

When considering any approach to Process modelling, there are a number of key features of Processes that must be taken into account and that are described as follows.

- Missing information. One very real danger that occurs when modelling anything, not just Processes, is that too much information may be inadvertently missed out. A Process model that is too simplified will not add the amount of value that an appropriately modelled one will and, likewise, a Process model that contains too much detail will be riddled with complexity and all its associated problems. Reaching the appropriate level of abstraction can be very difficult to achieve, therefore some guidance is required for obtaining the correct level of detail.

- Realistic Processes. Another problem that occurs with Process modelling is of ensuring the Process really reflects the actual practices carried out in real life. This occurs as Processes are usually modelled as abstract notions that are thought about theoretically before being put into practice. This is all well and good, but it is just as important to think about the real-life execution of such Processes that are referred to as Process instances or, to put it another way, real-life examples of the Processes being executed in the organisation.

- Process partitioning. Any Process model has the potential to contain a very large number of Processes and it is important to be able to partition them in some way. The approach to partitioning Processes into groups can take many forms. For example, many Organisations will take the structure of an international Standard as the basis for the main Process partitions. Rather than using an international Standard or best practice model, Processes are also often grouped in terms of their functionality, or in terms of areas of responsibility. The actual approach taken will depend on the Organisation and the nature of the applications of the Process, but somewhere this decision must be made and recorded in some way.

- Process iteration within a Process. When Processes have been identified and the key features defined, it is important to be able to define how the Activities in the Process are carried out – the order in which these Activities are executed, the conditions under which they are executed and any timing constraints that may come into play. Very often, the internal workings of a Process will be defined as a linear set of Activity, whereas in real life, many Processes will exhibit a high degree of looping. For example, most Processes will have decision points and, by the very nature of a decision point, there will be more than one option based on a decision. These different options will result in different paths of flow through a process resulting in a high degree of iteration. Caution must be exercised when identifying iteration as the more the iterations within a diagram, the higher the level of complexity.

- Process iteration with Process instances. In real life, it is possible to execute many instantiations of a single Process at the same time. Consider any transaction-processing system where it is a key feature of the System to be able to process transactions in parallel, rather than in a simple sequence.

- Complexity and interactions. Interactions exist at many levels in a Process model in both its structural definition and its behaviour. These interactions can be identified visually by looking at the graphical paths (lines) on any diagram that connect together the graphical nodes (shapes).
- Traceability. One of the most important goals for any quality system is that of traceability. It is essential to be able to trace from any point of any Life Cycle, right back to the original Needs of the Projects. For example, during an audit the auditor may point at any part of the system that is being developed and ask which of the original Needs that part of the System is meeting. The same is true for the Process model, it is essential that all the Artefacts are not only identified but that they are also fully traceable. For example, a delegate-booking Process may require an invoice to be produced and sent out to a customer, but if there is no traceability between the booking Process and an associated invoicing Process then the whole process will fail.

Any approach that is adopted to model Processes must take in account these points and be able to address them in some way. The approach that is advocated in this book, the so-called "seven views" approach, addresses all of these points through its Context-based approach to modelling.

7.2   Approach

The "seven views" approach to Process modelling has been used successfully in both industry and academia for over a decade. The approach is truly model-based and uses a Context-based approach to create the various Views. The "seven views" approach is defined using the basic 'Ontology, Framework and Views' style that has been adopted throughout this book.

The "seven views" approach to Process modelling may be realised using any suitable modelling notation, such as BPMN [1,2], UML [4,5], and flowcharts [3]. For the purposes of this book, the SysML will be used to visualise each of the Views, but for a more complete discussion on other visualisation techniques, see Reference 6.

7.2.1   The MBSE Ontology (revisited)

A subset of the MBSE Ontology may now be considered that is related directly to Process modelling.

The diagram in Figure 7.2 shows the subset of the MBSE Ontology that has been identified as being relevant for Process modelling. Most of the Ontology Elements shown here should not come as any real surprise as they may be clearly identified as relating to Process engineering simply by their proximity to the 'Process' element from the MBSE Ontology. There is one element, however, that is not obviously shown as being related to the MBSE Ontology, and that is the concept of the 'Process Context', which is one type of 'Context'. The concept of a 'Core Element' from the MBSE Ontology was introduced and discussed in

Chapter 2, which was defined as being an 'Ontology Element' that applies to one or more 'Basic Element' from the ontology. As 'Context' is identified as a 'Core Element' it actually applies to more Ontology Elements, which is shown in the standard MBSE Ontology, and one of these un-shown relationships is between 'Process' and 'Context' using the concept of the 'Process Context'. This is the relationship that can be seen in this diagram.

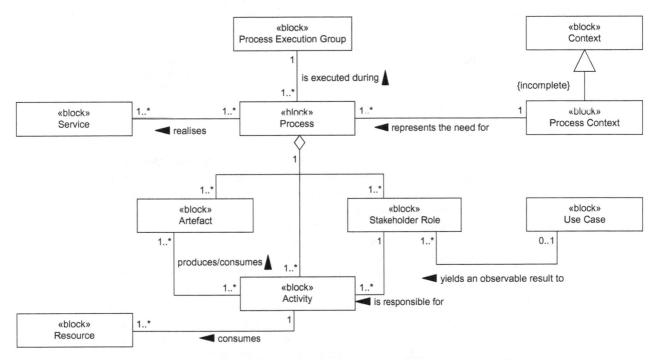

Figure 7.2 Subset of the MBSE Ontology focused on Process modelling

7.2.2   The Framework

The "seven views" Framework comprises a number of Viewpoints that will be used to define a number of Views. These Viewpoints are identified in the diagram in Figure 7.3.

The diagram here shows the main Views that are needed according to the "seven views" approach Framework. It should be noted that for each of these Views, an associated Viewpoint will need to be defined that describes its structure. The seven basic Views that have been defined are:

- The 'Requirement Context View' (RCV). The 'Requirement Context View' defines the Context for the Process, or set of Processes. It will identify a number of Use Cases, based on the Needs for a Process and any relevant Stakeholder Roles that are required.

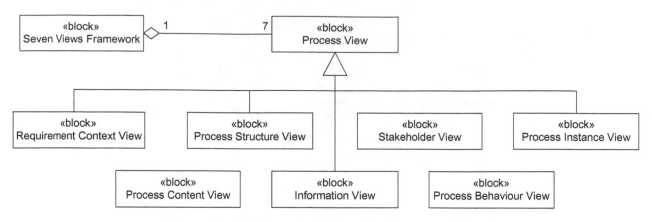

Figure 7.3   The Framework Views for Process modelling

- The 'Stakeholder View' (SV). The 'Stakeholder View' identifies the Stake-holder Roles that have an interest in the Processes being defined. It presents Stakeholder Roles in a classification hierarchy and allows additional relation-ships, such as managerial responsibility.
- The 'Process Structure View' (PSV). The 'Process Structure View' specifies concepts and terminology that will be used for the Process modelling in the form of an Ontology. If the Process modelling is taken as part of a larger MBSE exercise, then the Process Structure View will be a subset of the MBSE Ontology.
- The 'Process Content View' (PCV). The 'Process Content View' identifies the actual Processes, showing the Activities carried out and the Artefacts produced and consumed. The Process Content View may be considered as the library of Processes that is available to any Process-related Stakeholder Roles.
- The 'Process Behaviour View' (PBV). The 'Process Behaviour View' shows how each individual Process behaves in terms of the order of Activities within a Process, the flow of Artefacts through the Process, Stakeholder Role responsibilities and, where relevant, Resource usage.
- The 'Information View' (IV). The 'Information View' identifies all the Artefacts produced or consumed by Activities within a Process and the inter-relationships between them.
- The 'Process Instance View' (PIV). The 'Process Instance View' shows instances of Processes in the Process Execution Groups.

These Views are expanded upon in the following sections, using an example Process model. This is a bespoke process model that is compliant with ISO 15288 and that was originally developed as an educational tool for teaching and training purposes. The process is known as STUMPI – STUdents Managing Process Intel-ligently and it has been used very successfully for over a decade.

7.2.3   The Views

7.2.3.1   The Requirement Context View

View rationale

As with all aspects of systems engineering, it is essential that everything that we do adds value to our work activity. In order to ensure that we are adding value, it is essential that we understand what it is we are setting out to achieve. Process modelling is no different, so it is crucial that we understand what we want from the Process in the first place or, in other words, we need to understand the Needs for that Process.

The Requirement Context View actually shows the Context of the Process. The techniques used to model this Context are exactly the same as the techniques used to perform model-based requirements engineering, as detailed in Chapter 9 where the ACRE (Approach to Context-based Requirements Engineering) is introduced. The Requirement Context View that is presented in this section is analogous to the Requirement Context View using ACRE.

The Requirement Context View forms the basis for the validation activities for the Process modelling as it is essential that we can demonstrate that the Process model is fit for purpose. If the purpose is unknown, then it is impossible to validate. The Process model may actually work as a functional set of Processes (it may be verified), but unless it satisfies a set of defined Needs, then the Process model is not demonstrably useful.

To summarise, therefore, there must always be a Requirement Context View for a Process. A Process without any defined need may be verified but may never be validated.

View definition

The subset of the MBSE Ontology that relates to Process modelling is shown in Figure 7.4, with the relevant Ontology Elements highlighted.

The diagram here shows that the Ontology Elements that are important for model-based Process engineering are: the 'Stakeholder Role', the 'Use Case' and the 'Process Context'.

This whole View shows a single Context that relates to a Process or set of Processes.

View relationships

The diagram in Figure 7.5 shows the relationships between the Requirement Context View and other Views in the "seven views" approach. The diagram here is actually a subset of the MBSE Process Framework, which will be shown in its entirety later in this chapter.

The 'Requirement Context View' has relationships with the 'Process Content View' and the 'Process Instance View'. These relationships lead to the definition of the following Rules, which may be used to enforce compliance with the "seven views" approach.

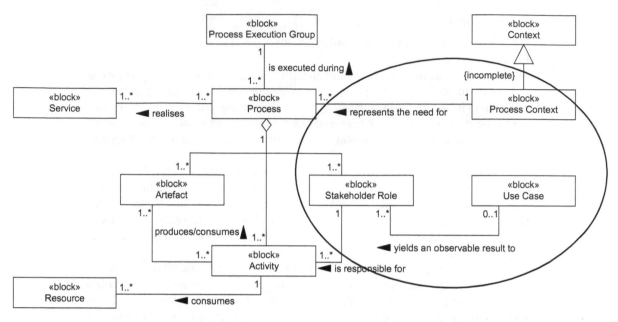

Figure 7.4   Definition of the Requirement Context View

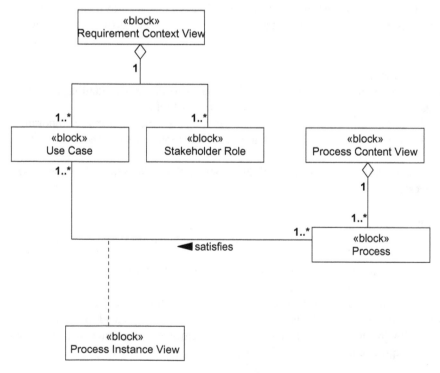

Figure 7.5   Relationships between the Requirement Context View and other Views

- At least one Requirement Context View must exist for the Processes.
- At least one Process Instance View must exist for each *use case* in the Process Context View that needs to be validated.
- Each Stakeholder Role on the Process Context View, represented as a SysML *actor*, must exist on the accompanying Stakeholder View.

These Rules may be used as a basis for automation for the "seven views" approach.

View visualisation

The Requirement Context View is visualised in SysML using a *use case diagram*, as shown in Figure 7.6.

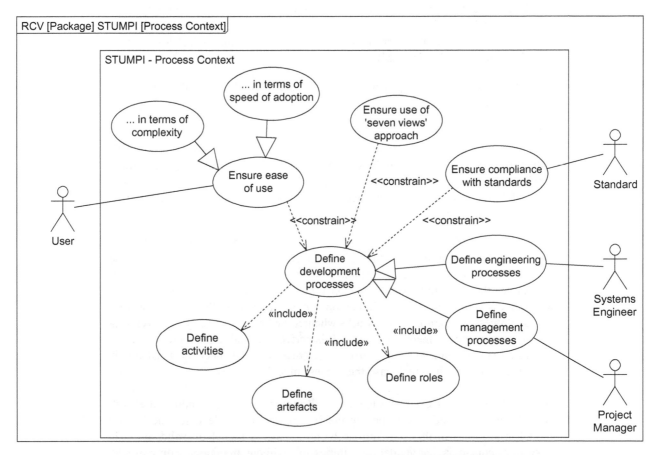

Figure 7.6   Example Requirement Context View for the STUMPI Process

Figure 7.6 shows the 'Requirement Context View' for the STUMPI Process. The main aim of the STUMPI Context is to allow a set of Processes for systems engineering development to be defined ('Define development processes'), which can be used for both engineering ('Define engineering processes') and management

('Define management processes') processes. This definition of Processes must allow the user to:

- Define Activities ('Define activities') that allow the Process to be executed.
- Define Artefacts ('Define artefacts') that will allow the inputs and outputs for the Process to be specified.
- Define roles ('Define roles') that will allow the Stakeholder Roles for the Process to be identified and defined.

The main constraints on the process definition are to:

- Ensure that the approach can be taught, learned and adopted quickly ('Ensure ease of use').
- Ensure that the approach complies with best practice ('Ensure compliance with standards')
- Ensure that the approach promotes the "seven views" approach ('Ensure use of '"seven views"' approach')

This Process Context View provides the basis against which the resultant Processes may be validated.

View discussion

The Requirement Context View is very important as it will form the basis for validating each Process. It is quite often the case that a set of Processes is defined that is fully verified, but that is not validated. The difference between verification and validation can never be repeated enough, so here it is again, but this time relating to Processes.

- Process verification. Process verification is concerned with ensuring that the Process works properly — that it is correct, consistent and will respond to a set of inputs in a predictable fashion. Verification, generally speaking, demonstrates that something can be demonstrated to meet a specification.
- Process validation. Process validation is more subtle than Process verification, as Process validation basically asks whether the Process actually achieves what it is supposed to (meets its Needs). It is perfectly possible for a Process model to be correct and working (verified) but that does not meet the need for the Process model, in which case the Process model is useless.

It is the Requirement Context View that will provide an understanding of exactly why the Process model is needed in the first place. If the Need for the Process model is not known, then how on earth can a Process model be validated? The answer, of course, is that validation is impossible without an understanding of what the basic Needs are.

One of the features of a robust Process model is its ability to remain valid over a long period of time. In order to do this, the Process model must evolve to react to the changing environment in which it lives. As time goes on, changes will occur in surrounding environment, so it is important that this can be captured in some way, and it is the Requirement Context View that achieves this. Examples of changes include:

- Changes to Stakeholder Roles, realised by *actors*. By the very definition of the term *actor*, they each have some sort of interest in the system; therefore, if one of the *actors* changes in some way, then there is a potential impact on the System which requires investigation.
- Changes in related Process models. This is actually a variation of the point above, but is worthy of its own discussion. Invariably, a Process model will not exist in isolation and will have to co-exist with a number of other Process models, such as related Standards, and procedures. It is quite possible and, indeed quite common, for these external Process models to change in some way and to render elements of the actual Process model redundant, incorrect or simply out of date.
- Changes in the Organisation. Organisations are living entities and, as such, are subject to change due to any number of factors, such as technology changes, best practice changes, new business areas opening up, and automation of production. As the Organisation evolves so must the Process model to reflect this.

These changes are nothing new but, in many instances, they often go unnoticed as the Process model still functions in a correct fashion, but it can no longer meet its new purpose. It is quite common for a Process model to be verified and validated when it is first defined. However, as time goes on, the basic Needs change, as discussed above, which leads to a non-validated, yet still-verified Process model. It is the fact that the Process model remains verified that leads to complacency. Therefore, it is crucial that any Process model is continuously assessed on a regular basis, maybe once or twice per year, in order to make sure that: the Needs for the Process model are still accurate and that the Process model itself can be validated against these Needs.

The Requirement Context View, therefore, is essential for ensuring that the Process model is correct and can be validated over a period of time, and that it evolves to reflect any changes in the environment.

7.2.3.2 The Stakeholder View

View rationale

In order to understand the value that any Process adds to our work activities, it is essential that we can identify and understand any Stakeholder Roles that have an interest in the Process.

The Stakeholder View identifies the Stakeholder Roles that have an interest in the Processes being defined. It presents Stakeholder Roles in a classification hierarchy and allows additional relationships, such as managerial responsibility, to be added. The Stakeholder Roles appearing on the Stakeholder View must be consistent with those shown on the Requirement Context View in the form of *actors*.

View definition

The subset of the MBSE Ontology that relates to modelling Processes is shown in Figure 7.7, with the relevant Ontology Elements highlighted.

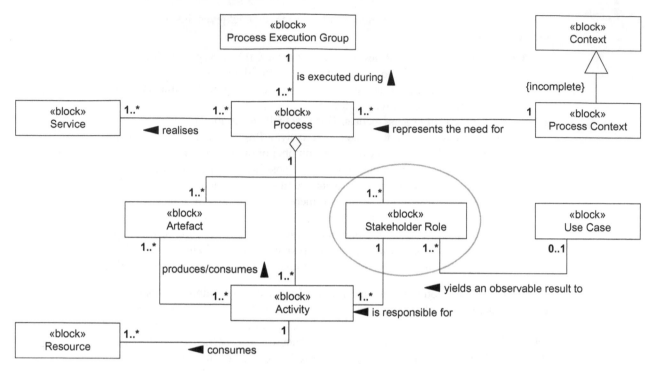

Figure 7.7   Definition of the Stakeholder View

The diagram here shows that the Ontology Element that is important for modelling Processes is the 'Stakeholder Role'.

View relationships

The diagram in Figure 7.8 shows the relationships between the Stakeholder View and other Views in the "seven views" approach. The diagram here is actually a subset of the MBSE Process Framework that will be shown in its entirety later in this chapter.

The 'Stakeholder View' has relationships with the 'Process Content View', the 'Process Behaviour View' and the 'Requirement Context View'. These relationships lead to the definition of the following Rules, which may be used to enforce compliance with the "seven views" approach.

- Each Stakeholder Role on the Stakeholder View must exist as a *swim lane* owner on a Process Behaviour View.
- Each Stakeholder Role represented as an *actor* on the Process Context View must exist as a Stakeholder Role on the Stakeholder View.

These Rules may be used as a basis for automation for the "seven views" approach.

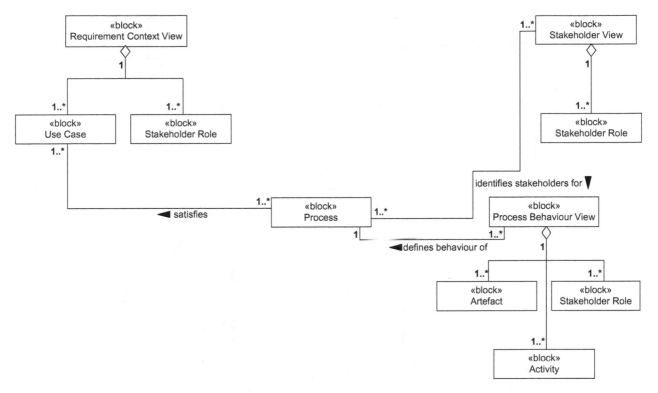

Figure 7.8   Relationships between the Stakeholder View and other Views

View visualisation

The Stakeholder View is visualised in SysML using a *block definition diagram*, as shown in Figure 7.9.

The diagram here shows the 'Stakeholder View' for the STUMPI Process, where a single *block* represents each Stakeholder Role.

View discussion

The Stakeholder View represents a simple classification of the different types of Stakeholder Roles that are involved with the Process. The Stakeholder View is realised in SysML with a *block definition diagram*, with each Stakeholder Role being represented by a single *block*.

It is typical for a single Stakeholder View to be drawn up that represents many or, in some cases, all Stakeholder Roles in an Organisation, rather than creating one on a project-by-project basis. This is a tremendous help when it comes to trying to get an idea of the big picture of an Organisation and can be invaluable when it comes to making sure that Processes are consistent with one another.

The biggest mistake made by people when defining Stakeholder Roles is that they refer to them by individual names, such as the name of a Person of an

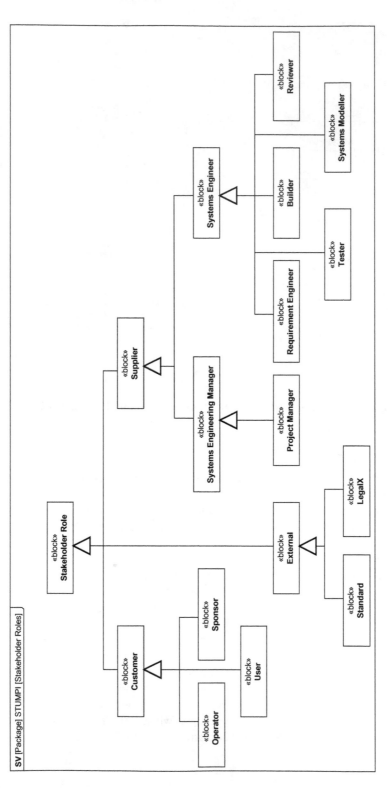

Figure 7.9 Example Requirement Context View for the STUMPI Process

Organisation. It is the role of the Person or Organisation, rather than the actual name, that is of interest from the modelling point of view. There are several reasons for this:

- Multiple roles. It is possible and, indeed, very common for a single Person to have more than one Stakeholder Role. Consider the roles taken on by any single Person in an Organisation and, in the vast majority of cases, each Person will play more than one role. This is important as the roles played by an Organisation, for example, can be wildly different, yet have the same name associated with them. This becomes particularly relevant when considering Competences, which will be discussed in Chapter 3.2, which discusses advanced process modelling.
- Multiple names. It is equally common for a single Stakeholder Role to have many names associated with it. In some cases, particularly when it comes to users of a system, there can be millions of names associated with a single Stakeholder Role.
- Robustness. By thinking of roles, rather than names, a model that is robust towards change is generated. Imagine how unmanageable the model would be – if every time the name associated with a Stakeholder Role changed then the model had to be changed! Not only is this impractical simply from people moving jobs (particularly in large organisations), but it is also possible that the number of names associated with a single Stakeholder Role will increase as the Project progresses through the development Life Cycle.

Therefore, always think of the role, rather than names, when thinking of Stakeholder Roles.

When generating a list of Stakeholder Roles, it is very easy to get things wrong and for two totally different reasons. The first reason is that, invariably, if one was to write down a list of Stakeholder associated with a Process, then there would be something missing. On the other hand, there will also be some Stakeholder Roles on the list who are not involved at all with the Project! The only way to have any confidence that the Stakeholder Role list is correct is to look at how and where the Stakeholder Roles occur on the different Views of the approach.

There are three main types of 'Stakeholder': 'Customer', 'External' and 'Supplier'. This three-way split is typical for many systems and can be a very good place to start thinking. These terms are defines as follows:

- The 'Supplier' Stakeholder Role refers to all the roles that are associated with providing a Service or Product that relates to the development of the System.
- The 'External' Stakeholder Role refers to all the roles that are not Supplier roles, that have an interest in the System, but that cannot be argued with.
- The 'Customer' Stakeholder Role refers to all the roles that receive the Service or Product associated with the System and that may be reasoned with in some way and compromises reached.

In terms of the 'Customer' Stakeholder Roles, three have been identified here:

- 'User', this Stakeholder Role represents all the end users of a System. In the case of a transport system, this role would represent the passengers and, hence, there may be millions of names associated with this role. Likewise, in a healthcare system, this role would represent the actual patients who are retrieving treatment.

- 'Operator', this Stakeholder Role represents the people who will be configuring, controlling and operating the System. In the case of the transport system, this role would cover a range of roles ranging from tickets sales, to driving the vehicles, to controlling the position of vehicles, route planning, etc. In the case of the healthcare system, this role would again cover a number of other roles including doctors, nurses, surgeons, and administrators.
- 'Sponsor', This Stakeholder Role represents whoever is providing the financial backing for the System. In the case of the transport system this may be government-related, private or some combination of the two. Similarly, the healthcare system may have a number of different names associated with it.

In terms of the 'External' Stakeholder Roles, two main roles have been identified:

- 'Standard', this Stakeholder Role represents standards and standard bodies that may constrain the development and operations of a System in some way. This may relate to safety standards, security, etc.
- 'Legal', this Stakeholder Role relates to legal roles that may impact the System in some way, for example, data protection laws, and health and safety legislation.

In terms of 'Supplier', three main Stakeholder Roles have been identified:

- 'Systems Engineer', this role represents technical roles, such as engineers and scientists.
- 'Systems Engineering Manager', that includes all management-related roles, such as project managers, process managers, and configuration managers.

The Stakeholder View is the same as the Stakeholder Context Definition View that is used as part of the ACRE approach to model-based requirements engineering, in that it identifies Stakeholder Roles. However, the purpose behind the two is subtly different. The Stakeholder View is intended to identify Stakeholder Roles in order that they can be used as part of the larger Process model (for responsibilities, competencies, etc.), whereas the Stakeholder Context Definition View identifies Stakeholder Roles in order to help to define a number of Contexts based on these roles.

7.2.3.3 The Process Structure View

View rationale

It has already been mentioned several times in this book why understanding the concepts and terms associated with any aspect of systems engineering is so important. Indeed, one of the main philosophies of this book is to ensure that there is always an Ontology in place that identifies and defines the concepts and terms. The Process Structure View is essentially the Ontology for the Process. If the Process modelling is being carried out as part of a larger systems engineering activity (which it should!), then the MBSE Ontology may be used for the Process Structure View. In the event that the Process modelling is being carried out as its own activity, a Process Structure View must be created.

View definition

As the Process Structure View is itself an Ontology, the Ontology for the View actually sits at the meta-model level, as discussed in Chapter 2, and as shown in the diagram in Figure 7.10.

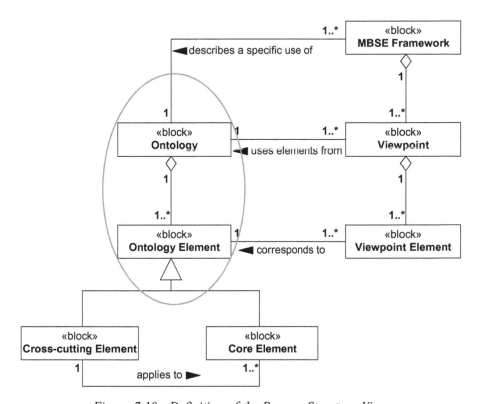

Figure 7.10   Definition of the Process Structure View

The diagram shows that the 'Process Structure View' is focused on the 'Ontology' and, hence, one or more 'Ontology Element' that make up the 'Ontology'. Again, it should be stressed that this view may very well exist in the form of the MBSE Ontology.

View Relationships

The Process Structure View actually has relationships with all the other Views, as it forms the Ontology and, therefore, defines the concepts and terms used in all of the other six Views.

View visualisation

The Process Structure View is visualised in SysML using a *block definition diagram*, as shown in Figure 7.11.

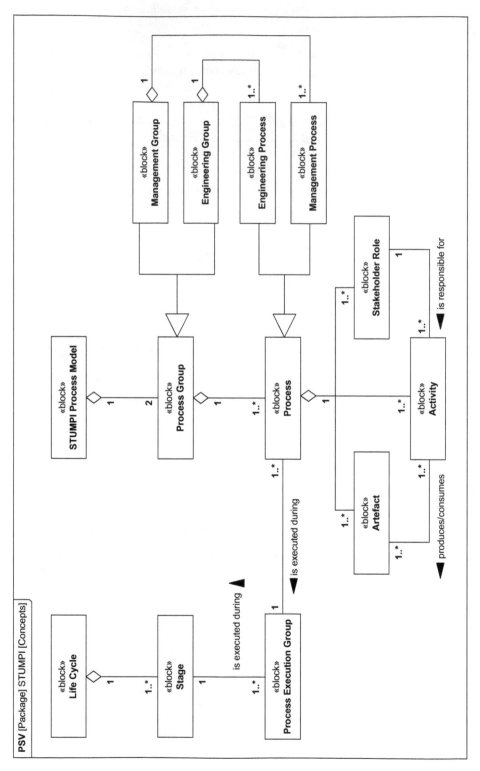

Figure 7.11   Example Process Structure View for the STUMPI process

The diagram in Figure 7.11 shows the 'Process Structure View' for the STUMPI processes. Note that the 'Process Structure View' shown in Figure 7.11 considers Process-related concepts that are used for additional modelling, such as the 'Life Cycle', 'Stage' and 'Process Execution Group'.

- A Process Structure View, or Ontology, must exist for each Process model.
- Each element in the Process Structure view must be instantiated to form the other six Views.

The Process Structure View is unusual as it sits at a higher conceptual level than the other Views and, therefore, does not have the same type of consistency checks with the other Views, as it provides the concepts and terminology for all Views.

View Discussion

The Process Structure View specifies the structure of concepts and the terminology used when defining Processes. The Process Structure View defines this vocabulary in order to ensure that consistency of terminology is used. If many different Processes have to be mapped to each other, then the Process Structure Views for each set of Processes form the basis for this process mapping, allowing the terminology used in one Process model to be related to the terminology used in another.

The Process Structure View may also be used as a basis for complexity analysis. This is an interesting area that does not fall within the scope of this book, but a full discussion can be seen in Reference 6.

7.2.3.4   The Process Content View

View rationale

When a number of Processes have been identified and defined, it is natural for them to form some sort of Process library, which presents the available Processes to potential users. The library of Processes is represented in the "seven views" approach as the Process Content View.

The Process Content View identifies the Processes available, showing the Activities carried out and the Artefacts produced and consumed. It may show general associations and dependencies between Processes. It is important to understand that the Process Content View only identifies Processes. It does not show how they are carried out, which is the role of the Process Behaviour View.

View definition

The subset of the MBSE Ontology that relates to process modelling is shown in Figure 7.12, with the relevant Ontology Elements highlighted.

The diagram in Figure 7.12 shows that the Ontology Elements that are important for modelling Process are: the 'Process', the 'Activity' and the 'Artefact'.

View relationships

The diagram in Figure 7.13 shows the relationships between the Process Content View and other Views in the "seven views" approach. The diagram is actually a subset of the MBSE Process Framework, which will be shown in its entirety later in this chapter.

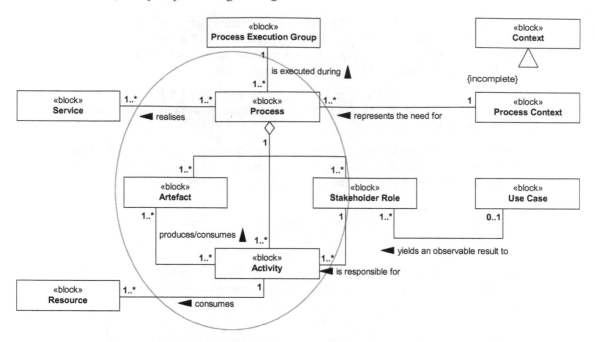

Figure 7.12   View definition of the Process Content View

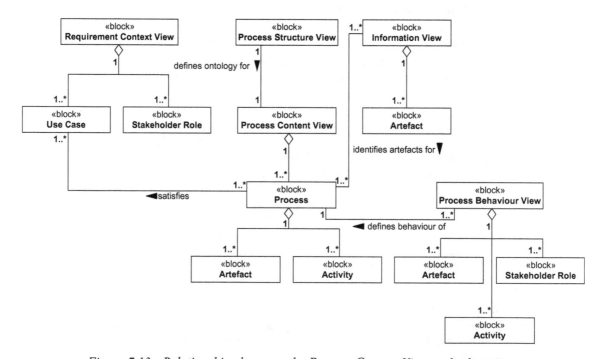

Figure 7.13   Relationships between the Process Content View and other views

The 'Process Content View' has relationships with the 'Process Behaviour View', the 'Requirement Context View', the 'Information View' and the 'Process Instance View'. These relationships lead to the definition of the following Rules, which may be used to enforce compliance with the "seven views" approach.

- Each Process in the Process Content View must have at least one Process Behaviour View to define its behaviour.
- Each Artefact in the Process Content View (represented as a *property* on its parent *block*) must exist as an Artefact (represented by a *block*) in the Information View.
- Each Process Instance (represented by a *life line*) in the Process Instance View must be an instance of a Process (represented by a *block*) on the Process Content View.
- Each Artefact in the Process Content View (represented as a *property* on its parent *block*) must exist as an Artefact (represented by an *instance specification*) on its associated Process Behaviour View.
- Each Activity in the Process Content View (represented as a SysML *operation* on its parent *block*) must exist as an Activity (represented by a SysML *activity*) on its associated Process behaviour View(s).

These Rules may be used as a basis for automation for the "seven views" approach.

View visualisation

The Process Content View is visualised using a *block definition diagram*, as shown Figure 7.14.

The diagram here shows the 'Process Content View' for the STUMPI processes. Each Process is represented by a single *block* with each Artefact represented by a *property* and each Activity by an *operation*.

View discussion

The Process Content View shows the actual content, in terms of Activities and Artefacts by representing each Process as a single *block*. Due to the large number of Processes within an Organisation, it is usual to produce a Process Content View for each classification, or Process grouping, from the Process Content View. The STUMPI process model, for example, has two main process groups ('Engineering' and 'Management'), each of which will have its own Process Content View.

By adopting this presentation style, it is possible to represent an entire Process by a single *block*, while showing all of its Artefacts and Activities. This notation not only is simple and concise, but also allows an idea of the complexity of each Process to be ascertained, albeit at a very high level, simply by looking at the number of *properties* and *operations* and the ratio of their numbers.

An ideal *block* that represents a Process should contain around seven *properties* (plus or minus two) and *operations* for a well-balanced Process. This is because the number of things that a human can remember at any one time is defined as 7, plus or minus 2 — quite by coincidence, this is also the number of Views in the

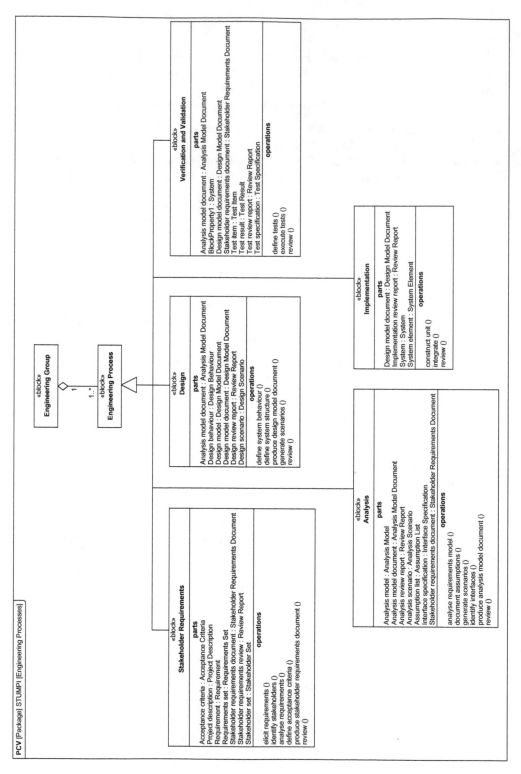

Figure 7.14   Example Process Content View for the STUMPI Process showing the 'Engineering Group' Processes

MBSE Process Framework. Bearing this simple rule in mind, there are a number of issues to look for when analysing Processes:

- Too many Activities. If a Process exists with far more than nine (seven plus two) Activities, then the chance of someone being able to understand this Process begins to diminish as the higher number of Activities increases. There are simply too many steps involved in this task, which will, potentially, lead to complexity when the Process is executed. This high number could be due to the fact that the Activities represent very small steps of behaviour, which means that the level of granularity of the Activities should be changed so that fewer Activities represent the same behaviour. This high number could also be due to the fact that there is simply too much going on in this single Process, and maybe the Process should be broken down into two or more simpler Processes that describe the same behaviour. As to which of these two reasons is the cause, this will become more apparent when another View — the Process Behaviour View — is looked at for a Process.
- Too many Artefacts. The same principles can be applied when the number of Artefacts, represented by *properties*, is excessive. An excessive number of Artefacts may be due to the fact that the individual Artefacts are too detailed and that the level of granularity of information needs to be raised.
- Too few Artefacts. Following on from the previous point, too few Artefacts result in exactly the same problems but, this time, the danger lies in over-simplifying the Artefacts of the Process.
- Too few Activities. The situation where the number of Activities defined is very low, typically one or two, can mean one of three things. The first is that the Activities will be identified at a very high level. The second possibility is that the Process itself may be too detailed and it maybe needs to be abstracted into another, related Process. The third possibility is, of course, that the diagram is correct, but this is quite unlikely, bearing in mind the first two possibilities.
- No Activities or no Artefacts. If the situation arises where the number of Artefacts or the number of Activities is zero, then alarm bells should start to go off immediately. This is simply wrong! Consider the situation where Activities exist, yet there are no Artefacts. In this case it means that it is impossible to demonstrate that a Process has been executed – there is no evidence identified for any of its Activity execution. Also consider the situation where there are Artefacts but no Activities – where do the Artefacts come from? It may be the Artefacts are part of a data store, in which case the owner-*block* is not a Process, but some sort of storage element. It should be noted that this does not apply to an abstract *block* that will sometimes simply represent a grouping of lower level Processes.
- Out-of-balance ratio. A quick, yet often accurate way to judge how well balanced a Process is to consider the ratio of the Artefacts to Activities on the *block*. Although there are no hard rules for this, an ideal Process should have between five and nine of both Artefacts and Activities. It is also possible to gain an appreciation of how well thought-out a Process is by looking at the ratio.

The Process Content View encapsulates all of the Processes that exist within the Process model and, therefore, gives a good overview of the scope of the capability of an Organisation in the various Process groups.

7.2.3.5 The Process Behaviour View

View rationale

The "seven views" approach allows for a library of Processes to be identified in the form of the Process Content View where each Process is defined in terms of its Artefacts and Activities. The Process Content View does a good job of defining the structure of each Process, but does not attempt to define the internal behaviour of the Process, which is the purpose of the Process Behaviour View.

View definition

The subset of the MBSE Ontology that relates to Process modelling is shown in Figure 7.15, with the relevant Ontology Elements highlighted.

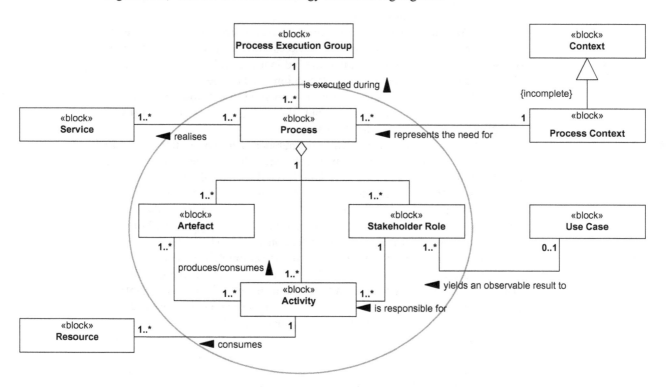

Figure 7.15   Definition of the Process Behaviour View

The diagram here shows that the Ontology Elements that are important for modelling Processes are: the 'Stakeholder Role', the 'Artefact' and the 'Activity'.

View relationships

The diagram in Figure 7.16 shows the relationships between the Process Behaviour View and other Views in the "seven views" approach.

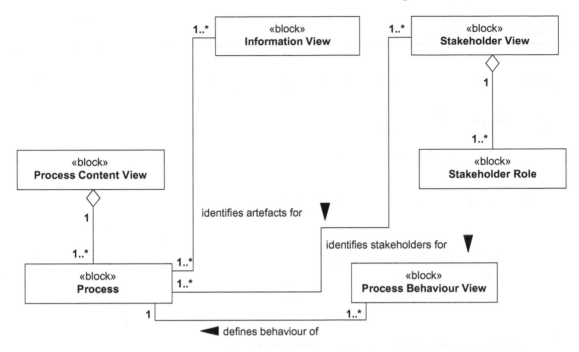

Figure 7.16 Relationships between the Process Behaviour View and other Views

The 'Process Behaviour View' has relationships with the 'Process Content View', the 'Information View', the 'Stakeholder View' and the 'Process Instance View'. These relationships lead to the definition of the following Rules, which may be used to enforce compliance with the "seven views" approach.

- Each Process (represented by a *block*) in the Process Content View that exhibits behaviour (Activities represented as *operations*) must have one or more Process Behaviour View associated with it that defines its behaviour.
- Each Artefact in the Process Content View (represented as a *property* on its parent *block*) must exist as an Artefact (represented by an *instance specification*) on its associated Process behaviour View.
- Each Activity in the Process Content View (represented as an *operation* on its parent *block*) must exist as an Activity (represented by an *activity*) on its associated Process behaviour View.
- Each Stakeholder Role on the Stakeholder View must exist as a *swim lane* owner on a Process Behaviour View.

These Rules may be used as a basis for automation for the "seven views" approach.

View visualisation

The Process Behaviour View is visualised in SysML using an *activity diagram*, as shown in Figure 7.17.

The diagram here shows the 'Process Behaviour View' for the STUMPI 'Design' Process.

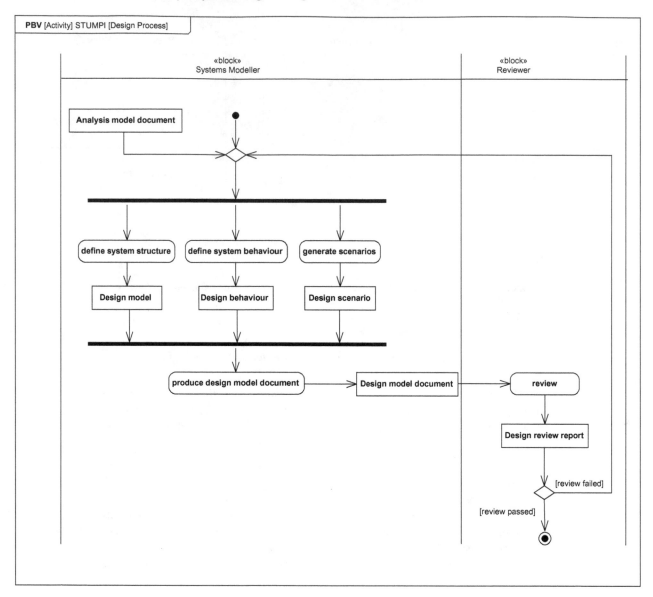

Figure 7.17   Example Process Behaviour View for the STUMPI Process showing the 'Design' Process

View discussion

The Process Behaviour View shows how an individual Process behaves and each Process identified on the Process Content View should have a Process Behaviour View that defines its behaviour. A Process Behaviour View shows the order of Activities within a Process, the flow of information through the Process (i.e., the flow of Artefacts around the Process) and the responsibilities, in terms of Stakeholder Roles, for carrying out the Activities. The Activities and Artefacts shown on a Process Behaviour View must be consistent with those shown for the Process on a Process Content View, and the Stakeholder Roles indicating responsibility must appear on both the Stakeholder View and the Requirement Context View.

The Process Behaviour View should be as simple as possible while still adding value to the process model. There are a few warning signs to look out for, however:

- A single *swim lane*. Although this is certainly possible, it can often be an indication that the Stakeholder Role identified is either the name of a Person (rather than the Stakeholder Role name) who holds many roles, or the role that has been taken from too high in the hierarchy of the Stakeholder View.
- Too many possible execution paths. Remembering that complexity manifests itself through relationships rather than the nodes in the diagram, a diagram that is too messy or looks like a spider's nest should be avoided. In many cases this is the sign of a poorly understood or uncontrolled Process. Bear in mind that some structure should exist within the Process, so having every *activity* related to every other one can be needless.
- Single execution path. Some Processes are truly linear in their behaviour with no possible deviation from the single thread of execution defined. Although this is possible, it is very unlikely in all, but the most trivial of Processes. Bear in mind that many Processes will have at least one decision point involved – certainly in any Process that contains any sort of review, checking or testing activity will have at least two possible outcomes in each case. Where this is the case, there will be different paths of execution and iterations.

It is also possible to show any other Stakeholder Roles that are involved, yet not responsible. This is done by showing participating roles in the *activity* in brackets – for example '(Project manager)' or may even be indicated by an *actor* with an *association* to the relevant *activity*.

7.2.3.6   The Information View
View rationale
The "seven views" approach requires that Processes are defined in terms of their Activities, Artefacts and Stakeholder Roles. It is very important to understand which Artefacts are produced and consumed by which Activities, as shown on the Process Behaviour View but it is equally important to understand the Artefacts themselves form a structural point of view. This structural view may take the form of looking at the internal structure of a single Artefact or may consider the relationships between the various Artefacts. This structure is captured in the Information View.

View definition
The subset of the MBSE Ontology that relates to modelling Processes is shown in Figure 7.18, with the relevant Ontology Elements highlighted.

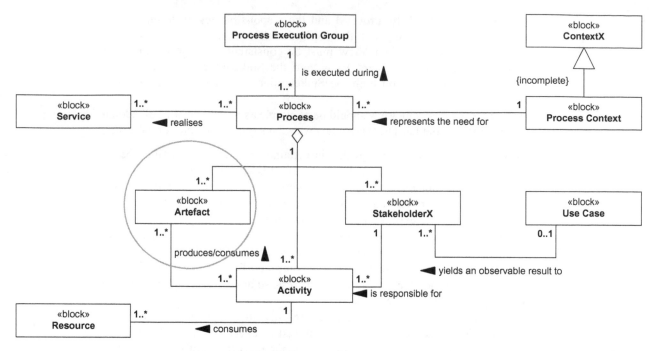

Figure 7.18   Definition of the Information View

The diagram here shows that the Ontology Element that is important for modelling processes is the 'Artefact'.

View relationships

The diagram in Figure 7.19 shows the relationships between the Information View and other Views in the "seven views" approach.

The 'Information View' has relationships with the 'Process Content View' and the 'Process Behaviour View'. These relationships lead to the definition of the following Rules that may be used to enforce compliance with the 'seven views' approach.

- Each Artefact, represented as a *block*, on the Information View must exist as an Artefact, represented as a *block instance* on at least one Process Behaviour View.
- Each Artefact, represented as a *block*, on the Information View must exist as an Artefact, represented as a *property* on at least the Process Content View.

These Rules may be used as a basis for automation for the 'seven views' approach.

View visualisation

The Information View is visualised in SysML using a *block definition diagram*, as shown in Figure 7.20.

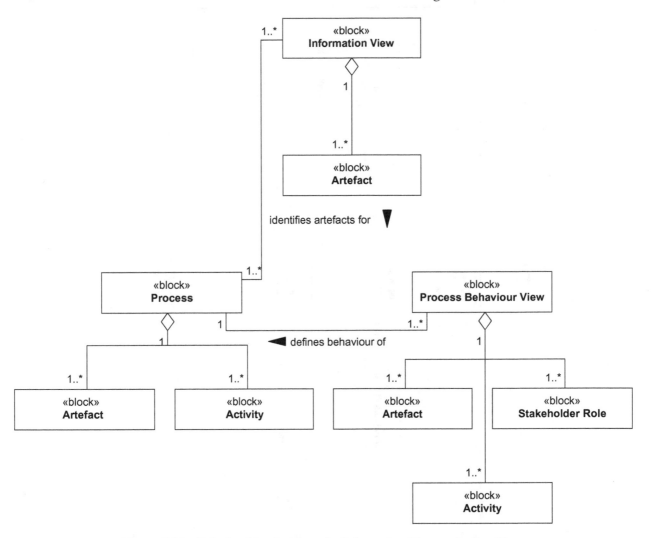

Figure 7.19 Relationships between the Information View and other Views

The diagram here shows a high-level Information View for the STUMPI Process set that emphasises the relationships between Artefacts from different Processes. This is useful in terms of traceability across the entire Process set.

The diagram in Figure 7.21 shows the Information View for the 'Analysis' Process. Note how the structure of the 'Analysis Model Document' is shown together with its relationships to Artefacts from other STUMPI Processes.

View discussion

The Information View identifies all the Artefacts produced or consumed by a Process or set of Processes, showing the relationships between them. An Information View can be created at both a high level or a low level. A high-level

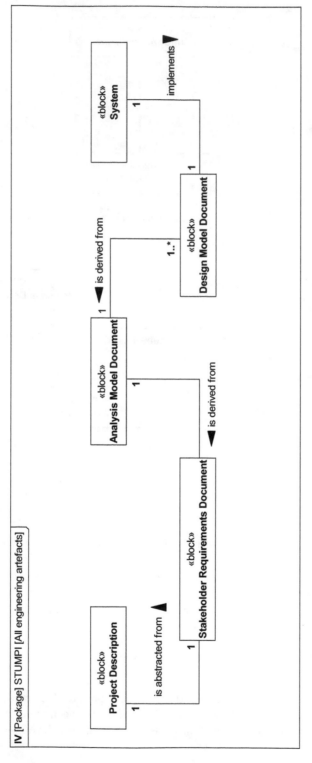

Figure 7.20 Example Information View for the STUMPI Process showing traceability paths

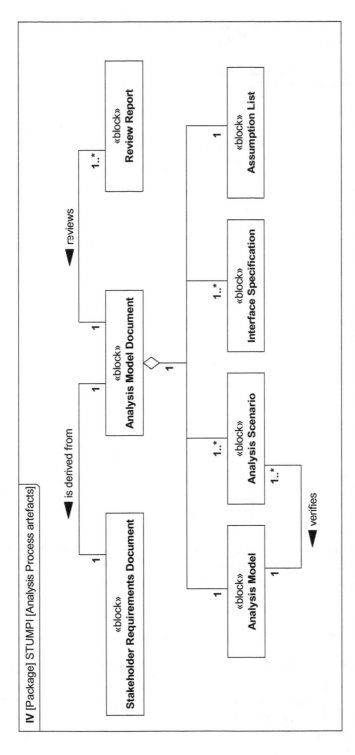

Figure 7.21   Example Information View for the STUMPI Process showing Artefact structure

Information View will typically identify Artefacts and relationships, whereas a low-level Information View will typically show the detailed structure and content of individual Artefacts.

The Information View is concerned with identifying the key Artefacts from the system and then identifying their inter-relationships. This viewpoint is crucial for two main reasons:

- Inter-process consistency. A large part of the complexity involved with Process models is derived from the interactions between the Processes, rather than the internal working of each Process. In order to make sure that Processes are compatible (e.g. that their respective inputs and outputs match up) it is vital to have an understanding of both the main Artefacts of the Processes and their inter-relationships.
- Process automation. If the Process model is going to be used at a practical level by a group, or several groups, of people, then process automation will be a point worth considering. In order to automate Processes, it is important to understand what each Artefact looks like (maybe a template will be defined for each one) and how these Artefacts relate to one another. In fact, very often it will be individual parts of each Artefact that relate to their parts of Artefacts, rather than the entire Artefacts relating to one another.

The Information View may be modelled at several levels of abstraction in order to represent the elements and their inter-relationships, and also the individual structure of each Artefact.

7.2.3.7   The Process Instance View

View rationale

The "seven views" approach allows for the Needs for the Process to be understood (using *use cases* in the Requirement Context View) and the Processes that satisfy those Needs to be defined (using the Process Content View), but is essential that it can be shown that the Processes do, indeed, satisfy these original *use cases*. This is achieved using the Process Instance View.

View definition

The subset of the MBSE Ontology that relates to modelling Processes is shown in Figure 7.22, with the relevant Ontology Elements highlighted.

The diagram here shows that the Ontology Elements that are important for Process modelling are: the 'Process Execution Group' and the 'Process'.

View relationships

Figure 7.23 shows the relationships between the Process Instance View and other Views in the seven views approach. The diagram here is actually a subset of the MBSE Process Framework, which will be shown in its entirety later in this chapter.

The 'Process Instance View' has relationships with the 'Process Content View' and the 'Requirement Context View'. These relationships lead to the definition of the following Rules that may be used to enforce compliance with the "seven views" approach.

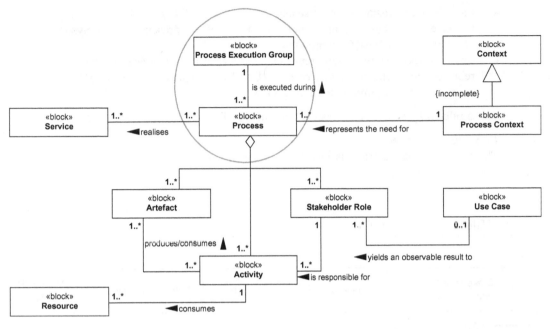

Figure 7.22 Definition of the Process Instance View

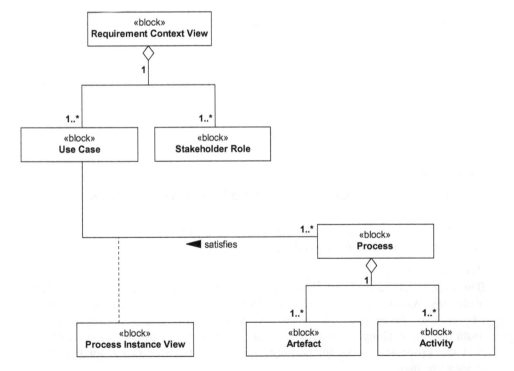

Figure 7.23 Relationships between the Process Instance View and other Views

- Each Process Instance (represented by a SysML *life line*) in the Process Instance View must be an instance of a Process (represented by a SysML *block*) on the Process Content View.
- Each Process Instance View (represented as a SysML *sequence diagram*) must represent an instance of one or more Use Case (represented as SysML *use cases*) on the Requirement Context View.

These rules may be used as a basis for automation for the "seven views" approach.

View visualisation

The Process Instance View is visualised in SysML using a *sequence diagram*, as shown in Figure 7.24.

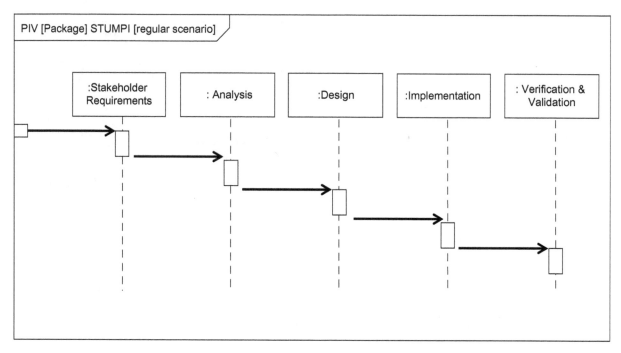

Figure 7.24   Example Process Instance View for the STUMPI Process

The diagram here shows the 'Process Instance View' for the STUMPI Processes, where the emphasis is on the interactions between Process instances.

View discussion

The Process Instance View shows instances of Processes and the Stakeholder Roles involved in order to validate the Processes by relating the execution of a sequence of Processes back to the Use Case for the Process. Each Process Instance View along with its associated Requirement Context View ensures that the Processes are fit for purpose and that all the Use Cases for the Processes are met.

The Process Instance View is a set of diagrams that provides the main validation for the Process model. It is the Process Instance View that relates the actual Processes that are specified back to the source *use cases* and validates that each *use case* has been met. The basic elements of the Process Instance View are executions of (or instances of) individual Processes. For each *use case* from the Requirement Context View, it should be possible to execute a number of Scenarios in order to validate that *use case*.

The Process Instance View is realised by a *sequence diagram*, with the main elements being executions of processes (represented by *life lines*) and their interactions (represented by SysML *interactions*).

The Process Instance View looks very similar to the Validation Views used in the ACRE approach to requirements modelling, but their application, however, is subtly different. The Process Instance Views are used to validate a set of Processes against their Use Cases. The Validation Views, on the other hand, are used to explore a number of possible Scenarios related to a specific Use Case.

7.3   The Process Modelling Framework

The complete MBSE Process modelling Framework for the "seven views" approach to Process modelling is shown in the diagram in Figure 7.25.

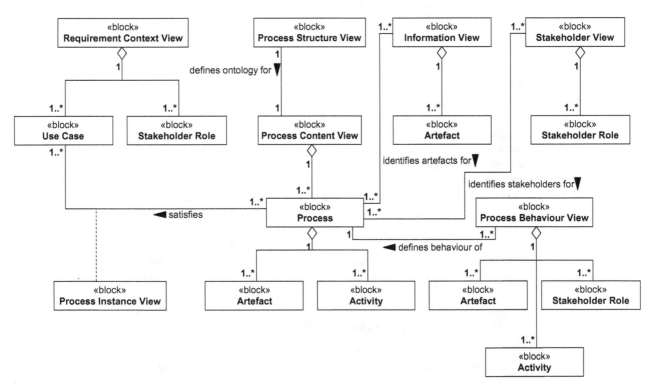

Figure 7.25   Complete Framework for Process modelling

The diagram here shows the complete MBSE Process modelling Framework for the "seven views" approach to Process modelling. Notice that this diagram brings together each of the diagrams that was used previously to show relationships between Views.

7.4   Using the process modelling framework

There are a number of ways that the "seven views" can be used to add value to any Process modelling exercise. This section introduces several different Scenarios that describe how the approach may be used and then discusses the advantages of its use for each Scenario. This is not intended to be an exhaustive list of possible Scenarios, but presents a good spread that illustrates the flexibility of the approach itself.

7.4.1   Analysing existing processes

In many cases, it is desirable to look at and analyse existing Processes. Some possible reasons for wanting to do this include:

- As part of a Process improvement exercise. A Process model is a living entity and, as such, it needs to be constantly monitored and, where necessary, changed and improved.
- To identify the causes of failure in the Process. It is relatively easy to simply define a Process but rather more difficult to ensure that it is an accurate reflection of real life and that it is effective. Therefore, these modelling techniques can be used to capture and analyse existing Processes. This is particularly effective when trying to understand why something has gone wrong and can be a very powerful tool for examining the causes of failures and disasters.
- To gain an appreciation of an undocumented or complex Process. In many cases, Processes are represented as text descriptions, which can be very long and verbose. In such cases, it is desirable to have a simplified version of the Process description so that an appreciation of how the Process fits together and works can be gained. This is particularly powerful for looking at Standards, Processes and procedures that are out of the control of the actual Organisation, such as mandated standards, government initiatives.
- As a part of audit or assessment. When carrying out any sort of process-based audit or assessment, it is crucial to have an understanding of both the Process under review and the Standard to which the Process is being audited or assessed. This is actually a powerful combination of the first two points in this section – the Process being audited must be modelled to gain an appreciation and the Standard being audited against must also be modelled.

In terms of how the approach would be used for the previous points, Figure 7.26 shows an example scenario of the order in which the various Views in the approach may be created.

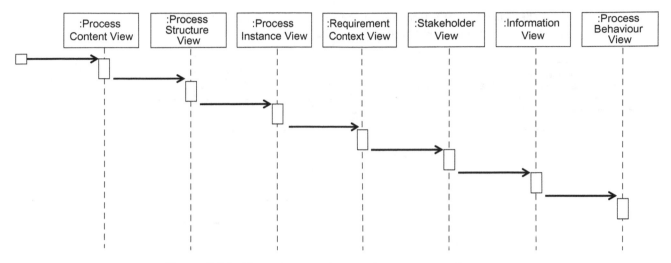

Figure 7.26 Example scenario – analysing existing Processes

The diagram in Figure 7.26 shows an example Scenario that represents the order of creation of the Views when analysing an existing process model. The first View that is created is the 'Process Content View' as, in cases where a Process model exists and is well documented, this is often the easiest View to construct first. The 'Process Content View' may then be used as a basis for abstracting the 'Process Structure View', as the structure can be most easily extracted from existing content. The next View to be created is the 'Process Instance View' as, in many cases, examples of Scenarios will be given as part of the Process description. From the 'Process Content View' for the Process and the 'Process Instance View', it is then possible to abstract right back up to the top-level 'Requirement Context View'. A natural progression from the 'Requirement Context View' and the 'Process Instance View' is the 'Stakeholder View', as many of the Stakeholder Roles will have been identified between each of these two Views. The Artefacts of the Process, which have been identified from the 'Process Content View' and the information flow in the 'Process Instance View', can now form the basis of the 'Information View'. Finally, the 'Process Behaviour View' may be extracted from the low-level Process descriptions.

7.4.2   Creating a new process document from scratch

In some cases, such as the start of a new business or perhaps the creation of a brand new Process description for an impending audit or assessment, it is desirable to start a Process description from scratch with, in effect, a blank sheet of paper. Although this situation does not occur very often in real-life industry, it is a very good exercise to get the feel for Process modelling, whether it is to understand the how the modelling works or, indeed, to understand Process models in the first place.

The generation of information in the situation of creating a Process document from scratch can be summarised in Figure 7.27.

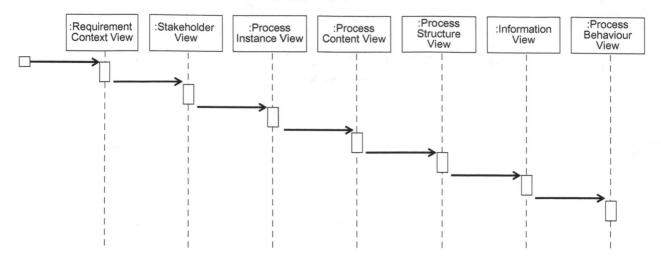

Figure 7.27   Example scenario – creating a process model from scratch

The diagram in Figure 7.27 shows a simple Scenario to represent creating a Process document from scratch. As with all the situations, or Scenarios, described in this section, the order of generation of the Views is by no means carved in stone, but gives an idea of how the information in the Process model may be used in different ways.

In a situation like this, a good first step is to think about the Needs of the Processes themselves. For example, the main Need for a Process may be to 'protect human life' in the case of a safety standard, or to 'process' applications in the case of a patient admission system. This highest level Need can then be broken down into lower level Needs that can relate directly to Processes. Also, it is usual for the highest level Needs to have a number of constraints associated with them, for example meeting another Standard, working in a particular environment or Context, or even working with an existing System. It is also usual to start thinking about the Stakeholder Roles that interact with the Processes at this point. When these Needs are put into Context, they become Use Cases (represented as SysML *use cases*) on the 'Process Context View' and *actors* may be used to represent the Stakeholder Roles.

Once the 'Requirement Context View' has been established, it is then possible to think about how its Use Cases could possibly be realised, by identifying a number of Scenarios in the form of one or more 'Process Instance View'. Each Scenario represents the execution of a number of Processes that satisfy a specific Use Case. From the 'Process Instance View' it is possible to create a list of Processes that are needed along with the dependencies between them. Once the Processes have been identified, there are a number of possible routes, such as defining the 'Process Content View', 'Process Structure View' or even the 'Information View'.

7.4.3   *Abstracting tacit process knowledge for a new System*

It is often the case that the Process knowledge that is required in order to create the Process model only exists inside people's heads. In such a situation, it is necessary to both observe the Process in action and talk to the relevant Stakeholder Roles to try to gain any complex knowledge that may not be immediately perceived when observing. Caution must be exercised, however, as it is often easy to be misdirected and miss some aspects of the Process under investigation. An incomplete and inaccurate Process description is often more harmful than no Process at all.

It should be stressed here that there are many reasons why such misdirection may occur:

- Deliberate misdirection. This often occurs in a working environment where the staff are unhappy – perhaps they don't take their job seriously, are worried about being replaced, or are simply mischievous! In such cases, it is important to know what questions to ask the relevant stakeholders and to compare the answers with other answers from the same stakeholder or maybe from other stakeholders. The MBSE Process Framework and MBSE Ontology provide the information required to know which questions to ask which Person holding which Stakeholder Roles at what time.
- Misdirection by assumption. Assumption, as the old adage goes, is the mother of all foul-ups and the basic problem here is that the Activities carried out by the Stakeholder Roles seem so obvious that they are never mentioned. For example, when it comes to testing a TV set, before any tests can be carried out the TV set must have the power to be switched on. It is this type of obvious information that is often omitted as people simply assume that it is known or done.
- Misdirection by ignorance. It may be that the Person who is describing the Process does not fully understand the Process in the first place. In such situations, it is unlikely that an accurate Process description will be provided.

The diagram in Figure 7.28 shows the order of creation of the Views for this situation.

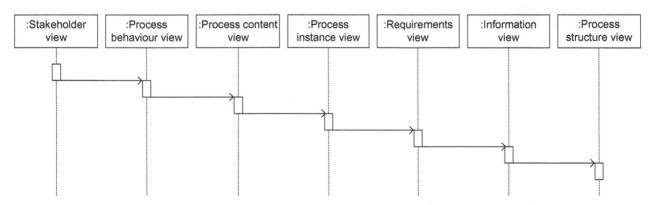

Figure 7.28   Process Instance View for abstracting tacit Process knowledge for a new System

The diagram in Figure 7.28 shows the order that the Views are created in for this situation. The first View that is generated is the 'Stakeholder View', as this will identify which Stakeholder Roles exist and provide a basis for knowing who to talk to concerning the Process behaviours. Therefore, the second View to be generated is the 'Process Behaviour View', which will consist of a number of diagrams – one for each Process that exhibits behaviour in the form of *activities*. Once the process behaviours have been created, it is then possible to abstract the 'Process Content View' from them and, from there, the 'Process Instance View'. From the 'Process Instance View' and the 'Process Content View', it is then possible to create the 'Requirement Context View' and the 'Information View'. Finally, the 'Process Structure View' may be abstracted.

7.4.4   Abstracting tacit process knowledge for an existing System

This situation is similar to the previous one except, in this case, there is some recorded Process information already in existence. Therefore, any Process knowledge may be realised by written information, Standards, existing Process models, etc.

The diagram in Figure 7.29 shows the order of creation of the Views for the situation for abstracting tacit Process knowledge for an existing system. In this case, the 'Process Structure View' is created first, based on the limited Process knowledge available. It is then possible to generate the 'Process Content View' and, from this, the 'Information View'. The 'Stakeholder View' is generated next which, again, is abstracted from existing documentation. Now that the Stakeholder Roles and the Processes have been identified, it is possible to put them together into scenarios and to generate the 'Process Instance View'. As the 'Process Instance View' and the 'Process Content View' have been identified, the 'Requirement Context View' can be abstracted. Finally, the detailed 'Process Behaviour View' may be generated.

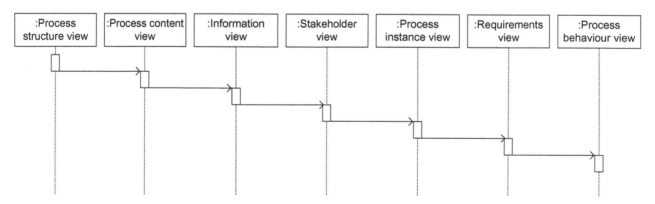

Figure 7.29   Process Instance View for abstracting tacit Process knowledge for an existing system

7.4.5   Process improvement for existing Processes

This situation occurs when there is an existing Process model that has been well defined and well documented. As part of the continuous Process improvement exercise, a basic review is carried out on a regular basis, say every 6 months, and rather than a full Process model analysis as shown in Figure 7.28, this time a partial analysis is carried out.

The diagram in Figure 7.30 shows the situation for Process improvement. The first View that is generated here is the 'Requirement Context View'. This is done to check that the original Needs for the Process have not changed in any way. Once the Needs have been checked and any new ones added, the 'Process Structure View' is generated to check that the basic Ontology for the Process is unchanged. The main part of this exercise is then to look at the 'Process Content View' to identify all the existing Processes. Finally, the 'Process Instance View' is created that validates the 'Requirement Context View'.

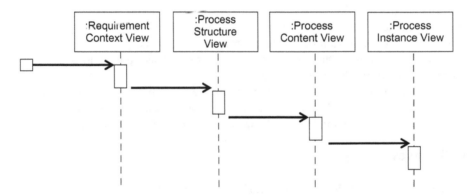

Figure 7.30   Process Instance View for Process improvement

The example shown here does not need to include all of the Views in the approach as everything has gone according to plan in the Process improvement exercise – there are no changes to be made.

Consider now what would happen if the Process Instance View has been used as a basis for a gap analysis to ensure that the existing Processes meet their original Needs. Where gaps are found, the new Processes must be added to the Process Content View. This would then entail creating the remainder of the Views as there has been a major change to the Process model and, hence, all views must be revisited.

7.4.6   Summary

It should be stressed that the examples discussed here are just that – examples. Do not feel constrained by the Scenarios provided here as each one could be changed, as long as there is some rationale behind the order that is specified in the Process Instance Views.

In terms of the order of creation of the Views, it should be clear by now that there is no strict order that is carved in stone, as the actual order will depend on the situation at hand. There are, however, a few common patterns in the various Process Instance Views shown here, which is only natural as they are based on the structural consistency checks that were described earlier in this chapter as part of the definition of each View. The structural checks are based on the *associations* in the MBSE Process Framework and the MBSE Ontology; therefore, if the Process Content View and the Requirement Context View are known, then the Requirement Context View is an obvious place to go next. Likewise, if the Process Instance View and the Stakeholder View are known, then the Requirement Context View could be a good next move.

Keep in mind that the more that the MBSE Process Framework is understood and becomes ingrained as a natural part of Process modelling, then the more natural these scenarios will become, and the more robust the final Process will be.

7.5   Summary

This chapter has introduced an approach to model Process in the form of the "seven views". The development of "seven views" follows the same 'Ontology, Framework and Views' approach that is used throughout this book.

The application of the "seven views" approach was applied to a bespoke Process model in the form of STUMPI.

Chapter 8 goes on to show how the "seven views" approach may be expanded and used in a number of other applications, including modelling Standards, showing compliance, Life Cycle modelling, Competence modelling and Project planning.

References

1. *Business Process Model and Notation*. Available from http://www.omg.org/cgi-bin/doc?bmi/2007-6-5
2. White S.A., Goldstine D.M. *BPMN Modeling and Reference Guide: Understanding and Using BPMN*. Florida, USA: Herman; 1972
3. ISO. *Information Processing – Documentation Symbols and Conventions for Data, Program and System Flowcharts, Program Network Charts and System Resources Charts*. International Organization for Standardization; 1985. ISO 5807:1985
4. Holt J., *UML for Systems Engineering – Watching the Wheels*. 2nd edn. Stevenage, UK: IEE publishing; 2004
5. Rumbaugh J., Booch G., Jacobson I. *The UML 2.0 Reference Manual*. Boston, USA: Addison Wesley publishing; 2004
6. Holt, J., *A pragmatic guide to business process modelling. Second Edition*. Swindon, UK: BCS Publishing; 2009

Chapter 8

Expanded Process modelling

The universe itself keeps on expanding and expanding,
In all of the directions it can whizz.

The Galaxy Song, Monty Python

8.1 Introduction

This chapter considers how the "seven views" approach that was introduced in the previous chapter may be used as a basis for various model-based systems engineering (MBSE) applications.

8.1.1 Background

The basic Context for Process modelling that was introduced in the previous chapter contained a number of constraints that were not discussed in detail. The Process modelling context is shown again in the diagram in Figure 8.1.

The diagram here shows the Context for Process modelling, most of which was discussed in the previous chapter. The main *use case* that was considered was 'Define approach to Process modelling' and its three inclusions, and the approach that was proposed to satisfy these *use cases* was the "seven views" approach to Process modelling. The basic "seven views" approach is very flexible and may be used for more applications than traditional Process-related activities. This chapter considers how this basic approach may be expanded for a number of areas, in particular:

- Expanding Process modelling with Standards modelling ('Be applicable to different levels of process . . . standards'), where the application of the "seven views" approach to established Standards, in particular ISO 15288.
- Expanding Process modelling with compliance mapping ('Allow mapping between processes'), where showing the relationships between any two (or more) process models will be discussed.
- Expanding Process modelling with competence ('Be expandable . . . for competence'), where Competence and competency-related views are discussed.
- Expanding Process modelling with life cycles ('Be expandable . . . for life cycles), where Life Cycles and Life Cycle Model Views are discussed.
- Expanding process modelling with project management ('Be expandable . . . for projects), where Project management-related Views are discussed.

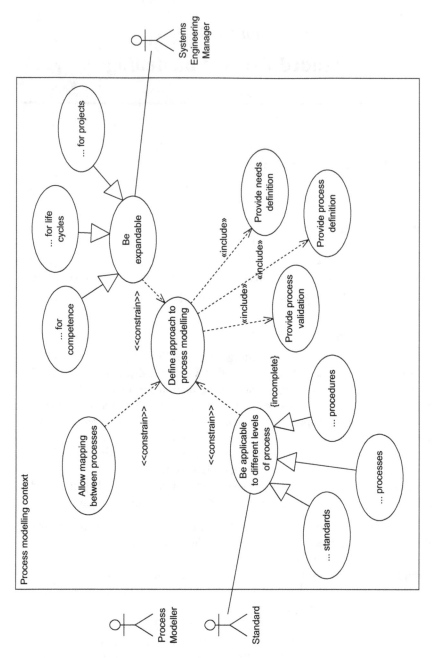

Figure 8.1   Process modelling context

These expanded uses of Process modelling are not intended to be exhaustive but are intended to provide examples of how the modelling can, and should, be applied to areas that may not be traditionally associated with MBSE. These examples also provide some good examples of how some Views may be visualised using non-SysML notation yet, through the use of the 'Ontology, Framework and Views' approach, remain consistent with the overall MBSE approach. This is achieved by expanding the MBSE Ontology and, therefore, providing the mechanism for additional Views to be defined.

8.2   Expanded process modelling – standards modelling

An excellent application for Process modelling and, in particular, the "seven views" approach is that of modelling Standards.

The standard that is used here as an example is 'ISO/IEC 15288:2008 – software and systems life cycle processes' (abbreviated to 'ISO 15288') [2]. The ISO 15288 standard is the most widely used standard in the world and, as such, is a staple reference in any systems engineering endeavour.

This is a straightforward application of the "seven views" approach and does not, therefore, require the Ontology and Framework to be defined, as it is the same as the basic approach discussed in the previous chapter. One general comment to bear in mind, however, is that the full set of "seven views" does not exist for ISO 15288. This is because high-level standards, such as international standards and industry standards, tend to focus more on what needs to be achieved rather than exactly how it should be achieved. The Views that are shown here are the Requirement Context View, Process Structure View, Stakeholder View and Process Content View.

The "seven views" process model is shown here at a high level and some general comments are made. For reasons of clarity, the Process Content View does not show the Task level of detail but stops at the Activity level. For the full, detailed model, see Appendix E.

8.2.1   Views
8.2.1.1   ISO 15288 – Requirement Context View
The Requirement Context View for a Standard will be typically abstracted from the overview of the Standard at the beginning of the document. Every Standard begins with a definition of its purpose and aims and so this is perfect information for creating the Requirement Context View (Figure 8.2).

The diagram here shows the Requirement Context View for ISO 15288. The main *use case* is to 'Establish common framework for describing the life cycle of systems'. This has three main inclusions and a single constraint, which are:

–   'Define Processes' that then has four *specialisations* that reflect the different process areas that are required by the Standard.
–   'Define terminology' that identifies the need for a common vocabulary.

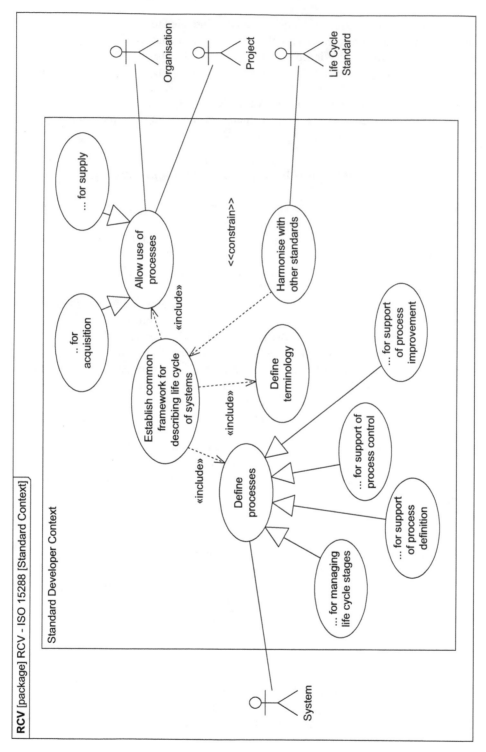

Figure 8.2   ISO 15288 – Requirement Context View

- 'Allow use of processes' that states that the Processes should be suitable for both acquisition and supply (shown by the specialisations).
- 'Harmonise with other standards' that requires that other Standards should be complied with, where appropriate.

It should be clear from these high-level *use cases* that there is a natural link between the Standard and the "seven views".

8.2.1.2 ISO 15288 – Stakeholder View

The ISO 15288 Standard identifies a number of Stakeholder Roles that are shown in the diagram in Figure 8.3.

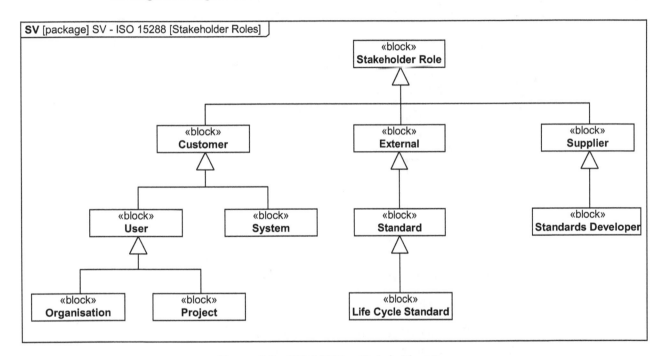

Figure 8.3 ISO 15288 – Stakeholder View

The diagram shows the various Stakeholder Roles in ISO 15288. The first thing to notice is that there are not very many of them, which is typical for a high-level standard. The Stakeholder Roles that are identified tend to be very high level ones that provide very broad categories for compliance.

8.2.1.3 ISO 15288 – Process Structure View

The Ontology for ISO 15288 is shown in the Process Structure View. This View has been used previously, as it was one of the references for the MBSE Ontology that is used throughout this book.

The diagram here shows the Ontology for ISO 15288 (Figure 8.4). It is interesting to see that the Standard basically defines one or more 'Process' and proposes a 'Life

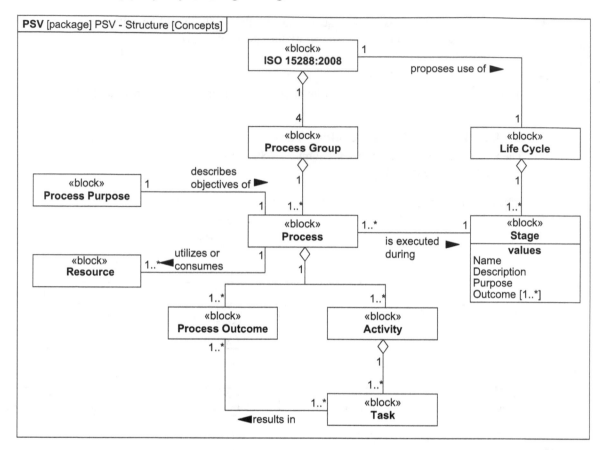

Figure 8.4   ISO 15288 – Process Structure View

Cycle', and that the terminology used in the Ontology reflects that. This is a typical pattern that can be seen in many Standards as many quality standards are essentially process-based and, hence, the emphasis will be solely on Processes and Life Cycles.

The Ontology is extended on the next diagram to emphasise the types of 'Stage' that make up the 'Life Cycle' (Figure 8.5).

The diagram here shows a slightly different aspect of the overall Ontology for ISO 15288. In this view, the emphasis is on the different types of Life Cycle Stages and also the concept of the 'Decision Gate'.

There are six Stages that are identified in the Standard, which are:

– The 'Conception' Stage, which covers the identification, analysis and specification of all the Needs for the Project. This may also include prototyping, trade studies, research or whatever is necessary to formalise the requirements set.
– The 'Development' Stage, which covers all the analysis and design for the Project and results in the complete System solution.

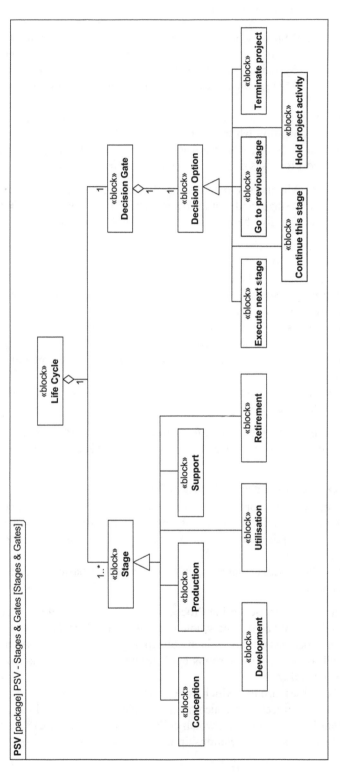

Figure 8.5   ISO 15288 – Process Structure View showing 'Stage' and 'Gate'

- The 'Production' Stage, which covers the production of the System of Interest, either as a one-off in the case of bespoke systems or full manufacture in the case of volume Systems. This Stage also includes the transition to operation.
- The 'Utilisation' Stage, which covers the operation of the System at the target environment.
- The 'Support' Stage, which provides the maintenance, logistics and support for the system of operation while it is being operated.
- The 'Retirement' Stage, which covers the removal of the System of Interest and all related Processes or support mechanisms from service.

A 'Decision Gate' will usually manifest itself as some sort of review that takes place at the end of a 'Stage' and that makes a decision ('Decision Option') on what action to take next. The five basic types of 'Decision Option' are:

- 'Execute next stage' where the current Stage has gone according to plan and the Project may progress.
- 'Continue this stage' where more work needs to be carried out before the Project can progress to the next Stage. This will often require another 'Decision Gate' review to be executed.
- 'Go to previous stage' where something has happened that results in rework and going back to a previous Stage.
- 'Hold project activity' where all work on the Project is halted, pending further investigations.
- 'Terminate project' where, for whatever reason, it has been decided that the Project will be killed off.

Again, it should be stressed that the information in the Standard is there to provide recommendations and suggestions as to how the Life Cycle should be executed.

8.2.1.4　ISO 15288 – Process Content View

The Process Content View for ISO 15288 is by far and away the most populated of the "seven views". Again, this is because one of the main requirements for the standard, from the Requirement Context View, was to define a set of Processes in four areas (Figure 8.6).

The first of the Process Content Views shows the four basic types of 'Process Group', which are:

- 'Organisational Project-enabling Processes Group', which collects together all Processes that apply across the whole Organisation, all staff and all Projects.
- 'Technical Processes Group', which collects together the Processes that most people will associate with systems engineering and that cover areas such as requirements and design.
- 'Project Processes Group', which collects together Processes that are applied on a project-by-project basis, such as project planning and risk management.
- 'Agreement Processes Group', which collects together Processes that describe the customer and supplier relationship in the Project.

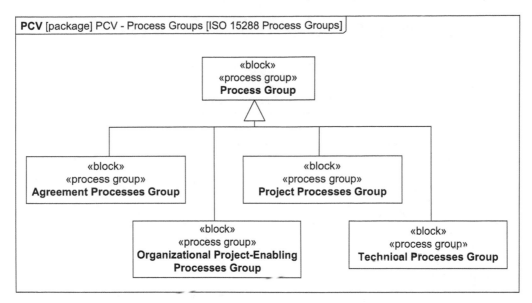

Figure 8.6   ISO 15288 – Process Content View showing types of 'Process Group'

Some of these Process Groups are shown in more detail in the following Process Content Views (Figure 8.7) and the whole model for the Standard is presented in Appendix E.

The diagram shows the two high-level Processes that are suggested for the 'Agreement Processes Group'. The Process Outcomes are shown as block *properties* and the Process Activities are shown as block *operations*. It should be noted that each of the Activities on this diagram are broken down into more detail, in the form of one or more 'Task'. These Tasks are not shown in this diagram for the sake of brevity and readability, but are fully defined in Appendix E.

One of the first things to notice is that there are only two Processes in the Agreement Processes Group. This reflects where the emphasis of this standard lies – in the technical areas rather than agreement. This is an area where the use of other, complementary standards comes into play. When compared to some of the other Process Groups, for example the 'Technical Processes Group', it can be seen that there is far more of an emphasis in other areas.

The Views that have been introduced so far can now be used as a start point for compliance mapping between two or more Standards and/or process models.

8.2.2   Summary

This section has shown how the "seven views" approach to Process modelling can be applied to a Standard – in this case ISO 15288. Due to the nature of the standard, only a subset of the Views was produced as the standard itself and does not cover detailed aspects of each Process.

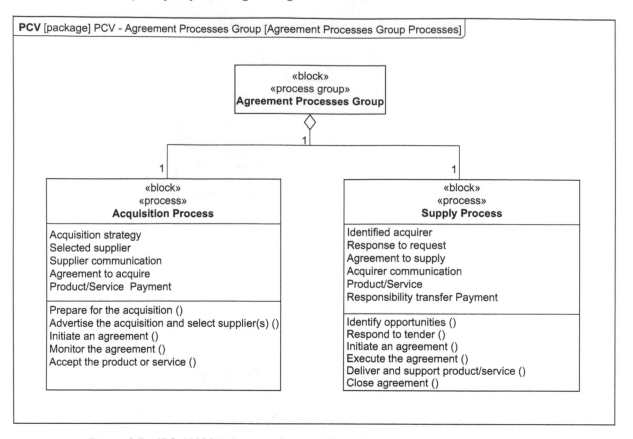

Figure 8.7　ISO 15288 – Process Content View showing 'Agreement Processes Group'

Performing this Process modelling on a Standard is a very interesting and useful exercise and provides a number of benefits:

– Increased understanding of the Standard. The very fact that the Standard is being modelled means that some thought and analysis need to be carried out. Also, relationships between different aspects of the Standards will be highlighted that provides a more complete understanding of the big picture of the Standard.

– Identification of problem areas of the Standard. By applying the modelling to a Standard, an increased understanding of any problems associated with the Standard is gained, for example inconsistencies within the Standard (such as differences in terminology), areas of complexity and whether or not the Standard achieves what it sets out to do.

– Basis for compliance. Demonstrating compliance with a Standard is an essential part of any quality system, audit or assessment. These models of Standards can be used as an integral part of these activities.

An example of using the Standard process model is provided in the next section, where compliance mapping will be discussed.

8.3   Expanded Process modelling – compliance mapping

One way to inspire other people's confidence in your business is to demonstrate that the approach taken by your organisation is compliant with an established best practice approach. In other words, it is very beneficial to be able to map your own processes back to source standards.

This section, therefore, is concerned with the 'Allow mapping between processes' *use case* from Figure 8.1.

The way that an approach is demonstrated is usually carried out in one of two ways, through an assessment or through an audit. The process model that is being audited against (usually a Standard) will be referred to as the source, whereas the process model under review will be referred to as the target. In both audits and assessments, there are three aspects of the process model that are being examined:

- Source standard compliance. The first thing to look for is whether or not there is a basic mapping between the source Standard and the target Process.
- Process implementation. The next thing to look for is whether or not the target Process is being implemented on real Projects. Examples of the use of Processes being used on Projects, or process instances as they are known, are sought and then these are either audited or assessed.
- Process effectiveness. The third thing that is looked for is whether or not the target Process is effective. Are any metrics being taken and the Process improved as time goes on? Are the requirements for the Process correct and up to date? And so on.

Although both assessments and audits share the same basic aims, they are executed in very different ways:

- Audit. An audit tends to be more formal than an assessment. An audit is usually carried out by a third-party, independent body to enforce the source Standard. This source Standard, for example ISO 9001, must be well understood and the audit will often make use of specific checklists that enable each part of the Standard to be checked against the target Process. For an audit, a documented Process model must exist; otherwise the full audit cannot take place. The output of an audit is typically a straight pass or fail result with an indication of which specific parts of the source Standard were not met – or non-compliances as they are often known.
- Assessment. An assessment tends to be more informal that an audit and may be carried out either by independent third parties or by suitably qualified people inside the Organisation. Examples of assessment Standards include ISO 15504 (software process assessment) (ISO 15504) and CMM (capability maturity model) (CMM). An assessment starts out with a blank sheet of paper and the target Process is then abstracted and the results of this abstraction are then assessed. This means that the target Process may be well documented, in which case the abstraction is relatively simple, or there may be no documentation whatsoever (the process exists purely in someone's head), in which case the abstraction is not so straightforward. Of course, one advantage of this is that any target Process may be effectively assessed, even if it is not formally

documented. The output of an assessment is typically a profile, rather than a simple pass or fail that provides effective feedback about how mature each process is. There is usually a scale of five or so levels that indicates the maturity – a low number indicating an immature and uncontrolled Process and a high number indicating a mature and controlled Process.

A common aspect of both approaches is being able to demonstrate basic compliance between the source Standard and the target Process, and this is where, initially, Process mapping comes in.

There are several inherent problems associated with Process mapping:

–   Terminology differences. Perhaps the most common problem between different standards or process models is one of communication – the actual terminology is very different. For example, consider the different words that may be employed to indicate the Activities (using the terminology adopted in this book) within a Process, such as task, step, practice and action. Although these seem like minor differences, what about the situation where the same word is used, such as process, but has different definitions in each Process model. It is essential, therefore, that these differences in language can be identified and clarified.

–   Volume of data. In many cases, it is desirable to map, not just between two Processes but between many. It is not uncommon to find a list of relevant Standards, either in a requirements specification or in a Project contract that forms a formal obligation for the Project. It should be borne in mind, however, that realistically if there are 50 Standards listed, then this means, potentially, 50 audits or assessments must be carried out. The sheer volume of data involved here, not to mention the time and effort involved, would be phenomenal.

–   Meaningful metrics. There is an old adage that anything that can't be measured, can't be controlled [1], therefore it is important that measurements and, hence, metrics can be applied to the Process mapping in order to demonstrate how effective the mapping is. However, coming up with meaningful metrics is often difficult, so any effective Process mapping should be capable of being measured in some way.

The remainder of this section defines an example of a Process for Process mapping that meets all of the requirements laid out above. Of course, this Process is merely an example and is not the only approach that can be taken to perform Process mapping, but it is one that has proven to be simple yet effective for real-life situations.

8.3.1   Process Mapping Process (PoMP)

This section introduces a simple Process for Process mapping, known as PoMP (Process for Mapping Processes) which is, of course, defined using the "seven views" approach. For reasons of clarity, not all of the "seven views" are shown here. However, a full definition of the Processes can be found in Appendix E.

8.3.1.1   PoMP – Process Structure View

The process structure view will be a subset of the MBSE Ontology with a focus on Process (shown in Figure 7.2) that is used in this book.

8.3.1.2 PoMP – Requirement Context View

The first View that will be considered here will be the 'Requirement Context View' that will look at why we are defining the Process mapping Process in the first place. This is realised in the *use case diagram* (Figure 8.8).

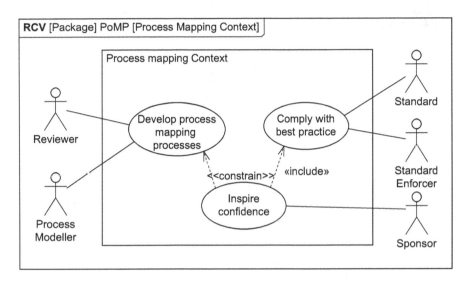

Figure 8.8 PoMP – Requirement Context View

The diagram in Figure 8.8 shows a simple Requirement Context View for a mapping Process. Note that one of the main *use cases* is stated quite simply as 'Develop process mapping processes' which has two *actors* associated with it – the 'Process Modeller' which represents the person or group of people who will be developing the Process and the 'Reviewer'. There is one single constraint on this *use case*, which is to 'Inspire confidence' and is related to the 'Sponsor' and the 'Standard Enforcer'. In this case, the exercise is being carried out at the request of Sponsors who require some confidence that their processes map onto the relevant standards, shown as the 'Comply with best practice' use case. The 'Standard Enforcer' is involved as any mapping that is produced and any compliance issues discovered will need to be approved by the appropriate authority. The 'Standard' represents the model to be mapped against.

8.3.1.3 PoMP – Stakeholder View

The Stakeholder View can be abstracted from the *actors* that were identified in the Requirement Context View, and then arranged into a classification hierarchy, as shown in Figure 8.9.

The diagram in Figure 8.9 identifies the Stakeholder Roles that are relevant to the Project. These Stakeholder Roles are consistent with the *actors* on the Process Context View and also the names that govern each swim lane in the

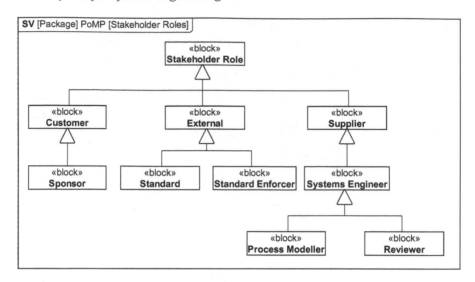

Figure 8.9   PoMP – Stakeholder View

Process Behaviour View. The Stakeholder Roles that have been identified are as follows:

–   'Sponsor' – the role of the Person or Organisation who is paying for the Process mapping exercise, maybe as part of an audit or assessment.
–   'Standard Enforcer' – the role of the Person or people who will be carrying out the audit or assessment. In the case of an audit, these people will be independent of the target Organisation or, in the case of an assessment, these people may be either internal or external to the target Organisation.
–   'Process Modeller' – the role of the Person or people who are defining the Process mapping approach.
–   'Standard' – this represents the role of the source Standard. It may seem a little odd to have a Standard as a Stakeholder Role but it meets all the requirements of being one – it is outside the boundary of the System and has an interest in the Project.
–   'Reviewer' – the role of the Person or people who are responsible for the review Activities in the Process.

Now that the Context and the Stakeholder Roles have been identified, it is time to look at the actual Processes that need to be defined in order to meet the original Needs.

8.3.1.4   PoMP – Process Content View

The Process Content View for process mapping consists initially of three Processes as shown in Figure 8.10.

The diagram in Figure 8.10 shows the Process Content View that identifies the Processes that have been created along with their relevant Artefacts (represented by *properties*) and Activities (represented by *operations*). These are the three Processes that will be executed in order to meet the *use cases* from Figure 8.8.

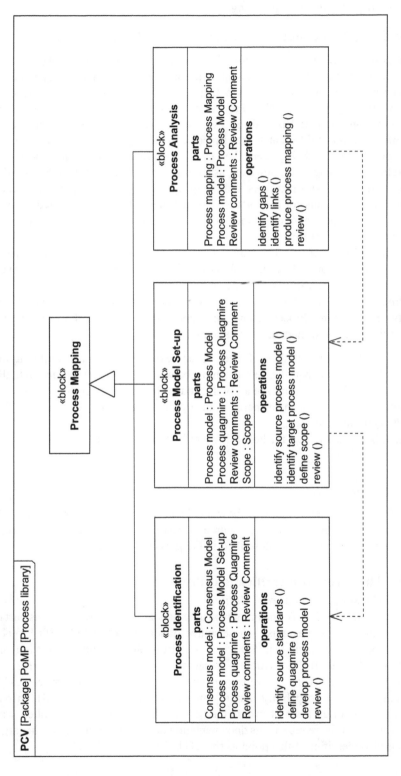

Figure 8.10   PoMP – Process Content View

The three processes that have been identified are described as follows:

−　'Process Identification'. The aim of this process is to identify all the relevant source Processes that are applicable to the mapping exercise. The source Processes here are the Processes that are being assessed against. One of the main outputs here is the 'Process quagmire' which is a variation of the Information View and is realised by a *block definition diagram* where each *block* represents a different source Process. In the situation where only a single source Standard is being used, then this quagmire is quite simple (more of a puddle than a quagmire); however, as soon as more than one source Standard is used, the complexity increases and the quagmire becomes deeper and deeper. The Process models for each source Process are also either identified (if they already exist) or generated (if they do not exist). Note that the target Processes is also identified at this point.

−　'Process Model Set-up'. The main aim of this Process is to define the scope of the assessment or audit (which Processes in the target Process will be evaluated) and then to identify the relevant parts of each source Process.

−　' Process Analysis'. The aim of this process is to actually perform the mapping between the source Processes and the target Process. This involves looking for both links between them as well as gaps.

In terms of the way that these Processes are executed, they are quite tightly coupled. This means that the relationships between the Processes are actually *dependencies* and, hence, does not allow for much freedom in terms of variation of execution. This can be seen in the diagram by the *dependency* relationships that exist between the Processes.

The full Process model for PoMP is described in Appendix F and shows all of the remaining Views.

8.3.2　Using PoMP

This section provides an example of how the PoMP Processes may be executed. In this example, there are a number of source Standards and a single target Process, which is STUMPI, which was described in the previous chapter.

8.3.2.1　The 'Process Identification' Process

The 'identify source standards' Activity

This Activity aims to identify one or more source standards that will be used as part of the compliance mapping exercise. These source standards will include ISO 15504 – software process assessment [6], ISO 15288 – software and systems life cycle management [2], ISO 9001:2008 Quality management systems – Requirements [3], ISO/IEC 12207 Systems and software engineering – software life cycle processes [4] and, finally, CMMI – capability maturity model integration [5] (CMMI). In real projects, there is often a set of pre-defined standards that must be complied with provided as part of the requirements documentation or project description. The target Process is also identified at this point as the STUMPI Process Model.

The 'define quagmire' Activity

The quagmire identifies any related Standards or Processes that may have an influence on the Process mapping exercise. The quagmire has been constructed and is shown in Figure 8.11.

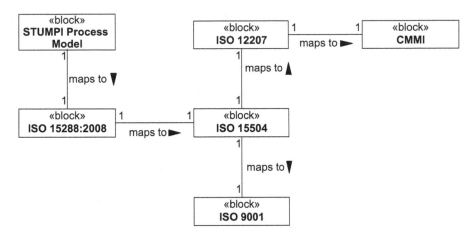

Figure 8.11   Process quagmire

The diagram in Figure 8.11 shows a Process quagmire for the exercise, where 'ISO 15288:2008' maps to 'ISO 15504' which maps to both 'ISO 12207' and 'ISO 9001'. Also, 'ISO 12207' maps to 'CMMI'. The target Process is also shown here, as 'STUMPI Process Model' that maps to 'ISO 15288:2008'.

For the sake of clarity and brevity, the purpose of this exercise is to focus on the relationship between 'STUMPI Process Model' (the target) and 'ISO 15288:2008' (one of the sources). If this exercise was taken further, it would be possible to provide a full mapping between all of these standards based on the relationships between them in the quagmire.

The 'develop process model' Activity

In this Activity, any necessary Process models will be produced. The two main Views that will be used as a basis for the basic Process mapping are the Process Structure View and the Process Content View. The purpose of producing the Process Structure Views is to provide a basis for mapping terminology between the source and target Processes. The purpose of producing the Process Content Views is to provide a basis of mapping between the Processes and their relevant parts (Activities, Artefacts and Stakeholder Roles) between the source and target Processes.

The diagram in Figure 8.12 shows the Process Structure View for both the source (ISO 15288 – shown on the left) and target Process (STUMPI – shown on the right). There are some immediate similarities in terms of the patterns of *blocks* in the diagram and also in terms of the names that are being used. These will be discussed later when the 'Process Analysis' Process is executed.

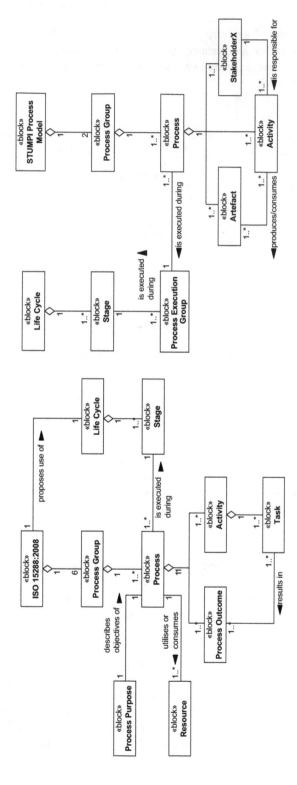

Figure 8.12 Showing compliance of the Ontologies using the Process Structure View

Along with the main concepts that are shown here, it is also possible to drop down a level of detail and examine the two concepts of 'Process Group' that exist in each Process model using the Process Content View.

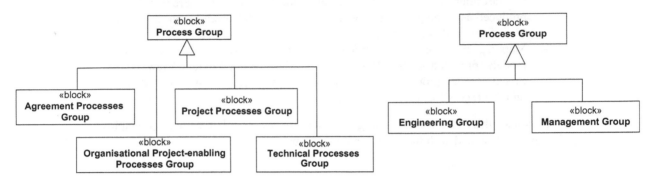

Figure 8.13   Compliance of process groups using the Process Content View

The diagram in Figure 8.13 shows part of the Process Content View for both the source and target Processes. This is not the entire Process Content View but is the subset of the target Process model that will be defined by the scope. Again, the basic patterns look quite different, but this will be explored during the 'Process analysis' process.

The 'review' Activity
At this point, there would be a review of the Artefacts that have been produced so far in the process. Once this review has been completed satisfactorily, the next process can be invoked.

8.3.2.2   The 'Process Model set-up' Process
The 'identify source process model' Activity
Based on the Process quagmire, the source Process model has been identified as 'ISO 15288 – software and systems life cycle management'. Depending on the number of process models involved, this activity may be almost trivial, as in this example. This is because there is only a single mapping being investigated. In the situation where there are many process mapping being investigated, this activity becomes more complex.

The 'identify target process model' Activity
Based on the Process quagmire, the target Process model has been identified as 'STUMPI Process Model'. Again, in this example, this Activity is quite trivial.

The 'define scope' Activity
The next step is to look at the target Process model and to identify which elements of the terminology will be mapped and which Processes are to be involved in the

mapping exercise. For the sake of brevity for this example, the exercise will be limited to:

– Mapping between the terminology used in both process models, provided by the development of the Process Structure Views in the Process Model, produced as an output of the 'develop process model' Activity on the Process Identification Process.
– Mapping between the requirements-related processes in the two process models, provided by the development of the Process Content Views in the Process Model, produced as an output of the 'develop process model' Activity on the Process Identification Process.

Of course, this scope will be far larger in a real-life scenario, but the main principles may be illustrated with the very limited scope presented here.

The 'review' Activity

As with many Processes, there is a review Activity at the end of the Process that must be passed before progress can be made to the next Process form the Process Instance View.

8.3.2.3   The 'Process analysis' Process

The 'identify gaps' Activity

This Activity will use the information in Figure 8.12 to try to identify any gaps in the mapping between the two Standards. Therefore, the question that will be asked will be 'are there any features of the source Process model that do not map onto the target Process model' and vice versa.

The 'identify links' Activity

This Activity will use the information in Figure 8.12 to try to identify any links in the mapping between the source and target. Therefore, the question that will be asked will be 'for each feature of the target Process model, which features of the source Process model map onto it'.

The 'produce process mapping' Activity

This is the Activity where the actual results of the previous two Activities are recorded. This can be done using any appropriate mechanism and simple tables will be used here to capture the results. This mapping will occur at different levels.

The information in Table 8.1 shows the basic mapping between the two views shown in Figure 8.12. This highlights the differences in the basic language being used in both source and target. At this level there are several one-to-one mappings along with some minor inconsistencies and one non-mapped concept.

The same approach to mapping may be carried out at the next level down, by looking at the types of 'Process Group'.

The information in Table 8.2 shows the mapping between the two Views shown in Figure 8.13. This establishes the mapping between the terms used for the Process Groups.

Table 8.1   Basic terminology mapping

ISO 15288 (source)	STUMPI (target)	Comment
Process Group	Process Group	*Exact match of terminology and concepts*
Process	Process	*Exact match of terminology and concepts*
Process Outcome	Artefact	*'Process Outcome' and 'Artefact' are not directly analogous, although they are related. Artefacts and deliverables of the process contribute towards achieving the overall outcome that is defined in ISO 15288*
Activity	Activity	*Match of terminology and concepts, although 'Activity' in ISO 15288 is described at a higher level and has its details defined by one or more 'Task'*
Task		*There is no analogous concept for 'Task' in STUMPI, but a mapping will exist between the tasks in ISO 15288 and the description of activities in STUMPI*
Life Cycle	Life Cycle	*Exact match of terminology and concepts*
Stage	Stage	*Exact match of terminology and concepts*
Purpose		*There is no analogous concept for 'Purpose' in STUMPI, but a property of 'Stage' is 'Purpose' that provides the mapping*
Resource		*There is no analogous concept for 'Resource' in STUMPI*

Table 8.2   Process grouping terminology mapping

ISO 15288 Process Group (source)	STUMPI Process Group (target)	Comment
Agreement Processes Group		*No mapping*
Organisational Project-enabling Processes Group		*No mapping*
Project Processes Group	Management Group	*Mapping exists – specifically, the mapping is from STUMPI to the 'Project Management Process'*
Technical Processes Group	Engineering Group	*Mapping exists*

The next step is to look at the Processes that exist within the Process Groups. Remember that the scope of this mapping exercise is limited to the requirements-related Processes. These Processes exist in the 'Technical Processes Group' in ISO 15288 (source) and in the 'Engineering Group' in STUMPI (target). Therefore, the following table is limited to only investigating these Processes. Care must be exercised, however, as it was highlighted earlier in Figure 8.12 that there is an extra level of detail in the ISO 15288 process model when it comes to describing Processes, which is shown in Table 8.3.

Table 8.3 Process terminology mapping

ISO 15288 (source)		STUMPI Activity (target)	Comment
Requirements Analysis Process		**Stakeholder Requirements**	
Activity	**Task**		
Define systems requirements	Define functional boundary of system	Analyse requirements	Part of defining the context if a model-based approach is adopted
	Define each system function	Analyse requirements	Part of defining the use cases as part of the context if a model-based approach is adopted
	Define implementation constraints	Analyse requirements	Part of defining the use cases as part of the context if a model-based approach is adopted
	Define technical and quality metrics		*Not covered*
	Specify requirements/functions that relate to critical qualities	Analyse requirements	Part of defining the use cases as part of the context if a model-based approach is adopted
Analyse and maintain system requirements	Analyse integrity of system requirements	Analyse requirements	Part of analysing use cases in the context if a model-based approach is adopted
	Feedback analysed requirements	Review	Customer involvement in the review
	Demonstrate traceability between system/stakeholder requirements		*Not covered*
	Maintain system requirements		
Stakeholder Requirements Definition Process		**Stakeholder Requirements**	
Activity	**Task**		
Elicit stakeholder requirements	Identify stakeholders	Identify stakeholders	Part of defining a stakeholder view if a model-based approach is adopted
	Elicit stakeholder requirements	Elicit requirements	Initial list of requirements
Define stakeholder requirements	Define solution constraints	Analyse requirements	Part of analysing use cases in the context if a model-based approach is adopted
	Define activity sequences	Define acceptance criteria	Part of defining scenarios if a model-based approach is adopted
	Identify user/system interactions	Define acceptance criteria	Part of defining scenarios if a model-based approach is adopted
	Specify requirements and functions relating to critical qualities	Analyse requirements	Part of analysing use cases in the context if a model-based approach is adopted
Analyse and maintain stakeholder requirements	Analyse elicited requirements	Analyse requirements	Part of analysing use cases in the context if a model-based approach is adopted
	Resolve requirements problem	Analyse requirements	Part of analysing use cases in the context if a model-based approach is adopted
	Feedback analysed requirements	Review	Customer involvement in the review
	Confirm stakeholder requirements	Review	Customer involvement in the review
	Record stakeholder requirements	Produce stakeholder requirements document	
	Maintain requirements traceability		*Not covered*

The information in Table 8.3 shows the mapping between the process terms that are being used in the source and target. Note where there are gaps in the mapping and also the many cases where more explanation is required. This could be because the target Process model, in this case STUMPI, is defined at a very high level (which is the case) or it could be because the target process does simply not comply with the source Process.

Notice that a lot of the comments here relate to the qualifier of 'if a model-based approach is adopted'. This is particularly interesting as there is a model-based approach that is advocated in Chapter 9, known as the Approach to Context-based Requirements Engineering, or ACRE. One of the claims made by ACRE is that its View-based approach can be used with a number of different Processes. If this is the case, then surely the ACRE views can be mapped to the STUMPI which should answer the queries raised above. This is taken further in Chapter 15 where a more complex mapping is explored.

The 'review' Activity
Once more, there is a review Activity before the process is completed.

8.3.3   Summary

This section has discussed how Process modelling can be used as an enabler for compliance mapping between any two or more Processes or Standards. The examples used here were the STUMPI as the target, which was introduced in Chapter 7, and ISO 15288 as the source that was introduced earlier in this chapter.

8.4   Expanded Process modelling – competence

One of the main themes of this book is stressing the importance of 'People, Process and Tools' and, clearly, the previous chapter dealt extensively with modelling Processes. This Process modelling may be extended to include extra views that allow Competence to be modelled.

For a full definition of the Processes that relate to competency assessment, including Competency Frameworks, see Chapter 14, Annex F and Annex G.

8.4.1   The expanded MBSE Ontology

The MBSE Ontology already includes elements that represent competence and its related concepts and terms. The subset of the MBSE Ontology identified for model-based process engineering has its scope expanded and is shown in Figure 8.14.

The diagram here shows the MBSE Ontology expanded to include concepts relating to Competence. These concepts have already been covered in detail in Chapter 3 and are expanded upon on in Chapter 14, so no further discussion will be entered into here.

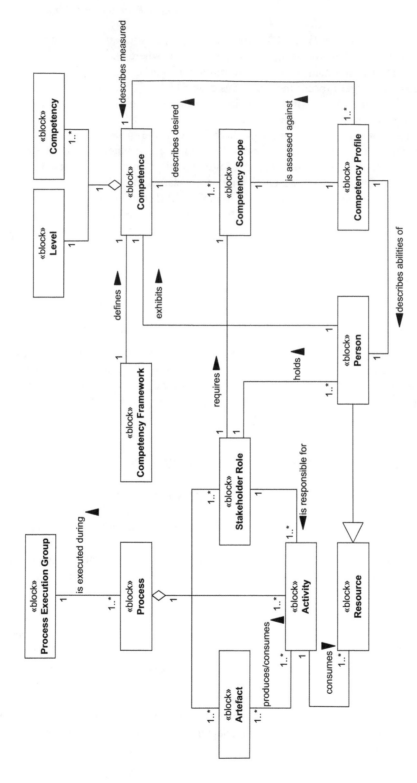

Figure 8.14 Expanded MBSE Ontology focussed on Competence

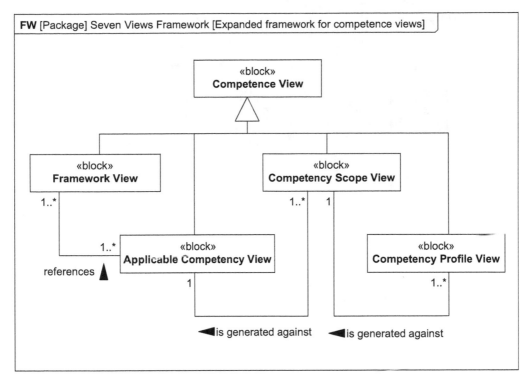

Figure 8.15 The Framework Views for Competence

8.4.2 The Framework

Four new Views associated with Competence are shown in the diagram in Figure 8.15.

The diagram here shows that there are four types of 'Competence View' that have been identified: the 'Framework View', the 'Applicable Competency View', 'Competency Scope View' and the 'Competency Profile View' both of which are described in the next four sections.

8.4.3 Views

8.4.3.1 The Framework View

View rationale

The main aim of the Framework View is to provide an understanding of any source Frameworks that are intended to be used as part of the competency assessment exercise. The Framework View is composed of a number of models of source frameworks that can then be mapped to a generic framework.

View definition

The elements of the MBSE Ontology that are concerned with the 'Framework View' are highlighted in the diagram in Figure 8.16.

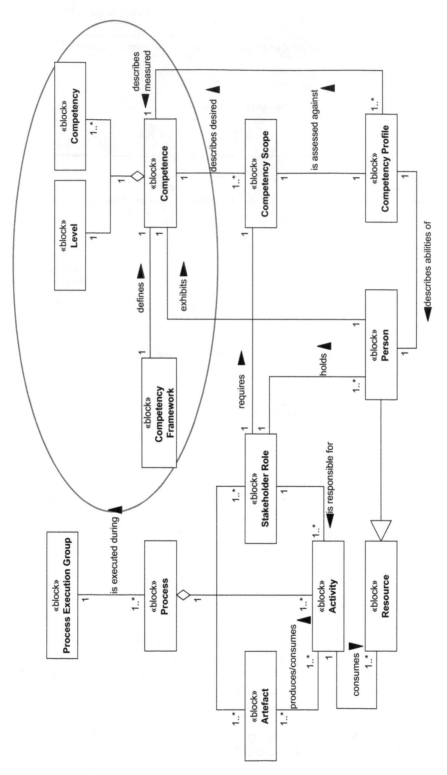

Figure 8.16 View definition for Framework View

Figure 8.16 shows that the main element that is of interest for the 'Framework View' is the 'Competency Framework'. As the 'Competency Framework' defines one or more 'Competence', this is also of interest.

View relationships
The Framework View is mainly related to the 'Applicable Competency View' as this is actually a subset of the 'Framework View' and references the frameworks in it.

View visualisation
The Framework View may be visualised by a SysML *block definition diagram* as shown in the diagram in Figure 8.17.

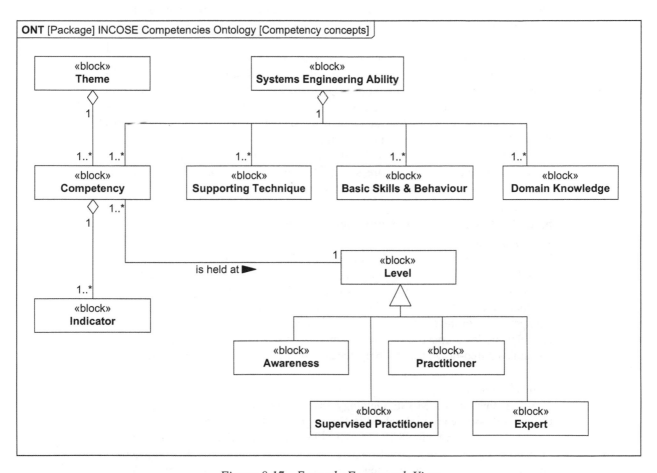

Figure 8.17   Example Framework View

The diagram in Figure 8.17 shows a 'Framework View' for a specific competency framework, in this case the INCOSE Systems Engineering Competencies Framework [8]. The 'Framework View' is essentially an Ontology for a specific Competency Framework. This may then be used as a basis for generating the 'Applicable Competency View' and, hence, for traceability back to source Competency Frameworks.

The following Rule apply to the 'Framework View':

–   The 'Applicable Competency View' must be a subset of one or more of the frameworks contained in the 'Framework View'.

This relationship may be used as a basis for process automation.

View discussion

The Framework View is an Ontology for a specific Competency Framework. One or more of these Views may then be used as the basis for generating the Applicable Competency View which forms the basis of a competency assessment exercise.

When analysing any Competency Framework, we can actually employ the "seven views" approach to create the models. With this in mind, the creation of a Framework View may be thought of as generating the Process Structure View and the Process Content View, where the Process Structure View would show the Ontology and the Process Content View would show the detail of the Competencies that make up the Competency Framework.

Again, notice how we are using the same techniques, in this case the "seven views" approach, for different areas of modelling which increases the value of the model and the techniques we use to create them.

8.4.3.2   The Applicable Competency View

View rationale

The main aim of the Applicable Competency View is to define a subset of one or more Competencies that are applicable for a particular Organisation unit. When we create models of Competency Frameworks, it allows us to understand the specific Competencies and the relationships between them. In almost all cases, the set of Competencies in the source Framework will be greater than the Competencies that are relevant for a specific business; therefore, the Applicable Competency View contains a pared-down set of Competencies from one or more source Framework.

View definition

The elements of the MBSE Ontology that are concerned with the Applicable Competency View are highlighted in the diagram in Figure 8.18.

The diagram in Figure 8.18 shows the elements of the MBSE Ontology that are of interest for the 'Applicable Competency View'. A set of one of 'Competence' and, hence one or more 'Competency' and 'Level' are defined as part of this View.

View relationships

The 'Applicable Competency View' is related to both the 'Framework View' and the 'Competency Scope View'. The 'Framework View' provides the source Competencies that make up the 'Applicable Competency View'. The 'Competency Scope

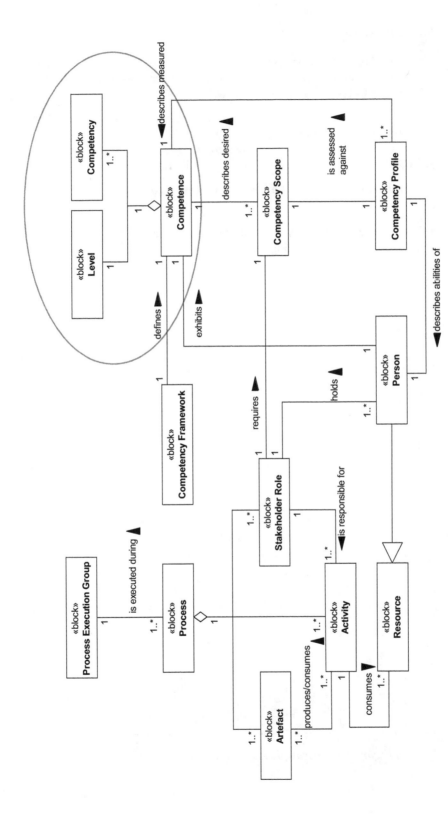

Figure 8.18 Definition of the Applicable Competency View

View' takes the 'Applicable Competency View' and defines the Levels, Evidence Types, and so on that are required for the input to a competency assessment exercise. The following Rules apply to the 'Framework View':

–   The 'Applicable Competency View' must be a subset of one or more of the frameworks contained in the 'Framework View'.
–   The 'Competency Scope View' must be a copy of the 'Applicable Competency View' that has the Levels and Evidence Types defined.

These relationships may be used as a basis for process automation.

View visualisation

The Applicable Competency View is visualised using a simple table, an example of which is shown in the diagram in Figure 8.19.

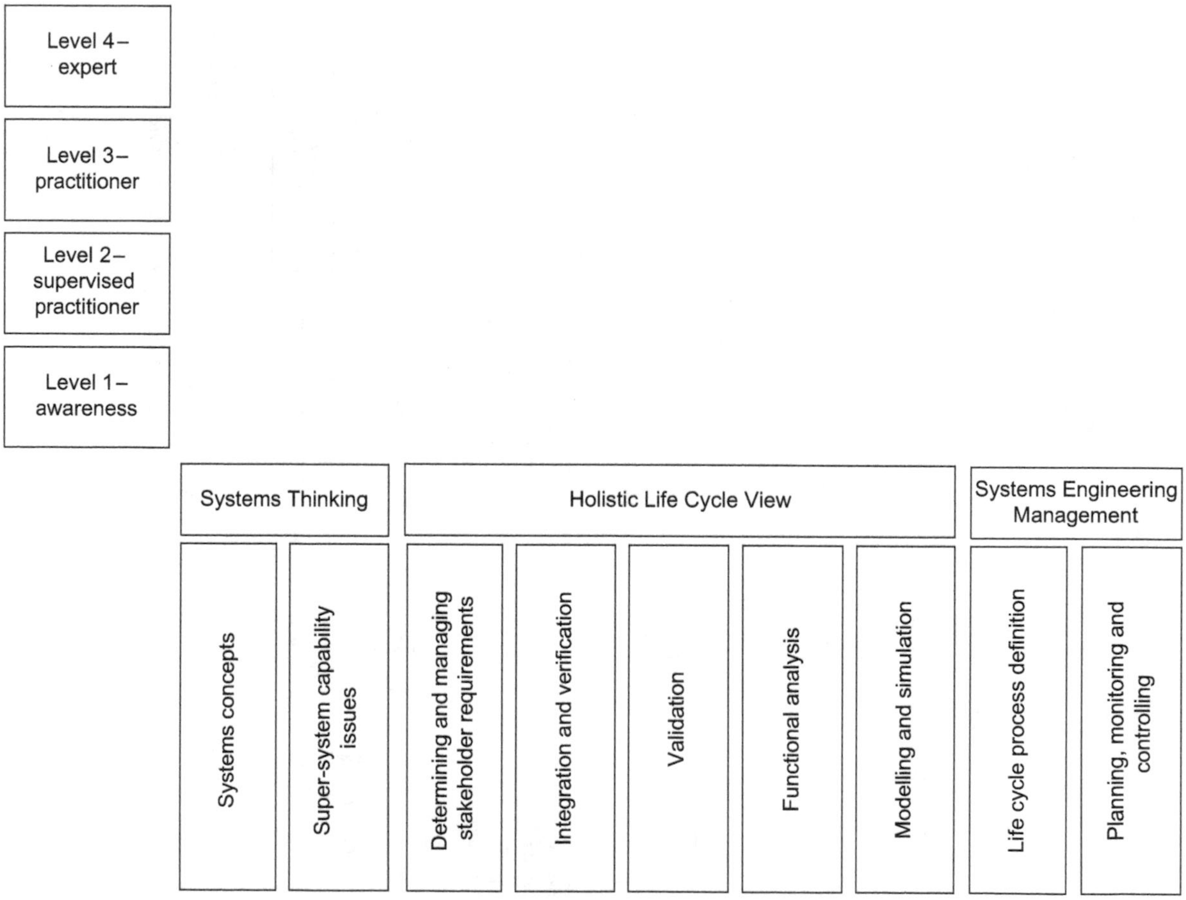

Figure 8.19   Example Applicable Competency View

The diagram in Figure 8.19 shows an example of an 'Applicable Competency Set'. The view itself is a table where the horizontal axis shows one or more 'Competency Area' and their component 'Competency'. The vertical axis shows the one or more 'Level' that has been defined. This vertical axis does not need to be shown here as the Levels do not form any part of the Applicable Competency Set, but it does make life simpler when the Competency Scope if defined as the same table may be used. In this case, the 'Applicable Competency View' is based on the example MBSE Competency Framework that is described in Appendix G.

View discussion

Possibly the first thing to notice about this view is that it is not visualised using SysML. It is possible to show this View using, for example, a *block definition diagram* but the simple table is more straightforward and intuitive to understand. As has been discussed previously in this book, the notation used to visualise any View is not restricted to SysML; however, the View must be consistent with the rest of the model. In this example, it can be seen clearly that both axes of the table relate directly to elements in the MBSE Ontology, hence it is consistent with the rest of the model.

8.4.3.3 The Competency Scope View

View rationale

The Competency Scope View is concerned with identifying and defining a Competency Scope for a specific Stakeholder Role. This is needed as the main input to any competency assessment exercise and provides a definition of the required Competencies and the Levels at which they must be held. This is covered in far greater detail in Chapter 14.

View definition

The areas of the MBSE Ontology that are of specific interest for the 'Competency Scope View' are shown in the diagram in Figure 8.20.

The diagram here shows that the areas of the Ontology that are of specific interest are the 'Competency Scope' that describes the desired 'Competence' for a specific 'Stakeholder Role'. The 'Competence' is defined in terms of one or more 'Competency' along with the 'Level' at which it is held.

View relationships

It can be seen that one or more 'Competency Profile View' shows the output of an assessment against a 'Competency Scope View'. The 'Competency Scope View' is also related to the 'Applicable Competency View' as it is generated against it – the Competency Scope is based entirely on the applicable competency set.

The following Rules apply to the 'Framework View':

– The 'Competency Scope View' must be a copy of the 'Applicable Competency View' that has the Levels and Evidence Types defined.
– The 'Competency Profile View' must have at least one 'Competency Scope View' that is created as a result of a competency assessment exercise.

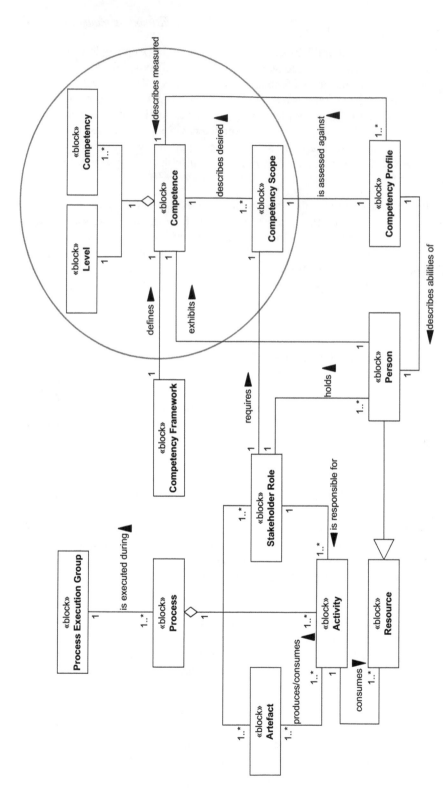

Figure 8.20 Definition of the Competency Scope View

These relationships may be used as a basis for process automation.

View visualisation
The 'Competency Scope View' is visualised using a simple table with shaded cells, as shown in the diagram in Figure 8.21.

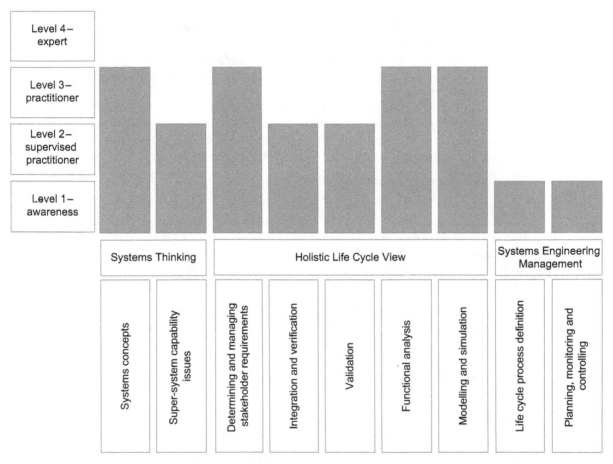

Figure 8.21 Example Competency Scope View showing the 'Requirements Engineer' Stakeholder Role

The first thing that stands out about the diagram here is that it is not realised using the SysML. As has been said several times in this book already, this is perfectly fine, provided that the view remains consistent with the Ontology, Framework and other Views in the model.

The relationships between the visual elements and the MBSE Ontology are as follows:

– The concept of the 'Level' is represented by a row on the table. Note that there are four rows – one for each of the four Levels that were defined on the MBSE Ontology.
– The concept of the 'Competency Area' is represented by the grouping of columns, shown as the last horizontal text on the table (e.g. 'Systems thinking'). Each of these groupings refers to one of the Competency Areas that was defined as part of the MBSE Ontology.
– Each individual 'Competency' is shown as a single column in the table, each of which corresponds to a 'Competency' in the MBSE Competency Framework and MBSE Ontology.
– Each of the cells is shaded to show at which Level each Competency must be assessed to. It is also possible to show extra information in these cells, such as 'Evidence Type', as discussed in Chapter 12. Of course, any additional information like this must be included on the Ontology that defines the view.

This is just one possible interpretation of how the View may be visualised.

View discussion

The 'Competency Scope View' allows the required Competencies for a specific Stakeholder Role to be defined. In terms of exactly what information goes into the View, this is up to the modeller. As has been discussed above, it is possible to keep the scope as simple as Levels and Competencies, but it is also possible to add more detail, for example:

– It is possible to show the Competency Areas that each Competency belongs to. Although in one sense this actually makes no difference to the Competency Scope itself, it can make a difference to how easy the Competency Scope is to read.
– Likewise, it may be desirable to show the Evidence Types that are acceptable for each Competency at each Level (the cells), in which case the Ontology would show the Evidence Types.

This is also an interesting view as it shows a non-SysML visualisation in the form of a table. It does not matter what notation is used to realise each view, provided that it is consistent with the model. The use of the 'Ontology, Framework, Views' approach allows the rigour of MBSE to be enforced regardless of the notation used.

In order to visualise any view, it is essential that the relevant elements from the MBSE Ontology can be realised in a consistent way. Therefore, provided that you can realise each element of the MBSE Ontology in at least one way, it is possible to retain the consistency of the model.

8.4.3.4   The Competency Profile View

View rationale

The Competency Scope View is concerned with identifying the Competencies and their associated Levels for a specific Stakeholder Role, whereas the 'Competency Profile View' is concerned with the actual competencies and the levels that have been measured for a Person. A simple way to think about the two is that the Competency Scope View is the main input to a competency assessment exercise, whereas the Competency Profile View is the output of such an exercise.

View definition

The areas of the MBSE Ontology that are of specific interest for the 'Competency Profile View' are shown in the diagram in Figure 8.22.

The diagram here shows that the elements of the MBSE Ontology that are important for this view are the 'Competency Profile' and its associated 'Competence'. The 'Competence' as in the previous view has two main elements that define it, the 'Competency' and its associated 'Level'. Note how the 'Competency Profile View' is associated with a 'Person' whereas the 'Competency Scope View' is associated with a 'Stakeholder Role'.

View relationships

There is a relationship between the 'Competency Scope View' that describes Competency Scopes and the 'Competency Profile View' that describes Competency Profiles. It can be seen from Figure 8.15 that one or more Competency Profile shows the output of an assessment against a Competency Scope.

These two Views are very closely related together, which is only to be expected as they both describe the concept of a 'Competence' but from two different points of view – one as desired 'Competence' for a 'Stakeholder Role' and the other as measured 'Competence' of a 'Person'.

The following Rules apply to 'Competency Profile View'.

– Each 'Competency Profile View' must be directly related to a single 'Competency Scope View'.
– Each 'Competency Profile View' must be directly related to a single instance of 'Person'.

These rules may be used as a basis for automation.

View visualisation

The diagram in Figure 8.23 shows a specific visualisation of the 'Competency Profile View', in this case using a non-SysML notation.

The first thing that stands out about the diagram here is that, as in the previous view, it is not realised using the SysML.

The relationships between the visual elements and the MBSE model are as follows:

– The concept of the 'Level' is represented by a row on the table. Note that there are four rows – one for each of the four Levels that were defined on the MBSE Ontology.
– The concept of the 'Competency Area' is represented by the grouping of columns, shown as the last horizontal text on the table ('Systems thinking', etc). Each of these groupings refers to one of the Competency Areas that was defined as part of the MBSE Ontology.

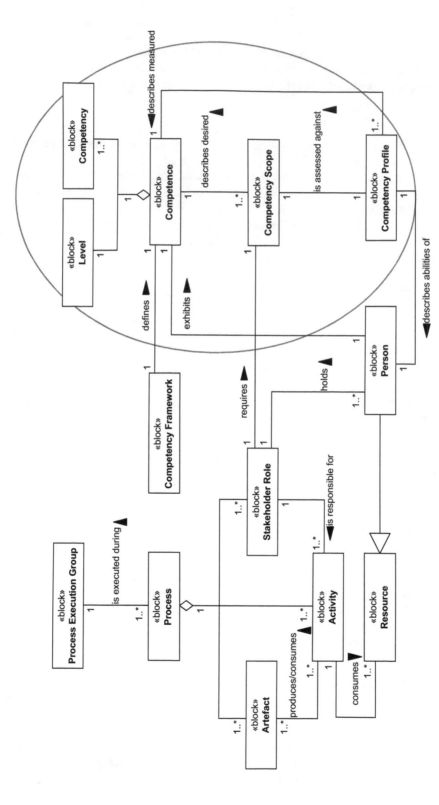

Figure 8.22   Definition of the Competency Profile View

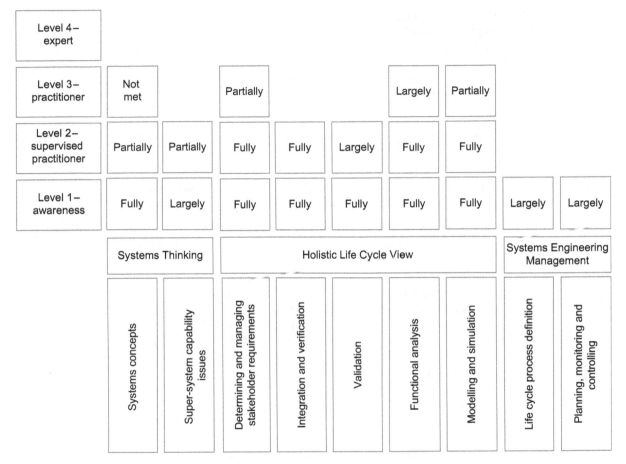

Level 4–expert									
Level 3–practitioner	Not met		Partially			Largely	Partially		
Level 2–supervised practitioner	Partially	Partially	Fully	Fully	Largely	Fully	Fully		
Level 1–awareness	Fully	Largely	Fully	Fully	Fully	Fully	Fully	Largely	Largely
	Systems Thinking		Holistic Life Cycle View					Systems Engineering Management	
	Systems concepts	Super-system capability issues	Determining and managing stakeholder requirements	Integration and verification	Validation	Functional analysis	Modelling and simulation	Life cycle process definition	Planning, monitoring and controlling

Figure 8.23   Example 'Competency Profile View' showing the 'Requirements Engineer' Stakeholder Role

- Each individual 'Competency' is shown as a single column in the table, each of which corresponds to a 'Competency' in the MBSE Competency Framework and Ontology.
- Each of the cells is shaded to show at which level each Competency was assessed to as part of the assessment – the 'Competency Scope View' in fact.
- The actual levels that were achieved are shown as the thick black line that shows the actual profile. All competency levels shown with a level rating in the cell demonstrate the actual granulated score for the Competency.

This is just one possible interpretation of how the view may be visualised.

View discussion
The Competency Profile View is interesting as it shows all of the information that have been shown on the 'Competency Scope View', and it also shows extra

information concerning the result of the assessment. This may be thought of as overlaying the results of the assessment over the original scope, which can be very useful for gap analysis. For a full discussion on how to interpret and use this view, see Chapter 14.

Again, this view uses a non-SysML notation for its visualisation, so the same discussion points as raised above will apply.

8.5   Expanded Process modelling – Life Cycle modelling

Processes have an inherent relationship with Life Cycles, but the nature of this relationship and, indeed, the nature of Life Cycles are often misunderstood. There are many different types of Life Cycle that exist, including, but not limited to:

- Project Life Cycles. Project Life Cycles are perhaps, along with Product Life Cycles, one of the most obvious examples of applications of Life Cycles. We tend to have rigid definitions of the terminal conditions of a Project, such as start and end dates, time scales, budgets and resources and so a Project Life Cycle is one that many people will be able to identify with.
- Product Life Cycles. Again, another quite obvious one is to consider the Life Cycle of a Product. It is relatively simple to visualise the conception, development, production, use and support and disposal of a Product.
- Programme Life Cycles. Most Projects will exist in some sort of higher-level Programme. Each of the Programmes will also have its own Life Cycle and, clearly, this will have some constraint on the Life Cycles of all Projects that are contained within it.
- System procurement Life Cycles. Some Systems may have a procurement Life Cycle that applies to them. From a business point of view, this may be a better way to view a Product, or set of Products, than looking at the Product Life Cycle alone.
- Technology Life Cycles. Any technology will have a Life Cycle. For example, in the world of home computers, the accepted norm for removable storage was magnetic tapes. This was then succeeded by magnetic discs, then optical discs, then solid-state devices and then virtual storage. Each of these technologies has its own Life Cycle.
- Equipment Life Cycles. Each and every piece of equipment will have its own Life Cycle. This may start before the equipment is actually acquired and may end when the equipment has been safely retired. Stages of the equipment life cycle may describe its current condition, such as whether the equipment is in use, working well, degrading and so on.
- Business Life Cycle. The business itself will have a Life Cycle. In some cases, the main driver of the business may be to remain in business for several years and then to sell it on. Stages of the Life Cycle may include expansion or growth, steady states, controlled degradation and so on.

These different types of Life Cycle not only exist, but often interact in complex ways. Also, each of these Life Cycles will control the way that Processes are executed during each Stage in the Life Cycle.

8.5.1   The expanded MBSE Ontology

The MBSE Ontology already includes elements that represent Life Cycles and its related concepts and terms. The subset of the MBSE Ontology that has been identified for model-based process engineering has its scope expanded and is shown in Figure 8.24.

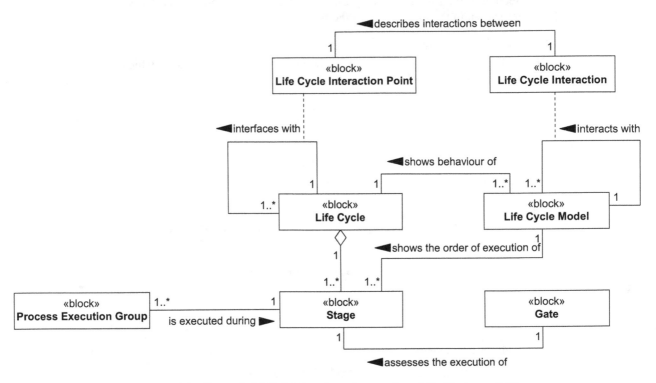

Figure 8.24   Expanded MBSE Ontology focussed on Life Cycle modelling

The diagram here shows the MBSE Ontology expanded to include concepts relating the Life Cycles. These Ontology Elements are defined as:

— 'Life Cycle' – a set of one or more 'Stage' that can be used to describe the evolution of 'System', 'Project', etc. over time.
— 'Life Cycle Model' – the execution of a set of one or more 'Stage' that shows the behaviour of a 'Life Cycle'.
— 'Stage' – a period within a 'Life Cycle' that relates to its realisation through one or more 'Process Execution Group'. The success of a 'Stage' is assessed by a 'Gate'.
— 'Gate' – a mechanism for assessing the success or failure of the execution of a 'Stage'.
— 'Life Cycle Interface Point – the point in a 'Life Cycle' where one or more 'Life Cycle Interaction' will occur.

-    'Life Cycle Interaction' – the point during a 'Life Cycle Model' at which they interact, which will be reflected in the way that one or more 'Stage' interact with each other.
-    'Process Execution Group' – an ordered execution of one or more 'Process' that is performed as part of a 'Stage'.

This section of the MBSE Ontology forms the basis of the content of all the Views that are shown in the Framework in the following section.

8.5.1.1   The Framework

The MBSE Process Life Cycle Framework comprises four main Views which are shown in the diagram in Figure 8.25.

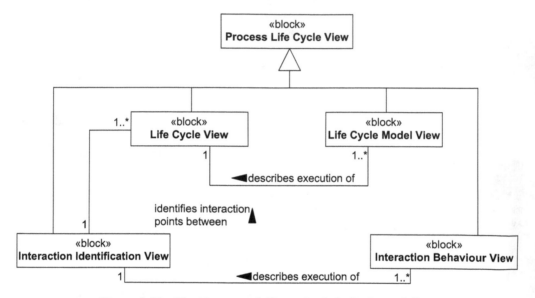

Figure 8.25   The Framework Views for Life Cycle modelling

The diagram here shows that there are four main views:

-    The 'Life Cycle View', which identifies one or more 'Stage' that exists in the 'Life Cycle'.
-    The 'Life Cycle Model View', which describes how each 'Stage' behaves in relation to one or more other 'Stage'.
-    The 'Life Cycle Interaction View', which identifies one or more 'Life Cycle Interaction Point' between one or more 'Life Cycle'.
-    The 'Life Cycle Model Interaction View', which shows the behaviour of each 'Life Cycle Interaction Point' in relation to one or more other 'Life Cycle Interaction Point' as identified in the previous view.

Each of these Views will now be described and discussed in the subsequent sections.

8.5.1.2   The Life Cycle View

View rationale

The aim of the Life Cycle View is to simply identify one or more Stage that may exist within a specific Life Cycle.

It should be stressed that this is a structural View and does not contain any behaviour – it simply identifies the Stages. This is very important as there is often a lot of confusion between the concepts of a Life Cycle and the concept of a Life Cycle Model. For the purposes of this book, the difference is as follows:

– A Life Cycle is a structural construct that shows one or more Stage that makes up a Life Cycle.
– A Life Cycle Model is a behaviour construct that shows how one or more Stage behaves within the execution of a Life Cycle.

Indeed, as was shown in Chapter 3, several standards and source references use these two terms interchangeably.

View definition

The elements of the MBSE Ontology that are concerned with Life Cycle modelling are highlighted in the diagram in Figure 8.26.

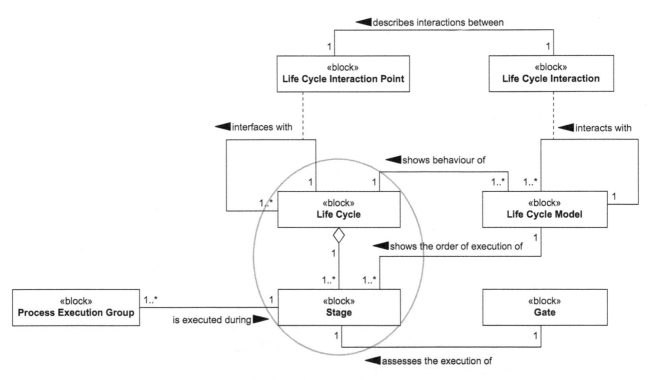

Figure 8.26   Definition of Life Cycle View

The diagram here shows that the elements that are of interest for the 'Life Cycle View' are the 'Life Cycle' itself and one or more 'Stage'. This view is a relatively simple view that shows the structure of a 'Life Cycle'.

View relationship

The Life Cycle View is strongly related to two of the other views. The Life Cycle View identifies the Stages that exist in the Life Cycle, whereas the Life Cycle Model View shows the execution of these Stages. The Life Cycle View may be thought of as the structural view of the Life Cycle, whereas the Life Cycle Model View may be thought of as the behaviour; therefore, the two are very strongly linked.

The Interaction Identification View shows the points at which a number of Life Cycles interact and, therefore, uses information from the Life Cycle View.

The following Rules apply to the Life Cycle View:

– The 'Life Cycle View' must consist of at least one 'Stage'.
– Each 'Life Cycle Model View' must be based on a Life Cycle View that shows the Stages.
– Each 'Life Cycle Interaction Point' must relate to a 'Stage' or 'Gate' from the 'Life Cycle View'.

These relationships may be used as a basis for process automation.

View visualisation

The Life Cycle View may be realised in SysML using a *block definition diagram*, an example of which is shown in the diagram in Figure 8.27.

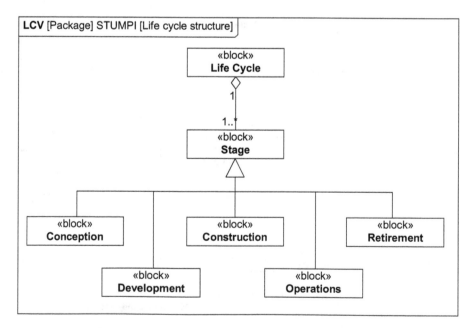

Figure 8.27   Example Life Cycle View for STUMPI

The diagram here shows the 'Life Cycle View' for the STUMPI Process Model that was introduced in Chapter 7. This view uses *blocks* to represent both the Life Cycle and its associated one or more Stage. Here a *block* has been used to explicitly show the concept of a Stage and then its associated Stages are shown as *specialisations*. This may also be shown without the Stage *block* by using SysML *stereotypes*.

View discussion

The Life Cycle View is an essential view for any real-life Projects. One of the biggest problems concerning Life Cycles is the lack of appreciation of the different types of Life Cycle that exist. For example, many people will just use the term life cycle without providing any real context to it. The danger here is that everyone will agree that they understand the term, but each person may very well have a different idea about what it exactly means. The Project Life Cycle and Product Life Cycle are very often confused but very often do not even reflect the same time frames, and one may exist within the other. Consider the example of a passenger train – the typical time to develop a train may be two years, whereas its in-service life may last up to 30 years. This means that the Product Life Cycle may be spread over 32 years, whereas there will be many, many Project Life Cycles that exist within it. There will not only be the original development Project, but also maintenance projects, upgrades, etc.

Another important aspect of Life Cycles to be clear about is the difference between the Life Cycle and the Life Cycle Model – one is structural and the other behavioural, which will be discussed in more detail in the next section.

8.5.1.3   The Life Cycle Model View

View rationale

The aim of the Life Cycle Model View is to show the potential behaviour of the execution of Stages that have been identified in the Life Cycle View. The Life Cycle Model View is a behavioural view, whereas the Life Cycle View is structural.

The Life Cycle Model View may be used to specify required behaviour of a Life Cycle, predicted anticipated behaviour or actual behaviour.

View definition

The elements of the MBSE Ontology that are concerned with Life Cycle modelling are highlighted in the diagram in Figure 8.28.

The 'Life Cycle Model View' is concerned with examining the execution of the 'Stage' and 'Gate' that make up the Life Cycle.

View relationships

The Life Cycle Model View is very strongly related to the Life Cycle View as it shows one or more behaviours for each Life Cycle. Each Stage and Gate shown on the Life Cycle Model View is actually an instance based on the elements in the Life Cycle.

The Life Cycle Model View is also closely related to the Interaction Behaviour View that effectively combines elements of one or more Life Cycle Model View.

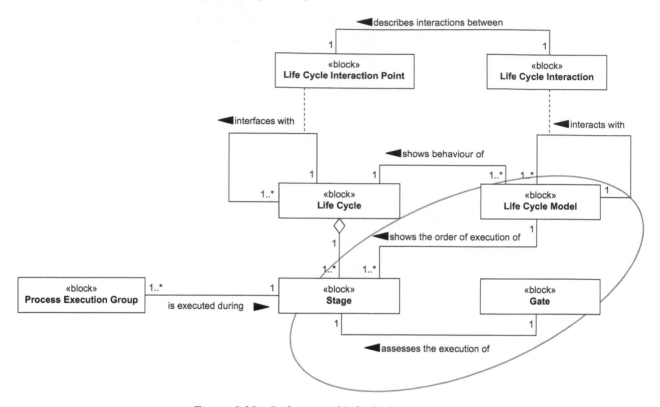

Figure 8.28   Definition of Life Cycle Model View

The following Rules apply to the Life Cycle Model View:

–   Each 'Life Cycle Model View' must be based on a Life Cycle View that shows the Stages.
–   Each instance of a 'Stage' and 'Gate' in the 'Life Cycle Model View' must be directly instantiated from the 'Life Cycle View'.
–   Each 'Life Cycle Model View' may be used as a basis for the 'Project Schedule View' – see the following section on Project-related Process modelling.

These relationships may be used as a basis for process automation.

View visualisation
The 'Life Cycle Model View' is realised using a SysML *sequence diagram,* as shown in the diagram in Figure 8.29.

The diagram here shows the 'Life Cycle Model View' for the STUMPI process model that was introduced in Chapter 7. Each *life line* is an instance of a *block* that represents a 'Stage' on its corresponding 'Life Cycle View' that is shown in Figure 8.27. Each *life line* may also show an *execution specification* that may be used to relate timing constraints or parallelism between various stages. Notice also

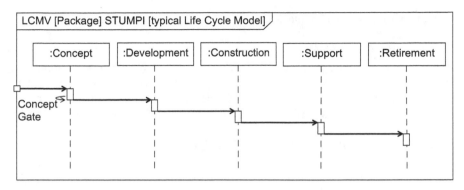

Figure 8.29   Example Life Cycle Model View for STUMPI

that a 'Gate' is shown here as an internal *message* to indicate where the 'Concept Gate' takes place.

View discussion

The Life Cycle Model View is another essential View that must exist for each relevant application, whether this is Project, Product, etc.

One important feature of this view is its flexibility. Bearing in mind that the View is visualised using a *sequence diagram*, it follows that it is possible to show a number of different Scenarios. This basically means that there are potentially many Life Cycle Model Views for each Life Cycle View, each of which will show a different Scenarios. These Scenarios may be grouped into three broad categories:

– Intended behaviour. These Scenarios represent the ideal situation where all Stages in the Life Cycle are executed according to some pre-determined plan. When Life Cycles are discussed in many domains, it is typical to show these desired life Cycle Models, such as the classic Waterfall, Iterative and Spiral. An important point to note here is that these ideals are often referred to as life cycles whereas, using the terminology adopted in this book in the MBSE Ontology, these are actually examples of the Life Cycle Model.
– Predicted behaviour. These Scenarios are more related to how it is actually anticipated that the Life Cycle will be executed, rather than the ideal norm. These may be thought of as being analogous to project schedules in the project management world.
– Actual behaviour. These Scenarios may be constructed based on what has actually occurred during a Project and form an excellent basis for project monitoring.

Clearly, it is possible to have any number of Life Cycle Models for any single Life Cycle which allows different approaches, such as Waterfall and Spiral to be visualised by the different Life Cycle Model Views.

It should be apparent from the above discussion that there are some strong links with the world of project management. This will be discussed in more detail later in this chapter when the MBSE Process Ontology is expanded for project management.

The Life Cycle Model View may also be applied at different levels of abstraction, rather than just looking at the execution of Stages. For example, the Life Cycle Model View may be used to explore scenarios for the execution of Process Execution Groups within a Life Cycle Stage. Examples of the use of the Life Cycle Model Views used at lower levels will be provided later in this chapter.

8.5.1.4   The Interaction Identification View

View rationale

The main aim of the Interaction Identification View is to identify one or more Life Cycle Interaction Point that may exist between multiple Life Cycles. In reality, Life Cycles rarely exist in isolation but they interact with one another in a potentially complex manner. The idea of this view, in conjunction with the Interaction Behaviour View, is to manage and control these complex relationships and interactions between Life Cycles.

View definition

The elements of the MBSE Ontology that are concerned with life cycle modelling are highlighted in the diagram in Figure 8.30.

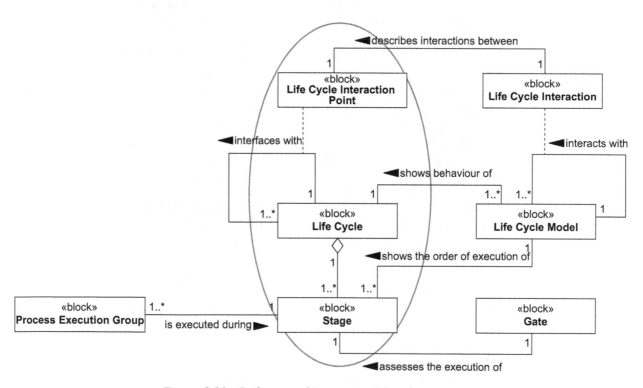

Figure 8.30   Definition of Interaction Identification View

The diagram here shows that the main elements that are of interest here are focused on the 'Life Cycle Interaction Point' that may exist on the relationships between one or more 'Life Cycle'. The aim here is simply to identify these points, rather than examine the behaviour between them.

View relationships

The Interaction Identification View is closely related to both the Life Cycle View and the Interaction Behaviour View. Each Life Cycle Interaction Point that is identified relates together two elements from one or more Life Cycle View, specifically, one or more of Stage, Gate or Life Cycle.

The Interaction Identification View is a structural view that is purely concerned with identification and not with behaviour. It is the Interaction Behaviour View that shows its respective behaviours and, therefore, there are very close links between them.

The following Rules apply to the 'Interaction Identification View':

- Each Life Cycle Interaction Point must relate to a Stage or Gate from the Life Cycle View.
- Each Interaction Behaviour View must have an Interaction Identification View associated with it.

These relationships may be used as a basis for process automation.

View visualisation

The Interaction Identification View is visualised using a *block definition diagram*, an example of which is shown in the diagram in Figure 8.31.

The diagram here shows an example of an 'Interaction Identification View' that shows relationships between three different Life Cycles. Each Life Cycle is represented by a *package*, in this case there are three: 'Development Life Cycle', 'Acquisition Life Cycle' and 'Deployment Life Cycle'. Each *package* that represents a Life Cycle contains one or more Stage using *blocks*. Each Life Cycle Interaction Point is represented as a *dependency* that has been stereotyped as «interaction point». Therefore, there is a Life Cycle Interaction Point between 'Delivery' and 'Concept' that is represented by the «interaction point» dependency between them. Note that the full-term Life Cycle Interaction Point is not used here purely for reasons of clarity and presentation.

View discussion

The relationships and subsequent interactions between different elements of different Life Cycles are areas that are very often overlooked, but one that require some effort to understand, manage and control.

There are several main problems associated with these interactions:

- Many people do not know that there are many types of Life Cycle.
- Many people who do know this do not realise that they interact.
- Many people who understand these first two points do not appreciate the complexity involved.

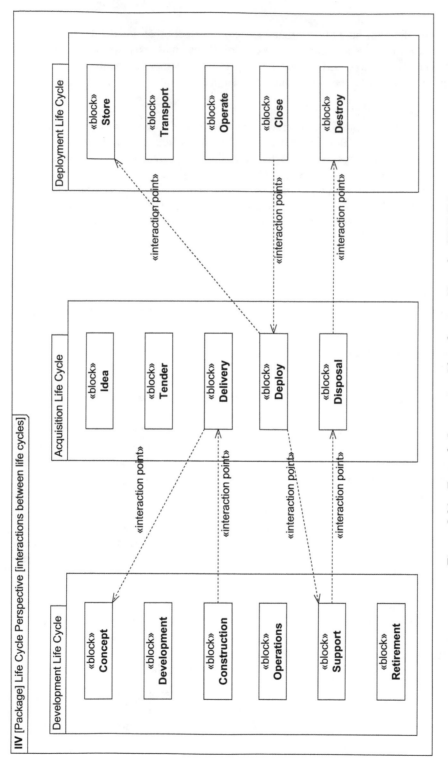

Figure 8.31   Example Interaction Identification View for STUMPI

Of course, in many cases, there may be no issues with interacting Life Cycles particularly for short simple Projects. The problem occurs frequently, however, when considering:

- Programmes, where many Projects, and hence Life Cycles, will interact.
- Systems of Systems, where many Constituent Systems interact to provide System of System Capabilities. In this case there will be not only System Life Cycles, but also System of Systems Life Cycles.
- Systems that have a long shelf life, such as the train example discussed previously, where the System Life Cycle may have multiple Project Life Cycles associate with it.

Each Interaction Identification View will have a number of Interaction Behaviour Views associated with it that define different executions of the Stages.

8.5.1.5   The Interaction Behaviour View

View rationale

The main aim of the Interaction Behaviour View is to explore the different possible behaviours of interacting Life Cycles, by considering a number of Scenarios. The Interaction Behaviour View is a behavioural View, whereas the Interaction Identification View is a structural View.

The Interaction Behaviour View may be used to specify the required behaviour of Life Cycle Interaction points whether these are predicted anticipated behaviour or actual behaviour.

View definition

The elements of the MBSE Ontology that are concerned with Life Cycle interaction behaviour are highlighted in the diagram in Figure 8.32.

The diagram here shows that the 'Interaction Behaviour View' is concerned primarily with the 'Life Cycle interaction' and its associated 'Life Cycle Interaction Point'. Each 'Life Cycle Interaction' describes the behaviour between one or more 'Life Cycle Interaction Point'.

View relationships

The Interaction Behaviour View is very closely related to the Interaction Identification View as it shows the behaviour of the interaction points. The Interaction Behaviour View shows a behavioural View, whereas the Interaction Identification View shows a structural View.

The following Rule applies to the Interaction Identification View:

- Each 'Interaction Behaviour View' must be an 'Interaction Identification View' that shows the structure.

These relationships may be used as a basis for process automation.

View visualisation

The Interaction Behaviour View is visualised using a number of *sequence diagrams* that may be used in two different ways, examples of which are shown in the diagrams in Figures 8.33 and 8.34.

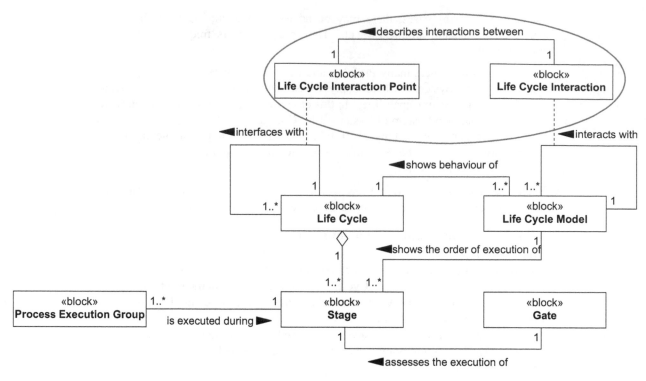

Figure 8.32   Definition of Interaction Behaviour View

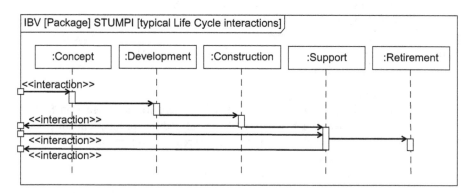

Figure 8.33   Example Interaction Behaviour View for STUMPI showing interactions using Gates

The diagram shown here explores the interactions between Life Cycle Interaction Points where the emphasis is on a Specific Life Cycle. The whole *sequence diagram* represents the behaviour of a single Life Cycle with each Stage being represented as a *life line*. The basis of internal Life Cycle behaviour is the same as shown in a

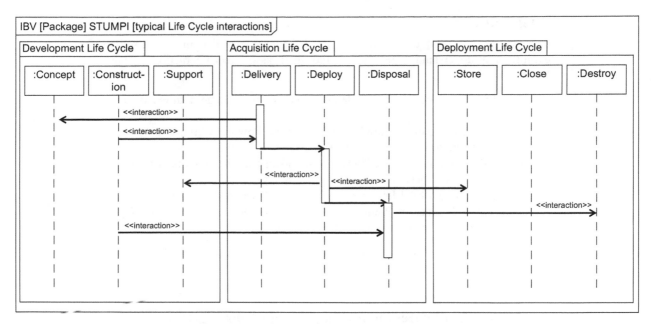

Figure 8.34 Example Interaction Behaviour View for STUMPI showing full interactions

Life Cycle Model View (e.g., see Figure 8.29). Each interaction is represented by a *message* that has been stereotyped as «interaction point» which enters and exits the *sequence diagram* via a *gate.*

When using this type of visualisation it should be noted that the other life cycles that are interacted with are not shown, simply the interaction points and *gates.* Of course, it is possible to augment the gates by indicating which Life Cycles the *gates* are related to. This may be done using either *notes* or *tag values* associated with the *gates.* If the relationships between the different Life Cycle Models are particularly important, then the following alternate visualisation may be considered (Figure 8.34).

The diagram shown here has a similar visualisation to that shown in Figure 8.33 but this time the interaction points to not enter and exit the diagram anonymously, but interact with specific Life Cycles. Each Life Cycle is shown as a *package* with each Stage visualised as a *life line.* This time, however, the interaction points do not end in a *gate* but go to other stages (*life lines)* within other life cycles (*packages).*

View discussion
The Interaction Behaviour View shows the behaviour of interactions that were identified on the Interaction Identification View.

Each Interaction Behaviour View in a similar fashion to the Life Cycle Model View may show behaviour that is ideal, predicated or actual.

8.5.2   Summary

This section has introduced a number of different Views that may be used to explore and understand Life Cycles and their associated interactions. These Views are:

- The 'Life Cycle View', which identifies one or more 'Stage' that exists in the 'Life Cycle'.
- The 'Life Cycle Model View', which describes how each 'Stage' behaves in relation to one or more other 'Stage'.
- The 'Life Cycle Interaction View', which identifies one or more 'Life Cycle Interaction Point' between one or more 'Life Cycle'.
- The 'Life Cycle Model Interaction View', which shows the behaviour of each 'Life Cycle Interaction Point' in relation to one or more other 'Life Cycle Interaction Point' as identified in the previous view.

Each of these Views was described and examples provided, using SysML, of how they may be visualised.

8.6   Expanded Process modelling – project management

This section looks at another way that the "seven views" approach can be expanded and used and this time we consider its potential use in an Organisation for managing Projects.

Any Project requires an element of planning and the generation of some sort of schedule. A Project schedule is usually realised in some sort of Gantt chart or Pert chart which are, themselves, a form of visual modelling. However, such schedules are often wildly inaccurate when it comes to representing the actual activities that are carried out by the workers involved with the Project and are often regarded as a work of fiction by the people doing the work. Consider the horrific examples concerning project overruns in the field of, for example, IT systems. It is possible to pick up any newspaper in any given week of the year and find examples of projects that have been absolute disasters. For detailed examples of these see Reference 7.

Such cost and time overruns are quite common but, in many cases, this is not necessarily a fault of the people carrying out the work but more a case of the Project not meeting the initial expectations of the schedule. One indicator of the expectations of the Project can be found in the schedule which, if very unrealistic, will by its very nature result in time and hence cost overruns. Therefore, where does the fault lie – with the people carrying out the work to the best of their ability or in the unrealistic expectations of the Project Managers who set unrealisable goals?

These inaccurate estimates of times, costs and resources are inexcusable, and mostly avoidable, when a full knowledge of the Processes in an Organisation is held.

8.6.1   The expanded MBSE Ontology

The MBSE Ontology includes the concept of a Project and Programme but does not explicitly cover the concept of a schedule. The MBSE Ontology may be easily and simply expanded to include these concepts as shown in the diagram in Figure 8.35.

The diagram here shows the MBSE Ontology and how it may be expanded to include concepts related to project management. Basic project management tells us that the 'Project Schedule' manages the execution of a 'Project', and that the 'Project Schedule' is divided up into one or more discrete 'Task' that represent very high level project activity. Each high-level 'Task' may then be further broken down, for example:

—   Each 'Task' may be broken down into one or more 'Subtask' that shows a more detailed view of what project activity is occurring.
—   Each 'Subtask' may be broken down into one or more 'Subsubtask' that shows a more detailed view of what project activity is occurring.
—   Each 'Subsubtask' may be broken down into one or more 'Subsubsubtask' (no, really!) that shows a more detailed view of what project activity is occurring.

This decomposition may be taken further, but for this example, we will stop at four levels of decomposition below the 'Project Schedule' as this provides a convenient mapping onto our established MBSE Ontology.

Also, other information, such as key milestones, dates and resources, may be indicated on the expanded MBSE Ontology and related to MBSE Ontology elements, such as each milestone may map onto an Artefact, and so on. This is left deliberately vague at this point as there are many different ideas and terminologies in the world of project management, but the basic principle holds up here. Indeed, the correct approach to defining these mappings would be to model the project management Processes using the "seven views" and then map them onto the MBSE Ontology. The basic mapping that we can derive here is summarised as follows:

—   'Life Cycle Model' in the MBSE Ontology maps onto the 'Project Schedule'.
—   'Stage' in the MBSE Ontology maps onto the 'Task'.
—   'Process Execution Group' in the MBSE Ontology maps onto the 'Subtask'.
—   'Process' in the MBSE Ontology maps onto the 'Subsubtask'.
—   'Activity' in the MBSE Ontology maps onto the 'Subsubsubtask'.

Based on this expanded MBSE Ontology, the Framework may now be defined.

8.6.2   The Framework

The MBSE Process Project Framework comprises a single View that can be seen in the diagram in Figure 8.36.

The diagram here shows that there are two Views identified in the Framework, which are the 'Project Schedule View' and the 'Programme Structure View'. In reality, there will be more views than this but this will depend on the nature of the project management Processes. One View that is ubiquitous to just about every Project is that

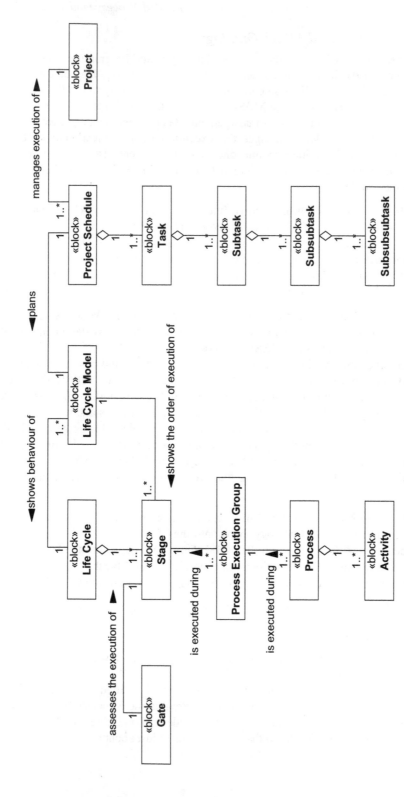

Figure 8.35   Expanded MBSE Ontology focussed on project management

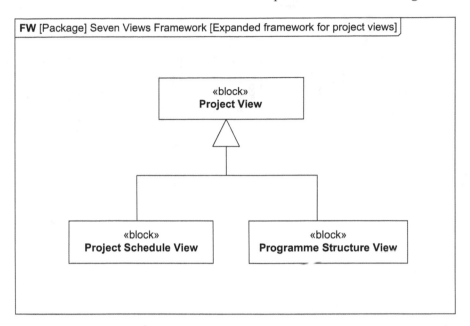

Figure 8.36 The Framework View for project management-related Views

of the Project Schedule, which is why it is included here. Other potential views may include resource identification views and resource allocation views.

It should be noted here how closely these Views may be related to some of the Process and Competency views.

8.6.3 Views

8.6.3.1 The Project Schedule View

View rational

The basic aim of the 'Project Schedule View' is to provide an overview of the execution of the Project over time. This type of View may be used in a number of ways:

– To show the ideal Project execution.
– To show the predicted Project execution.
– To show the actual Project execution.

The Project execution, in the form of the Project Schedule, is typically broken down into a number of Tasks, Subtasks, etc. and it is also possible to show timings, resources, milestones, etc.

View definition

The elements of the MBSE Ontology that are concerned with Project scheduling are highlighted in the diagram in Figure 8.37.

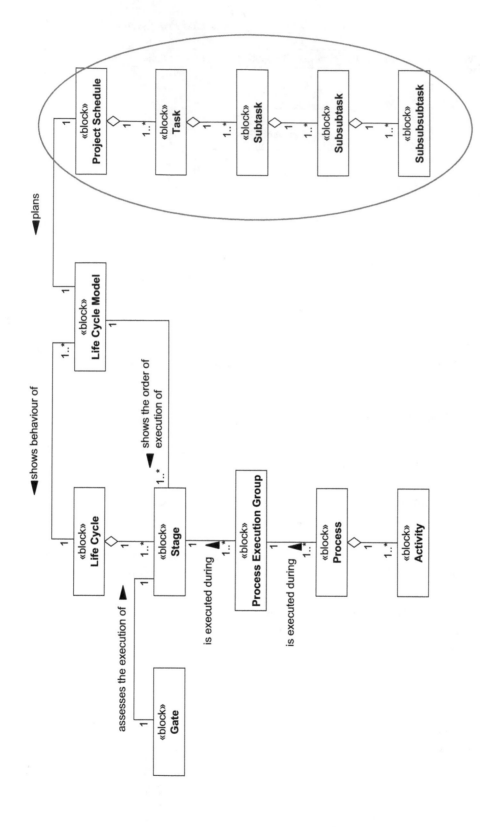

Figure 8.37 Definition of Project Schedule View

The diagram here shows that the 'Project Schedule View' is concerned with the 'Project Schedule' and its decompositions.

View relationships

The 'Project Schedule View' has relationships with many other views, depending on the level of detail that is required of the schedule. Even when simply looking at the Project activity, there are clear links to the Life Cycle Views and Process Views.

The following rules apply to the 'Project Schedule View':

– The order of execution of each 'Task' in the 'Project Schedule' must map directly onto a 'Life Cycle Model View' that shows the behaviour of the Life Cycle in terms of the interactions between Stages.

– The order of execution of each 'Subtask' in each 'Task' must map directly onto a 'Life Cycle Model View' that shows the behaviour of a Stage in terms of the interactions between Process Execution Groups.

– The order of execution of each 'Subsubtask' in each 'Subtask' must map onto a 'Life Cycle Model View' that shows the behaviour of the Process Execution Group.

– The order of execution of each 'Subsubsubtask' in each 'Subsubtask' maps directly onto a 'Process Behaviour View' for a specific 'Process'.

These relationships may be used as a basis for process automation.

View visualisation

The rules in the previous section actually show how the entire Project can potentially be mapped out by using Views that have already been defined as part of the Life Cycle and Process Views. This would be a great idea from the point of view of a SysML model, but not a good idea in terms of getting Project Managers to buy in to the approach and follow the schedules. In almost every instance of project management, Project Managers will produce and expect to see a Project Schedule in the form of a Gantt chart. The diagram in Figure 8.38 shows how the Project Schedule View may be visualised using a standard Gantt chart.

The diagram in Figure 8.38 shows a typical Gantt chart that represents the 'Project Schedule View'.

A typical Gantt chart will show more information as just the Project activity breakdown (Task, Subtask, etc.), but these project management concepts can be very easily mapped onto the MBSE Ontology, for example:

– The concept of a 'Responsibility' shown on the Gantt chart could map directly onto the concept of a 'Stakeholder' from the MBSE Ontology.

– The concept of a 'Milestone' shown on the Gantt chart could map directly onto the concept of 'Artefact' from the MBSE Ontology.

In fact, any concept from the project management Processes can and should be mapped onto the MBSE Ontology to make it an integral part of the overall MBSE approach.

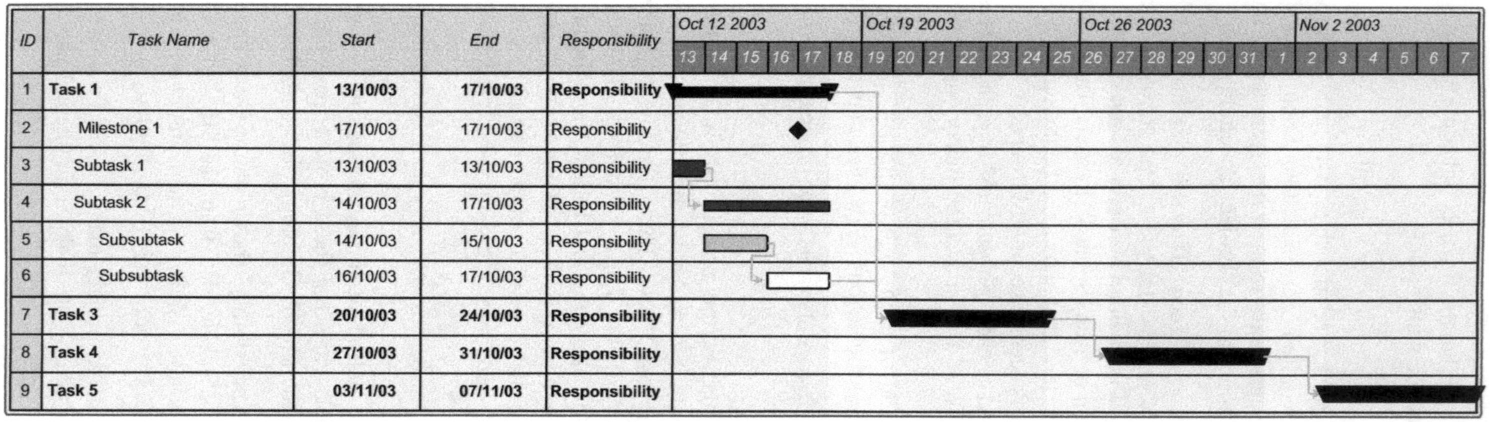

ID
Task Name
Start
End
Responsibility
Oct 12 2003
Oct 19 2003
Oct 26 2003
Nov 2 2003
13 14 15 16 17 18 19 20 21 22 23 24 25 26 27 28 29 30 31 1 2 3 4 5 6 7
1 Task 1 13/10/03 17/10/03 Responsibility
2 Milestone 1 17/10/03 17/10/03 Responsibility
3 Subtask 1 13/10/03 13/10/03 Responsibility
4 Subtask 2 14/10/03 17/10/03 Responsibility
5 Subsubtask 14/10/03 15/10/03 Responsibility
6 Subsubtask 16/10/03 17/10/03 Responsibility
7 Task 3 20/10/03 24/10/03 Responsibility
8 Task 4 27/10/03 31/10/03 Responsibility
9 Task 5 03/11/03 07/11/03 Responsibility

Figure 8.38 Example Project Schedule View

View discussion

There is no denying that a Gantt chart is seen as an essential part of any project management activity but, in real life, these often bear no relation to what is actually happening on the Project or what Processes are being followed.

The approach shown here of making the Project Schedule part of the overall MBSE approach is both common sense and good practice. A good Project Schedule must reflect the work activities that are carried out on the Project and the creation of such a schedule should be a relatively simple piece of work. Bear in mind that we potentially already have the following information, as discussed previously in this chapter:

- The highest-level breakdown of any project in the form of the Life Cycle View and the Life Cycle Model View.
- The execution of many projects that make up a programme in the form of the Interaction Identification View and Interaction Behaviour View.
- The definition and execution of every level under the Life Cycle Views in the form of the Life Cycle Model Views.
- A complete set of responsibilities in the form of the Stakeholder View.
- All skills required for each responsibility in the form of the Competency Views.

In fact, almost all the views discussed in this chapter may be used to contribute to a Project Schedule and ensure that it is correct and accurate.

This use of Views for management activities also re-enforces the reuse of the model. The more that we can use each View that we generate, the more value we can get from each View.

8.6.3.2   The Programme Structure View

View rational

The basic aim of the 'Programme Structure View' is to identify a number of Programmes and their associated Projects. This View may be used to identify any dependencies between Programmes and/or Projects that may be useful when planning, monitoring and executing Projects and Programmes.

View definition

The elements of the MBSE Ontology that are concerned with Programmes are highlighted in the diagram in Figure 8.39.

The diagram here shows that the 'Programme Structure View' is concerned with one or more 'Programme' and one or more 'Project'. This View also emphasises relationships between Projects and between Programmes.

View relationships

The 'Programme Structure View' has relationships with many other Views, including the Project Schedule View, Life Cycle Views and Process Views.

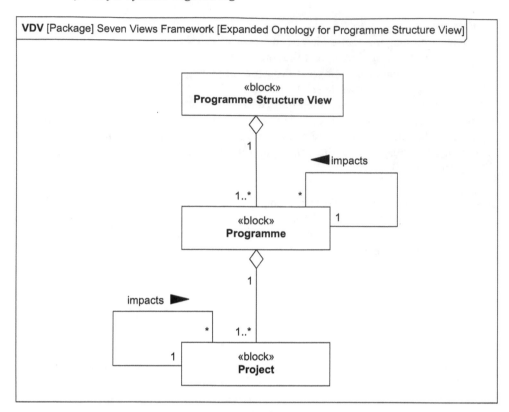

Figure 8.39   Definition of Programme Structure View

The following Rules apply to the 'Programme Structure View':

- Each Programme will have an associated Life Cycle View that identifies the Stages for the Programme.
- Each Programme will have an associated Life Cycle Model View that describes the execution of the Stages in the Programme.
- Each Project will have an associated Life Cycle View that identifies the Stages for the Project.
- Each Project will have an associated Life Cycle Model View that describes the execution of the Stages in the Project.
- Each Project will have an associated Project Schedule View.

These relationships may be used as a basis for process automation.

View visualisation

The Programme Structure View may be realised using the *block definition diagram*. In this case, the visualisation is quite straightforward and *blocks* are used to represent both Programmes and Projects.

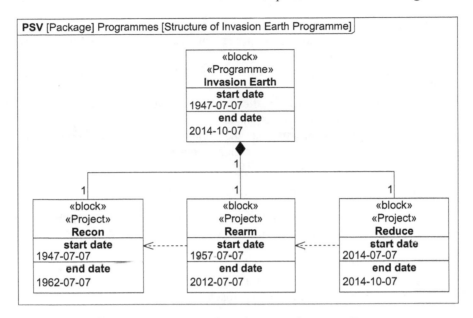

PSV [Package] Programmes [Structure of Invasion Earth Programme]

«block»
«Programme»
Invasion Earth
start date
1947-07-07
end date
2014-10-07

«block»
«Project»
Recon
start date
1947-07-07
end date
1962-07-07

«block»
«Project»
Rearm
start date
1957-07-07
end date
2012-07-07

«block»
«Project»
Reduce
start date
2014-07-07
end date
2014-10-07

Figure 8.40   Example Programme Structure View

The diagram in Figure 8.40 shows a *block definition diagram* used to visualise a 'Programme Structure View'. Each Project and Programme is visualised by a standard *block* that has a *stereotype* applied to indicate whether it represents a Programme or Project. Each Programme actually owns a number of Projects, so note the explicit use of a *composition* relationship here. Several relationships between the Projects are shown here using *dependencies*. Notice how additional properties have been shown here to indicate the 'start date' and 'end date' of the Projects.

This View may also include multiple Programmes, rather than just the single Programme shown here and, of course, relationships between Programmes may also be shown using *dependencies*.

View discussion

The Programme Structure View is quite a simple View but, nevertheless, is a very important one. Relationships between Projects and Programmes are often overlooked and are incredibly important in real life. Some of these dependencies will be explored on the Life Cycle Views that are associated with the Programme Structure View, which explicitly show exactly where the Life Cycles interact in terms of the Stages, Process Execution Groups and the Processes.

8.7   Summary

This chapter has taken the basic "seven views" approach to Process modelling that was described in Chapter 7 and has shown how it can be expanded to cover many different and diverse application areas. The areas covered here are:

- Modelling standards, in this case ISO 15288.
- Showing compliance between process models, in this case ISO 15288, STUMPI and ACRE.
- Competency modelling, which enforces the relationship between people and Process in MBSE.
- Life Cycle modelling, which allows different types of Life Cycle to be modelled along with the interactions between them.
- Project management, in particular the project schedule, which uses aspects of the model from the previous points to define a Project Schedule and a Programme Structure View.

There are two key points to take away from this chapter:

- That the "seven views" approach is very flexible and can be applied in a variety of different situations and is not even limited to the examples provided here.
- That the Process is such an important part of MBSE, as each example provided here is derived from a basic process model, yet provided a lot of value and contributed to the overall MBSE approach.

The Process modelling and its expansions will be used throughout the entirety of this book.

References

1. De Marco T. *Controlling Software Projects: Management, Measurement & Estimation*. NJ, USA: Yourdon Press; 1982
2. ISO. *ISO/IEC 15288:2008 Systems and Software Engineering – System Life Cycle Processes*. 2nd edn. ISO Publishing; 2008a
3. ISO. *ISO 9001:2008 Quality Management Systems – Requirements*. ISO Publishing; 2008b
4. ISO. *ISO/IEC 12207 Systems and Software Engineering – Software Life Cycle Processes*. ISO Publishing; 2008c
5. CMMI. *CMMI for Development, Version 1.3*. CMMI-DEV (Version 1.3, November 2010). PA, USA: Carnegie Mellon University Software Engineering Institute; 2010. http://www.sei.cmu.edu/library/abstracts/reports/10tr033.cfm (retrieved 16 February 2011)
6. ISO. *ISO/IEC 15504 Information Technology – Process Assessment, Parts 1–9*. ISO Publishing; 2006–2011
7. Flowers S. *Software Failure: Management Failure*. Wiley Series in Software Engineering Practice. Chichester, UK: Wiley; 1996
8. INCOSE. *INCOSE Competencies Framework*. INCOSE, 2007. http://www.incoseonline.org.uk/Groups/SE_Competencies/Main.aspx?CatID=Groups

Chapter 9

Requirements modelling with MBSE

All you need is ignorance and confidence and the success is sure.

Mark Twain

9.1 Introduction

This chapter introduces a model-based approach to requirements engineering. This approach is known as ACRE – Approach to Context-based Requirements Engineering [6]. The approach uses the 'Ontology, Framework and Views' techniques that are used throughout this book.

9.1.1 Background

The basic need for model-based requirements engineering is captured in Figure 9.1, which describes the Needs in the form of Use Cases in the ACRE Context.

The diagram here shows that the basic Need for the ACRE Context is to define an approach for requirements engineering ('Define requirements engineering approach'). There are two main constraints in this Use Case, which are:

– The approach that is defined must be model-based ('Must be model-based'), clearly because this is part of the larger MBSE effort described in this book.
– The approach must be realisable by any appropriate tools ('Must be realisable by tools'). This means that not only it must be possible to realise the approach in tools, but also that the approach should be flexible enough to allow realisation in different tools from different Tool Vendors.

There are three main inclusions that make up the main Use Case.

There is an obvious need to actually define the Process ('Define process') as the Process will form the heart of the definition of any approach. This is constrained in three ways:

– The Processes that are defined must comply with Standards ('Comply with standards'). This compliance refers to anything that may be thought of as a Standard, for example an international standard, an industry standard and an in-house standard.

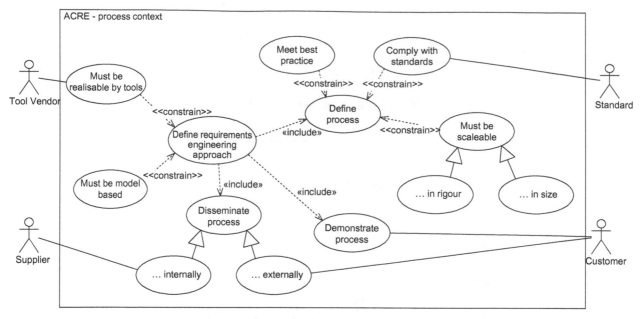

Figure 9.1   Requirements modelling Context

- The Processes that are defined must comply with best practice models ('Meet best practice'). This is very similar to the previous point but has a wide scope and will include methodologies, legislation, and proprietary models.
- The Processes that are defined must be scaleable ('Must be scaleable') in two ways. The Processes must be scaleable in terms of the size of the Project ('... in size') so that the Processes may be applied to very short Projects of just a few days, right up to long-term Projects of many years. The Processes must be scaleable in terms of the levels of rigour of the Project or System ('... in rigour') so that it may be applied to non-critical systems, mission critical systems and anywhere in between.

Part of the definition of the approach also includes the ability to demonstrate the Process to a Customer ('Demonstrate process'). This is vital in terms of inspiring the Customer and also facilitates audits and assessments significantly.

The Process must also be disseminated so that people are aware of it and how it is to be used ('Disseminate process'). This must be done both internally to the business ('... internally') and externally to the Customer ('... externally').

9.2   Approach

9.2.1   The MBSE Ontology (revisited)

Figure 9.2 shows the MBSE Ontology with an emphasis on the Need-related elements using a SysML *block definition diagram*.

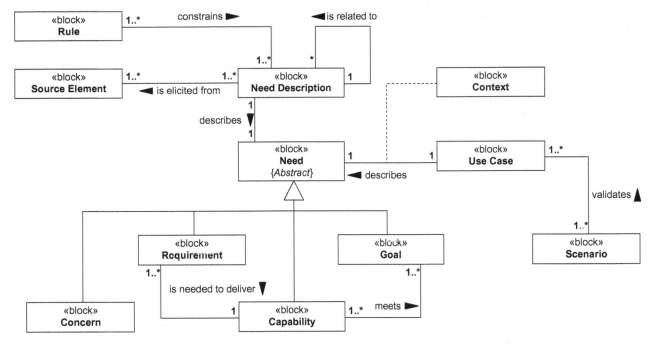

Figure 9.2   Subset of the MBSE Ontology focused on Requirements modelling

The diagram here shows that there is an abstract concept of a 'Need' that has four types: 'Capability', 'Requirement', 'Goal' and Concern. One or more 'Requirement' is needed to deliver each 'Capability', a number of which, in turn, meet one or more 'Goal'. A 'Need Description' describes each 'Need' and one or more 'Need Description' is elicited from one or more 'Source Element'. One or more 'Rule' constrains one or more 'Need Description'.

One or more 'Use Case' describes the context of each 'Need' via the 'Context' and one or more 'Scenario' validates one or more 'Use Case'.

Each of these elements will now be described in more detail.

9.2.1.1   The 'Need' concept

The prime concept in any requirements engineering approach is that of the Need. The Need is an abstract concept that describes a Requirement, Capability, Goal or Concern of a System or Project. Every System will have a set of Needs, whether they are formally defined or just exist tacitly inside someone's head. The artefacts that we see when we capture, analyse and document Needs are *not* the Needs themselves, but are representations of each Need. Of course, a Need may be represented in any number of different ways, and it is these different interpretations that form the basis of the Views that will be used in the ACRE Framework.

A Need is an abstract and non-tangible concept. Needs exist as ideas or thoughts and it is essential, therefore, that we formalise them in some ways so that we can capture and reason about them. A well-defined Need should be identifiable, clear, non-solution-specific, owned, have an origin, be able to be verified, be able to be validated and must be prioritised. There are many different types of Need that may exist which are often classified into a number of groups using a Needs taxonomy, which is simply a classification hierarchy. There is no definitive view on exactly what these types of Needs are and it may vary depending on the project, the industry or the company. For the purposes of this book, the Needs taxonomy that will be adopted is shown in the diagram in Figure 9.3, which expands on Figure 9.2.

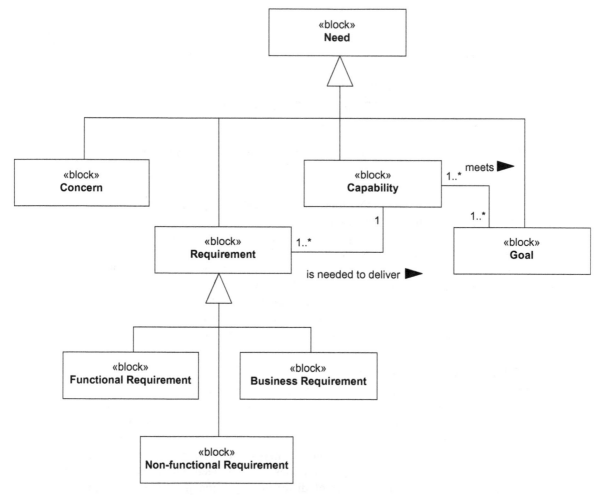

Figure 9.3   Subset of the MBSE Ontology focused on Requirements modelling showing types of Need

The diagram here shows that there are four types of 'Need', which are:

- 'Goal'. A special type of 'Need' whose Context will typically represent one or more Organisational Unit (as an Organisational Context). Each 'Goal' will be met by one or more 'Capability'. Examples of this type of Need will be discussed in more detail in Chapter 10 and Part 4 of the book.
- 'Capability'. A special type of 'Need' whose Context will typically represent one or more Project (as a Project Context) or one or more Organisational Unit (as an Organisational Context). A 'Capability' will meet one or more 'Goal' and will represent the ability of an Organisation or Organisational Unit. Examples of this type of Need will be discussed in more detail in Chapter 10 and Part 4 of the book.
- 'Requirement'. A property of a system that is either needed or wanted by a Stakeholder Role. Also, one or more 'Requirement' is needed to deliver each 'Capability'. Examples of this type of Need will be discussed in more detail in Chapter 9 and Part 4 of the book.
- 'Concern'. A special type of 'Need' whose Context will represent an Architecture, an Architectural Framework or a Viewpoint. Examples of this type of Need will be discussed in more detail in Chapter 11 and Part 4 of the book.

The concept of the Requirement may also be further classified as follows:

- 'Business Requirement'. A Business Requirement is used to state the Needs of a business. This will include business drivers that impact the entire Organisation and all the Projects within it. Business Requirements should drive every Project in the Organisation and, as such, every Project must contribute either directly or indirectly to meeting the Business Requirements.
- 'Functional Requirement'. Functional Requirements, in their essence, yield an observable result to someone, or something, that is using the System. By their very definition, Functional Requirements affect the performance of an action and result in some sort of function being performed. Functional Requirements are usually what are referred to when people misuse the term user requirements.
- 'Non-functional Requirement'. A 'Non-functional Requirement' will constrain, or limit in some way, the way that a Functional Requirement may be realised. It should be noted that the term constraint is often used rather than 'Non-functional Requirement'.

Again, it should be stressed that the terms used here are the ones used in this book and that your own terminology may well differ in this area.

9.2.1.2 The 'Need Description' concept

The Need Description is an essential element of any requirements engineering approach, but it is one that is very often misunderstood. The Need Description is exactly what it says – it is a description of a Need. The Need Description is not the Need itself but is a way to describe the abstract concept of the Need. This is necessary because, as described in the previous section, there are a number of features that make up a good Need and it is the Need Description that captures these.

Again, it must be stressed that the Need Description is not the Need but a representation of it. Of course, each Need must have a Need Description, but the fact that each Need has an associated description does not mean that the Need itself is understood – in fact far from it. The Need Description provides a high-level description of each Need, but this does not mean that the Need has been given meaning. A Need has not been given a meaning until it has been put into a Context.

The Need Description has many uses, which are to describe the Need, to provide a basis for traceability, to provide a basis for measurement and to provide a basis for contractual agreements.

All Need Descriptions describe Needs and must be abstracted from source information, which is discussed in the next section.

9.2.1.3   The 'Source Element' concept

Each Need must originate from somewhere and this is where the Source Element comes into play. A Source Element represents the source of a Need. In terms of what a Source Element actually is, the list of examples is almost endless as a Source Element can be just about anything, such as requirement lists, conversations, emails, workshop outputs, Business Requirements, standards, existing systems, specifications or designs, information sources and higher level Needs.

The key point here is that Needs can be abstracted from almost anything but, regardless of what they are, it is essential that there is traceability established between these Source Elements and the Need Descriptions.

In order for a Source Element to be usable, it must be a configurable item. This means that it must be identifiable in terms of its version number and findable in terms of its location.

9.2.1.4   The 'Rule' concept

When describing any Need there is a lot of room for ambiguity and mis-interpretation. In order to minimise these problems, it is quite common to see a number of Rules defined that are applied to describing Needs.

These Rules may apply to the Need itself or, more usually, to the attributes of a Need. If a Need is represented by a SysML *block*, then its attributes may be represented using *properties*. Examples of Rules include:

– The way that the wording in a Need Description must be applied. One of the most common examples of wording rules concerns the use of words such as 'shall', 'may', 'should' and 'can'.
– The complexity of the text that forms the Need Description. There are many best practice complexity measures that can be used to assess the complexity of a sentence or paragraph of text. One of the most widely used is the Flesch Reading Ease Score [1] that indicates how easy text is to read.

– The value of an attribute of a Need Description is constrained. For example, this may take the form of an enumerated list where an attribute of 'Priority' may only take on one of four values, 'Essential', 'Desirable', 'Bells and whistles', or 'Unknown'. The value that an attribute may take on may also be constrained by defining a special type for the value, for example the value of an 'Owner' attribute may be constrained to be defined as a reference to one of a number of Stakeholder Roles.

The previous three examples of Rules show how various attributes of Need Descriptions may be constrained by Rules, but these Rules may also apply to the set of Need Descriptions. For example, the total number of Needs may be measured.

The examples of Rules that are shown here were chosen to make a specific point: the Rules themselves can take on many different forms and can be applied to either the attributes of the Need Descriptions or the Need Descriptions themselves. These Rules can be realised in many ways, ranging from simple text-based constraints to SysML parametric *constraint blocks*, through to formal methods. It is also possible to use Rules to constrain the wordings, or text descriptions, that lie behind a *use case*.

9.2.1.5   The 'Scenario' concept

The original Needs must be given meaning by putting each into Context using Use Cases. It is essential that we can demonstrate that we have met the original Need, but this must be achieved by demonstrating that we can satisfy the relevant Use Cases. The way that Use Cases are validated is by considering various Scenarios for each Use Case.

The diagram in Figure 9.4 shows that there are two types of 'Scenario' – 'Semi-formal Scenario' and 'Formal Scenario'.

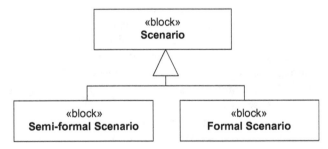

Figure 9.4   Subset of the MBSE Ontology focused on Requirements modelling showing types of Scenario

A Scenario is defined in this book as an exploration of a 'what if' for a Use Case. Each Use Case will give rise to a number of different situations that may arise when it is being satisfied.

The Semi-formal Scenarios will be realised by SysML *sequence diagrams* that show interactions between elements in the System. These interactions will usually exist at two levels:

- Stakeholder-level Scenarios, which treat the System as a black box and analyse the interactions between the Stakeholder Roles and the System.
- System-level Scenarios, which look at the interactions between System Elements within the System.

These Scenarios allow a Use Case to be analysed by considering different what ifs and representing them with the *sequence diagram*.

The Formal Scenarios will be realised by SysML parametric *constraint blocks* and their use on *parametric diagrams*. This allows a more mathematical-based approach to be taken for understanding the Use Cases. The *constraint properties* are connected together into different networks that allow what if analysis and are particularly powerful when considering trade-offs.

All of these Scenarios may be used for two purposes:

- Understanding, to allow each Use Case to be analysed.
- Validation, to allow each Use Case to be satisfied in a demonstrable way.

Scenarios provide a very powerful mechanism that is essential for any Needs exercise.

9.2.1.6 The 'Context' concept

The idea of the Context is fundamental to the approach taken in this book and hence it is very important that the concept is well-understood. In its simplest form, a Context may be thought of as a point of view. It is essential, however, that it is well-understood from what point of view each Context is taken. It is possible to view the Needs of a System from any number of different points of view, so it is essential that the origins of these points of view are well-defined. The diagram in Figure 9.5 shows several common Contexts that are possible.

Figure 9.5 shows that there are several types of 'Context' which are the 'Organisational Context', 'System Context', 'Project Context', 'Stakeholder Context', 'Process Context', 'Viewpoint Context' and 'Architectural Framework Context'. The diagram also shows that the full set of Contexts shown here is incomplete (indicated by SysML {incomplete} *constraint*), so there are many other types of Context that are not shown here.

Rather than discuss all these in great detail, only the 'Stakeholder Context' and the 'System Context' will be discussed in the following sections, but it should be stated that the points raised here apply to all the other Contexts shown in the diagram.

9.2.1.7 Stakeholder Context

The first type of Context that will be considered is the Stakeholder Context. The Stakeholder Context is a set of points of view that is defined by looking at a set of Needs from the point of view of different Stakeholder Roles. Key to getting this

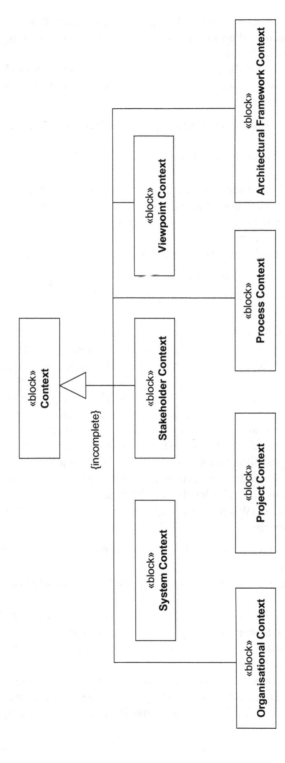

Figure 9.5 Subset of the MBSE Ontology focused on Requirements modelling showing types of 'Context'

right is being able to identify what the various Stakeholder Roles are. A Stakeholder Role is defined as the role of any Person, Organisation or thing that has an interest in or is impacted by a System.

Once the Stakeholder Roles have been identified, then it is possible to create a set of Contexts. When considering Contexts, the following basic facts should be considered:

- The Stakeholder Roles identified here form the basis for defining a number of Contexts.
- Each one of these Stakeholder Roles will have their own point of view, or Context.
- Each Context will be used to express the Needs of a System from the point of view of a single Stakeholder Role, in the form of Use Cases.
- Each Context will potentially conflict with other Contexts, as they represent different points of view.
- All Contexts must be consistent with one another to form a model.

The identification of Stakeholder Roles is only one way to help to define a number of Contexts and it is common that several types of Context are developed.

9.2.1.8   System Contexts

The second type of Context that will be considered is a set of Contexts based on a System or, more specifically, the level of hierarchy of a System. This type of Context is particularly relevant where a System is being developed that can be broken down into many subsystems, assemblies and components. This is very often the case where manufactured Systems are concerned, such as in the automotive and rail industries.

When considering such a System, it is quite common to have a number of different types of Need defined that exist at the various levels in the hierarchy.

By considering the different levels of hierarchy, it is possible to identify Contexts at each level. In other words, each level of the hierarchy has its own point of view.

Once the System hierarchy levels have been identified, then it is possible to create a set of Contexts. When considering System-driven Contexts, the following basic facts should be considered:

- The System hierarchy levels identified here form the basis for defining a number of Contexts.
- Each one of these System hierarchy levels will have their own point of view, or Context.
- Each Context will be used to express the Needs of a System from the point of view of a single System hierarchy level, in the form of Use Cases.
- Each Context will potentially conflict with other Contexts, as they represent different points of view.
- All Contexts must be consistent with one another to form a model. By looking at the various Contexts together and applying the modelling techniques discussed in Chapter 2.2 it is possible to identify conflicts, overlaps, similarities and so on.

The identification of System hierarchy levels is one way to help to define a number of Contexts that form the heart of the Needs model.

9.2.1.9   The 'Use Case' concept

The concept of a Use Case is one that is very often misunderstood. Many people assume that a Use Case is the same as a Need but this is not the case. The definition of a Use Case that will be used in this book is that a Use Case is a Need that has been given meaning by putting it into Context. Any single Need may be interpreted in different ways depending on the point of view, or Context, that it is viewed from. The previous section described how a number of Contexts may be identified for any System, and it is the Use Case that looks at each Need in these different Contexts.

In order to illustrate the concept of the Use Case, let us consider two examples.

For the first example, consider a passenger airline system. In this example imagine that there is a Need, and hence a Need Description, that is defined as 'Save money'. This seems quite straightforward and easy to understand as almost everybody can understand the idea of saving money. However, depending on the role that we are taking (which Stakeholder Role we are) the Need will take on different meanings (different Use Cases).

–   From the passenger's point of view, this Need may be interpreted as saving money on the fare paid to make a journey. Therefore, the Need is 'Save money', the Context is from the point of view of the 'User' Stakeholder Role and the Use Case may be 'save money on cost of fare'.
–   From the airline owner's point of view, this Need may be interpreted as saving money on the cost of providing a flight, in terms of fuel costs, staff costs, food costs and so on. Therefore, the Need is 'Save money', the Context is from the point of view of the 'Sponsor' Stakeholder Role and the Use Case may be 'save money on the cost of providing a flight'.

This simple example just goes to show how the Context considered can completely alter the meaning of the original Need. It should also be noted that in the example here that the two Use Cases will potentially conflict, as the passenger doesn't want to pay much money, but the owner doesn't want to spend any money either. By considering the various Use Cases, it is possible to identify any areas of potential conflict, overlaps, gaps in understanding and so on.

For the second example, let us consider a car System. Imagine that there is a Need, and hence a Need Description, to 'conserve fuel'. Again, this may seem quite straightforward, but depending on the Context, this time based on the level of hierarchy, it will take on different meanings.

–   From the System's point of view, this Need may be interpreted as conserving fuel to save on running costs of the car. Therefore, the Need is 'Conserve fuel', the Context is from the point of view of the 'System' level and the Use Case may be 'conserve fuel to minimise the running costs of the car'.

- From the fuel injection unit's point of view, this Need may be interpreted as conserving fuel to optimise the engine performance, which was derived from the engine's needs. Therefore, the Need is 'Conserve fuel', the Context is from the point of view of the 'Assembly' and the Use Case may be to 'conserve fuel to optimise engine performance'.

In the example here, the Use Cases do not conflict, but they do have quite different, yet complementary, meanings.

When it comes to demonstrating that the original Needs can be met, known as validation, then it is the Use Cases that must be validated, which, in turn, will validate the original Needs.

9.2.2   The Framework

The concepts introduced in the MBSE Ontology must be realised in some way. The ACRE Framework identifies and defines a number of Viewpoints that are used to describe the structure and content of the Views. It is these Views that combine to form the model.

The ACRE Framework defines a number of Viewpoints that are shown in the diagram in Figure 9.6.

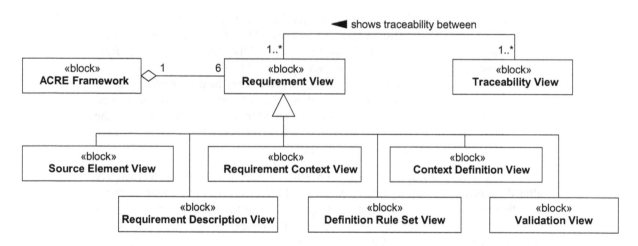

Figure 9.6   The Framework Views for Requirements modelling

The diagram here shows that there are six main ACRE Viewpoints that are needed to define the Views, which are:

- 'Source Element View'. This View contains all the Source Elements that are required in order to get the Needs right.
- 'Requirement Description View'. This View contains structured Need Descriptions. These Need Descriptions are considered individually and will usually have a number of attributes, or features, associated with each one.

- 'Definition Rule Set View'. This View contains any Rules that may have to be applied to each Need Description. For example, these may be complexity Rules in the form of equations or more general text-based Rules.
- 'Requirement Context View'. This View takes the Needs and gives them meaning by looking at them from a specific point of view by putting them into Context.
- 'Context Definition View'. This View identifies the points of view that are explored in the Requirement Context View.
- 'Validation View'. These Views provide the basis for demonstrating that the Needs can be satisfied by defining a number of Scenarios. These Views can describe Semi-formal Scenarios or Formal Scenarios.
- 'Traceability View'. Alongside these core Views there is an additional set of support Views known as the Traceability Views. These Views allow traceability between different elements of the model to be explicitly shown. These traceability links may exist between Views or between View Elements.

It should be stressed that not all Views are always necessary on a given Project as this will depend upon the level of rigour of the Project, the scale of the Project and the tools available. This is discussed in more detail in Part 5 of the book.

9.2.3 Views

This section looks at each of the Views that was introduced in the previous section. These views are not presented in any particular order, as it is the process that is being followed that will define this. Examples of such processes can be found in Appendix E.

9.2.3.1 The Source Element View

View Rationale

The Source Element View contains all relevant source information that is required to get the Needs right. It is essential that the origin of each Need is known and this is what this View allows us to define. This View is used primarily as a mechanism to establish traceability and provide links between the Needs and any other aspect of the System.

As to what these Source Elements can be, then the list is almost limitless. A Source Element can range from a single utterance to a full system specification or design. Examples of some typical Source Elements include conversations, emails, informal documents, formal requirements documents, systems specifications, designs, processes, existing systems, brainstorming sessions, structured workshops, and standards.

The list presented here simply shows some typical Source Elements and is not intended to be exhaustive. Do not feel constrained in any way by this list but use it as a starting point to consider where each Source Element may come from.

View definition

The Source Element View focuses on the subset of the original MBSE Ontology that is shown in the diagram in Figure 9.7.

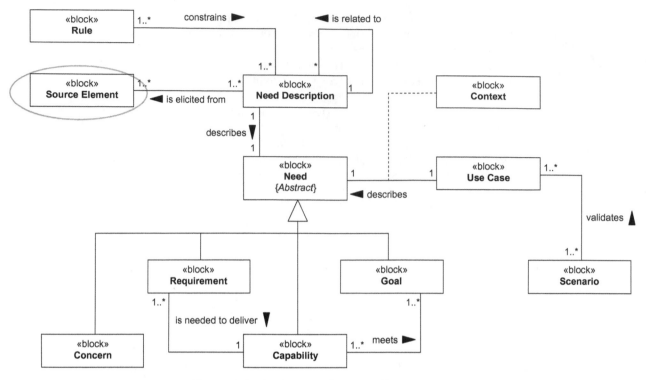

Figure 9.7   Definition of Source Element View

The Source Element View focuses on the 'Source Element' from the MBSE Ontology, as shown in the diagram here. This View is perhaps the simplest of all the Views in the Framework, as reflected in its simple structure consisting as it does of one or more 'Source Element'. Due to the varied nature of the structure and format of the Source Elements, and given the fact that this View is really just a collection of such elements that can be linked back to, the structure of this View is very simple indeed.

It should be borne in mind that the structure of the Source Element itself may be highly complex, such as the case when the Source Element is a system specification. However, this View is used primarily as a basis for traceability and as such the information in the View may be thought of as a list-like collection of elements.

View relationships
The Source Element View is related to one other View in the Framework and, hence, there will be consistency checks that must be applied to ensure that these relationships are valid.

The diagram in Figure 9.8 shows that the 'Source Element View' is related to the 'Requirement Description View' via its elements. The Need Descriptions in the

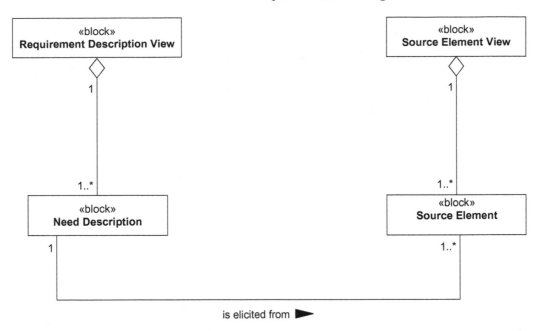

Figure 9.8 Relationships between Source Element View and other Views

Requirement Description Views are related back to the Source Elements. Each Need Description must be related to at least one Source Element and vice versa. The following Rules must be enforced:

– Rule – Each Source Element in the Source Element View must be traceable to one or more Need Description in the Requirement Description View.
– Rule – Each Need Description in the Requirement Description View must be traceable to one or more Source Element in the Source Element View.

In order to maximise the benefits of a true MBSE approach, these Rules should be automated rather than being manually applied to the model.

Stakeholder Scenario View

This view may be realised in SysML using a *block definition diagram*, with each Source Element being represented as a single *block*, as shown in the diagram in Figure 9.9.

Figure 9.9 shows a collection of *blocks* that are used in a very simple fashion. Each *block* is used only as a reference point to specific external Source Element. The example here shows a number of different types of Source Element that have number of properties defined, which are:

– 'type', which describes the basic type of the Source Reference. The various types that are allowed may be defined as a separate part of the MBSE Ontology, as shown in Figure 9.10.

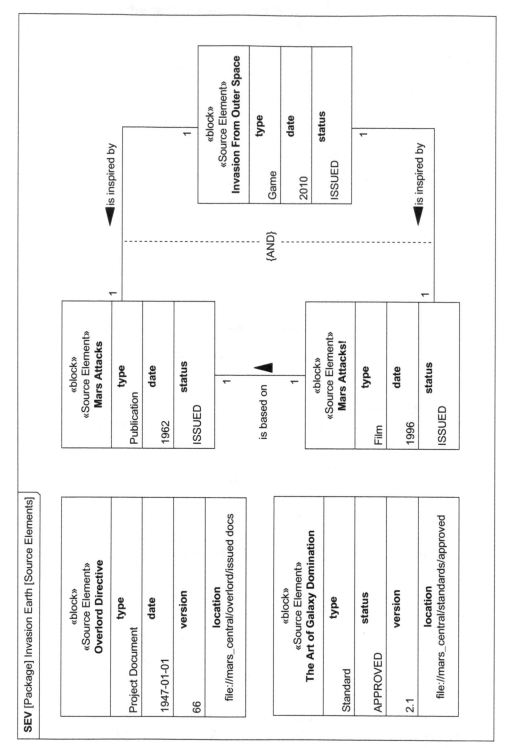

Figure 9.9 Example Source Element View

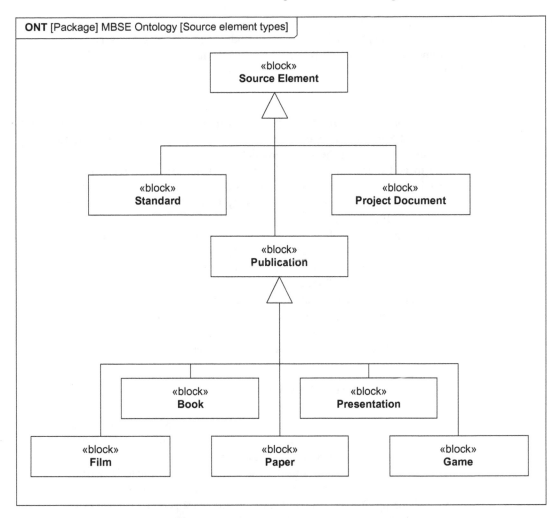

Figure 9.10   Example Source Element View showing types of Source Element

- 'status', which describes the current state of Source Element in terms of configuration control. For example, the 'status' may take on a number of values, such as 'APPROVED', 'DRAFT', 'ISSUED' and 'ARCHIVED'
- 'date', which may be a full calendar date or year.
- 'version', which defines the current version of the Source Element according to the version control system.
- 'location', which shows where the Source Element may be found.

It can easily be argued that the use of a SysML diagram here is "overkill" and that the Source Elements could simply be listed, but there is a good reason way this has been done. One of the benefits of a model-based approach is that traceability is inherent in the model. This traceability can only exist for elements that are either part of the model or explicitly linked to the model, and this diagram serves this single, but important purpose – to provide an explicit link between external Source Elements and the model itself.

View discussion

The Source Element View is both the simplest view in terms of its structure and the loosest in terms of what it may look like. This View is present to provide solid traceability back to the rest of the system model.

One way to add more value to this View is to make use of *stereotypes* and *tagged values* in order to define some basic types of Source Element. An example of some of the types of Source Elements that may be considered is shown in the diagram in Figure 9.10.

The example here shows how the Source Element may have a number of *specialisations* defined that help to define typical types of Source Element. Each of these may have a number of *tagged values* defined that show how to locate the Source Element. For example, Publications may have *tagged values* defined that show the name, author, publisher, date, etc. for each type.

This is particularly useful for validation Source Elements and it is also possible to define a Rule that states that each Source Element must have a *stereotype* based on the Source Element classification hierarchy shown here.

9.2.3.2   Requirement Description View

View rationale

This View contains structured descriptions of each Need in the form of Need Descriptions. These Need Descriptions are considered individually and will usually have a number of attributes, or features, associated with each one.

The main purpose of this View is to consider each individual Need Description according to a pre-defined set of attributes. These attributes will vary depending on the process that is being followed, the industry that the work is being carried out in, any standards or best practice models that may be used and any other number of factors — see [9] for an example of this.

This View is primarily used for managing the Need Descriptions of a System and is often the basis of implementation for many of the commercial requirements management tools that are on the market today.

Each Need Description provides a non-contextual description of a Need. When a Need is put into Context, it is known as a Use Case and, hence, there is a very strong relationship between the Need Descriptions and the Use Cases from the Requirement Context Views.

View definition

The Requirement Description View focuses on the subset of the MBSE Ontology that is shown in the diagram in Figure 9.11.

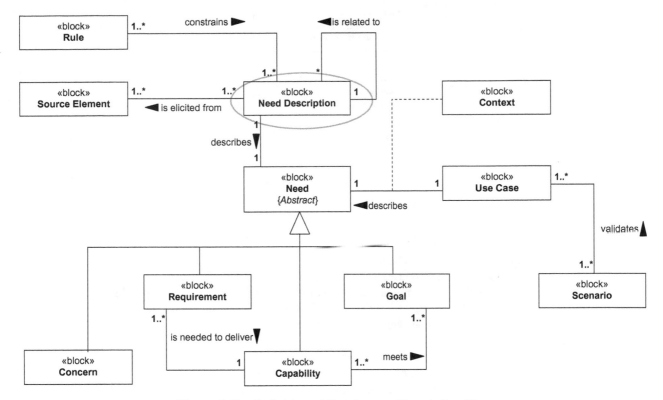

Figure 9.11   Definition of Requirement Description View

The Requirement Description View focuses on the 'Need Description' from the MBSE Ontology, as shown here. This View is one of the simplest (bearing in mind that simple does not imply easy) of all the Views in the Framework, along with the Source Element View, as reflected in its simple structure in that the 'Requirement Description View' is made up of one or more 'Need Description'. It is important to remember that the 'Need Description' shown here is not the Need itself but an abstraction of that Need that describes it using a number of features or attributes. The Need Description will be realised in SysML using a *requirement block* that has a default set of *properties* already defined but that, in reality, will usually have a number of other *properties* defined. An example of this is shown in the diagram in Figure 9.12.

The diagram in Figure 9.12 shows a set of *properties* that are defined for the concept of a Need Description. The *properties* that are defined as part of the SysML are:

– 'id#'. The unique identifier for the Need Description. Need Descriptions on any real Project will evolve during the Life Cycle of the Project and hence the

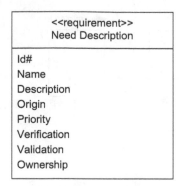

Figure 9.12   Definition of a Need Description

names and Need Descriptions may change beyond all recognition. In order to ensure that each Need Description can always be located, regardless of how it has evolved, each Need Description has a unique identifier. This can be used to locate the Need Description and also is used as a basic mechanism for trace-ability in the system. The id# will be used primarily by automated services, such as software management tools, as it will be non-memorable to most people who read it.

– 'Name'. The name is a simple label that should have some intuitive meaning that can be used to identify the Need Description by human eyes. In some ways this serves the same role as the id#, but from a human point of view. It should be remembered, however, that the Name may evolve as the Project progresses, whereas the id# may not.

– 'Description'. The description is a piece of text that describes the Need Description. This should be kept as simple and unambiguous as possible but, in reality, this is often ignored and long, verbose descriptions are often defined. This text is often supported by the definition of a number of Rules.

This is a very brief list that is based on the SysML modelling standard and should be seen as an absolute minimum set of attributes, defined as *properties*. In any real-life System several other attributes should also be considered, such as:

– 'Origin'. Any Need Description must have an origin – it must have originated from somewhere. This information is recorded as part of the Need Description. This source will be taken directly from the Source Element View. For example, this may be a conversation with a Stakeholder Role, level of hierarchy on the System, or a Source Element.

– 'Priority'. Each Need Description will often have a level of priority asso-ciated with it. For example, it may be decided that a Need may be essential in that it is always required, desirable in that it would be strongly recom-mended that it is met, or bells and whistles in that it is a nice idea, time permitting.

- 'Verification criteria'. It is essential that each Need can be proven to work – verification, which is recorded in the Need Description. The verification aspect is often omitted, whereas the validation criterion is usually deemed essential.
- 'Validation criteria'. It is essential that for each Need it can be proven that it does what it is supposed to do – validation, which is recorded in the Need Description. The verification aspect is often omitted whereas the validation criterion is usually deemed essential. The validation criterion is related directly to the Validation Views.
- 'Ownership'. Each Need must be owned and hence has a Stakeholder Role who is responsible for delivering the Need, which is recorded in the Need Description. This attribute should reference one of the Stakeholder Roles identified in the System directly. Note that this attribute differs from the 'Origin' attribute despite the fact that they are often both referring to Stakeholder Roles. The 'Origin' is related to the origin of the Need, whereas the 'Ownership' relates to who is responsible for delivering the Need.

There are many other attributes that may be considered for a Need Description as the list shown here is only intended to show a generic best practice list that may need to be tailored for specific applications.

View relationships

The Requirement Description View is related to other Views in the framework and hence there will be consistency checks that must be applied to ensure that these relationships are valid.

The diagram in Figure 9.13 shows that the Requirement Description View is related to the following other Views from the Framework:

- Source Element View. Each Need Description must be traceable back to a Source Element. This is essential for traceability and for enforcing validation of each Need.
- Definition Rule Set View. The attributes that make up the Need Description may be checked by applying a number of Rules. For example, complexity Rules may be enforced on the 'Description' attribute to ensure that the text is legible.
- Requirement Context View. Each Need Description will be related to a number of Use Cases. Each Use Case takes one or more Need and gives them meaning by putting it into Context.

These relationships may be enforced by applying the following Rules:

- Rule – Rules, when they exist, must apply to a Need Description.
- Rule – Each Need Description must relate back to a Source Element.
- Rule – Each Need Description must be related to at least one Use Case.
- Rule – The Need Description Views must relate to a Requirement Context View.
- Rule – Each Need Description must have a full set of attributes defined.

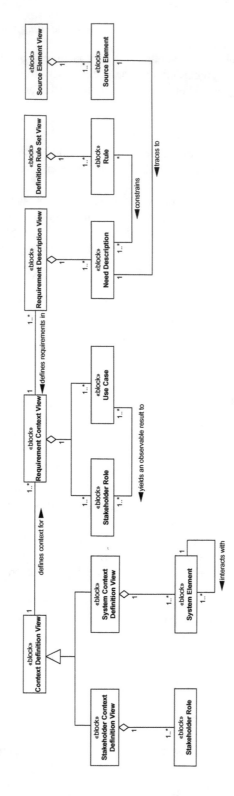

Figure 9.13   Relationships between the Requirement Description View and other Views

Rules are also needed for each of the additional attributes, such as:

- Rule – The 'Origin' attribute of any Need Description must refer to a Source Element.
- Rule – The 'Validation criteria' attribute must reference Validation Views.

In order to maximise the benefits of a true MBSE approach, these Rules should be automated rather than being manually applied to the model.

System Scenarios View

This view may be realised in SysML using a *requirement diagram* where each Need Description is shown in the diagram in Figure 9.14 using the SysML *requirement block*, indicated by the «requirement» *stereotype*.

The diagram here shows a SysML representation of a single Need Description. Notice that the *property* values have been defined here to show the 'id#', the 'txt' and the name of the Requirement. In this example, only a basic set of *properties* has been shown.

View discussion

It should be noticed here that the Need Descriptions in this View have a flat structure, whether they are visualised using lists or SysML *requirement blocks*. This is quite deliberate. There is a temptation among requirements engineers to group Needs based on their functionality or type and to create a Needs taxonomy (classification hierarchy). This goes fundamentally against the context-based approach. One of the key points of the context-based approach is that needs should be grouped together based on Context and *not* functionality or type.

Many historical approaches to requirements engineering and, indeed, many requirements documents have been obsessed with putting Needs into strict classifications. At a high level, many documents will often split up Functional Requirements and Non-functional Requirements. This is fine if the Requirements are being described, but holds no meaning in the real world. In the reality, and by the very nature of a Non-functional Requirement, they constrain Functional Requirements. It is essential, therefore, that these constraining relationships are identified. These constraining relationships can only be defined when looked at in Context. The same holds true for inclusions, extensions and generalisations – it is the Context that gives them meaning.

The same idea holds for when people want to group Needs because they appear to have similar functionality. This is fundamentally wrong because the functionality of a given Need may change depending on the Context.

Needs must be grouped according to their Context, which forms the basis of the whole approach advocated in this book. If Needs are going to be classified based only on type or functionality, then it would be as well to group them alphabetically.

This View may also be used to identify and define relationships between Requirement Descriptions and, hence, *requirements*. For example, it may be desirable to show derived Requirement Descriptions using a «derive» *dependency* in SysML. The use of such relationship will be dependent on the process and approach being followed. Chapter 5 contains a full discussion on the different types of *relationships* that may be used between *requirements*.

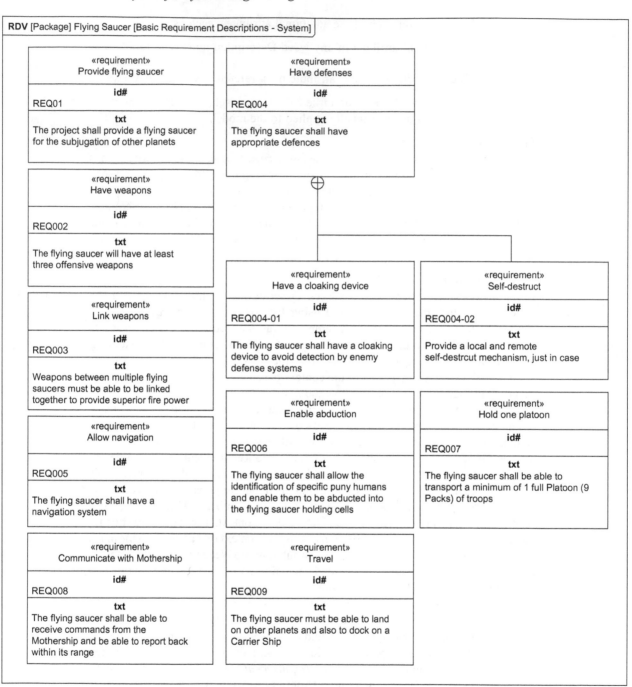

Figure 9.14   Example Requirement Description

9.2.3.3   Definition Rule Set View

View rationale

This View contains Rules that may have to be applied to each Need Description. For example, these may be complexity Rules in the form of equations of more general text-based Rules.

When defining individual Need Descriptions it is often desirable to put constraints on either the values of their *properties* or on measurable aspects of the values. These constraints are enforced by applying one or more Rule to the Need Description values. These Rules must be defined somewhere and the relevant attributes of the Need Descriptions must be identified. The purpose of this View is to capture this information.

View definition

The Definition Rule Set View focuses on the subset of the MBSE Ontology that is shown in the diagram in Figure 9.15.

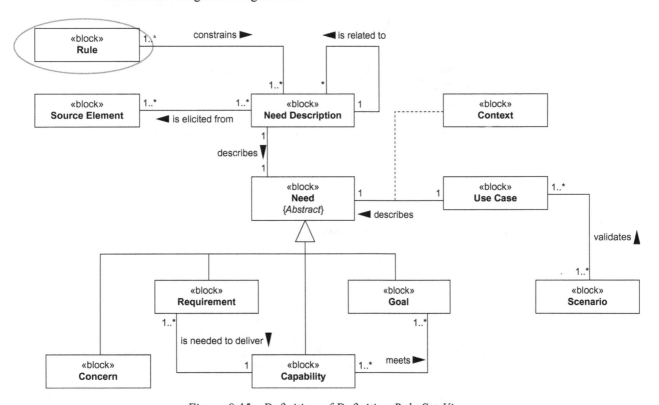

Figure 9.15   Definition of Definition Rule Set View

This View is concerned with the 'Rule', one or more of which constrains one or more 'Need Description'. Notice that the Rules are related to the Need Descriptions, rather than the Needs themselves, as the Need Description is one of the ways that the abstract Need is manifested in the model.

The 'Definition Rule Set View' is made up of one or more 'Rule'. Each 'Rule' is, in turn, made up of a 'Rule Definition', an optional 'Parameter Set' and 'ID' (not shown in the diagram):

- The 'Rule Definition' defines the Rule itself in some form. These Rules may take a number of different forms, for example equations, heuristics, enumerated lists, tables, graphs and so on. A number of examples of these are shown in the discussion below.
- The optional 'Parameter Set' defines the elements that will be used by the Rule itself, in other words the parameters of each Rule. This allows the rules to be applied in a uniform and consistent manner. In instances where the Rule Definition is, for example, a mathematical equation, then the Parameter Set must be defined. In other cases, such as the use of words to be used, the parameter Set may not exist.

These Rules will be used as the basis for automation as part of the overall MBSE approach.

View relationships

The Definition Rule Set View is related to other Views in the Framework and hence there will be consistency checks that must be applied to ensure that these relationships are valid.

It can be seen in Figure 9.16 that one or more 'Rule' from the 'Definition Rule Set View' constrains one or more 'Need Description' from the 'Requirement Description View'.

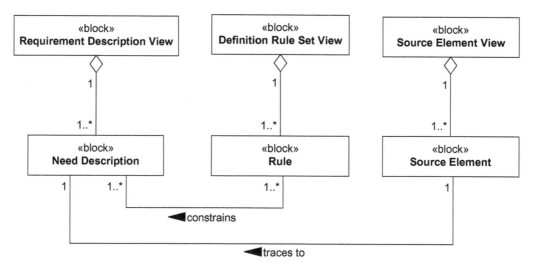

Figure 9.16   Relationships between the Definition Rule Set View and the other Views

These relationships result in the following process Rules:

- Rule – Each Rule must apply to at least one Need Description attribute or the Need Description itself.
- Rule – Each Need Description may be constrained by zero or more Rules.

In order to maximise the benefits of a true MBSE approach, these rules should be automated rather than being manually applied to the model.

Constraint Validation View

This View may be visualised in SysML using a *block definition diagram* to specify a number of Rules using either regular *blocks* or special *constraint blocks*. These *blocks* may be used in a number of different ways, depending on the type of constraint that needs to be applied, for example:

- The Rule may be realised using formal techniques, such as mathematics, in which case the SysML notation that is applied will be the *constraint block*.
- The Rule may be quite abstract and as such not require the full *constraint block* notation, in which case a regular *block* may be applied.

An example of using formal mathematics for defining a Rule using a *constraint block* constraint is shown in the diagram in Figure 9.17.

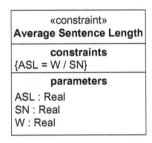

Figure 9.17   Example Definition Rule Set View showing a single Rule

The diagram here shows how a Rule may be defined using a SysML parametric *constraint block*. The Rule that is being defined forms part of a standard set of rules for complexity measurement of sentences.

The Rule here is made up of three main elements:

- The Rule name. This is shown in the top box in the diagram and has the word «constraint» above it to indicate that this is a SysML *constraint block*. The name for the Rule in this case is defined as 'Average Sentence Length' which is a standard measurement for text.
- The Rule definition. This is shown in the middle box and has the word 'constraints' above it to indicate that this is part of the standard SysML *constraint block*. The rule itself is shown in curly brackets and, in this instance, is defined in terms of a mathematical equation. The various *parameters* that are used as part of the equation are defined in the next box.

–   The *parameter* definitions. This is shown in the lowest of the three boxes and has the word 'parameters' above it to indicate that this is part of the standard SysML *constraint block*. In this instance, there are three *parameters*: 'ASL' which is the 'Average Sentence Length' and is a 'Real' number, 'SN' which is the 'Syllable Number' and is an 'Integer' and 'W' which is the 'number of words' and is also an integer.

Clearly, these Rules must be verified, which can be done in any way seen fit, such as using a mathematical proof, a software package and so on.

The same Rule, however, may also be defined in a more abstract and less formal way, as shown in the diagram in Figure 9.18.

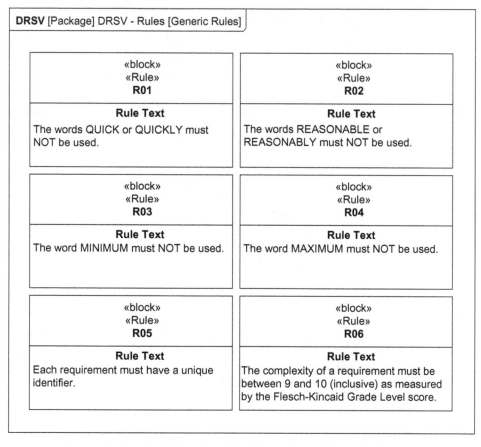

Figure 9.18   Definition Rule Set View using abstract techniques

The Definition Rule Set View in Figure 9.18 is realised as a *block definition diagram* with each Rule represented using a *stereotyped block*. The «Rule» *stereotype* has the *tag* "Rule Text" defined with it, allowing the text to be displayed in a separate, named *compartment* of the *block*. The information shown in Figure 9.2

is a minimum: a name or identifier for a Rule, along with descriptive text. Additional *tags*, for example, could be added to capture the justification and source of each Rule.

It is often the case that the Rules themselves are made up of a number of other Rules. This is the case in the example shown in Figure 9.18, and a complete set of Rules for performing the text description complexity measure is shown in Figure 9.19.

The diagram here shows the complete set of Rules for calculating the complexity of text descriptions. These Rules are based on the so-called Flesch–Kincaid grade level test and the Flesch reading ease test [1,2].

Where a number of Rules are defined that are dependent on one another, for example in the order that they must be calculated, it is also important to show a network of these Rules and their inter-dependencies. This can be achieved in SysML by using the *parametric diagram*, an example of which can be seen in Figure 9.20.

Figure 9.20 shows how the Rules that have been defined can be strung together in a network to provide the ultimate end result that is required for the complexity measure. There are four main Rules here that are used to calculate the complexity using mathematical equations ('Average Sentence Length', 'Flesch Reading Ease Test', 'Average Number of Syllables Per Word' and 'Flesch–Kincaid Grade Level Test') and then a single rule in the form of a heuristic ('Requirement Complexity Rule') that is used to make the decision of whether or not the attribute satisfies the ultimate Rule.

View discussion

The Definition Rule Set View is quite an odd view in the way that it is frequently used. In many cases, this view is simply never considered, and the individual Need Descriptions can be written in an ad hoc fashion providing that they are in the correct place in the requirement document.

Another way that this view is often badly used is when its importance is overemphasised. It must be made clear that this View is very important, particularly when the Project is concerned with a mission-critical or safety-critical system, However, in many cases all that is presented for a complete set of Needs is the Requirement Description View (or equivalent) and, provided that the rules in the Definition Rule Set View have been applied, then this is deemed as acceptable. Again, it should be stressed that the main emphasis should be on the Context of the needs and, hence, the set of all the Views.

9.2.3.4 Requirement Context View

View rationale

This View takes the Needs and gives them meaning by looking at them from a specific point of view. This is known as putting the Needs into Context and forms the basis of the approach presented in this chapter. The Needs have only been described so far by defining a number of Need Descriptions in the Requirement Description View. This is all well and good and an essential part of any requirements exercise, but this is by no means complete. The problem arises that these Need Descriptions

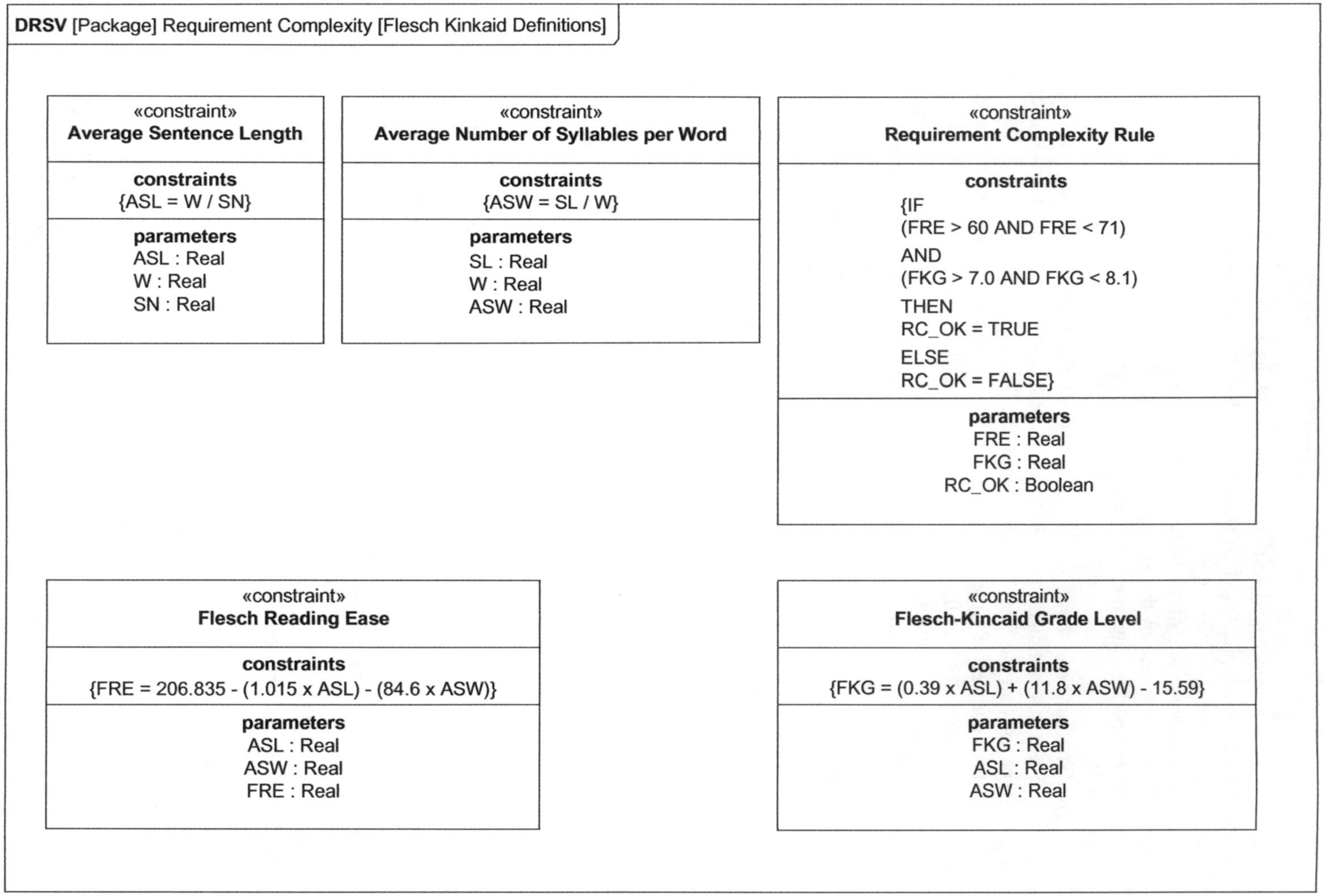

DRSV [Package] Requirement Complexity [Flesch Kinkaid Definitions]

«constraint»
Average Sentence Length

constraints
{ASL = W / SN}

parameters
ASL : Real
W : Real
SN : Real

«constraint»
Average Number of Syllables per Word

constraints
{ASW = SL / W}

parameters
SL : Real
W : Real
ASW : Real

«constraint»
Requirement Complexity Rule

constraints

{IF
(FRE > 60 AND FRE < 71)
AND
(FKG > 7.0 AND FKG < 8.1)
THEN
RC_OK = TRUE
ELSE
RC_OK = FALSE}

parameters
FRE : Real
FKG : Real
RC_OK : Boolean

«constraint»
Flesch-Kincaid Grade Level

constraints
{FKG = (0.39 x ASL) + (11.8 x ASW) - 15.59}

parameters
FKG : Real
ASL : Real
ASW : Real

«constraint»
Flesch Reading Ease

constraints
{FRE = 206.835 - (1.015 x ASL) - (84.6 x ASW)}

parameters
ASL : Real
ASW : Real
FRE : Real

Figure 9.19   Example Definition Rule Set View showing complete Rule set

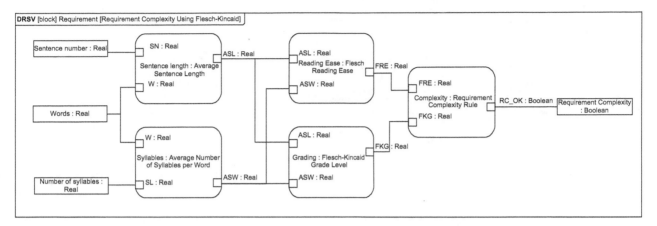

Figure 9.20   Example Rule Set Definition View showing constraint usage

may be interpreted in different ways depending on the viewpoint of the reader of the Need Description. It is essential then that each Need is looked at from different points of view, or in different Contexts. It will also be found that different Contexts are concerned with different sets of Needs, all of which will be related together in some way. When a Need is put into Context it is known as a Use Case, and by considering these Use Cases and the relationships between them and other Use Cases or Stakeholder Roles, it is possible to generate a complete point of view, or Context.

View definition

The Requirement Context View focuses on the subset of the MBSE Ontology that is shown in the diagram in Figure 9.21.

The diagram here shows that the Requirement Context View is primarily concerned with one or more 'Context' of the System that is concerned with using one or more 'Use Case' to describe the context of a 'Need'.

A number of these Requirement Context Views will exist, the number of which will be determined by the information contained in the Context Definition Views.

View relationships

The Requirement Context View is related to other views in the Framework and, hence, there will be consistency checks that must be applied to ensure that these relationships are valid.

It can be seen from the diagram in Figure 9.22 that the one or more 'Requirement Description View' describes the Needs in each 'Requirement Context View'. This reflects the very strong relationship between each 'Need Description' and one or more associated 'Use Case'. One or more 'Validation View' validates each 'Use Case'. This is a very important relationship as every Need in the System must be demonstrated to be achievable and that it has been satisfied, which is the purpose of the Validation Views. Notice, however, that it is the Use Cases that are the subject of

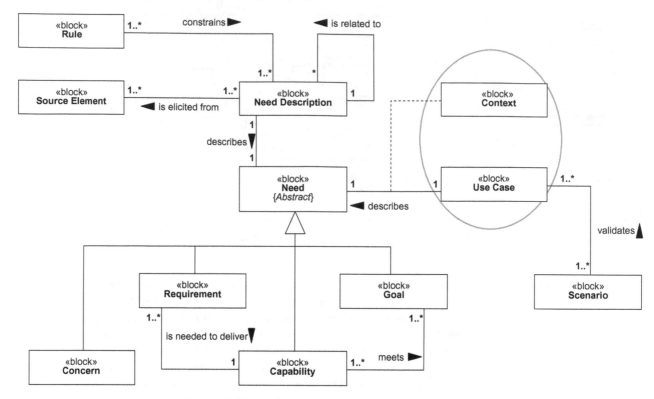

Figure 9.21   Definition of Requirement Context View

the validation, rather than the Need Descriptions. This is because a single Need Description may be interpreted in a number of different ways depending on the Context of the Need.

A 'Context Definition View' defines the context for one or more 'Requirement Context View' which may result in quite a number of diagrams that represent the Requirement Context Views.

It should be clear from this diagram that the Requirement Context View forms the heart of the whole Framework possessing, as they do, direct relationships to almost all other Views in the Framework. The following Rules should be applied:

- Rule – Each Requirement Context View must have a related element on a Context Definition View that defines the Context.
- Rule – Each Use Case must be related to at least one Need Description.
- Rule – Each and every Need Description must have at least one Use Case.
- Rule – Each Stakeholder Role on the Requirement Context View must have an associated element form a Context Definition View, such as a Stakeholder Role or System Element.
- Rule – Each Context Definition View must be related to at least on Requirement Context View.

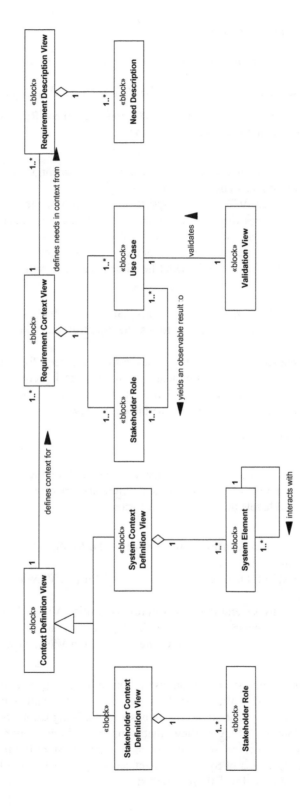

Figure 9.22   Relationships between the Requirement Context View and the other Views

–   Rule – Each Use Case must be related to either another Use Case or a Stakeholder Role.
–   Rule – Each Use Case must have at least one Validation View associated with it.

In order to maximise the benefits of a true MBSE approach, these Rules should be automated rather than being manually applied to the model.

View visualisation

This view will be visualised in SysML using the *use case diagram*, which has been a cornerstone of requirements engineering for many years.

The diagram in Figure 9.23 shows a SysML visualisation of the Requirement Context View using a *use case diagram*. In this diagram the Use Cases from the MBSE Ontology are shown as SysML *use cases*. This is slightly confusing as the term use case is used twice here, once to refer to the concept of a Use Case (a Need in Context) and once to refer to the SysML *use case* element (the ellipse in the diagram).

View discussion

This View focuses on the Contexts of the Needs that are described in the Requirement Description View and, as such, it forms the heart of the whole approach advocated in this book.

The Requirement Context View really does enforce the need for applying an effective modelling notation to requirements engineering as it demonstrates the sheer number and also the complexity of the relationships between the various Views in the Framework and the elements within each View.

9.2.3.5   Context Definition View

View rationale

This View identifies the points of view that are explored in the Requirement Context View. These points of view, or Contexts, may take many forms including Stakeholder Roles and levels of hierarchy in a System.

View definition

The Source Element View focuses on the subset of the MBSE Ontology that is shown in the diagram in Figure 9.24.

The area of the MBSE Ontology that is focused on for this View is the various types of 'Context'.

There are potentially several types of 'Context Definition View' dependent on the Contexts that are considered. For example, Figure 9.4 shows a number of Contexts, each of which will have its own Context Definition View. Two examples of this are:

–   The 'Stakeholder Context Definition View' that is made up of one or more 'Stakeholder Role'. This View identifies a number of Stakeholder Roles in a classification hierarchy that are used as a basis for defining Contexts.
–   The 'System Context Definition View' that is made up of one or more 'System Element', each of which relates to one or more other 'System Element'. This View identifies a number of System Elements, usually in a structural hierarchy that are used as a basis for defining Contexts.

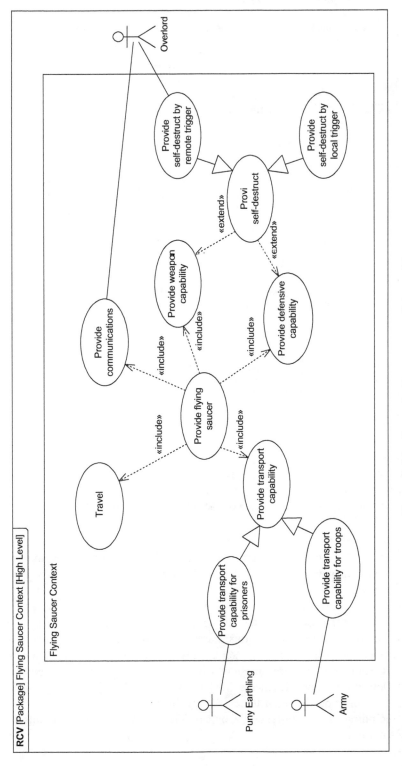

Figure 9.23 Example Requirement Context View

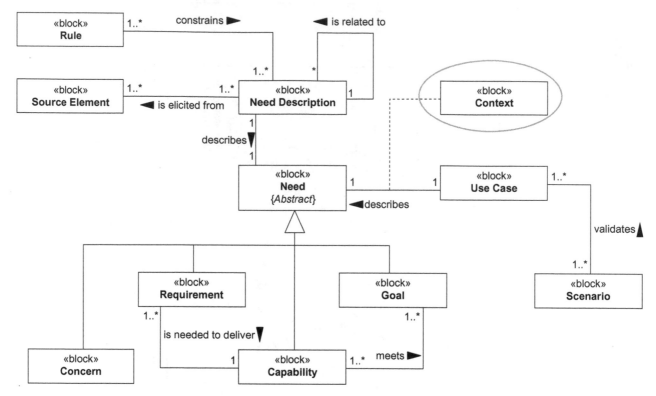

Figure 9.24   Definition of Context Definition View

It should be remembered that there may very well be more different types of View identified here, which will depend on the application of the modelling and the Project. The two shown here are two of the most common types.

View relationships

The Context Definition View is related to other Views in the Framework and hence there will be consistency checks that must be applied to ensure that these relationships are valid.

The main relationship shown in Figure 9.25 is between this View and one or more 'Requirement Context View' as the main purpose of this View is to define the Contexts. As a consequence of this, there will be several diagrams that realise the Requirement Context View for each Context Definition View. There will also be other relationships that are not shown in this diagram from the 'Stakeholder Context Definition View'. Elements from the Context Definition View, such as Stakeholder Roles or System Elements, may be used and referenced in other Views, including the Requirement Context View, where these elements may appear as *actors*.

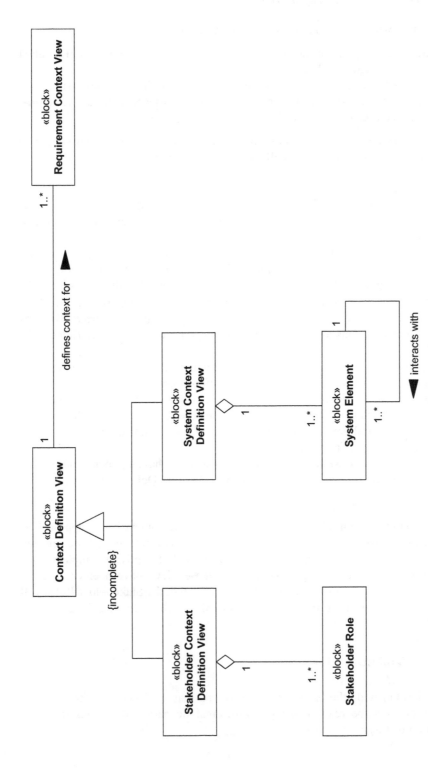

Figure 9.25   Relationships between the Context Definition View and the other Views

The following Rules may be applied to these Views:

- Rule – Each element in each Context Definition View may define an individual Requirement Context View.
- Rule – Each element on a Stakeholder Context Definition View, such as a Stakeholder Role or System Element, may appear as a Stakeholder Role on a Requirement Context View.

In order to maximise the benefits of a true MBSE approach, these Rules should be automated rather than being manually applied to the model.

View visualisation

The Context Definition View is visualised in SysML using *block definition diagrams* to show the Stakeholder Roles, System hierarchy, or whatever the source of the Contexts is.

The diagram in Figure 9.26 shows the SysML visualisation of both the Stakeholder Context Definition View and the System Context Definition View.

This diagram here shows how the Stakeholder Context Definition View may be realised using a *block definition diagram*. The Stakeholder Roles on this View are usually shown as taxonomy, or classification hierarchy, using the *generalisation* (has types) relationship. This allows a number of categories of Stakeholder Roles to be defined.

Each one of these Stakeholder Roles will potentially have its own Context and, hence, require the creation of a Context Definition View.

The diagram in Figure 9.27 shows how the System Context Definition View may be realised using a *block definition diagram*. The various System Elements are shown as *blocks* and are expressed in the form of a structural hierarchy using the SysML *composition* relationship.

Each one of these System Elements will potentially have its own Context and, hence, will require the creation of an associated Context Definition View.

View discussion

The Context Definition Views are crucial to the whole context-based approach as they are the Views that allow us to identify the various Contexts that are relevant for the System or Project at hand. The Views can look deceptively simple as they can be very difficult to get right. Indeed, once these Views have been created and then the Requirement Context Views have been created, the Stakeholder Roles will often be refined, resulting in another iteration of modelling for the Context Definition Views.

9.2.3.6   Validation View

View rationale

These Views provide the basis for demonstrating that the Needs can be satisfied. These Views can be realised using Semi-formal Scenarios at various levels of abstraction or Formal Scenarios.

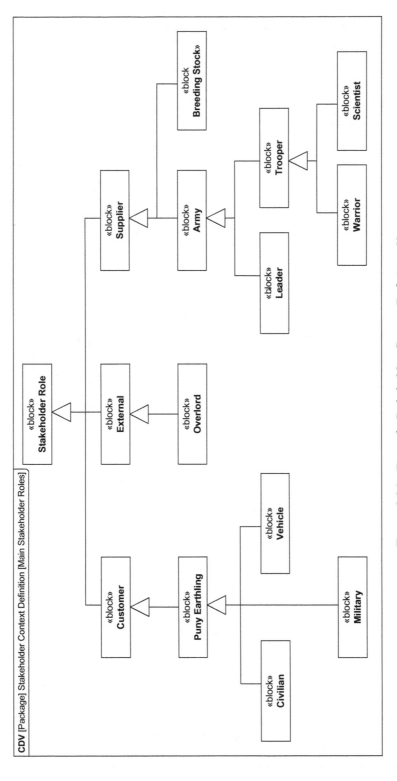

Figure 9.26 Example Stakeholder Context Definition View

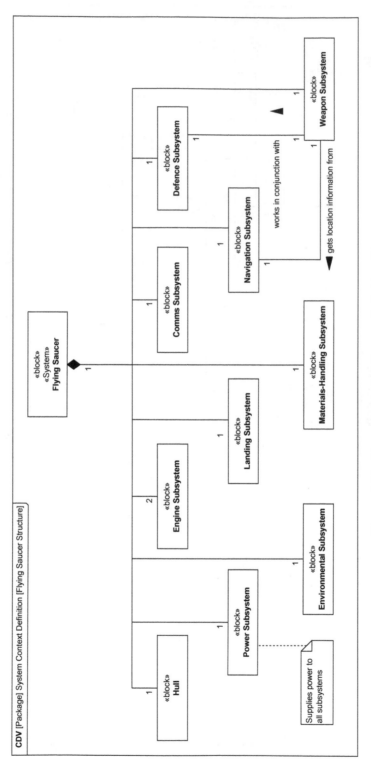

Figure 9.27 Example System Context Definition View

View definition

The Validation View focuses on the subset of the MBSE Ontology that is shown in the diagram in Figure 9.28.

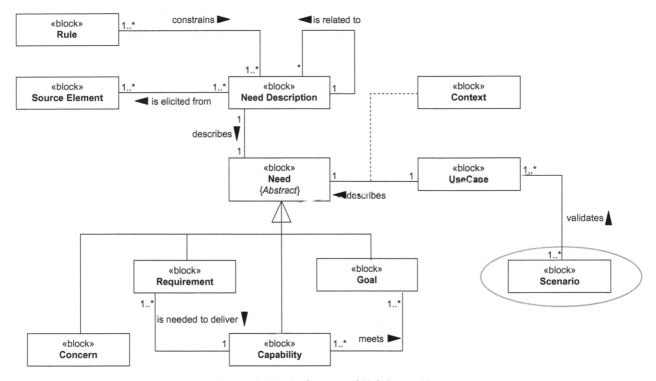

Figure 9.28   Definition of Validation View

This View focuses on the Scenarios that are used to validate the Use Cases and, hence, the original Needs. Two main types of Scenario, shown in Figure 9.4, are considered:

- Semi-formal Scenarios. These Scenarios explore various what-if situations by considering the relationships between entities in the System, for example by looking at how the various Stakeholder Roles interact with the System in order to satisfy a particular Use Case. These Scenarios will be visualised using, primarily, SysML *sequence diagrams*.
- Formal Scenarios. These Scenarios explore various what-if situations by considering how the *values* of various *properties* vary and, hence, impact the System. These Scenarios will be visualised using SysML *constraint blocks* and their associated diagrams.

There are three possible types of 'Validation View', which are the 'Stakeholder Scenario View', the 'System Scenario View' and two types of 'Constraint Validation view'.

View relationships

The Validation View is related to other Views in the Framework and hence there will be consistency checks that must be applied to ensure that these relationships are valid.

It can be seen from the diagram in Figure 9.29 that one or more 'Validation View' validates each 'Use Case'. The validation of all the original Needs is achieved through validating each Use Case.

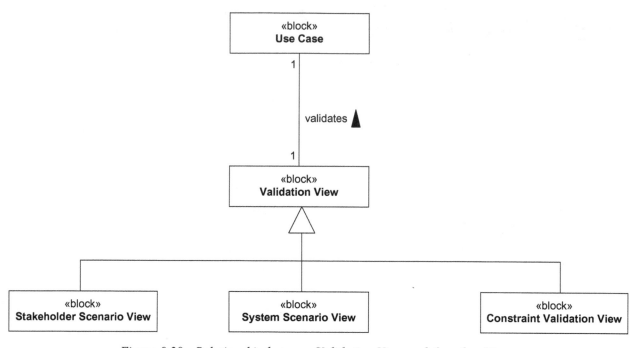

Figure 9.29   Relationship between Validation View and the other Views

The following Rules may be applied:

–   Each Use Case must have one or more Validation View associated with it.
–   Each Constraint Validation View must use *properties* that exist on the System Context Definition View.

In order to maximise the benefits of a true MBSE approach, these Rules should be automated rather than being manually applied to the model.

View visualisation

The first of the Validation Views that will be considered is the 'Stakeholder Scenario View'.

This View is concerned with looking at Scenarios using the *sequence diagram*. The *sequence diagram* looks at the *interactions* between sets of *life lines* which, in this View, will be the System itself and a number of *actors* representing Stakeholder Roles.

In order to generate a Scenario, the first step is to select a specific Use Case, visualised by a *use case,* from a Context. Next, the Context itself, or the System, is visualised using a single *life line*. The Stakeholder Roles that relate to the selected Use Case are then identified by seeing which *actors* relate to the *use case*, either directly or indirectly. An example of this is shown in the diagram in Figure 9.30.

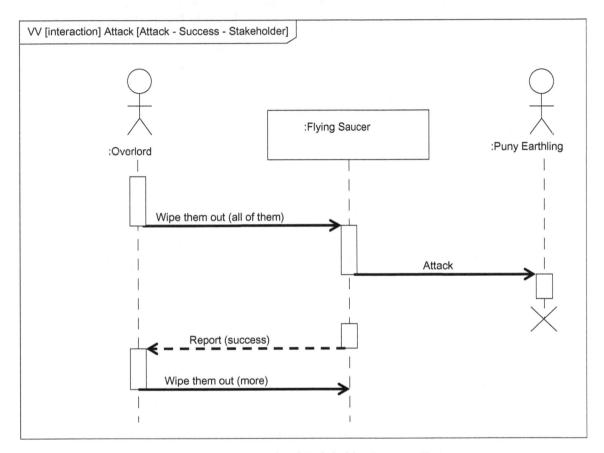

Figure 9.30   Example of Stakeholder Scenario View

Figure 9.30 shows a Scenario that has been described for the *use case* 'Provide ground attack capability', an inclusion of 'Provide weapon capability' from the System Context. In this case, the scenario shown is one where the Overlord provides an instruction to the Spaceship to attack the Puny Earthlings. This attack is successful and the Overlord then orders the Spaceship to wipe out some more.

View visualisation

This View also looks at Scenarios and also visualises them using the *sequence diagram*. In this case, however, the *life lines* are realised by System Elements and the *interactions* between them are analysed for a specific *use case*.

These System-level Scenarios must be consistent with the higher-level Stakeholder Role-level Scenarios, should they exist. One way to think about these two types of Scenario and the differences between them is to think of the Stakeholder Role-level Scenarios as black box Scenarios where the System is treated as a single entity with no details on what goes on inside. The System-level Scenarios, however, may be thought of as white box Scenarios where the inner workings of the System are considered by looking at the System Elements and the interactions between them.

An example of a System Scenario View is shown in the diagram in Figure 9.31.

The diagram here shows the same Scenario that was considered for the 'Stakeholder Scenario View' in Figure 9.30 but this time using a 'System Scenario View'. It can be seen that, in essence, the two diagrams show exactly the same information, but from two different points of view. While the Stakeholder Scenario View focused on the interactions between the Stakeholder Roles and the System, the System Scenario View focuses on the interactions between System Elements within the System.

View visualisation

The Constraint Validation View actually has two Views associated with it, the Constraint Definition View and the Constraint Usage View. The Constraint Validation Views allow Formal Scenarios to be considered. While the previous Semi-formal Scenarios looked at interactions between various elements, the Formal Scenarios allow different properties of the System to be measured and reasoned about.

The approach taken is the same as previously, in that a single Use Case, visualised by a *use case* from a Context is chosen, but this time a series of parametrics from the model will be looked at reasoned about. This reasoning will take the form of applying equations, logic, heuristics, look-up table and any number of other mathematical-type techniques. These techniques are defined using *constraint blocks*, as shown in the diagram in Figure 9.32.

The diagram here shows an example of a set of *constraint blocks* that have been defined. These *parametric constraints* form a library of calculations that can be applied to the System but, as yet, how they are applied to the System has not been defined. This usage of the *constraint blocks* is shown in the following view, the 'Constraint Usage View'.

Visualising the 'Constraint Usage View'

The Constraint Usage View shows how the *parametric constraints* defined in the Constraint Definition View are applied to the model itself. This view is visualised using the SysML *parametric diagram*.

The diagram in Figure 9.33 shows how the *constraint blocks* that have been defined previously may be applied to the System Elements. The *constraint properties* representing the usage of each *constraint block* are connected together in the form of a network, and then the *parameters* that are required for each *constraint property* are taken either from other *constraint properties* or directly from *properties* on the model.

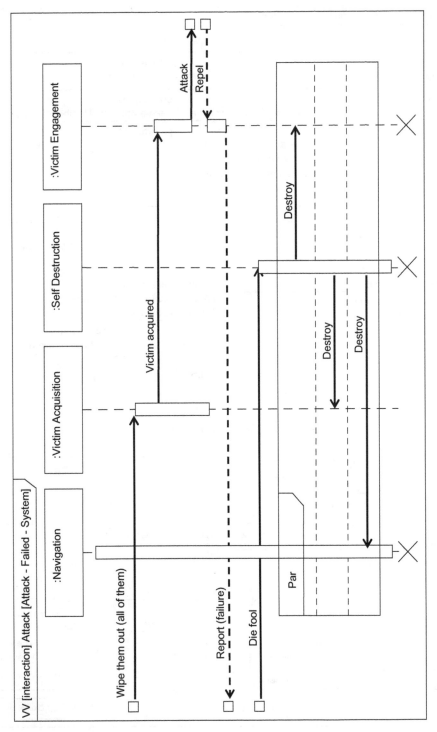

Figure 9.31   Example of System Scenario View

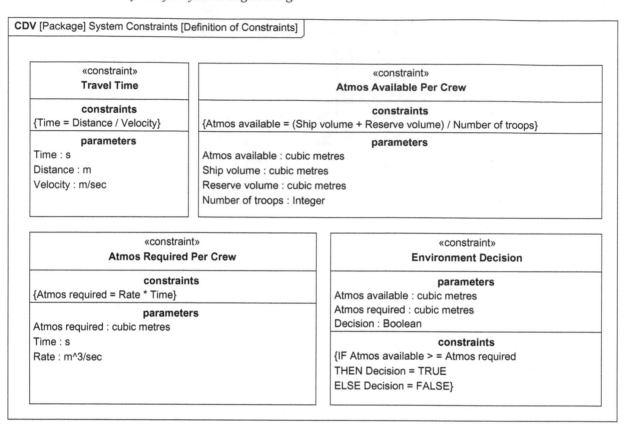

Figure 9.32   Example Constraint Definition View

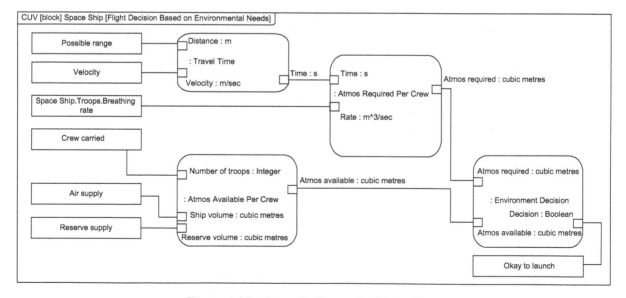

Figure 9.33   Example Constraint Usage View

View discussion

The various Validation Views are an essential part of the Framework. Needs are not Needs if they cannot be satisfied. In order to satisfy a Need, it is necessary to understand its Context by considering its Use Cases. These Use Cases may then be validated by the Scenarios. The original Needs, therefore, are validated via their Use Cases.

The Validation Views have many uses. The obvious use is that they allow us to demonstrate how we can satisfy each Need. As a result of this, it is possible to use these Validation Views as a basis for acceptance tests. Acceptance tests are the only means by which the end customer can assess whether or not the Project has been successful and are based solely on the original Needs.

These Validation Views are also used to ensure that the Use Cases are actually correct. Not only do they allow us to satisfy the Needs, but they also force us to understand the Use Cases and, hence, understand the source Needs better. This understanding allows conflicts to be identified, gaps to be spotted, overlaps and identical needs to be highlighted and other analysis techniques to be applied – see Chapter 5 for a discussion on such analysis techniques.

Another use for these Validation Views is to allow us to reason about the Needs at a business level. Business analysts often use terms like measures of effectiveness (MOEs) and measures of performance (MOPs). The clue to the relationship between these measures and the Scenarios is the word measure. When using *constraint blocks* and *parametric diagrams*, this is exactly what we are doing. As a result of this, the formal Validation Views can be used to provide both measures of effectiveness and measures of performance. In the same way that the Semiformal Scenarios can be applied at either the Stakeholder Role level or System level, the same is true for the formal validation. By applying Formal Scenarios at the Stakeholder Role level, we can provide measures of effectiveness, and by applying them at the System-level, we can provide measures of performance.

Applying the same thought processes, it is also possible to perform trade studies on the Needs set. This takes a very similar form, where different Formal Scenarios are considered and the results then analysed.

9.2.3.7   The traceability Views

View rationale

The Views that have been looked at so far form the heart of the context-based approach; however, a key part of any requirements engineering endeavour is to provide traceability both to and from the original Needs. This is essential for both quality and validation reasons and provides a level of rigour and, hence, confidence to any Needs set.

Establishing traceability can be a long, tedious and error-prone activity, especially when Needs must be traced by hand. There are many types of relationships that may exist between Needs and defining what these are and where they exist is no simple task. One of the big benefits of adopting a model-based approach is that all of this traceability is inherent in the model and, therefore, may be easily automated, given a Tool of sufficient capability.

There are two levels of traceability relationships that exist in the model: implicit and explicit relationships. The implicit relationships are the ones that are inherent in the modelling language itself. One of the advantages of using a standard model notation, such as the SysML, is that there is an underlying meta-model beneath the notation that specifies exactly how each of the modelling elements relates to one another. For example an *operation* on a *block* will be related to an *activity* on a *state*, hence traceability will exist. The explicit relationships are those that are not inherent in the modelling notation but that are dependent on the application of the modelling. These relationships can be identified directly from the MBSE Ontology and its associated Frameworks. For example, one or more Validation View validates one or more Use Case.

View definition

In the area of requirements engineering, these traceability relationships can take on many different forms. For example, just consider the Source Element and the number of different things that can be a Source Element. These range from conversations, to higher-level Needs, to specifications to entire Systems. It is often necessary, therefore, to define exactly where the traceability relationships exist. Indeed, it is possible to trace between almost any System Element and any element in the Framework. It is also often desirable to trace between the Views themselves. This is shown in the diagram in Figure 9.34.

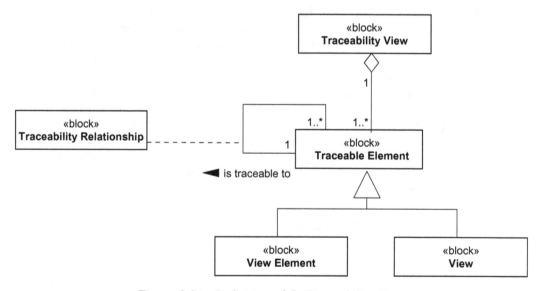

Figure 9.34   Definition of the Traceability View

The diagram here shows that the 'Traceability View' is made up of one or more 'Traceable Element' of which there are two types:

– The 'View Element' that represents any element that exists within the MBSE Ontology.
– The 'View' that represents any View from the Framework.

Each 'Traceable Element' is traceable to one or more other 'Traceable Element' via a 'Traceability Relationship'. It should also be noted that the concept of a 'Traceable Element' is defined as a Cross-cutting Element, as described in Chapter 2.

View relationships

The very nature of this View is to relate other Views and View Elements together; therefore, it can potentially relate to all of the core Views in the Framework.

View visualisation

This View can be visualised using a number of different techniques, such as:

— Tables – simple tables to show relationships between elements.
— Spread sheets – similar to the previous point, but using a spread sheet.
— In a database, using a requirements management tool – many requirements management tools allow traceability to be established using the underlying database and then visualised in different ways.
— SysML diagrams – any relationships may be defined in the model. This may be achieved using, for example, *block definition diagrams* to show relationships between System Elements and *requirement diagrams* to show relationships between Needs and Use cases.

As has been mentioned several times already, when a true model is produced then the traceability is inherent and, therefore, many of these views may be automated.

The diagram in Figure 9.35 shows an example of how traceability may be set up in the model. In this case, the traceability between Use Cases (shown as *use cases*) and Needs (shown as *requirements*) is shown using the *refine* dependency.

The diagram in Figure 9.36 shows another approach to showing traceability. In this case the traceability is shown in a number of ways:

— The validation of Use case (shown as *use cases*) is shown by using the '«validate»' *stereotype* of a *dependency* that has been specially defined. In this case, *testCases* are shown that apply to each *use case*.
— The traceability between Use Cases (shown as *use cases*) and needs (shown as *requirements*) is shown using the *refine dependency* in the same way that it has been shown in Figure 9.35.
— The traceability between Source Elements (represented by *blocks*) and Needs (represented by *requirements*) is shown using the *refine dependency*.
— The traceability between System Elements (shown here by the 'Weapon Subsystem' *package*) and the Use Cases (shown by *use cases*) that they relate to is shown using the *trace dependency*.
— The traceability between System Elements (shown here by the 'Weapon Subsystem' *package*) and Needs (shown as *requirements*) is shown using the *satisfy dependency*.

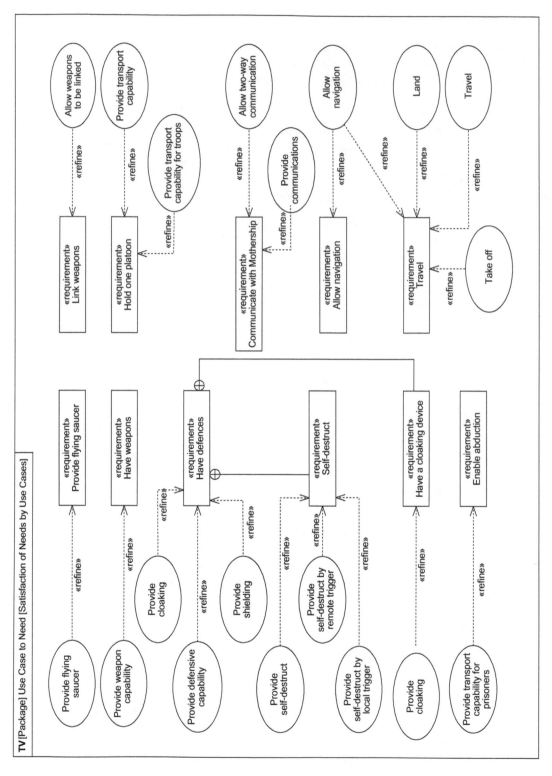

Figure 9.35 Traceability View showing refinement of Needs by Use Cases

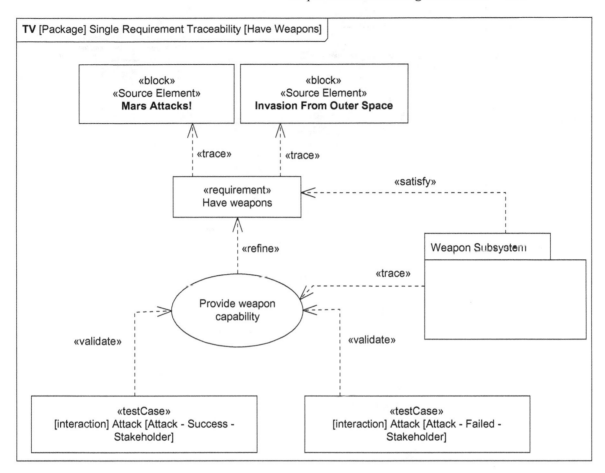

Figure 9.36   Traceability View showing traceability for a single Requirement Description

The traceability shown here is not carved in stone and may be tailored depending on the specific approach adopted by the Organisation. The point here is to show that all of the traceability paths may be set up in the model and, once this has been done, all traceability artefacts (such as tables and matrices) may then be potentially generated by a Tool.

9.3   The Requirements modelling Framework

It is now possible to define the full ACRE Framework, based on all of the Views defined in this chapter.

The diagram in Figure 9.37 shows the full ACRE Framework with all the Views shown and the relationships between them.

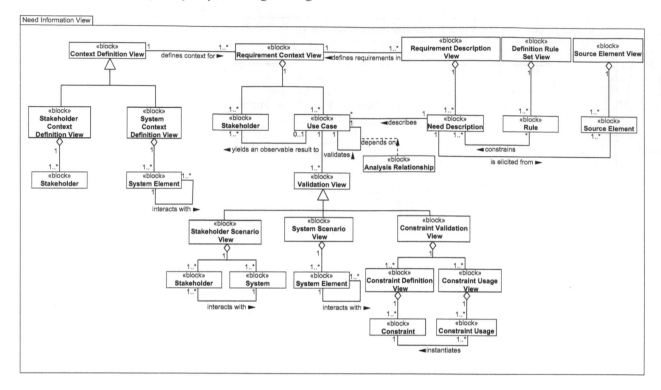

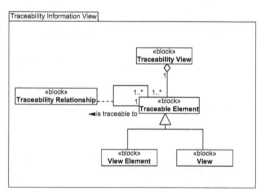

Figure 9.37   Complete Framework for Requirements modelling

9.4   Using the Requirements modelling Framework

The ACRE Framework was deliberately created so that its use was flexible, which was one of the original Use Cases from the Context. This section shows an example of how the ACRE Framework may be used by presenting a simple, high-level Process that allows the Views to be created.

The description of this Process is shown, of course, using the "seven views" approach [4].

9.4.1   The ACRE Process – Process Content View

This section presents the rather simple Process Content View for the ACRE Process, as shown in the diagram in Figure 9.38.

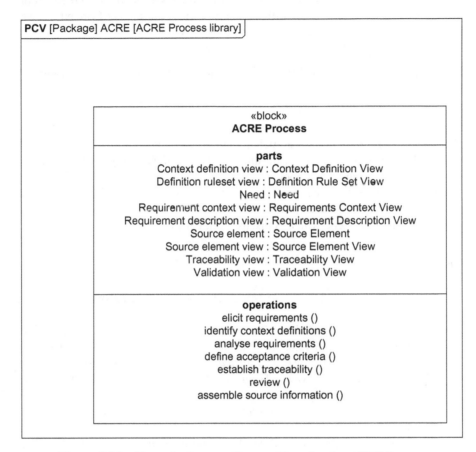

Figure 9.38   Example Process Content View for the ACRE Process

The diagram in Figure 9.38 shows the Process Content View for the ACRE Process. Note that there is only a single Process here, named the 'ACRE Process'.

The *properties* on the *block* represent the Process Artefacts, as usual, and it can be seen that these are all typed to either elements from the MBSE Ontology (such as 'Need') that make up Views or the actual Views from the ACRE Framework.

The *operations* on the *block* represent the Process Activities, which may be described briefly as:

– 'assemble source information', where the Source Element Views are created.
– 'elicit requirements', where the Needs are elicited from the Source Elements in the form of the Requirement Description View.
– 'identify context definitions', where the Context Definition Views are identified from Needs.

- 'analyse requirements', where the Requirement Context Views are created, based on the Context Definition Views and based on the Requirement Description View.
- 'define acceptance criteria', where the Validation Views are created based on the Use Cases that were identified as part of the Requirement Context Views.
- 'establish traceability', where the Traceability Views are created.
- 'review', where all the ACRE Views are reviewed.

This simple Process is defined fully with all the remaining Views in Appendix F.

9.5   Summary

This chapter has introduced the ACRE Framework that comprises a number of Views. The Views are based on realisations of the MBSE Ontology that has formed the core of everything in this book.

A simple Process for using ACRE has then been very briefly introduced. The next logical step is to look at how the Framework may be used to implement the approach on real projects, which is discussed in Chapter 15.

References

1. Flesch R. 'A new readability yardstick'. *Journal of Applied Psychology*. 1994; 32:221–33
2. Kincaid J.P., Fishburne R.P. Jr, Rogers R.L., Chissom B.S. *Derivation of New Readability Formulas (Automated Readability Index, Fog Count and Flesch Reading Ease Formula) for Navy Enlisted Personnel)*. Research Branch Report 8-75, Millington, TN: Naval Technical Training, U.S. Naval Air Station, Memphis, TN; 1975
3. Holt J. *A Pragmatic Guide to Business Process Modelling*. 2nd edn. Swindon, UK: BCS; 2009
4. Holt J., Perry S., Brownsword M. *Model-based Requirements Engineering*. Stevenage, UK: IET Press; 2011
5. IEEE. *IEEE Standards Style Manual*. IEEE; 2005. http://www.science.uva.nl/ research/csa/Presentations/2005Style.pdf

Chapter 10

Expanded requirements modelling – systems of systems

'One more thing.'

Lt Columbo

10.1 Introduction

This chapter looks at expanding the approach to context-based requirements engineering (ACRE) introduced in Chapter 9 so that it can be applied to Systems of Systems.

The adoption of the naming notation defined in Chapter 2 applies throughout the whole book to every term – except one! This term is System of Systems and the confusion comes into play with the plural of term. Therefore, when referring the standard term from the MBSE Ontology, the usual term System of Systems will be used. However, when this term is used in the plural, the term Systems of Systems will be used (note the plural of the first word).

10.1.1 Background

The basic Needs for expanding the ACRE Process for Systems of Systems are shown in the Context in Figure 10.1.

The diagram in Figure 10.1 shows that the main Use Case is to 'Provide SoS requirements approach' that must be applicable to different types of Systems of Systems (the constraint 'Apply to different types of SoS') and also across the whole Life Cycle (the constraint 'Apply across life cycle').

There is one main Use Case that helps to realise this, which is to 'Provide SoS requirement engineering processes'. This may at first appear a little odd as there is only single *include* relationship shown here, but this leaves room for future expansion, for example to define Processes for Requirements management. This has three main inclusions, which are:

- 'Understand context', which applies to both the System of Systems level ('Understand SoS context') and the Constituent System level ('Understand CS context').

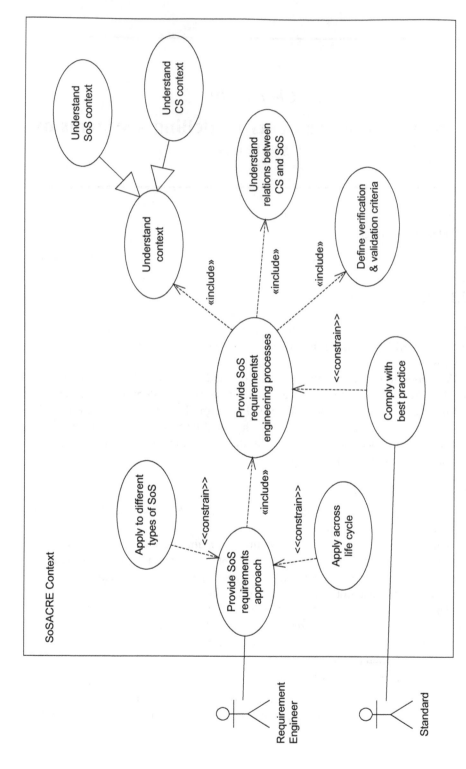

Figure 10.1 Expanded Requirements modelling – Systems of Systems Context

- 'Understand relations between CS and SoS', which provides the understanding of the interfaces and interactions between the Constituent Systems and their System of Systems.
- 'Define verification & validation criteria', which ensures that the System of Systems both works and satisfies its original Needs.

All of this is constrained by the need to meet current best practice ('Comply with best practice').

This chapter is concerned with applying the ACRE approach to Systems of Systems; therefore, it is appropriate to re-visit the subset of the model-based systems engineering (MBSE) Ontology that is concerned with Systems and Systems of Systems, which is shown in Figure 10.2.

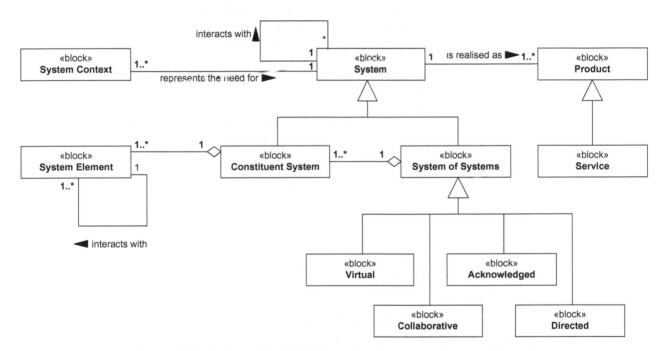

Figure 10.2 Subset of the MBSE Ontology focused on System of Systems

The diagram in Figure 10.2 shows the MBSE Ontology with a focus on System of System-related elements. These concepts are defined as follows:

- 'System' – set of interacting elements organised to satisfy one or more 'System Context'. Where the 'System' is a 'System of Systems', its elements will be one or more 'Constituent System', and where the 'System' is a 'Constituent System', its elements are one or more 'System Element'. A 'System' can interact with one or more other 'System'.
- 'Constituent System' – a special type of 'System' whose elements are one or more 'System Element'.

- 'System of Systems' – a special type of 'System' whose elements are one or more 'Constituent System' and which delivers unique functionality not deliverable by any single 'Constituent System'.
- 'System of Interest' – a special type of 'System' that describes the system being developed, enhanced, maintained or investigated.
- 'Enabling System' – a special type of 'System' that interacts with the 'System of Interest' yet sits outside its boundary.
- 'System Element' – a basic part of a 'Constituent System'.
- 'Product' – something that realises a 'System'. Typical products may include, but are not limited to, software, hardware, processes, data, humans, and facilities.
- 'Service' – an intangible 'Product' that realises a 'System'. A 'Service' is itself realised by one or more 'Process'.
- 'Virtual' – a special type of 'System of Systems' that lacks central management and resources, and no consensus of purpose.
- 'Collaborative' – a special type of 'System of Systems' that lacks central management and resources, but has consensus of purpose.
- 'Acknowledged' – a special type of 'System of Systems' that has designated management and resources, and a consensus of purpose. Each 'Constituent System' retains its own management and operation.
- 'Directed' – a special type of 'System of Systems' that has designated management and resources, and a consensus of purpose. Each 'Constituent System' retains its own operation but not management.

Some of these terms will be discussed in more detail in the following sections.

10.1.2   Defining a System of Systems

The previous section defined a System of Systems as a special type of System whose elements are Constituent Systems and which delivers unique functionality not deliverable by any single Context. Therefore, another way to decide whether a System is a System of Systems or not is to ask whether it has its own Context, or is merely a sum of the Contexts of its Constituent Systems. Any true System of Systems will have its own Context, thereby satisfying the part of the definition that it must deliver unique functionality that will not occur on its Constituent Systems' Contexts.

It is possible to identify and define the Context of a System of Systems, and of its Constituent Systems, using the ACRE approach that was described in Chapter 9. Indeed, this chapter will demonstrate that these Contexts can be analysed for consistency by adding a few additional views to the ACRE approach that will allow it to be extended for Systems of Systems.

10.1.3   Types of Systems of Systems

Most definitions concerning Systems of Systems will inevitably end up discussing various types of Systems of Systems. These are well described and often referenced; indeed, these four basic types of System of Systems have made it into the

MBSE Ontology to show how important they are. System of Systems is, according to Reference 1, divided into the following four types:

- 'Virtual' – A Virtual System of Systems will comprise an often-disparate set of Constituent Systems. There is no central management and no overarching agreed-upon purpose. This will result in there being no consistent configuration or maintenance of the System of Systems as a whole, although the individual Constituent Systems will typically be well configured and managed.
- 'Collaborative' – In a Collaborative System of Systems, the Constituent Systems interact with one another to deliver Capability. There will be a number of key Stakeholder Role Roles involved who will collaborate and agree a general consensus of what the System of Systems Needs should be that form the basis of the Capability. The Constituent Systems in a Collaborative System of Systems will typically be owned by different Stakeholder Roles.
- Acknowledged – Acknowledged Systems of Systems have a defined and acknowledge purpose and some kind of centralised management for the System of Systems as whole. Each Constituent System retains its independence and will have well-defined relationships and interactions with other Constituent Systems.
- Directed – Directed Systems of Systems have well-defined, specific purposes and are centrally managed throughout their Life Cycle. The Constituent Systems operate independently but share a common purpose.

These classifications of Systems of Systems are very useful for helping us think about the characteristics of Systems of Systems, but caution must be exercised. There is a temptation to think of these four broad categories as being distinct groups, but this is simply not the case. Trying to classify a System of Systems into one of these categories can often be an exercise in futility as it is rare that real life is that clear cut.

For example, consider the Internet, and ask yourself which category this fits into? Is it Virtual or Collaborative?

It is essential not to fall into the trap of trying to classify a System of Systems exactly and specifically into one of these groups.

Another way to consider Systems of Systems is to consider the main characteristics of a System of Systems. There is much discussion on what the key characteristics of a System of System should be, such as Refs. 2 and 3. For the purposes of this book, the following characteristics will be considered:

- Independence. One problem with Constituent Systems is that they may already exist, have a purpose of their own and be managed by their own authority. This can give rise to conflicts when a Need for the System of Systems in which the Constituent System is taking part conflicts with its own Needs. This is also compounded as it should be borne in mind that a Constituent System can belong to more than one System of Systems, which could lead to conflicting Needs for the Constituent System in relation to different Systems of Systems. Independence means operational as well as managerial independence of the Constituent Systems. For the purposes of this book, managerial independence means that the

Constituent Systems can operate independently, whereas operational independence means that the Constituent Systems do operate independently. This implies that new capabilities, requirements and changes must be dealt with at two levels, the System of Systems level and the Constituent Systems level.

–   Emergence. The concept of emergent behaviour forms part of the definition of a System of Systems and, therefore, applies only at the System of Systems level. This emergent behaviour arises as a result of the interaction between a number of Constituent Systems and which cannot be achieved by, or attributed to, any of the individual Constituent Systems. In practical terms, this means that this emergent behaviour should be captured on the Context for the System of Systems.

–   Evolution. Whereas emergent behaviour only applies at the System of Systems level, the concept of system evolution applies both at the System of Systems level and at the Constituent Systems level. A System of Systems and its Constituent Systems may have long Life Cycles, with each Constituent System often in a different Stage of its individual Life Cycle. Evolution is a natural phenomenon that will apply at all levels of the System of Systems.

Any System of Systems requirements engineering processes must, therefore, support a continuous development Life Cycle model, where new Needs (Capabilities, Goals, Requirements and Concerns) and changes to existing Needs are to be handled by the Process at either the System of Systems-level or the CS-level throughout the Life Cycle of the System or System of Systems.

10.2   Approach

10.2.1   The MBSE Ontology (revisited)

This section presents the extensions to the basic ACRE Framework that allows it to be used for Systems of Systems, hereafter known as SoSACRE.

The diagram in Figure 10.3 takes the original ACRE Ontology that was introduced in Chapter 9 and extends it to cover the additional concepts needed when dealing with Systems of Systems.

The key change is the differentiation between types of 'System'. Two types of 'System' have been introduced, the 'Constituent System' and the 'System of Systems' that itself is made up of one or more 'Constituent System'.

Although two types of 'System' have been introduced, this does not directly impact the creation of a 'System Context', which still represents the need for a 'System'.

When engineering a System of Systems, then one such System Context that must be produced is that for the System of Systems. Such a System of Systems-level Context is a set of points of view that shows the Needs that do not exist in any single System, but exist for the System of Systems. When dealing with System of Systems Needs they often represent the Goals of the System of Systems often stated as Capabilities.

In addition to the System of Systems Context, Contexts are also produced for each individual Constituent System. In a System of Systems, some of the Needs in the Contexts of the Constituent Systems will trace back to and be derived from

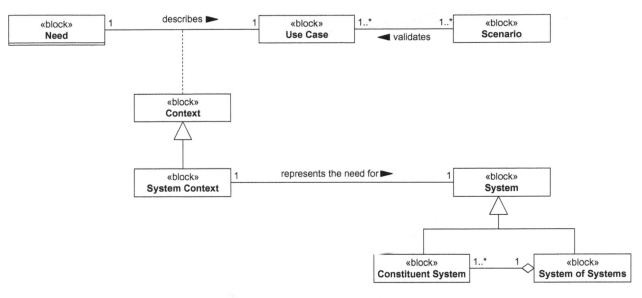

*Figure 10.3   subset of the MBSE Ontology focused on Requirements modelling
showing System of Systems*

the overarching System of Systems Needs, but not all. Only those Needs of the Constituent System that are needed to support the System of Systems in which it partakes will be traced. In this way the Constituent Systems will have their own Needs that are not relevant to their participation in the System of Systems.

For example, consider a System of Systems, 'Invasion', that is made up of two Constituent Systems 'Spaceship System' and 'Army'. A Context Definition View could be drawn for this as shown in Figure 10.4.

Given the Context Definition View in Figure 10.4, three Requirement Context Views would then be expected: one for 'Invasion' and one for each of the two Constituent Systems, 'Spaceship System' and 'Army'. The Requirement Context View for the 'Invasion' System of Systems from the point of view of the 'Overlord' Stakeholder Role is given in the diagram in Figure 10.5.

The *use cases* shown on the diagram in Figure 10.5 represent those Needs, in Context, for the System of Systems as a whole. It should be noted here that as this Context sits at the System of Systems level, then the Needs represented by the *use cases* are Goals and Capabilities, rather than Requirements. Indeed, there is a single Goal of 'Rule Galaxy', whereas the other *use cases* represent Capabilities that meet this Goal.

While there are no Needs for any of the individual Constituent Systems, one of the *use cases*, 'Subjugate races', indicates that it may need participation from 'Flying Saucer' and 'Army'; therefore, both Constituent Systems will be involved with the System of Systems.

There are many kinds of 'Spaceship System' involved in the invasion. One kind is the 'Flying Saucer'. The Requirement Context View for 'Flying Saucer' is shown in Figure 10.6.

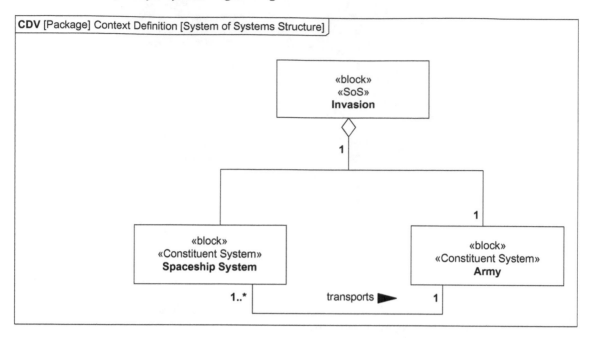

Figure 10.4   Example Context Definition View for a System of Systems

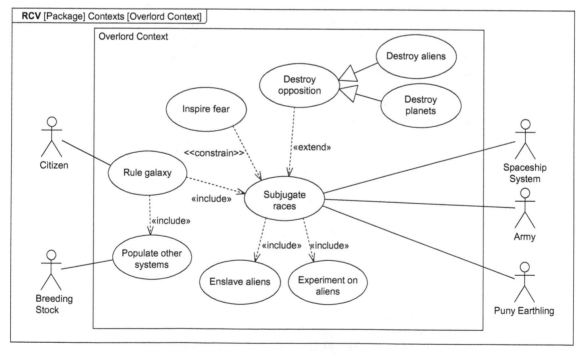

Figure 10.5   Example Requirement Context View for System of Systems 'Invasion'
from the point of view of the 'Overlord' Stakeholder Role

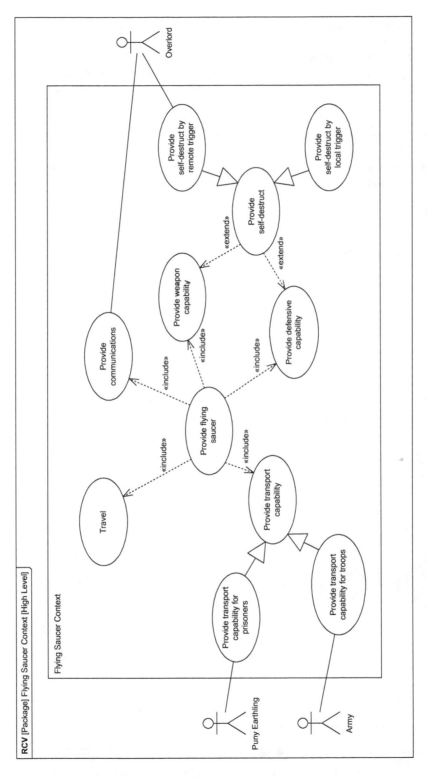

Figure 10.6 Example Requirement Context View for Constituent System 'Flying Saucer'

The *use cases* shown on the diagram in Figure 10.6 represent the Needs, in Context, for the Constituent System 'Flying Saucer'. Most of the *use cases*, those not directly related to the 'Overlord' *actor*, represent the *use cases* that are relevant to 'Flying Saucer' as a System in its own right and not as a Constituent System of the System of Systems. The *use cases* 'Provide communications' and 'Provide self-destruct by remote trigger' represent a Use Case for supporting the System of Systems. The fact that these *use cases* are relevant to the System of Systems can be seen by their link to the 'Overlord' *actor*. The implication here is that these *use cases* are somehow related to *use cases* 'Subjugate races' and 'Inspire fear' from the 'Overlord' Context in Figure 10.5.

A similar diagram would be created for 'Army', as shown in Figure 10.7.

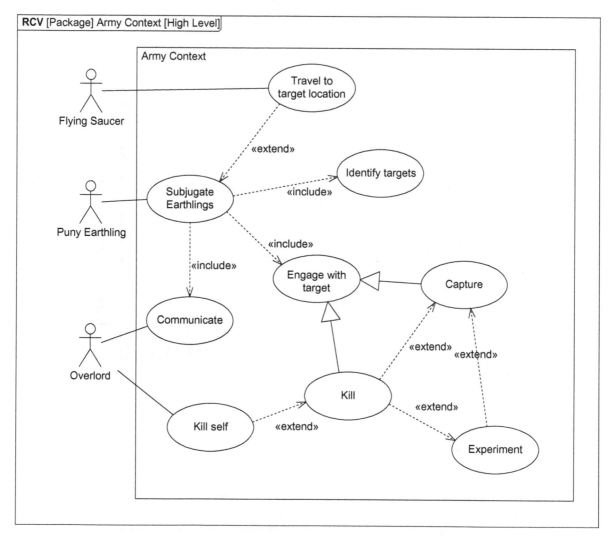

Figure 10.7   Example Requirement Context View for Constituent System 'Army'

Again, most of the *use cases* in Figure 10.7 represent those Use Cases that are relevant to 'Army' as a System in its own right and not to it as a Constituent System of the System of Systems. The *use cases* 'Communicate' and 'Kill self' will somehow relate to the 'Subjugate races' and 'Inspire fear' *use cases* from the 'Overlord' Context shown in Figure 10.5.

It is important to be able to capture the links between *use cases* in the Context of Constituent Systems that relate back to *use cases* for the System of Systems. In SysML, use of the *trace dependency* can be used to capture such links (Table 10.1).

Table 10.1　*Traceability from Constituent System to System of Systems Use Cases*

System of System use case	Constituent System use case	Constituent System use case
'Overlord' Context use cases	'Flying Saucer' Context use cases	'Army' Context use cases
'Subjugate races'	'Provide communications'	'Communicate'
'Inspire fear'	'Provide self-destruct by remote trigger'	'Kill self'

In summary, the key change to the MBSE Ontology to incorporate the additional concepts needed when dealing with System of Systems is the differentiation between types of System, the System of Systems that is made up of one or more Constituent System.

Although no new type of View is needed to capture the System of Systems Context differently from its Constituent System Contexts, there are additional Views needed when modelling the Needs for a System of Systems. These new Views are discussed in the next section.

10.2.2　The Framework

10.2.2.1　Changes to the Framework

When applying MBSE to Requirements modelling, Chapter 9 introduced the ACRE Framework that proposed the use of six Views to fully represent a set of Needs.

When considering Systems of Systems, these six Views, together with the Traceability View, are sufficient for modelling the Needs for the Constituent Systems that make up a System of Systems. As discussed in Section 10.2.1 they are also sufficient for modelling most aspects of the Needs for a System of Systems. However, two additional Views are needed. These extensions to the ACRE Framework are shown in Figure 10.8.

The two additional views in the extended ACRE Framework are the 'Context Interaction View' and the 'Validation Interaction View'.

These two additional Views are described in the following sections.

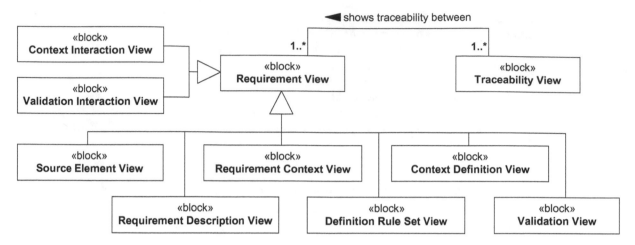

Figure 10.8   The Framework Views for Requirements Modelling for Systems of Systems

10.2.3   The Views

10.2.3.1   The Context Interaction View

View rationale

The Context Interaction View is intended to provide an overview of the relationships between the Contexts of the various Constituent Systems that make up a System of Systems.

Each Constituent System Context is related to any other Constituent System Context by considering the System of Systems Context and identifying the key relationships, as described in the previous section.

View definition

The subset of the MBSE Ontology that focuses on the Context Interaction View is shown in the diagram in Figure 10.9.

The diagram here shows the subset of the MBSE Ontology that focuses on the Context Interaction View. Notice here how, just as with the Requirement Context View from the ACRE Framework, the Context Interaction View is primarily concerned with showing Needs in Context as Use Cases. Rather than showing a single Context, as is the case with each Requirement Context View, the Context Interaction View combines the Requirement Context Views of each Constituent System into what is, essentially, an expanded Requirement Context View for the entire System of Systems.

View relationships

The relationships between the Context Interaction View and the other Views are shown in Figure 10.10.

The diagram in Figure 10.10 shows the relationships between the Context Interaction View and the other Views. It can be seen that this View has two relationships with the 'Requirement Context View, in that it expands the 'Requirement

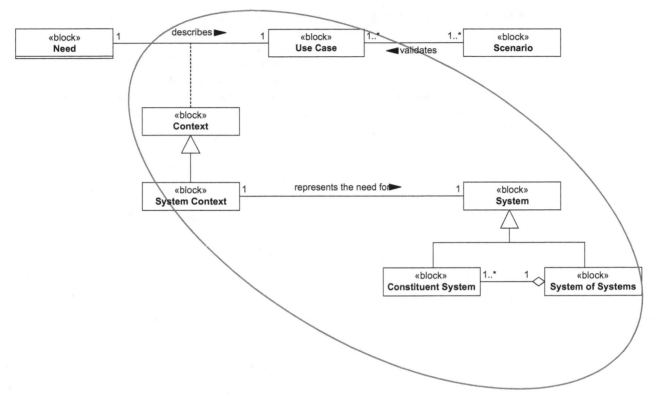

Figure 10.9   Definition of Context Interaction View

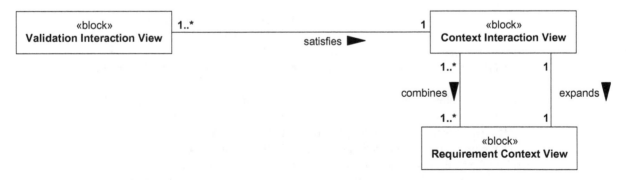

Figure 10.10   Relationships between Context Interaction View and other Views

Context View' by considering it from the System of Systems level of abstraction and in relation to other 'Requirement Context Views' for various Constituent Systems.

However, although the Context Interaction View can be thought of as an expanded Requirement Context View for the entire System of Systems, it is showing the Contexts from the perspective of the Constituent Systems and so, as discussed in Section 10.2.1, will show the various *use cases* of the System of Systems from the point of view of the Constituent Systems, rather than from that of the System of Systems. It will typically also show *use cases* of the Constituent Systems that are not involved in the System of Systems. Although these can be omitted, it is often useful to leave them in as this can allow common functionality to be identified by comparing *use cases* across the Contexts shown.

The following consistency checks apply to the Context Interaction View:

- When modelling Needs for a System of Systems, a Context Interaction View must be created.
- The Context Interaction View must include the Requirement Context Views for all of the Constituent Systems of the System of Systems.
- Each use case on a Context Interaction View that is involved in the System of Systems (linked to the System of Systems Stakeholder Role) must have at least one Validation Interaction View associated with it.

In order to maximise the benefits of a true MBSE approach, these Rules should be automated rather being manually applied to the model.

View visualisation

The Context Interaction View is visualised in SysML using a *use case diagram*, an example of which is shown in Figure 10.11.

The Context Interaction View in Figure 10.11 is based on the Requirement Context Views for the Constituent Systems 'Flying Saucer' and 'Army' that were discussed previously and which are shown in Figures 10.5 and 10.6. It was created by simply taking those two Requirement Context Views and combining them on a single diagram.

View discussion

The Context Interaction View shows the relationships between the Requirement Context Views of all the Constituent Systems of the System of Systems. Unsurprisingly, the main link between the contexts will be through the Stakeholder Role representing the System of Systems, as can be seen in Figure 10.11 via the 'Overlord' *actor*. This will be the case on any Context Interaction View; all the Constituent System Contexts will be related through System of Systems Stakeholder Role, which, in this case, is the 'Overlord' *actor*.

However, bear in mind that the individual Requirement Context Views will often have been created in isolation (if, indeed, at all) by different organisations, and therefore the Context Interaction View may well be the first time that the Contexts of the two Constituent Systems have been considered together. This can be very useful for identifying other areas of linkage between Constituent Systems.

For example, in Figure 10.11 it can be seen that both 'Flying Saucer' and 'Army' interact with 'Puny Earthling', which is *not* a Constituent System of the System of Systems. 'Flying Saucer' and 'Army' may not even be aware of this shared connection. Knowing this, one could then investigate whether, for example, 'Puny Earthling' provides functionality that could or should be part of the System of Systems. It is also very useful when conducting impact analysis.

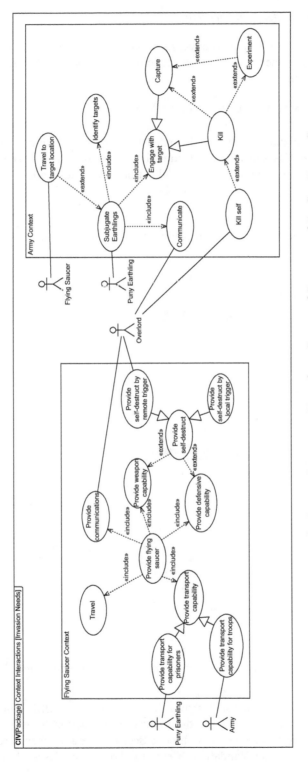

Figure 10.11 Example Context Interaction View for a System of Systems and its Constituent Systems

Also, the use case 'Travel to target location' does not form part of the overall System of Systems; therefore, any changes to it are unrelated to the fact that it is a Constituent System.

10.2.3.2   The Validation Interaction View

View rationale

The Validation Interaction View is intended to provide a combined view of the Scenarios for Use Cases that are involved in the System of Systems. Therefore, this View combines information from the Validation Views for various Constituent Systems.

View definition

The subset of the MBSE Ontology that focuses on the Validation Interaction View is shown in Figure 10.12.

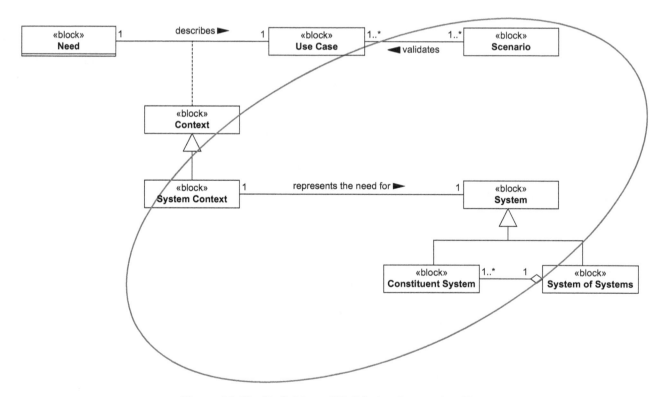

Figure 10.12   Definition of Validation Interaction View

The diagram in Figure 10.12 shows the subset of the MBSE Ontology that focuses on the elements required for the Validation Interaction View.

The Validation Interaction View shows a Scenario for a number of related Use Cases by combining the Validation Views of those Use Cases. A number of

Validation Interaction Views would be created in order to show that the Context Interaction View can be satisfied.

View relationships

Not all of the *use cases* that appear on a Context Interaction View will have associated Validation Interaction Views, only those *use cases* that are involved in the System of Systems. These *use cases* can be identified from the Context Interaction View as those that are linked to the Stakeholder Role represent the System of Systems – the Overlord. Thus, for example, from Figure 10.11 the *use cases* 'Provide communications' and ('Provide self-destruct') 'Provide self-destruct by remote trigger' from the Context of 'Flying Saucer' and 'Communicate' and 'Kill self' from the context of 'Army' can be seen to be those for which Validation Interaction Views will be needed.

The following Rules apply to the Validation Interaction View:

- Each *use case* on a Context Interaction View that is involved in the System of Systems (linked to the System of Systems Stakeholder Role) must have at least one Validation Interaction View associated with it.
- Validation Views can only be combined into a Validation Interaction View if they validate *use cases* that trace to the same System of Systems-level *use case*.
- Validation Views can only be combined into a Validation Interaction View if they represent the same (or aspects of the same) Scenario.

Where a single *use case* at the Constituent System level traces to a single *use case* at the System of Systems level, the Validation Interaction Views for the *use case* will be the same as its Validation Views. This is the case for the *use case* 'Communicate' from the 'Army' Context. However, where *uses cases* in more than one Constituent System can be traced back to single *use case* in the System of Systems, or where multiple *use cases* in single Constituent System can be so traced, then the appropriate Validation Views are combined. This is the case for the *use cases* 'Provide self-destruct by remote trigger' in 'Flying Saucer' and 'Kill self' in 'Army'. Both of these *use cases* have potential impacts on other *use cases* and, therefore, changes to them may result in changes to other *use cases*.

View visualisation

Two related Validation Views for these *use cases* are shown in Figures 10.13 and 10.14. These both treat the two Constituent Systems 'Flying Saucer' and 'Army' as black boxes, but there is no reason why this should be the case. It is done here simply for clarity. One or both could be Scenarios that treat their Systems as white boxes, showing their internal System Elements.

The diagram in Figure 10.14 shows an existing Validation View for the *use case* 'Kill self' from the Context from the 'Army' System. This is the Scenario where the Army is instructed to engage with the enemy ('Wipe them out (all of them)'), which is subsequently acted upon shown by the 'Attack' *message*. Unfortunately, the Puny Earthlings prove too much for the Army ('Repel') resulting in the Army having to report back to the Overlord with the bad news ('Report(failure)'). The response from

View relationships

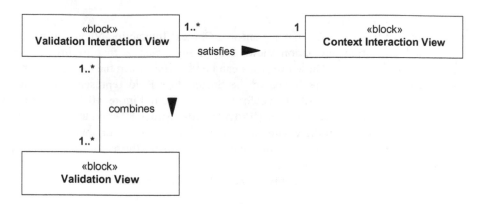

*Figure 10.13   Relationships between the Validation Interaction View
and the other Views*

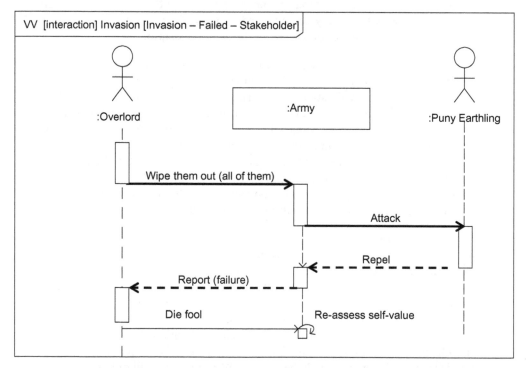

*Figure 10.14   Example Validation View for Use Case 'Kill self' for Constituent
System 'Army'*

the Overlord is both swift and merciless ('Die fool') resulting in a brief moment of reflection on behalf of the Army ('Re-assess self-value') before being eradicated by their own self-destruct mechanism.

The diagram in Figure 10.15 shows an existing Validation View for the 'Provide self-destruct by remote trigger' from the Context from the 'Flying Saucer'. This is the Scenario where the Army is instructed to engage with the enemy ('Wipe them out (all of them)'), which is subsequently acted upon shown by the 'Attack' *message*. Unfortunately, the Puny Earthlings prove too much for the Army ('Repel'), once more resulting in the Army having to report back to the Overlord with the bad news ('Report(failure)'). The response from the Overlord is equally swift and merciless ('Die fool') leaving no time for brief moments of reflection before being eradicated by their own self-destruct mechanism.

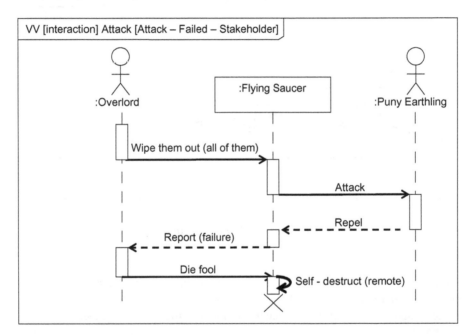

Figure 10.15 Example Validation View for the 'Provide self-destruct by remote trigger' Use Case

These two Validation Views can be combined to provide a single Validation Interaction View as shown in Figure 10.15. The Validation Views can be combined in this way only if they represent the same (or aspects of the same) Scenario.

The diagram in Figure 10.16 shows the Validation Interaction View for the combined use cases of 'Provide self-destruct by remote trigger' from the Context of the 'Flying Saucer' and the 'Kill self' use case from the Context from the 'Army' System.

Just as with the Requirement Context Views for Constituent Systems often being created in isolation, the same is true for the various Validation Views.

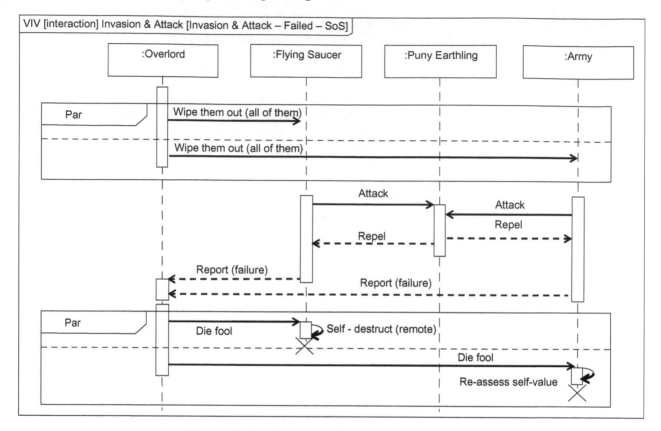

Figure 10.16   Example Validation Interaction View

Combining them together into Validation Interaction Views may be the first time that the Scenarios have been looked at together at the level of the Constituent Systems and may reveal inconsistencies to the Requirements Engineer.

View discussion

The resulting Validation Interaction Views should also be compared to the corresponding Validation Views for the use case at the System of Systems level. For example, the Validation Interaction View above should be compared to the Validation View (for the same scenario) for *use case* 'Inspire fear' from the Overlord Context. Such a comparison may again reveal inconsistencies between the Scenarios modelled at the System of Systems level and the corresponding combined Scenarios at the Constituent System level.

They are related to the other views as shown in Figure 10.17.

The diagram in Figure 10.17 shows that the first of the new Views, the 'Context Interaction' has two relationships with the 'Requirement Context View' in that it both combines and expands the 'Requirement Context View'.

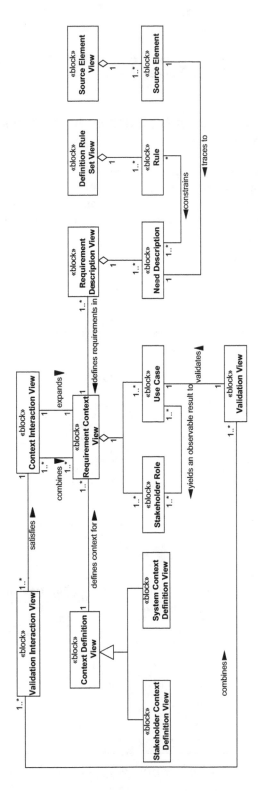

Figure 10.17   The complete Framework for Requirements modelling for Systems of Systems

The second of the new Views, the 'Validation Interaction View' satisfies the 'Context Interaction View'. The 'Validation Interaction View' also combines one or more 'Validation View'.

10.3   Using the Requirements modelling for Systems of Systems Framework

In order to create the additional Views required for SoSACRE, a set of example Processes has been defined using the seven views approach. The complete set of Processes is shown in Appendix E, but the diagram in Figure 10.18 provides the Process library, in the form of a Process Content View for the SoSACRE Processes.

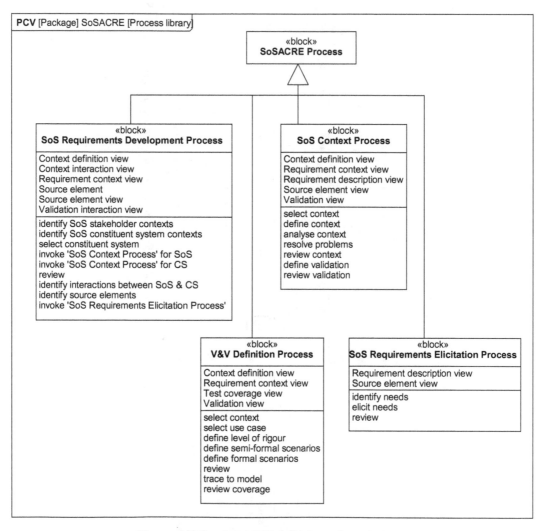

Figure 10.18   SoSACRE – Process Content View

The diagram in Figure 10.18 shows the there are four types of 'SoSACRE Process' that are described as follows:

- 'SoS Requirements Development Process', which is the overarching Process that interacts with the other Processes. The main aim of this Process is to identify the Stakeholder Roles and Constituents Systems and then invokes the Context Process for both the System of Systems and its associated Constituent Systems. The Process then identifies the interactions between the System of Systems and its Constituent Systems.
- 'SoS Context Process', which defines the Context for either the System of Systems or a Constituent System, depending on which point it is invoked from the SoS Requirements Development Process.
- 'V&V Definition Process', which defines a number of Scenarios, both Formal Scenarios and Semi-formal Scenarios, which are then used to demonstrate that the original Use Cases can be validated.
- 'SoS Requirements Elicitation Process', which identifies the basic Needs for the System of Systems.

The Processes themselves may be executed in a variety of sequences to represent different Scenarios, some examples of which are shown in the Process Instance Views.

10.4 Summary

In summary, the two additional Views are needed to model System of Systems requirements, the 'Context Interaction View' and the 'Validation Interaction View'. The Context Interaction View is intended to provide an overview of the relationships between the Contexts of the various Constituent Systems that make up a System of Systems. The Validation Interaction View is intended to provide a combined View of the Scenarios for *use cases* that are involved in the System of Systems.

References

1. Dahmann J.S., Rebovich G. Jr. 'Systems engineering for capabilities'. *CrossTalk – The Journal for Defense Software Engineering*. 2008 (November): 4–9
2. Maier M.W. 'Architecting principles for systems-of-systems'. *Systems Engineering*. 1998; 1(4):267–84
3. DeLaurentis D.A., Callaway R.K. 'A system-of-systems perspective for future public policy decisions'. *Review of Policy Research*. 2004; 21(6(November)): 829–37

Chapter 11

Architectures and Architectural Frameworks with MBSE

Of course I know very little about architecture,
and the older I get the less I know.

Richard Rogers

11.1   Introduction

This chapter considers two essential enabling concepts for model-based systems engineering: the Architecture and the Architectural Framework (AF). After considering the basic Context for Architectures and Architectural Frameworks, the chapter describes a model-based approach to the definition of an AF. This defines a framework for the definition of an architectural framework, FAF (Framework for Architectural Frameworks). The definition of FAF follows the basic Ontology, Framework and Views approach that is used throughout the book. A set of Processes are also introduced that can be used, along with FAF, to define an Architectural Framework. These Processes are briefly described in this chapter and the full model is given in Appendix F.

11.1.1   Background

Architectures and Architectural Frameworks are now considered to be fundamental to model-based systems engineering. The basic Needs behind these two areas are given in the Context in Figure 11.1.

The diagram in Figure 11.1 shows the overall Context that describes the Use Cases for Architectures and Architectural Frameworks.

The main Use Case is concerned with defining an approach to modelling Architectures and Architectural Frameworks ('Define approach to modelling architectures & architectural frameworks'). This has two main inclusions:

- Any approach must support the definition of Architectures ('Support definition of architectures'). Such support must allow Architectures to be defined that model both the structural aspects ('...for structure') and the behavioural aspects ('...for behaviour') of the System being represented by the Architecture. When defining an Architecture, it is essential that an established

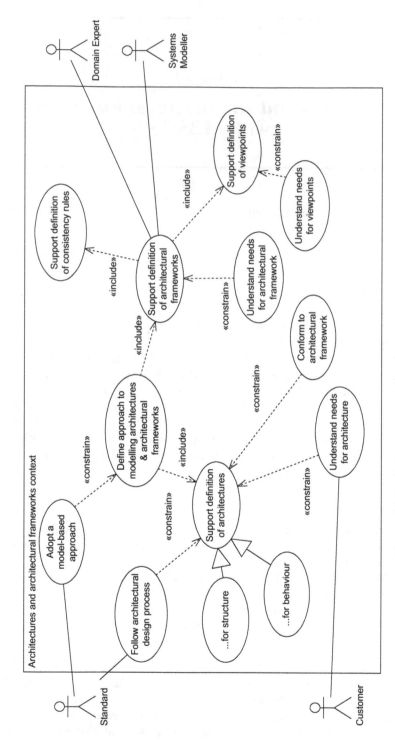

Figure 11.1   Architectures and Architectural Frameworks Context

architectural design process is followed ('Follow architectural design process') and that any Architecture conforms to a defined Architectural Framework ('Conform to architectural framework'). Too often Architectures are produced seemingly simply for the sake of producing an Architecture. For this reason it is essential that the Needs of the Customer are understood ('Understand needs for architecture') so that the Architecture is produced for a defined purpose and so that it can be validated.

• Any approach must support the definition of architectural frameworks ('Support definition of architectural frameworks'). Any Architectural Frameworks should be defined in terms of a number of Viewpoints ('Support definition of viewpoints') and should have Rules defined to ensure consistency ('Support definition of consistency rules'). Just as with an Architecture, it is essential that the reasons why the Architectural Framework is being created are understood ('Understand needs for architectural framework'). Similarly, the Needs for each Viewpoint defined as part of an Architectural Framework must also be understood ('Understand needs for viewpoints').

Whatever the approach to modelling Architectures and Architectural Frameworks, it should be a model-based one ('Adopt a model-based approach'), using all the techniques described in this book.

The Context presented in Figure 11.1 covers Architectures and Architectural Frameworks in general and is the guiding Context for this chapter. However, when it comes to the definition of an approach to the creation of Architectural Frameworks, then we can define a more focused Context. This has been done, and is shown in Figure 11.2.

Figure 11.2 shows the Context for the definition of an approach for the definition of Architectural Frameworks. The main Use Case that must be fulfilled is to 'Define an architectural framework for creating architectural frameworks', constrained by 'Comply with best practice' such as Architectural Framework Standards (e.g., ISO42010). In order to 'Define an architectural framework for creating architectural frameworks' it is necessary to:

• 'Allow needs that the AF is to address to be captured' – When defining an Architectural Framework, it is important that the Needs that the Architectural Framework is to address can be captured, in order to ensure that the Architectural Framework is fit for purpose.

• 'Support definition of ontology for AF domain' – When defining an Architectural Framework, it is essential that the concepts, and the relationships between them, are defined for the domain in which the Architectural Framework is to be used. This is the Ontology that forms the foundational basis of the definition of the Architectural Framework's Viewpoints. Such an Ontology ensures the consistency of the Architectural Framework. The Architectural Framework must support such a definition of an Ontology.

• 'Support identification of required viewpoints' – The Viewpoints that make up the Architectural Framework need to be identified. As well as supporting such an identification, the Architectural Framework must also 'Support

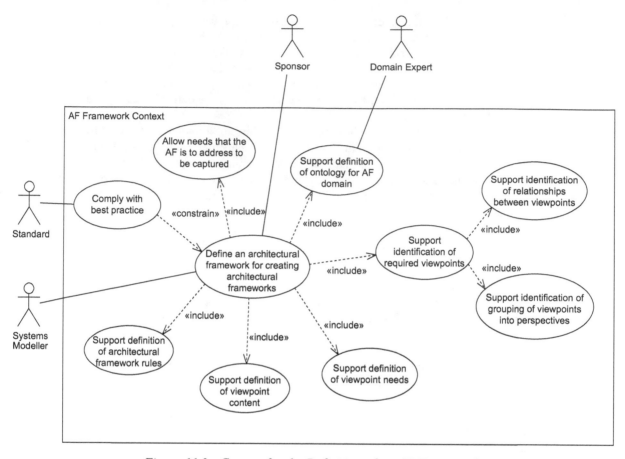

Figure 11.2   Context for the Definition of an AF Framework

identification of relationships between viewpoints' and 'Support identification of grouping of viewpoints into perspectives'.

- 'Support definition of viewpoint needs' – In order to define the Viewpoints that make up an Architectural Framework, it is essential that the Needs of each Viewpoint be clearly understood in order to ensure each Viewpoint is fit for purpose and that the Viewpoints defined meet the overall Needs for the Architectural Framework.
- 'Support definition of viewpoint content' – An Architectural Framework is essentially a number of Viewpoints that conform to an Ontology. Therefore, when defining an Architectural Framework it is essential that each Viewpoint can be defined in a consistent fashion that ensures its conformance to the Ontology.
- 'Support definition of architectural framework rules' – Often, when defining an Architectural Framework, it is often necessary to constrain aspects of the

Architectural Framework through the definition of a number of constraining Rules. It is therefore essential that a Framework for the definition of an AF supports the definition of such Rules.

The key Stakeholder Roles involved are:

- 'Sponsor' – the role involved in sponsoring the creation of the Architectural Framework.
- 'Systems Modeller' – the role involved in the modelling and definition of an Architectural Framework.
- 'Standard' – the role of any appropriate Standard for Architectural Frameworks. An example of a Standard that could fill this role would be ISO42010.
- 'Domain Expert' – the role of an expert in the domain for which the Architectural Framework is to be used.

This Context is the basis of the approach described in the following section and of the processes described in Section 11.4.

11.2 Approach

The FAF is a simple Architectural Framework that is intended to be used as an aid to the production of an Architectural Framework. It is a meta-AF – an Architectural Framework Framework. This is a bit of a mouthful, and so rather than call the Framework AFF, FAF was felt to be a better name (and more appropriate!). This section defines FAF through the familiar 'Ontology, Framework and Views approach' used throughout the book.

Although the FAF is defined using SysML, an Architectural Framework based on FAF may be realised using any suitable modelling notation, such as the Unified Modelling Language (see Reference 1) and Business Process Modelling Notation (see Reference 4).

11.2.1 The MBSE Ontology (Revisited)

The FAF uses the concepts from the subset of the MBSE Ontology that was presented in Chapter 3 and which is repeated here for ease of reference.

Given that the FAF is itself an Architectural Framework, only those concepts relating directly to the 'Architectural Framework' element in Figure 11.3 are relevant to the definition of FAF. Thus, the FAF is based directly around those concepts highlighted in Figure 11.3: 'Architectural Framework', 'Rule', 'Standard', 'Architectural Framework Concern', 'Viewpoint Concern', 'Ontology', 'Ontology Element', 'Viewpoint', 'Viewpoint Element' and 'Perspective'. FAF does not cover the concepts of 'Architecture', 'View' and 'View Element'. These concepts are realised by any 'Architecture' that conforms to a defined 'Architectural Framework'.

11.2.2 The Framework

The FAF defines six Viewpoints that are needed when defining an Architectural Framework. The Viewpoints are shown in the diagram in Figure 11.4.

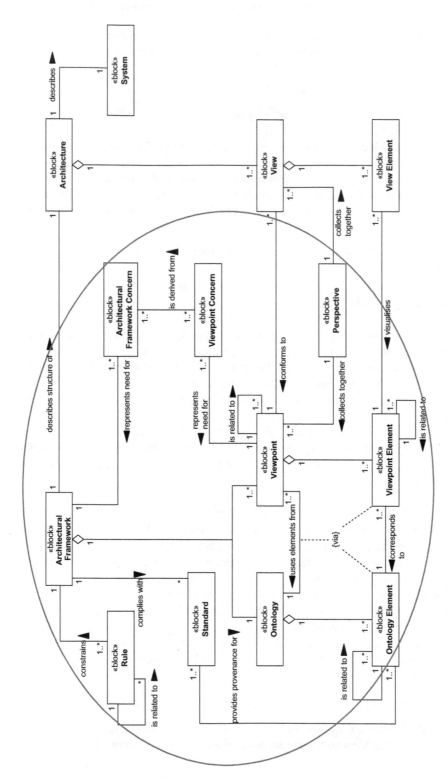

Figure 11.3   Subset of the MBSE Ontology focused on Architectures and Architectural Frameworks

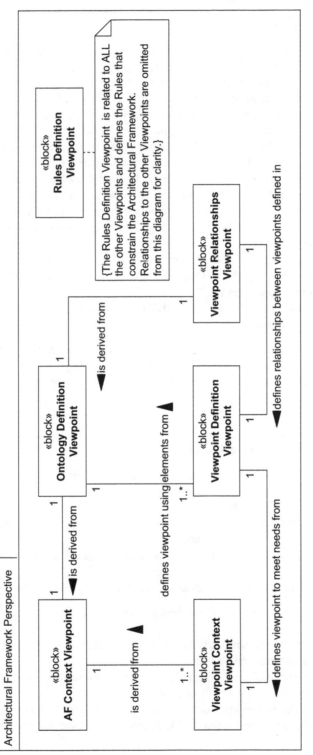

Figure 11.4   The Framework Viewpoints for Architectural Frameworks

The six Viewpoints are:

- The 'AF Context Viewpoint' (AFCV), which defines the Context for the Architectural Framework. That is, it represents the Architectural Framework Concerns in Context, establishing why the Architectural Framework is needed.
- The 'Ontology Definition Viewpoint' (ODV), which defines the Ontology for the Architectural Framework. It is derived from the 'AF Context Viewpoint' and defines the concepts that can appear on a Viewpoint.
- The 'Viewpoint Relationships Viewpoint' (VRV), which shows the relationships between the Viewpoints that make up an Architectural Framework and groups them into Perspectives. It is derived from the 'Ontology Definition Viewpoint'.
- The 'Viewpoint Context Viewpoint' (VCV), which defines the Context for a particular Viewpoint. That is, it represents the Viewpoint Concerns in context for a particular Viewpoint, establishing why the Viewpoint is needed. It is derived from the 'AF Context Viewpoint'.
- The 'Viewpoint Definition Viewpoint' (VDV), which defines a particular Viewpoint, showing the Viewpoint Elements (and hence the Ontology Elements) that appear on the Viewpoint.
- The 'Rules Definition Viewpoint' (RDV), which defines the various Rules that constrain the Architectural Framework.

The six Viewpoints are collected into a single Perspective, the 'Architectural Framework Perspective', as shown by the enclosing *package* in Figure 11.4.

Each of these Viewpoints is expanded upon in the following section.

11.2.3   The Viewpoints

The six FAF Viewpoints are defined and discussed in the following subsections. For each Viewpoint there are five subsections:

- Viewpoint Rationale, which discusses the rationale for the Viewpoint.
- Viewpoint Definition, which identifies the parts of the MBSE ontology that are shown on each Viewpoint.
- Viewpoint Relationships, which defines the Viewpoint and identifies its relationships to other Viewpoints.
- Viewpoint Visualisation, which gives an example of a View that visualises the Viewpoint.
- Viewpoint Discussion, which discusses issues and aspects of the Viewpoint.

It is worth re-emphasising here the difference between a Viewpoint and a View:

- An Architectural Framework is made up of a number of Viewpoints that define the information that can be presented.
- An Architecture is based on an Architectural Framework. It is made up of Views, with each View a realisation of a Viewpoint.
- Viewpoints define the information that can be presented; it is a definition of what can be produced when an Architecture is based on an Architectural Framework.

- A View is an artefact, produced as part of an Architecture. It describes an aspect of that Architecture. If the Architecture is created using an Architectural Framework, then every View will conform to a Viewpoint in the Architectural Framework.

When using FAF things get interesting. Because FAF is a meta-Architectural Framework, the result of using FAF will be both an Architecture (since an Architecture is essentially the realisation of an Architectural Framework) and an Architectural Framework (since FAF is a meta-Architectural Framework).

For example, when using FAF to define an AF, one can produce a Viewpoint Definition View for a particular Viewpoint of the AF being defined. This conforms to the FAF Viewpoint Definition Viewpoint (see Section 0 below) since it defines a Viewpoint made up of a number of Viewpoint Element. It is a View (when looked at from the point of view of FAF) that conforms to a FAF Viewpoint. However, it is also a Viewpoint of the Architectural Framework that is being developed using FAF, since it will be realised by a View in an Architecture based on the defined Architectural Framework.

For example, Chapter 12 defines parts of an AF for use in the case study. This AF is defined using FAF. There is a Viewpoint Definition View (a View conforming to the FAF Viewpoint Definition Viewpoint) that defines the System Identification Viewpoint (a Viewpoint of the defined AF).

This discussion of Viewpoints and Views has been included here because of a convention that has been adopted by the authors in the 'Relationships with Other Viewpoints' subsections of each of the six Viewpoints. Although the diagrams in these subsections show relationships between Viewpoints, the explanatory text will discuss the relationships in terms of Views, since the relationship actually holds between the Views that conform to the Viewpoints. If this all sounds too confusing, don't worry about it. The examples in Chapters 12 and 13 will make things clear.

11.2.3.1 The AF Context Viewpoint

The AF Context Viewpoint (AFCV) defines the Context for an Architectural Framework. That is, it represents the Architectural Framework Concerns in context, establishing why the Architectural Framework is needed.

Viewpoint Rationale

The Viewpoint Concerns that the AF Context Viewpoint is intended to address are shown in the diagram in Figure 11.5.

Figure 11.5 shows the Viewpoint Concerns (a type of Need) that the AF Context Viewpoint must address shown in context as Use Cases, together with relevant Stakeholder Roles. The main Use Case, taken from the Context for the definition of an AF framework (see Figure 11.2), is to 'Allow needs that the AF is to address to be captured'; the AF Context Viewpoint exists solely to capture the Needs (in fact, the Architectural Framework Concerns, which are types of Needs) of the Architectural Framework being defined.

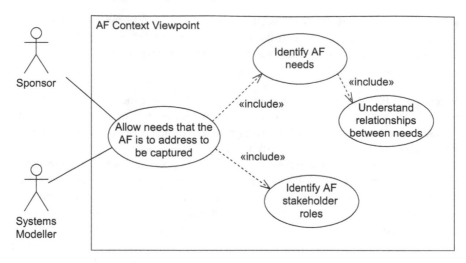

Figure 11.5   AF Context Viewpoint Context

In order to do this, it is necessary to be able to:

- 'Identify AF needs' – Identify the Needs that the Architectural Framework is being created to address.
- 'Understand relationships between needs' – Understand any relationships between the Needs that the Architectural Framework is being created to address.
- 'Identify AF stakeholder roles' – Identify the Stakeholder Roles involved in definition of the Architectural Framework and that have an interest in or are impacted by the identified Needs.

As identified in Figure 11.2, the two key Stakeholder Roles involved are (through the «include» *relationships* from 'Define an architectural framework for creating architectural frameworks'): the 'Sponsor' and the 'Systems Modeller'.

Viewpoint Definition
The subset of the MBSE Ontology that relates to Architectural Frameworks is shown in Figure 11.6, with the relevant Ontology Elements highlighted.

The diagram in Figure 11.6 shows that the Ontology Elements relevant to the AF Context Viewpoint are the 'Architectural Framework' and the 'Architectural Framework Concern'.

Viewpoint Relationships
The AF Context Viewpoint is defined in the diagram in Figure 11.7.

Figure 11.7 defines the content of the 'AF Context Viewpoint'. The 'AF Context Viewpoint' is a type of 'Context' and is made up of a 'Boundary', one or more 'Stakeholder Role', that are outside the 'Boundary', and one or more 'Use Case' that are inside the 'Boundary'.

Each 'Use Case' describes an 'Architectural Framework Concern' (a type of 'Need') in a 'Context' for the 'Architectural Framework', which yields observable

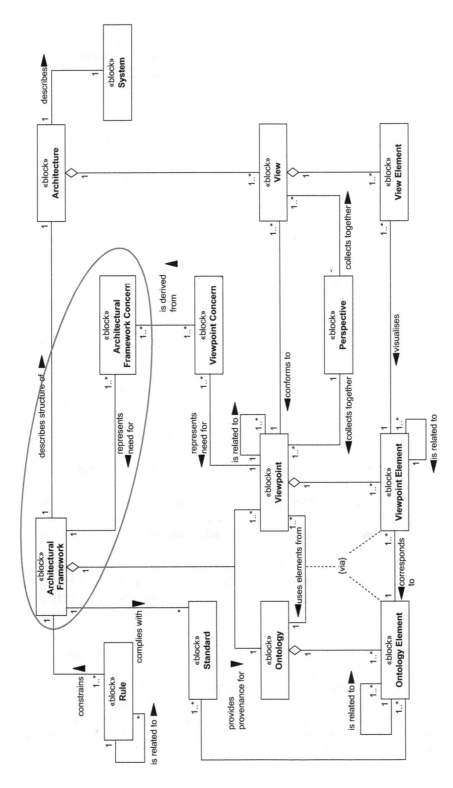

Figure 11.6 Definition of the AF Context Viewpoint

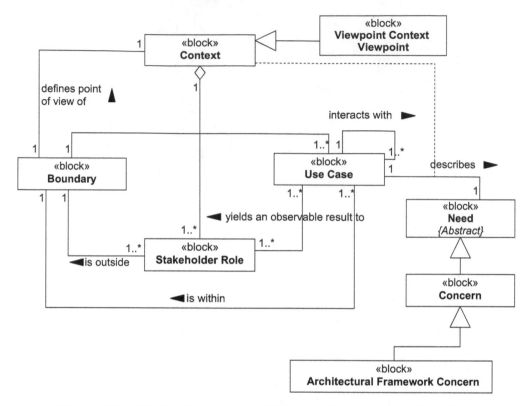

Figure 11.7   Relationships between AF Context Viewpoint and other Views

results to one or more 'Stakeholder Role'. Each 'Use Case' may interact with a number of other 'Use Case'.

Note that Figure 11.7 makes use of Ontology Elements that do not appear in Figure 11.3. These Ontology Elements (such as Context) do appear on the full MBSE ontology discussed in Chapter 3. For a full discussion of the concepts behind the 'Context' see Chapter 9.

The 'AF Context Viewpoint' is the cornerstone of the FAF and as such does not relate to any other Viewpoint, although there are a number of other Viewpoints that relate to it (as will be seen in the descriptions of the other Viewpoints later in this section).

Viewpoint Visualisation

The AF Context Viewpoint is usually visualised using a *use case diagram*. An example AF Context View is shown in Figure 11.8.

Figure 11.8 is an example AF Context View. Note here the use of View rather than Viewpoint. Figure 11.8 is the realisation of an AF Context Viewpoint and hence is a View, as shown in the *diagram frame*. Note also the use of the Viewpoint ID as the *frame tag* in the *diagram frame*. This is consistent with the diagramming guidelines described in Chapter 6.

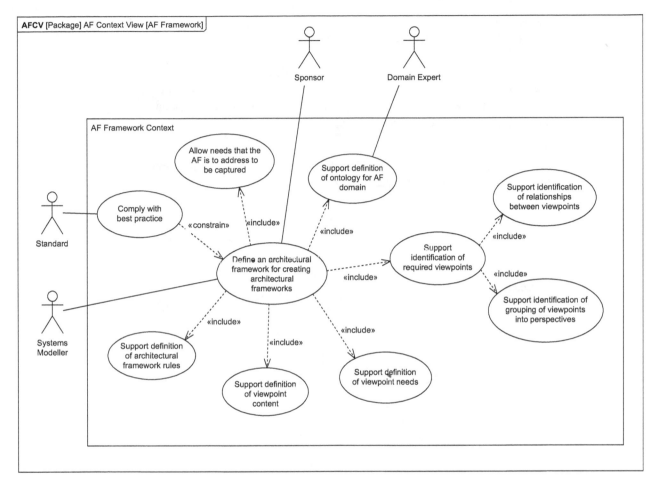

Figure 11.8 Example AF Context View for an Architectural Framework
Framework

Note also that the AF Context View shown is, in fact, the Context that was presented for the definition of an Architectural Framework shown in Figure 11.2. This is because the FAF was itself defined using FAF.

Viewpoint Discussion

The AF Context Viewpoint is central to the FAF. Any Architectural Framework that is defined using FAF must be based on documented Architectural Framework Concerns. The purpose of the AF Context Viewpoint is to capture Use Cases that represent such Concerns in Context. An AF Context View that realises the AF Context Viewpoint documents those Architectural Framework Concerns.

In the section titled **'Viewpoint Visualisation'** earlier in this section, the example AF Context View was visualised using a *use case diagram*. This is the minimum visualisation that is needed. Given that the AF Context View essentially captures

Needs, it would be possible to use the entire ACRE approach as described in Chapter 9, producing a number of different Views to visualise the AF Context Viewpoint.

11.2.3.2 The Ontology Definition Viewpoint

The Ontology Definition Viewpoint (ODV) defines the Ontology for the Architectural Framework. It is derived from the AF Context Viewpoint and defines the concepts that can appear on a Viewpoint.

Viewpoint Rationale

The Viewpoint Concerns that the Ontology Definition Viewpoint is intended to address are shown in the diagram in Figure 11.9.

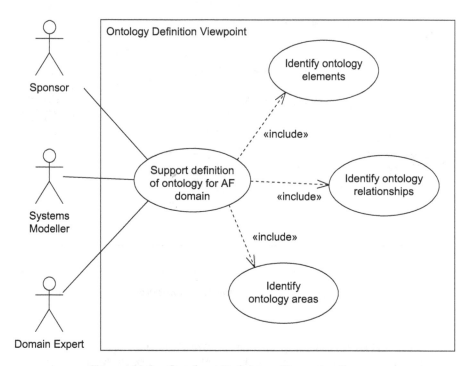

Figure 11.9   Ontology Definition Viewpoint Context

Figure 11.9 shows the Viewpoint Concerns (a type of Need) that the Ontology Definition Viewpoint must address shown in context as Use Cases, together with relevant Stakeholder Roles. The main Use Case, taken from the Context for the definition of an AF framework (see Figure 11.2), is to 'Support definition of ontology for AF domain'; the Ontology Definition Viewpoint exists to define the Ontology that defines all the concepts and terms (Ontology Elements) that relate to any Architecture structured according to the Architectural Framework that is being defined.

The main Use Cases that must be addressed are to:

- 'Identify ontology elements' – Identify the Ontology Elements for the domain in which the Architectural Framework will be used.
- 'Identify ontology relationships' – Identify the relationships between the Ontology Elements. Such relationships are equally as important a part of the Ontology defined using this Viewpoint as are the Ontology Elements.
- 'Identify ontology areas' – When defining an Ontology it is often useful to group together related Ontology Elements. For example, when defining an Ontology for systems engineering, one could expect to see groupings of Ontology Element related to the concepts of System, Life Cycle, Process, Project, etc. Such groupings are useful when defining an Architectural Framework, as they help to identify the Perspectives into which the Viewpoints, and the Views based on them, are grouped.

As identified in Figure 11.2, the three key Stakeholder Roles involved in the main need to 'Support definition of ontology for AF domain' are (through the «include» *relationships* from 'Define an architectural framework for creating architectural frameworks' and directly): the 'Sponsor', the 'Systems Modeller' and the 'Domain Expert'.

Viewpoint Definition
The subset of the MBSE Ontology that relates to Architectural Frameworks is shown in Figure 11.10, with the relevant Ontology Elements highlighted.

The diagram in Figure 11.10 shows that the Ontology Elements relevant to the 'Ontology Definition Viewpoint' are the 'Ontology' and the 'Ontology Element'.

Viewpoint Relationships
The Ontology Definition Viewpoint is defined in the diagram in Figure 11.11.

Figure 11.11 shows that the 'Ontology Definition Viewpoint' is made up of an 'Ontology' that is itself made up of one or more 'Ontology Element' that are related to each other. It is important to note that the relationships between any 'Ontology Element' are themselves an important part of the 'Ontology'.

While not directly related to any elements that appear on an 'AF Context View', an 'Ontology Definition View' is nonetheless derived from the information described by an 'AF Context View'.

Viewpoint Visualisation
The Ontology Definition Viewpoint is usually visualised using a *block definition diagram*. An example Ontology Definition View is shown in Figure 11.12.

Figure 11.12 is an example Ontology Definition View. Note here the use of View rather than Viewpoint. Figure 11.12 is the realisation of an Ontology Definition Viewpoint and hence is a View, as shown in the *diagram frame*. Note also the use of the Viewpoint ID as the *frame tag* in the *diagram frame*. This is consistent with the diagramming guidelines described in Chapter 6.

Note also that the Ontology Definition View shown is, in fact, the Ontology that was presented for Architectures and Architectural Frameworks in Chapter 3

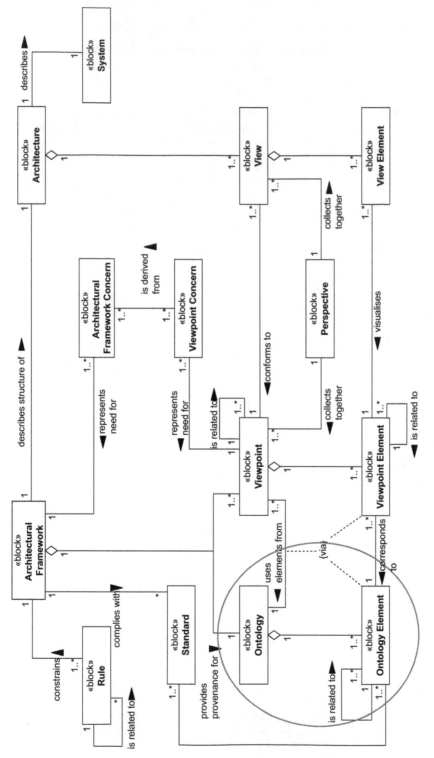

Figure 11.10 Definition of the Ontology Definition Viewpoint

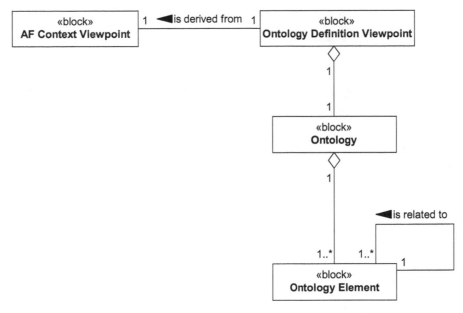

*Figure 11.11   Relationships between Ontology Definition Viewpoint and
other Views*

and also shown in Figure 11.3. This is because the FAF was itself defined
using FAF.

Viewpoint Discussion

Whenever an Architectural Framework is defined, it is essential that the concepts
that can appear on the Viewpoints are clearly documented. This helps to ensure that
each Viewpoint is defined using a consistent and related set of concepts. These
concepts and the relationships between them form an Ontology and the Ontology
Definition Viewpoint is used to visualise this Ontology. Whereas the AF Context
Viewpoint is essential to establish the Needs for the Architectural Framework (so
we know why we are defining an AF and know what Needs it has to address), the
Ontology Definition View is essential to establish the consistency between
Viewpoints.

Although the Ontology Definition View in Figure 11.12 is shown as a single
block definition diagram, this does not mean that only a single *block definition
diagram* needs be produced. If necessary the Ontology Definition View can be
visualised using a number of diagrams, showing different Ontology Elements or
showing Ontology Elements at different levels of detail.

11.2.3.3   The Viewpoint Relationships Viewpoint

The Viewpoint Relationships Viewpoint (VRV) shows the relationships between
the Viewpoints that make up an Architectural Framework and groups them into
Perspectives. It is derived from the Ontology Definition Viewpoint.

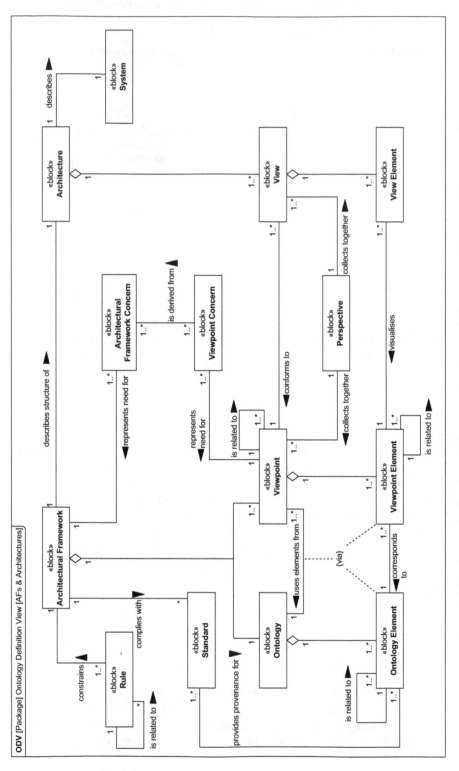

Figure 11.12   Example Ontology Definition View for an Architectural Framework Framework

Viewpoint Rationale

The Viewpoint Concerns that the Viewpoint Relationships Viewpoint is intended to address are shown in the diagram in Figure 11.13.

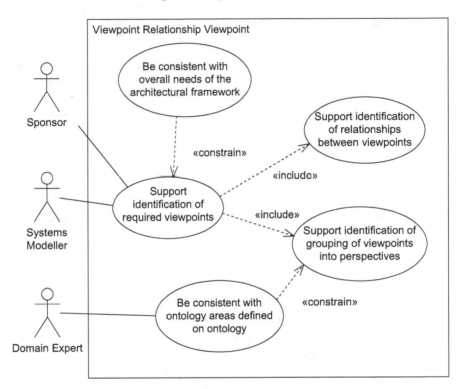

Figure 11.13   Viewpoint Relationship Viewpoint Context

Figure 11.13 shows the Viewpoint Concerns (a type of Need) that the Viewpoint Relationships Viewpoint must address shown in context as Use Cases, together with relevant Stakeholder Roles. The main Use Case, taken from the Context for the definition of an AF framework (see Figure 11.2), is to 'Support identification of required viewpoints', which includes 'Support identification of relationships between viewpoints' and 'Support identification of grouping of viewpoints into perspectives'. The Viewpoint Relationships Viewpoint exists to identify the Viewpoints that make up the Architectural Framework, to show how they are related to each other and to show how they are grouped into Perspectives.

The Use Cases for this Viewpoint are subject to two constraints:

- 'Support identification of required viewpoints' is constrained by the Need to 'Be consistent with overall needs of the architectural framework'. The Viewpoints identified as being required in the Architectural Framework must meet the Needs for the Architectural Framework as defined on the AF Context Viewpoint.
- 'Support identification of grouping of viewpoints into perspectives' is constrained by the need to 'Be consistent with ontology areas defined for

ontology'. While it is not essential that the Perspectives identified on the Viewpoint Relationships Viewpoint should be the same as the groupings of Ontology Elements, as identified on the Ontology Definition Viewpoint, keeping them in accord with each other can help with consistency and to ensure that the Viewpoints defined cover the whole of the Ontology.

As identified in Figure 11.2, the two key Stakeholder Roles involved in the main need to 'Support identification of required viewpoints' are (through the «include» *relationships* from 'Define an architectural framework for creating architectural frameworks'): the 'Sponsor' and the 'Systems Modeller'. The 'Domain Expert' is also a key Stakeholder Role with an interest in the need to 'Be consistent with ontology areas defined on for ontology'.

Viewpoint Definition

The subset of the MBSE Ontology that relates to Architectural Frameworks is shown in Figure 11.14, with the relevant Ontology Elements highlighted.

The diagram in Figure 11.14 shows that the Ontology Elements relevant to the 'Viewpoint Relationships Viewpoint' are the 'Viewpoint' and the 'Perspective'.

Viewpoint Relationships

The Viewpoint Relationships Viewpoint is defined in the diagram in Figure 11.15.

Figure 11.15 shows that the 'Viewpoint Relationships Viewpoint' is made up of one or more 'Viewpoint' and one or more 'Perspective'. It shows how a 'Viewpoint' may be related to others and also shows how one or more 'Viewpoint' can be collected into a 'Perspective'.

A 'Viewpoint Relationships View' (an actual instance of a 'Viewpoint Relationship Viewpoint') is derived from an 'Ontology Definition View' (an actual instance of an 'Ontology Definition Viewpoint'), which informs the identification and grouping of each 'Viewpoint' that appear on the 'Viewpoint Relationships View''. Each 'Viewpoint' identified on a 'Viewpoint Relationships View' must have been defined on a 'Viewpoint Definition View'.

Viewpoint Visualisation

The Viewpoint Relationships Viewpoint is usually visualised using a *block definition diagram*. An example Viewpoint Relationships View is shown in Figure 11.16.

Figure 11.16 is an example Viewpoint Relationships View. Note here the use of View rather than Viewpoint. Figure 11.16 is the realisation of a Viewpoint Relationships Viewpoint and hence is a View, as shown in the *diagram frame*. Note also the use of the Viewpoint ID as the *frame tag* in the *diagram frame*. This is consistent with the diagramming guidelines described in Chapter 6.

Note also that the Viewpoint Relationships View shown is, in fact, the diagram identifying Viewpoints and Perspectives that was presented in Figure 11.4. This is because the FAF was itself defined using FAF.

Viewpoint Discussion

The purpose of the Viewpoint Relationships Viewpoint is threefold. It can be used to show all the Viewpoints in an Architectural Framework; it shows the relationships between the Viewpoints (important for establishing consistency in the

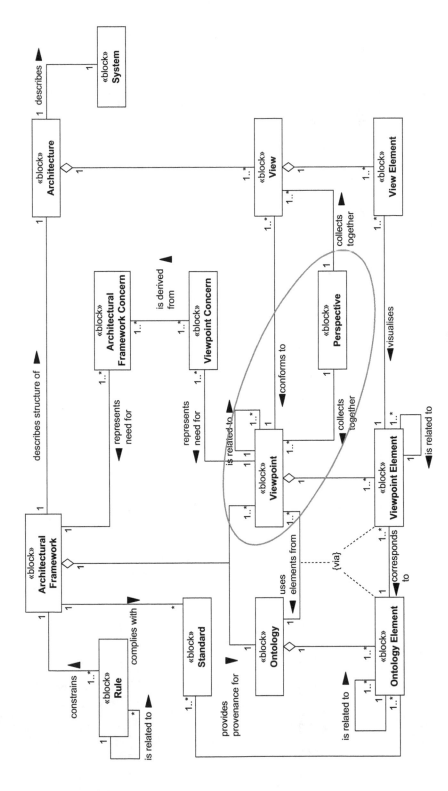

Figure 11.14   Definition of the Viewpoint Relationships Viewpoint

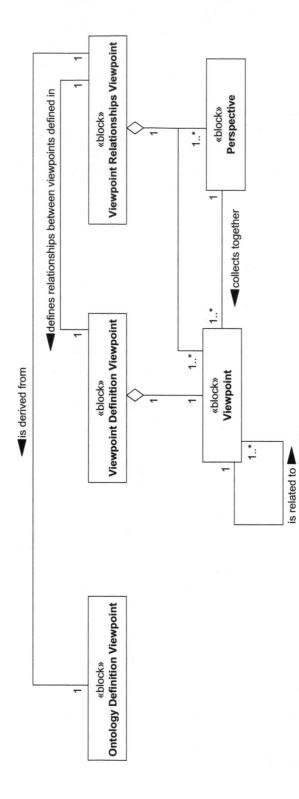

Figure 11.15   Relationships between Viewpoint Relationships Viewpoint and other Views

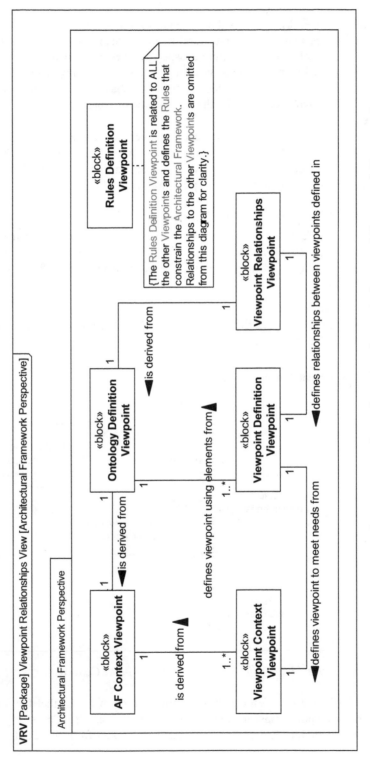

Figure 11.16 Example Viewpoint Relationships View for an Architectural Framework Framework

Architectural Framework); it shows the grouping of Viewpoints into Perspectives (often useful for presentation of Architectural Frameworks, particularly if issued as documents, where each Perspective can be issued as a separate document).

The example in Figure 11.16 shows a single Perspective, simply because the Architectural Framework that it relates to (the FAF) has a single concern. The Architectural Framework defined for the case study in Chapter 12 has multiple Perspectives.

Each Perspective and its Viewpoints can be represented as separate *block definition diagrams* or multiple Perspectives can be shown on a single *block definition diagram*. Such a Viewpoint Relationships View is often hard to read and is known to some systems engineers as the viewpoint quagmire. See References 5 and 9.

11.2.3.4   The Viewpoint Context Viewpoint

The Viewpoint Context Viewpoint (VCV) defines the Context for a particular Viewpoint. That is, it represents the Viewpoint Concerns in context for a particular Viewpoint, establishing why the Viewpoint is needed. It is derived from the AF Context Viewpoint.

Viewpoint Rationale

The Viewpoint Concerns that the Viewpoint Context Viewpoint is intended to address are shown in the diagram in Figure 11.17.

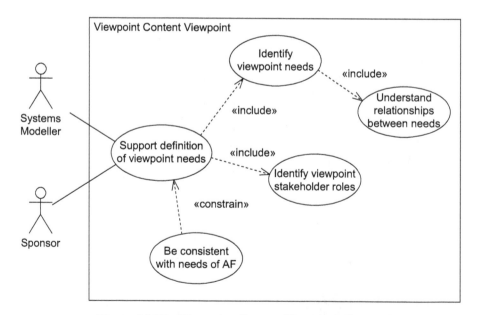

Figure 11.17   Viewpoint Context Viewpoint Context

Figure 11.17 shows the Viewpoint Concerns (a type of Need) that the Viewpoint Context Viewpoint must address shown in context as Use Cases, together with relevant Stakeholder Roles. The main Use Case, taken from the Context for the definition of an AF framework (see Figure 11.2), is to 'Support definition of viewpoint needs'; the Viewpoint Context Viewpoint exists to capture the Needs (in fact, the Viewpoint Concerns, which are types of Needs) of a Viewpoint being defined. In order to do this, it is necessary to 'Be consistent with needs of AF' and to be able to:

- 'Identify viewpoint needs' – Identify the Needs that the Viewpoint is being created to address.
- 'Understand relationships between needs' – Understand any relationships between the Needs that the Viewpoint is being created to address.
- 'Identify viewpoint stakeholder roles' – Identify the Stakeholder Roles involved in the definition of the Viewpoint and that have an interest in or are impacted by the identified Needs.

As identified in Figure 11.2, the two key Stakeholder Roles involved are (through the «include» *relationships* from 'Define an architectural framework for creating architectural frameworks'): the 'Sponsor' and the 'Systems Modeller'.

Viewpoint Definition

The subset of the MBSE Ontology that relates to Architectural Frameworks is shown in Figure 11.18, with the relevant Ontology Elements highlighted.

The diagram in Figure 11.18 shows that the Ontology Elements relevant to the 'Viewpoint Context Viewpoint' are the 'Viewpoint' and the 'Viewpoint Concern'.

Viewpoint Relationships

The Viewpoint Context Viewpoint is defined in the diagram in Figure 11.19.

Figure 11.19 defines the content of the 'Viewpoint Context Viewpoint'. The 'Viewpoint Context Viewpoint' is a type of 'Context' and is made up of a 'Boundary', one or more 'Stakeholder Role' that are outside the 'Boundary', and one or more 'Use Case' that are inside the 'Boundary'.

Each 'Use Case' describes a 'Viewpoint Concern' (a type of 'Need') in 'Context' for the 'Viewpoint', which yields observable results to one or more 'Stakeholder Role'. Each 'Use Case' may interact with a number of other 'Use Case'.

Note that Figure 11.19 makes use of Ontology Elements that do not appear in Figure 11.3. These Ontology Elements (such as Context) do appear on the full MBSE discussed in Chapter 3. For a full discussion of the concepts behind the 'Context' see Chapter 9.

Each 'Viewpoint Context Viewpoint' is derived from the 'AF Context Viewpoint'.

Viewpoint Visualisation

The Viewpoint Context Viewpoint is usually visualised using a *use case diagram*. An example Viewpoint Context View is shown in Figure 11.20.

Figure 11.20 is an example Viewpoint Context View. Note here the use of View rather than Viewpoint. Figure 11.20 is the realisation of a Viewpoint Context Viewpoint and hence is a View, as shown in the *diagram frame*. Note also the use of the Viewpoint ID as the *frame tag* in the *diagram frame*. This is consistent with the diagramming guidelines described in Chapter 6.

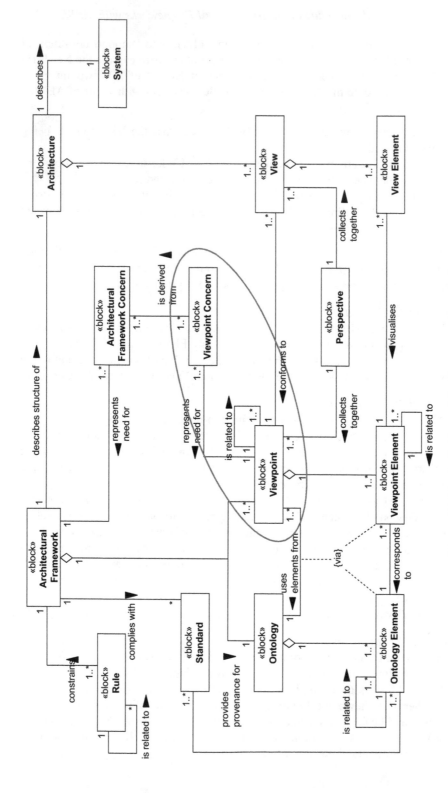

Figure 11.18 Definition of the Viewpoint Context Viewpoint

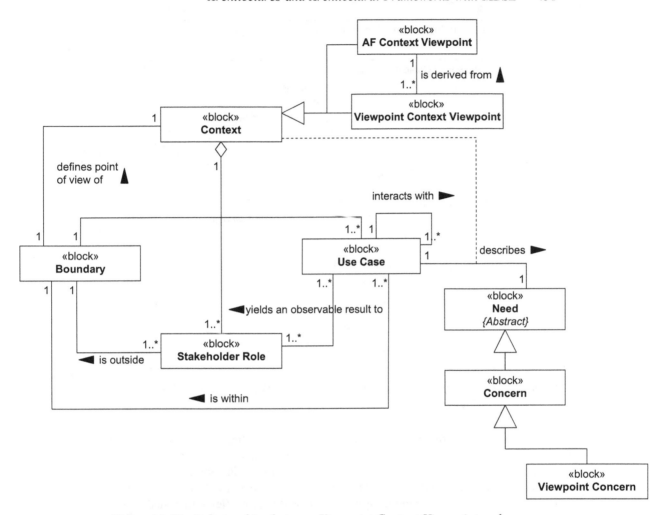

Figure 11.19   Relationships between Viewpoint Context Viewpoint and other Views

Note also that the example Viewpoint Context View shown is, in fact, that for the Viewpoint that the View realises. It is the Viewpoint Context View for the Viewpoint Context Viewpoint. This is because the FAF was itself defined using FAF, and thus every Viewpoint must have a Viewpoint Context View, including the Viewpoint Context Viewpoint itself!

Viewpoint Discussion

The Viewpoint Context Viewpoint is central to the definition of any Viewpoint. The purpose of the Viewpoint Context Viewpoint is to capture Viewpoint Concerns that a Viewpoint must address, so that the purpose of the Viewpoint is understood. A Viewpoint Context View that realises the Viewpoint Context Viewpoint documents those Viewpoint Concerns.

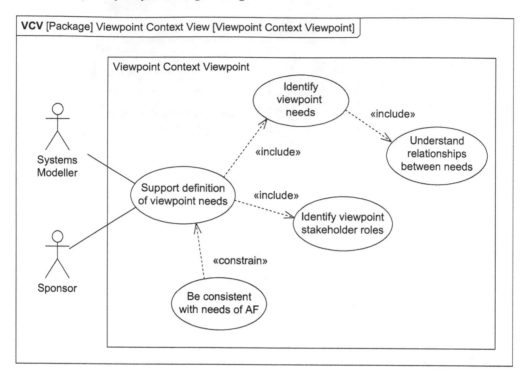

Figure 11.20   Example Viewpoint Context View for the Viewpoint Context Viewpoint

In the section titled 'Viewpoint Visualisation' earlier in this section, the example Viewpoint Context View was visualised using a *use case diagram*. This is the minimum visualisation that is needed. Given that the Viewpoint Context View essentially captures Needs, it would be possible to use the entire ACRE approach as described in Chapter 9, producing a number of different Views to visualise the Viewpoint Context Viewpoint.

11.2.3.5   The Viewpoint Definition Viewpoint

The Viewpoint Definition Viewpoint (VDV) defines a particular Viewpoint, showing the Viewpoint Elements (and hence the Ontology Elements) that appear on the Viewpoint.

Viewpoint Rationale

The Viewpoint Concerns that the Viewpoint Definition Viewpoint is intended to address are shown in the diagram in Figure 11.21.

Figure 11.21 shows the Viewpoint Concerns (a type of Need) that the Viewpoint Definition Viewpoint must address shown in context as Use Cases, together with relevant Stakeholder Roles. The main Use Case, taken from the Context for the definition of an AF framework (see Figure 11.2), is to 'Support definition of viewpoint content'; the Viewpoint Definition Viewpoint exists to define the contents

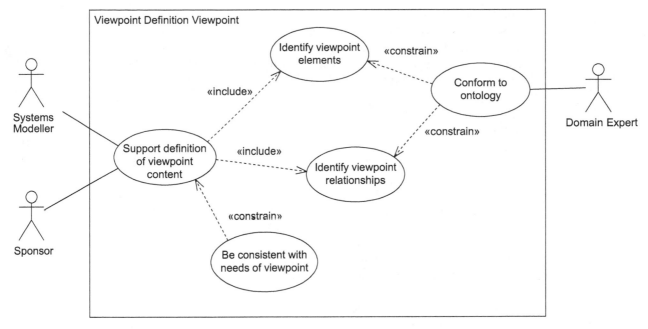

Figure 11.21   Viewpoint Definition Viewpoint Context

of a Viewpoint. In order to do this, it is necessary to 'Be consistent with needs of viewpoint'. That is, the Viewpoint must be defined in such a way that it meets its Needs (or, more precisely, its Viewpoint Concerns), described on its associated Viewpoint Context Viewpoint.

The main needs that must be addressed are to:

- 'Identify viewpoint elements' – Identify the Viewpoint Elements that will appear on the Viewpoint.
- 'Identify viewpoint relationships' – Identify any relationships between the Viewpoint Elements that appear on the Viewpoint.

Both of these Needs are constrained by:

- 'Conform to ontology' – Every Viewpoint Element (and relationship) that can appear on a Viewpoint must correspond to an Ontology Element (or relationship) from the Ontology. Nothing can appear on a Viewpoint that does not exist on the Ontology.

As identified in Figure 11.2, the two key Stakeholder Roles involved in the main need to 'Support definition of viewpoint content' are (through the «include» *relationships* from 'Define an architectural framework for creating architectural frameworks'): the 'Sponsor' and the 'Systems Modeller'. The 'Domain Expert' role is also involved, given the constraint imposed by the need to 'Conform to ontology'.

Viewpoint Definition

The subset of the MBSE Ontology that relates to Architectural Frameworks is shown in Figure 11.22, with the relevant Ontology Elements highlighted.

The diagram in Figure 11.22 shows that the Ontology Elements relevant to the 'Viewpoint Definition Viewpoint' are the 'Viewpoint', 'Viewpoint Element' and the 'Ontology Element'.

Viewpoint Relationships

The Viewpoint Definition Viewpoint is defined in the diagram in Figure 11.23.

Figure 11.23 shows that the 'Viewpoint Definition Viewpoint' defines a 'Viewpoint' that is made up of one or more related 'Viewpoint Element'. A 'Viewpoint' has a 'Name', an 'ID' and a 'Description'. The 'ID' property of a 'Viewpoint' is typically used as a shorthand abbreviation by which the 'Viewpoint' can be named. For example, the 'ID' of the 'Viewpoint Definition Viewpoint' is 'VDV'.

Every 'Viewpoint Definition View' (an actual instance of a 'Viewpoint Definition Viewpoint') is directly related to an 'Ontology Definition View' (an actual instance of an 'Ontology Definition Viewpoint'), as a 'Viewpoint' uses elements from an 'Ontology' through each 'Viewpoint Element' making up the 'Viewpoint'. Each 'Viewpoint Element' must correspond to an 'Ontology Element' from the 'Ontology' that is realised by an 'Ontology Definition View'. Each 'Viewpoint Definition Viewpoint' defines a Viewpoint to meet the Needs described on its corresponding 'Viewpoint Context Viewpoint'.

Viewpoint Visualisation

The Viewpoint Definition Viewpoint is usually visualised using a *block definition diagram*. An example Viewpoint Definition View is shown in Figure 11.24.

Figure 11.24 is an example Viewpoint Definition View. Note here the use of View rather than Viewpoint. Figure 11.24 is the realisation of a Viewpoint Definition Viewpoint and hence is a View, as shown in the *diagram frame*. Note also the use of the Viewpoint ID as the *frame tag* in the *diagram frame*. This is consistent with the diagramming guidelines described in Chapter 6.

Note also that the example Viewpoint Definition View shown is, in fact, that for the Viewpoint that the View realises. It is the Viewpoint Definition View for the Viewpoint Definition Viewpoint. This is because the FAF was itself defined using FAF, and thus every Viewpoint must have a Viewpoint Definition View, including the Viewpoint Definition Viewpoint itself!

Viewpoint Discussion

The Viewpoint Definition Viewpoint is used to define a Viewpoint, showing which Ontology Elements can appear on the Viewpoint. Often it is possible to realise a Viewpoint in a number of ways. For example, a Rules Definition Viewpoint could be realised as text in a document, text in a spread sheet, a SysML *block definition diagram* or a UML *class diagram*, etc. If it is important that the realisation for a Viewpoint be constrained, then the Viewpoint Definition Viewpoint can be annotated to show how it should be realised. An example is shown in Figure 11.25.

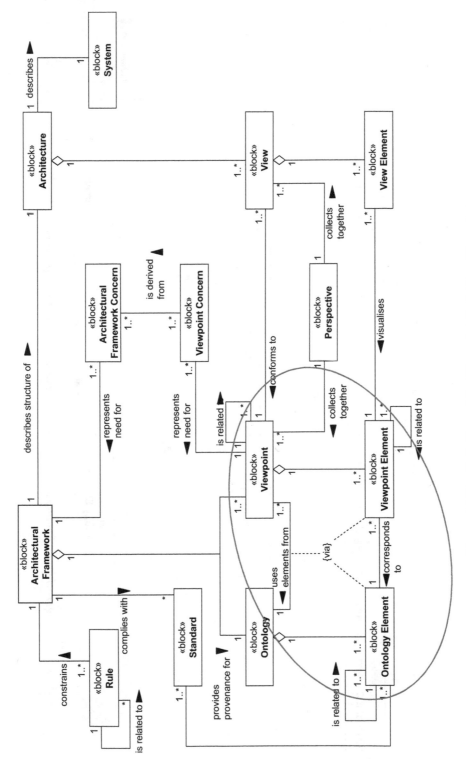

Figure 11.22 Definition of the Viewpoint Definition Viewpoint

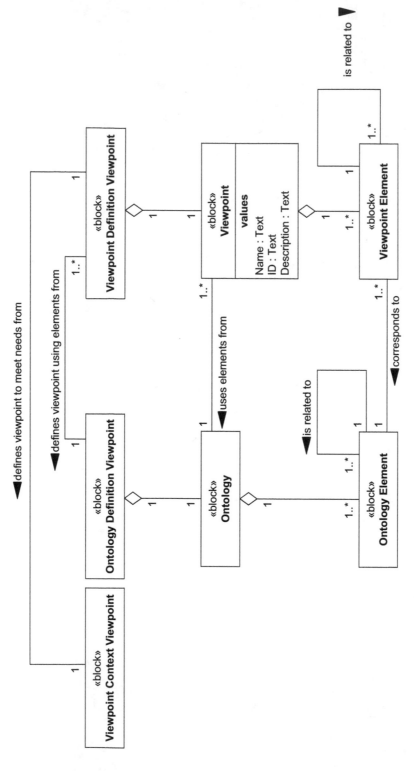

Figure 11.23   Relationships between Viewpoint Definition Viewpoint and other Views

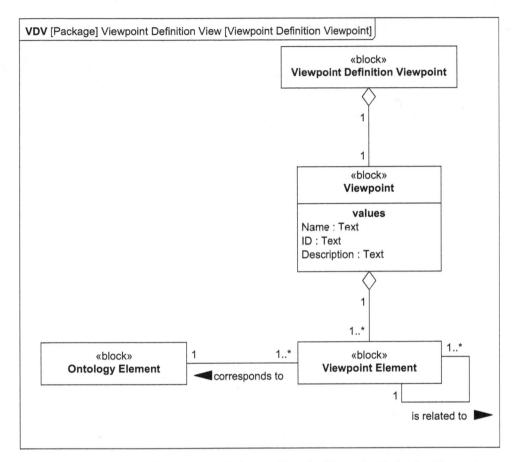

Figure 11.24   Example Viewpoint Definition View for Viewpoint Definition Viewpoint

Figure 11.25 shows the Viewpoint Definition View for the Rules Definition Viewpoint. It has been annotated using *comments* with the «realisation» *stereotype* to show how the Viewpoint is to be realised. It can be seen from the diagram that the 'Rules Definition Viewpoint' is to be realised as a spread sheet, with Rules and relationships defined in the spread sheet rows as described.

The authors would go so far as to say that realisation of all Viewpoints should be defined. This ensures that all Views conforming to a Viewpoint will be realised in the same way, helping to ensure consistency of approach and presentation by all working on an Architecture based on the Architectural Framework. It is also possible to show a number of different visualisation options, rather than just a single one, which provides more possibilities for different applications and projects.

11.2.3.6   The Rules Definition Viewpoint

The Rules Definition Viewpoint (RDV) defines the various Rules that constrain the Architectural Framework.

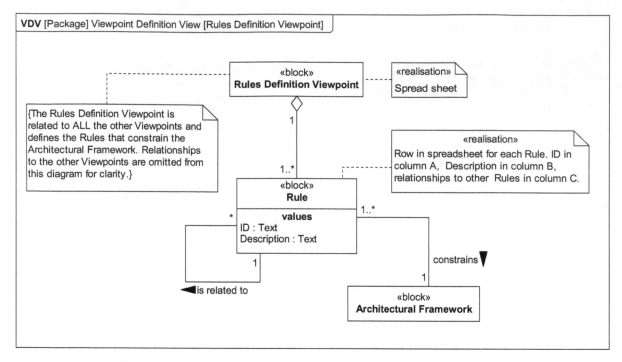

Figure 11.25   Example Viewpoint Definition View showing realisation

Viewpoint Rationale

The Viewpoint Concerns that the Rules Definition Viewpoint is intended to address are shown in the diagram in Figure 11.26.

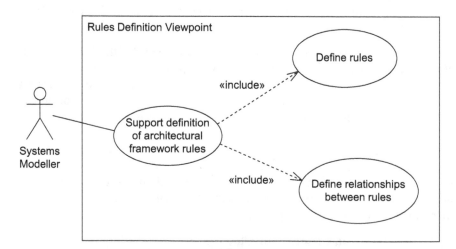

Figure 11.26   Rules Definition Viewpoint Context

Figure 11.26 shows the Viewpoint Concerns (a type of Need) that the Rules Definition Viewpoint must address shown in context as Use Cases, together with relevant Stakeholder Roles. The main Use Case, taken from the Context for the definition of an AF framework (see Figure 11.2), is to 'Support definition of architectural framework rules'; the Rules Definition Viewpoint exists to define any Rules that constrain the Architectural Framework. Note that such Rules can constrain any aspect of the Architectural Framework.

The main Use Cases that must be addressed are to:

- 'Define rules' – Define any Rules that constrain the Architectural Framework.
- 'Define relationships between rules' – Define any relationships between the Rules. This allows complex Rules to be built up.

As identified in Figure 11.2, the key Stakeholder Role involved in the main need to 'Support definition of architectural framework rules' is (through the «include» *relationships* from 'Define an architectural framework for creating architectural frameworks'): the 'Systems Modeller'.

Viewpoint Definition

The subset of the MBSE Ontology that relates to Architectural Frameworks is shown in Figure 11.27, with the relevant Ontology Elements highlighted.

The diagram in Figure 11.27 shows that the Ontology Elements relevant to the 'Rules Definition Viewpoint' are the 'Architectural Framework' and the 'Rule'.

Viewpoint Relationships

The Rules Definition Viewpoint is defined in the diagram in Figure 11.28.

Figure 11.28 shows that the 'Rules Definition Viewpoint' is made up of one or more 'Rule'. Each 'Rule' has an 'ID' and a 'Description and may be related to one or more other 'Rule'. A 'Rule' can constrain any aspect of an 'Architectural Framework'.

No explicit links are shown to the other parts of the framework, as is stated in the *constraint note* on the diagram. A 'Rule' can constrain any aspect of an 'Architectural Framework'. Explicitly showing this would require *associations* to every other Viewpoint and Viewpoint Element.

Viewpoint Visualisation

The Rules Definition Viewpoint can be visualised in a number of ways, depending on how the Rules are to be defined. Common representations use text, *block definition diagrams* and *parametric* diagrams. An example Rules Definition View is shown in Figure 11.29.

Figure 11.29 is an example Rules Definition View that is realised using a *block definition diagram*. Each *block* has the *stereotype* «Rule» to distinguish it from a normal *block*. The Rule ID is used to name the *block* and the Rule Description is represented as text, shown in the 'Rule Text' *compartment* of each *block*.

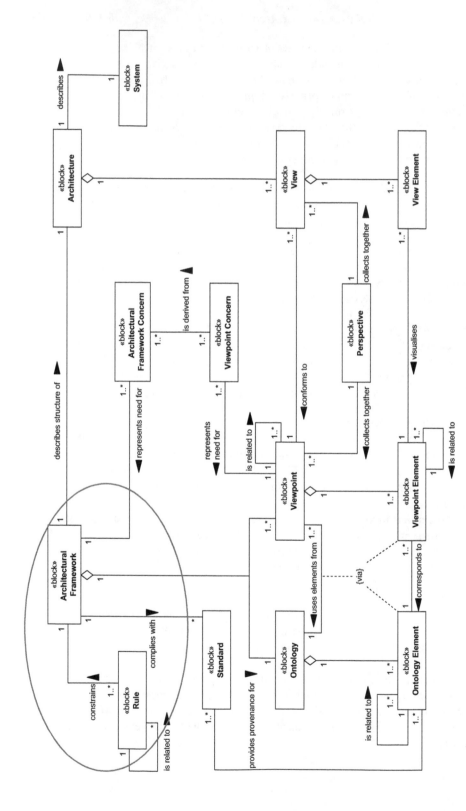

Figure 11.27 Definition of the Rules Definition Viewpoint

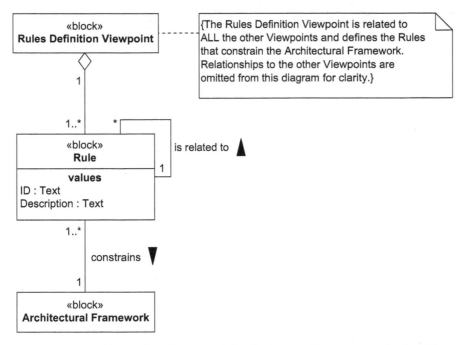

Figure 11.28   Relationships between Rules Definition Viewpoint and other Views

Note here the use of View rather than Viewpoint. Figure 11.29 is the realisation of Rules Definition Viewpoint and hence is a View, as shown in the *diagram frame*. Note also the use of the Viewpoint ID as the *frame tag* in the *diagram frame*. This is consistent with the diagramming guidelines described in Chapter 6.

Viewpoint Discussion
When defining an Architectural Framework it is often useful to define a number of Rules that can help to enforce the consistency both of the AF and of any Architecture that is created based on it. This can be particularly useful when using 'sharp' tools to model the Architecture. Such tools often allow user-defined consistency checks to be defined. The Rules on a Rules Definition View can form the basis of such definition.

Note that the Rules Definition Viewpoint in Figure 11.28 shows the Description property of a Rule as being text. This text could be a simple natural language description (as in the example in Figure 11.29), could be a formal modelling language such as VDM or Z or any mixture as necessary. If more complex Rule definitions are needed, then rather than representing them as simple *blocks,* as in Figure 11.29, Rules could be represented using SysML *constraint blocks* and *parametric diagrams.*

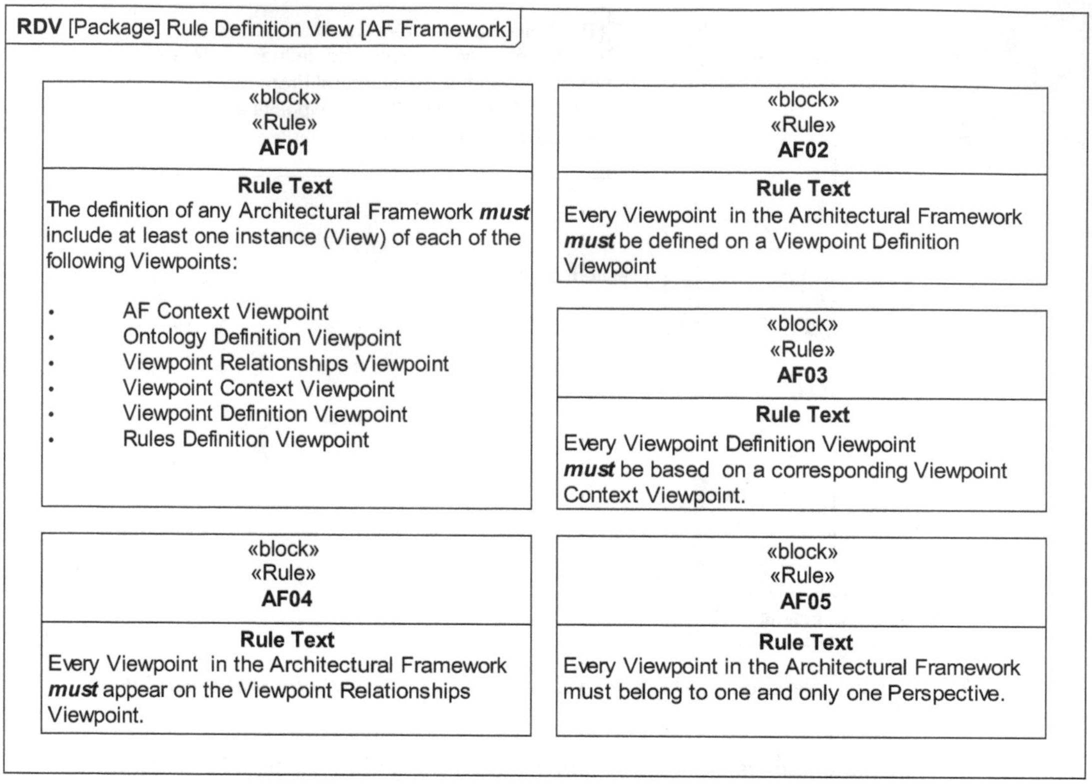

RDV [Package] Rule Definition View [AF Framework]

«block»
«Rule»
AF01

Rule Text
The definition of any Architectural Framework **must** include at least one instance (View) of each of the following Viewpoints:

- AF Context Viewpoint
- Ontology Definition Viewpoint
- Viewpoint Relationships Viewpoint
- Viewpoint Context Viewpoint
- Viewpoint Definition Viewpoint
- Rules Definition Viewpoint

«block»
«Rule»
AF02

Rule Text
Every Viewpoint in the Architectural Framework **must** be defined on a Viewpoint Definition Viewpoint

«block»
«Rule»
AF03

Rule Text
Every Viewpoint Definition Viewpoint **must** be based on a corresponding Viewpoint Context Viewpoint.

«block»
«Rule»
AF04

Rule Text
Every Viewpoint in the Architectural Framework **must** appear on the Viewpoint Relationships Viewpoint.

«block»
«Rule»
AF05

Rule Text
Every Viewpoint in the Architectural Framework must belong to one and only one Perspective.

Figure 11.29   Example Rules Definition View for an Architectural Framework Framework

11.3   The Framework for Architectural Frameworks

The complete framework for the definition of architectural frameworks is shown in the diagram in Figure 11.30.

The diagram in Figure 11.30 shows the complete FAF, illustrating the Ontology Elements that can appear on each Viewpoint and the relationships between the Viewpoints. An example of using the FAF for the definition of an Architectural Framework is given in Chapter 12. The example AF so defined is then used in Chapter 13.

11.4   Using the FAF

As discussed in Section 11.1.1, Architectures and Architectural Frameworks are an essential part of systems engineering and system of systems engineering.

While there are a number of widely used Architectural Frameworks, this does not necessarily mean that they are suitable for all systems engineering and SoS

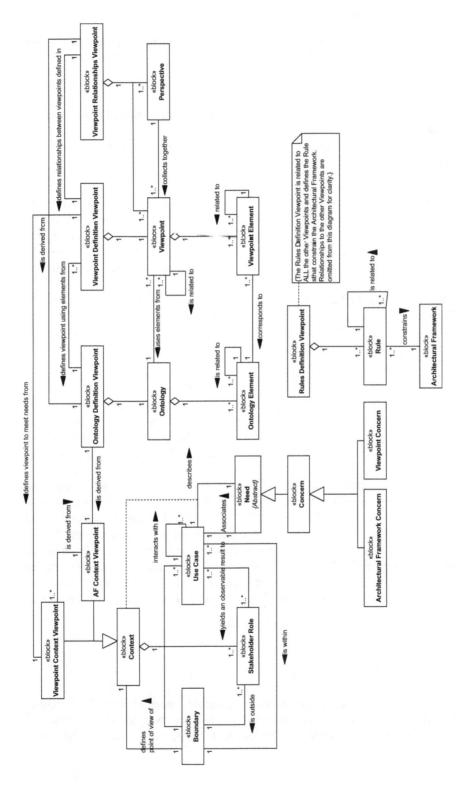

Figure 11.30 Complete Framework for Architectural Frameworks

engineering projects; it is important that the correct AF, fit for purpose, be used. For example:

- Defence frameworks, such as MODAF [10], are intended to be used in the acquisition of systems.
- TOGAF [11] is intended to provide an approach for developing IT Architectural Frameworks.
- Zachman [12] is a framework approach for defining IT-based enterprise architectures.

For a discussion of these frameworks see [5].

The use of an Architectural Framework is a prerequisite for the development of a robust Architecture. Before any existing Architectural Frameworks can be assessed for suitability, it is essential that the Needs for the Architecture, and hence it's guiding Architectural Framework, are understood. If an existing Architectural Framework is not suitable, then a project will have to define its own.

The FAF, described earlier, forms the heart of such an approach. In order to use FAF a set of Processes are needed to ensure consistency of application. One such set is ArchDeCon (**Arch**itecture **De**finition and **Con**struction), a set of Processes for the definition of an Architectural Framework. The Processes are shown in Figure 11.31.

The Processes may be summarised as:

- 'AF Definition Process' – The aim of this Process is to understand the underlying need for the AF. It uses the other three ArchDeCon Processes to: identify Architectural Framework Concerns for the Architectural Framework and put them into Context; define an Ontology; and define Viewpoints, Perspectives and Rules.
- 'Ontology Definition Process' – The aim of this Process is to identify and define the main concepts and terms used for the AF in the form of an Ontology.
- 'Viewpoint Definition Process' – The aim of this Process is to identify and define the key Viewpoints and to classify them into Perspectives. It also defines any Rules that constrain the Viewpoints and Architectural Framework.
- 'Context Process' – The aim of this Process is to create a Context that can be used to create either an 'AF Context View' or a 'Viewpoint Context View' (see Section 11.2.2 for a description of these Views and their defining Viewpoints).

These processes are fully defined in Appendix F.

11.5 Summary

This chapter has discussed the principles and essential concepts behind Architectures and Architectural Frameworks, informed by best practice found in influential texts and international standards. The essential Needs surrounding Architectures

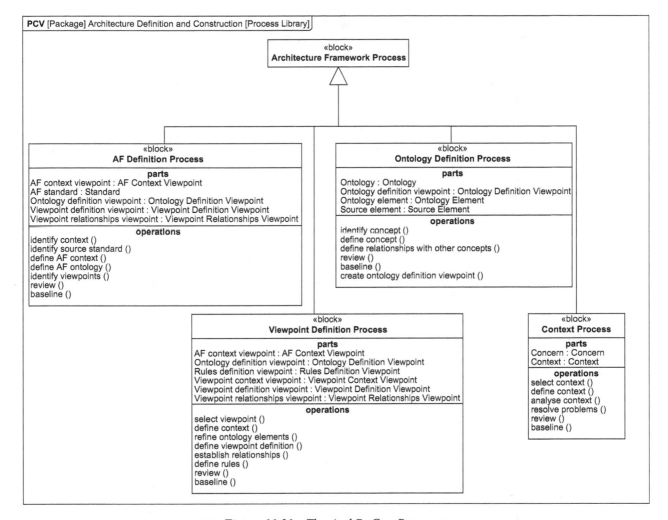

Figure 11.31   The ArchDeCon Processes

and Architectural Frameworks were considered and any approach to modelling Architectures and Architectural Frameworks must support the definition of Architectures, allowing Architectures to be defined that model both the structural aspects and the behavioural aspects of the System represented by the Architecture. When defining an Architecture, it is essential that an established architectural design process is followed and that any Architecture conforms to a defined Architectural Framework.

Too often Architectures are produced seemingly simply for the sake of producing an Architecture. For this reason it is essential that the Needs of the Customer are understood so that the Architecture is produced for a defined purpose and so that it can be validated.

Given that any Architecture should be defined based on an Architectural Framework, there is also the need to be able to define such frameworks. An Architectural Framework should be defined in terms of a number of Viewpoints and should have Rules defined to ensure consistency. Just as with an Architecture, it is essential that the reasons why the Architectural Framework is being created are understood. Similarly, the Needs for each Viewpoint defined as part of an Architectural Framework must also be understood.

Whatever the approach to modelling Architectures and Architectural Frameworks, it should be a model-based one, using all the techniques described in this book.

These Needs were used to guide the definition of a set of processes (ArchDeCon) and an Architectural Framework (FAF) that can be used by anyone who has to define their own Architectural Framework.

References

1. Holt J. *UML for Systems Engineering: Watching the Wheels*. 2nd edn. London: IET Publishing; 2004
2. Dickerson C.E., Mavris D.N. *Architecture and Principles of Systems Engineering*. Boca Raton, USA: CRC Press; 2009
3. Office of the Deputy Under Secretary of Defense for Acquisition and Technology, Systems and Software Engineering. *Systems Engineering Guide for Systems of Systems'. Version 1.0*. Washington, DC: ODUSD(A&T)SSE; 2008
4. Object Management Group. *BPMN Website* [online]. Available from http://www.bpmn.org [Accessed March 2013]
5. Holt J., Perry S. *Modelling Enterprise Architectures*. Stevenage, UK: IET publishing; 2010
6. ISO/IEC. *ISO/IEC 15288:2008 Systems and Software Engineering – System Life Cycle Processes*. 2nd edn. International Organisation for Standardisation; 2008
7. ISO/IEC. *ISO/IEC 42010:2011 Systems and software Engineering – Architecture Description*. International Organisation for Standardisation; 2011
8. Kleppe A., Warmer J., Bast W. *MDA Explained – The Model Driven Architecture: Practice ad Promise*. Boston, USA: Addison-Wesley; 2003
9. Sheard, S. 'The frameworks quagmire, a brief look'. *Proceedings of the Seventh Annual International Symposium of the International Council on Systems Engineering*. Los Angeles, CA: INCOSE; 1997
10. MoD. *The Ministry of Defence Architectural Framework*. Ministry of Defence; 2010. Available from https://www.gov.uk/mod-architecture-framework [Accessed March 2013]
11. The Open Group. *The Open Group Architectural Framework (TOGAF), Version 9.1*. Available from http://www.opengroup.org/architecture/togaf9-doc/arch [Accessed March 2013]
12. Zachman J.A. *Concise Definition of the Zachman Framework*. Zachman International; 2008. Available from http://www.zachman.com/about-the-zachman-framework [Accessed March 2013]

Part 4

Case study

P4.1   Overview

Chapter 12

Case study introduction and Architectural Framework

There is nothing so annoying as a good example!!

Mark Twain, 1835–1910

12.1 Introduction

In order to demonstrate the concepts, principles and notation in Parts 1–3, a case study will be used. This case study is presented in Chapter 13. The current chapter sets the case study in Context by considering the Needs that it addresses in Section 12.1.1. This is followed, in Section 12.2, by the definition of an Architectural Framework that will be used as the main means of presentation of the case study in Chapter 13. This is followed by a discussion of the use of SysML auxiliary constructs in the definition of Viewpoints. Finally, the chapter concludes with a summary and references.

12.1.1 Background

The Needs that the case study is intended to address are shown in Figure 12.1.

The main Need that the case study must address is to 'Demonstrate MBSE concepts covered in book'. Chapters 12 and 13 exist specifically to provide a more in-depth example of the concepts discussed so far. When covering these concepts it is important that both the approach taken throughout ('Demonstrate use of ontology, framework & view approach') and the SysML notation used ('Demonstrate use of SysML') are covered by the case study.

It is also important to ensure that all the areas of MBSE discussed in the book are covered by the case study, as shown by the 'Cover key areas' Use Case and its specialisations. Finally, it is essential that the consistency of approach and notation be highlighted and in such a way that it can be seen as a whole rather than as a collection of piecemeal examples. This is captured in the final Use Case in Figure 12.1, 'Demonstrate consistency through extended example'. The Need captured by this Use Case is considered by the authors to be very important. It would be possible to demonstrate all the key concepts through a number of unconnected examples. However, this makes it harder to see how all the concepts relate to and reinforce each other and how consistency can come out of a robust

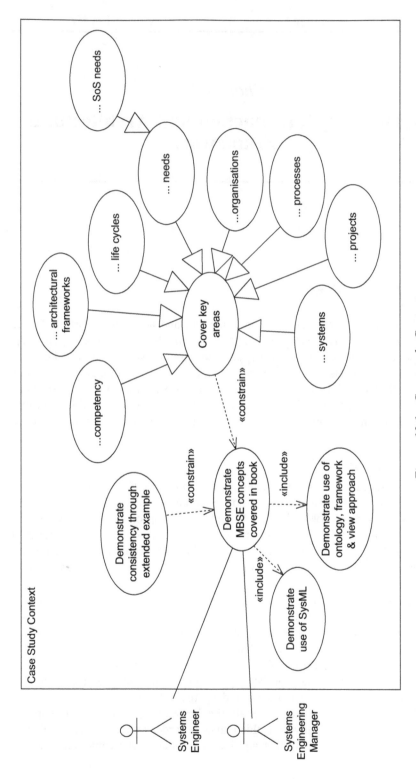

Figure 12.1   Case study Context

MBSE approach since each example exists either in isolation or as part of a very small collection of diagrams. So to fulfil this Need, the case study is a single, extended example, that is presented as an Architecture of a System. The remainder of this chapter defines the Architectural Framework that will be used as the basis of this Architecture. The subject of the case study will be revealed in Chapter 13.

12.2   The MBSE Architectural Framework

This section presents the MBSE Architectural Framework (MBSEAF) that forms the basis of the example Architecture presented in Chapter 13. The MBSEAF has been defined using the Framework for Architectural Frameworks (FAF) and ArchDeCon Processes that are described in Chapter 11. For this reason, the MBSEAF is defined and presented as a set of Views that conform to the six Viewpoints defined in the FAF. An AF Context View is presented first to detail the Architectural Framework Concerns that the MBSEAF is intended to address. This is followed by an Ontology Definition View to define the concepts that will be used in the MBSEAF and two Viewpoint Relationship Views that define the Perspectives that are found in the MBSEAF together with the Viewpoints in each Perspective. A Rules Definition View comes next, giving an illustration, but not a complete definition, of the types of Rules that should be defined for the MBSEAF. A number of Viewpoints are then defined using a Viewpoint Context View and a Viewpoint Definition View. Again, this is not done for all the Viewpoints in the MBSEAF, but for a sample in order to give an additional example, in addition to that found in Chapter 11, of the way that Viewpoints are defined using the FAF approach.

12.2.1   The AF Context View

The AF Context View for the MBSEAF is shown in Figure 12.2. The underlying Needs behind the Use Cases shown in Figure 12.2 are Architectural Framework Concerns, as opposed to Requirements, Goals or Capabilities. See Chapter 11 for a discussion of Concerns.

Figure 12.2 shows that the main Architectural Framework Concern that the MBSEAF must address is to 'Provide architectural framework for modelling a system'. The types of modelling that the Architectural Framework must support are indicated by the four Use Cases that constrain the main Concern:

- 'Must support acquisitions, development & deployment' – the Architectural Framework must be suitable for use throughout the whole of a System's Life Cycle, from acquisition, through development and onto deployment. Many Architectural Frameworks only support part of a Life Cycle necessitating the use of multiple Architectural Frameworks, or even worse, attempting to use an Architectural Framework for purposes for which it was not intended. An example of this is the MODAF. This is an Architectural Framework intended for use in the acquisition of Systems but often used, with varying degrees of success, for the development and deployment of Systems.

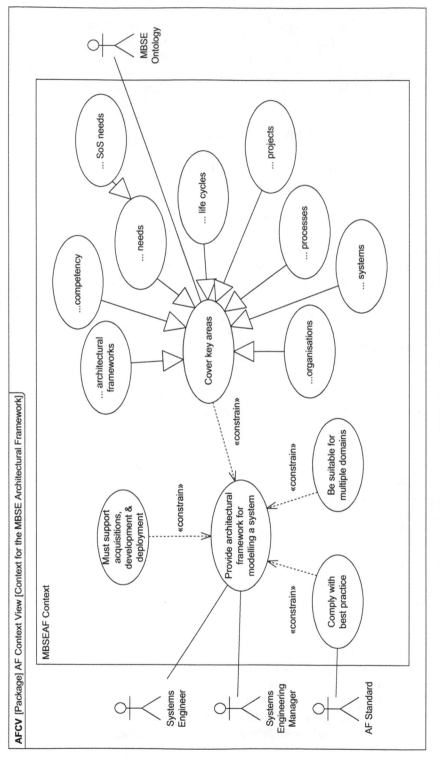

Figure 12.2 AF Context View for the MBSEAF

- 'Comply with best practice' – as with anything we do in systems engineering, it is important that the work complies with best practice in order to ensure the quality of the work undertaken. The same holds for any Architectural Framework we define; it must comply with best practice in the form of Architectural Framework Standards.
- 'Be suitable for multiple domains' – defining an Architectural Framework is a time-consuming activity. An Architectural Framework that can be used in multiple domains means that new frameworks need not be defined for every new domain encountered. In addition, having an Architectural Framework that can be used across multiple domains means that the framework can be used across an Organisation and across multiple Projects; the more widely a framework is used within an Organisation, the more the return on investment placed on its initial creation and, more importantly, the better the communication between those involved in developing Systems since the Architectural Framework with its defined Viewpoints and underlying Ontology establishes a common vocabulary throughout the Organisation.
- 'Cover key areas' – given that this book defines a number of key areas that are important to model-based systems engineering, through the MBSE Ontology, any Architectural Framework should also cover these areas.

The Concerns that are represented by the Use Cases in Figure 12.2 have guided the definition of the MBSEAF, but tempered with the pragmatic understanding that the MBSEAF is an example Architectural Framework only. Defining a full MBSE Architectural Framework would require more space than is available in this chapter. Nonetheless, for those readers who want to define an Architectural Framework for their own Organisation and who don't want to adopt existing Architectural Frameworks such as MODAF or TRAK, the MBSEAF is a good place to start.

12.2.2   The Ontology Definition View

The Ontology Definition View for the MBSEAF is shown in Figure 12.3.

Given that the case study is intended to demonstrate all the concepts covered so far, the Ontology that the MBSEAF is based on is the MBSE Ontology previously presented and used throughout the book. It is presented again in Figure 12.3, with a *frame* that identifies it as an Ontology Definition View through the 'ODV' *frame tag*.

This ODV forms a starting point; when defining Viewpoints below any additions will be noted in the relevant Viewpoint Definition View for Viewpoints that require additional concepts.

12.2.3   The Viewpoint Relationships View

The Viewpoint Relationships View for the MBSEAF is shown in Figure 12.4.

The MBSEAF has nine Perspectives that are defined to cover all the concepts found on the ODV in Figure 12.3. Eight of the Perspectives are shown in Figure 12.5. The ninth Perspective is the Architectural Framework Perspective and is the same as

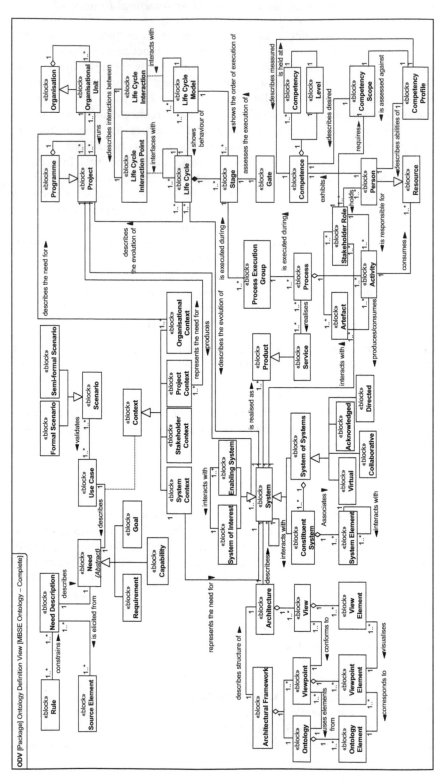

Figure 12.3   Ontology Definition View for the MBSEAF

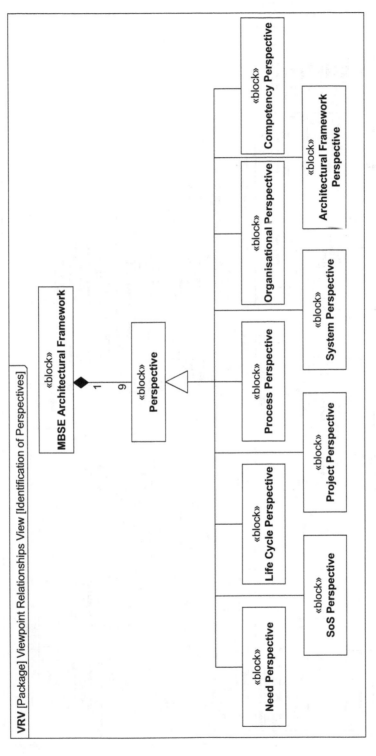

Figure 12.4 Viewpoint Relationships View for the MBSEAF showing the Perspectives

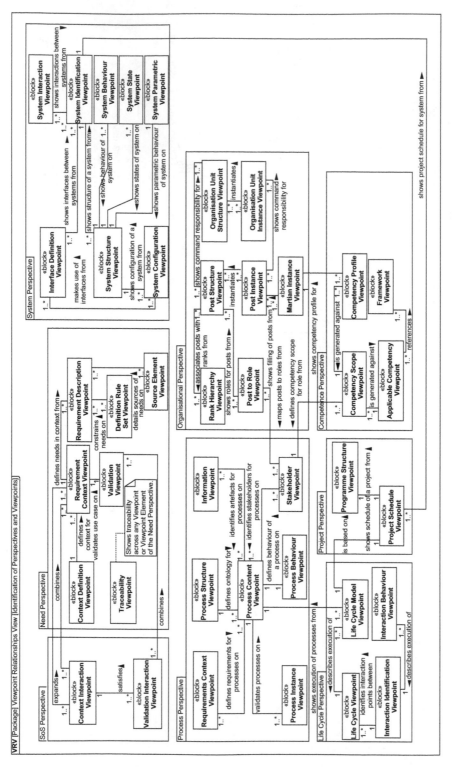

Figure 12.5 Viewpoint Relationships View for the MBSEAF showing Viewpoints in each Perspective

the FAF described in Chapter 11. This Perspective is not shown in Figure 12.5 since it is a meta-Perspective that is used to define the MBSEAF itself; an Architecture based on the MBSEAF, for example that is presented in Chapter 13, would not contain any Views based on the Viewpoints in the Architectural Framework Perspective, since this Perspective is used to define the MBSEAF. The current chapter shows a number of Views, produced using the Architectural Framework Perspective (i.e., the FAF from Chapter 11), that define the Perspectives and Viewpoints of the MBSEAF that is used to produce the Architecture covered in Chapter 13.

The Viewpoints within each Perspective are shown in the Viewpoint Relationships View (VRV) in Figure 12.5.

There are a number of points to note about the Perspectives in Figure 12.5:

- The 'SoS Perspective' includes all the Viewpoints of the 'Need Perspective'
- The 'Need Perspective' can represent Needs for any of the other Perspectives
- The 'Context Definition Viewpoint' and 'Validation Viewpoint' of the 'Needs Perspective both have a number of *sub-types* (*specialisations* of the Viewpoints). These are omitted from Figure 12.5

Seven out of the nine Perspectives are based directly on the Frameworks described in Part 3 and so are not described further in this chapter. Table 12.1 provides a cross-reference from the various Perspectives to the relevant chapters.

Table 12.1   Cross-reference to descriptions of the MBSEAF Perspectives

Perspective	Described in...
Process Perspective	Chapter 7
Project Perspective	Chapter 8
Life Cycle Perspective	Chapter 8
Competence Perspective	Chapter 8
Need Perspective	Chapter 9
SoS Perspective	Chapter 10
Architectural Framework Perspective	Chapter 11
System Perspective	See description later in this section
Organisational Perspective	See description later in this section

The remaining two Perspectives are described briefly below:

- 'System Perspective' – defines Viewpoints that allow aspects of System structure and behaviour to be captured.
- 'Organisational Perspective' – defines Viewpoints that allow aspects of the structure of Organisations and Organisational Units to be captured, as well as Posts and their relationships to Stakeholder Roles, the Person filling the roles and associated Competencies.

The Viewpoints that are contained in these two Perspectives are described in Section 12.2.5.

12.2.4   The Rules Definition View

The Rules Definition View defines those Rules that constrain an Architectural Framework in some way. There are three types of Rules that are usually defined for an Architectural Framework:

- Rules that define the minimum set of Views that have to be present in an Architecture based on the Architectural Framework
- Rules that define consistency checks between Viewpoints and the Views based on them
- Rules that define consistency checks within Viewpoints and the Views based on them

Rather than defining all the possible rules that apply to the MBSEAF, Figure 12.6 shows an example of each of the three types.

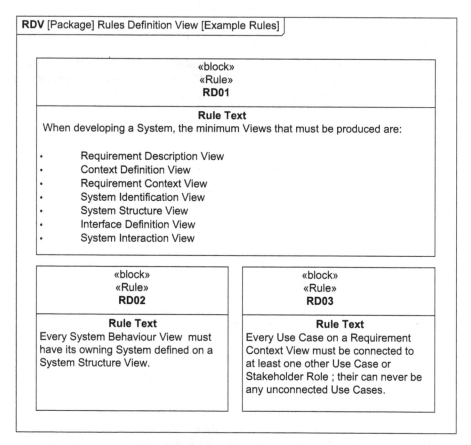

Figure 12.6   Rules Definition View for the MBSEAF showing example Rules

Rule 'RD01' is an example of a Rule that defines a minimum set of Views that an Architecture based on the MBSEAF must contain. Note that the Rule makes it clear that it applies when developing a System. If the MBSEAF is being used for another purpose, for example, defining a set of Processes for an Organisation, then this Rule would not apply. There would be a similar Rule defining a minimum set of Views to be produced when developing Processes.

Rule 'RD02' is an example of a Rule that applies between Viewpoints and their realising Views. When developing a System Architecture, the Rule says that you must have modelled both the structure of a System and its behaviour; you can't model just behaviour.

Rule 'RD03' is an example of a Rule that applies within a Viewpoint and its realising View. When looking at Requirements in Context – modelling them as Use Cases on a Requirement Context View – then none of the Use Cases can exist in isolation. They must be related to a Stakeholder Role or to another Use Case.

12.2.5   *Viewpoint Definitions*

The Viewpoints in seven of the nine Perspectives shown in Figures 12.4 and 12.5 have already been described in this book, as shown in Table 12.1 (see Section 12.2.3). For this reason, they will not be defined here. The new Viewpoints shown in Figure 12.5 are briefly described in Table 12.2.

Careful reading of Table 12.2 will show a number of capitalised terms that aren't found on the Ontology Definition View in Figure 12.3, namely: Post and Rank. This indicates that the Ontology needs expansion to include these terms. Don't forget, nothing can appear on a Viewpoint that is not present on the Ontology. The expansion of the Ontology to include these terms is discussed in Section 12.2.5.1, where one of the Viewpoints that makes use of these new concepts is defined.

Two of these Viewpoints, the Post Structure Viewpoint from the Organisational Perspective and the System Structure Viewpoint from the System Perspective, are defined fully in the following sections. In a full definition of the MBSEAF, the same approach would be applied to all the Viewpoints in these Perspectives. Examples of all the Viewpoints in Table 12.2, and indeed of all the Viewpoints in the MBSEAF, will be presented in Chapter 13.

Table 12.2   New Viewpoints and their purpose

Perspective	Viewpoint	Purpose
Organisational Perspective	Organisation Unit Structure Viewpoint	Used to show the typical structure of an Organisation, broken down into Organisational Units, which can be further subdivided.
	Organisation Unit Instance Viewpoint	Used to show the structure of an actual Organisation, conforming to the structure in the Organisation Unit Structure Viewpoint.
	Rank Hierarchy Viewpoint	Used to show Ranks and their hierarchy.
	Post Structure Viewpoint	Used to show typical Posts and lines of command between Posts and between a Post and an Organisational Unit. Also shows the minimum Rank that can fill a Post.

(Continues)

Table 12.2   (Continued)

Perspective	Viewpoint	Purpose
	Post Instance Viewpoint	Used to show actual Posts, the actual Organisational Units that the Posts command and the actual Ranks of the Person filling each Post.
	Post to Role Viewpoint	Used to show the Stakeholder Roles that are required by each Post.
	Martian Instance Viewpoint	*** SPOILER ALERT! *** Used to show the actual Person (and in the case study, Martians (!)) that fill each Post.
System Perspective	System Identification Viewpoint	Used to identify Systems and the relationships between them.
	System Structure Viewpoint	Used to define the structure of a System, showing how it is composed of System Elements. Shows relationships between System Elements, their properties and behaviours.
	System Configuration Viewpoint	Used to show a System is actually configured based on its structure, together with the Interfaces between the System Elements.
	Interface Definition Viewpoint	Used to define Interfaces between Systems and between System Elements within a System.
	System Interaction Viewpoint	Used to define interactions between Systems and between System Elements within a System.
	System State Viewpoint	Used to define state-based behaviour of a System and its System Elements.
	System Behaviour Viewpoint	Used to define the behaviour of a System and its System Elements.
	System Parametric Viewpoint	Used to define parametric behaviour of a System and its System Elements.

12.2.5.1   The Post Structure Viewpoint

Viewpoint Context View

The Viewpoint Context View for the Post Structure Viewpoint is shown in Figure 12.7.

The Viewpoint Concerns that the Post Structure Viewpoint is intended to address are shown as Use Cases on the Viewpoint Context View in Figure 12.7. The main Use Case is to 'Define posts'. This is the primary aim of the Viewpoint – to allow Posts within an Organisation to be modelled. There are two inclusions that allow extra information to be captured. The first is 'Define minimum rank for a post' that allows the minimum military Rank that is required by a Post to be defined. The second is 'Define lines of command' with two specialised Use Cases, '. . . between posts' and '. . . between post and an organisational unit'. Fulfilling these Use Cases allow lines of command to be modelled, showing which Posts command other Posts and which Posts command which Organisational Units.

Viewpoint Definition View

As discussed earlier in this section, the Organisational Perspective introduces two new concepts, Post and Rank, which are not found on the ODV in Figure 12.3. These concepts could be added to that diagram, but for the sake of clarity a separate

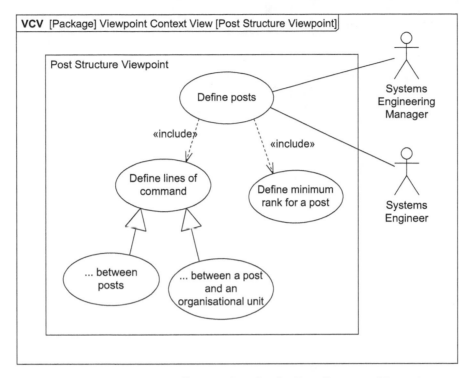

Figure 12.7   Viewpoint Context View for the Post Structure Viewpoint

ODV showing how these relate to existing concepts has been produced. This is shown in Figure 12.8.

The ODV in Figure 12.8 shows that a 'Post' commands zero or more 'Post' and zero or more 'Organisational Unit' and that each 'Post' requires a minimum 'Rank'. Each 'Rank' is subordinate to zero or one other 'Rank'. Each 'Post' requires one or more 'Stakeholder Role' (which then links through to 'Competency Scope'). One or more 'Person' fill a 'Post'.

This extended Ontology is used to define each of the Viewpoints of the Organisational Perspective. For reference, the annotated diagram in Figure 12.9 shows which parts of the Ontology in Figure 12.8 appear on which of the Viewpoints.

The Viewpoint Definition View for the Post Structure Viewpoint is shown in Figure 12.10.

The VDV in Figure 12.10 shows that the 'Post Structure Viewpoint' is made up of one or more 'Post', one or more 'Rank' and zero or more 'Organisational Unit'. For each 'Post' it shows the minimum 'Rank' required by the 'Post', any other 'Post' that a given 'Post' commands and any 'Organisational Unit' that a given 'Post' commands.

It is worth noting here that the Post Instance Viewpoint will have a similar (if not identical) definition. The difference between them is that the Post Structure Viewpoint is intended to be used to define typical Posts, for example 'Pack Leader' commanding a 'Pack'. The Post Instance Viewpoint is intended to define actual Posts, for example '1138-11 Pack Leader' commanding 'Pack 1138-11'.

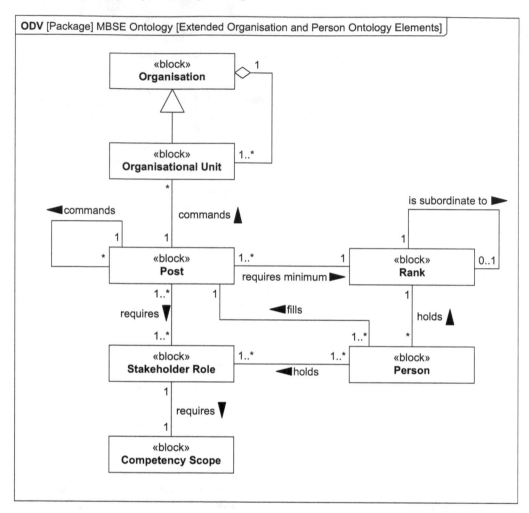

Figure 12.8   Ontology Definition View showing extended concepts related to Organisation and Person

12.2.5.2   The System Structure Viewpoint

Viewpoint Context View

The Viewpoint Context View for the System Structure Viewpoint is shown in Figure 12.11.

The Viewpoint Concerns that the System Structure Viewpoint is intended to address are shown as Use Cases on the Viewpoint Context View in Figure 12.11. The main Use Case is to 'Show system structure'; the Viewpoint is intended to allow the structure of a System to be modelled. The main Use Case also has a number of inclusions:

- 'Show relationships between system elements' – the Viewpoint must be able to capture the relationships between System Elements.

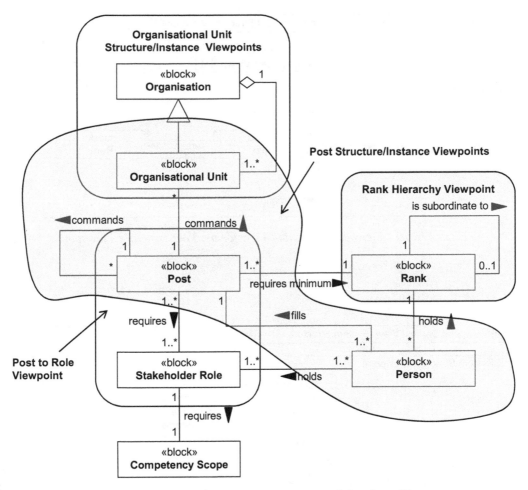

Figure 12.9 Annotated Ontology showing mapping of Ontology Elements to Viewpoints of Organisational Perspective

- 'Show system elements' – the Viewpoint must be able to show the System Elements that a System is made up of.
- 'Identify properties' – the Viewpoint must be able to show the properties of both the System (as stated by the specialised Use Case 'Identify properties for system') and for its System Elements (as stated by the specialised Use Case 'Identify properties for system elements').
- 'Identify functionality' – the Viewpoint must be able to show the functionality that can be provided (but not how it is provided) of both the System (as stated by the specialised Use Case 'Identify functionality for system') and for its System Elements (as stated by the specialised Use Case 'Identify functionality for system elements').

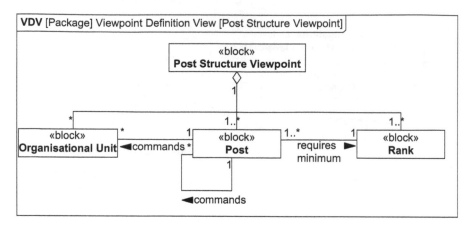

Figure 12.10   Viewpoint Definition View for the Post Structure Viewpoint

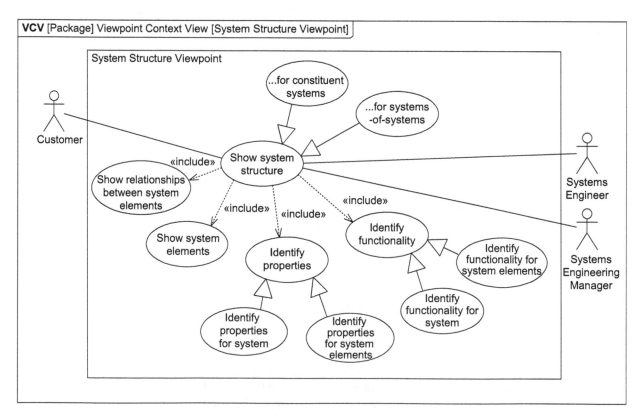

Figure 12.11   Viewpoint Context View for the System Structure Viewpoint

The main Use Case has two specialised Use Cases '... for constituent systems' and '... for systems of systems'; the Viewpoint can be used to model the structure of an independent System, the Constituent System of an SoS or the structure of an SoS.

Viewpoint Definition View

The Viewpoint Definition View for the System Structure Viewpoint is shown in Figure 12.12.

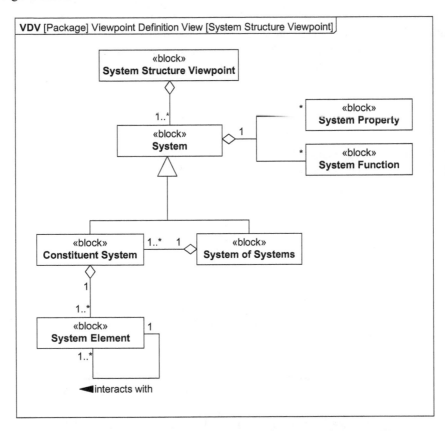

Figure 12.12   Viewpoint Definition View for the System Structure Viewpoint

Figure 12.12 shows that a 'System Structure Viewpoint' shows a one or more 'System' that can be a 'Constituent System' or a 'System of Systems' made up of one or more 'Constituent System'. For a 'Constituent System' the Viewpoint will show one or more 'System Element' that make up each 'Constituent System' together with the interactions between them, which would be modelled as high-level relationships between each 'System Element'. For each 'System', zero or more 'System Property' and zero or more 'System Function' are shown.

There are two points worth noting about this Viewpoint. First, it introduces two new MBSE Ontology elements: System Property and System Function. Remember that a Viewpoint can show only elements that appear on the MBSE Ontology, so these two additions could be added to the ODV in Figure 12.3.

The second point concerns the level of abstraction at which the Viewpoint is used. If used to model a System of Systems then the System Elements that are shown on a View that realises the Viewpoint will be Constituent Systems. Remember that what constitutes a System is often a matter of perspective: one Organisation's System Element will be another Organisation's System and vice versa. For this reason, System Property and System Function are shown as being parts of a System. The Viewpoint Context View in Figure 12.11 shows that properties and functions can be shown for both Systems and System Elements, and so these concepts could also be linked to System Element in Figure 12.12 by aggregation relationships. However, this has not been done as it would make the diagram overly complicated and also, since we can look at Systems and System Elements from different levels of abstraction, it is sufficient to show this via the relationships to System.

12.3   Defining Viewpoints using SysML Auxiliary Constructs

So far, all Viewpoints have been defined using *block definition diagrams*, with the Concerns that they address and the Stakeholder Roles involved defined using *use case diagrams*. An alternative is to use the SysML *viewpoint* auxiliary construct, as shown in Figure 12.13.

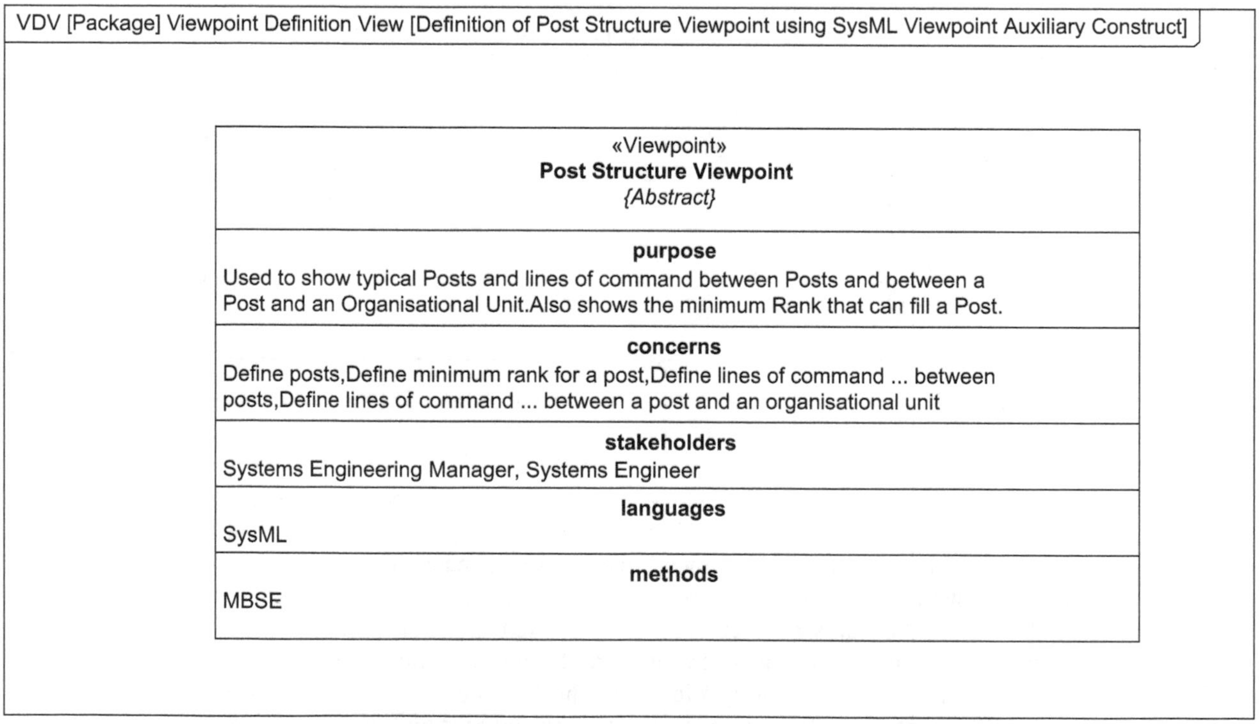

VDV [Package] Viewpoint Definition View [Definition of Post Structure Viewpoint using SysML Viewpoint Auxiliary Construct]

«Viewpoint»
Post Structure Viewpoint
{Abstract}

purpose
Used to show typical Posts and lines of command between Posts and between a Post and an Organisational Unit.Also shows the minimum Rank that can fill a Post.

concerns
Define posts,Define minimum rank for a post,Define lines of command ... between posts,Define lines of command ... between a post and an organisational unit

stakeholders
Systems Engineering Manager, Systems Engineer

languages
SysML

methods
MBSE

Figure 12.13   Viewpoint Definition View for the Post Structure Viewpoint using SysML viewpoint auxiliary construct

A SysML *viewpoint* is a special kind of *block* that has the *stereotype* «Viewpoint» and a number of associated *tags* that hold information about the *viewpoint*:

- *stakeholders* – Set of stakeholders
- *purpose* – The purpose addresses the stakeholder concerns
- *concerns* – The interest of the stakeholders
- *languages* – The languages used to construct the viewpoint
- *methods* – The methods used to construct the views for this viewpoint

The above descriptions are taken from the SysML specification, see Reference 1. In the specification these *tags* are defined simply to contain strings of text. In the example in Figure 12.13 the 'concerns' *tag* has been populated with the names of the Uses Cases from the Viewpoint Context View in Figure 12.7. If the Viewpoint Concerns that these Use Cases represent are not modelled in this way, then the 'concerns' *tag* could contain much more descriptive text.

While the *viewpoint* construct is useful as a summary of a Viewpoint and while it does require the Concerns that a Viewpoint is to address to be considered and explicitly stated, it doesn't allow the definition of the Viewpoint to be modelled. One possible use for them is in the initial development of an Architectural Framework; they can be useful when considering the Viewpoints that are required and in producing what is essentially a text-based definition of a Viewpoint. They might also be useful in the production of the Viewpoint Relationships View, being used instead of *blocks*. However, this will vary depending on the SysML tool that you are using. The SysML specification is unclear whether or not a *viewpoint* can take part in relationships with other *viewpoints*. If your Tool does allow them to be used just like *blocks* in terms of the allowed relationships that they can take part in, then they could very usefully be used on a Viewpoint Relationships View. If, as is the case with some Tools, they cannot be used in this way, then the Viewpoint Relationships View is better modelled using *blocks*. If using both *viewpoints* and *blocks* in this way, then the *block* representing a Viewpoint could be linked to the *viewpoint* representing the same via a *refines dependency*, for example. This could then be shown explicitly as in Figure 12.14.

The choice of a *refine dependency* in Figure 12.14 is somewhat arbitrary. The weaker *traces dependency* could have been used or an *allocate dependency* in the opposite direction. Whatever notation chosen, the choice should be consistent and included in the kind of diagramming and modelling guidelines discussed in Chapter 6.

12.4 Summary

This chapter has defined an Architectural Framework, the MBSE Architectural Framework (MBSEAF), which is used in Chapter 13 as the basis of the example Architecture presented there. The MBSEAF has nine Perspectives that cover all the concepts found in the Ontology Definition View defined earlier in this section.

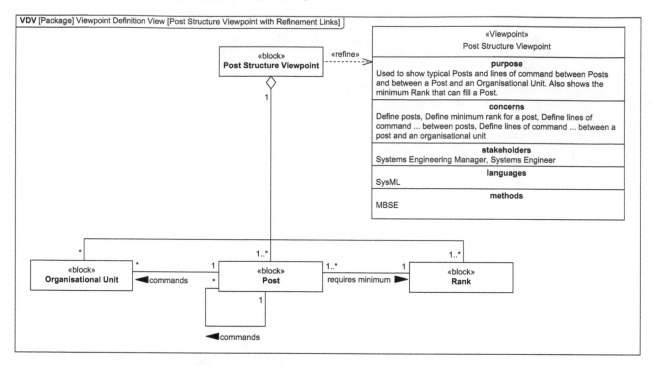

*Figure 12.14   Viewpoint Definition View for the Post Structure Viewpoint
showing* refine dependency *to associated* viewpoint

This ODV is itself based on the MBSE Ontology given in Chapter 3 and used throughout the book since the intention of the case study presented here and in Chapter 13 is to provide an extended example that covers all of the concepts found in this book. Eight of the Perspectives are used to develop the Architecture in Chapter 13. The remaining Perspective, the Architectural Framework Perspective, has been used in this chapter to define the MBSEAF.

An example was also given of the use of the standard SysML *viewpoint* auxiliary construct that can be used to define Viewpoints. While useful, its limitations will be clearer when compared with the extended FAF approach described in Chapter 11 and used as a basis of the Architectural Framework Perspective used in this chapter.

Reference

1.   Object Management Group. *SysML Specification* [Online]. Available from http://www.omgsysml.org [Accessed April 2013]

Chapter 13

The Case Study

Ack ack ack ack-ack!
Don't run, we are your friends!

Unnamed Martian, Mars Attacks! 1996

13.1   Introduction

This chapter presents an extended example that, as discussed in Chapter 12, is intended to demonstrate the Model-Based Systems Engineering (MBSE) concepts covered in this book using the SysML as the main means of presentation.

Rather than trying to retrospectively apply the many and varied techniques, concepts, Frameworks and Views to an actual Project and System, we have chosen to model a System from scratch. There is always a danger when doing this that, if a real System is chosen, there will always be those readers who know more about the System than the authors. This can have a serious impact on the learning experience as the reader inevitably notices mistakes in the modelling of the System which detracts from the learning experience.

For this reason, we have chosen a fictional example, albeit one that allows all the Perspectives defined in the MBSE Architectural Framework in Chapter 12 to be explored. The example we have chosen is one from popular culture that can be traced back to at least 1898 when H.G. Wells published one of his most famous novels. Our example, though, is inspired by more recent examples from the 1960s onwards. The example we have chosen is the Martian invasion of Earth. If you are interested in our sources, see References 1–3.

Each of the Perspectives defined in Chapter 12 is considered, with at least one example of each View from each Perspective given. The intention in this chapter is not to describe the thinking behind each View, which can be found in the relevant chapter of the book on which the Perspective is based. Rather, the discussion will focus on aspects of each View that are worthy of discussion, as well as a commentary on the way each View is realised.

13.2   The Need Perspective

The Need Perspective is perhaps the most important of all the Perspectives, being concerned with the modelling of Needs for a System: capturing the Needs, relating them to their Source Elements, defining any constraining Rules that apply to the description of the Needs, putting them into Context, establishing how to validate the Needs and establishing traceability.

This section contains the Views that make up the Need Perspective: the Source Element View, the Definition Rule Set View, the Requirement Description View, the Context Definition View, the Validation View and the Traceability View. For a full description of the Viewpoints in this Perspective and the concepts behind them, see Chapter 9.

13.2.1   The Source Element View

The Source Element View is used to capture all relevant source information that is required to get the Needs right when undertaking Model-Based Requirements Engineering (MBRE). An example Source Element View for the Martian invasion of Earth is shown in Figure 13.1.

The Source Element View is realised using a *block definition diagram*, with each Source Element modelled using a *block*. In Figure 13.1 these *blocks* have had the *stereotype* «Source Element» applied to emphasise that they represent Source Elements. This *stereotype* has a number of *tags* defined for it, allowing additional information about each Source Element to be captured such as the type of Source Element, its status, date, version and location. The diagram also shows how *associations* can be used to relate different Source Elements together.

13.2.2   The Definition Rule Set View

The Definition Rule Set View is used to define Rules that may have to be applied to each Need Description. The Definition Rule Set View can be as simple as a table of text to complex mathematical equations. An example of a Definition Rule Set View is shown in Figure 13.2.

The Definition Rule Set View in Figure 13.2 is realised as a *block definition diagram* with each Rule represented using a *stereotyped block*. The «Rule» *stereotype* has the *tag* "Rule Text" defined with it, allowing the text to be displayed in a separate, named *compartment* of the *block*. The information shown in Figure 13.2 is a minimum: a name or identifier for a Rule, along with descriptive text. Additional *tags* could be added to capture the justification and source of each Rule, for example.

The Rules defined in Figure 13.2 could just as easily have been defined in a table. However, defining them as *blocks* within a SysML model means that they exist as Model Elements and hence can be the target (or indeed, source) of *trace relationships* within the model if required, something that is not possible if represented as a simple textual table in a document.

Rule 'R06' in Figure 13.2 makes reference to a complexity measure that has to be calculated. This Rule might be further expanded on another Definition Rule Set View diagram that shows how the calculation is performed. This could be realised as a textual description of the method or through SysML diagrams such as the *activity diagram* or the *parametric diagram* that show how the calculation is performed.

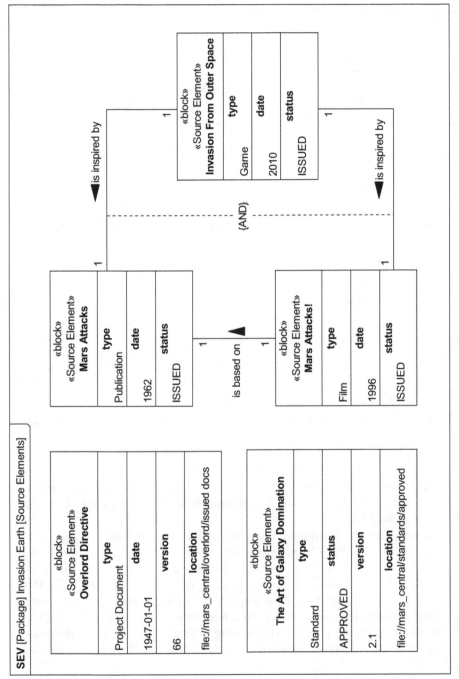

Figure 13.1   Source Element View showing Source Elements, relationships between them and properties

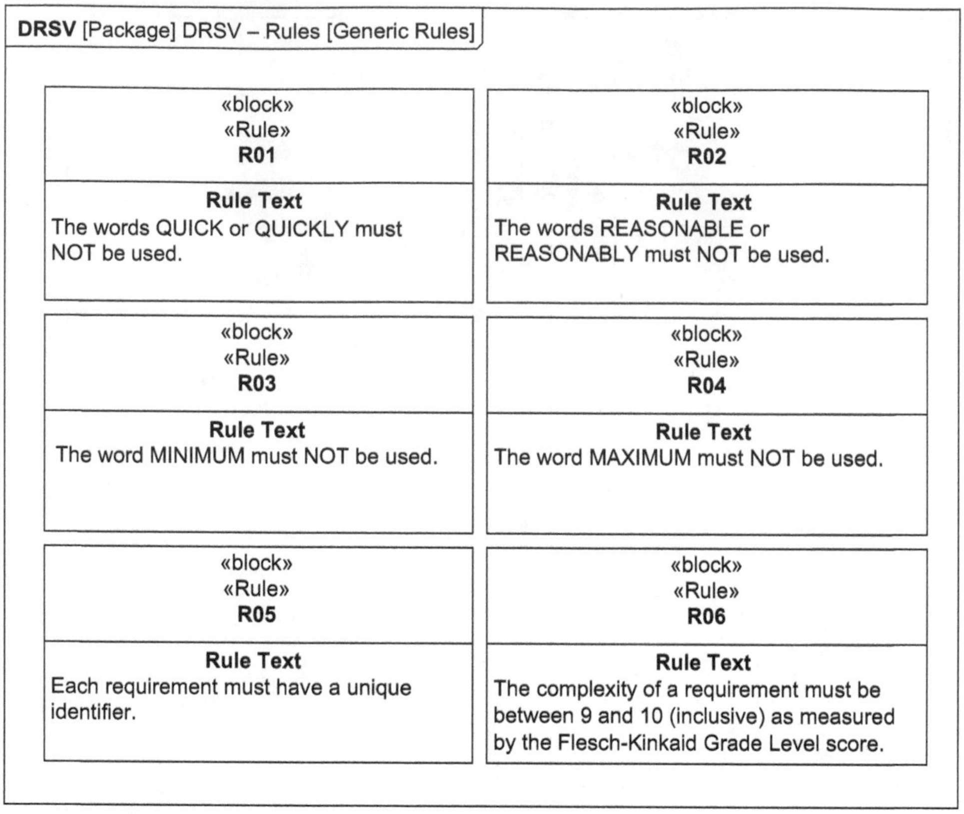

DRSV [Package] DRSV – Rules [Generic Rules]

«block» «Rule» **R01**	«block» «Rule» **R02**
Rule Text The words QUICK or QUICKLY must NOT be used.	**Rule Text** The words REASONABLE or REASONABLY must NOT be used.
«block» «Rule» **R03**	«block» «Rule» **R04**
Rule Text The word MINIMUM must NOT be used.	**Rule Text** The word MAXIMUM must NOT be used.
«block» «Rule» **R05**	«block» «Rule» **R06**
Rule Text Each requirement must have a unique identifier.	**Rule Text** The complexity of a requirement must be between 9 and 10 (inclusive) as measured by the Flesch-Kinkaid Grade Level score.

Figure 13.2   Definition Rule Set View showing Rules represented using blocks

13.2.3   The Requirement Description View

The Requirement Description View is used to capture structured descriptions of each Need in the form of Need Descriptions. Two examples are shown in Figures 13.3 and 13.4.

The Requirement Description View is realised as a *requirement diagram* as shown in Figure 13.3. Each Need Description is realised as a SysML *requirement* and has, as a minimum, a name, unique identifier and descriptive text. These are shown for all the Need Description in Figure 13.3, but most SysML tools will allow the *id#* and *txt* to be turned off on a diagram if required. Relationships between Need Descriptions can also be shown on a Requirement Description View. Only two are shown in Figure 13.3, showing *nesting* to emphasise that 'Have defences' is made up of two additional Needs Descriptions: 'Have a cloaking device' and 'Self-destruct'.

Of course, on a real Project there will be many more Need Descriptions than this, requiring many Requirement Description Views to be produced. When

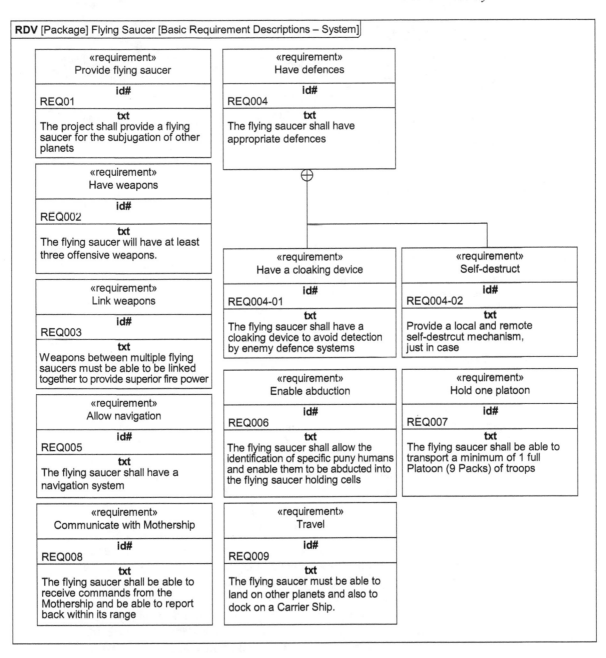

Figure 13.3   Requirement Description View showing high-level Need Descriptions for 'Flying Saucer' System

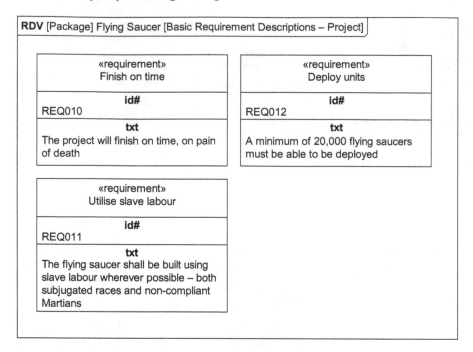

Figure 13.4   Requirement Description View showing high-level Need Descriptions for 'Flying Saucer' Project

creating multiple Views in this way it is useful to separate unrelated Need Descriptions on to separate Views. This has been done, in a small way, in Figures 13.3 and 13.4. Whereas Figure 13.3 shows high-level Need Descriptions for the 'Flying Saucer' System, those related more to the overall Project have been modelled separately in Figure 13.4.

13.2.4   The Context Definition View

The Context Definition View is used to identify the Contexts that are explored in the Requirement Context View. These Contexts may take many forms including Stakeholder Roles and System Elements from different levels of hierarchy in a System. An example of each is given in Figures 13.5 and 13.6.

The Context Definition View is realised using a *block definition diagram* with *blocks* used to represent each relevant Context. If Stakeholder Roles are being considered as Contexts, then the *blocks* will be Stakeholder Roles, as shown in Figure 13.5. If desired, the *blocks* could have the *stereotype* «Stakeholder Role» applied to make it clear that they are Stakeholder Roles, rather than any other type of Ontology Element.

The Context Definition View in Figure 13.6 is one based on System Contexts rather than Contexts based on Stakeholder Roles. You will encounter this same

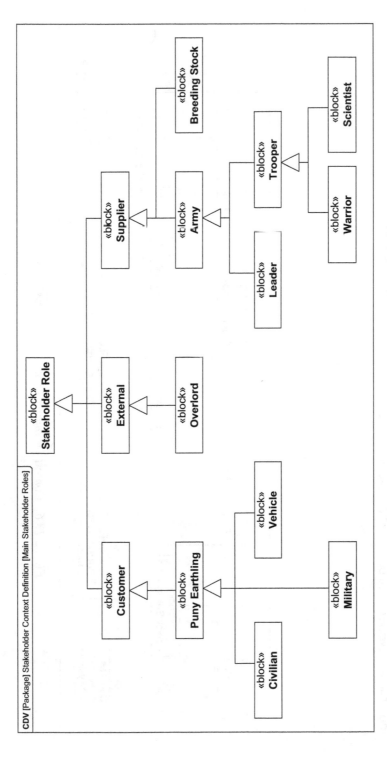

Figure 13.5 Context Definition View showing possible Stakeholder Contexts

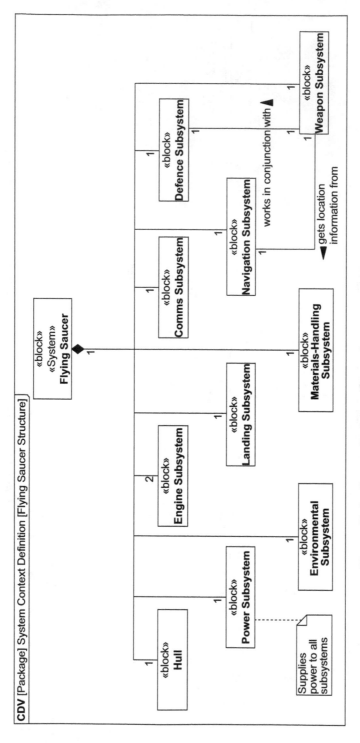

Figure 13.6   Context Definition View showing possible System Contexts

diagram in Section 13.9.1, albeit with a different *frame tag*, where it forms one of the System Identification Views. This is an example of low-level model reuse, where the content of a diagram is reused on multiple Views.

13.2.5 The Requirement Context View

The Requirement Context View is used to give Needs meaning by looking at them from a particular Context. Each Context identified on a Context Definition View will, potentially, have their own Requirement Context View, otherwise why are they on the Context Definition View at all?

A Requirement Context View is realised as a *use case diagram*. When an abstract Need, modelled as a concrete Need Description on a Requirement Description View is looked at from a particular Context it becomes a Use Case and is realised on a Requirement Context View as a *use case*.

Figure 13.7 shows a Requirement Context View for the 'Army' Stakeholder Role. Each of the Use Cases appearing on this View will correspond to Need Descriptions on a Requirement Description View. Another Requirement Context View, this time for the 'Flying Saucer' Context identified on the Context Definition View in Figure 13.6, is shown in Figure 13.8.

The Requirement Context View in Figure 13.8 shows a high-level Context for the 'Flying Saucer' System. It shows the high-level Use Cases for the 'Flying Saucer' Context, only expanding the central 'Provide flying saucer' Use Case to the next level along, with any related *extending* Use Cases or *specialisations* of Uses Cases. It is good practice to create such high-level Contexts for any System and such a Requirement Context View should, wherever possible, conform to the "7 ± 2" rule of complexity (which in practice is often more like "9 ± 5"). Even the most complex System can often be summarised in double handful of Use Cases.

The high-level Requirement Context View from Figure 13.8 has been expanded in Figure 13.9, with many of the Use Cases expanded to the next level. This diagram is really as complex as it is useful. Any more levels of expansion will make the diagram very cluttered. If this level of detail is needed, then consider creating a Requirement Context View at a lower level in the System hierarchy. For example, suppose 'Provide weapon capability' and its related Uses Cases need to be expanded to a lower level. From the Context Definition View in Figure 13.6 it can be seen that the 'Weapon Subsystem' is a possible Context and therefore can have its own Requirement Context View. This would be the place to expand on the 'Provide weapon capability' and its related Uses Cases.

A final point to make here concerns the *actors* on the Requirement Context Views, representing Stakeholder Roles that are outside the Context under consideration. Look at Figure 13.7 which shows the Context for the 'Army'. This diagram has an *actor* 'Flying Saucer'. This means that when the Requirement Context View for the 'Flying Saucer' is created, it must have an *actor* 'Army' on it. This is the case. This holds for any Stakeholder Role and Context. The 'Invasion' Context will have an 'Army' *actor*, as will the 'Puny Earthling' Context.

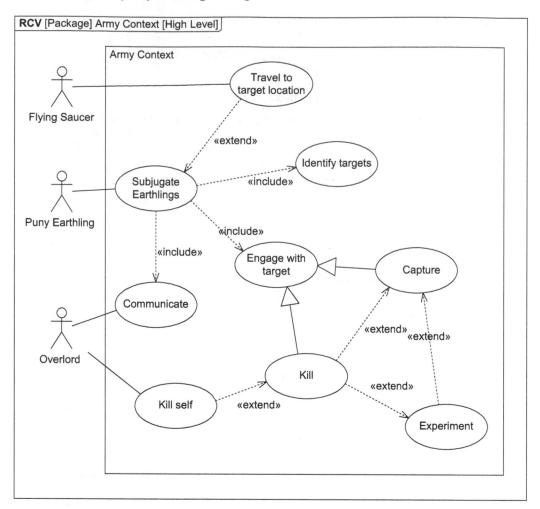

*Figure 13.7   Requirement Context View showing high-level Context for the
'Army' Stakeholder Role*

13.2.6   The Validation View

The Validation View is used for demonstrating that Needs can be satisfied by the
System. Such Validation Views can be both informal Scenario-based Views and
more mathematical-based Views. Examples of both are given in this section.

When creating Scenario-based Validation Views, they are realised using
sequence diagrams. Such Validation Views, like Context Definition Views, can be
created at the Stakeholder Role level, System level, etc. When creating at the
Stakeholder Role level, the emphasis is on interactions between the Stakeholder Roles,
with the System treated as a black box. Each such Validation View is intended
to validate a Use Case. An example of a Validation View created at the Stakeholder

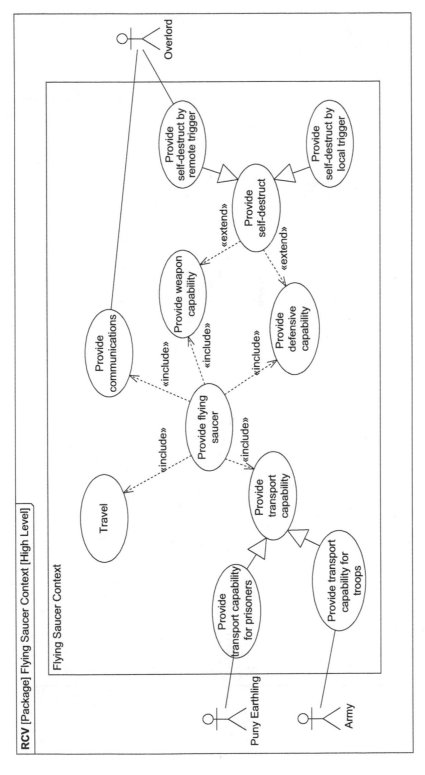

Figure 13.8 Requirement Context View showing high-level Context for 'Flying Saucer' System

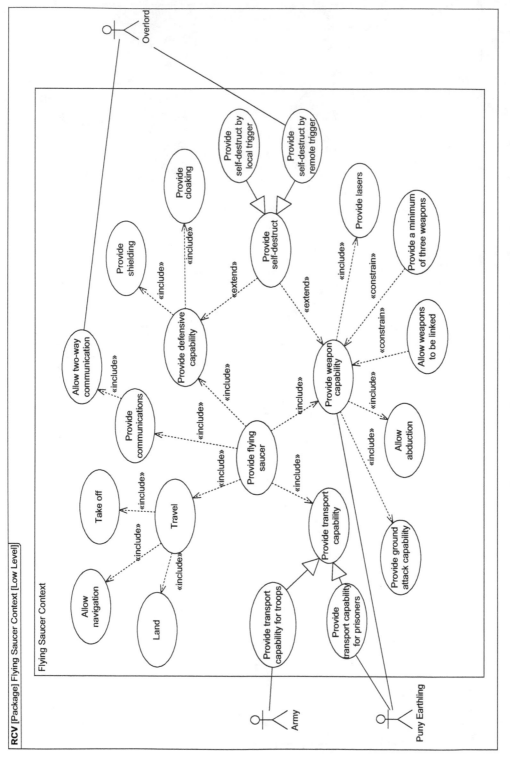

Figure 13.9 Requirement Context View showing low-level Context for 'Flying Saucer' System

Role level is shown in Figure 13.10, a Scenario for the 'Provide ground attack capability' Use Case from the Requirement Context View in Figure 13.7. Typically multiple Validation Views are created, considering both "success" and "failure" Scenarios.

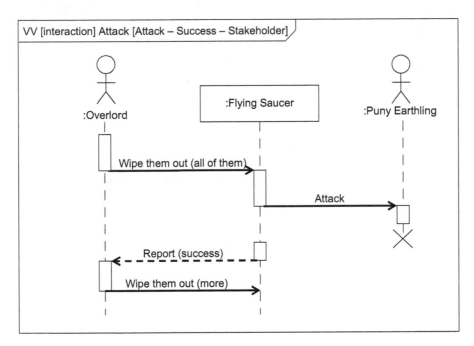

Figure 13.10   Validation View showing successful Scenario at Stakeholder Role level for 'Flying Saucer' System

A "failure" Scenario for the same Use Case is shown in Figure 13.11. This starts the same way, but ends differently. The common behaviour could be abstracted out into a separate diagram that is referenced using SysML's *interaction use* mechanism. An example of this is given in Section 13.9.7, where *sequence diagrams* are used for the System Interaction View. This Scenario also addresses aspects of the 'Provide self-destruct by remote trigger' Use Case and as such, can be considered the "success" Scenario for that Use Case.

Having created a Validation View representing a Stakeholder Role Scenario, it is possible to detail this at a lower level of abstraction by opening the black box and creating a white box System level Scenario. This has been done in Figure 13.12.

The Validation View in Figure 13.12 shows the same Scenario as that in Figure 13.11, but this time at the System level. Here, the emphasis is on the interactions between System Elements. The interactions that were shown to and from the *life lines* representing Stakeholder Roles on Figure 13.11 are now shown connected to *gates* on the enclosing diagram *frame*.

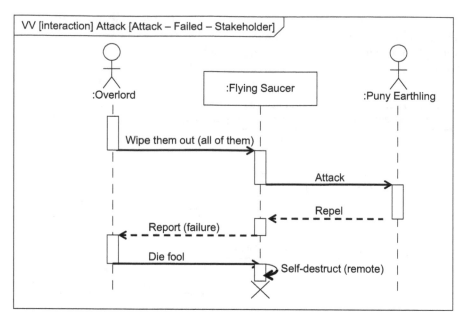

Figure 13.11   *Validation View showing failure Scenario at Stakeholder Role level for 'Flying Saucer' System*

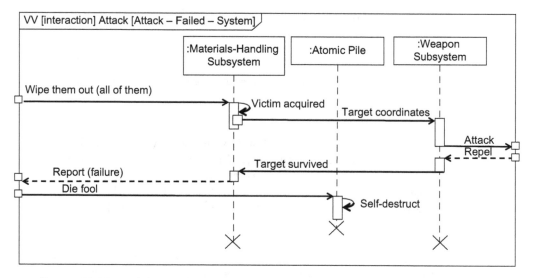

Figure 13.12   *Validation View showing failure Scenario at System level for 'Flying Saucer' System*

Sometimes it is necessary to take a more mathematical approach to validation. One way of doing this in SysML is to create Validation Views that make use of parametric *constraint blocks* and *parametric diagrams*. Examples are given in Figures 13.13 and 13.14 which address the Use Case 'Travel to target location' from the Requirement Context View in Figure 13.7.

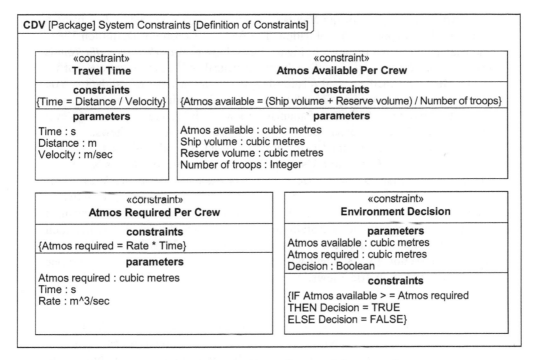

Figure 13.13   Constraint Definition View showing definition of parametric constraint blocks

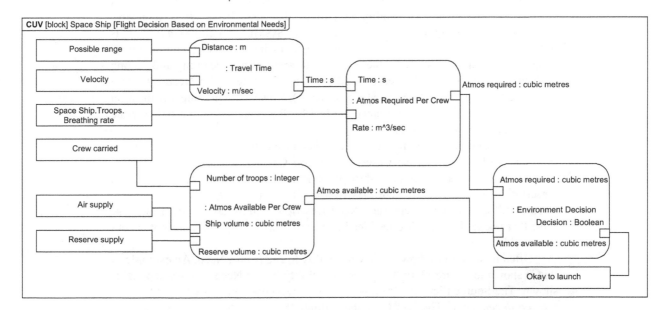

Figure 13.14   Constraint Usage View showing use of parametric constraint blocks (constraint properties) for determining flight decision based on ship air supply

Two *specialisations* of the Validation View need to be created when using a constraint-based approach to validation. The first is a Constraint Definition View, and example of which is shown in Figure 13.13. Here a *block definition diagram* is used with *constraint blocks* to define the mathematical and logical equations that are used to define the mathematical relationships that form the basis of validation. You will encounter this same diagram in Section 13.9.8, albeit with a different *frame tag*, where it forms one of the System Parametric Views. This is an example of low-level model reuse, where the content of a diagram is reused on multiple Views.

The way that the defined constraints are used is modelled on the second *specialisation*, the Constraint Usage View. An example of this is shown in Figure 13.14, where a *parametric diagram* is used to realise the View. This relates the defined constraints to System Properties in a parametric network. Such a network can be implemented in a mathematical tool, from a spreadsheet to a mathematical simulation system, in order to execute the network with actual values for the various System Properties. Again, you will encounter this same diagram in Section 13.9.8, albeit with a different *frame tag*, where it forms one of the System Parametric Views.

13.2.7   The Traceability View

The Traceability View is used to show traceability both to and from Needs (actually to and from their concrete representation as Need Descriptions). It can be used in many different ways, showing all the traceability of a certain type or showing all the traceability for a particular Need. Examples of both approaches are given in Figures 13.15 and 13.16.

The Traceability View is often realised on a *requirement diagram* since, at least when considering traceability as part of the Need Perspective, it always involves Need Descriptions, which are realised in SysML as *requirements*. This is not to say that other realisations are not possible; indeed, one common representation is as a table showing the source and target of a traceability link, along with the type of traceability represented (such as refinement of a Need by a Use Case and validation of a Use Case by a Scenario). However, a graphical realisation is often very useful to give an immediate feel for the degree of connectedness due to the traceability relationships.

The Traceability View in Figure 13.15 is an example that concentrates on the refinement of Needs by Use Cases. Every Use Case created on a Requirement Context View must be traced, through a refinement relationship, to a Need Description from a Requirement Description View, otherwise why does the Use Case exist? Conversely, every such Need Description must have at least one Use Case that refines it, otherwise the Need that the Need Description represents is not being addressed.

Often it is useful to show all the traceability to and from a Need. An example of this is shown in Figure 13.16. Here, the traceability for the Need 'Have weapons' is shown. The Source Elements from which 'Have weapon' comes are traced through a *trace dependency*. The Use Case that refines 'Have weapon' is shown through a *refine dependency*. The Scenarios that validate the Use Case are also shown,

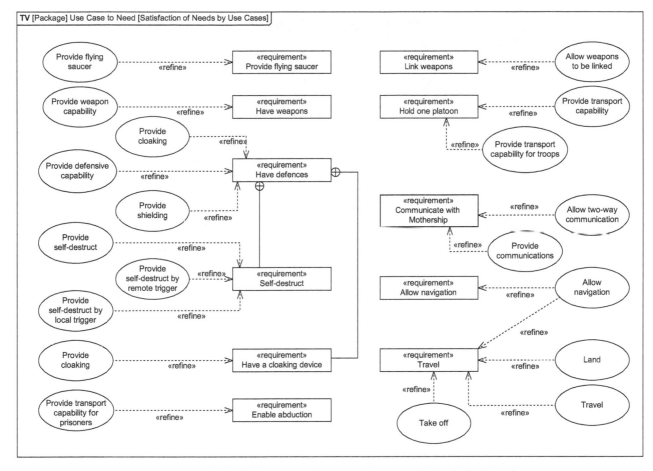

Figure 13.15   Traceability View showing refinement of Needs by Use Cases

connected through a *validate dependency*. These Scenarios have the SysML *stereotype* «testCase» applied. Finally, a *package*, representing the part of the model containing the 'Weapon Subsystem' is shown, with a *trace dependency* to the 'Provide weapon capability' and a *satisfy dependency* to the 'Have weapons' Need. This is done to show which part of the model addresses the 'Have weapon' Need and 'Provide weapon' Use Case. A *trace dependency* is used between the *package* and the *use case* rather than a *satisfy dependency* simply because SysML only allows a *satisfy dependency* to be connected to a *requirement*.

13.3   The System of Systems Perspective

The System of Systems Perspective expands on the Need Perspective to add additional Viewpoints that are required when modelling the Needs for a System of

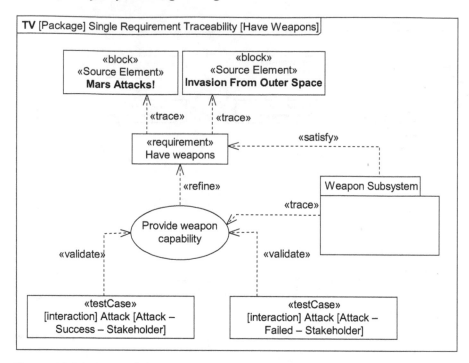

*Figure 13.16   Traceability View showing traceability for a single Requirement
Description*

Systems. It includes all the Viewpoints of the Need Perspective, used at the System
of System level.

The additional Views provide an overview of the relationships between the
Contexts of the various Constituent Systems that make up a System of Systems and
provide a combined view of the Scenarios for Use Cases that are involved in the
System of Systems.

This section contains the additional Views that make up the System of Systems
Perspective: the Context Interaction View and the Validation Interaction View.
Only the additional Views will be discussed, along with some necessary supporting
Views. For a full description of the Viewpoints in this Perspective and the concepts
behind them, see Chapter 10.

Before looking at examples of the additional Views, it is first necessary to
define the Contexts for the System of Systems. This is done in Figure 13.17.

The Context Definition View in Figure 13.17 shows a System of Systems,
'Invasion', made up of two Constituent Systems, 'Spaceship System' and 'Army'.
Because this Context Definition View is for the System of Systems it is entirely
possible that it is produced by a different Organisational Unit, which is responsible
for the design of the individual Constituent Systems. For this reason, the names
used for the Constituent Systems might not match exactly with those used by other

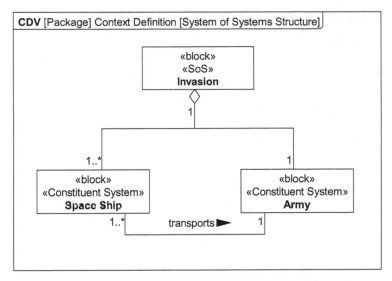

Figure 13.17   Context Definition View showing System of System and its Constituent Systems

Organisational Units tasked with design of the Constituent Systems. For example, Figure 13.17 has 'Spaceship System' but in the System Perspective (see Section 13.9) the corresponding System is called 'Spaceship' (with a number of sub-types). In addition, the term 'Army' in Figure 13.17 is used generically as a branch of the military, whereas in the Organisational Perspective (see Section 13.7) an 'Army' is just part of an 'Army Group' and thus represents an Organisational Unit rather than a branch of the military. Such difference in terms is quite common on real projects and can be a source of confusion if not handled carefully. One way of addressing this would be to use the various traceability relationships or even *allocations* to map one term to another.

Given the Context Definition View in Figure 13.17, three Requirement Context Views would then be expected: one for 'Invasion' and one for each of the two Constituent Systems, 'Spaceship System' and 'Army'. The Requirement Context View for the 'Invasion' System of Systems from the point of view of the 'Overlord' Stakeholder Role is given in Figure 13.18. Those for 'Army' and 'Spaceship System' were given in Figures 13.7 and 13.8. Note that Figure 13.8 is actually that of a 'Flying Saucer' but, as discussed in above and in Section 13.9, the 'Flying Saucer' is a particular kind of 'Spaceship System'.

The Requirement Context View for the 'Invasion' System of Systems in Figure 13.18 is drawn from the point of view of the 'Overlord' Stakeholder Role. Other Stakeholder Roles might be involved at the System of Systems level, and would therefore have their own Requirement Context View. In a similar way, the 'Invasion' System of Systems would have a Requirement Context View created for

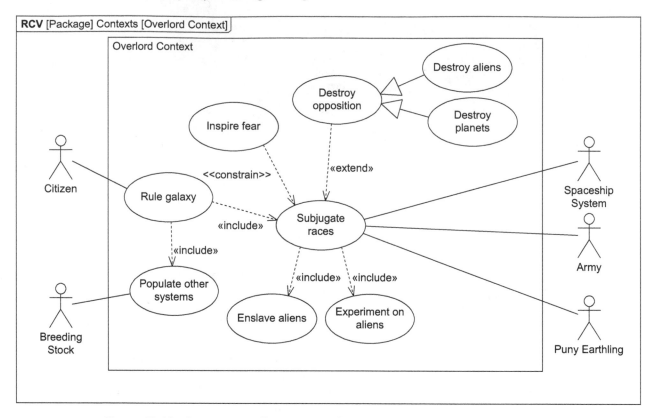

Figure 13.18   Requirement Context View for 'Invasion' System of Systems from point of view of 'Overlord' Stakeholder Role

it as a System. The same comments apply to Figure 13.18 regarding the terms used as were made for Figure 13.17.

13.3.1   The Context Interaction View

The Context Interaction View is used to provide an overview of the relationships between the Contexts of the various Constituent Systems that make up a System of Systems. An example Context Interaction View showing the interactions between the 'Flying Saucer' and 'Army' Contexts is shown in Figure 13.19.

The Context Interaction View is realised as a *use case diagram*. The Context for each Constituent System is shown on the diagram, joined via any *actors* representing the System of Systems (in this case the 'Overlord' *actor*). When creating a Context Interaction View be on the lookout for other *actors* that appear in multiple contexts. For example, 'Puny Earthling' appears twice on Figure 13.19 and so could have been replaced with a single copy that is connected to both Contexts, as has been done with the 'Overlord' actor. This would show that the two Constituent Systems, 'Flying Saucer' and 'Army', both interact with 'Puny Earthling'. We know

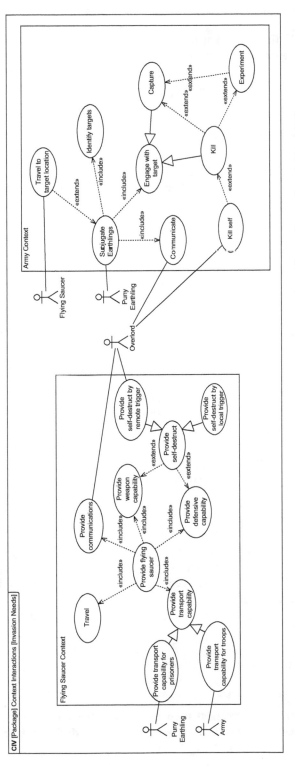

Figure 13.19 Context Interaction View showing interactions between the 'Flying Saucer' and 'Army' Contexts

from Figure 13.17 that 'Puny Earthling' is not part of the System of Systems; it is not a Constituent System. Questions can then be asked regarding the nature of these connections and whether 'Puny Earthling' provides any functionality that could or should be part of the System of Systems, i.e. that would make it a Constituent System.

13.3.2   The Validation Interaction View

The Validation Interaction View is used to provide a combined view of the Scenarios for Use Cases that are involved in the System of Systems; it combines information from the Validation Views for various Constituent Systems. An example is given in Figure 13.20.

The Validation Interaction View is used to combine Validation Views if they represent the same (or aspects of the same) Scenario. The diagram in Figure 13.20 shows the Validation Interaction View for the combined Use Cases of 'Provide self-destruct by remote trigger' from the Context of the 'Flying Saucer' (see Figure 13.11) and the 'Kill self' Use Case from the Context of the 'Army' System. The latter is shown below in Figure 13.21.

Since the Validation Interaction View is used to combine Validation Views, it will typically be realised as a *sequence diagram*. The key when producing Validation Interaction Views is to ensure that they are drawn for related Scenarios. Their intent is to allow Validation of Scenarios for the System of Systems that are realised by behaviour in multiple Constituent System and hence modelled as Use Cases and Scenarios on Requirement Context Views and Validation Views for those Constituent Systems. When the Validation Views for those Use Cases are combined and compared, are they consistent with the corresponding Use Case at the System of Systems level? Do they reveal common behaviour in multiple Constituent Systems that could, perhaps, be pushed out to a new Constituent System or up to the System of Systems itself?

13.4   The Life Cycle Perspective

The Life Cycle Perspective is very important yet one that is often ignored in real-life systems engineering Projects. One of the main reasons for this is that there are many types of Life Cycles, as discussed previously in this book and it is crucial to be able to differentiate between them and see how they interact with one another. The Life Cycle Perspective contains a number of Views that enable this understanding: the Life Cycle View, the Life Cycle Model View, the Interaction Identification View and the Interaction Behaviour View. For a discussion on the definition of the Life Cycle Perspective Views, see Chapter 8.

13.4.1   Life Cycle View

The Life Cycle View is a structural View that very simply identifies the Stages that exist within a specific Life Cycle. Examples of three different Life Cycles are provided in Figures 13.22 to 13.24.

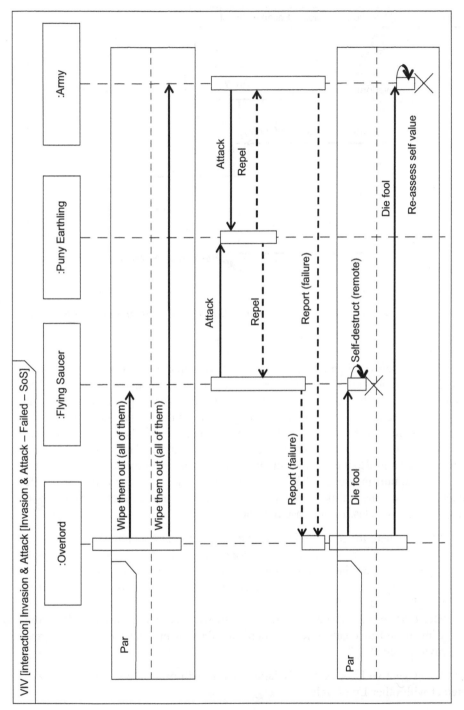

Figure 13.20 Validation Interaction View showing interacting System-level Scenarios

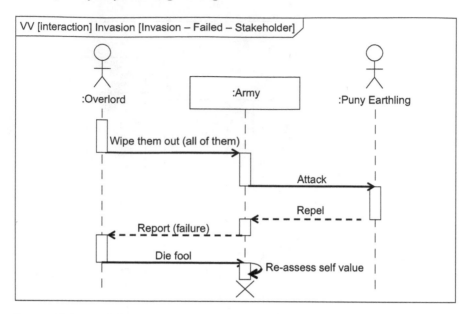

Figure 13.21   Validation View for Use Case 'Kill self' for Constituent System 'Army'

The diagram in Figure 13.22 shows the Stages that exist in the Development Life Cycle. Notice that these Stages have been named as 'Development Stage' to avoid confusion with Stages in other Life Cycle. This Development Life Cycle is one that will be familiar to most system engineers and the Stages shown here have been taken directly from ISO 15288. It was stated previously in this book that ISO15288 is the most widely used systems engineering Standard in the world – it turns out that it is also the most widely used systems engineering Standard on Mars!

The diagram in Figure 13.23 shows a Life Cycle View for a different Life Cycle, this time one that describes the deployment of materiel, such as equipment, weapons and vehicles. In this case the Stages cover:

- 'Store', where the materiel is held in a safe and secure location.
- 'Transport', where the materiel is transported to wherever it will be deployed.
- 'Operate', where the materiel is actually used in (extreme) anger.
- 'Close', where, once the materiel has reached the end of its usefulness, it is closed down and left.
- 'Destroy', where whatever is left is destroyed to prevent anyone else from using it and to create one last moment of mayhem. Martians are not great environmentalists.

This Life Cycle will not exist in isolation and, as will be seen on later Views, will interact with other Life Cycles.

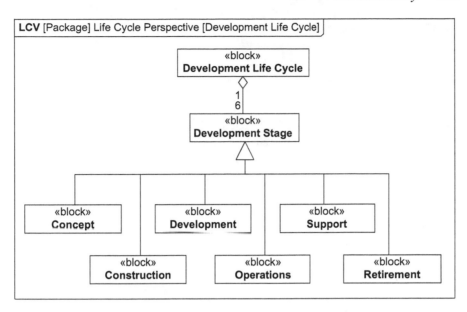

Figure 13.22   Life Cycle View for Development Life Cycle

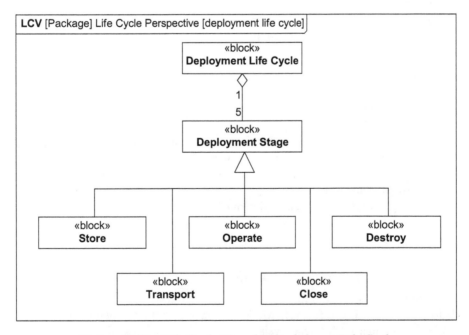

Figure 13.23   Life Cycle View for Deployment Life Cycle

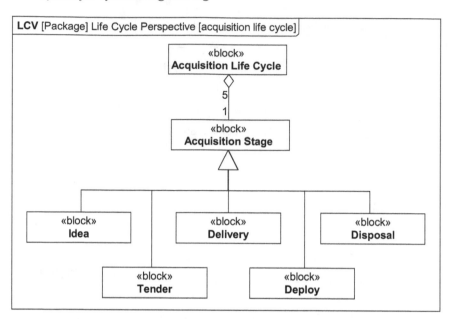

Figure 13.24   Life Cycle View for Acquisition Life Cycle

The diagram in Figure 13.24 shows a Life Cycle View for an Acquisition Life Cycle. Notice that the Views in this case reflect the acquisition of a System, rather than its development or deployment, that were shown in the previous two diagrams. These Stages are:

- 'Idea', where the initial idea for the System is dreamt up and the requirements are generated.
- 'Tender', where the tender information, including a number of Contexts, such as System Context and Project Context is put out to potential Suppliers who then respond to the tender. On the basis of these submissions, a preferred Supplier is selected to deliver the System.
- 'Deliver', where the System is delivered by the Supplier and is accepted, or not, by the Customer.
- 'Deploy', where the System is deployed in its target environment.
- 'Disposal', where the System is finally disposed of.

Again, this Life Cycle will not exist in isolation and will interact with other Life Cycles.

13.4.2   The Life Cycle Model View

The Life Cycle View showed the structure of a number of Life Cycles and identified their Stages. The Life Cycle Model Views shows the behaviour of each Life Cycle at a number of different levels:

- Showing the interactions between the Stages.
- Showing the interactions between Process Execution Groups within each Stage.

- Showing the interactions between the Processes within each Process Execution Group.

An example of each of these levels will be shown in the following diagrams.

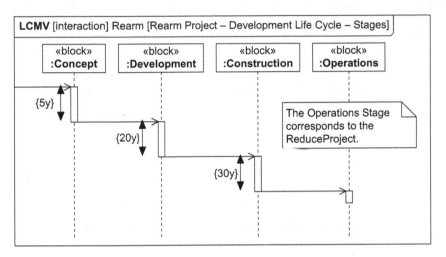

Figure 13.25   Life Cycle Model View showing development life cycle Stages

The diagram in Figure 13.25 shows the Life Cycle Model View at a high level by showing the interactions between the Stages in the Development Life Cycle. Notice here that the *life lines* on this diagram are instances of the Stages from Figure 13.22. Also, it is not necessary to show all of the Stages from the Life Cycle View, as is the case here. It should be remembered that the Life Cycle Model View is, in essence, just a Scenario and therefore will show a possible sequence, which may or may not include every Stage.

The diagram in Figure 13.26 shows the next level of detail which focuses on the behaviour within a Stage. According the MBSE Ontology, there are a number of Process Execution groups that are executed within each Stage. Therefore, each *life line* in this diagram corresponds to a Process Execution Group, rather than a Stage. Exactly the same principles hold in that the diagram shows a single Scenario.

The diagram in Figure 13.27 drops down another level and focuses on the Processes that are executed within a specific Process Execution Group. In this case, each *life line* corresponds to a development Process (it looks like the Martians have adopted STUMPI) and the diagram shows a single Scenario for a number of Process executions.

It should be noted that this View is the same as the Process Instance View from the Process Perspective in that it shows the execution of Processes, but it is used for different purposes. The Process Instance View is concerned with validation of Use Cases and their associated Needs, whereas the Life Cycle Model View is more concerned with exploring different possible Scenarios that may be executed on a Project.

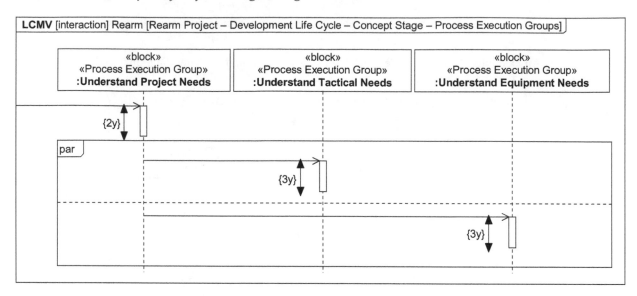

Figure 13.26   *Life Cycle Model View showing breakdown of a Stage into Process Execution Groups*

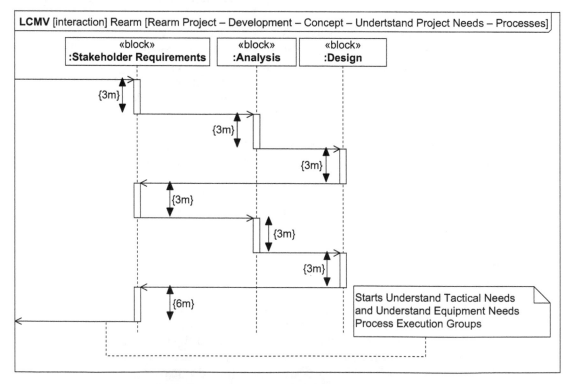

Figure 13.27   *Life Cycle Model View showing breakdown of a Process Execution Group into Processes*

13.4.3 Interaction Identification View

The Interaction Identification View is a structural View that focuses on identifying the Interaction Points that exist between different Life Cycles. It should be clear from the Life Cycle Views that there are clear relationships between the different Life Cycles and this View makes those relationships explicit.

The diagram in Figure 13.28 shows the three Life Cycles that were shown previously, the Development Life Cycle, the Deployment Life Cycle and the Acquisition Life Cycle. In this View each Interaction Point is shown by using a *dependency* stereotyped as «interaction point» that crosses the boundaries, represented by *packages*, between each Life Cycle.

As this is a structural View, there is no behaviour of the interactions shown, but they are shown in the following View.

13.4.4 Interaction Behaviour View

The Interaction Behaviour View shows how the various Life Cycles interact with one another. In essence, this shows a number of Life Cycle Model Views and how they behave towards one another.

The diagram in Figure 13.29 shows the same three Life Cycles as discussed previously but this time focuses on their behaviour. Each package on the diagram corresponds to a Life Cycle Model View and the interactions between these Views correspond to the Interaction Points that were identified on Figure 13.28.

13.5 The Process Perspective

The Process Perspective is concerned with identifying, analysing and defining Processes that may be used for any activity within the Organisation. This is the aspect of MBSE that has been used the most throughout this book as a number of Processes have been defined (indeed, the whole Case Study is the output of the Processes shown in Appendix F) and, therefore, the descriptions for each View will be minimal and are included here for completeness. The "seven views" approach to Process Modelling has been used so much that even the Martian Overlord has mandated it for all domination and invasion Projects, as will be shown on the Process Context in the Requirement Context View. The Process Perspective is made up of the following Views: Process Structure View, Requirement Context View, Process Context View, Stakeholder View, Information View, Process Behaviour View and Process Instance View.

13.5.1 Process Structure View

The Process Structure View identifies and defines the concepts and terminology used for the MBSE activities within the Organisation. This View is essentially an Ontology, so that MBSE Ontology will be used for this Case Study, and is described in great detail in Chapter 3 and Appendix A, so will not be repeated here.

13.5.2 Requirement Context View

The Requirement Context View defines the Context for the Processes. This View is exactly the same as the Requirement Context View form the ACRE approach and,

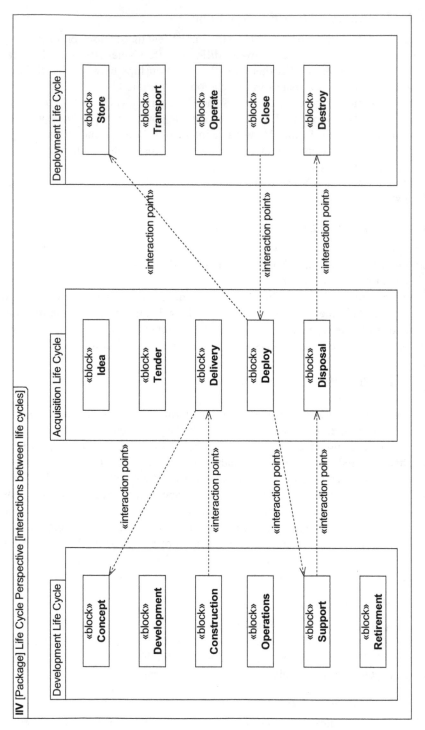

Figure 13.28 Interaction Identification View between Life Cycles

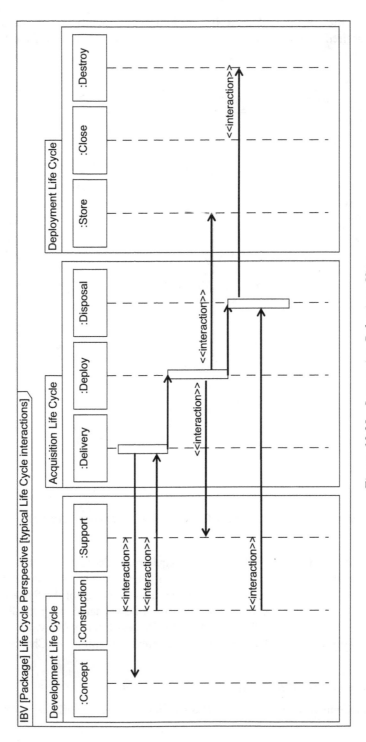

Figure 13.29   Interaction Behaviour View

indeed, the entire set of ACRE Views may be used to specify the Needs of the Process as desired. In most cases, however, it is sufficient to only create the Views described here.

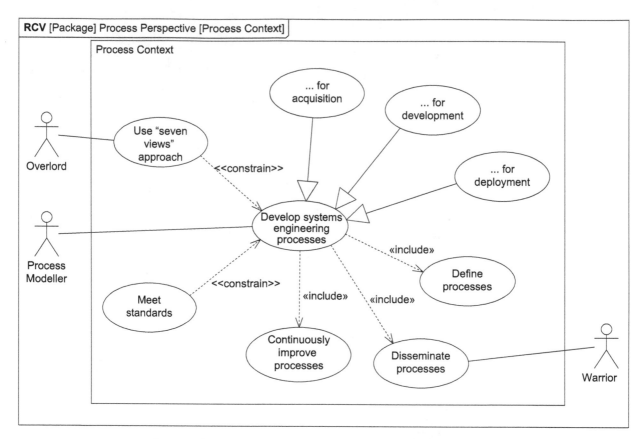

Figure 13.30   Requirement Context View for Process Context

The diagram in Figure 13.30 shows the Requirement Context View that shows the Process Context. Note that the *use cases* on this diagram are focused on the Needs of the Processes that need to be developed, rather than the Needs of the System.

Each of the *use cases* shown on this View must be validated using the Process Instance View that instantiates Processes from the Process Content View.

For a full discussion on the finer points of Context modelling, see Chapters 5, 9 and 10.

13.5.3   Process Content View

The Process Content View shows the Process library for a specific aspect of the Organisation.

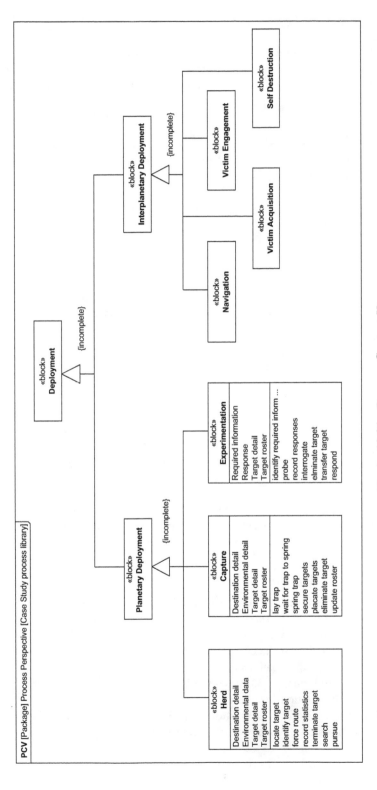

Figure 13.31 Process Content View

The diagram in Figure 13.31 shows the Process Content View for the Case Study. Notice that only a few Processes are shown on this diagram and that many more would exist in reality. These Processes are kept to a minimum for the sake of legibility and brevity.

13.5.4   Stakeholder View

The Stakeholder View shows the Stakeholder Roles that are associated with the Processes in the form of a classification hierarchy.

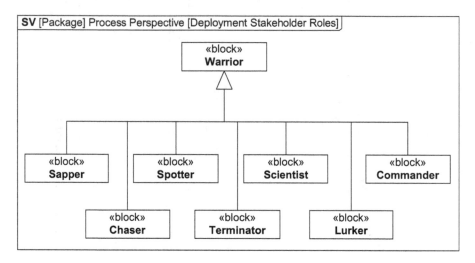

Figure 13.32   Stakeholder View for deployment Stakeholder Roles

The diagram in Figure 13.32 shows a simple Stakeholder View for the Stakeholder Roles associated with deployment. Again, this is only a subset of the overall Stakeholder View that focuses on the 'Warrior' Stakeholder Role.

13.5.5   Information View

The Information View identifies the Artefacts associated with the Processes and the relationships between them. These can be used to define the structure of a specific Artefact or may show the relationships between the Artefacts at a higher level. The Information View may also be created at a detailed level for each Process or at a higher level, showing the relationships between all Artefacts.

The diagram in Figure 13.33 shows the Information View for the Herd Process that focuses on the relationships between each Artefact.

The diagram in Figure 13.34 shows the Information View for the Capture Process that focuses on the relationships between each Artefact.

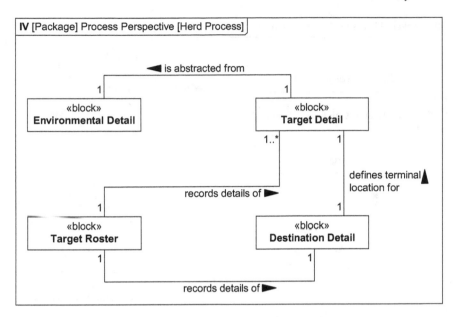

Figure 13.33 Information View for Herd Process

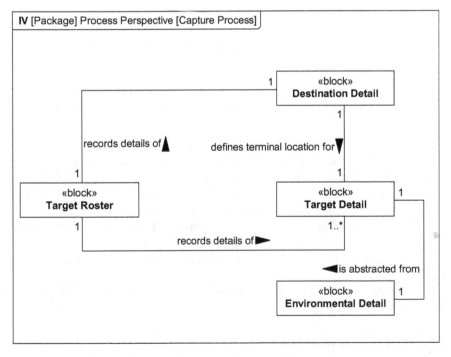

Figure 13.34 Information View for Capture Process

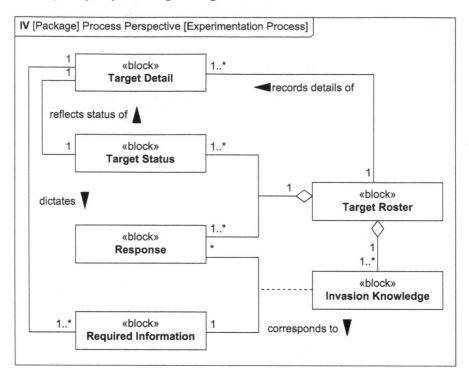

Figure 13.35   Information View for Experimentation Process

The diagram in Figure 13.35 shows the Information View for the Experimentation Process that focuses on the relationships between each Artefact.

13.5.6   Process Behaviour View

The Process Behaviour View shows how each Process behaves internally. The order of execution of Activities (using *operations*) is shown along with the production and consumption of Artefacts (using *objects*). The responsibility of Activities is also shown by allocating Stakeholder Roles to *operations* using *swim lanes*.

The diagram in Figure 13.36 shows the Process Behaviour View for the Herd Process.

The diagram in Figure 13.37 shows the Process Behaviour View for the Capture Process.

The diagram in Figure 13.38 shows the Process Behaviour View for the Experimentation Process.

13.5.7   Process Instance View

The Process Instance View shows the execution of Processes in a specific Scenario. These are used specifically to validate the Use Cases from the Requirement Context View to ensure that the Processes satisfy their original Needs.

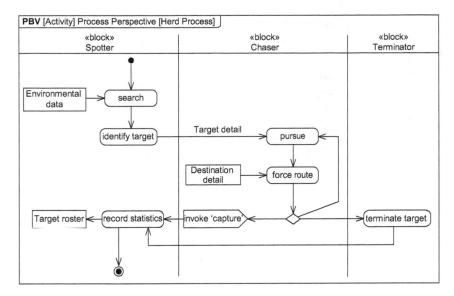

Figure 13.36   Process Behaviour View for Herd Process

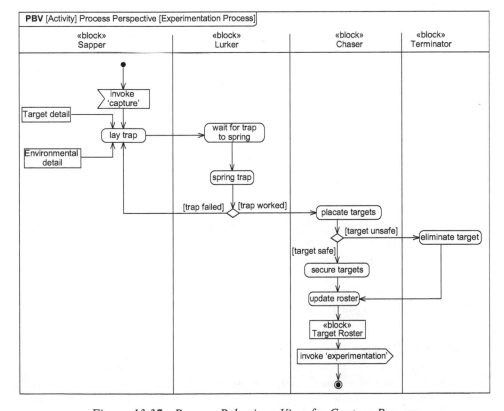

Figure 13.37   Process Behaviour View for Capture Process

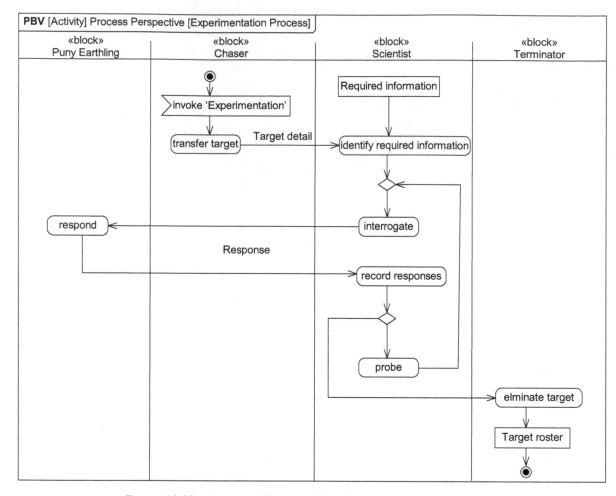

Figure 13.38   Process Behaviour View for Experimentation Process

The diagram in Figure 13.39 shows a Process Instance View that provides the validation for the '...for deployment' *use case* from Figure 13.30.

This View looks the same as the Life Cycle Model View, as discussed previously, but is exactly analogous with a Validation View from the ACRE Processes. The Process Instance View is a Validation View that is used specifically for validating that Processes satisfy their original Needs.

13.6   The Project Perspective

The Project Perspective is used to capture aspects of Projects and Programmes that are executed in order to deliver Systems. It allows the structure of Programmes of

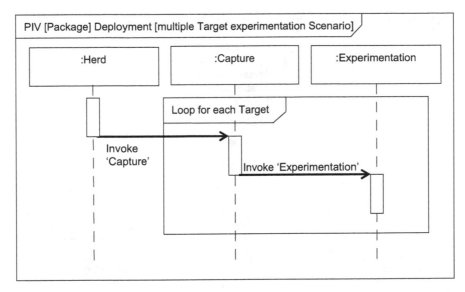

Figure 13.39   Process Instance View for Deployment with multiple Targets and experimentation

related Projects to be defined as well as the schedule for an individual project. For details, see Chapter 8.

This section contains the Views that make up the Project Perspective: the Programme Structure View and the Project Schedule View.

13.6.1   The Programme Structure View

The Programme Structure View is used to show how a Programme is made up of a number of related Projects. An example is given in Figure 13.40 which shows a single Programme, 'Invasion Earth', which is made up of three Projects: 'Recon', 'Rearm' and 'Reduce'.

In Figure 13.40 a *block definition diagram* has been used to realise the Programme Structure View, with *blocks* used for both Programmes and Projects. These are differentiated from each other through the use of *stereotypes*. Associated with each of these *stereotypes* are the *tags* 'start date' and 'end date' to hold additional information for the Programme and Projects. The relationships between the Projects are shown using *dependencies*; these show that the 'Reduce' Project depends on the 'Rearm' Project which, in turn, depends on the 'Recon' Project.

There are a number of points related to the realisation that are worthy of discussion.

- *Composition* has been used to show how the Projects are related to the orga-nising Programme. This means that each of the three Projects shown are part of the 'Invasion Earth' Programme only. Should one of the Projects also form part

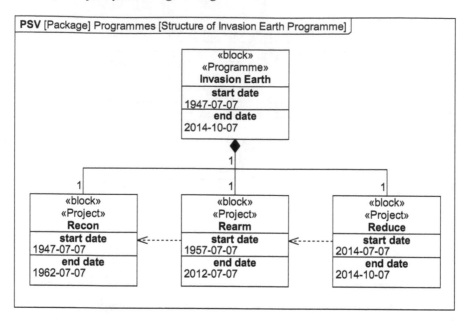

Figure 13.40   Programme Structure View showing dependencies between Projects

of another Programme, then *aggregation* could be used for that Project, rather than *composition* in order to emphasise the shared nature of such a Project.

- Additional *tags* could be added to both the Programme and Project *stereotypes* in order to hold additional information, such as responsible Organisation.
- Although Projects are shown with a single *dependency* there is nothing to prevent a Project being dependent on multiple Projects. If the dependency is to a Project in a different Programme, then the Programme Structure View allows for the display of multiple Programmes. This would then also allow relationships between Programmes to be shown.

If required, additional concepts could be added, such as milestones or lines of development. Remember, if you find you need to add additional information to a View, you must ensure that its definition (i.e. its Viewpoint) is updated. This might also require changes to the underlying Ontology.

13.6.2   The Project Schedule View

The Project Schedule View is used to provide an overview of the execution of a Project over time. An example is given in Figure 13.41.

A Gantt chart is used to realise the Project Schedule View in Figure 13.41. This is the Project Schedule View for the 'Rearm' Project that is part of the 'Invasion Earth' Programme. The example is necessarily simplified for presentational

ID	Task Name	Start	End	Duration	Responsibility
1	**Concept**	**08/07/1957**	**08/07/1962**	**261w**	
2	**Understand Project Needs**	**08/07/1957**	**05/07/1959**	**104w**	
3	Stakeholder Requirements	08/07/1957	06/10/1957	13w	Requirement Engineer; Reviewer
4	Analysis	07/10/1957	05/01/1958	13w	Systems Modeller; Reviewer
5	Design	06/01/1958	06/04/1958	13w	Systems Modeller; Reviewer
6	Stakeholder Requirements	07/04/1958	06/07/1958	13w	Requirement Engineer; Reviewer
7	Analysis	07/07/1958	05/10/1958	13w	Systems Modeller; Reviewer
8	Design	06/10/1958	04/01/1959	13w	Systems Modeller; Reviewer
9	Stakeholder Requirements	05/01/1959	05/07/1959	26w	Requirement Engineer; Reviewer
10	Understand Tactical Needs	06/07/1959	01/07/1962	156w	
11	Understand Equipment Needs	06/07/1959	08/07/1962	157w	
12	Development	09/07/1962	07/06/1987	1300w	
13	Construction	08/06/1987	06/05/2012	1300w	

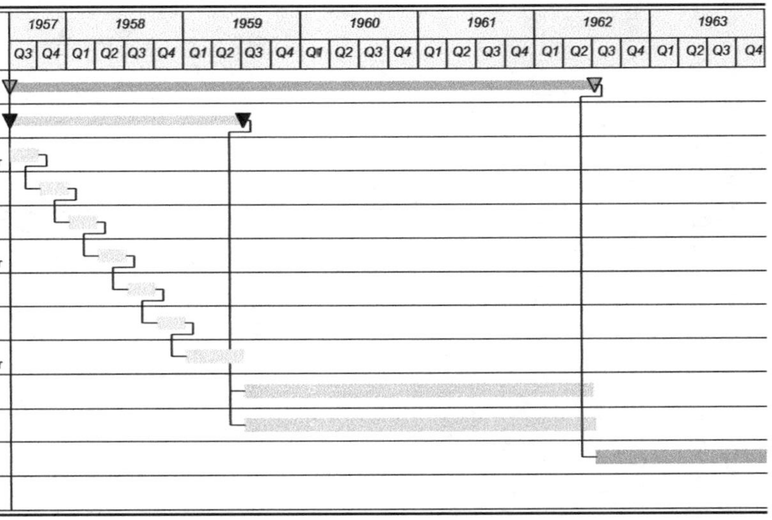

Figure 13.41 Project Schedule View showing part of the 'Rearm' Project

purposes: only the Concept stage is broken down, and then only one of its Process Execution Groups is broken down as far as the Processes inside it. These Processes could be broken down into Tasks if desired.

Remember that the Project Schedule View is very closely related to the Life Cycle Model View of the Life Cycle Perspective and also to the Processes defined in the Process Perspective. See, for example, the Life Cycle Model Views in Section 13.4.2. The Project Schedule View in Figure 13.41 is consistent with the three Life Cycle Model Views presented there. The information in the 'Responsibility' column in Figure 13.41 is taken from the Process Behaviour Views for the corresponding STUMPI Processes found in Appendix F.

See Chapter 8 for a detailed discussion on the Project Schedule View. Also, don't forget that a Programme is just a special kind of Project and, as such, can have its own Project Schedule View (and associated Life Cycle Model Views).

13.7   The Organisational Perspective

The Organisational Perspective is concerned with modelling aspects of an Organisation's structure, the Posts that need to be filled in the Organisation, the Stakeholder Roles that are relevant to each Post, the Rank (or Grade) that is required to fill a Post and the actual Person (or Martian!) that fills each Post.

This section contains the Views that make up the Organisational Perspective: the Organisation Unit Structure View, the Organisation Unit Instance View, the Rank Hierarchy View, the Post Structure View, the Post Instance View, the Post to Role View and the Martian Instance View.

13.7.1   The Organisation Unit Structure View

The Organisation Unit Structure View is used to show the typical structure of an Organisation, broken down in to Organisational Units which can be further subdivided. For the Martian army, an example is shown in Figure 13.42, with Martian terms translated into the nearest Human terms.

In Figure 13.42 a *block definition diagram* has been used to realise the Organisational Unit Structure View, with *blocks* used to represent Organisational Units and *composition* relationships used to show the structure. A *stereotype* is used to show that the *blocks* represent Organisational Units.

The final Organisational Unit on the diagram, the 'Pack', is shown as being composed of three 'Martians'. These are, however, not Organisational Units but rather have the *stereotype* «Person» to show that the 'Martian' *block* represents a Person. This raises two points. One of these is shown in the diagram in a *note*, namely that the Ontology that forms the basis of the MBSE Architectural Framework (see Chapter 12) could be updated to replace the concept of Person with that of Martian. The second point is that the Ontology defined on the Ontology

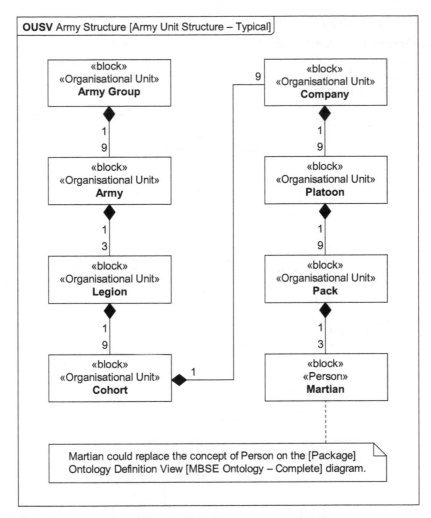

Figure 13.42   Organisational Unit Structure View showing typical army unit structure

Definition View in Chapter 12 is inconsistent with the Organisational Unit Structure View in Figure 13.42 from which we can infer that an Organisational Unit can be made up of one or more Person. However, such a relationship is not found in the Ontology Definition View and would need to be added to that View to ensure consistency. Of course, we have not formally defined the Organisational Unit Structure View in Chapter 12. Had we done so, this inconsistency would have been discovered and addressed as part of the definition of the Organisational Unit Structure Viewpoint.

13.7.2   *The Organisation Unit Instance View*

The Organisation Unit Instance View is used to show the structure of an actual Organisation, conforming to the structure defined in the Organisation Unit Structure Viewpoint. An example of an Organisation Unit Instance View for the Martian army is shown in Figure 13.43.

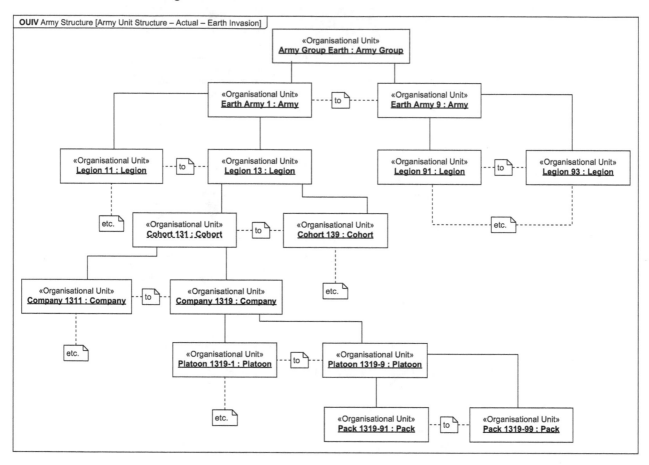

Figure 13.43   Organisational Unit Instance View showing structure of invading army

The Organisation Unit Instance View in Figure 13.43 shows "actual" instances of Organisational Units corresponding to the typical structure found in Figure 13.42. Since the intention of the Organisation Unit Instance View is to show instances of Organisational Units it makes sense to use *instance specifications* on a *block definition diagram*. This has been done here, with *stereotypes* again being used to show that the *instance specifications* represent Organisational Units. Thus we can see that 'Army Group Earth' is an actual 'Army Group' and is made up of 'Earth Army 1' to

'Earth Army 9', each an actual 'Army'. The *stereotypes* show that these are all Organisational Groups. The rest of actual structure is modelled in a similar fashion, with *notes* being used to elide information and show the range of Organisational Units and how they are named.

Here it is worth remembering that the Organisation Unit Instance View must correspond to an Organisation Unit Structure View. For example, if 'Earth Army 9' was made up of only two 'Legions', then there would be an inconsistency between the Organisation Unit Instance View and its Organisation Unit Structure View in Figure 13.42, which would have to be changed to show that an 'Army' is composed of two or more 'Legions' (or perhaps even one or more in order to allow maximum flexibility).

13.7.3   The Rank Hierarchy View

The Rank Hierarchy View is used to show Ranks and their hierarchy. An example showing Martian army Ranks is shown in Figure 13.44, with Martian Ranks translated into Human equivalents where there is no other suitable translation.

A *block definition diagram* is used to realise the Rank Hierarchy View, with *blocks* representing Ranks. Again, *stereotypes* are used to show that the *blocks* represent Ranks. The subordination of one Rank to another is shown via *associations*. The use of the '{incomplete}' *constraint* on the *generalisation* between the 'Rank' and the 'Army Rank' *blocks* shows that Figure 13.44 is incomplete and that other high-level Ranks are omitted (e.g. 'Navy Rank' and 'Science Rank'). These would need to be defined on their own Rank Hierarchy Views. If the equivalence of Ranks needs to be modelled, then the Ontology Definition View for the MBSE Architectural Framework could be extended to show that a Rank is equivalent to another. The definition of the Rank Hierarchy View (i.e. the Rank Hierarchy Viewpoint) could then be extended to allow relationships to be added showing such Rank equivalence.

13.7.4   The Post Structure View

The Post Structure View is used to show typical Posts and lines of command between Posts and between a Post and an Organisational Unit. It also shows the minimum Rank that can fill a Post. An example defining typical Posts in the Martian army is given in Figure 13.45.

A *block definition diagram* has been used in Figure 13.45 to realise the Post Structure View. Each Post is represented using a *block* with a *stereotype* marking the *blocks* as being Posts. As with the Rank Hierarchy View, the use of the '{incomplete}' *constraint* shows that not all Posts are shown in this diagram. Lines of command were deliberately omitted from Figure 13.45 in order not to clutter the diagram. They are shown in Figure 13.46, along with minimum Rank required for each Post.

The Post Structure View in Figure 13.46 now shows the minimum Rank required for each Post, as well as the lines of command between Posts and

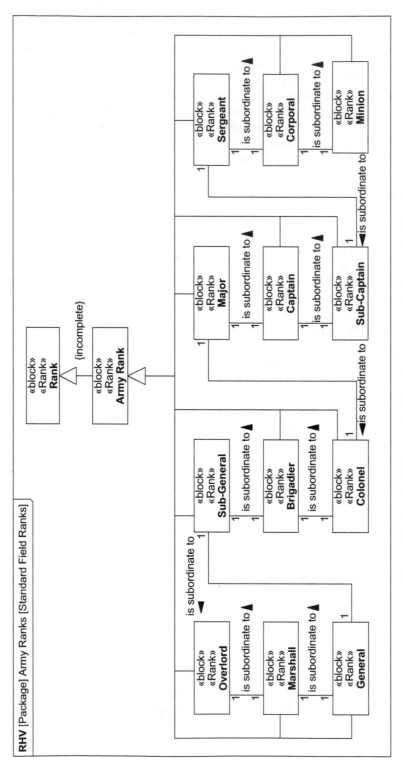

Figure 13.44   Rank Hierarchy View showing standard army field ranks

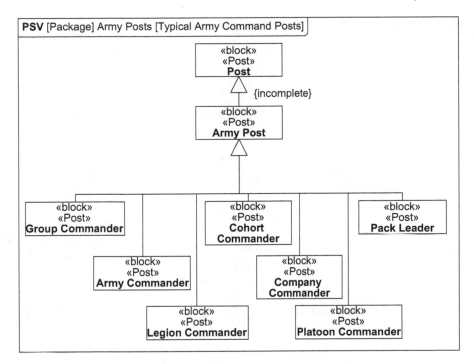

Figure 13.45 Post Structure View showing typical army posts

between Posts and Organisational Units. Note the use of *packages* to provide a visual grouping of the Ranks, Posts and Organisational Units. Lines of command are shown using *stereotyped dependencies* and minimum Ranks using *associations*. *Dependencies* or *associations* could be used for either or both. The realisations used in Figure 13.46 were chosen to illustrate the two possibilities. Note also how the use of *stereotypes* in this diagram also helps to differentiate between the different Ontology Elements being represented by the *blocks*.

Remember that the Post Structure View must be consistent with other Views. For example, the Ranks shown on Figure 13.46 must appear on a Rank Hierarchy View. Similarly the Organisational Units must appear on an Organisational Unit Structure View.

If your Organisation is less militaristic than that modelled in this section, then think Grade rather than Ranks, 'manages' rather than 'commands' and 'requires grade' rather than 'requires rank'. For example, the Post of 'Team Leader' manages a 'Team' Organisational Unit, manages a 'Team Member' Person and requires a 'G6' Grade.

Not all Posts have command responsibility. Such Posts could be shown on a separate Post Structure View, again to avoid cluttering diagrams. An example is shown in Figure 13.47.

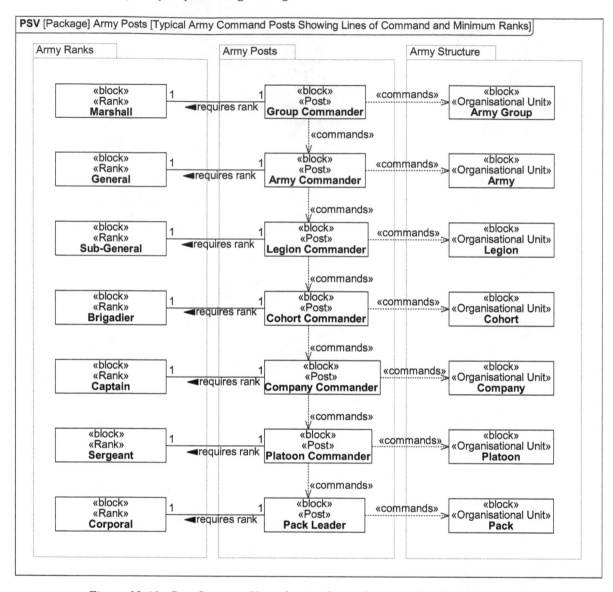

Figure 13.46   Post Structure View showing lines of command and minimum ranks

Figure 13.47 shows three Posts that all require the same minimum Rank but which have no command responsibility. This is in agreement with the Ontology Definition View showing extended concepts related to Organisation and Person in Chapter 12, which shows that a Post commands zero or more Posts and zero or more Organisational Units.

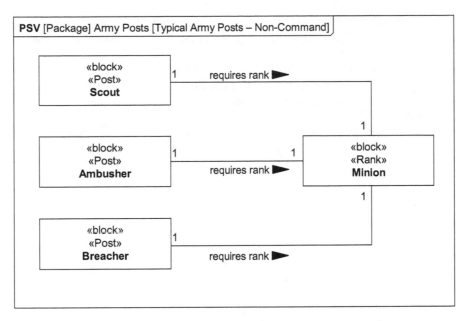

Figure 13.47   Post Structure View showing non-command posts

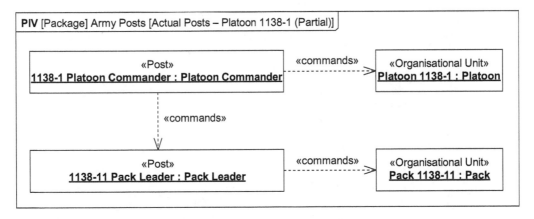

Figure 13.48   Post Instance View showing examples of actual Posts, actual Organisational Units and lines of command

13.7.5   The Post Instance View

The Post Instance View is used to show actual Posts, the actual Organisational Units that the Posts command and the actual Ranks of the Person filling each Post. A small example is shown in Figure 13.48.

Given that the Post Instance View shows actual Posts, etc. it should be no surprise that a *block definition diagram* is used with *instance specifications* showing instances of each Post and Organisational Unit. Again, these *instance specifications* are marked with *stereotypes* to show that they represent Posts and Organisational Units. In a diagram with more Posts and Organisational Units than shown here, *packages* could again be used to provide a visual grouping if required, in a similar way to their use in Figure 13.46.

Again, remember that the instances of Posts shown on the Post Instance View must correspond to defined Posts on a Post Structure View.

13.7.6   The Post to Role View

The Post to Role View is used to show the Stakeholder Roles that are required by each Post. A small example for the Martian army is shown in Figure 13.49.

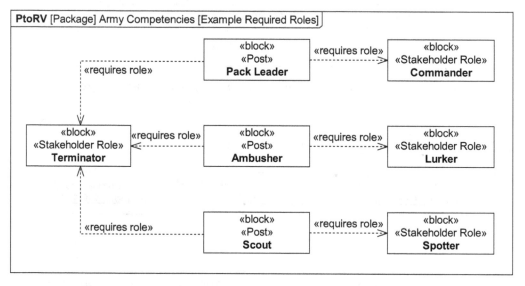

Figure 13.49   Post to Role View showing required Stakeholder Roles for typical Posts

A *block definition diagram* is used in Figure 13.49 to realise the Post to Role View. As with the other Views in the Organisational Perspective, *stereotypes* are used to help distinguish between the different uses the *blocks* are put: Posts and Stakeholder Roles. The mapping from a Post to the required Stakeholder Roles has been realised using a *stereotypes dependency*. Again, this relationship could also be modelled using an *association* instead. In circumstances where one modelling element has no real benefit over another, then often the decision as to which to use is a matter of personal (and often aesthetic) choice. However, whatever choice of realisation is made must be used consistently throughout the architecture. One way of enforcing this is to annotate the Viewpoint Definition View for each Viewpoint so that the realisation to be used for each Viewpoint Element is defined.

13.7.7   The Martian Instance View

The Martian Instance View is used to show the actual Person (and in this case, Martians) that fill each Post. A small example showing two Persons and their Posts is shown in Figure 13.50.

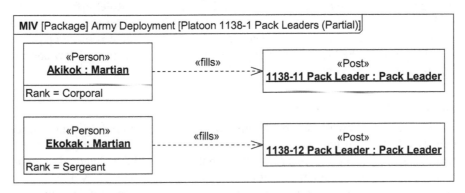

Figure 13.50   Martian Instance View showing actual Martians assigned to actual Posts

Since the Martian Instance View is showing instances of Person and Post, *instance specifications* on a *block definition diagram* are again used to realise the Martian Instance View. The filling of Posts is modelled using a *stereotyped dependency*. As before, an *association* could have been used as an alternative.

From the point of view of consistency, any instance of a Post that appears on a Martian Instance View must appear on a Post Instance View. The Post '1138-11 Pack Leader : Pack Leader' appears on the Post Instance View in Figure 13.48; presumably the Post '1138-12 Pack Leader: Pack Leader' appears on a different Post Instance View.

Note the assignment of values to the *slots* in the *instance specifications* for the Person *blocks*. A *slot* in an *instance specification* corresponds to a *property* in the *block* that types the *instance specification*. It is, in effect, an instance of a *property*. Two points are worth noting regarding their use here. Firstly, Figure 13.46 shows that the minimum 'Rank' for a 'Pack Leader' is 'Corporal'. However, in Figure 13.50 it can be seen that 'Ekokak' has 'Rank' of 'Sergeant'; he (she? It?) is actually over-qualified. Either there is not an available 'Platoon' for him to command, or he is deemed unsuitable in some way. This is just as true in "real" Organisations; a person can get promoted to a Rank or Grade that makes them suitable for holding a higher Post, but such a Post may not be available. The MBSE Architectural Framework allows for such situations to be captured. The second point is that the 'Rank' *slot* shown means that the 'Martian' *block* must have a *property* named 'Rank'. This is not shown on the Organisation Unit Structure View in Figure 13.42 where it has been omitted for clarity.

13.8   The Competency Perspective

The Competency Perspective is concerned with ensuring that Each Person has the appropriate set of Competencies to perform their Stakeholder Roles effectively. All of the Views that make up the Competency Perspective may be used as part of a Competency Assessment exercise. The Competency Perspective is made up of the following Views: the Framework View, the Applicable Competency View and the Competency Scope View.

13.8.1   Framework View

The Framework View is concerned with providing an understanding of the source Framework that will be used as a basis for demonstrating Competence. This will typically be some sort of Standard, such as a publically available Standard or an in-house Standard. The Framework View will typically be visualised by a number of diagrams as Competency Frameworks can be very large and can require quite a lot of modelling – see Chapter 14 for examples of this.

The diagram in Figure 13.51 shows one diagram that makes up the Framework view. In this case, the focus of the diagram is on the various Competency Areas that make up the Framework and their associated Competencies. The View itself takes the form of a simple Classification Hierarchy and it should be noted that not all of the possible Competencies are shown here as the full View will be larger and potentially more complex.

Note how stereotypes are used to show extra information about which *block*s are representing Competency areas and which are representing Competencies. This is not absolutely necessary but it does simplify the diagram.

This View identifies the basic Competencies that will be used as part of the other Competency Perspective Views. These Competencies will also map to other parts of the overall MBSE model, such as the MBSE Ontology and the MBSE Processes. This is discussed in more detail in Chapter 14.

13.8.2   Applicable Competency View

The Applicable Competency View identifies the subset of the Competencies that were defined in the Framework view that is relevant for the set of Stakeholder Roles that are being assessed as part of the Competency Assessment exercise.

The diagram in Figure 13.52 shows the Applicable Competency View for a specific Competency Assessment exercise. This is clearly not a SysML diagram but a simple graphical, chart-type representation. This is not the only graphical representation that could be used but has been adopted because it makes the Competency Scope View easier to generate as it looks very similar.

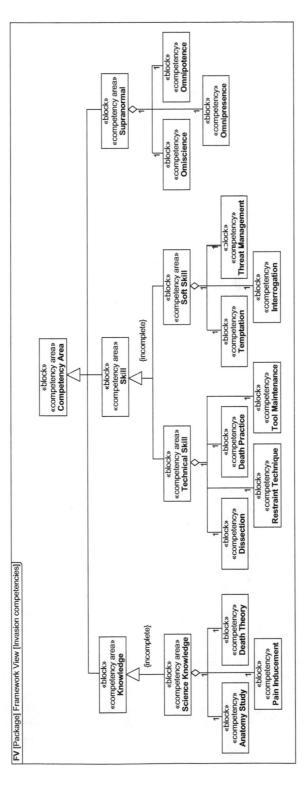

Figure 13.51 Framework View for Invasion case study

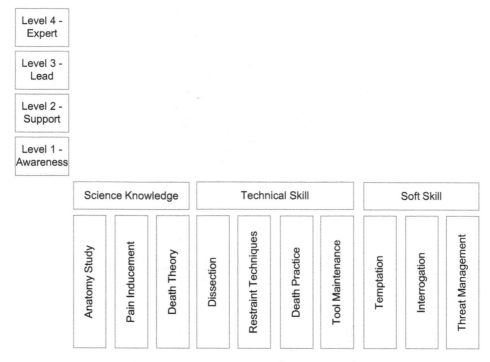

Figure 13.52   Applicable Competency View

It does not matter what graphical notation is adopted and the View may even be realised as a simple text list but, whatever the format adopter, it must form part of the overall model in that it must be consistent with the other Views. For example, the y-axis on the chart shows the Levels that were defined as the part of the MBSE Ontology that focused on Competency. Likewise, the x-axis shows landscape-oriented boxes that represented the Competency Areas from the Framework View and portrait-oriented boxes that represent the Competencies from the Framework View.

13.8.3   Competency Scope View

The Competency Scope View comprises a single diagram for each Stakeholder Role that is to be assessed as part of the competency Assessment exercise. The Competency Scope View takes the Applicable Competency View and then identifies which Competencies are relevant for the Stakeholder Role and defines at what level each should be held.

The diagram in Figure 13.53 shows the competency Scope View for the Scientist Stakeholder Role. Note the similarities between this View and the Applicable Competency View shown in Figure 13.52.

The diagram in Figure 13.54 shows the competency Scope View for the Terminator Stakeholder Role. Note the differences between the Competencies required for this Stakeholder Role and that of the Scientist shown in Figure 13.53.

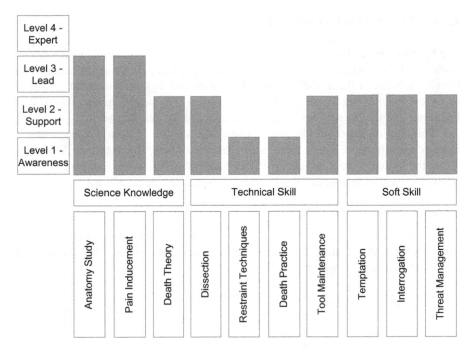

Figure 13.53 Competency Scope View for Scientist Stakeholder Role

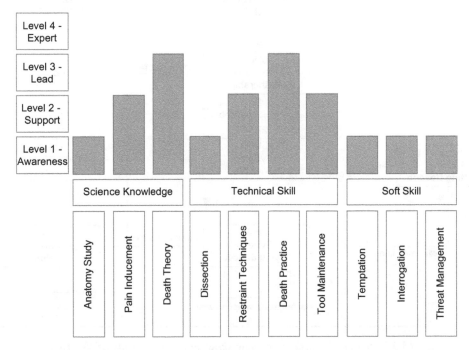

Figure 13.54 Competency Scope View for Terminator Stakeholder Role

13.9   The System Perspective

The System Perspective is concerned with capturing the structure and behaviour of a System or System of Systems. It captures the Systems and their System Elements, the Interfaces between them, their System Properties and System Functions and their behaviour in terms of internal behaviour in a System or System Element or its System Functions and the interactions between Systems and System Elements.

This section contains the Views that make up the System Perspective: the System Identification View, the System Structure View, the Interface Definition View, the System Configuration View, the System State View, the System Behaviour View, the System Interaction View and the System Parametric View.

13.9.1   System Identification View

The System Identification View is used to identify Systems and the relationships between them. An example showing the main elements of the Martian invasion fleet is shown in Figure 13.55.

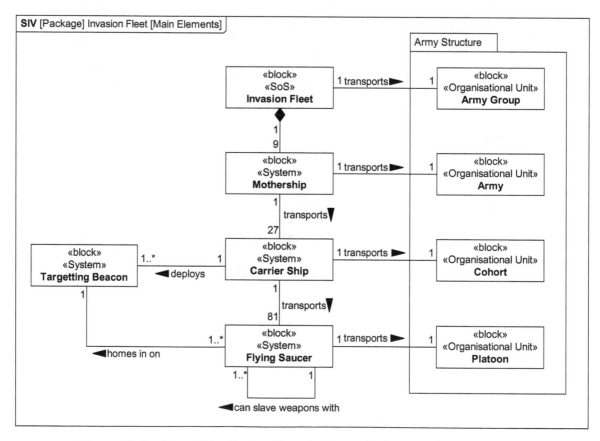

Figure 13.55   System Identification View showing main elements of 'Invasion Fleet'

The System Identification View has been realised using a *block definition diagram* as shown in Figure 13.55. The main element shown is a System of Systems, the 'Invasion Fleet', composed of nine 'Mothership' Systems. Note the use of *stereotypes* to show the types of Ontology Elements represented by the various *blocks*. The main Systems involved are shown, as are the relationships between them. Note the relationships between Systems, the System of Systems and Organisational Units and the use of a *package* to visually differentiate the Organisational Units from the Systems and System of Systems.

The System Identification View in Figure 13.55 deliberately omits System Functions and System Properties in order to keep the diagram uncluttered. Such information can be added to more detailed, specific System Identification Views, as has been done in Figure 13.56.

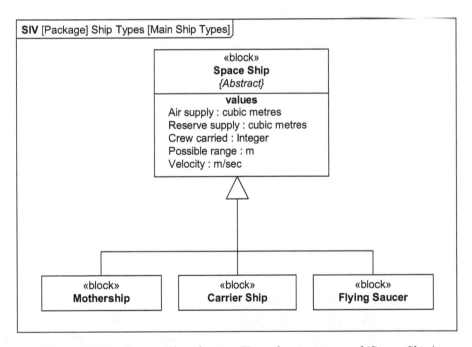

Figure 13.56   System Identification View showing types of 'Space Ship'

The System Identification View in Figure 13.56 focuses on the 'Mothership', 'Carrier Ship' and 'Flying Saucer' from Figure 13.55. These all share a number of System Properties that are abstracted to an *abstract block* 'Space Ship' that they are all *specialisations* of.

Each System can also be broken down into its main System Elements on a System Identification View. An example of this is shown in Figure 13.57.

In Figure 13.57, the 'Flying Saucer' has been broken down into its System Elements, with the major relationships between them shown. Again, System

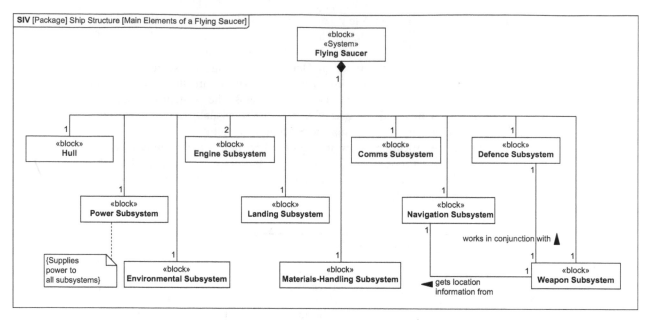

Figure 13.57   System Identification View showing main elements of 'Flying Saucer'

Properties and System Functions are omitted, both for reasons of clarity and because the System Structure View (covered in the next section) is more suited to the modelling of System Properties and System Functions. Some relationships have been omitted for clarity, as shown by the *note* attached to the 'Power Subsystem'. One addition that could be made to the diagram, and which would bring the modelling approach and style in line with what has been done with Systems, System of Systems, etc. would be to use a *stereotype* to mark the other *blocks* in Figure 13.57 as «System Element».

13.9.2   System Structure View

The System Structure View is used to define the structure of a System, showing how it is composed of System Elements. It shows the relationships between System Elements, their System Properties and System Functions. A number of examples follow.

The System Structure View in Figure 13.58 has been realised using a *block definition diagram* with *blocks* representing Systems and System Elements. As with the System Identification View, additional *stereotypes* could be used to mark those *blocks* that represent System Elements. This, however, raises an interesting point. The 'Power Subsystem' is a System Element since it is part of the 'Flying Saucer' System as shown on the System Identification View in Figure 13.57. However, it is itself further decomposed as shown in an 'Atomic Pile' and a 'Power Conduit' so can also, from a different level of abstraction, be considered to be a System in its own right, which would make the 'Atomic Pile' and 'Power Conduit' System Elements. This was discussed in Chapter 12 in the discussion of

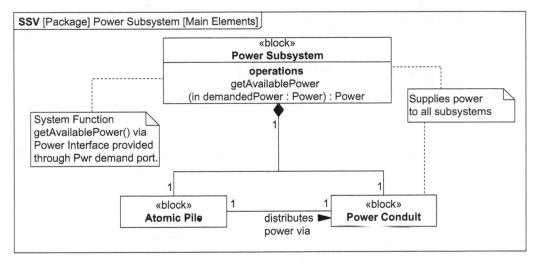

Figure 13.58   System Structure View showing high-level structure of 'Power Subsystem'

the definition of the System Structure Viewpoint. The need to work and model at different levels of abstraction in this way is very common in systems engineering. In Figure 13.58, 'Power Subsystem' is being treated as a System in this way.

The 'Power Subsystem' has a single System Function, modelled as an *operation*: 'getAvailablePower'. However, this System Function is not provided directly by the 'Power Subsystem' but rather via an Interface 'Power Interface' provided by 'Power Subsystem'. A *note* has been used in the diagram to clarify this aspect of the model. The Interface itself is defined on an Interface Definition View (see Figure 13.61 in the following subsection) and its use is shown on a System Configuration View (see Figure 13.62 in the System Configuration View subsection). Again, this emphasises the consistency between the various Views that must exist if an Architecture is to be more than just a set of pictures.

A further example of a System Structure View is given in Figure 13.59, this time for the 'Defence Subsystem'. Again, a *note* is used to indicate that some (but not all) of the System Functions provided by the 'Ray Shield' are provided by the Interface 'Shield Interface'; the other System Functions are those provided directly by the 'Ray Shield'. In this example, a number of System Properties are also shown for 'Ray Shield', modelled as SysML *properties* (and in this case, as *value properties*). Note also the use of a *role name* (the 'RS') on the *composition* between 'Defence Subsystem' and 'Ray Shield'. This is used to name the 'Ray Shield' when it is realised as a *part* on the System Configuration View in Figure 13.63.

The final System Structure View presented in Figure 13.60 shows the main System Elements of the 'Weapon Subsystem'. Some System Properties and System Functions are also shown, as are the relationships to other Systems and System Elements, with *packages* used to provide a clear graphical boundary to these other

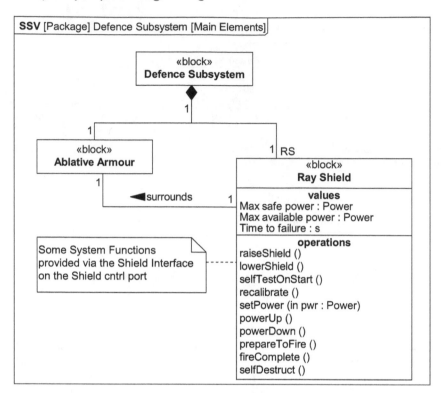

Figure 13.59   System Structure View showing high-level structure of 'Defence Subsystem', along with System Properties and System Functions

Systems. Note again the use of *role names* on the *composition* from 'Weapon Subsystem'. These are again used so that the System Elements ('Fire Control' and 'Laser Cannon') can be named when used on a System Configuration View, such as that in Figure 13.63. Because each of the three 'Laser Cannon' that form part of the 'Weapon Subsystem' are to be referred to individually, it is necessary to use three separate *compositions*, each with its own *role name* and a *multiplicity* of one, rather than a single *composition* with a single *role name* and a *multiplicity* of three. The latter option is valid from a SysML point of view, but would not allow the three separate *roles* of 'Cannon1', 'Cannon2' and 'Cannon3' to be distinguished on a System Configuration View. This is a limitation of the SysML. There is no easy way to represent a *multiplicity* greater than one as separate *parts* on an *internal block diagram*. As a modeller, it would be useful to say that the 'Weapon Subsystem' is composed of three 'Laser Cannon' (via a single *composition*) and associate three different *role names* with this single *composition*, allowing the *roles* to be represented as distinct *parts* on an *internal block diagram*. Unfortunately, to date, the SysML does not allow this.

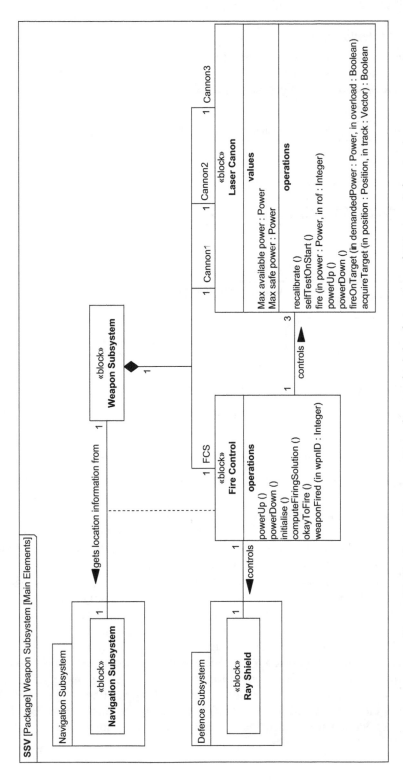

Figure 13.60   System Structure View showing high-level structure of 'Weapon Subsystem'

13.9.3 Interface Definition View

The Interface Definition View is used to define Interfaces between Systems and between System Elements within a System. The Interfaces used in the Systems and System Elements of the 'Flying Saucer' are shown in Figure 13.61.

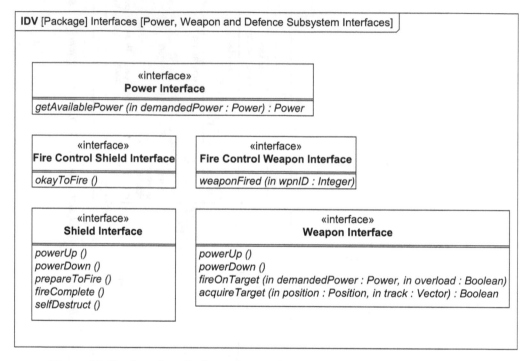

Figure 13.61 Interface Definition View showing interfaces used by subsystems

The Interface Definition View is realised as a *block definition diagram* with *interface blocks* (unsurprisingly) being used to model Interfaces. Five different Interfaces are shown on Figure 13.61. In this example (and in the intent behind the Interface Definition Viewpoint), these Interfaces are all of an operational or service-based nature and so can easily be realised as *operations* of an *interface block*. The way that the Interfaces are used is shown on a System Configuration View.

Other types of Interface, such as those based on the transfer of energy, data or material, are not identified explicitly on an Interface Definition View (in the MBSEAF) but, rather, are implied through connections via *item flows* between *ports* on a System Configuration View. The MBSEAF could be extended to allow such Interfaces to be explicitly modelled, as well as allowing more advanced aspects of an Interface to be captured, such as protocol and behaviour. The Interface Definition View as defined for MBSEAF is the minimum that is required. The definition of additional Interface Views is left as an exercise for the reader.

13.9.4 System Configuration View

The System Configuration View is used to show that a System is actually configured based on its structure, together with the Interfaces between the System Elements. Two examples follow in Figures 13.62 and 13.63.

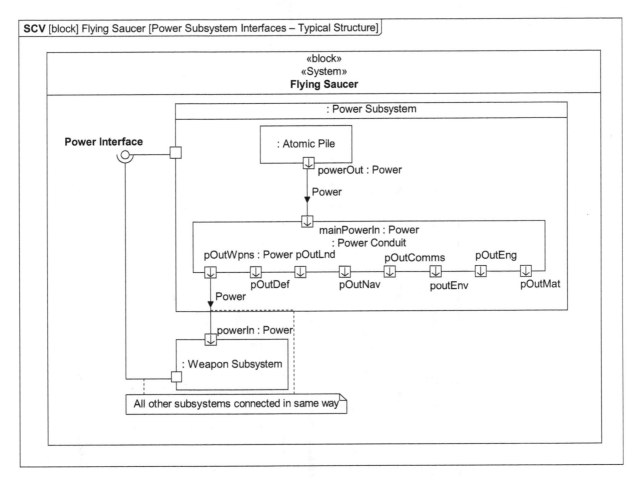

Figure 13.62   System Configuration View showing 'Power Subsystem' and its Interfaces to other subsystems

The System Configuration View is realised using an *internal block diagram* with System Elements represented using *parts* connected together via *interfaces* (defined on an Interface Definition View) and *item flows*. The connection points for the *interfaces* and *item flows* are shown using *ports*. Figure 13.62 shows the System Configuration View for the 'Power Subsystem' of the 'Flying Saucer', and is intended to show how the various System Elements (the 'Weapon Subsystem',

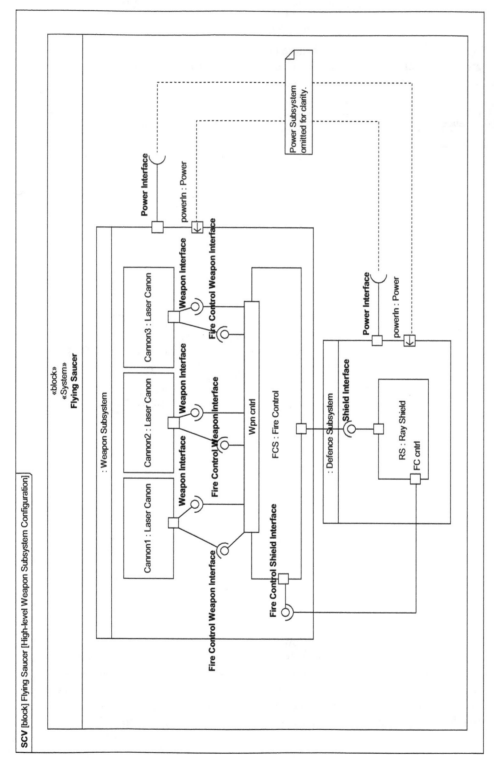

Figure 13.63   *System Configuration View showing 'Weapon Subsystem' and Interfaces to the 'Defence Subsystem'*

'Defence Subsystem', etc.) of the 'Flying Saucer' System are connected to the 'Power Subsystem'.

In this example, an explicit Interface, the 'Power Interface' that is modelled on the Interface Definition View in Figure 13.61, is used to model the control aspects of the Interface between the 'Weapon Subsystem' and the 'Power Subsystem'. From the way that the connection has been modelled using a *provided interface* on the 'Power Subsystem' and a *required interface* on the 'Weapon Subsystem' it can be inferred from Figures 13.61 and 13.62 that the 'Weapon Subsystem' makes requests of the 'Power Subsystem'. The possible nature of such requests can be seen by looking at the definition of 'Power Interface' on the Interface Definition View in Figure 13.61. The way in which the Interface is used can be seen by looking at the various System Interaction Views in their subsection below.

The transfer of 'Power' from the 'Power Subsystem' is also shown on Figure 13.62, via the 'Atomic Pile' and 'Power Conduit', through the use of *item flows*. The direction of the flow can be seen from the arrows on the various *ports*. A *note* attached to the *interface* and *item flow* connections is used to remove clutter from the diagram and to avoid duplication of what would be essentially the same diagram, by stating that all the various subsystems connect to the 'Power Subsystem' in that same way.

Note that in Figure 13.62, none of the System Elements are named and that the *type* of most of the *ports* has been omitted from the diagram.

The System Configuration View in Figure 13.63 does feature named System Elements. For example, 'Fire Control' has the name 'FCS'. Remember that these names correspond to the *role names* used on the *composition relationships* in the System Structure Views in Figures 13.59 and 13.60. This diagram also shows that a *port* can have both *required* and *provided interfaces* attached, and attached multiple times. Again, the System Configuration View in Figure 13.63 should be read in conjunction with the Interface Definition View in Figure 13.61 and the various System Interaction Views in their subsection below in order to understand the nature of the connections shown.

13.9.5   System State View

The System State View is used to define state-based behaviour of a System and its System Elements. A simple example for the 'Ray Shield' is shown in Figure 13.64.

The System State View is realised as a *state machine diagram* and will have close links to the System Structure View, the Interface Definition View, the System Configuration View and the System Interaction View. This can be seen in Figure 13.64.

Firstly, consider the *events* that trigger *transitions* between *states*. From the diagram, it can be seen that a *transition* can be triggered by the following: 'powerUp', 'prepareToFire', 'fireComplete', 'powerDown' and 'selfDestruct'. These correspond to the *operations* of the Interface 'Shield Interface' that is defined on the Interface Definition View in Figure 13.61. But are they available to the 'Ray Shield'? Looking at the System Configuration View in Figure 13.63 it can be seen that 'Shield Interface' is a *provided interface* of 'Ray Shield'. Therefore these *operations* can be invoked to

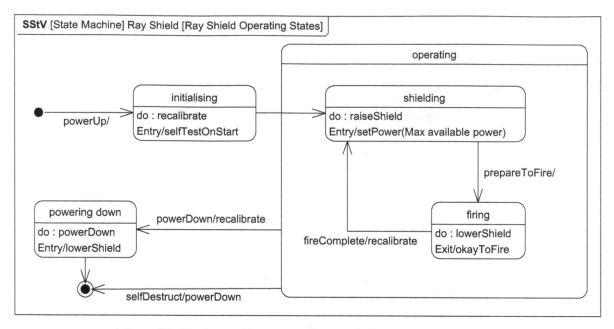

Figure 13.64   System State View showing behaviour of 'Ray Shield'

cause such transitions. Thus we have consistency between the System State View and the Interface Definition View and System Configuration View.

Secondly, consider the System Functions that are executed on entry to or within the *states* or as part of the *transitions*. From Figure 13.64 these can be seen to be: 'recalibrate', 'selfTestOnStart', 'raiseShield', 'setPower', 'lowerShield' and 'powerDown'. Where are these defined? They are the System Functions that are provided directly by the 'Ray Shield', rather than via the 'Shield Interface', as can be seen in the System Structure View in Figure 13.59. Thus we have consistency between the System State View and the System Structure View.

The only behaviour not so far considered is the invocation of the 'okayToFire' System Function on exit from the *state* 'firing'. This again corresponds to an *operation* defined on an *interface block*, in this case that defined on the 'Fire Control Shield Interface'. This Interface is *provided* by 'Fire Control' and *required* by 'Ray Shield' as can be seen on the System Configuration View in Figure 13.63. It is defined on the Interface Definition View in Figure 13.61. Thus we have consistency again between the System State View and the Interface Definition View and System Configuration View.

Finally, the System State View must be consistent with the Scenarios explored through System Interaction Views. This can be checked by looking at the possible *transitions* and their triggers and *send events* on a System State View and comparing these with the *messages* on a System Interaction View. For example, looking at the System State View in Figure 13.64 and considering the *transitions* from the *initial state* to the 'shielding' *state*, the following sequence of System Functions should be invoked: 'powerUp', 'selfTestOnStart', 'recalibrate', setPower' and 'raiseShield'. Comparing this sequence to the interactions with the 'Ray Shield' on the System Interaction View in Figure 13.68 we do, indeed, see that they are consistent. However, Figure 13.68 shows an additional *message*, 'getAvailablePower', between the 'Ray Shield' and the 'Power Subsystem'. This is not an inconsistency, but rather an interaction that is not directly part of the state-based behaviour modelled on the System State View, part of the internal behaviour of the 'recalibrate' System Function and as such would be modelled on a System Behaviour View. It is worth noting here that such a check between the System State Views and System Interaction Views should also be made in the opposite direction: abstract the sequence of *messages* from a System Interaction View and check that they correspond to the *transitions* on the relevant System State View.

As a final comment on the example System State View shown in Figure 13.64, note the use of a *sequential composite state*, 'operating', containing the *states* 'shielding' and 'firing'. This was used as the 'powerDown' and 'selfDestruct' *transitions* apply to both these contained *states*. Using the *composite state* makes the diagram and its intent clearer.

13.9.6   System Behaviour View

The System Behaviour View is used to define the behaviour of a System and its System Elements. It is usually used to model the behaviour of a System Function. An example, for the 'fireOnTarget' System Function of the 'Laser Cannon', as provided through its *provided interface* 'Weapon Interface', is given in Figure 13.65.

The System Behaviour View is realised using an *activity diagram*. In Figure 13.65, the *parameters* to the 'fireOnTarget' *operation* of the 'Weapon Interface' are shown in the rectangles in the upper right of the diagram. After the initial *decision node*, the two *actions* both invoke the 'getAvailablePower' System Function that is defined in the 'Power Interface' provided by the 'Power Subsystem' (see Figures 13.61 and 13.62). SysML doesn't define a format or notation for the text inside an *action*, but that chosen and used in Figure 13.65 is in common use. It would also have been possible to use the *signal* notation here, rather than *actions*, as the behaviour represents and invocation of external behaviour. Again this is a matter of modelling style and preference, but must be used consistently. The 'getAvailablePower' System Function would be expected to have its own System Behaviour View, as indeed would all the System Functions in the model.

A *merge node* is used following these initial *actions* simply to make it clear graphically that there is a single flow of control through the rest of the diagram. The invocation of the 'fire' System Function is not preceded by the name of its System or System Element, as was done with the invocation of 'getAvailablePower', since 'fire' is a System Function provided by the same System Element (the 'Laser Cannon') as the 'fireOnTarget' System Function that is being modelled on the System Behaviour View.

The behaviour as modelled does not allow for any kind of interruption to the behaviour. However, this is a very common requirement when modelling the

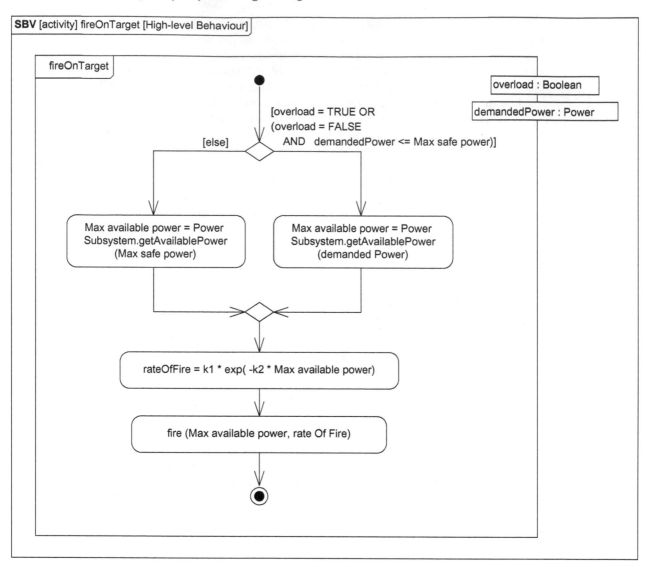

*Figure 13.65   System Behaviour View showing high-level behaviour of
'fireOnTarget' System Function*

behaviour of a System and can be achieved through the use of an *interruptible region* as shown in Figure 13.66.

The System Behaviour View in Figure 13.66 is the same as that in Figure 13.65 except for the addition of an *interruptible region* and a corresponding interrupting *event*. Now, the 'fireOnTarget' System Function can be interrupted on receipt of the 'Abort' *event,* which will immediately terminate any *action* in the *interruptible region* and cause the System Function to terminate.

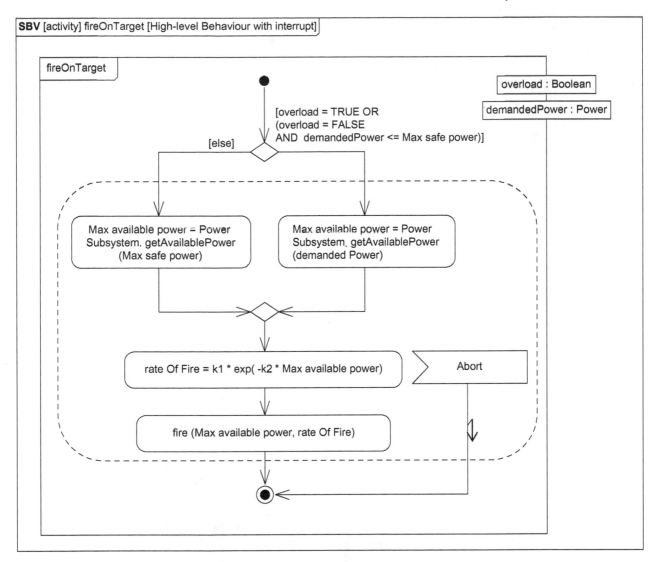

SBV [activity] fireOnTarget [High-level Behaviour with interrupt]

fireOnTarget

overload : Boolean

demandedPower : Power

[overload = TRUE OR
(overload = FALSE
AND demandedPower <= Max safe power)]

[else]

Max available power = Power
Subsystem. getAvailablePower
(Max safe power)

Max available power = Power
Subsystem. getAvailablePower
(demanded Power)

rate Of Fire = k1 * exp(-k2 * Max available power)

Abort

fire (Max available power, rate Of Fire)

*Figure 13.66   System Behaviour View showing high-level behaviour of
'fireOnTarget' System Function with interrupt*

Again, there are consistency checks that can be made. Does the behaviour modelled on the System Behaviour View agree with that modelled on the System Interaction Views, for example. From Figure 13.65 it can be seen that once the 'fireOnTarget' System Function is invoked on a 'Laser Cannon', it should invoke the 'getAvailablePower' System Function on the 'Power Sub-system' and then invoke 'fire' on its owning 'Laser Cannon'. According to the System Interaction View in Figures 13.67, 13.69 and 13.70 this is exactly what happens.

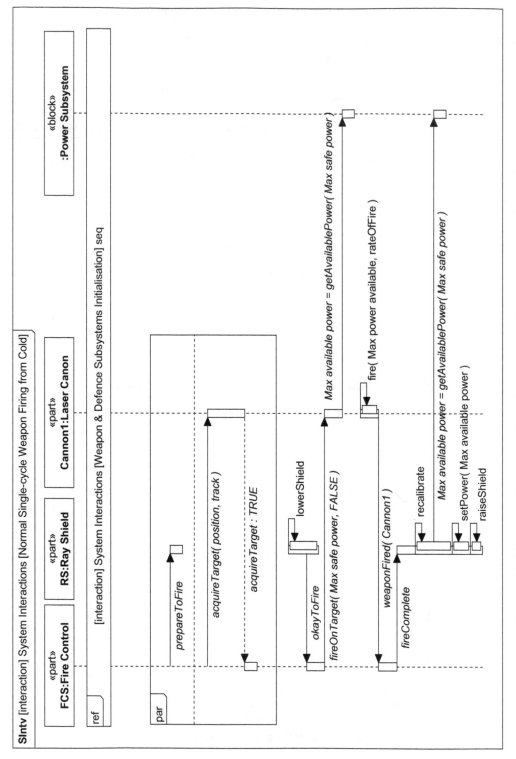

Figure 13.67 System Interaction View showing normal weapon firing with initialisation

13.9.7 System Interaction View

The System Interaction View is used to define interactions between Systems and between System Elements within a System. They are typically used to explore operational Scenarios for the System during analysis and design and can also be used as Validation Views (System Scenario Views – see Chapter 9) as part of the MBRE work on a System. An example of a System Interaction View is shown in Figure 13.67.

The System Interaction View is realised as a *sequence diagram* as shown in Figure 13.67, and is used to explore Scenarios by considering the interactions between Systems and System Elements. As discussed previously in the sections covering the System State View and the System Behaviour View, the System Interaction View does not exist in isolation but is deeply related to these other behavioural Views. In order to reinforce the understanding of the relationship between these Views (and indeed of the underlying SysML diagrams used to realise them), the reader is encouraged to check for themselves how the different aspects of the System's behaviour are modelled using these Views.

There are two things worthy of note on Figure 13.67: the use of an *interaction use* and a *parallel combined fragment*. The *interaction use* is represented by the first rectangle overlaying the *life lines*, containing the *keyword* 'ref'. This tells the reader that the rectangle represents another System Interaction View (actually another SysML *sequence diagram*) that is identified by the name in the main part of the rectangle. Such an *interaction use* enables common behaviour that would otherwise appear identically on multiple diagrams, to be abstracted and referenced indirectly in the manner shown. The diagram represented by this *interaction use* can be seen in Figure 13.68. The *parallel combined fragment* is used to represent possibly parallel behaviour. In the example above it shows that 'Fire Control' can send the 'prepareToFire' *message* to the 'Ray Shield' (i.e. invoke the 'prepareToFire' System Function provided by the 'Ray Shield') in parallel with sending the 'acquireTarget' *message* to the 'Laser Cannon' with name 'Cannon1'.

The diagram referenced by the *interaction use* is shown in Figure 13.68. Here, two nested *parallel combined fragments* are used. The outer *parallel combined fragment* could have been drawn with four compartments and the nested *parallel combined fragment* expanded into the additional compartments with no real change in meaning. Nested *parallel combined fragments* were used here for two reasons: firstly, purely to illustrate that *combined fragments* can be nested in this way and secondly, to emphasise that the powering up of all three 'Laser Cannon' is conceptually a single piece of behaviour that takes place in parallel with the powering up of the 'Ray Shield'.

Typically when producing System Interaction Views a number of related scenarios will be created. For example, the diagram in Figure 13.69 is closely related to that in Figure 13.67. The latter models a "normal" Scenario and the former a related "failure" Scenario.

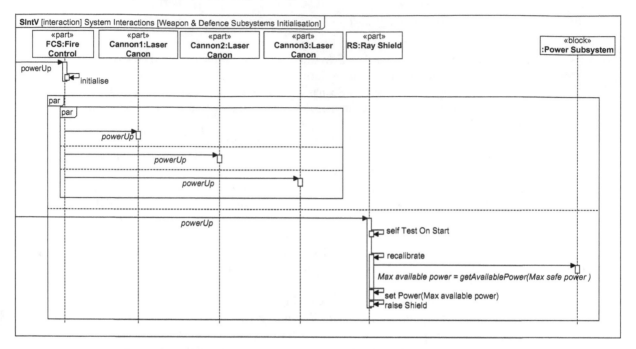

Figure 13.68   System Interaction View showing weapon and defence subsystem initialisation

In the System Interaction View in Figure 13.69 the bulk of the modelled Scenario is the same. However, in this Scenario the 'Laser Cannon' is fired in "overload" mode, resulting in its destruction. This is explicitly shown in the diagram through the truncated *life line* for the 'Laser Cannon' which is marked with the large X to signify its destruction. From this point on the rest of the Scenario is the same.

When two (or more Scenarios) are so closely related, it is possible to combine them on a single System Interaction View, this time using the *alternative combined fragment*. This has been done for the Scenarios in Figures 13.67 and 13.69. The resulting diagram is shown in Figure 13.70.

The Scenario in the System Interaction View shown in Figure 13.70 combines the two previous Scenarios through the *alternative combined fragment*. The two start and end in the same way, differing only in the behaviour when the 'Laser Cannon' is fired, as shown by the behaviour in the two compartments in the *combined fragment*.

While showing multiple Scenarios on a single System Interaction View is tempting, modellers are advised to use caution. Diagrams showing multiple Scenarios lessen the number of diagrams needed, but can result in diagrams that are very hard to read. Remember, one of the key aims of modelling is to aid

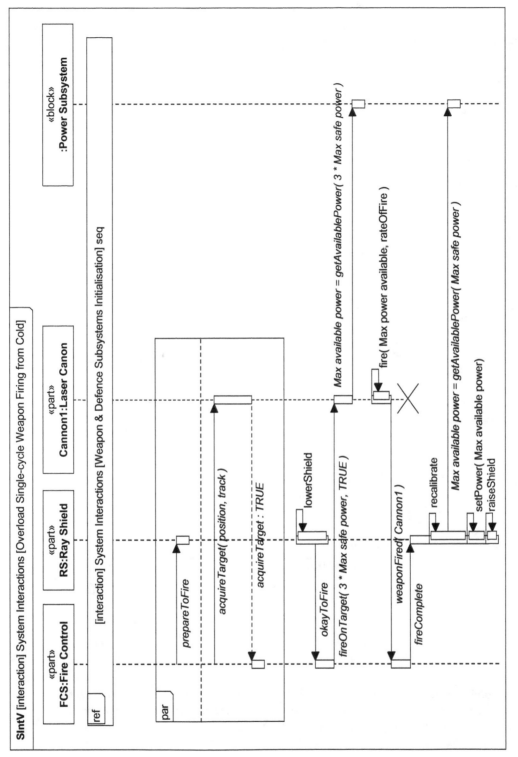

Figure 13.69   System Interaction View showing overload weapon firing with initialisation

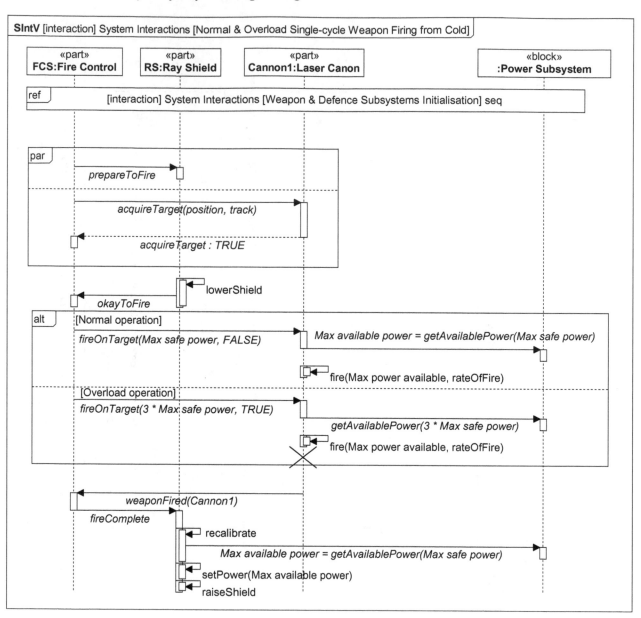

Figure 13.70   System Interaction View showing normal and overload weapon
firing with initialisation

communication. Sometimes multiple, simple diagrams are easier to work with than
one very complex diagram that makes sophisticated use of the available notation
but which is impenetrable to all except the person who drew it. As a rule of thumb,
the authors never create Scenarios with more than two or three alternative paths and

then only do so when each alternative differs only by a small amount. They never combine radically different Scenarios in a single diagram.

13.9.8   System Parametric View

The System Parametric View is used to define parametric behaviour of a System and its System Elements. That is, it is used to define behaviour that is best expressed by a network of mathematical and logical constraints between the System Properties of a System and its System Elements. The System Parametric View actually consists of two parts, examples of which are given in Figures 13.71 and 13.72.

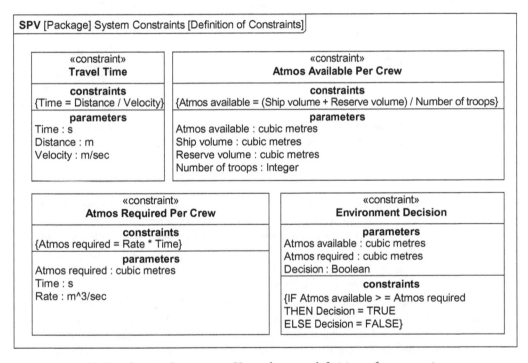

Figure 13.71   System Parametric View showing definition of parametric constraint blocks

The first part of a System Parametric View that has to be created is a definition of the constraints that will be used in the definition of the constraining network. An example of such a diagram is shown in Figure 13.71. This is a *block definition diagram* that uses *constraint blocks* to define the appropriate constraints.

Typically on all but the smallest of Projects, a number of such diagrams would be needed. Also, the types of constraint defined typically fall into one of two types: either generic constraints that can apply across multiple Projects and Systems, such as mathematical or physical laws, or specific constraint that only apply to that

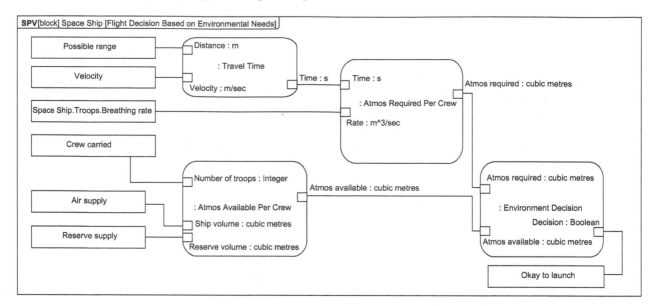

Figure 13.72   System Parametric View showing use of parametric constraint blocks (constraint properties) for determining flight decision based on ship air supply

particular Project and System. Figure 13.71 contains a single example of the former (the 'Travel Time' constraint) and three examples of the latter. Normally, the two types would be captured on separate diagrams, one for generic constraints and one for specific. In order to save space this has not been done here. The generic constraints would eventually form a defined "library" of such constraints that can be reused on multiple Projects and Systems.

Defining such constraints is an essential first step, but the definitions have to be used for them to be of value. This is the second part of a System Parametric View that has to be created, showing a particular network of such constraints connected to each other and to System Properties. An example of such a diagram is shown in Figure 13.72.

In order to show how the constraints can be used to constrain System Properties, a System Parametric View is defined using a *parametric diagram*. Each such diagram is created for a specific purpose and the defined constraints can be used multiple times on a single diagram and also on multiple diagrams. The diagram in Figure 13.72 shows a System Parametric View created specifically to explore the "go/no go" launch design for one of the Martian space ships based on its velocity, the distance to travel, amount of air on board and number of crew carried.

The System Parametric View is closely related to the System Identification and System Structure Views since it connects the defined constraints to System Properties that are defined on these Views. Indeed, often when creating a

System Parametric View new System Properties will be identified that are needed in order to define the network so it is very common to find that the creation of a System Parametric View also involves an iteration through a number of System Identification Views and System Structure Views until all are consistent.

As a final comment on this View, it would be perfectly reasonable to define two separate Viewpoints given the difference in nature of the two kinds of diagrams needed. Perhaps a System Parametric Definition Viewpoint and a System Parametric Usage Viewpoint could be defined. This has been done in this book in the ACRE Framework discussed in Chapter 9 and used to define the Views in Section 13.2 of the current chapter. In ACRE, parametrics can be used in the definition of Validation Views and for this purpose a Constraint Definition Viewpoint and a Constraint Usage Viewpoint are defined.

13.10   Summary

This chapter has provided an extended example in which all of the concepts covered in the book have been exercised and discussed. It has been presented as extracts from a System Architecture that is based on a defined Architectural Framework, the MBSEAF that is defined in Chapter 12. Although the System modelled is fictional, it is rich enough to provide examples for all of the Views from every Perspective of MBSEAF.

References

1.   Burton, T. (director). *Mars Attacks!* Film. Warner Bros. Pictures; 1996
2.   Hill, J.C. *Invasion from Outer Space.* Game. Flying Frog Productions; 2010
3.   Saunders, Z., The Topps Company & Brown, L. *Mars Attacks: 50th Anniversary Collection.* Abrams ComicArts; 2012

Part 5

Deploying MBSE

P5.1 Overview

This part of the book is structured according to the diagram in Figure P5.1.

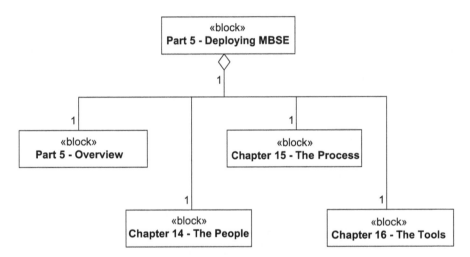

Figure P5.1   Structure of 'Part 5 – Deploying MBSE'

Part 5 considers the practical issues involved with deploying MBSE into an Organisation. There are three essential elements to deploying MBSE: 'People, Process and Tools', each of which is discussed in the chapters that make up this part of the book.

– 'Chapter 14 – The People'. This chapter considers how to ensure that the people in your Organisation have the right skills for the Stakeholder' Roles that they hold. This covers education and how to teach MBSE, how to define Competencies for MBSE and how to perform Competency assessment.
– 'Chapter 15 – The Process'. This chapter focuses on the underlying Process that is necessary for a rigorous approach. The basic Needs for a Process are discussed along with how to deploy such a process in a scalable manner, in terms of the rigour and size of the Project.

–   'Chapter 16 – The Tools'. This chapter looks at how Tools may be deployed on Projects. This includes looking at how they will be deployed, different types of Tool and Tool chains and how to perform a rigorous, repeatable evaluation of Tools.

This part of the book covers aspects of MBSE that are, arguably, the most difficult to get right in any MBSE endeavour.

Chapter 14

The 'People'

'I'm not left-handed either.'

Wesley, Man in Black, Dread Pirate Roberts

14.1 Introduction

This chapter looks at the pragmatic issues involved when trying to realise the model-based systems engineering (MBSE) approach in this book in any Organisation or business. In particular this chapter looks at how it is possible to ensure that the right people are in the right place, doing the right job – in other words, competent people.

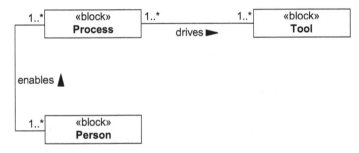

Figure 14.1   Pragmatic issues with implementing MBSE

By way of a recap, the diagram in Figure 14.1 shows the three main elements that must be in place in order to realise successful MBSE, in particular:

- The 'Person', by which we mean *competent* people, rather than just any people.
- The 'Process', which is in place in order to realise the approach.
- The 'Tool', which may range from a whiteboard or log book, to standard office tools, to a full-blown automated tool set, to any combination of these.

In order to understand the basic needs for providing competent people, the 'People Context' shown in Figure 14.2 was generated.

The diagram in Figure 14.2 shows the Context for the people aspect of MBSE. An essential element of having competent people is 'Provide resource' that is needed to carry out the MBSE activities, which may cover their '...for

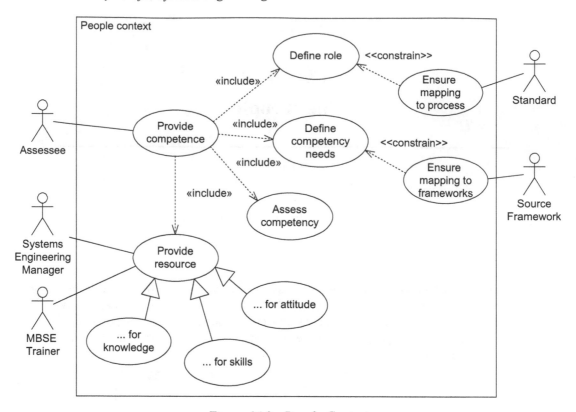

Figure 14.2 People Context

knowledge', '...for skills' and '...for attitude'. This chapter, therefore, contains a teaching guide that may be used to develop a bespoke teaching or training course based around many of the ideas in this book. It must be appreciated that MBSE is a very large subject; therefore, the ideas presented here should be seen as a good starting point for course development, rather than covering every aspect of the subject.

Being competent, however, involves far more than just training people to give them the right skill-set as it must also be ascertained what the Person's role will be ('Define role'), which will depend on the processes that describe the capability of the Organisation. Therefore, it is essential that the Stakeholder Roles define map onto ('Ensure mapping to process') whatever source Process ('Standard') is required. This section also contains, therefore, a set of Competency Scopes ('Define competency needs') that reflect current best practice ('Ensure mapping to frameworks') for the MBSE Stakeholder Roles identified in this book. These Competency Scopes may then be used as a basis for assessing the Competence ('Assess competency') of people who are required to work in MBSE. In order to assess Competence, a set of Processes will be introduced that can be used to carry out assessments.

In order to satisfy these Needs, it is first necessary to revisit the people aspects of the MBSE Ontology.

14.2 The MBSE Ontology (revisited)

The diagram in Figure 14.3 shows the subset of the MBSE Ontology that focuses on people-related concepts.

The diagram here shows the MBSE Ontology for the main concepts that are related to Competence. These are defined as follows:

- 'Person' – a special type of 'Resource', an individual human, who exhibits 'Competence' that is represented by their 'Competency Profile'. A 'Person' also holds one or more 'Stakeholder Role'.
- 'Competence' – the ability exhibited by a 'Person' that is made up of a set of one or more individual 'Competency', held at a specific 'Level'.
- 'Competency' – the representation of a single skill that contributes towards making up 'Competence'. Each 'Competency' is held at a 'Level' that describes the maturity of that 'Competency'. There are four 'Level' defined for the MBSE Ontology. One or more 'Competency' is collected together into a 'Competency Area'.
- 'Indicator' – the measurable unit that represents a single skill, one or more of which make up a 'Competency'. Indicators are assessed by comparing evidence provided by the person under assessment with predefined criteria, known as evidence types – see Chapter 8 for a full discussion.
- 'Competency Profile' – a representation of the actual measured 'Competence' of a 'Person' and that is defined by one or more 'Competencies'. An individual's 'competence' will usually be represented by one or more 'Competency Profiles'. A 'Competency Profile' is the result of performing a competence assessment against a 'Competence Scope'.
- 'Competency Scope' – representation of the desired 'Competence' required for a specific 'Stakeholder Role' and that is defined by one or more 'Competencies'.
- 'Stakeholder Role' – the role of anything that has an interest in a 'System'.

The Competence-related concepts are strongly related to the Process-related concepts.

14.3 Teaching guide

One of the main concerns that arise when presenting information regarding MBSE is that of how to teach or train people. There is no single correct way to do this, so this chapter provides a discussion on communicating the modelling approach in this book to people using teaching and training techniques. The information contained in this chapter is intended for guidance only and is based on the authors' years of experience teaching at both undergraduate and postgraduate levels as well as developing and delivering professional training courses for major industries.

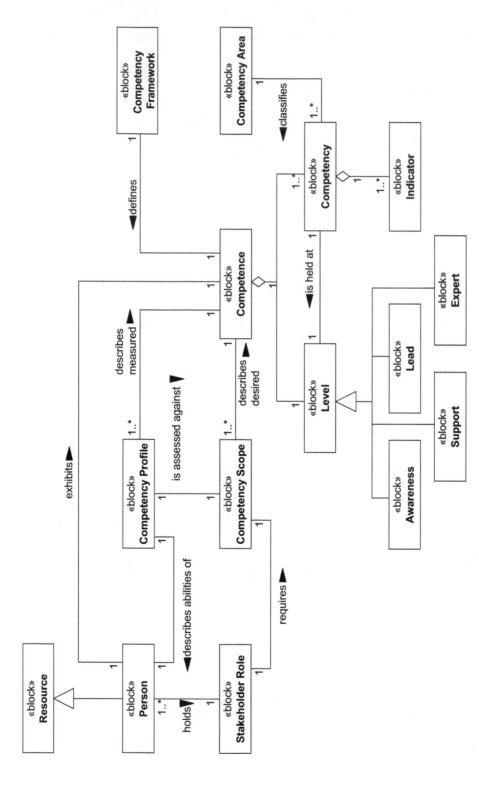

Figure 14.3 Subset of the MBSE Ontology focused on people-related concepts

This chapter also suggests a course structure for teaching at university level that is fully referenced back to in this book.

The main aim of this section is not to provide a full course that can simply be lifted out of the book and taught, and therefore no slides are provided. The intention is that this chapter, along with supporting CASE tools and models, can be used as a tool kit for someone to create an MBSE course, based on the contents of this book. Therefore, it is intended that this book is used as the recommended course text that provides lots of additional information and many more fully-worked examples.

So, please feel free to use this chapter and the models as the start point your own course – make the course your own!

14.3.1 Different types of teaching

There is no definitive way to teach MBSE, so this chapter provides a few examples of how teaching may be approached, depending on the audience. One key part of any teaching or training is to know and understand the audience and by this what we really mean is understanding the Needs of each Stakeholder Role. The point here is that teaching MBSE will differ depending on who the target audience is, and this will be discussed in some detail.

The diagram in Figure 14.4 shows a generic 'Teaching context' that will be used as a basis for discussion. It should be borne in mind, however, that this context will need to be tailored, or even started again from scratch, to fit the reader's Needs. It is strongly recommended that if you are interested in teaching or training, then this short Requirements modelling exercise is carried out, as it will really improve your own understanding of the teaching and help to ensure that the course that is

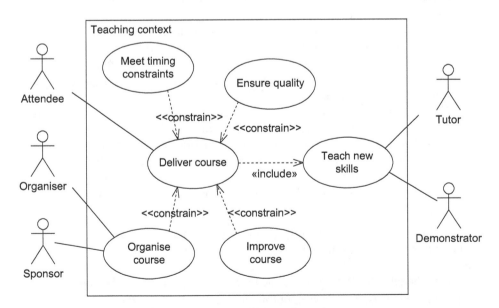

Figure 14.4   Generic Teaching Context

developed actually satisfies the Context. This will clearly result in a better course and, hopefully, a better learning experience for the teaching subjects. This exercise should be treated as a regular Requirements modelling exercise and it is recommended to follow the approach defined in Chapter 9.

The diagram shown in Figure 14.4 shows the generic Teaching Context for delivering training or teaching courses. The *use cases* are described in more detail below, along with a few suggestions for each as to how the basic needs may be tailored.

- 'Deliver course'. This is the overall *use case* that sets the scene for the Context. This could be tailored by adding different 'types of' (*specialisation*) *relationships* to the diagram to show Needs for different types of courses.
- 'Teach new skills'. Note that this is the only inclusion in the overall *use case* of 'Deliver course' and hence will form the basis of the course. This could be expanded upon by adding in more included *use cases*. For example, there may be a need to provide examples or to set course work – these could be added in as new *use cases*.
- 'Organise course'. This *use case* could mean almost anything, depending on the nature of the course being taught. For example, it may be as simple as making sure that a room is booked, to something as complex as making travel arrangements, renting facilities, hiring equipment, etc.
- 'Ensure quality'. This is a constraint on delivering the course and may include issues such as making sure that the course material is printed out and bound nicely, making sure that the facilities for the course are suitable and so on. This may also be extended to include other concerns, such as making sure that the presenters wear suits and appear smart before the course or whatever else is deemed important.
- 'Improve course'. It is always important to continuously improve everything that we do in our work and, therefore, this should be a *use case* that is always present in the Context. This may include collecting feedback from the course, making notes of any corrections or enhancements that could be made to the course afterwards, and so on.
- 'Meet timing constraints'. This *use case* is very important as this will limit what can be delivered and when. Understanding the timing constraints can often be the difference between a successful and an unsuccessful course and its importance cannot be stressed strongly enough. For example, if a course is to be taught for 10 sessions, each of 1 h duration, then the course will have a different structure from a course that will be taught over 8 h on a single day.

Due to the space limitation of this book, the emphasis for the example provided in this chapter will focus mainly on providing a course as part of a university syllabus.

The Stakeholder Roles that are shown on the diagram will differ significantly, depending on the type of teaching or training and will be discussed in more detail in the following two sections.

14.3.2 *Professional training*

This section looks at the whole area of professional training. The term 'professional training' is used here to refer to training that is provided commercially within industry as opposed to being aimed at academia.

Interestingly, the basic Context for teaching remains the same as for academic teaching; however, as the next section will discuss, the instances of the Stakeholder Roles and *use cases* that make up the Context are very different.

14.3.2.1 Teaching Context – Stakeholder Roles

When considering a professional training course, the core *use cases* are still those shown in Figure 14.2. With regard to the Stakeholder Roles that have been identified, the following shows a typical list of names that may be associated with each:

- 'Attendee', this Stakeholder Role represents the actual delegates on a training course. It may be useful for the case of professional courses to record information such as name, organisation, position, and contact details.
- 'Organiser', this may be the training company or the client company, depending on how the training is set up. This is a very important Stakeholder Role to consider as the possible scenarios for each will differ significantly.
- 'Tutor', this will be the primary trainer for the course.
- 'Demonstrator', this will be the demonstrator or secondary trainer of the course. In some cases, the Stakeholder Role of the tutor and the demonstrator may be taken on by single person.
- 'Sponsor', this is the Stakeholder Role representing whoever is paying the bill and may be a company or a number of individuals, depending on the nature of the course.

In terms of the Needs for the course, there are some Use Cases that must be considered.

- 'Organise course'. This Use Case can vary massively, depending on who is taking on the Stakeholder Role of the Organiser, as discussed previously. One of the big differences will be dependent on whether the Organiser is part of the training or the client Organisation. For example, if the course is being organised by the client company, then the onus on the training provider may be to simply turn up and deliver the course. If the organisation of the course is, on the other hand, being managed by the training organisation, then a number of logistical Processes will start to be come necessary, such as arranging the event venue, refreshments and meals, and accommodation. This is a good example of where a Project will vary depending on the nature of the people or Organisations that map onto the generic Stakeholder Roles from the Requirement Context View.
- 'Teach new skills'. This represents the main core Use Case for any training or teaching. In the case of a professional course, this may be related directly back to staff assessments, Competency Profiles or Standards of some description.

- 'Ensure quality'. When considering a professional training Organisation, the quality of the course may be driven by an external source, such as an independent or industry-driven endorsement from a recognised body. Another aspect of quality here relates to mapping the course content to recognised Competency Frameworks.
- 'Improve quality'. This will entail capturing any problems or mistakes on the course notes, capturing and addressing any comments that are made by the Attendees of the course, updating course materials, ensuring that best practice is being adhered to with regard to the course content, etc.
- 'Meet timing constraints'. The timing constraints for a professional training course will usually be concerned with making sure that the course is delivered over the duration of perhaps 2 or 3 working days. There may also be some client-specific constraints that come into play here. For example, some Organisations allow training only on particular days of the week or it may be desirable to avoid school holidays.

There are a lot of considerations to bear in mind with regard to professional training. Interestingly, depending on which of the above Use Cases and Stakeholder Roles apply to your Organisation, the diagram itself will change. For example, new Stakeholder Roles may be introduced that represent, say, a professional body that accredits trainers.

14.4   Teaching as part of an undergraduate or postgraduate course

This section considers the situation where MBSE needs to be taught as part of a university or college course. The generic Use Cases will be revisited and discussed in more detail within the Context of an educational establishment. It is interesting to note that the Teaching Context for this section is the same one that was used in the previous section for professional training. The instances of the Use Cases and the Stakeholder Roles will differ significantly, but the fundamental Need is the same.

14.4.1   Teaching Context – Stakeholder Roles and Use Cases

The generic Stakeholder Roles remain the same as discussed previously, but the following points need to be borne in mind.

- 'Attendee', this Stakeholder Role represents the actual students who are enrolled in the course.
- 'Organiser', this will be the department who offers the course.
- 'Tutor', this will be the actual lecturer for the course.
- 'Demonstrator', this may be the lecturer or any assistants who may supervise example classes and laboratory sessions.
- 'Sponsor', this will be whoever pays the university fees for the students.

In terms of the Use Cases for the course, there are some specific needs that must be considered.

– 'Organise course'. This will involve ensuring that the rooms are booked and available and that any necessary Resources are available. In the case of a college or university, however, this will also include ensuring that the information regarding the course is disseminated to students, such as the time and location of the course.
– 'Teach new skills'. In the case of a university environment, there may be a specific set of skills that is required to be taught.
– 'Ensure quality'. This will involve making sure that the course maps onto any generic teaching Need, such as Bloom's taxonomy that is often used in the UK [1,2,4] or any Competency Frameworks.
– 'Improve quality'. This will entail capturing any problems or mistakes on the course notes, capturing and addressing any comments that are made by the students of the course, updating course materials, ensuring that best practice is being adhered to with regard to the course content, etc. In fact, most universities will have an established means of student feedback that will apply to all courses.
– 'Meet timing constraints'. The timing constraints for a university course are very strict and will rely on the number of teaching and access hours with students, the structure of the timetable, holidays, etc. For example, some courses may be taught in intensive 2-week modules, whereas another course may be 1 h per week over a 20-week duration.

Based on the Context presented here, it is possible to generate a generic course structure that may be used as a start point for defining MBSE courses.

14.4.2   A generic course structure

It is possible to identify several key elements that should be considered when defining a course structure. The structure provided here is intended as a guide only and should be used as a starting point for developing a full course and its associated resources. The structure presented here is based primarily on the experience of the authors in presenting material to students in a university environment.

The diagram in Figure 14.5 shows a generic structure for a university-type course and each of the main elements are explained in more detail in the following sections.

14.4.2.1   The 'Introduction' section

The introduction section of the course contains three main elements, as detailed below:

– 'Background'. It is important to put the course into context and to get the students to understand where the course has come from and why it is necessary. For example, the course may form part of a whole module in a larger course. This may be, for example, a part of a larger systems engineering course, or an engineering course or IT course.
– 'Aims and Objectives'. It is important that the teaching aims of the course are identified early on. A good way to think about this is to generate a Context in the form of a *use case diagram* that will have the teaching aims and objectives

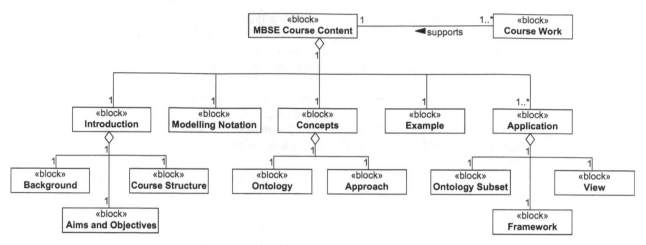

Figure 14.5   Generic course structure for a university-type course

represented as the Use Cases (represented as *use cases*) and the main Stakeholder Roles (represented as the *actors*). One important consideration here is to identify any constraints that may come into play with regard to source Standards or information. For example, it may be that the course needs to map onto the teaching objectives of Bloom, in which case the Standard (realised by the actual Bloom taxonomy) would be represented as an *actor* and there would be an associated *use case*, named something along the lines of 'Meet source standards' or similar. Of course, the *use cases* will also reflect the more functional aims and goals. In fact there is an almost endless set of aims for a course such as this, but it is crucial to identify what they are and then to ensure that course content addresses these aims.

−   Course Structure. This section is relatively straightforward as it simply states the major elements of the course and the relationships between them. In the case of using the information in this chapter, the course structure is simply the diagram in Figure 14.5 along with some explanatory notes.

It is important to use this section to make the course your own and to make sure that it meets all the Needs of the Stakeholder Roles.

This section can use some of the material from Chapter 1, but really should be bespoke to the specific course being taught.

14.4.2.2   The 'Modelling Notation' section

When introducing the modelling notation, it should be stressed that any notation deemed suitable for systems modelling may be used here. In the context of this book, the notation that is chosen is the SysML for reasons that have been discussed previously. It is also worth considering that the notation chosen should not rely on any specific tool or application and that students should be able to work out as much as possible, in the first instance, using a PAPS (pen and paper system) tool. This is for very pragmatic reasons. When attending a course, students will potentially be learning about a number of new ideas and concepts simultaneously. For example, they will be learning about systems engineering, modelling and, in this case, SysML for the first time. It is important to try to isolate each of these initially when communicating the information to the students and then bring them together to form a complete knowledge. If any tool is introduced too early, then students will immediately dive into trying to use the tool, which adds another layer of complexity and shifts the students' focus away from understanding to trying to do.

It is suggested that the actual notation is underplayed and to concentrate on examples and emphasise the consistency checks that are contained in the various frameworks that are presented here, rather than the individual parts of the notation. The notation should be correct and should also be kept to a minimum.

The use of summary sheets is also highly recommended, such as the ones found in the Appendix B of this book. This forms an excellent quick-reference guide for all students. See Part 2 for a full description of the SysML notation and Appendix B for notation summary information.

14.4.2.3   The 'Concepts' section

There are two main conceptual areas that need to be introduced here, the MBSE Ontology and the approach.

–   The MBSE Ontology should provide a clear indication of exactly what the concepts and definitions that will be used in the world of MBSE are. These will form the basis for the rest of the course. These concepts relate directly to the information in Chapter 3.
–   The approach will describe the basic 'Ontology, Framework and Views' approach adopted throughout this book. It should be stressed that the Framework will elaborate on all the concepts introduced in the MBSE Ontology. Simple examples of each View should be provided along with a clear definition of why the View is required. This basic approach is described fully in Chapter 2. Also, a Framework for modelling Architectural Frameworks is defined in Chapter 11.

Of course, the Ontology referred to in this book is the MBSE Ontology and it may be necessary to adopt this to meet your own requirements. Naturally, this will have an impact of referencing Chapter 3.

In terms of teaching people the concepts of the MBSE Ontology, full definitions are provided in Chapter 3, with expanded discussions being presented throughout the book. With regards to remembering the terms in the MBSE Ontology, there is a "memory palace" provided in Appendix H, which provides a memorable story that can be used to recall any of the terms in the MBSE Ontology.

14.4.2.4   The 'Example' section

Examples are best worked out as a group, rather than just providing detailed case studies. Another approach is to provide partial models and then get the students to fill in the gaps in the model. This is a good way to emphasise the consistency between the Views and, if used sensibly, can be an excellent way to show how the SysML model may be navigated by asking the right questions at the right time.

The best types of examples are ones that are based on either real-life situations or situations that most people would have some knowledge of, such as films and books. There are two excellent examples provided in this book that should be considered: the Coffin Escape Stunt application that is discussed in Chapter 5 and the Martian Invasion example discussed in the case study in Part 4. Students should be encouraged to look how they can make the model their own, and see how small changes to any aspect of the model may result in quite large changes to the System as a whole.

The subject of specific examples is left to readers to decide which are most appropriate to the course being taught.

14.4.2.5   The 'Application' section

This section covers the actual application of MBSE to particular work activities. There are a number of such areas covered in Part 3.

All applications should adopt the same style of the basic approach that was introduced in the Approach section and that was described in Chapter 2.

14.4.2.6   Developing 'Course Work'

It is suggested that any course work that is given out is phrased using the terminology of the MBSE Ontology. An example of a generic Project description that is aimed at Requirements modelling with MBSE and uses the Approach to Context-based Requirements Engineering (ACRE) approach that is defined in Chapter 9 is provided in the following box.

Project description:

Choose any example project, such as the development of a robot, and produce the following information, in line with the ACRE process:

– *Requirement Description Views (RDV). These should use SysML requirement diagrams to describe a set of individual requirement.*
– *Context Definition View (CDV). This should take the form of a SysML block definition diagram to show a taxonomy of stakeholder roles.*
– *Requirements Context Views (RCV). These should be SysML use case diagrams that relate back to the stakeholder roles that were identified in the context definition view.*
– *Validation Views (VV). These should be generated using SysML sequence diagrams and relate directly back to the use cases from the requirement context views.*

> – *Traceability Views (TV). These should show the traceability relationships that can be derived from the ACRE ontology.*
>
> *Each diagram should be accompanied with a short textual description, no more than half a page.*
>
> *Please note that marks will only be awarded for the information requested above. Any missing views will lose marks and any additional diagrams will not warrant extra marks. Most of the marks will be awarded for consistency of the diagrams as discussed in the lectures and shown on the summary sheet.*
>
> *Also, do not choose: a cash point machine (ATM), any library system (or variations thereof) or a petrol pump.*

This Project description should be treated purely as a guide. For example, this example asks for some of the ACRE Views (described in Chapter 9) but not others. It is also worth putting some constraints on the solutions, such as not allowing ATMs or library systems, as these are standard examples used in many, many text books. If you don't want 30 copies of a petrol pump submitted, then please consider these constraints seriously!

14.4.2.7 Marking schedules

Due to the rigorous nature of the Project description, it is possible to have an equally rigorous marking schedule. The bulk of the marks should be awarded based directly on the Views that were asked for in the Project description, which will include both the Views and the relationships between the Views and their various elements.

In fact, if a true MBSE approach is applied to the teaching of the course, then it would be possible to automate many of the mundane aspects of the marks, such as consistency checking, by using appropriate tools. This could be achieved by having the students submit their models and then having a bespoke set of rules that represent the marking in the tool. Students could also be asked to submit a written report that must be generated from the tool.

14.4.3 Summary

This section has provided a start point for developing teaching courses and material, whether it is for professional training or university-based teaching. Much of teaching is subjective and will depend upon the nature of the person who is teaching, the format of the courses, the type of Attendees or students, etc. Carrying out a proper Requirements modelling exercise is deemed, therefore, an essential part of ensuring that a quality course is delivered. The information contained in this section is based on many years' experience of teaching and training at many levels and is offered to promote thought, rather than to be prescriptive.

14.5   Competence

When considering individuals for a specific Stakeholder Role, it is essential that they have the right knowledge, skills and attitude required to perform the activities required for the Stakeholder Role. Before their suitability can be assessed, it is important that the knowledge domain and Processes that they will be involved in, in particular the Activities that they will be responsible for and contributing towards, have been identified and are well understood. Once this domain and these Process Activities have been identified, it is then possible to consider which Competencies are necessary for the Stakeholder Role.

Before progressing any further, it is worth defining and differentiating between a few terms that will be used when discussing Competence. These are shown graphically in the diagram in Figure 14.6, which is the same as that in Figure 14.3 but which is worth revisiting to emphasise some of the definitions and differences between terms.

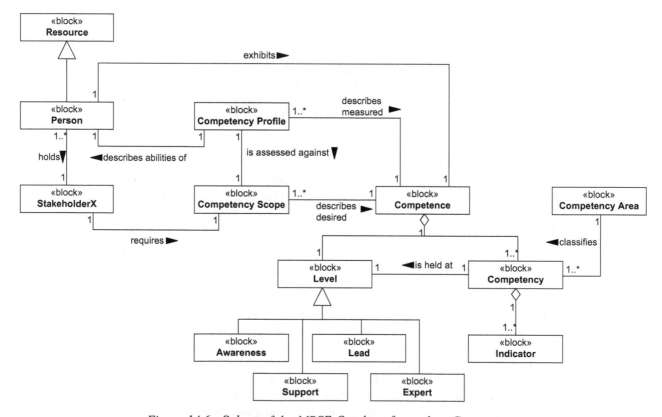

Figure 14.6   Subset of the MBSE Ontology focused on Competence

The diagram here shows that a 'Person' exhibits 'Competence'. The measured ability of a 'Person' is defined as their 'Competency Profile', and the required ability for a specific 'Stakeholder Role' is defined by its 'Competency Scope'.

These terms can be quite confusing, so the following observations should be noted:

- The term 'Competence' is used to refer to the total ability of an individual (Person), rather than a single element. Therefore, each Person in an Organisation has an overall Competence.
- The term 'Competency' refers to a single element of Competence that can be measured and, hence, assessed. The totality of a person's Competencies forms their Competence.
- The term 'Competency Scope' refers to the defined set of Competencies that are required for a specific Stakeholder Role. This Competency scope forms one of the major inputs to a Competency assessment exercise.
- The term 'Competency Profile' refers to a defined set of Competencies that is held by a Person and that relates directly to the Competencies required for a Stakeholder Role, as defined in the Competency Scope. The Competency Profile forms the main outcome of a Competency assessment exercise.

In order to illustrate how Competencies can be used to assess the suitability of a Person, some examples of Competency scopes will be presented in the following sections. It should be stressed that these are shown here for illustrative purposes and, although they may suit your assessment needs exactly, in many cases they will need to be tailored to meet your specific needs.

Competencies may exist on different levels. For example, it is possible to define a set of competencies that are based on an accepted industrial best practice or standard that can be used at a generic level. Competencies may also be defined at a very specific level. The next section (Section 14.7) will discuss the former, generic competencies, while the section following will discuss the latter, more specific competencies. Each approach has its own set of advantages and disadvantages that will be presented as part of the discussion.

14.6   The MBSE Stakeholder Roles

There are a number of key stakeholder roles that may be identified for MBSE. In the context of this book, a suggested start point for looking at the 'Supplier' roles may be based on the diagram in Figure 14.7.

The diagram here shows a Stakeholder View for MBSE using a *block definition diagram*. The Stakeholder Roles are shown in the form of a simple taxonomy used as part of the Processes that are defined and used in Part 3, and that are summarised in Appendix F.

It was shown previously that there are three main types of 'Stakeholder Roles': 'Customer', 'External' and 'Supplier'. As we are looking at the Stakeholder Roles

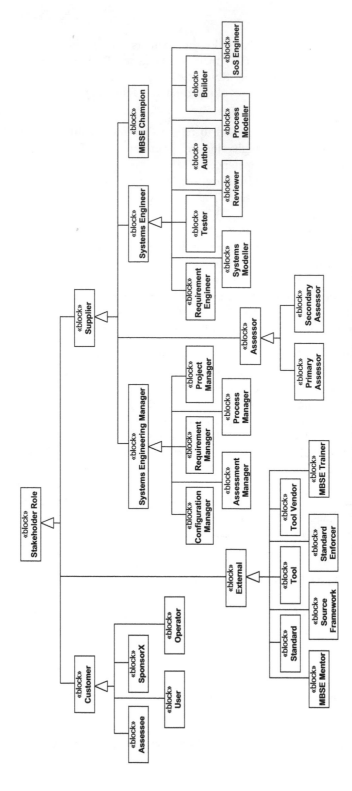

Figure 14.7 Stakeholder view for MBSE Stakeholder Roles

involved with implementing MBSE, the emphasis here is on the 'Supplier' roles rather than the 'Customer' and 'External' roles. There are several examples in previous chapters where such roles have been discussed in some detail.

The main 'Supplier' roles fall into three sub-categories, 'Systems Engineering Manager', 'Assessor' and 'Systems Engineer', plus a single role of 'MBSE Champion'.

The 'Systems Engineer' roles represent the Stakeholder Roles of people who are involved with the engineering activities associated with MBSE, and are described below:

- 'Requirement Engineer'. The area of Requirements engineering is one that is fundamental to systems engineering and, hence, MBSE. The Stakeholder Role here has an emphasis on the understanding of the modelling of Requirements and, therefore, will include Competencies that relate to Context modelling, Use Cases, Scenarios, validation and traceability. Unlike a traditional Requirements engineering Stakeholder Role, there is a strong need for modelling skills as well as understanding the fundamentals of Requirements engineering.
- 'Systems Modeller'. This Stakeholder Role covers a multitude of activities and will, in reality, usually be split into a number of sub-types. Areas of expertise that must be covered here include understanding: Architectures, interfaces, specification, design, testing, traceability, etc. This is perhaps the most loosely defined of all the Stakeholder Roles here as the scope is so large. Having said this, however, it should be pointed out that the Systems Modeller requires very strong modelling skills and these skills may be applied to any of the aforementioned activities. Therefore, it is possible for the Systems Modeller to require a high level of Competence in almost any area, depending on the nature of the work.
- 'Process Modeller'. Having a well-defined Process is crucial when defining any approach to work and, in keeping with the MBSE philosophy, this Stakeholder Role requires good modelling skills as well as an understanding of Process concepts and the business. The Stakeholder Role of the Process Modeller will also require a good understanding of any areas in which the Processes will be either defined or applied; therefore, it is possible for the Process Modeller to require a large number of Competencies.
- 'SoS Engineer'. The Stakeholder Role of the SoS Engineer is one that may be used in conjunction with any of the other Systems Engineering Stakeholder Roles in order to elevate it to the level of Systems of Systems. Key skills here will include integration, understanding of Requirements and verification and validation.
- 'Reviewer'. This Stakeholder Role is essential for all aspects of MBSE. Interestingly, there are two main variations on this Stakeholder Role (not shown in the diagram) that cover "mechanical reviews" and "human reviews". A mechanical review is a straightforward verification review that does not require any real human input but simply executes a predefined rule. Examples of these include SysML syntactical checks and checks based on a Process.

These mechanical reviews tend to be quantitative in that they can be measured in terms of numbers or values and, very importantly, they may be automated. This is essential for MBSE as it is one of the benefits that was discussed in Chapter 1. The human reviews require reasoning and will tend to be qualitative and are typically very difficult, if not impossible, to automate using a tool. The Reviewer Stakeholder Role will require a good understanding of any area in which they are involved with reviewing.

- 'Tester'. This Stakeholder Role is primarily involved with the verification and validation activities that are applied throughout the Life Cycle. Again, the Competencies necessary for this Stakeholder Role may differ depending on the type of testing activities required.
- 'Author'. This Stakeholder Role is concerned with taking models and turning them into beautiful text. Caution needs to be exercised however, as the vast majority of the text generated by the Author will form part of the model; therefore, good modelling skills will be necessary for this Stakeholder Role.
- 'Builder'. This Stakeholder Role is concerned with taking the model and turning it into a real System. This will include building System Elements, integrating them into the System itself, installation and so on. Of course, this is another Stakeholder Role that on real Projects may be broken down into a set of lower level Stakeholder Roles with different skill-sets and, hence, different Competency Scopes.

The 'Systems Engineering Manager' is a generic type of Supplier Stakeholder Role that may be defined as:

- 'Requirements Manager'. This Stakeholder Role will require good management skills but also an understanding of the Requirements engineering activities that are being used on Projects. The manager need not be an expert in this field but certainly needs to understand the fundamentals of the work being carried out. This may seem quite obvious but, in real life, it is worryingly common to find managers who understand very little of what they are managing.
- 'Configuration Manager'. This Stakeholder Role is responsible for ensuring that the model and all the other System Artefacts are correctly controlled, managed and configured. This will require a basic understanding of modelling, as it is the model itself as well as the Artefacts that are generated from it that will be held under configuration control. These artefacts may take on many different forms, such as models, documents, hardware, and software.
- 'Process Manager'. This Stakeholder Role is responsible for the definition, creation and consistency of Processes. This will involve understanding the Need for the Processes and, where necessary, setting up Processes, for example.
- 'Assessment Manager'. This Stakeholder Role describes the role of the Person who is responsible for defining, setting up and managing Competency Assessments.
- 'Project Manager'. This Stakeholder Role describes the role of the Person who will be in charge of the Project as a whole. Note that this Stakeholder Role

requires, quite obviously, good management skills, but will also require that they have a basic understanding of any areas that they will be managing. For example, if the Project Manager is overseeing a Project where an Architecture is being generated, then it is essential that the Person playing this Stakeholder Role has an understanding of what Architecture is.

The third general category of the Supplier Stakeholder Role is the 'Assessor' group that has two variations:

- 'Primary Assessor', this is the Stakeholder Role of the Person who will be leading the Competency Assessment, and therefore will require very good inter-personal skills in order to make the assessment flow in a comfortable and consistent fashion. The Primary Assessor must also have very good working knowledge of all of the Competencies that are being assessed. This is for very pragmatic reasons as anyone who is leading the assessments needs to be able to make judgement calls about whether the assessee truly understands the subject matter and their interpretation of it.
- 'Secondary Assessor', this Stakeholder Role is a Support role associated with the Primary Assessor. A basic knowledge of the Competencies being assessed is required, although not to the level of the Primary Assessor. Good communication skills are also required for this Stakeholder Role, especially good writing skills.

The final Supplier Stakeholder Role that will be discussed is that of the 'MBSE Champion'. Unlike all of the other Stakeholder Roles that are described here, this one may not be immediately familiar to most readers. Nonetheless, it is a crucial Stakeholder Role for the successful implementation of MBSE in an Organisation.

- 'MBSE Champion'. This Stakeholder Role is essential when it comes to implementing MBSE into an Organisation. The MBSE Champion needs to have strong modelling skills but need not be an expert. The MBSE Champion must be visible in the business, have good communication skills and be able to address any MBSE-related queries that arise. The key word here is "address" as it is not the role of the MBSE Champion to solve all the problems. In many instances, it may be that the MBSE Champion can solve issues, in which case all is well and good. The MBSE Champion, however, does need to know who the people holding the appropriate Stakeholder Roles are so that they can help to solve the particular problem. For example, if a tool-related issue arises, then the MBSE Champion may not have the specific expertise to solve the problem outright. On the other hand, they must be able to understand the nature of the problem and then relate this to an expert who can solve it. The Stakeholder Role of MBSE Champion, therefore, will often be one of a go-to Person for all MBSE-related things. The effective use of an MBSE Champion is also one way to ensure that the MBSE knowledge and experience within a business is captured, controlled and used so that the same mistakes are not always repeated.

Example Competency Scopes for all of these Supplier Stakeholder Roles are provided in Appendix G.

The diagram in Figure 14.8 focuses on the 'External' Stakeholder Roles.

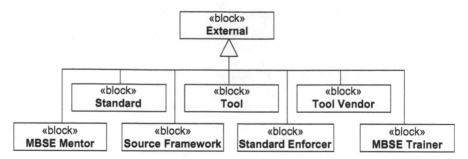

Figure 14.8   The 'External' Stakeholder Roles

The diagram shows the 'External' Stakeholder Roles that have been identified. Many of these are self-explanatory and so will only have brief descriptions, as follows:

— 'Standard', which refers to any commonly accepted reference, such as Standards, best practice models, and Processes, that may be used as part of an MBSE activity.
— 'Standard Enforcer', which refers to the role of ensuring that a Standard has been complied with auditors, etc.
— 'Source Framework', which refers to any accepted Framework, such as Competency Framework and Architectural Framework, that may be used as part of an MBSE activity.
— 'Tool', which refers to any Tool, such as CASE tool, mathematical tool, and management tool, that may be used as part of the MBSE activity.
— 'Tool Vendor', which refers to the provider of such a 'Tool'.

Two of the Stakeholder Roles shown on this diagram are very important for implementing MBSE – the 'MBSE Trainer' and the 'MBSE Mentor'. It may seem at first glance that these roles may be able to be filled on the Supplier side of the business but, as will be discussed later, there are some very important reasons why they are defined here as external to the business.

— 'MBSE Mentor'. The MBSE Mentor must be an expert in the field of MBSE or the specific area of MBSE as necessary. The MBSE Mentor, unlike the MBSE Trainer, must build up an excellent working relationship with the Organisation. This will involve getting to know and understand the nature of the Organisation, getting to know and understand specific issues and getting involved with Projects. Indeed, the MBSE Mentor should be a valuable member of any Project team where they are contributing to a Project. This does not mean that they need to work full-time on the Project, but they must be known to the team and able to be called upon by the team or the MBSE Champion at any point. Continuity is a key to being a good MBSE Mentor, so it should not be the case that every time there is an issue that a different person turns up as the MBSE Mentor. Continuity is essential for a good working relationship.

–   'MBSE Trainer'. The MBSE Trainer must be an established and recognised expert in the field of MBSE. They must possess excellent theoretical knowledge of the subject but also have practical experience of applying MBSE on real projects. Unlike the MBSE Mentor, the MBSE trainer does not need an in-depth understanding of the Organisation nor necessarily need to form an ongoing relationship with the Organisation.

In reality, it may often be the case that the two roles of MBSE Trainer and MBSE Mentor are filled by the same Person. This is perfectly acceptable, and in some cases often desirable to establish continuity. It should be remembered, however, that there are two separate Organisations involved here.

These two Organisations are deliberately defined as External Stakeholder Roles rather than Supplier Stakeholder Roles and this is mainly for pragmatic reasons. Even if the skills exist within the Organisation, it is often a good idea to have these Stakeholder Roles filled by external people for the following reasons:

–   Credibility. Having an established and recognised Person associated with a business lends instant credibility to it.
–   Acceptability. People will accept the opinions and advice of an established "name" far more readily than someone internal to the Organisation. This is even the case when the advice being given is the same!
–   Confidence. Having someone from the outside world coming into a Project and advising, assessing and encouraging the workers provides a tremendous boost to Project team confidence and morale. It provides reassurance that the work is being carried out in the right way and also that the maturity of the business and the individuals (Capability and Competence) is progressing.

Now that the basis for the Stakeholder Roles has been established, it is time to look at the Competencies that are required for each Stakeholder Role. This will be done by looking at the generic Competencies that are related to international Standards and specific Competencies that are related to this book.

14.7   Generic Competencies

This section looks at generic Competencies that are based on industrial best practice. There are many sources available when it comes to defining Competencies, most of which may be described as Competency Frameworks. The concept of a Competency Framework is shown on the MBSE Ontology and can be seen in Figure 14.3. A Competency Framework defines a set of Competencies that is usually specific to a particular industry or technology. In the example presented here, the Framework chosen is a systems engineering best practice model that is known as the "INCOSE Systems Engineering Competencies

Framework" (see [3]). The International Council on Systems Engineering (INCOSE) is an international body that is committed to furthering the discipline of systems engineering. This Framework has been chosen as INCOSE has defined a set of Competencies that is associated with the world of systems engineering, so this is a good choice for a generic Framework to be used as a basis for Competency assessment.

The focus of the Framework is concerned with the concept of 'Systems Engineering Ability', which is described in the diagram in Figure 14.9.

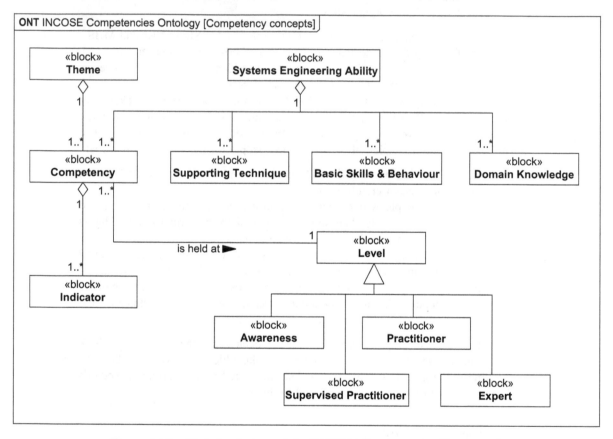

Figure 14.9 High-level view of the INCOSE Competencies Framework

The INCOSE Competencies Framework has a concept of 'Systems Engineering Ability' that may be broken down into four main areas:

- 'Supporting Technique'. A Supporting Technique is a specific technique that is used to support the main Competencies. For example: failure analysis, decision analysis, the use of specific notations and languages, etc. These techniques are very important but are not much of value by themselves as it is when they are used to support and enable Competencies that they start to add true benefits. These supporting techniques tend to be of a more technical nature and, therefore, easier to teach and measure. Due to the sheer number of these different techniques, the INCOSE Framework does not go into any detail in this area, but simply provides a checklist that one may want to refer to when considering such techniques.

— 'Basic Skills & Behaviour'. These represent the soft skills that are required in order to be a systems engineer. This includes skills such as: abstract thinking and communication (verbal/non-verbal, listening, writing, etc.). These softer skills tend to be less easy to teach or, indeed, to measure and can often rely on the objectivity of an Assessor. Again, the INCOSE Framework does not enter into much detail in this area and only provides a simple list of suggested areas that may be considered.

— 'Domain Knowledge'. This knowledge is related directly to the domain in which the Person is working. As systems engineering is a multi-disciplinary subject it can cover, potentially, any domain. As the scope of "any domain" is so wide, it is not covered in any detail in this framework.

— 'Competency'. The INCOSE Framework has managed to side-step all three of the areas covered so far, but the focus of the Framework is very much what is referred to as 'Competency' that refers to the core skills required for a systems engineer. These will be discussed in more detail in the remainder of this section.

Any Competency may be held at a particular Level. The INCOSE Framework identifies four levels of Competency:

— Level 1, 'Awareness'. The Awareness Level indicates that the Person is able to understand basic concepts, to understand how the System fits into their enterprise and to be able to ask relevant questions associated with each Competency. It may be that the Person has no actual experience of the Competency but does display some theoretical knowledge and understanding of it.

— Level 2, 'Supervised Practitioner'. An individual who has Competencies held at the Supervised Practitioner Level will have some real experience of the Competency. They will be able to display true understanding through the application of systems techniques and concepts as part of their work. Also, as the name would imply all this work is carried out under supervision.

— Level 3, 'Practitioner'. An individual who has Competencies held at the Practitioner Level will provide guidance and lead activity in this area. They will be able to supervise people at lower Levels of Competency and may very well lead teams or groups of people.

— Level 4, 'Expert'. The Expert Level represents those rare individuals who truly lead the field in a particular area. They are able to display what they experience by defining best practice, policy or Process within an organisation or industry.

Each Competency may be held at any of these four Levels. At each of the Levels and for each Competency, there are a number of Indicators defined, and it is these

Indicators that are actually assessed. Each Indicator is a simple statement of what must be demonstrated to contribute towards meeting a Competency. The Indicator should be measurable in some accepted form. The way that these Indicators are measured is by looking for evidence that is provided by the assessee. The evidence that may be accepted as valid is defined by Evidence Types. Examples of such Evidence Types are provided later in this chapter when bespoke Competency Scopes are discussed.

14.7.1   Example Competency Scope

The MBSE Ontology states that each Stakeholder Role has its desired abilities defined by a Competency Scope. Therefore, there will a Competency Scope for each of the Stakeholder Roles that has been described so far in this Chapter. An example Competency Scope for the Requirements Engineer is shown in Figure 14.10, based on the INCOSE Systems Engineering Competencies Framework.

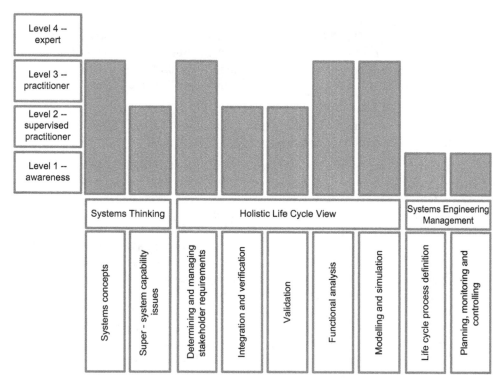

Figure 14.10   The Competency Scope for the Requirements Engineer Stakeholder Role

The chart here shows the Competency Scope for the Requirements Engineer Stakeholder Role. The relevant Levels for each of the Competencies are shown by shading the relevant cells.

There are some interesting features to this Competency Scope when the shape itself is considered. First of all, notice that it is not a "flat" shape, but has highs and lows. The highest Level on this Competency Scope is 'Level 3 – Practitioner', which is typical for most engineers. The areas in which the requirement for Level 3 is present are related to the Stakeholder Role name. Anyone who is involved in Requirements engineering would be expected to have good appreciation of systems engineering generally (the Systems Thinking-themed Competencies) and would be expected to be at the same level for Requirements-related Life Cycle Competencies. This includes 'Determining and managing stakeholder requirements', which is the obvious Competency, but also two other Competencies that require this high Level are closely related: 'Functional analysis' and 'Modelling and simulation'.

Looking at the 'Systems Engineering Management' theme, there is an interesting pattern there also. Both 'Life cycle process definition' and 'Planning monitoring and controlling' are required Competencies, but only at 'Level 1 – Awareness'. This is quite typical as the scope is asking that the individual understands management (Level 1) but is not expecting any relevant experience in this area.

14.7.2 Generic Competency Scope – Evidence Types

When dealing with a standard Framework, such as the INCOSE Systems Engineering Competencies Framework, it is almost impossible to define any Evidence Types as this is far too prescriptive. The best that can be achieved is for some guidelines to be available for defining Evidence Types, an example of which is presented later in this chapter.

14.8 Bespoke Competencies

This section is very similar to the previous one. However, rather than using a standard Framework, a bespoke MBSE Competency Framework will be introduced, based on the contents of this book.

The main concepts associated with the MBSE Competency Framework are based on those of the MBSE Ontology that was discussed previously in this chapter. The concept of the Competency Area from the MBSE Ontology is now expanded to show a taxonomy of Competency Areas and can be seen in the diagram in Figure 14.11.

The diagram here shows an example set of 'Competency Area' that forms the basis for the Competencies that will make up the MBSE Competency Framework, which is defined below. This high-level view of the MBSE Competency Framework is intended to be used as a start point for people to define their own Competency Framework, and there are a few generic pointers that apply to all Frameworks, which are:

– The 'MBSE Concepts Competency Area'. This Competency Area applies to generic concepts and its equivalent can be found in many source Frameworks – for example in the INCOSE Competencies Framework, this is known as 'System Concepts'. When following the MBSE approach defined in this book, this becomes quite simple, as this Competency area is based directly on the

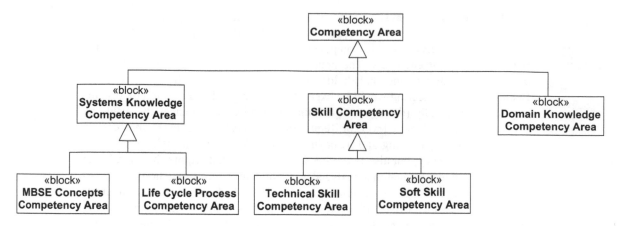

Figure 14.11   Taxonomy of Competency Area types

MBSE Ontology. The MBSE Ontology defines all the concepts for MBSE; therefore, it makes sense that this should be used as a basis for assessing people's understanding of MBSE concepts.

– The 'Life Cycle Process Competency Area'. This Competency Area applies to the Life Cycle Processes that are used within an Organisation and, again, examples of this can be found in many source Frameworks. For example, in the INCOSE Framework, this is known as 'Holistic Life Cycle Activities'. Again, these Competencies will be based on the MBSE Model, especially the MBSE Ontology, the MBSE meta-model and the Processes.

– The 'Technical Skill Competency Area'. This Competency Area applies to specific techniques that are necessary to carry out the MBSE activities in the business. In the context of this book, many of these skills are described in their own chapters or sections, such as ACRE, "seven views", and Modelling Tool Evaluation (MonTE). When following the MBSE approach defined in this book, this becomes quite straightforward, as the Competencies are based directly on the Processes that are summarised in Appendix F.

– The 'Soft Skill Competency Area'. This is a Competency Area that is absolutely essential for all systems engineers, yet the one that is covered the least in the source Frameworks. This Competency Area will often be covered by in-house human-resource Processes and Frameworks rather than stemming from technical areas.

– 'Domain Knowledge Competency Area'. This Competency Area is directly related to the field in which the business operates and will usually be an in-house Framework that maps onto some industry-specific source.

The MBSE Ontology identifies four Levels of Competence at which individual Competencies may be held. These levels will be discussed in more detail later in this chapter but for the sake of the following Competency Scope, these levels are: 'Level 1 – Awareness', 'Level 2 – Support', 'Level 3 – Lead' and 'Level 4 – Expert'.

14.8.1   Example Competency Scope

The MBSE Ontology states that each Stakeholder Role has its desired abilities defined by a Competency Scope. Therefore, there will be a Competency Scope for each of the Stakeholder Roles that have been described so far in this Chapter. An example of a Competency Scope for the Requirements Engineer Stakeholder Role is shown in Figure 14.12, based on the MBSE Competency Framework.

The Stakeholder Role of Requirements Engineer needs a strong, practical background in all three of the bespoke Competency Areas. In an ideal world, these should all be held at 'Level 3 – Lead', as shown here. However, if there is a team of Requirements Engineers, then it may be possible to have one Stakeholder Role held at 'Level 3 – Lead' supported by a number of people who hold 'Level 2 – Support' so that their combined profiles match the Competency Scope shown here. Notice also how this Stakeholder Role requires a basic, Level 1 understanding of many of the other Competencies.

This Competency Scope may be compared to the one described in Figure 14.8 that shows the Competency Scope for the same role based on the generic Competencies from the INCOSE Competencies Framework.

14.8.2   Bespoke Competency Scope - Evidence Types

One of the advantages of a bespoke Framework is that it is indeed possible to define Evidence Types that relate to the Competencies in the Framework. These Evidence Types will reflect the individual business and the way that they work. An example of these for the MBSE Competency Framework will be presented later in this chapter.

14.9   Generic vs. specific Competencies

Each of the two approaches described in the previous sections has its own set of advantages and disadvantages. One of the main advantages of using the generic Framework is acceptance. One of the main reasons to use an industry best practice model or Standard is that they will be recognised in the industry and, in the case of some, at an international level. Of course, this can be very advantageous as it provides a common way that a Person's Competence can be assessed that will be recognised in more than one Organisation. This has a lot of attraction from an individual's point of view as it provides a mechanism to demonstrate one's own Competence that may be used in a number of Organisations and, hence, it will make moving between Organisations simpler. From a company's point of view this is also good because it makes the whole area of recruitment far simpler. Indeed, when recruitment is based (either wholly or partly) on Competency assessments, it is possible to define a set of Competency Scopes that represent the Stakeholder Roles that make up the post and issue them to potential employees.

The downside of using the generic approach is that, because the Competencies are defined at a high level, the definitions may not map onto the way that an

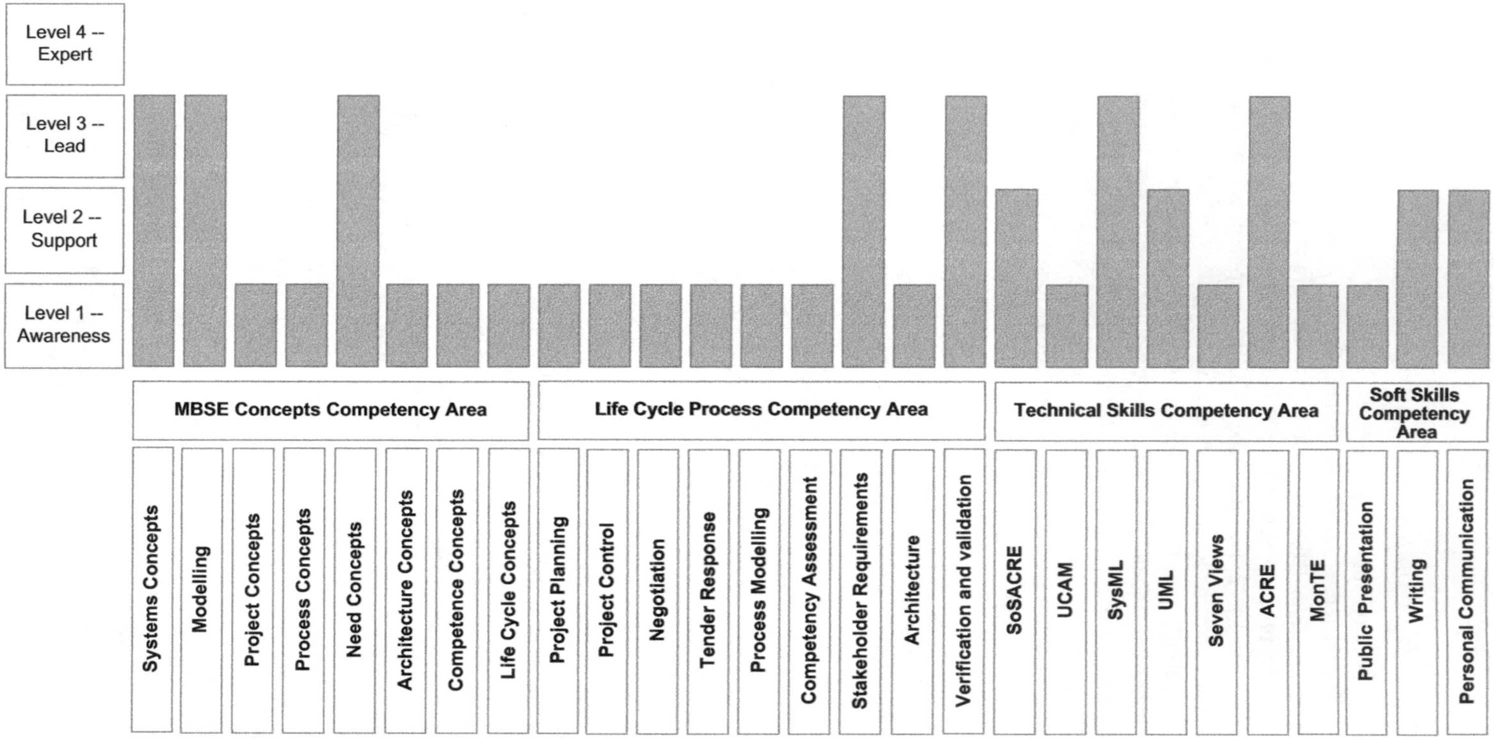

Figure 14.12 Example Competency Scope for the Requirements Engineer Stakeholder Role

Organisation does their business. Nor will they reflect any specific techniques, Processes or Tools that may be required by the company. Indeed, this is one of the main strengths of the bespoke approach described in the MBSE Competency Framework. When defining specific Competencies it is possible to get an exact match on the skills required by the Organisation. This also relates to the ability to be able to define Evidence Types that are specific to the business, whereas this is impossible for the generic Framework.

Therefore, in summary:

– The generic approach is good for establishing a common baseline for Competencies that are recognised by different Organisations.
– The specific approach is weak in terms of recognition, as it is tailored to a particular Organisation.
– The generic approach is weak when it comes to specific Tools, techniques and methodologies, as it is, by its nature, aimed at the high level.
– The specific approach is strong in meeting the exact requirements of an Organisation.
– The specific approach enables the definition of explicit Evidence Types.

The use of Competencies is very important when it comes to getting the right Person for a Stakeholder Role – for a far more detailed discussion, see Reference 5.

14.10   Defining a bespoke Competency Framework

This section looks at some of the practical issues involved with defining a bespoke set of Competencies, in the form of a Framework, and how to define the individual Competencies along with their associated Indicators.

The approach to defining a bespoke Competency Framework is to use the MBSE approach that has been introduced and discussed within this book. It is possible and, indeed, desirable to use as much as the model as possible when defining the Competencies. In particular, the following parts of the model will be used:

– The MBSE Meta-model, which defines the fundamental building blocks that make up the MBSE model.
– The MBSE Ontology, to identify and define the concepts and terms. The Competency activity should be part of a wider MBSE activity and, if so, then this should build upon the existing MBSE Ontology.
– The various frameworks, which define the Views that are required in the form of Viewpoints. An example of this was provided in Chapter 8 that was concerned with expanded Process modelling.
– Views, which define the key Artefacts required to carry out Competency assessment, such as Competency Scope (the 'Competency Scope View') and its resulting Competency Profiles (the 'Competency Profile View').

– A set of Processes will also be required if you want to actually perform assessments. Again, this should be part of a wider MBSE activity and form part of the overall Process library. An example set of Competency assessment Processes, known as the Universal Competency Assessment Model (UCAM), is provided in Appendix F.

When it comes to defining the Competencies and their associated Indicators, then the MBSE approach can be of great help and can significantly shorten the time taken to define the content of the Framework.

The set of Processes provided in this book relates to the field of competence, in particular Competency assessment, and this approach is known as UCAM. This set of Processes also contains two Processes that relate to pre-assessment activities, in particular to creating a bespoke Competency Framework. These two Processes are shown in the diagram in Figure 14.13.

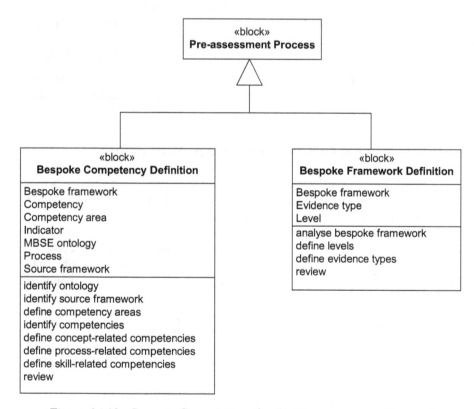

Figure 14.13   Process Context View for the 'Pre-assessment Process'

The diagram in Figure 14.13 shows the two 'Pre-assessment Process' Processes that are the 'Bespoke Competency Definition' Process and the 'Bespoke Framework Definition' Process. Each of these is described in more detail in the following sections.

14.10.1 The 'Bespoke Competency Definition' Process

This Process is concerned with identifying and defining the Competency Areas, Competencies and Indicators associated with a bespoke Framework. The Activities in the Process are described in the following sub-sections.

14.10.1.1 The 'identify ontology' Activity

This Activity is relatively straightforward and consists of identifying the Ontology that will underlie the bespoke Framework. In this example, this will be the MBSE Ontology.

14.10.1.2 The 'identify source framework' Activity

The main aim of this Activity is to identify any source Competency Frameworks that may be used as an input to create the bespoke Competency Framework. An example of this would be the INCOSE Competencies Framework that has been used elsewhere in this book.

14.10.1.3 The 'identify competencies' Activity

The MBSE Competency Framework that was introduced previously in this chapter has a number of Competency Areas that have been defined and that allow the individual Competencies to be classified into groups. These Competency Areas are shown in the diagram in Figure 14.14.

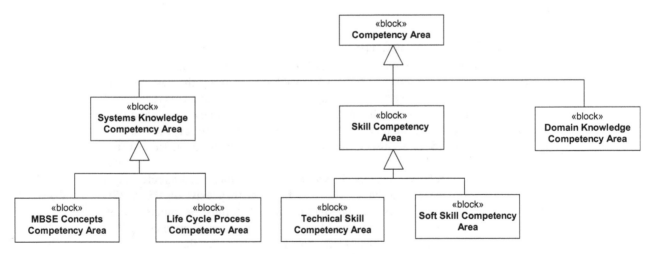

Figure 14.14 Defining 'Competency Area'

The diagram in Figure 14.14 shows the taxonomy of the various types of 'Competency Area' that was introduced previously in this Chapter and that is recapped here mainly for consistency.

Each Competency Area was identified based on the overall MBSE Model.

The next step is to define a set of Competencies that will make up the Framework and form the basis of any Competency Assessment Activities.

In a typical Framework there will be groupings of Competencies. When the source Frameworks are considered, there are a number of standard classifications that can be identified. The terminology used here is based on the MBSE Ontology and its associated Competency Framework (described in more detail in Appendix G). These standard groupings, represented in the MBSE Competency Framework by the 'Competency Area' concept, are:

- General or specific concepts, represented in the MBSE Competency Framework as the 'MBSE Concepts Competency Area'.
- Process- and Life Cycle-related concepts, represented in the MBSE Competency Framework as the 'Life Cycle Process Competency Area'.
- Technical skill-related concepts, represented in the MBSE Competency Framework as the 'Technical Skill Competency Area'.
- Soft skill-related concepts, represented in the MBSE Competency Framework as the 'Soft Skill Competency Area'.

In all of these areas, with the exception of the 'Soft Skill Competency Area', the information required to define the Competencies is already known and exists already within the model. The MBSE model (including the MBSE Ontology, Framework and Views) could be expanded to include the soft skills, but this is beyond the scope of this book.

14.10.1.4   The 'define concept-related competencies' Activity

This competency area is based on the MBSE Ontology and is defined in order to determine if the assessee holds sufficient knowledge concerning the key concepts that make up the Ontology. For example, consider the 'Systems Concepts' competency that forms part of the 'MBSE Concepts Competency Area', and then determine which areas of the ontology apply. In the MBSE Ontology, the concepts shown in Figure 14.15, as a subset of the MBSE Ontology, were identified as being relevant.

Each of the Ontology Elements shown here has been identified as relevant to the Systems Concepts Competency. The very fact that they exist on the MBSE Ontology means that they must be important concepts that must be understood by any Person who holds a Stakeholder Role that requires this Competency. The Indicators in the Competency, therefore, should identify areas that the assessee must understand.

An example of what the Systems Concepts Competency looks like is shown in Table 14.1.

Table 14.1 shows the name of the Competency along with a high-level description of that Competency. Alongside this is a set of Indicators that have been identified and that are based directly on the MBSE Ontology.

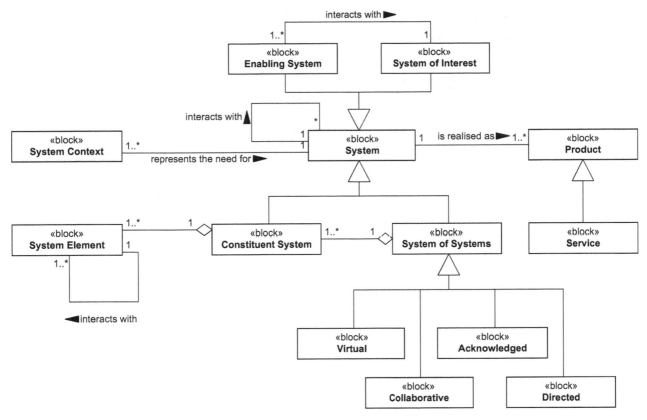

Figure 14.15   Subset of the MBSE Ontology focused on concepts relevant to the 'Systems Concepts' competency

14.10.1.5   The 'define process-related competencies' Activity

The competencies that exist in the Life Cycle Process Competency Area are, again, quite straightforward to define, as the information concerning the Processes is already part of the MBSE model. The information for the general Processes will relate to both the Ontology and the need for that particular Process.

The example in Table 14.2 shows the Competency definition for the Process Modelling Competency.

Table 14.2 has the same structure as the one shown in Table 14.1 but this time, rather than all of the Indicator descriptions deriving from the MBSE Ontology, the wider MBSE model is plundered for information. In general terms, the MBSE Ontology, the meta-model and the need for the Process will be prime sources. Table 14.3 shows which parts of the MBSE model the definitions of the Indicators are derived from.

As can be seen in this table, several parts of the MBSE model are used in order to define the Process-related concepts.

Table 14.1   Indicators for the 'Systems Concepts' Competency

Systems Concepts	This Competency relates to the concept of a 'System' and the related concepts that are necessary to demonstrate understanding of this concept.	• Understands the concept of a 'System' • Understands the concept of a 'System Context' and its relationship to a 'System' • Understands the concepts of 'System of Interest' and 'Enabling System' and the relationships between them • Understands the concepts of 'System of Systems' and 'Constituent Systems' and the relationships between them • Understands that there are different classifications of 'System of Systems' • Understands the concepts of 'System Element' and its relationship to 'Constituent System' • Understands that a 'System' is realised by one or more 'Product' • Understands the concepts of a 'Product' and a 'Service' and the relationship between them

Table 14.2   Definition for the Process Modelling Competency

Process Modelling	This Competency reflects the ability to model Processes	• Understands the need for Process • Understands what a Stakeholder Role is • Understands the drivers behind Process modelling (complexity, communication, lack of understanding) • Can define what a Process is, in terms of Activities, Artefacts and Stakeholder Roles • Is aware of different approaches or techniques to Process modelling • Is aware of the importance of Views • Understands how a good Process model may be used (assessment, audits, Process improvement, etc.)

Table 14.3   Origin of Indicator descriptions on the MBSE model

Indicator	Origin
Understands the need for Process	Framework view – 'Requirement Context View' for the Process
Understands what a Stakeholder Role is	MBSE Ontology for Process concepts
Understands the drivers behind Process modelling (complexity, communication, lack of understanding)	Framework view – 'Requirement Context View' for the Process
Can define what a Process is, in terms of Activities, Artefacts and Stakeholder Roles	MBSE Ontology for Process concepts
Is aware of different approaches or techniques to Process modelling	MBSE Process Model
Is aware of the importance of Views	MBSE Meta-model
Understands how a good Process model may be used (assessment, audits, process improvement, etc.)	Framework View – 'Process Content View' for the Process

14.10.1.6   The 'define skill-related competencies' Activity

When defining skill-related Competencies, then the Process model within the MBSE model is used as the main source. This is true for both Technical and Soft-Skill areas, but, as was stated previously, this book is focusing mainly on the Technical Skills, although examples of Soft-Skill-related Competencies are provided in Appendix G.

Table 14.4 shows an example of a Technical Skill-related Competency, in particular, the "Seven Views" Process modelling skill, that defines a specific technique.

The table here shows how the various Indicators of the "Seven Views Approach" Competency are described.

14.10.1.7   The 'review' Activity

Finally, the partial 'Bespoke Framework' that has been generated so far is reviewed and is then used as the main input to the next Process – the 'Bespoke Competency Framework Definition' Process.

14.10.2   The 'Bespoke Framework Definition' Process

This Process is concerned with identifying and defining the Levels and Evidence Types associated with a bespoke Framework. The Activities in the Process are briefly described in the following sub-sections.

14.10.2.1   The 'analyse bespoke framework' Activity

The main aim of this Activity is to take the partial Bespoke Framework from the previous Process and to consider different Competencies and their associated Indicators that will form a basis of the Levels and Evidence Types.

Table 14.4 Definition of a Technical Skill-related Competency

Seven Views	This Competency reflects the ability to use the "Seven Views" approach to Process modelling	• Must hold the 'Process Modelling' Competency • Must understand "seven views" Framework and each of the Views • Must understand the need for each View • Must understand the consistency relationships between the Views • Must understand how each View may be used • Must appreciate different Tools and techniques that can be used to realise the Views • Must understand that the Framework is tailorable • Must understand that Views may be created and developed in different orders depending on the application of Process modelling • Must understand how the Framework fits into the wider enterprise (such as Life Cycles and enterprise architecture)

14.10.2.2   The 'define levels' Activity

The main aim of this Activity is to define one or more Levels that each Competency may be held at. These may be based directly on one of the source Frameworks, such as the INCOSE Competencies Framework, or may be created specifically for the bespoke Framework, as defined in the MBSE Competency Framework that is used in this book.

These four Levels that form part of the MBSE Competency Framework are described in more detail below.

– *'Level 1 – Awareness'*. The main aim of this Level is for the assessee to demonstrate that they possess the ability to '*speak knowledgeably about a particular aspect of the competency. The main aim is for the assessee to demonstrate that they understand each indicator fully, and back this up with examples – either theoretical or real-life.*'
– *'Level 2 – Support'*. The main goal of this Level is for the assessee to demonstrate that they can '*reflect the ability to implement the concepts that were discussed at level 1 for this competency*'.

- *'Level 3 – Lead'*. The aim of this Level is for the assessee to demonstrate that they can *'reflect the ability to be able to lead the activity that was described at level 1 and implemented at level 2'*.
- *'Level 4 – Expert'*. The aim of Level 4 is for the assessee to demonstrate that they can *'reflect the ability to be a true, recognised expert in the field that is described by this competency'*.

The MBSE Ontology shows that each Competency is made up of one or more Indicators and they form the basis of assessing the Competency. Each Indicator states an aspect of the Competency that the Assessee must be able to demonstrate that they have met. This is achieved through the Assessee providing evidence and this being compared against one or more predefined Evidence Type.

In terms of what each Indicator looks like, this differs depending on the Level that the Competency is held at:

- Each Indicator at 'Level 1 – Awareness' will be a unique description of some aspect of knowledge, skill or attitude that must be met by the Assessee. Therefore, the Indicators will differ depending on the Competency.
- Each Indicator at 'Level 2 – Support' is the same for each Competency.
- Each Indicator at 'Level 3 – Lead' is the same for each Competency.
- Each Indicator at 'Level 4 – Expert' is the same for each Competency.

This approach of a unique set of Indicators at Level 1 and then generic (in that they are the same for each Level, regardless of the Competency) ones for each of the other Levels is one that is widely adopted in the world of Process maturity assessment – see References 7 and 8 for examples of this.

14.10.2.3   The 'define evidence types' Activity

For each Level that was defined in the previous Activity, it is now necessary to identify and define a number of acceptable Evidence Types. These Evidence Types will be entirely dependent on the Organisation and the way that they work. For example, Evidence Types that are suitable for a large multinational Organisation will not necessarily be the same as those defined for a small company with just a few employees.

The Evidence Types should also be considered alongside the rest of the MBSE Ontology and the MBSE Process Model, as Artefacts, Activities, the MBSE Ontology, etc., are excellent sources for the definition of Evidence Types.

In the MBSE Competency Framework, these Evidence Types are summarised as shown in Table 14.5.

Table 14.5 shows the Evidence Type that is acceptable at each of the four Levels, along with some examples of typical evidence that may be acceptable. A full definition of all of these terms can be found in Appendix G.

14.10.2.4   The 'review' Activity

Finally, the now-complete Bespoke Framework is now reviewed.

Table 14.5   Summary of Evidence Types for the MBSE Competency Framework

Level	Evidence type	Examples of evidence
Level 1 – Awareness	Tacit knowledge Informal training course	Ability to discuss terms and concepts Course attendance certificate
Level 2 – Support	Formal training course Activity	Course attendance certificate Contribution to artefact Sworn statement from manager Contributed Artefacts are formally reviewed
Level 3 – Lead	Educational qualification Lead activity Reviewer	Certificate of award Responsibility for Artefact Reviewed Artefacts
Level 4 – Expert	Professional qualification Publications Public speaking Activity definition	Certificate of award Papers, books Presentations, reviews of talk Policy, Process, etc.

14.10.3   Competency assessment

In order to put these Competency Scopes into practice, it is necessary to carry out a Competency assessment exercise. One approach to performing these assessments is the (UCAM) that is described in Chapter 8 and is defined in Appendix E. By using UCAM, it is possible to assess against any Competency Framework, as a model-based approach is taken, which means that as long as a source Framework can be modelled, it can be assessed.

14.11   Summary

One of the common themes of this book is that 'People, Process and Tools' are essential for realising any systems engineering Capability. This chapter has looked at how the People element of this may be addressed by discussing, in particular:

- The importance of teaching, training and education. This was achieved by discussing the requirements for education and providing a high-level teaching guide for anyone involved with model-based requirements engineering education.
- The definition of Competency Scopes. Two Competency Frameworks were discussed – one generic and one specific – and an example set of Competency Scopes is provided that may be used as a starting point for Competency assessment.

The issue of People is just one of the three main enablers, and Process and Tools will be discussed in Chapters 15 and 16.

The complete MBSE Competency Framework, including a complete set of Competency Scopes for the MBSE Stakeholder Roles, is presented in Appendix G.

References

1. Holt J. *A Pragmatic Guide to Process Modelling.* 2nd edn. Swindon, UK: BCS publishing; 2009
2. Bloom B.S. (ed.). *Taxonomy of Educational Objectives: The Classification of Educational Goals.* Susan Fauer Company, Inc; 1956. pp. 201–207
3. International council on systems engineering (INCOSE). *INCOSE Competencies Framework, Issue 2.0.* INCOSE; November 2006
4. Anderson L.W., Krathwohl D.R., Airasian P.W., Cruikshank K.A., Mayer R.E., Pintrich P.R., *et al.* (eds.). *A Taxonomy for Learning, Teaching, and Assessing — A Revision of Bloom's Taxonomy of Educational Objectives.* Boston, USA: Addison Wesley Longman, Inc; 2001
5. Holt J., Perry S. *A Pragmatic Guide to Competency: Tools, Frameworks and Assessment.* Swindon, UK: BCS publishing; 2011
6. *CMMI for Development, Version 1.3.* Carnegie Mellon University Software Engineering Institute; November 2010 [Accessed 16 February 2011]. http://www.sei.cmu.edu/library/abstracts/reports/10tr033.cfm
7. *ISO/IEC 15504 Information Technology — Process Assessment, Parts 1–9.* ISO Publishing; 2006–20011

Chapter 15

The 'Process'

'There are only two mistakes one can make along the road to truth; not going all the way, and not starting.'

Buddha

15.1 Introduction

This chapter looks at the pragmatic issues involved when trying to realise the model-based systems engineering approach in this book in any Organisation or business. In particular this chapter looks at how it is possible to ensure that the right approach is in place – in other words, the Process.

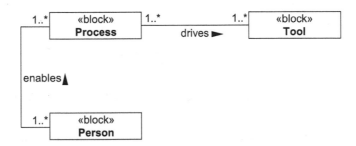

Figure 15.1 Pragmatic issues with implementing the approach

By way of a recap, the diagram in Figure 15.1 shows the three main elements that must be in place in order to realise successful MBSE, in particular:

– The 'Person', by which we mean *competent* people, rather than just any people.
– The 'Process', which is in place in order to realise the approach.
– The 'Tool', which may range from a whiteboard or log book, to standard office tools, to a full-blown automated tool set, to any combination of these.

In order to understand the basic needs for providing competent people, the 'Process Context' shown in Figure 15.2 was generated.

The diagram in Figure 15.2 shows the Context for the Process aspect of MBSE. Both systems engineering and MBSE describe an approach to realising successful Systems and at the heart of this approach is the concept of the Process ('Provide process').

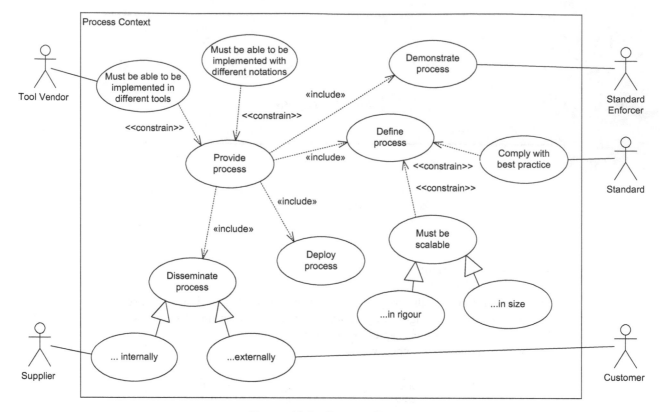

Figure 15.2   Process Context

Any Process that is defined ('Define process') needs to be flexible in a number of ways:

– The Process needs to be able to be realised using a number of different techniques ('Must be able to be implemented with different notations'). A good Process should be independent of any specific techniques. Of course, when considering model-based systems engineering, then there is an immediate constraint that modelling techniques must be used, but the Process should be flexible enough to allow the use of different modelling notations.

– The Process must be able to be realised using a number of different Tools ('Must be able to be implemented in different tools'). The Process should drive the Tools and not the other way around. With this in mind, it is essential that the Process may be implemented using any number of Tools.

– The Process must be scalable in terms of size and duration of Project ('Must be scalable' '...in size'). The Process must be able to be applied to very small Projects lasting only a few days or weeks, right up to long-term Projects lasting many years.

– The Process must be able to be applied at different levels of rigour ('Must be scalable' '...in rigour'). For example, it must be able to be applied to a

System where there are no safety concerns right up to a safety-critical or mission-critical System.

It is also essential that any Process that is defined is able to be mapped onto best practice ('Comply with best practice') and, related to this, it must be possible to demonstrate the Process ('Demonstrate process') in terms of an audit or assessment. Finally, it is crucial that the Process is deployed effectively. It does not matter how well a Process is defined, if it is not deployed effectively ('Deploy process') and if the people do not know about it ('Disseminate process') then the Process is potentially useless.

In order to satisfy these needs, it is first necessary to revisit the Process aspects of the MBSE Ontology.

15.2 MBSE Ontology revisited

The diagram in Figure 15.3 shows the subset of the MBSE Ontology that focuses on Process-related concepts.

The diagram here shows the MBSE Ontology for the main concepts that are related to the Process. These are defined as follows:

— 'Process' – a description of an approach that is defined by: one or more 'Activity', one or more 'Artefact' and one or more 'Stakeholder Role'. One or more 'Process' also defines a 'Service'.

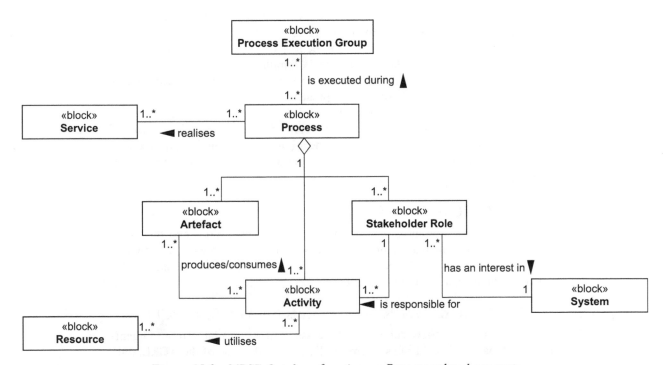

Figure 15.3   MBSE Ontology focusing on Process-related concepts

- 'Artefact' – something that is produced or consumed by an 'Activity' in a 'Process'. Examples of an 'Artefact' include documentation, software, hardware, and systems.
- 'Activity' – a set of actions that need to be performed in order to successfully execute a 'Process'. Each 'Activity' must have a responsible 'Stakeholder Role' associated with it and utilises one or more 'Resource'.
- 'Stakeholder Role' – the role of anything that has an interest in a 'System'. Examples of a 'Stakeholder Role' include the roles of a 'Person', an 'Organisational Unit', a 'Project', a 'Source Element', and an 'Enabling System'. Each 'Stakeholder Role' requires its own 'Competency Scope' and will be responsible for one or more 'Activity'.
- 'Resource' – anything that is used or consumed by an 'Activity' within a 'Process'. Examples of a 'Resource' include money, locations, fuel, raw material, data, and people.
- 'Process Execution Group' – a set of one or more 'Process' that are executed for a specific purpose. For example, a 'Process Execution Group' may be defined based on a team, function, etc.

The term 'System' has been defined previously and the link between Processes and Life Cycles is realised by the concept of the 'Process Execution Group'.

15.3   Defining the Process

The approach to Process modelling that is advocated in this book is the "seven views" approach [3] that was introduced and described in Chapter 7. The aim of this chapter is to discuss how Process may be realised effectively within an organisation, so it is assumed that the reader is familiar with the "seven views" approach. The example Process that is used in this chapter (and the next chapter that covers Tools) is defined using this approach.

The Process chosen is the one that describes the approach for requirements modelling (ACRE). A partial model will be presented in this chapter for the sake of brevity, but the full Process can be seen in detail in Chapter 9 and in Appendix F. For more information on the "seven views" approach see Chapters 7 and 8 and Reference 2.

15.3.1   The ACRE Process

The Views that are presented here are: the Process Content View and the Information View. The main reason for this is that the main discussion will focus on how various Activities in the Process can be realised and how the Artefacts vary, depending on the application of the Process.

15.3.2   The ACRE Process – the Process Content View (PCV)

The Process Content View defines the Processes that are available in an Organisation and may be thought of as a 'process library'. In the case of the ACRE, only single Process will be described here, but this is intended to be a start point for people to use when defining their own bespoke Processes for model-based requirements engineering (Figure 15.4).

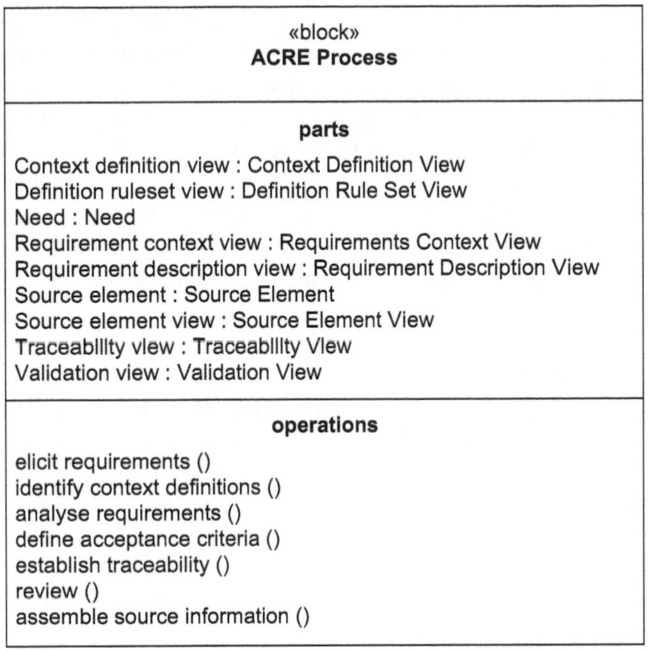

```
┌─────────────────────────────────────────────────────┐
│                     «block»                           │
│                   ACRE Process                        │
├─────────────────────────────────────────────────────┤
│                                                       │
│                     parts                             │
│ Context definition view : Context Definition View     │
│ Definition ruleset view : Definition Rule Set View    │
│ Need : Need                                           │
│ Requirement context view : Requirements Context View  │
│ Requirement description view : Requirement Description View │
│ Source element : Source Element                       │
│ Source element view : Source Element View             │
│ Traceabillty vlew : Traceabillty Vlew                 │
│ Validation view : Validation View                     │
├─────────────────────────────────────────────────────┤
│                   operations                          │
│ elicit requirements ()                                │
│ identify context definitions ()                       │
│ analyse requirements ()                               │
│ define acceptance criteria ()                         │
│ establish traceability ()                             │
│ review ()                                             │
│ assemble source information ()                        │
└─────────────────────────────────────────────────────┘
```

Figure 15.4   Process Content View for the ACRE Process

The Artefacts in the Process must all be consistent with the ACRE Framework. In this case, the Artefacts have been simplified and are defined as follows:

–   'Source Element'. This is taken directly from the MBSE Ontology and represents anything that is used as a source for the requirements engineering exercise.
–   'Requirement View'. This represents the set of all the Views that are used as part of ACRE, which are: the Source Element View, the Requirement Description View, the Definition Rule Set View, the Requirement Context View, the Context Definition View and the Validation View, which are summarised in Figure 15.5. For a full description of each View, see Chapter 9 and Appendix F.
–   'Need'. Again, this is taken directly from the MBSE Ontology and represents the fundamental Requirements behind the Process.

The Activities in the Process describe what actually needs to be done to execute the ACRE Process. These Activities are described as follows:

–   'assemble source information'. The main aim of this Activity is to identify the Source Elements and to create the Source Element View.
–   'elicit requirements'. The main aim of this Activity is to identify, gather and define the Source Elements that will be used as a basis for the Requirements.

In terms of the framework, this Activity will consume the Source Element View (containing Source Elements) as an input and produce the Requirement Description View (containing Requirement Descriptions).

- 'identify context definitions'. The main aim of this Activity is to identify and define the Stakeholder Roles and System Elements that will be used as a basis for the Context Definition Views. In terms of the framework, this Activity will consume the Source Element View (containing Source Elements) as an input and produce the Context Definition Views (the Stakeholder Context Definition View and/or the System Context Definition View).
- 'analyse requirements'. The main aim of this activity is to understand the Requirements of the System by looking at their Use Cases. Remembering that a Use Case is a Need (in this case a Requirement in Context), this Activity is mainly concerned with generating a number of Contexts, based on the Context Definition Views in order to understand the Needs. In terms of the framework, this activity will consume the Context Definition Views (the Stakeholder Context Definition View and/or the System Context Definition View) and the Requirement Description View as inputs and produce the Requirement Context Views (containing Stakeholder and Use Cases, along with all their inter-relationships).
- 'define acceptance criteria'. The main aim of this Activity is to consider how each Use Case will be validated. In terms of the framework, this Activity will consume the Requirement Context Views as an input and produce the Validation Views (a combination of Stakeholder Scenario Views, System Scenario Views and Constraint Validation Views).
- 'establish traceability'. The main aim of this Activity is to ensure that traceability between all the Views has been defined. In terms of the framework, this Activity will consume, potentially, all of the Views and will produce the Traceability Views.
- 'review'. The main aim of this Activity is to assess, consider and provide an indication of how fit for purpose the Process Artefacts are. In terms of the framework, this Activity will consume all of the Views that have been generated and will produce commented forms of the Views.

The way that these Activities are executed will depend on the way that the Process is being used, according to the type of Project that it is being applied to. The basic Activities will remain the same, but the techniques and Tools that are used to realise each Activity may differ enormously – this will be discussed later in this chapter along with the consideration of the use of the Process and the use of Tools, which will be covered in more detail in Chapter 16.

The Information View defines all of the Process Artefacts and the relationships and dependencies between them. Fortunately, this has already been done in great detail in this book in the form of the ACRE Framework. This is because the ACRE process is an information-driven process.

The diagram in Figure 15.5 shows that there are six different types of 'Requirement View' in the ACRE Process: the 'Source Element View', the 'Requirement

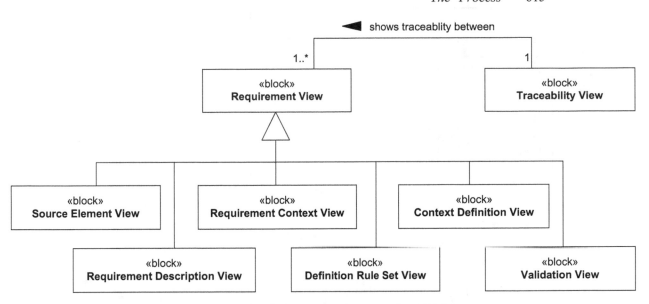

Figure 15.5 The different types of view in the ACRE process

Description View', the 'Definition Rule Set View', the 'Requirement Context View', the 'Context Definition View' and the 'Validation View'. One or more 'Traceability View' show the traceability between one or more 'Requirement View'.

Each of these Views is shown in more detail on the ACRE Framework, as shown in Figure 15.6.

The diagram here shows the main ACRE Framework. This Framework will form the basis of the Process implementation by highlighting different sets of the Views that may be implemented, depending on the scale and rigour of the Project.

15.4   Using the Process

The Process presented here may be used in a flexible way, in terms of the size and rigour of the Project. The Process may be used at any level of abstraction of the System and be used in a number of different ways. This section looks at three examples of how the Process may be implemented, although it can be implemented in many more ways.

When using the Process for different levels of rigour or for different scale Projects, the fundamental Process stays the same, but it is the number of Views produced that changes and the way in which they are realised. The way in which each view is realised will be discussed in more detail in Chapter 16 that discusses the Tool aspect of MBSE.

The complete set of Views needed to perform a complete requirement modelling exercise has been introduced previously in Chapter 9, but the number of Views produced may vary depending on the scale or rigour of the Project.

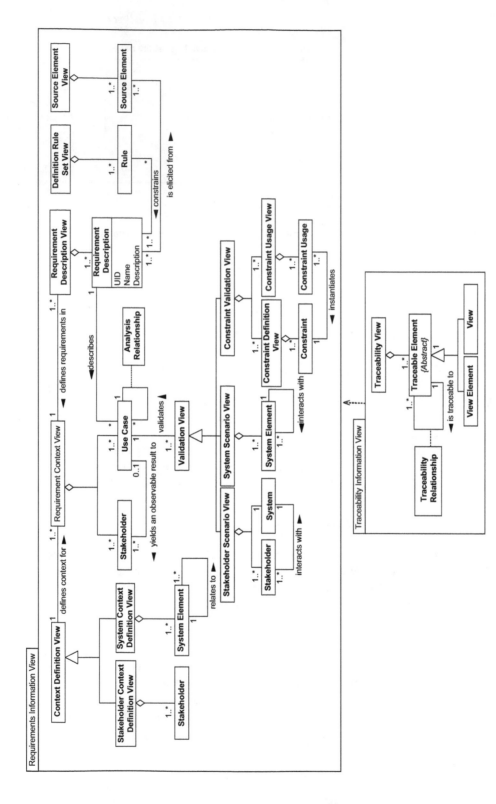

Figure 15.6   The ACRE Framework

When referring to the 'scale' of a Project we are really talking about the size of the Project in terms of the Resources. For example, a small Project may only last for a single week, which may only leave a morning, or even a few hours, to carry out all the requirements Activities. At the other end of the spectrum are Projects that may last many years and the requirements Activities themselves may initially take months or even years, and then they will also be re iterated throughout the Project.

When referring to the level of rigour of the Project, we are really talking about the criticality of the Project or System. For example, the Project may develop a System where, if it fails, lives are put at risk. Such safety-critical Systems will have a high level of rigour compared to, say, a System that allows someone to edit documents. Other Systems that have a high level of rigour include: mission-critical Systems (where the failure of the System may result in the failure of some critical activity (such as the navigations system on a missile or spaceship), real-time Systems (where the correctness of a result depends not only on the logical value, but also on the timing characteristics of the System) and business-critical Systems (where the failure of the System may result in the Organisation going out of business). The general term "critical system" will be used in this book to refer to any of the earlier described types of System.

For the purposes of the discussion in this chapter, three levels of scale (small, medium and large) and three levels of criticality (non-critical, semi-critical and critical) will be considered. For the purposes of the discussion, these are described further as:

–   Small-scale Project – a Project involving one or very few people, with a timescale that is measured in days or weeks and a very limited budget. Small Projects will often have very few Needs that are often poorly defined. Examples include proof-of-concept Projects, small proposals, and small bench top demonstrators.
–   Medium-scale Project – a Project involving one or a few small teams of people, with a timescale that is measured in months and a limited budget. Medium-scale Projects will often have a small, but quite well-defined set of initial Needs. Examples include many pure software Projects, and some manufacturing design Systems.
–   Large-scale Projects – a Project involving many teams of people, with a timescale measured in years and with a large and complex budget. Large-scale projects have a high number of Needs that, while being understood individually, have many complex relations between them. Examples of large-scale Projects include large complex programmes, Systems of Systems, and enterprise Systems.
–   Non-critical level – a Project where the correctness of operation of the developed System has no implication on the environment or human life. Examples include typical apps, office-type software, and library-type Systems.
–   Semi-critical level – a Project where the correctness of operation of the developed System may have implication on the environment or human life, depending on circumstances. Examples include design tools and satellite navigation Systems.

–   Critical level – a Project where the correctness of operation of the developed System has a large implication on the environment or human life. Examples include weapons Systems, direct control Systems, flight control Systems, and health Systems.

This section discusses which Views will be produced for three different types of application of the Process, but the emphasis is on the description of the Activities, rather than how each will be implemented – this is covered later in Chapter 16 in the Process deployment section.

In order to illustrate the flexibility of the Process, three different approaches to implementing the Process on different types of Project will be discussed, which are:

–   Quick and dirty Process implementation – the Process is implemented very quickly and informally with few Artefacts and limited configuration control.
–   Semi-formal Process – the Process requires more rigour in its implementation, requires good management and configuration control and requires traceability between Artefacts and audit trails.
–   Formal Process – the Process must be implemented as rigorously as possible with a high degree of control, configuration, traceability and mathematical rigour.

The next three sections relate these different approaches to different scales and levels of rigour. It should be noted that these are all provided for guidance only, but will make a good start point for your own Process implementation.

15.4.1   Example use – quick and dirty Process

The quick and dirty Process is often used on Projects that have a small-scale level and that have a non-critical level of rigour.

For example, consider a Project that has a timescale of single week for a proof-of-concept Project.

The diagram in Figure 15.7 shows the subset of Views that are realised when applying a quick and dirty Process. The Activities in the Process may be executed as follows:

–   'elicit requirements'. In this case, the Needs or Requirements would come from informal sources, indicated here by the lack of a Source Element View.
–   'Identify context definition'. In this case, only the Stakeholder Roles are being considered, so the 'System Context Definition View' is missing.
–   'Analyse requirements'. This will form the main Activity in this Process and will involve creating a Context for each of the Stakeholder Roles that have been identified.
–   'define acceptance criteria'. Not performed formally, indicated by the lack of Validation Views. In reality, however, many people may be considering validation as they are defining the Use Cases even if they are not documented.
–   'establish traceability'. Not performed formally, indicated by the lack of Traceability Views.
–   'review'. This may take the form of a simple, non-documented review where the model may be annotated with review comments.

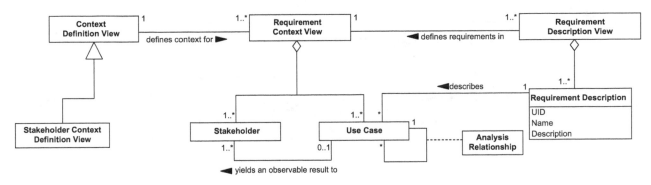

Figure 15.7 Example of a quick and dirty Process

As can be seen, we are still following the bones of the ACRE Process here, albeit in an informal way. Despite this informality, the type of Tools used to implement the Process will have a bearing on how rigorous these Artefacts are.

One of the main points that is being made here is that even when there not being much time or many Resources available, it is still possible to adopt a standard approach. Of course, the approach here is not formal and the tools that are being used may very well be pens and paper (PAPS) but the same fundamental approach is still being enforced.

15.4.2 Example use – semi-formal Process

The semi-formal Process is typically used on small-to-medium Projects of a non-critical nature.

The diagram in Figure 15.8 shows the subset of Views that are realised when applying a semi-formal Process. The Activities in the Process may be executed as follows:

– 'elicit requirements'. In this case, the Needs or Requirements would come from sources that can be formally identified and be represented as the Source Elements in the Source Element View.
– 'identify context definition'. In this case, only the Stakeholder Roles are being considered, so the 'System Context Definition View' is missing.
– 'analyse requirements'. This will form a major Activity in this Process and will involve creating a Context for each of the Stakeholder Roles that have been identified.
– 'define acceptance criteria'. For each of the Use Cases, a number of Validation Views will be generated. At the semi-formal level, these will be the Stakeholder Scenarios and will describe the Stakeholder Role interactions with the System.
– 'establish traceability'. This Activity will generate the Traceability Views. If the modelling is carried out properly, then this should be a straightforward Activity as all the traceability paths have already been identified in the model.
– 'review'. This may take the form of a formal review meeting where the ACRE Views that have been generated are assessed and commented on.

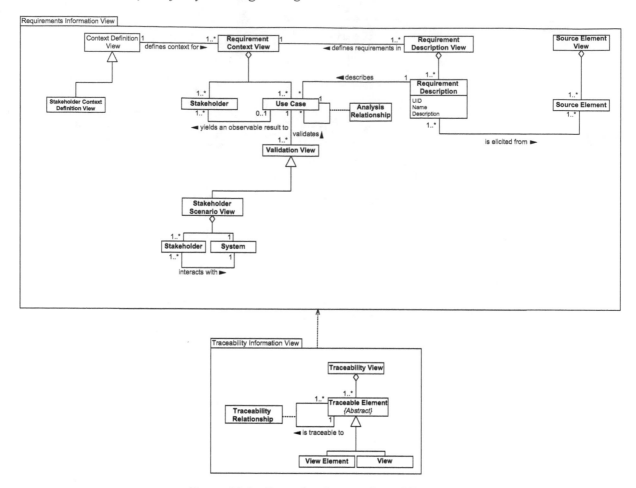

Figure 15.8   Example of a semi-formal Process

The Process here is starting to look a lot more like the full ACRE Process, with many of the Views being generated.

15.4.3   Example use – formal Process

The formal Process will be executed on Projects that are critical in some way, for example, on safety-critical Systems and for mission-critical Systems. The formal Process may also be used on long-term Projects and Projects that have a high cost associated with them.

The diagram in Figure 15.9 shows the subset of Views that are realised when applying a semi-formal Process. The Activities in the Process may be executed as follows:

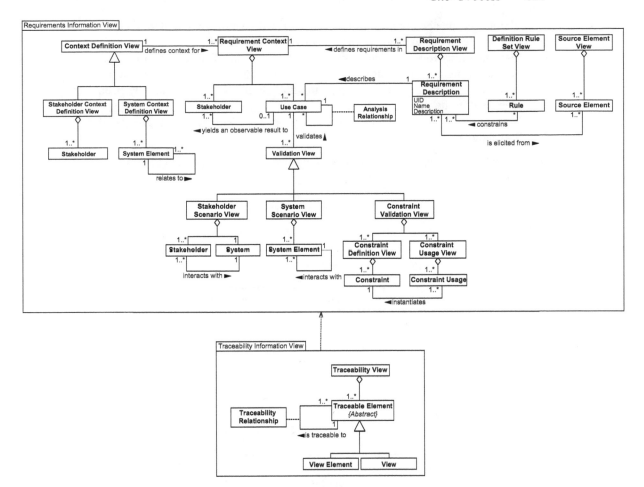

Figure 15.9   Example of a formal Process

- 'elicit requirements'. In this case this will be a major activity. All the Source Elements for the Needs will be formally identified and captured in the Source Element View. The Needs or Requirements themselves now have some limitations on the way that they can be defined as there is now the Definition Rule Set View to consider that will define Rules for how the Needs can be described.
- 'identify context definition'. In the formal Process, this will usually involve looking at both the Stakeholder Context Definition View and the System Context Definition View.
- 'analyse requirements'. There will be a large number of these Views generated and, of course, the more Views that there are, the more analyse that will be needed to be carried out.

- 'define acceptance criteria'. In this case this will be a massive undertaking, as all three levels of validation Scenarios will be considered.
- 'establish traceability'. This Activity will generate the Traceability Views. If the modelling is carried out properly, then this should be a straightforward if a very time-consuming Activity as all the traceability paths have already been identified in the model.
- 'review'. This will involve many formal reviews with different groups of Stakeholder Roles.

The formal Process represents all of the Views that can be considered in the ACRE Process.

15.4.4   Summary of process implementation

Table 15.1 summarises the discussions from the last few sections.

Table 15.1   Summary of Process implementation

Type of implementation	Scale	Rigour	Typical views
Quick and dirty	Small	Non-critical	Requirement Description View, Requirements Context View, Context Definition View
Semi-formal	Small, medium	Non-critical, semi-critical	Source Element View, Requirement Description View, Requirements Context View, Context Definition View, Validation View, Traceability View
Formal	Large	Semi-critical, critical	All views

Again, it should be stressed that the information provided here is for guidance only but can be used as an excellent start point for deciding the strategy and planning your own Process implementation.

Chapter 15 is concerned with Tools and has a discussion that is very closely related to this section, where Table 15.1 will be re-presented with examples of which Tools can be used for different implementations.

15.5   Deploying the Process

So far, we have discussed the Process itself and how the Process can be instantiated, depending on the level of scale or rigour required by the System. This is, of course, essential but all of this great work can still come to nothing if the Process is not deployed effectively. Deployment is not just a matter of providing people with a Process manual, but is a complex area in itself where a number of Needs must be considered. These Needs are summarised by the breakdown of the 'Deploy process' *use case* on the diagram in Figure 15.10.

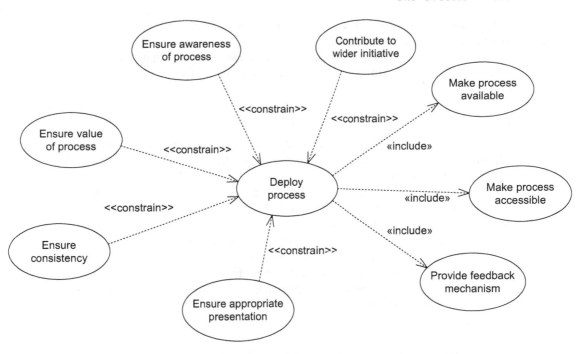

Figure 15.10   Breakdown of the 'Deploy process' use case

Each of the *use cases* in Figure 15.10 provides an important discussion point concerning the general issue of Process deployment. Each of these will now be discussed in more detail.

15.5.1   'Make process available'

The Process must be made available to each Person who is to use the Process. In the past, Process documentation and information has taken the form of large, printed and often very heavy documents, famous for gathering dust on shelves. In today's business, web-based approaches (whether they are intranets or the Internet) are far more efficient ways to store, update and disseminate information among workers.

There are other issues that come into play at this point, such as security issues and who should be permitted to have availability of different Processes. Some Processes may be proprietary or commercially sensitive, so it may be necessary to restrict availability. For example, it is a good idea, in principal, to make all of your Processes publically available so that people can have confidence in your approach. However, for many service-based companies, this can be a bad idea as it makes the Capability of the business open to third parties who may steal or unscrupulously copy the Process.

Another example of not allowing widespread availability of a Process may relate to security. For example, a lot of government Organisations may be concerned with matters that apply to national security such as defence, intelligence, and counter-terrorism. In such cases, again, it may be necessary to restrict the availability of Process information.

This point also comes into play when it comes to audits and assessments as it is impossible to perform either of these without having free access to the Process.

15.5.2   'Make process accessible'

The medium used to convey the information must be one that is accessible to all relevant users. Relating back to the previous point, the end users must be able to access the information easily.

It is possible to have a Process that is "available" to Process users, yet at the same time is not "accessible". It may seem quite a safe assumption that, for example, everyone has access to a web browser, but not everybody has access to the Internet. In many cases this may be because of security issues, such as no Internet connection at all or that a limited-access intranet is being used. Another example of Process users not having access to the Internet is for field engineers who may be working in remote locations where there is simply no access to a network. In such cases, it may be necessary to download Process information to portable devices, such as tablets or laptops. In extreme cases, one may even be forced to use physical media, such as paper and maybe go to such lengths as providing laminated sheets! (See Appendix B and fire up the laminator.)

Another issue to consider is that if a third-party product is being used as part of the deployment, then licencing will become an issue. If the Processes are deployed using a bespoke Process tool, then is it necessary to hold a licence for each end user? If this is the case then the cost of purchasing the licences may rocket and there may also be a danger of locking into a single Tool.

15.5.3   'Ensure awareness of process'

People must be aware that the Process exists. There is no point having the best Process in the world if nobody knows anything about it.

The classic problem of having a printed manual that nobody knows about is just as applicable in the digital age as it was decades ago. You may have a beautifully defined Process that is available and accessible to all, but it is essential that people are aware of the Process in the first place.

This is a problem that is particularly prevalent in large Organisations where there are a multitude of Processes in many forms (Standards, procedures, work instructions, etc.). Rather than people not being aware that a Process exists, the same problem may manifest itself because there are simply too many Processes, or there is too much Process information available to people.

It is essential that people know not only that a Process exists, but scope of the Process and the Context that it is intended to be used in. This information will exist if the Process has been modelled properly but, again, this has to be conveyed to the end users of the Process.

15.5.4 *'Ensure appropriate presentation'*

The format of the presentation of the Process must be one that people can understand. This may not necessarily be the same as the SysML modelling that was used to engineer the Process.

When developing any System, the techniques that are used to develop the Processes are not necessarily what will be used to communicate the Process information to the end users. Therefore, the Processes may be developed using a structured approach (such as the "seven views") and using a standard modelling notation (such as the SysML) but the final output may look very different.

Many people, especially non-technical folk, would be horrified to see the final Process definition in SysML, and many prefer text descriptions and simplified flow charts. The important point here is to ensure that the final format of the Process deployment is one that the target audience is both familiar and comfortable with. If this means text only, then so be it! If this means a less rigorous notation, such as flow charts, then so be it! If this means drawing odd symbols and colouring them in, then so be it! It is essential that the process information is communicated as efficiently and effectively as possible.

A word of caution here, however, as any format may be chosen, but this must be consistent with the Process model. Any alternate format or presentation must be treated as another view on the model rather than a stand-alone interpretation. Remember, it is the approach ("seven views") and the notation (SysML) that provide the rigour and confidence that the Process is correct, the medium of communication is irrelevant, proving it forms part of the model.

15.5.5 *'Ensure value of process'*

The use of the Process should make people's lives easier. This applies on two levels – both in terms of the added value of the Process and in terms of the ease of use of the Process.

One of the reasons why the whole area of Process gets a bad press is that on the occasions when people have been exposed to Process, the whole activity gets failed. One of the fundamental reasons behind this failure is: not understanding the need for the Process in the first place. Chapter 7 discusses this in more detail but, essentially, by ensuring that the Needs for the Process have been captured effectively, this can be avoided.

It must be also very easy to access the information. In fact, it should involve the minimum of effort and be less hassle than opening a book. The whole activity of accessing and navigating the Process should involve as few "clicks" as possible and be intuitive and quick. This may seem a little extreme, but if the information is very easy to access, then people will use it – if not, then they will not.

15.5.6 *'Provide feedback mechanism'*

The deployment should be a two-way activity in terms of information flow. Any Process will constantly evolve as time goes on and an essential part of this is being able to obtain feedback from the end users of the Process.

The application of Process modelling techniques and deployment techniques are very important, but there will always be room for improvement in the Process. This may not necessarily be caused by errors in the Process, but may simply reflect changes in the working environment, changes in Products or Services, changes in Tools, software changes, etc. The key point here is that the world is apt to change and providing an effective feedback mechanism is one way to begin to address this issue.

15.5.7 *'Ensure consistency'*

The deployment should be consistent with the underlying Processes. This could be in terms of the Project management or other Processes that are being used.

In too many cases it can be seen that an excellent job has been done of defining a Process, but then this flies out of the window when the Process is deployed. This may be due to complete ignorance of the underlying Process, misinterpretation of the Process model, lack of interoperability between Tools, etc.

The deployment of the Processes should be carried out in a structured and consistent fashion – in other words by following a Process.

15.5.8 *'Contribute to wider initiative'*

The deployment should contribute to wider initiatives within the enterprise. Any work involving Processes will be an ongoing activity if only for the simple fact that the world turns and things change. Therefore, Processes will need to be checked on an ongoing basis to ensure that they are fit for purpose. Any MBSE initiative will inherently include a large element of Process, so it is essential that the Processes are developed and deployed effectively.

The Process activity may involve contributing to a continuous Process improvement, such as CMMI and ISO 15504. Of course, this should fall under the umbrella of MBSE, but in many organisations Process improvement activities will be seen as being separate from MBSE.

The *use cases* described here are not intended to be exhaustive but, rather, to stimulate thought-about Process deployment. These use cases should be used as a start point for defining your own needs for Process deployment.

15.6   Compliance mapping with best practice

One of the constraints that were identified as part of the approach in Figure 15.2 was to ensure that the Process complies with best practice in the form of Standards, best practice models, etc. This section provides a simple example of how traceability back to source Standards, best practice models and other Processes may be defined.

The Standard that is used as a basis for this example is ISO 15288, 'Systems and software engineering – System life cycle processes' [4].

The approach taken to establish this mapping is the one used in the "seven views" approach to Process modelling as described in Chapter 7.

Before any of the Processes or Activities in the Process can be compared, it is essential that we can ensure that the two Processes can "speak" to one another. This requires making sure that the concepts and terms used in both the source Standard (ISO 15288) and the target Process (ACRE) can be mapped together. When using the "seven views" approach, this entails comparing the Ontologies in the Process Structure Views (PSVs) for each Process. This can be seen in the diagram in Figure 15.11.

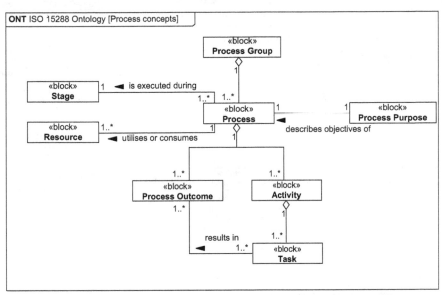

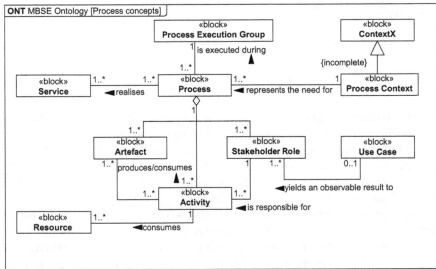

Figure 15.11   Mapping between two Process Ontologies using Process Structure Views

Figure 15.11 shows how the concepts and terms used in both Processes compare with one another. This is achieved by comparing and contrasting the Ontologies, or PSVs, for each Process and drawing up a mapping between them. This activity can then be repeated at a lower level by comparing the Processes, as shown in the diagram in Figure 15.12.

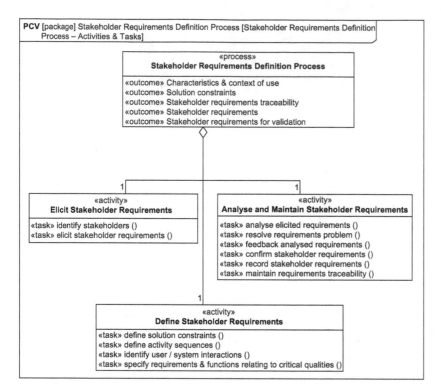

Figure 15.12   Mapping between Processes

The diagram in Figure 15.12 shows the Process Content Views for each Process and this then becomes the basis for a mapping exercise between the two. Based on the comparison of these two Views, it is now possible to draw up a table that maps between the Activities and Tasks in ISO 15288 and the Activities in ACRE.

The approach taken to define the mapping is the same as that introduced in Chapter 7 and that has its Process set defined in Appendix F.

The mapping shown in Table 15.2 shows not only the mapping for the Activities, but also the specific Views that are generated by each Activity. This is provided purely to show how the mappings can be tailored to show indirect mappings, in this case from the Standard to the Process Artefacts, by simply adding a new column.

Table 15.2 Compliance mapping between ISO 15288 and ACRE

ISO 15288		ACRE	
Stakeholder Requirements Definition Process		ACRE Process	ACRE View
Activity	**Task**		
elicit stakeholder requirements	identify stakeholders	identify context definitions	Stakeholder Context Definition View
	elicit stakeholder requirements	elicit requirements	Requirements Description View
define stakeholder requirements	define solution constraints	analyse requirements	Process Context View
	define activity sequences	define acceptance criteria	Validation Views
	identify user–system interactions	define acceptance criteria	Validation Views
	specify requirements as functions relating to critical qualities	analyse requirements	Process Context View
analyse and maintain stakeholder requirements	analyse elicited requirements	analyse requirements	Process Context View, Context Definition Views
	resolve requirements problem	analyse requirements	Process Context View
	feedback analysed requirements	review	All views
	confirm stakeholder requirements	review	All views
	record stakeholder requirements	baseline	All views
	maintain requirements traceability	baseline	Traceability Views

This can also be taken a step further as a mapping between STUMPI and ISO 15288 already exists (see Chapter 7). Therefore, we can very easily map between the three sources: STUMPI, ISO15288 and ACRE. These two sets of mapping may now be brought together, as shown in Table 15.3.

It is often desirable to demonstrate compliance to more than one source Standard that can add a large amount of complexity to the problem. This complexity, however, can be minimised by effectively developing new models of Standards or, even more preferable, reusing existing models for the source Standards. Indeed, part of the attraction of employing an MBSE approach is the idea of being able to reuse models or their parts. Therefore, all that is required is a set of source Standards or references that are related to MBSE that can be used to show further compliance. By sheer non-coincidence, this book already contains a rich source of models that represent these sources. In Chapter 3, the MBSE Ontology was developed and this was done partly by modelling existing sources of information and then abstracting the MBSE Ontology from them; therefore, we already have a ready store of source models. Indeed, it is possible to map between any or all of the information sources that were introduced and referenced in Chapter 3, which is exactly the approach that was taken to define the MBSE Ontology.

Table 15.3 Compliance mapping with ACRE Views

ISO 15288		STUMPI Activity	ACRE
Stakeholder Requirements Definition Process		**Stakeholder Requirements**	**ACRE Process**
Activity	**Task**		
elicit stakeholder requirements	identify stakeholders	identify stakeholders	identify context definitions
	elicit stakeholder requirements	elicit requirements	elicit requirements
define stakeholder requirements	define solution constraints	analyse requirements	analyse requirements
	define activity sequences	define acceptance criteria	define acceptance criteria
	identify user–system interactions	define acceptance criteria	define acceptance criteria
	specify requirements as functions relating to critical qualities	analyse requirements	analyse requirements
analyse and maintain stake-holder requirements	analyse elicited requirements	analyse requirements	analyse requirements
	resolve requirements problem	analyse requirements	analyse requirements
	feedback analysed requirements	review	review
	confirm stakeholder requirements	review	review
	record stakeholder requirements	produce stakeholder requirements document	baseline
	maintain requirements traceability		baseline

15.6.1 Automated compliance

When a true MBSE approach is taken to Process modelling that is then implemented using sharp Tools, then it is possible to automate the demonstration of compliance between Processes.

This actually becomes a relatively simple matter, provided that Traceability Views can be set up and then automated in the tool. To realise this, Traceability Views are set up between the MBSE Process model and any source Process models. In the example presented here, we mapped between ISO 15288 and the ACRE Process; therefore, a set of Traceability Views would be set up between the two that is based on the compliance exercise that was presented in the example.

On real Projects, all Artefacts that are produced can be easily shown to trace back to the Process, and then compliance tables, charts, matrices, etc., can be automatically produced by the Tool that can be used as evidence for part of an audit or assessment.

This is another example of a true benefit of MBSE but one that requires People, Process and Tools.

15.7 Summary

This section has shown how the ACRE Process can be used for real-life Projects and situations. This entailed the following:

- The use of the Process. It is important that the Process is flexible in terms of its scale and rigour and three examples of how the ACRE Process may be used were shown, along with which Views would be necessary. Again, these three Views are for information only based on previous experience and do not feel limited to them.
- The deployment of the Process. The Process may be very well defined, but if it is not deployed correctly, then the Process will fail. A number of key characteristics for Process deployment were discussed.

So far, the People and Process aspects of the ACRE have been discussed, which leaves the Tool aspect, which will be discussed in Chapter 16.

References

1. Holt J. *A Pragmatic Guide to Process Modelling*. 2nd edn. Swindon, UK: BCS Publishing; 2009
2. *INCOSE Competencies Framework, Issue 2.0*. International Council on Systems Engineering (INCOSE); 2006
3. ISO/IEC. *ISO/IEC 15288:2008 Systems and Software Engineering – System Life Cycle Processes*. 2nd edn. International Organisation for Standardisation; 2008

Chapter 16
The 'Tool'

'Any tool is a weapon if you hold it right.'

Ani DiFranco

16.1 Introduction

This chapter looks at the pragmatic issues involved when trying to realise the model-based systems engineering (MBSE) approach in this book in any organisation or business. In particular this chapter looks at how it is possible to ensure that effective Tools are in place.

This chapter is clearly heavily related to Chapters 14 and 15 and, as such, should not be read in isolation, but should bear in mind the totality of this part of the book.

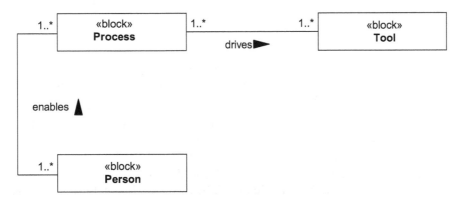

Figure 16.1   Pragmatic issues with implementing the approach

By way of a recap, the diagram in Figure 16.1 shows the three main elements that must be in place in order to realise successful MBSE, in particular:

−   The 'Person', by which we mean *competent* people, rather than just any people.
−   The 'Process', which is in place in order to realise the approach.
−   The 'Tool', which may range from a whiteboard or log book, to standard office tools, to a full-blown automated toolset, to any combination of these.

In order to understand the basic needs for providing effective Tools, the 'Tool Context' shown in Figure 16.2 was generated.

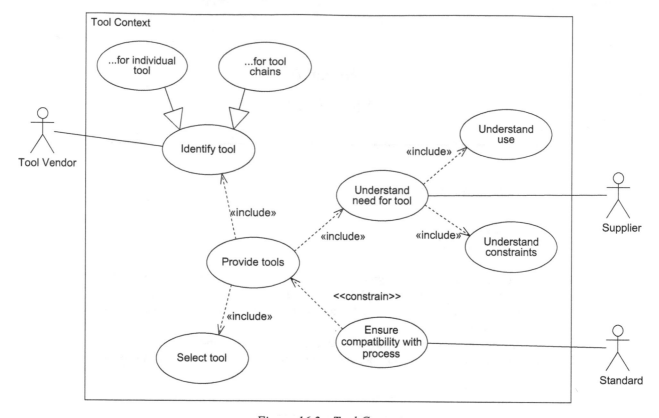

Figure 16.2   Tool Context

In order to realise the full benefits of MBSE, "sharp" tools are essential ('Provide tools'). There are four main issues that will be discussed in this section:

- Considering the types of Tools available ('Identify tool'). Before any sort of Tool selection may be performed, it is important to identify the types of Tools that may be applicable to MBSE whether these are individual Tools ('... for individual tool') or Tool chains ('... for tool chains').
- Understanding the need for the Tool ('Understand need for tool'). This includes considering how the Tools will be used ('Understand use') and what the major constraints on its use will be ('Understand constraints').
- Using Tools with existing processes ('Ensure compatibility with process'). This involves looking at which main Views in the Process each Tool will be used for, as well as how the Tools will be used in conjunction with one another.
- Considering Tool selection ('Select tool'). When the Tools have been identified and their usage is understood, then it is important to carry out a Tool selection exercise that will look at various aspects of each Tool, measure them and then use the results as a basis for deciding between Tools.

Each of these four issues will be discussed in detail in the following sections.

16.2 Considering the types of Tools available

There are many different types of Tools that can be used for MBSE that must be considered when performing any Tool selection. It is impossible to look at specific Tools within the context of a book like this, so general types of Tools will be considered. It should also be borne in mind that for successful MBSE we are not just looking at modelling Tools, but must also consider any Tool that may contribute to or support the MBSE activities.

A taxonomy of basic Tool types is shown in the diagram in Figure 16.3.

The diagram in Figure 16.3 shows a basic taxonomy of different types of 'Tool' and their related capabilities, shown by 'Tool Capability'. This is by no means intended to be exhaustive, nor is it intended to restrict the scope of Tools that may be used for MBSE, but it reflects Tools that may be used to support activities that are discussed in this book.

The concept of a 'Tool' has two basic types: 'Tool Chain' and 'Individual Tool', which will be discussed in more detail in the following sections.

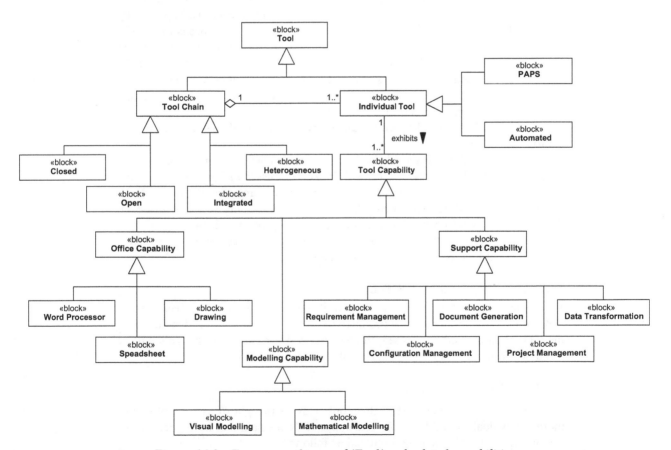

Figure 16.3   Taxonomy of types of 'Tool' and related capabilities

16.2.1   The 'Individual Tool'

This section discusses the two basic types of individual Tools that are considered in this book – the PAPS Tools and the automated Tools.

16.2.1.1   The 'PAPS' Tool

The PAPS (Pen And Paper System) is the oldest and most widely used Tool and still one that is used by almost every modeller today and the only Tool that is compatible with every other Tool on the market. The so-called PAPS Tools are available to anyone and everyone, have the advantage of being free (if you own a writing instrument and writing surface), are eminently portable and run on a number of different platforms – mainly paper and whiteboards.

The PAPS Tools are often overlooked or dismissed by many people, but they form a very important and necessary part of any professional systems engineer's toolkit. Regardless of the automated Tools available, the use of PAPS should be the first of the Tools touched by anyone until they have thrashed out their basic ideas and concepts.

With the advances in technology over the last few years, the PAPS tools are now no longer confined to their original pads of paper or whiteboards. The ubiquity of smartphones, smart boards and automated pen and paper pads means that PAPS Tools can truly form part of an MBSE toolset. One of the problems with a PAPS system has always been the reliance on pieces of paper, but this is no longer the case because as long as whatever is written can be captured digitally, and then it can become a configurable item. These configurable items may then be imported into automated tools and form part of a formal audit trail.

The PAPS Tools may be used to realise any or all of the Views required by any approach to MBSE.

Having said all this, it should also be borne in mind that in all but the simplest of Projects (see small-scale and non-critical Projects discussed in Chapter 15) a PAPS Tool alone is not sufficient. For any real-life Projects of any size, the PAPS Tools are perfect, and indeed recommended, for early brainstorming sessions; however, they fall down heavily when it comes to model management and automation.

Just to emphasise this last point – automated Tools are essential, but so is the PAPS Tool and its use should not be dismissed.

16.2.1.2   The 'Automated Tool'

When the term 'Automated Tool' is used, it is referring to software-based Tools that are intended to increase the productivity of the users. However, depending on the type of automated Tools used, the benefits will vary enormously. This will be discussed in more detail when Tool capabilities are considered.

16.2.2   The 'Tool Chain'

A 'Tool Chain', in the context of this book, may be thought of as a set of one or more 'Individual Tool'. There are four types of Tool Chain that have been identified in Figure 16.3, which are discussed as follows.

16.2.2.1 The 'Closed' Tool Chain

This term is used to refer to a set of Tools that can only be used in conjunction with a limited set of other Tools, usually from the same Tool provider. Closed Tool Chains comprise Tools that have bespoke or proprietary interfaces that cannot be accessed by all Tools, only a limited set. An advantage of the Closed Tool Chain that is often cited is that the Tools will integrate in a seamless fashion as they are produced by the same developer. In reality, however, this is often not the case. Increasingly it can be seen that the number of Tool providers is shrinking, which is typically not due to companies going out of business, but more usually because of company acquisition. What must be considered is that if one Tool vendor buys another, can it be assumed that these Tools will be compatible? In some cases, these are Tools that have historically been competitors, which, suddenly, become "seamlessly" integrated. Also, just because Tools are produced by a single vendor, it does not mean that the Tools have been developed by the same teams or even following the same Processes. It is quite common to outsource development activities to other companies, so again, the claim of seamless integration must be questioned.

16.2.2.2 The 'Open' Tool Chain

This Tool Chain is used to refer to a set of Tools that can be used, potentially, with any other Tool. Open Tool Chains comprise Tools that have open interfaces that are defined according to some sort of accepted norm or open Standard, and that may be accessed by any other Tool that complies with this Standard. This is a very interesting area and is surprisingly complex. One obvious way to achieve this integration is through the use of data exchange Standards but one has to consider only the number of these Standards and their history, which is often long and complex, to see that this can be a potential minefield.

Another factor that needs to be considered is the underlying technology. There are two main technological approaches that are adopted by most Tool vendors, either heterogeneous or integrated approaches (discussed in the next two subsections), so the question becomes pertinent as to which to choose. Are you going to end up being limited by the choice of Tools by this technology?

16.2.2.3 The 'Heterogeneous' Tool Chains

This term is used to refer to Tools that exist separately and are not able to communicate with other Tools without external help. Heterogeneous Tool Chains comprise Tools that may be from different or the same manufacturers but that cannot be easily integrated when they first come "out of the box".

16.2.2.4 The 'Integrated' Tool Chains

This term is used to refer to a set of Tools that exist separately but that can work together with no external help. Integrated Tools Chains comprise Tools that may be from different or the same Tool providers, but that will work together when fresh "out of the box".

Just to further complicate matters, these different types of Tool Chain may be mixed. For example, it may be possible that a Tool Chain exists that is both closed and integrated, another that is open and integrated, another that is open and heterogeneous and so on. This often results in data transformation Tools being necessary to enable the integration of Tools in these Tool Chains.

Now that the different types of Tools have been discussed, it is still not possible to choose between them, as it is first necessary to look at what capabilities may be offered by the various tools.

16.2.3 'Tool Capability'

This section looks at the different types of 'Tool Capability' that are exhibited by Tools. The concept of the Tool Capability has been split from the tool as many Tools are now very complex and offer many different types of capability. It would be difficult to classify types of Tool based on their capabilities as the mixture is so large and varied.

16.2.3.1 'Office Capability'

This capability is provided by standard office-based software that is available for free (or as good as free) in most Organisations. Office tools, such as word processors, spread sheets and drawing packages (even within other packages, such as presentation Tools) may be used to realise any or all of the Views required by any approach to MBSE. In an ideal world, people would use true modelling Tools but the reality is that many people rely on office-based Tools. Depending on the type of Project, this may be adequate. Like any Tool, it is important to understand the use that the Tool will be put to, but in some cases these somewhat primitive Tools (from a modelling point of view) may be perfectly adequate.

Word processors may be used for just about any View but, in particular, descriptive Views. A good example of this would be the Requirement Description View in the ACRE Process. Spread sheets are often used for management and Views related to traceability. An example of this would be the Traceability View in the ACRE Process.

Caution must be exercised when considering drawing capability as it can often be mistaken for modelling capability. Most people will have access to a basic drawing package, which may be a specific drawing Tool or may be an integral part of a presentation program or word processing application. When using established notations for modelling (such as SysML) it actually means that just about any Tool that offers basic shape-drawing capability and that can display ASCII text characters can visualise any diagram in the notation. Many dedicated drawing packages will come out-of-the-box with a set of SysML templates, but this does not mean that it is capable of SysML modelling. In order to realise many of the benefits of MBSE (automation, checking, etc.) any modelling capability must have an "understanding" of the notation in the form of an underlying meta-model that can be used as a basis for MBSE activities.

Drawing capability may be used to visualise any graphical Views in MBSE but remember that what comes out of a drawing package will be pictures rather than a model.

16.2.3.2 'Support Capability'

This category of capability contains many, many types. Only a few are discussed here, but this should be enough to provide a general idea of the sort of capability that may be used for MBSE.

One of the most widely used support Tools is one that provides the 'Requirements Management' capability. This is a capability that is usually quite simple in what can be done, yet very powerful in terms of its use and benefits. What this capability allows is the management and description of the Requirements in a System and the definition of relationships between them. This capability does not allow the modelling of the Requirements in a System. This is a simple yet much misunderstood belief about what this capability offers. Requirements management is often seen as a silver bullet for requirements engineering, so caution must be exercised that such Tools are being used properly. It is a myth that good requirements management promotes the understanding of Requirements – it does not. Many such capabilities that relate to Requirements are limited to requirements management, which is an essential part of MBSE but does not account for all Requirements activities.

Another type 'Support Capability is that of 'Document Generation'. Such capability is often offered as part of, or as a bolt-on, to modelling Tools but may also be seen as stand-alone. One of the benefits of MBSE is that it is an approach that can increase productivity and save vast amounts of time. One of the ways that these savings can be realised is through effective use of document generation. When any MBSE Process is understood, then it is possible to define templates for various Artefacts, all of which can be derived from the model. Document generation allows the user-friendly face of MBSE (text!) to be generated from any model. Interestingly, it is often the document generation capability that grabs the attention of senior management as it can be demonstrated to show an immediate and often quite striking example of automation and, hence, time saving. In order to sell MBSE to systems engineers, the benefits of automated consistency checks, confidence, integration, etc., are attractive. For many people who hold the purse strings, the fast generation of documents is very attractive.

While on the subject of managers, the next type of capability to be considered is 'Project Management'. There are only a few points to make here as most people are familiar (for better or worse) with Tools that offer Project scheduling and monitoring capabilities. Perhaps the most important point from an MBSE point of view is the compatibility with the Processes that exist in the business. In Chapter 8 we discussed how the Process should relate directly to the Project schedule and this point cannot be emphasised enough – for effective Project management, the Processes must form an inherent part of any schedules or plans. Following on from this, of course, comes the issue of Tool integration, which brings us rather neatly to the next type of Tool on the list.

The availability of the 'Data Transformation' capability is essential for any MBSE activity that uses multiple Tools from multiple vendors. It should be clear from looking at the plethora of capabilities that may be required that Tools integration may very well be an issue for many people. This is because, in reality, most Organisations will use a toolset that is made up of different Tools. As a result of this, there is often a need to be able to use data in more than one Tool that will, typically, require the use of a Tool to transform data from a format used in one Tool to a format used in another one. This may take the form of a dedicated Tool or, in some cases, a Tool may provide technology to allow data transformation with another Tool, such as an application programming interface (API).

The final type of capability under the umbrella of support Tools is 'Configuration Management'. In terms of MBSE, the capability made available by a good configuration management Tool is essential. One of the challenges of implementing MBSE in any business is that of controlling and managing the model and this is why the configuration management Tool is so important. Any model will evolve over time and may very well have multiple points where the model diverges down different paths. On larger Projects there will be a need for multiple users, multiple teams and the ability to work in different locations. A good configuration management capability will address these issues.

16.2.3.3 'Modelling Capability'

The capabilities associated with modelling Tools differ enormously and these will often be the deciding factors when deciding between Tools. Indeed, it will come as no surprise that modelling capability is arguably the most important capability of an MBSE tool. The modelling capability is divided into two types – visual and mathematical modelling.

When we refer to 'Visual Modelling' we are really concerned with capability that allows a diagrammatic representation of a View. There is often some confusion between modelling and drawing, but the distinction is quite clear and simple. Modelling Tools produce models, and drawing Tools produce pictures. The differences between modelling and drawing pictures are discussed elsewhere in this book.

When we refer to 'Mathematical Modelling' we are really concerned with Tools that allow formal specifications (such as formal methods) or mathematical analysis or reasoning to be performed. A mathematical modelling capability is really very important when considering critical Systems. Many Tools will focus on offering either visual modelling or mathematical modelling. Generally speaking, visual modelling tools are not good at mathematical modelling and, likewise, mathematical modelling Tools are not very good as visual modelling, so, in many cases, different Tools may be required to allow both capabilities.

16.2.4 Summary

This section has presented an overview of different types of Tools in two broad categories: Individual Tools and Tool Chains. The two main implementations of these Tools were discussed as being Automated Tools, which is what most people think of, and also the idea of the PAPS Tool was introduced, which is still judged as essential to successful MBSE.

A number of different Tool Capabilities were discussed that may be exhibited by Tools.

The next section looks at how the type of Tools introduced in this section may be used to realise different Views in a Process.

16.3   Understanding the Need for the Tool

This section presents some examples of how the various types of Tools and Tool Chains may be used to realise an MBSE Process. The example Process chosen is the ACRE Process that was used in the previous chapter and is fully defined in Chapter 9 and Appendix F.

The example Tool usage focuses on the three generic types of Process implementation that were discussed in the previous chapter and investigates what types of Tool may be used for each. By way of a recap, these three generic types of Process implementation were:

- Quick and dirty Process implementation – the Process is implemented very quickly and informally with few Artefacts and limited configuration control.
- Semi-formal Process – Process requires more rigour in its implementation, requires good management and configuration control, and requires traceability between Artefacts and audit trails.
- Formal Process – the Process must be implemented as rigorously as possible with a high degree of control, configuration, traceability and mathematical rigour.

The focus in the discussion will not be so much on which Tools are *possible* to be used for each example, but for which Tools are the *most appropriate* to be used for each example.

16.3.1   Pemberton's cooking analogy

The use of Tools may be considered as being analogous to the use of cooking equipment, in what is colloquially known as "Pemberton's Cooking Analogy". This analogy equates the maturity of a Person's cooking requirements to those of an Organisation's modelling.

Consider the first example, where a young student has just made the brave step of moving away from home and must, possibly for the first time, start to fend for themselves and cook their own meals. It is not difficult to imagine that a student may meet all of their dietary requirements with a toaster, a microwave oven and a kettle. This is perfectly adequate for them and the situation that they find themselves in. Indeed, to provide the student with a full range of pots, pans and cooking utensils would be a waste of time and effort as not only would the student not use them properly, but also they would have no appreciation whatsoever for what sophisticated and impressive cuisine they could create with such a fine set of Tools. Also, there is the potential danger of accidentally burning down the house. This is analogous to an Organisation that is just starting to implement MBSE and does not yet know how they will use the Tools, or what their Needs are for their use. For them, it is fine to simply make use of existing office-based Tools.

Consider now the same student who has graduated, started a career and now shares a flat or first house with a new partner. The classic "beans on toast" will no longer be sufficient for this new, more-mature life style and it will be necessary to expand the set of kitchen tools to include some basic pots, pans and utensils. They will probably be cheap and of sufficient quality to get by in day-to-day cooking. This situation is analogous to the situation where an Organisation has reached the limits of office-based Tools and will now be looking for more specific modelling Tools.

Consider again the same student who has now matured into a world-class chef who understands many nuances of the culinary world and can truly appreciate the difference that having a good set of Tools can make. The chef now sees the benefit of the high-quality Tools and the price now seems almost irrelevant as excellent result requires excellent Tools. This is the situation where an Organisation has a high maturity of modelling and can see the value in sophisticated Tools.

The point to remember here is that different Tools suit different people. A lot of this comes down to how mature the modelling in your Organisation is and how close you are to achieving MBSE.

16.4   Using Tools with existing Processes

This section looks at how the Tools that were discussed in the previous sections may be used in conjunction with an existing Process. The example Process what is used is the same as in the previous chapter – the ACRE Framework applied over a number of different implementations. By way of a recap, three levels of scale (small, medium and large) and three levels of criticality (non-critical, semi-critical and critical) will be considered. For the purposes of the discussion, these are described further as:

– Small-scale Project – a Project involving one or very few people, with a timescale that is measured in days or weeks and a very limited budget. Small Projects will often have very few Needs that are often poorly defined. Examples include proof-of-concept Projects, small proposals, and small bench top demonstrators.

– Medium-scale Project – a Project involving one or a few small teams of people, with a timescale that is measured in months and a limited budget. Medium-scale projects will often have a small, but quite well-defined set of initial Needs. Examples include many pure software Projects, and some manufacturing design systems.

– Large-scale Project – a Project involving many teams of people, with a timescale measured in years and with a large and complex budget. Large-scale projects have a high number of Needs that, while being understood individually, have many complex relations between them. Examples of large-scale Projects include large complex Programmes, Systems of Systems, and enterprise Systems.

– Non-critical level – a Project where the correctness of operation of the developed System has no implication on the environment or human life. Examples include typical Apps, office-type software, and library-type Systems.

- Semi-critical level – a Project where the correctness of operation of the developed System may have implication on the environment or human life, depending on circumstances. Examples include design tools and satellite navigation Systems.
- Critical level – a Project where the correctness of operation of the developed System has a large implication on the environment or human life. Examples include weapons Systems, direct control Systems, flight control Systems, and health Systems.

In order to illustrate the flexibility of the Process, three different approaches to implementing the Process on different types of Project will be discussed, which are:

- Quick and dirty Process implementation – the Process is implemented very quickly and informally with few Artefacts and limited configuration control.
- Semi-formal Process – this Process requires more rigour in its implementation, requires good management and configuration control and requires traceability between Artefacts and audit trails.
- Formal Process – the Process must be implemented as rigorously as possible with a high degree of control, configuration, traceability and mathematical rigour.

The next three sections (Sections 16.4.1–16.4.3) relate these different approaches to the different scales and levels of rigour and discuss the types of Tools that may be used for each approach. It should be noted that these are all provided for guidance only, but will make a good start point for your own Process implementation.

16.4.1   Example Tool realisation – quick and dirty Process

The quick and dirty Process was used when the system either is very simple or has a very limited set of timescales associated with it. Clearly, almost all of the Tools discussed previously may be used to realise this approach but, when time is against you on a Project, it may be that the quickest and (what is perceived as) the easiest-to-use Tools are more suitable than tools that may actually be far more powerful.

Two examples will be considered, the use of a PAPS Tool and the use of office-based Tools.

The diagram in Figure 16.4 shows that a PAPS Tool may be used to realise all of the Views that have been identified as essential for this Project. Note that this comes under the broad banner of a Heterogeneous Tool Chain, although, in reality the interface issue is an artificial one, due to the nature of a PAPS Tool.

In some cases, all of these Views may be created in a log book, for example:

- The 'Requirement Description View' may be a simple handwritten list of high-level descriptions for the Needs.
- The 'Requirements Context View' may be a set of *use case diagrams* that have been drawn in a log book.
- The 'Context Definition View' may be a *block definition diagram* that has been written into a log book.

These Views may either then stay in the log book, be transcribed into documents (see the next example) or make use of digital photography, or smart pen and pad

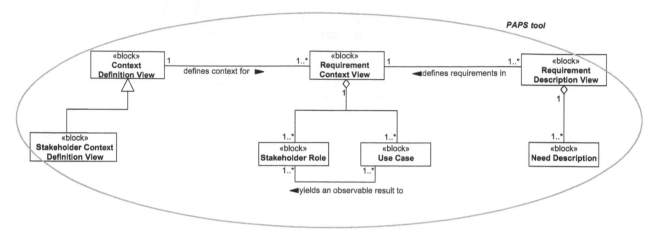

*Figure 16.4   Quick and dirty Process implementation example – PAPS tools in
a Heterogeneous Tool Chain*

to get the information into an electronic format that may be more easily communicated with the rest of the Project Stakeholder Roles.

The most immediate advantage to the PAPS approach is that it is free and
can be done almost anywhere. Also, provided that the Person doing the work is
competent in the approach and the modelling, there is no need for them to be
competent in the use of a specific Tool. This approach is also very well suited to
brainstorming sessions, far more suitable than using a sophisticated Tool, and it
should be considered as being used before any Tools are used.

Of course, the downside of the PAPS approach is quite steep, as there will be
no automation and hence, very few of the benefits of the MBSE approach in terms
of time-saving activities. For example, all consistency-checking must be carried out
manually and all documents must be generated by hand.

Bearing all of these constraints in mind, however, it is always worth
performing the modelling, even if it is only on a whiteboard for half an hour or so.
The increased level of understanding that can be achieved in such a short space of
time should not be underestimated.

Bearing the limitations of the PAPS Tool in mind, let us now look at how the
same quick and dirty Process may be realised using the first set of Automated Tools
– those that only exhibit office-type capabilities.

The example in Figure 16.5 shows Tools that exhibit office-type capabilities
may be used to realise the Views required for this Project. Note that, depending on
the office Tools selected, this Tool Chain can potentially fit into any of the four
categories of Tool Chain described previously. The Views may be realised in the
following way:

–   The 'Requirement Description View' may be defined as a word-processed
     document that describes the Needs in a list or in a table. Another way would be
     to represent the Needs in a table in a spread sheet.

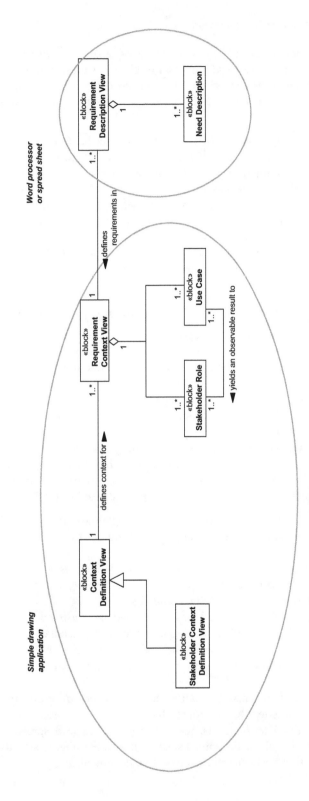

Figure 16.5   Quick and dirty Process implementation example – office-type Tools

–   The 'Requirement Context View' may be realised using *use case diagrams* in a simple drawing Tool in a word processor or even in a presentation application.
–   The 'Context Definition view' may be realised using a *block definition diagram* in a simple drawing Tool in a word processer or even a presentation application.

In many cases, the Tools here will be used to transcribe information that was generated using a PAPS Tool in order to get the Views into easily manipulated formats that can be communicated to other Stakeholder Roles on the Project.

The example shown here has the advantage of being quick and simple to implement. However, the downside of this approach is that the model, as it stands, is very difficult to manage and must be verified and validated entirely manually, which, of course, is both time consuming and prone to error. This is a perfectly valid approach, but not one that realises all the true benefits of MBSE as there is no automation between the Views and everything is carried out manually.

16.4.2   *Example tool realisation – semi-formal process*

The semi-formal variation of the Process was used where there was a need for a certain amount of rigour on the Project, or where the Project had quite a long timescale. Two realisations will be considered here, the first of which will be a Tool that exhibits office-type capabilities and the second of which will be using Tools that exhibit some modelling and support capabilities.

The diagram in Figure 16.6 shows a possible realisation of the semi-formal Process implementation.

The example here shows how Tools that exhibit office capabilities may be used to realise the Views required for this Project. Note that, depending on the office Tools selected, this Tool Chain can potentially fit into any of the four Tool Chain categories described previously. The Views may be realised in the following way:

–   The 'Source Element View' may be realised using almost any Tool or file type. For example: e-mails, digital photos, scans of log books, and word processor documents.
–   The 'Requirement Description View' may be defined as a word-processed document that describes the Needs in a list or in a table. Another way would be to represent the Needs in a table in a spread sheet.
–   The 'Requirement Context View' may be realised using *use case diagrams* in a simple drawing Tool in a word processor or even in a presentation application.
–   The 'Context Definition view' may be realised using a *block definition diagram* in a simple drawing Tool in a word processer or even a presentation application.
–   The 'Validation' views may be realised using *sequence diagrams* in a simple drawing Tool, or as text-based ordered lists in a word processor.
–   The 'Traceability View' may be realised using tables in a spread sheet. By using a hypertext links in the spread sheet, it is also possible to start to provide simple navigation between the various office documents.

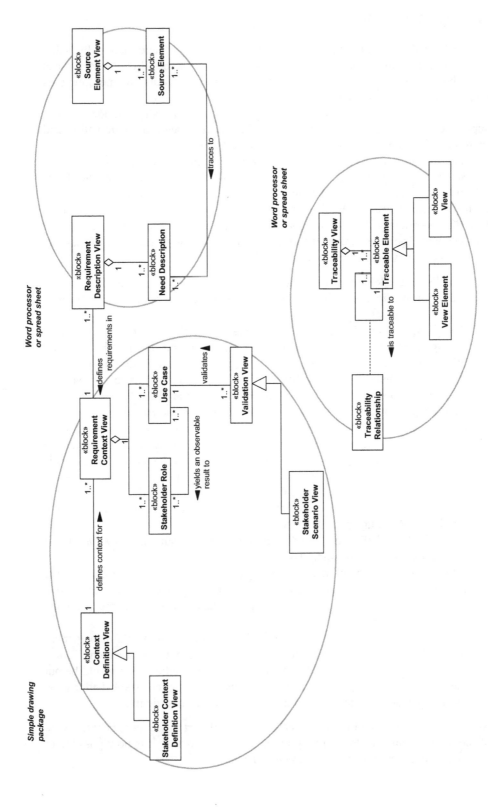

Figure 16.6 Semi-formal Process implementation – office-type Tools

Notice here that we are starting to see the beginnings of automation by using hypertext links. This is the tip of the iceberg in terms of the benefits that MBSE can offer, but it is a start point. Again, the more powerful the Tools, the more benefits will be realised by using the MBSE approach.

The next example uses more sophisticated Tools that exhibit modelling and support capabilities and, therefore, we would expect to see more automation and more benefits than when using the office-based Tools.

The example in Figure 16.7 shows how a proprietary Toolset may be used to realise the Views required for this Project. Note that, depending on the Tools selected, this Tool Chain can potentially fit into any of the four categories of Tool Chain described previously. For the purposes of this example, let us assume that this proprietary Toolset consists of a modelling Tool and a requirements management Tool that are being used in conjunction with standard office-type Tools. The Views may be realised in the following ways:

- The 'Source Element View' may be realised using almost any Tool or file type. For example: e-mails, digital photos, scans of log books, and word processor documents.
- The 'Requirement Description View' may be defined in the requirements management Tool. Most requirements management tools excel in this area and allow the user to define a set of attributes for each Requirement. Each Requirement here will be text-based, but it is also usually possible to paste in graphics and images, which will prove useful in some of the later Views.
- The 'Requirement Context View' may be realised using *use case diagrams* in the modelling Tool. This information may also be represented in the requirements Tool, depending on the sophistication of the Tool. At the very least, *each use case diagram* may be pasted into the management Tool as an image. This may then be used for the basis of traceability in the 'Traceability View' later. If the Tool is more powerful, then there may be an automated link between the modelling Tool and the requirements management Tool, which would have a number of advantages, as discussed later in this section.
- The 'Context Definition view' may be realised using a *block definition diagram* using the modelling Tool.
- The 'Validation View' may be realised using *sequence diagrams* in the modelling Tool. Again, depending on the level of sophistication of the Tools, there will be advantages to using the proprietary Toolset over the previous, office-based example.
- The 'Traceability View' will be realised using the requirements management Tool. This is one of the main uses for the requirements management Tool – establishing traceability. At the moment, these traceability links would be put into the requirements management Tool manually but, once established, can be used to perform impact analysis and other types of investigation.

Now that we are starting to use sharper tools, we will start to see more benefits. One of the main advantages to using a proprietary Toolset is that it is now possible to automate the interactions between the two Tools.

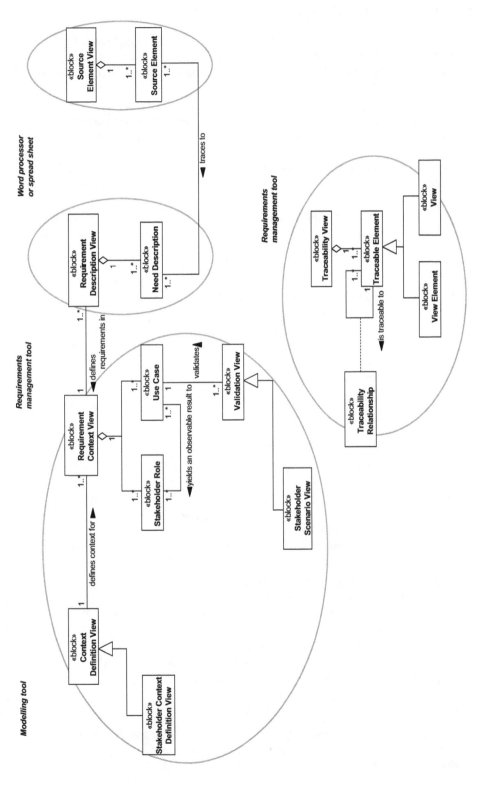

Figure 16.7 Semi-formal Process implementation – proprietary Tools

- First, the diagrams from the model and their representations in the management Tool will be linked, so that they can always be made consistent by simply pressing a button to update the information in the management Tool from the modelling Tool, or *vice versa*.
- Another advantage is that descriptions that are associated with elements in the model (such as *actors* or *use cases*) may then be used automatically in the requirements management Tool, avoiding the need for tiresome "cutting and pasting".
- Both Tools should allow documents, websites, etc., that exist outside the Tools to be linked to, which provides even more flexibility and power when it comes to traceability.
- The use of the two Tools together provides rigour in terms of both the technical correctness of the model (in the modelling tool) and the management of the requirements Artefacts (in the requirements management Tool).

There are, however, several disadvantages to using this approach:

- Very often the integration or communication between Tools is non-trivial and can entail quite a large piece of work. Of course, this should only need to be carried out once, and then it can be re-used as often as desired. This initial overhead should be taken into account when considering the semi-formal Tool implementation.
- On a related note, Tools from different providers may have different versions, so the configuration and version control of the Tools must be taken into account.

The semi-formal Process may be seen quite often in reality and can offer many benefits to a Project or Programme.

16.4.3 Example Tool realisation – formal Process

The formal Process was used where the System was a mission-critical System, or the Project was being conducted on a very large scale.

On Projects such as these, the initial cost of the Toolset being used is usually less of an issue as it tends to be a very small part of the overall Project budget. More importantly, the level of maturity of modelling of the Project should (emphasis the word "should") be higher and, therefore, all the benefits of a powerful Toolset may be realised.

Two examples of implementation will be looked at: the first with a Heterogeneous Tool Chain and the second with an Integrated Tool Chain.

The diagram in Figure 16.8 shows how the formal Process may be implemented using a Heterogeneous Tool Chain that exhibits modelling and support capabilities. In this case each Tool exists in its own right and will need some effort to be put into the integration of the Tools. Examples of Tools that may be used here are: a SysML modelling Tool, a requirements management Tool, simulation Tools, data exchange Tools, and spread sheets.

Other possible ways to realise the Views are as follows:

- The 'Source Element View' may be realised using almost any Tool or file type. For example: e-mails, digital photos, scans of log books, and word processor documents.

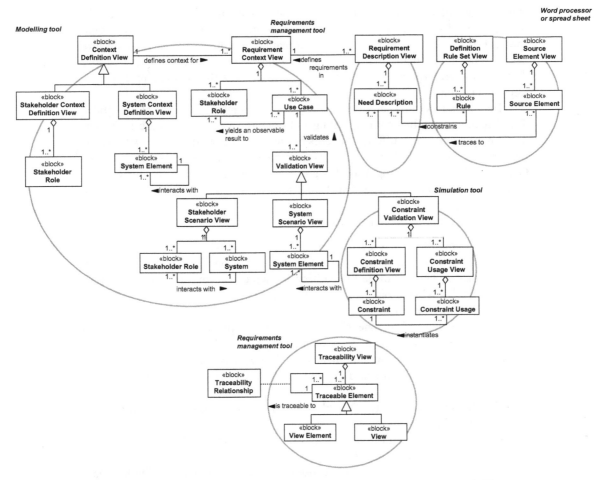

Figure 16.8   Formal Process implementation – Heterogeneous Tool Chain

- The 'Requirement Description View' may be defined in the requirements management Tool or in a modelling Tool that supports SysML *requirements diagrams*, or both.
- The 'Requirement Context View' may be realised using *use case diagrams* in the modelling Tool. This information may also be referenced or repeated in the requirements management Tool.
- The 'Context Definition view' may be realised using a *block definition diagram* using the modelling tool.
- The 'Validation View' may be realised using *sequence diagrams* in the modelling Tool. In the case of the formal Process a simulation Tool may be required to define the parametric *constraint blocks*.
- The 'Traceability View' will be realised using the requirements management Tool or with a separate traceability Tool, such as spread sheet or workbench-type environment.

With the use of more Tools, one would expect to see more benefits. In fact, the benefits and disadvantages are very similar to the ones discussed for the semi-formal Process. The main benefits are automation and the ability to generate Process Artefacts. The main disadvantages are again related to integrating the various Tools. These are problems that should be addressed with the next example of Tool implementation.

The second example of the formal Process implementation uses an Integrated Tool Chain that exhibits both modelling and support capabilities (Figure 16.9). The Tools may come from different vendors but all the hard work of Tool integration has already been carried out by the Tool provider. At the heart of Integrated Tool Chain will be the modelling Tool that provides interfaces to all of the other Tools, such as requirements management Tools, simulation Tools, checking Tools, and document generation Tools.

Other possible implementations of the Views are as follows:

– The 'Source Element View' may be realised using almost any Tool or file type. For example: e-mails, digital photos, scans of log books, and word processor documents. These will be linked back to elements within the model, or may even have SysML *blocks* to represent them.
– The 'Requirement Description View' is defined in the modelling tool using SysML *blocks*. If anyone should want to see the same information in a requirements management Tool, then a button is pressed and the management modules are generated automatically. These may then be edited in the requirements management Tool and re-imported back into the model – the model is the master.
– The 'Requirement Context View' may be realised using *use case diagrams* in the modelling tool.
– The 'Context Definition view' may be realised using a *block definition diagram* using the modelling Tool.
– The 'Validation View' may be realised using *sequence diagrams* in the modelling Tool. The *parametric constraints* may be defined using SysML *parametric diagrams* in the modelling Tool and then, at the push of button, they will be sent to the simulation Tool for formal validation.
– The 'Traceability View' will be generated automatically from the model. When the modelling is carried out properly, then traceability is inherent in the model and should not need to be entered again.

The true benefits of MBSE start to become apparent now. Just in terms of automating Artefacts, checking and simulation, the following benefits may be realised:

– Automatic verification of the model. This may take many forms as there may be standard checks and bespoke checks. When using SysML, there are a number of standard consistency checks that should be carried out on any model. However, in addition to these checks there may be bespoke checks associated with the Process that is being followed. For example, there were a number of consistency checks that were identified for the ACRE Process in Chapter 9 that can be automated. This automation of consistency checks is a

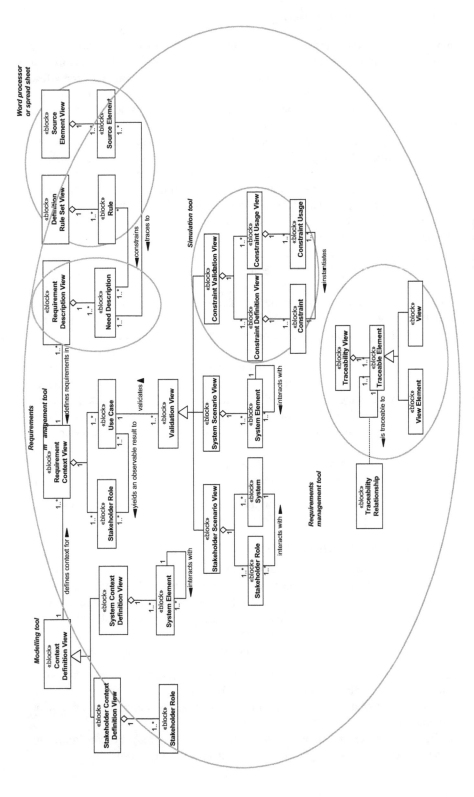

Figure 16.9 Formal Process implementation – Integrated Tool Chain

massive time-saver. Performing consistency checks manually takes a long time, is incredibly tedious and is very prone to human error. Just performing the consistency checks for the ACRE Process can take anything between a few hours, a few days and a few months, depending on the size of the Project. By automating this, the whole Process takes anywhere from a few seconds to just less than a minute.

- Automatic generation of documents. The modelling will allow the user to define document templates that may be used by standard word processors. Elements in the model are then used to populate the document, which is then produced as the word-processed document. This requires some effort to set up the templates but, once done, can save a lot of time. Apart from saving time, it also means that the word-processed document becomes a "throw-away" document in that if it ever needs to be changed then it is simply discarded. Any changes are made to the model and then the document is re-generated. This means that a document can be generated at any point in time that is guaranteed to be consistent with the model.
- Automated interface with simulation Tools. SysML modelling Tools are usually not very good at performing mathematical simulation as it is not what they are intended for. Therefore, a good interface between the modelling Tool and the simulation Tool can provide an excellent way to validate the *parametric constraints* that have been defined in the model.
- Requirements management automation. As was stated previously, if the model is correct, then traceability comes for free. There are many cases, however, where there is still a need for a separate requirements management Tool, whether this is a true or perceived need. Again, the model is the master and the management Tool information is simply automatically generated. Any changes made in the management Tool may then be imported back into the model, assuming that the interface is bidirectional.

Of course, these benefits will depend on the level of functionality of the Tools that are being used to implement the Process.

16.4.4   Guidance for using Tools

Once the Tool has been selected it is advisable to tie its use to your Organisation's Processes. This will often take the form of defining procedures that show how to implement the Processes using the Tools. The "seven views" approach to Process modelling can also be applied to defining procedures, which will ensure consistency with the overall MBSE approach.

This is the point where much of the automation may be defined. For example:

- Rules may be defined within the Tools that enforce the Process, allowing automated verification activities to be performed.
- Templates for Artefacts may be defined that allow automated document generation.
- Interfaces between different Tools in the Tool chains may be configured to allow (potentially!) seamless integration between various Tools.

There are many more ways that the Tools may be used to realise more MBSE benefits, such as automated test generation and automated Process measurement.

Another area where guidelines may be produced is in the use of the notation within the Tool and the structure, navigation and use of the model. This is an area that is covered extensively in Chapter 6 and it is recommended that this should be used as a start point for a style guide for modelling.

16.5 Considering Tool selection

The selection of the Tools for a Project or Organisation can be the most important decision that is made on a Project. Getting the right Tool is very important, but getting the wrong Tool is usually much worse than not getting any Tool at all.

It was seen in Figure 16.2 that 'select tool' was an essential *use case* of the overall 'Tool Context'. This section provides guidance on Tool evaluation and, in order to codify this, a set of Tool evaluation Processes known as MonTE (Modelling Tool Evaluation) is provided.

The main *use cases* that need to be satisfied when considering Tool evaluation are shown in the context in Figure 16.10.

The diagram in Figure 16.10 shows the Context for Tool evaluation and identifies a number of *use cases*. Note how the 'Evaluate CASE tool' *use case* is

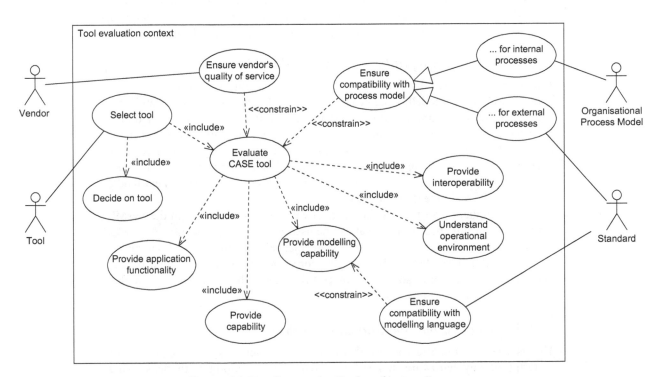

Figure 16.10   Context for Tool evaluation Processes

actually part of a higher-level 'Select tool' *use case*. There are a number of factors that should be borne in mind when selecting Tools, each of which will be represented as *use cases* and that are now discussed in further detail.

16.5.1   *'Provide modelling capability'*

This is probably the most obvious factor and one that most people will put a lot of effort into. First of all it needs to be decided if there is a need for mathematical modelling capability as well as the visual modelling capability.

The visual modelling capability describes the drawing, management and usability of a Tool. This is aimed primarily at modelling (and some drawing) Tools and should not be taken lightly or assumed.

There are some aspects, however, that are not so easy to quantify, such as the usability. The Tool should be easy to use in that it should have an intuitive interface. Unfortunately, what one Person thinks is perfectly intuitive (e.g. a programmer) may not seem at all intuitive to someone else (an end user). Therefore, it is often desirable to have a Tool that has a configurable user interface.

Another aspect of usability that should be considered is the navigation of the model. How easy is this? Are there search functions? Can one diagram be automatically navigated to from another? And so on.

The previous section discussed the use of style guides for modelling, which can be implemented by tailoring the Tool using profiles. The definition and application of profiles varies enormously between Tools but if style guides are to be followed, then this is a very important aspect of modelling capability for a Tool.

16.5.2   *'Ensure compatibility with modelling language'*

A large constraint on providing a good modelling capability is that of compliance with the underlying modelling language or notation. Many Tools claim compliance with a specific modelling notation, for example SysML, when in fact they do not meet the entire underlying Standard. This can be very important as it is not just a matter of how much of the Standard is implemented, but also to what degree is the notational meta-model implemented in the Tool. For example, if you want consistency-checking as part of your Tool, then the Tool needs to have a meta-model and not just be a simple drawing package.

The compliance for the Standard is relatively easy to quantify and the SysML Standard has a full specification that can be used for the comparison.

The same basic needs hold true for mathematical modelling – what languages are supported and to what level? It is quite common for Tools that exhibit mathematical modelling holds some sort of certification or has a formal proof that describes their internal Processes.

16.5.3   *'Understand operational environment'*

This is a very pragmatic concern that describes the actual system requirements in terms of any hardware and software requirements along with networking capabilities.

Some Tools, particularly more powerful ones, come with quite heavy installation requirements. For example, a Tool that uses a fully transactional database as its underlying technology will have very different system requirements compared to one that has a simple flat file structure as its technology.

This is also a problem that can be compounded when using multiple Tools from multiple vendors as the system requirements may require exclusive use of system resources that may clash when it comes to running on a single machine.

16.5.4 'Provide interoperability'

This is a key for MBSE and describes how a Tool that forms part of a Tool Chain may be required to operate with other Tools, technologies or clients. The previous sections have discussed how one of the biggest problems with Tool Chains is their integration.

It is important to look for what data formats may be used as outputs for compatibility of Tools, what interfaces are provided as standard, what interfaces may be programmed and so on.

Effective interoperability can be the difference between running a successful Project and having a Project fail. It is also very important that any interfaces or data exchange mechanisms are investigated thoroughly and are not just assumed to work on the basis of a data sheet. The use of Standards can be very important for ensuring interoperability, so compliance with data exchange standards may be an important issue for some users.

16.5.5 'Ensure vendor's quality of service'

This describes how to ensure that the vendors can meet all of your Needs. If you are working a Project that is in any way mission critical, expensive or scheduled to take a long time then it is important that good support is available from the Tool provider. Also, it is important that the Tool provider will still be in business when the Project ends. Generally speaking, large companies will have more chance of existing over the next 10 years, whereas a small provider may not. On the other hand, smaller companies tend to provide better, or certainly more personal and consistent support, as they can be far more pro-active and reactive in their support.

An essential aspect of any vendor is to decide whether they are providing a Product, Service or both. This becomes very important as many Tool vendors will also offer a number of professional Services, such as training, mentoring, telephone, and Internet support.

If a vendor is claiming to support MBSE then there are three very simple criteria that can be applied with some obvious questions:

- People – Assuming that the vendor develops its own Tool, do they have competent developers? In the event that the vendor is offering services, are their consultants, trainers and support staff competent? Use the techniques discussed in Chapter 14 and Appendix G to ascertain this.
- Process – Assuming that the vendor develops its own Tool, do they have effective development Processes in place? If they offer Services, do they have

effective customer-related Processes in place? Use the techniques in Chapter 15 and Appendix F to investigate this, along with Process assessment or audit techniques.

– Tools – Assuming again that the vendor develops its own Tool, do they use Tools, especially their own, to develop the Product? Consider some of the techniques discussed in this chapter and Appendix F to assess this.

In essence, it is important to ascertain whether the vendor "eats its own dog food" or whether they are simply paying lip-service to the principles of MBSE.

16.5.6 *'Ensure compatibility with the process model'*

This describes how the Tool may be required to fit in with a particular approach to working, which may put additional requirements on the Tool. This may be considered both internally and externally.

As an example of internal Processes, consider your own Processes (or the Processes that have been presented in this book and summarised in Appendix F), and ask yourself whether the Tool would support these Processes or seek to change the Process?

As an example of external Processes, consider any Standards that apply to your business (or Standards and best practice models that have been used in this book, for example ISO 15288, which is presented in Appendix E), and ask yourself whether the Tool would support these Processes or seek to change the process?

Remember that the Process must drive the Tool and not the other way around.

16.5.7 *'Provide capability'*

Every Tool will have its own unique selling points (USPs) and very often these will manifest themselves in additional capabilities that are offered by the Tool. Different Tool capabilities were discussed in the previous section, but some specific examples of these that many Tools offer are:

– Code generation, for automatically producing code from the models created in the Tool.
– Report generation, for automatically producing nice-looking documents directly from the model, without the need to create each document individually in a word processor.
– Reverse engineering, in the case of a Tool that is used for legacy systems that contain software, generating models (or model elements) from the code can be an attractive capability.
– Animation, in terms of SysML, in almost half of the diagrams is behavioural, which means that they can potentially be animated.
– Checking, not only in terms of the standard notational checks as found in SysML, but also the Tool, allows bespoke checks to be defined according to, for example, internal Processes

This list is not intended to be exhaustive, but should provide a good start point for considering other Tool capabilities.

One key question to ask here is whether you actually need these capabilities or not. It is very easy to be blinded by the flashing lights of a good sales demonstration, only to arrive back at work of the following week to realise that these capabilities are either not what you thought they were, or not of any practical use to you or the business.

16.5.8 *'Provide application functionality'*

Many Tools will be geared towards specific applications, such as real-time Systems, Process modelling, and enterprise modelling. Again, in a similar vein to the previous point, are these useful to you?

When specific application areas are covered, then the basic approach that is being used should be questioned. For example, is the approach based on genuine research (whether academic or industrial) or has it been fabricated? Is anyone in industry using the approach in anger, or does it have no user-base?

16.5.9 *'Decide on tool'*

The final *use case*, that sits alongside all the evaluation-related *use cases*, is that of making a decision for the Tool selection. Tool evaluation provides the evidence that is required in order to make an effective and informed decision that will be, ultimately, up to you.

It is impossible to advise everyone on how to make a decision, but it is possible to advise on how to perform an evaluation. The next section, therefore, introduces a set of Processes for Tool evaluation.

16.6 Tool evaluation

When evaluating Tools it is important that the results from each evaluation can be compared so that an informed decision can be made. If different Tools are evaluated using different techniques, then there is no common frame of reference, which will not allow a good decision to be made. This is also unfair to the Tool vendors who would not be competing on an even playing field.

With this in mind, there is a need for a defined set of evaluation Processes. These Processes will be introduced briefly here and are fully described in Appendix F.

The processes are known as MonTE (Modelling Tool Evaluation). This acronym is a little contrived but there is a hidden message in it, as the term "MonTE" is often associated with confidence tricks where you can't possibly hope to come out on top. Selecting Tools can sometimes seem a little like this.

16.6.1 *The MonTE Processes*

The MonTE Processes are defined using the "seven views" approach to Process modelling that was described in Chapter 7.

This section will introduce the Processes at a high level and focus on how they are applied, whereas the full definition can be found in Appendix F.

The Need for the Processes has actually already been described, as these Processes satisfy the Needs represented by the *use cases* in the 'Tool Context' in Figure 16.2. This Context, therefore, represents the Requirements Context View (RCV) for the MonTE Processes.

16.6.2   MonTE – the Process Content View

The Processes that make up MonTE are summarised in the Process Content View in Figure 16.11.

The diagram in Figure 16.11 shows the Processes that make up the MonTE Process set. These Processes are described as follows:

–   'Ideal Tool Requirement Capture'. The main aim of this Process is to capture the basic Needs of the ideal Tool. Essentially, this Process is concerned with carrying out a requirements engineering activity concerning the Tool needs and producing a model of what the ideal Tool should look like. The information presented previously in this chapter should be used as a guide for considering your needs for a tool and to understand how the Tool will be used with its relevant Processes. The 'Ideal Tool Evaluation' process will typically only need to be executed once for each Tool selection exercise.
–   'Evaluation Tool Capture'. The main aim of this Process is to take each candidate Tool and to produce a model that captures the Tool and its features, constraints and operation. This is then used to compare back to the model for the ideal Tool that was created in the previous Process.
–   'Tool Analysis' – 'Tool Verification'. The main aim of this Process is to compare the ideal Tool model with the model for a candidate Tool.
–   'Tool Analysis' – 'Tool Validation'. The main aim of this Process is to assess whether the candidate Tool satisfies the Needs for the Ideal tool.
–   'Result Definition'. The main aim of this Process is to take the outputs of the two 'Tool Analysis' Processes and to present them in some form of report that may then be used as an input to the decision-making Process (not shown here).

The basic way that these Processes work can be seen by considering the main Artefacts of the Processes in the form of the Information View (IV).

16.6.3   Information View

The Tool evaluation Processes rely on creating an ideal model and a number of evaluation models and then comparing the two. A high-level Information View of the final Artefact from the 'Result Definition' Process is shown in Figure 16.12.

The diagram in Figure 16.12 shows the main Artefacts for the 'Result Definition' Process. These may be described in more detail as follows.

–   'Ideal Tool Model' – this model is created based on an understanding of the main Needs of the Tool, represented by the 'Ideal Tool Context'. In order to support this Context an ideal set of Processes ('Ideal Process Model') is created that the Tool must either work with or comply with, and an ideal set of features

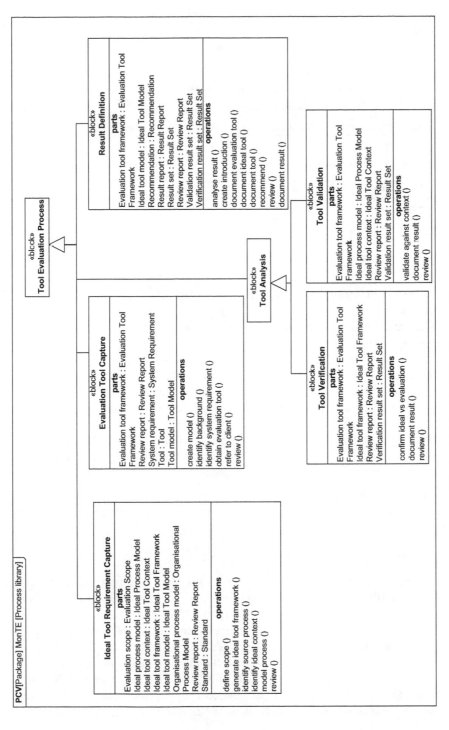

Figure 16.11 MonTE – Process Content View

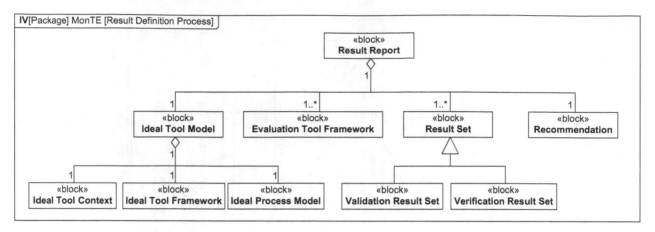

Figure 16.12   MonTE – Information View for 'Result Definition' Process

for the Tool ('Ideal Tool Framework') is created. This then forms the basis of the evaluation.

– 'Evaluation Tool Framework' – this is the model that represents each Tool that is being evaluated.

– 'Result Set' – this forms the main output of the evaluation, upon which the 'Recommendation' will be made. This is performed in two ways: by verification of the 'Evaluation Tool Framework' against the 'Ideal Tool Framework' and by validation of the 'Evaluation Tool Framework' against the 'Ideal Tool Context' and 'Ideal Process Model'.

– 'Recommendation' – this is generated based on the 'Result Set'. It should be noted that this is not the definitive decision on which Tool to select, but will form an input to that decision-making process.

The way that the Processes are executed and hence the number of these Artefacts that will be generated will vary depending on number of Tools being evaluated. This is discussed in the next section.

16.6.4   Process Instance View

The Processes shown in Figure 16.13 are executed in a simple sequence, but this will vary slightly depending on the number of Tools being evaluated. This is illustrated by the two Scenarios shown in Figures 16.13 and 16.14.

The diagram in Figure 16.13 shows a simple Scenario where only a single Tool is being evaluated. The Processes are executed in a straightforward linear fashion, with one Process instance (represented by a *life line*) for each Process. The 'Ideal Tool Requirement Capture' process needs only be carried out once and, likewise the 'Result Definition' Process. The 'Evaluation Tool Capture' and 'Tool Analysis' processes are executed once per tool. Thus, in the case of a single Tool, these are only executed once.

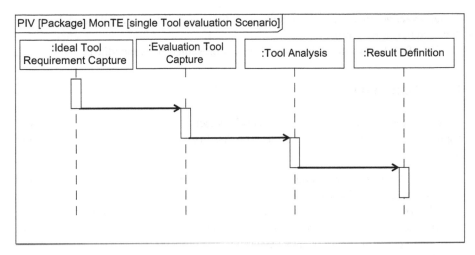

*Figure 16.13   MonTE – Process Instance View (PIV) – single Tool evaluation
Scenario*

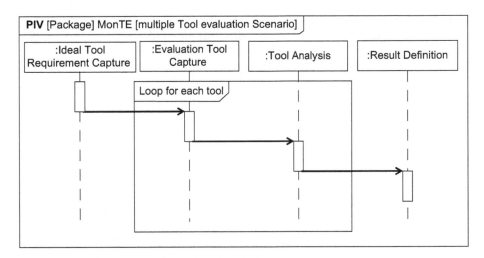

*Figure 16.14   MonTE – Process Instance View (PIV) – multiple Tool evaluation
Scenario*

The diagram in Figure 16.14 shows a second Scenario where multiple Tools
are being evaluated. Notice in this Scenario that the 'Ideal Tool Requirement
Capture' Process is only executed once, whereas the two tool analysis Processes
('Evaluation Tool Capture' and 'Tool Validation') are executed as many times as
there are Tools to be evaluated. A single instance of the 'Result Definition' Process

is then executed that takes all of the verification and validation results and, based on these, makes a recommendation.

The full definition of these Processes is presented in Appendix F.

16.7   Summary

This chapter has focused on the 'Tool' aspect of the 'People, Process, Tool' approach that is adopted in this book. This has been presented by considering these main areas:

–   Considerations for a Tool, which looked at different types of Tools, Tool Chains and Tool Capabilities.
–   Use of Tools for Processes, where an example Process was selected and then the use of various different types of Tools with different Tool Capabilities was considered for different implementations of the Process.
–   A set of Processes for Tool evaluation, where this set of Processes was introduced at a high level, the intention being to provide an overview of Tool evaluation.

This chapter is clearly heavily related to Chapters 14 and 15 and, as such, should not be read in isolation, but should bear in mind the totality of this part of the book.

Also, the full definition of the Processes that are used in chapter, both ACRE and MonTE, are presented in Appendix E.

Part 6

Annex

P6.1 Overview

This part of the book is structured according to the diagram in Figure P6.1.

This part of the book provides a wealth of information that can be used when employing MBSE in real Organisation, on real Projects in real life. This annex is intended to be used as a resource for MBSE practitioners, and comprises nine appendices.

– 'Appendix A – Ontology and Glossary'. This appendix provides a summary of the MBSE Ontology and definitions of all the concepts organised as a glossary, which was introduced in Chapter 3.
– 'Appendix B – Summary of SysML Notation'. This appendix provides a summary of the entire SysML notation, which was introduced in Chapter 5.
– 'Appendix C – Summary of Diagramming Guidelines'. This appendix summarises the style guide, which was introduced and discussed in Chapter 6.
– 'Appendix D – Using SysML Concepts in UML'. Do you want to use UML but are interested in also making use of the new concepts and constructs in SysML? Do not fear – this appendix shows how all of the SysML concepts can be realised using UML.

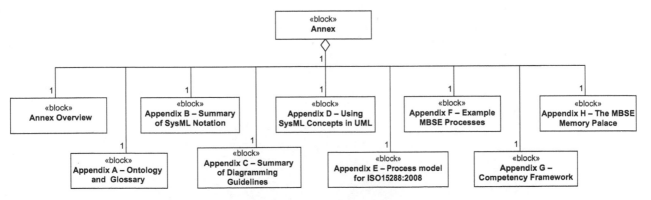

Figure P6.1   Structure of 'Annex'

–   'Appendix E – ISO 15288 Process Model'. This appendix defines the full model for the ISO standard that may be used for compliance or reference purposes.

–   'Appendix F – Example MBSE Processes'. This appendix provides the full models behind all of the Processes that have been used or referenced in this book.

–   'Appendix G – Competency Framework'. This appendix defines two complete sets of Competency Scopes, one for the INCOSE Competencies Framework and one for the MBSE Competency Framework, for each of the Stakeholders Roles that are used in all of the Processes described in this book.

–   'Appendix H – The MBSE Memory Palace'. This appendix contains a memory palace that provides an aid for enhancing the recollection of large amounts of information, in this case aimed at the MBSE Ontology.

All of the information presented in this annex is intended for reference only and, in many cases, this information will need to be tailored to suit your own organisational Needs. Having said this, however, the information here should certainly shorten the learning curve for MBSE and provide an excellent start point for any MBSE endeavour.

Appendix A

Ontology and glossary

Don't for heaven's sake, be afraid of talking nonsense!
But you must pay attention to your nonsense.

Ludwig Wittgenstein (1889–1951)

A.1 Introduction

This appendix provides a summary of the model-based systems engineering (MBSE) Ontology (Figure A.1) and the definitions of the concepts contained. For full details see Chapter 2; no explanation or additional details are given in this appendix.

A.2 Ontology

A.3 Glossary

Acknowledged System	A special type of System of Systems that has designated management and resources, and a consensus of purpose. Each Constituent System retains its own management and operation.
Activity	A set of actions that need to be performed in order to successfully execute a Process. Each Activity must have a responsible Stakeholder Role associated with it and utilises one or more Resource.
Architectural Framework	A defined set of one or more Viewpoint and an Ontology. The Architectural Framework is used to structure an Architecture from the point of view of a specific industry, Stakeholder Role set or Organisation. The Architectural Framework is defined so that it meets the Needs defined by one or more Architectural Framework Concern. An Architectural Framework is created so that it complies with zero or more Standard.
Architectural Framework Concern	Defines a Need that an Architectural Framework has to address.

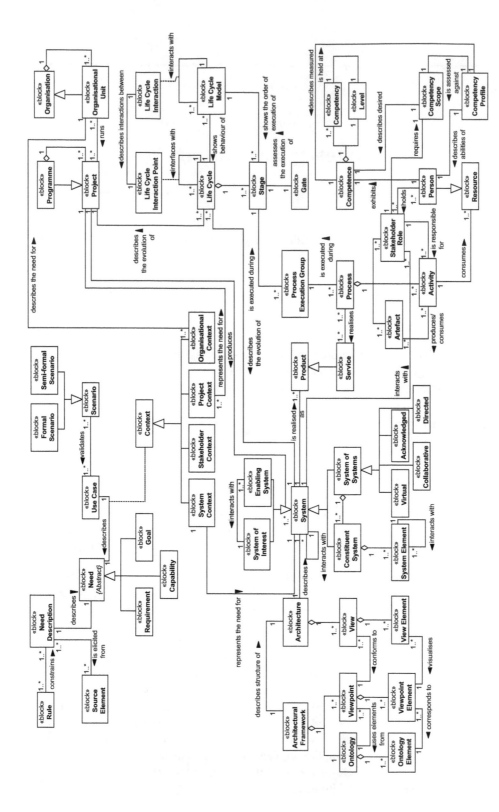

Figure A.1   The full MBSE Ontology

Architecture	A description of a System, made up of one or more View. One or more related View can be collected together into a Perspective.
Artefact	Something that is produced or consumed by an Activity in a Process. Examples of an Artefact include documentation, software, hardware, and systems.
Capability	A special type of Need whose Context will typically represent one or more Project (as a Project Context) or one or more Organisational Unit (as an Organisational Context). A Capability will meet one or more Goal and will represent the ability of an Organisation or Organisational Unit.
Collaborative System	A special type of System of Systems that lacks central management and resources, but has consensus of purpose.
Competence	The ability exhibited by a Person that is made up of a set of one or more individual Competency.
Competency	The representation of a single skill that contributes towards making up a Competence. Each Competency is held at a Level that describes the maturity of that Competency. There are four Level defined for the MBSE Ontology.
Competency Profile	A representation of the actual measured Competence of a Person and that is defined by one or more Competency. An individual's competence will usually be represented by one or more Competency Profile. A Competency Profile is the result of performing a competence assessment against a Competence Scope.
Competency Scope	Representation of the desired Competence required for a specific Stakeholder Role and that is defined by one or more Competency.
Constituent System	A special type of System whose elements are one or more System Element.
Context	a specific point of view based on, for example, Stakeholder Roles, System hierarchy level, and Life Cycle Stage.
Directed System	A special type of System of Systems that has designated management and resources, and a consensus of purpose. Each Constituent System retains its own operation but not management.
Enabling System	A special type of System that interacts with the System of Interest yet sits outside its boundary.
Formal Scenario	A Scenario that is mathematically provable using, for example formal methods.
Gate	A mechanism for assessing the success or failure of the execution of a Stage.
Goal	A special type of Need whose Context will typically represent one or more Organisational Unit (as an Organisational Context). Each Goal will be met by one or more Capability.

Indicator	A feature of a Competency that describes knowledge, skill or attitude required to meet the Competency. It is the Indicator that is assessed as part of competency assessment.
Life Cycle	A set of one or more Stage that can be used to describe the evolution of System, Project, etc., over time.
Life Cycle Interaction	The point during a Life Cycle Model at which one or more Stage interact with each other.
Life Cycle Interface Point	The point in a Life Cycle where one or more Life Cycle Interaction will occur.
Life Cycle Model	The execution of a set of one or more Stage that shows the behaviour of a Life Cycle.
Need	A generic abstract concept that, when put into a Context, represents something that is necessary or desirable for the subject of the Context.
Need Description	A tangible description of an abstract Need that is defined according to a predefined set of attributes.
Ontology	An element of an Architectural Framework that defines all the concepts and terms (one or more Ontology Element) that relate to any Architecture structured according to the Architectural Framework.
Ontology Element	The concepts that make up an Ontology. Each Ontology Element can be related to each other and is used in the definition of each Viewpoint (through the corresponding Viewpoint Element that makes up a Viewpoint). The provenance for each Ontology Element is provided by one or more Standard.
Organisation	A collection of one or more Organisational Units, it runs one or more Projects and will have its own Organisational Context.
Organisational Unit	A special type of Organisation that itself can make up part of an Organisation. An Organisational Unit also runs one or more Projects and will have its own Organisational Context
Person	A special type of Resource, an individual human, who exhibits Competence that is represented by their Competency Profile. A Person also holds one or more Stakeholder Role.
Perspective	A collection of one or more View (and hence also one or more defining Viewpoint) that are related by their purpose. That is, one or more View which address the same architectural needs, rather than being related in some other way, such as by mode of visualisation, for example.
Process	a description of an approach that is defined by: one or more Activity, one or more Artefact and one or more Stakeholder Role. One or more Process also define a Service.

Process Execution Group	A set of one or more Processes executed in order for a specific purpose as part of a Stage. For example, a Process Execution Group may be defined based on a team, function, etc.
Product	Something that realises a System. Typical products may include, but are not limited to: software, hardware, Processes, data, humans, facilities, etc.
Programme	A special type of Project that is itself made up of one or more Project.
Project	One or more Project is run by an Organisational Unit in order to produce one or more System.
Requirement	A property of a System that is either needed or wanted by a Stakeholder Role or other Context-defining element. Also, one or more Requirement is needed to deliver each Capability.
Resource	Anything that is used or consumed by an Activity within a Process. Examples of a Resource include money, locations, fuel, raw material, data, and people.
Rule	A construct that constrains the attributes of a Need Description. A Rule may take several forms, such as: equations, heuristics, reserved word lists, grammar restrictions, etc. Or A construct that constrains an Architectural Framework (and hence the resulting Architecture) in some way, for example by defining one or more Viewpoint that are required as a minimum.
Scenario	An ordered set of interactions between or more Stakeholder Role, System or System Element that represents a specific chain of events with a specific outcome. One or more Scenario validates each Use Case.
Semi-formal Scenario	A Scenario that is demonstrable using, for example, visual notations such as SysML, tables, and text.
Service	An intangible Product that realises a System. A Service is itself realised by one or more Process.
Source Element	The ultimate origin of a Need that is elicited into one or more Need Description. A Source Element can be almost anything that inspires, affects or drives a Need, such as a Standard, a System, Project documentation, a phone call, an e-mail, a letter, and a book.
Stage	A period within a Life Cycle that relates to its realisation through one or more Process Execution Group. The success of a Stage is assessed by a Gate.
Stakeholder Role	The role of anything that has an interest in a System. Examples of a Stakeholder Role include the roles of a Person, an Organisational Unit, a Project, a Source

	Element, and an Enabling System. Each Stakeholder Role requires its own Competency Scope and will be responsible for one or more Activity.
System	A set of interacting elements organised to satisfy one or more System Context. Where the System is a System of Systems, then its elements will be one or more Constituent System, and where the System is a Constituent System then its elements are one or more System Element. A System can interact with one or more other System. The artefact being engineered that an Architecture describes.
System Element	A basic part of a Constituent System.
System of Interest	A special type of System that describes the System being developed, enhanced, maintained or investigated.
System of Systems	A special type of System whose elements are one or more Constituent System and which delivers unique functionality not deliverable by any single Constituent System.
Use Case	A Need that is considered in a specific Context and that is validated by one or more Scenario.
View	the visualisation of part of the Architecture of a System that conforms to the structure and content defined in a Viewpoint. A View is made up of one or more View Element.
View Element	The elements that make up a View. Each View Element visualises a Viewpoint Element that makes up the Viewpoint to which the View, on which the View Element appears, conforms.
Viewpoint	A definition of the structure and content of a View. The content and structure of a Viewpoint uses the concepts and terms from the Ontology via one or more Viewpoint Element that make up the Viewpoint. Each Viewpoint is defined so that it meets the needs defined by one or more Viewpoint Concern.
Viewpoint Concern	Defines a Need that a Viewpoint has to address.
Viewpoint Element	the elements that make up a Viewpoint. Each Viewpoint Element must correspond to an Ontology Element from the Ontology that is part of the Architectural Framework.
Virtual System	A special type of System of Systems that lacks central management and resources, and no consensus of purpose.

Appendix B

Summary of SysML notation

It is worth noting that the notation facilitates discovery.
This, in a most wonderful way, reduces the mind's labour.

Gottfried Wilhelm Leibniz (1646–1716)

B.1 Introduction

This appendix provides a summary of the meta-model and notation diagrams for SysML that are used in Chapter 5. For each of the nine SysML diagram types, grouped into *structural* and *behavioural diagrams*, three diagrams are given:

- A partial meta-model for that diagram type.
- The notation used on that diagram type.
- An example of that diagram type.

The same information is also given for the SysML *auxiliary constructs*. The appendix concludes with a diagram that illustrates some of the main relationships between the SysML diagrams.

This appendix does *not* add further information to that found in Chapter 5 but is intended to provide a single summary section of the noted diagrams. See Chapter 5 for a discussion of each diagram.

B.2 Structural diagrams

This section contains diagrams for each of the five SysML *structural diagrams* (see Figure B.1):

- *Block definition diagrams* (Figures B.2–B.6)
- *Internal block diagrams* (Figures B.7–B.9)
- *Package diagrams* (Figures B.10–B.12)
- *Parametric diagrams* (Figures B.13–B.16)
- *Requirement diagrams* (Figures B.17–B.19)

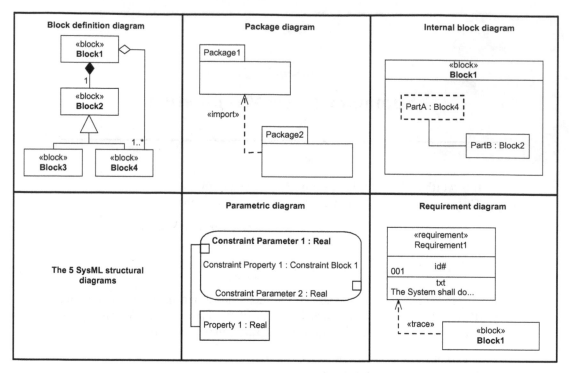

Figure B.1   Summary of structural diagrams

B.2.1   Block definition diagrams

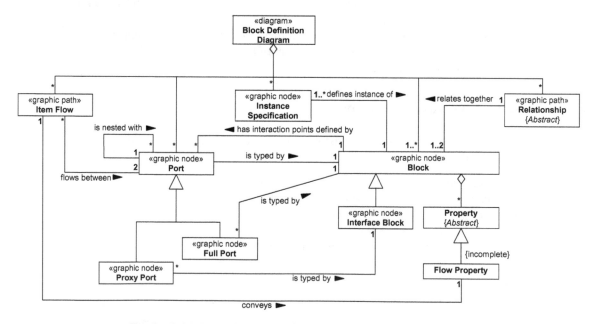

Figure B.2   Partial meta-model for block definition diagrams

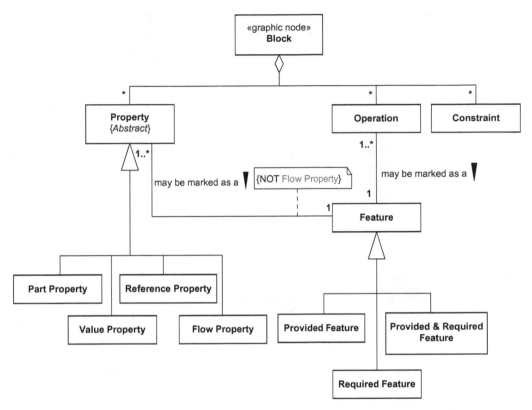

Figure B.3   Partial meta-model for the block definition diagram showing block elements

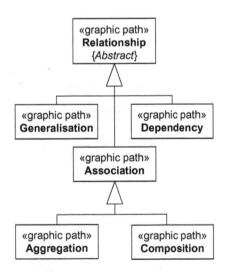

Figure B.4   Partial meta-model for the block definition diagram showing types of relationship

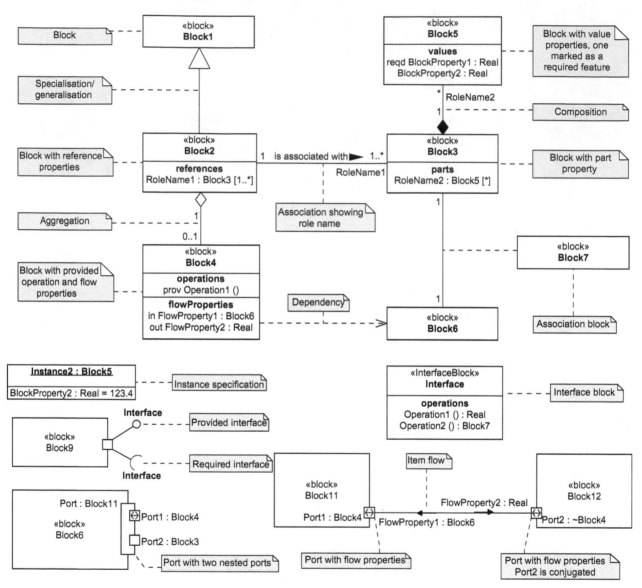

Figure B.5   Block definition diagram notation

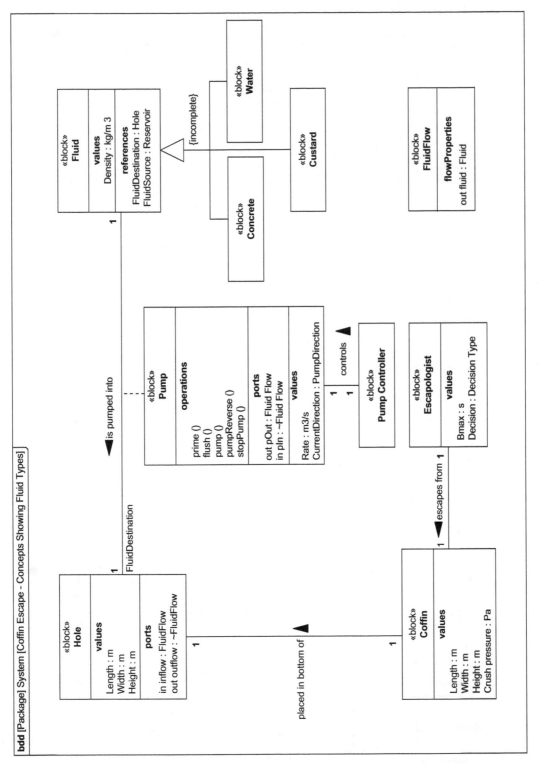

Figure B.6 Example of block definition diagram

B.2.2   Internal block diagrams

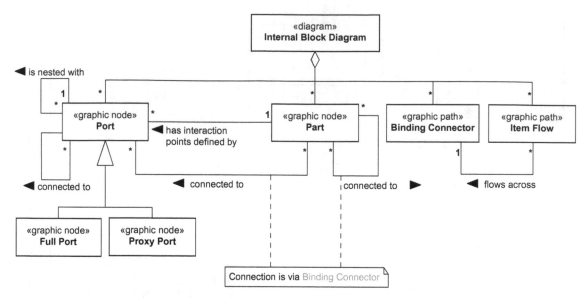

Figure B.7   Partial meta-model for the internal block diagram

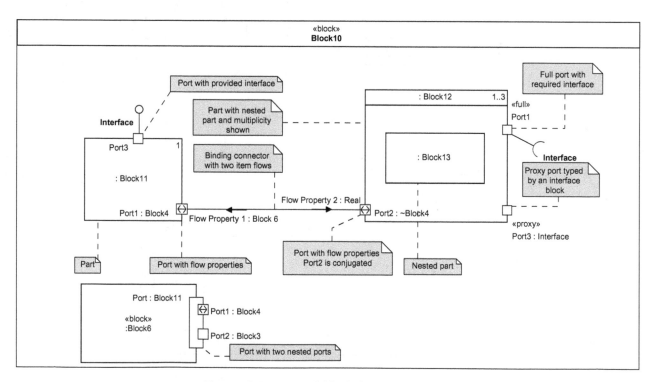

Figure B.8   Internal block diagram notation

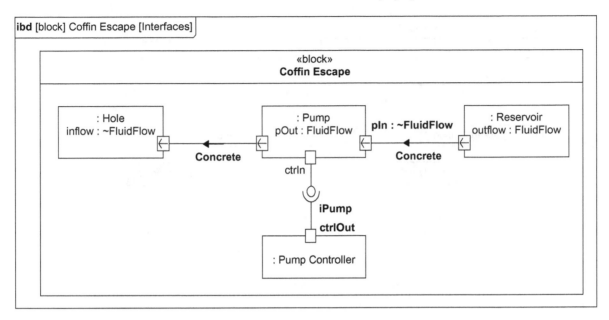

Figure B.9   Example of internal block diagram

B.2.3   Package diagrams

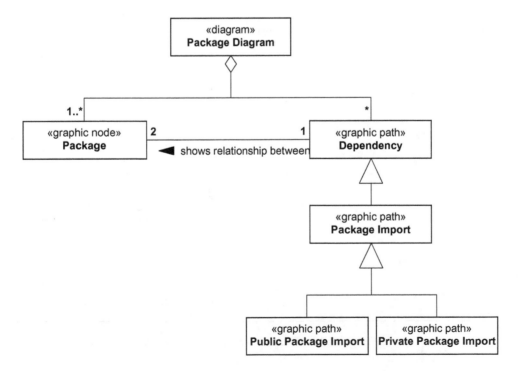

Figure B.10   Partial meta-model for the package diagram

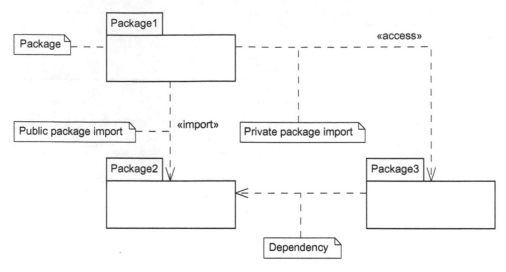

Figure B.11   Package diagram notation

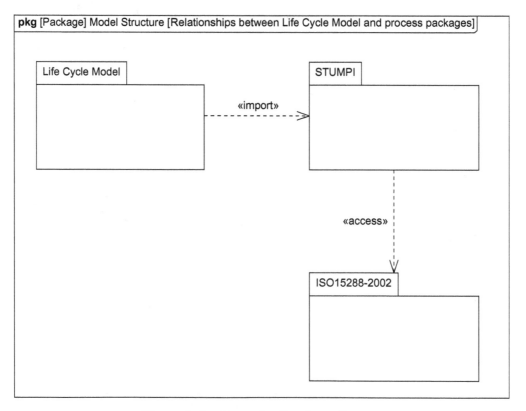

Figure B.12   Example of package diagram

B.2.4 *Parametric diagram*

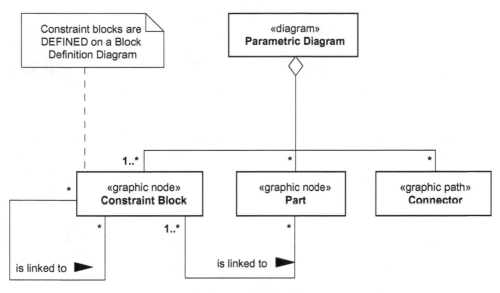

Figure B.13   Partial meta-model for the parametric diagram

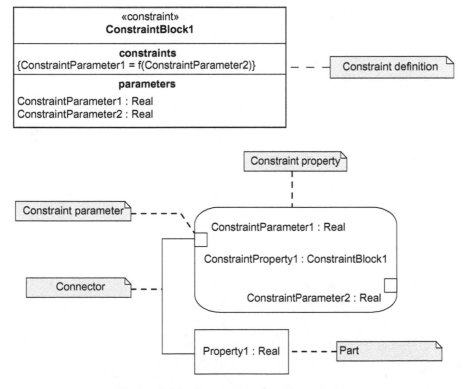

Figure B.14   Parametric diagram notation

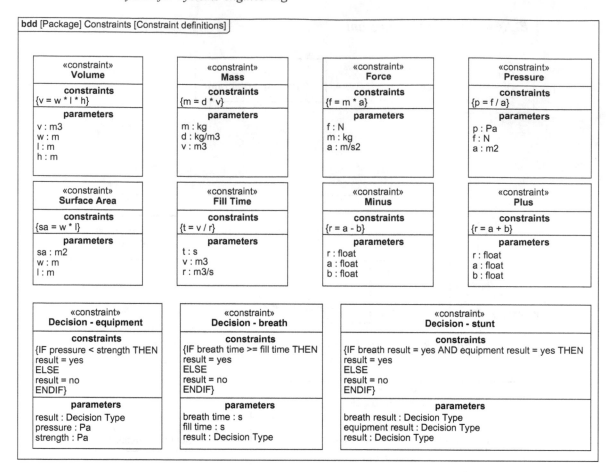

Figure B.15   Example of parametric diagram – definition

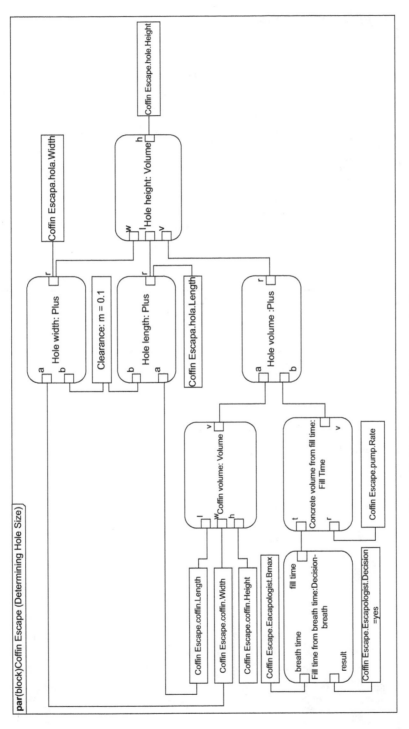

Figure B.16 Example of parametric diagram – usage

B.2.5   Requirement diagrams

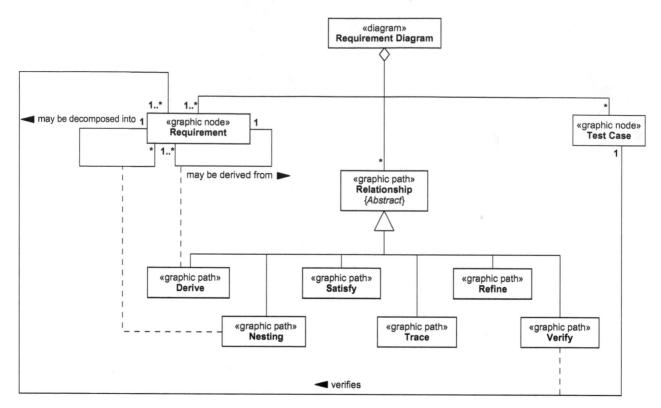

Figure B.17   Partial meta-model for the requirement diagram

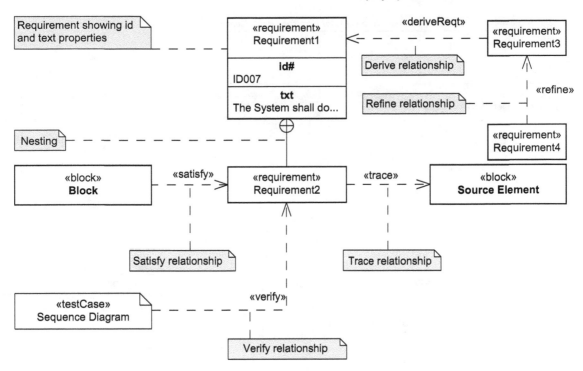

Figure B.18   Requirement diagram notation

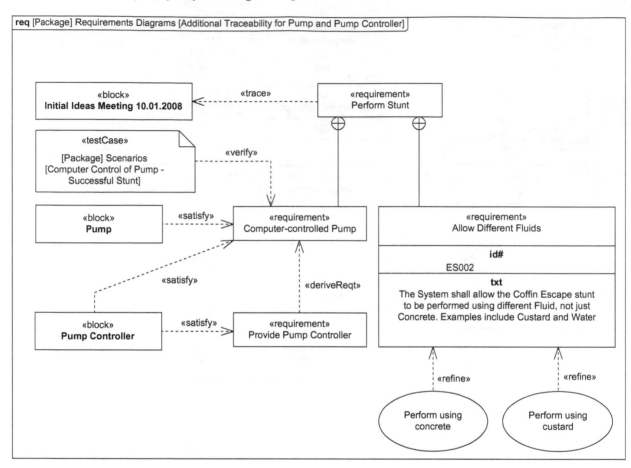

Figure B.19   Example of requirement diagram

B.3 Behavioural diagrams

This section contains diagrams for each of the four SysML *behavioural* diagrams (see Figure B.20):

- *State machine diagrams* (Figures B.21–B.23)
- *Sequence diagrams* (Figures B.24–B.26)
- *Activity diagrams* (Figures B.27–B.31)
- *Use case diagrams* (Figures B.32–B.34)

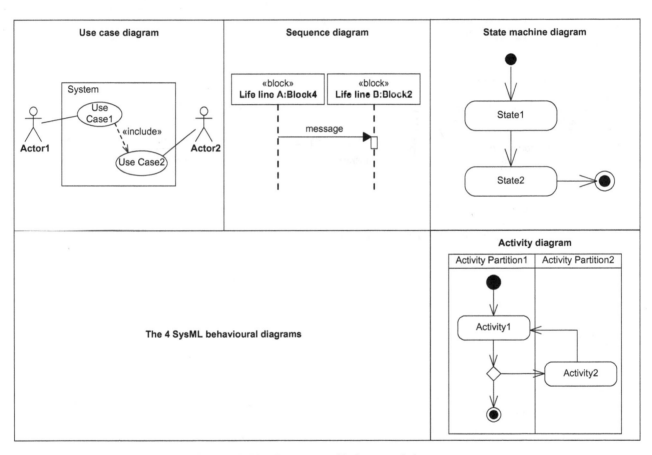

Figure B.20   Summary of behavioural diagrams

B.3.1   State machine diagrams

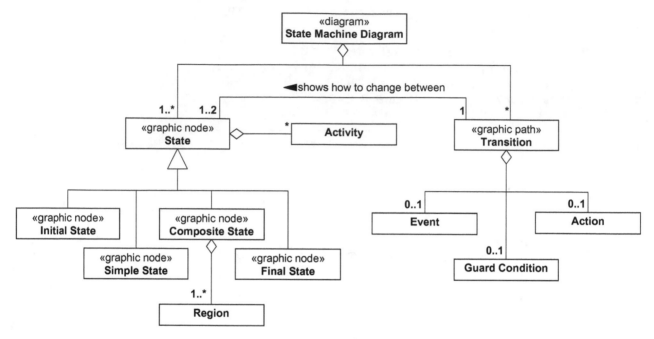

Figure B.21   Partial meta-model for the state machine diagram

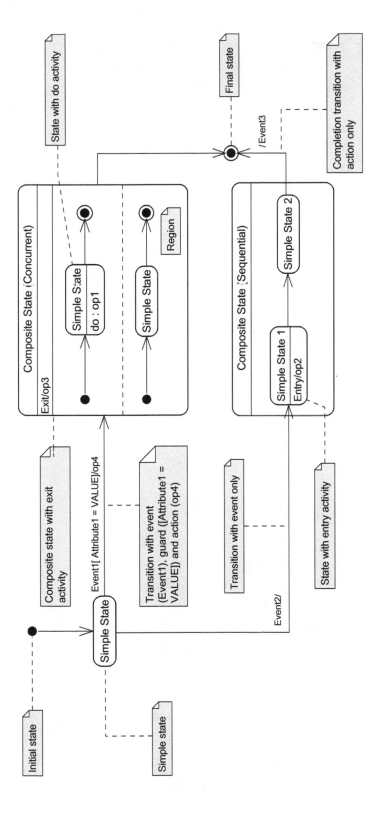

Figure B.22   State machine diagram notation

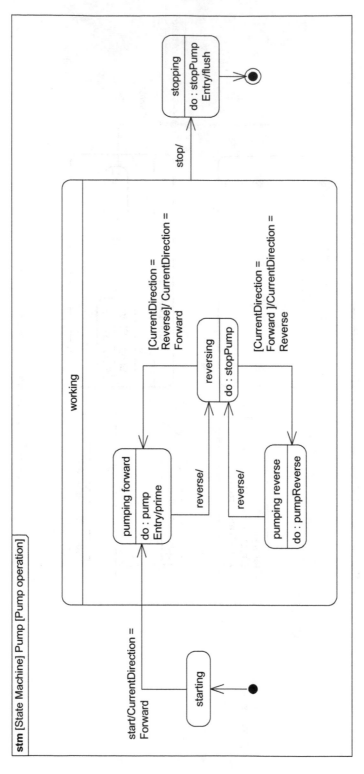

Figure B.23   Example of state machine diagram

B.3.2   Sequence diagrams

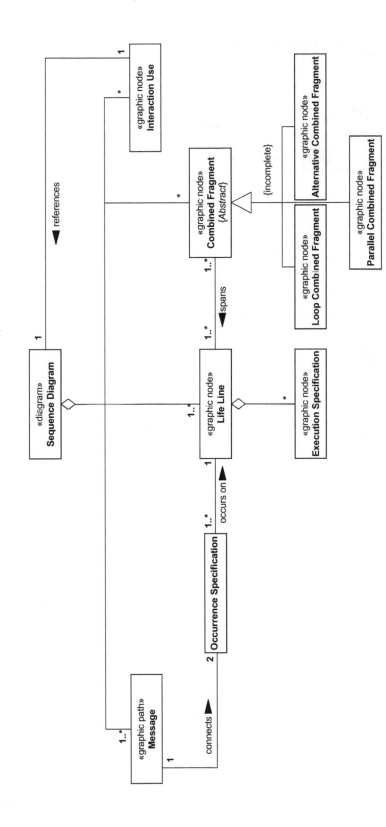

Figure B.24   Partial meta-model for the sequence diagram

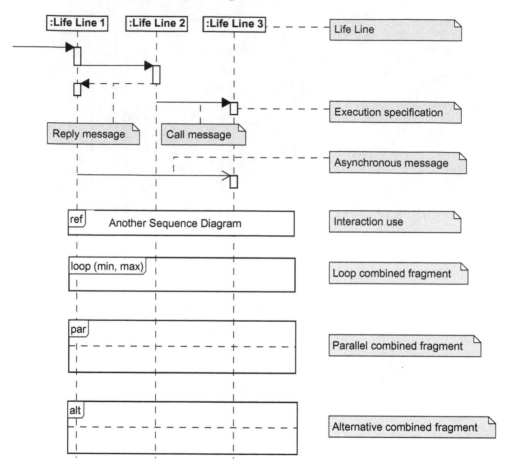

Figure B.25   Sequence diagram notation

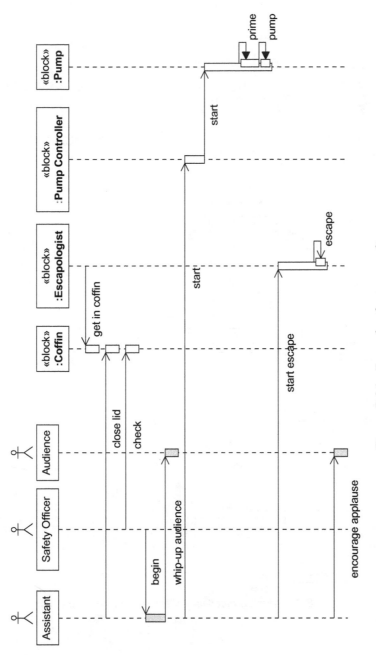

Figure B.26   Example of sequence diagram

B.3.3   Activity diagrams

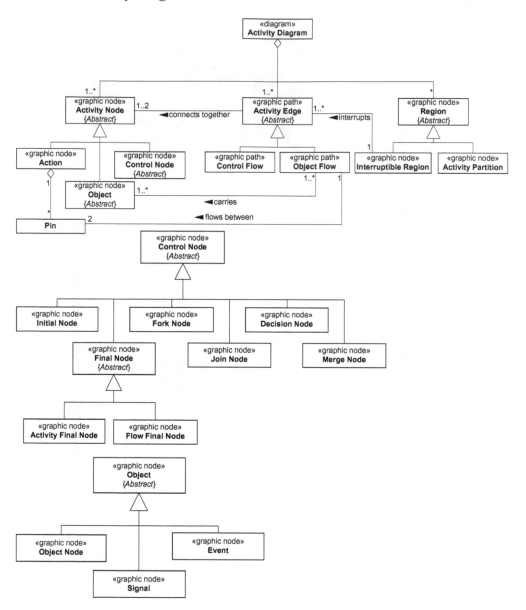

Figure B.27   Partial meta-model for the activity diagram

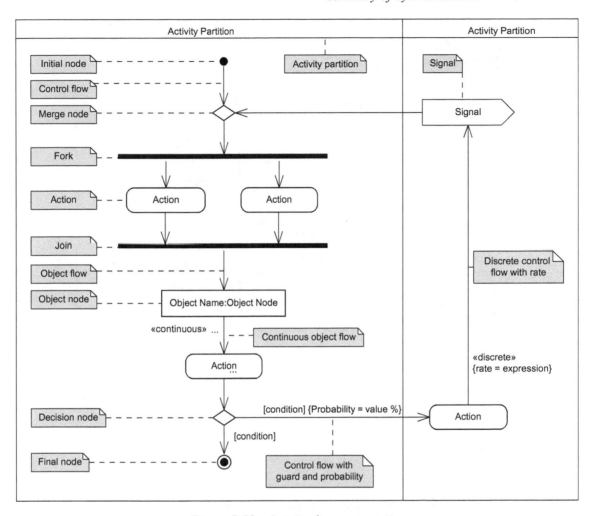

Figure B.28 Activity diagram notation

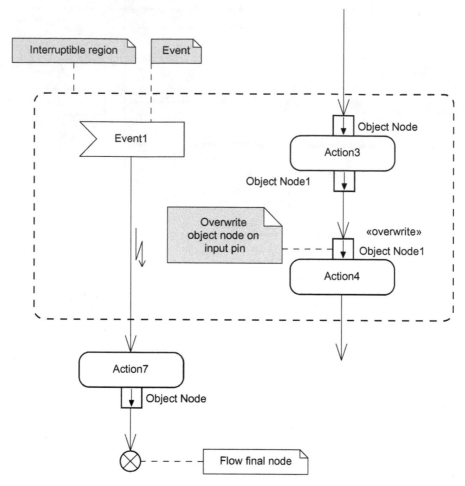

Figure B.29   Activity diagram notation for showing interruptible regions and use of pins rather than object nodes

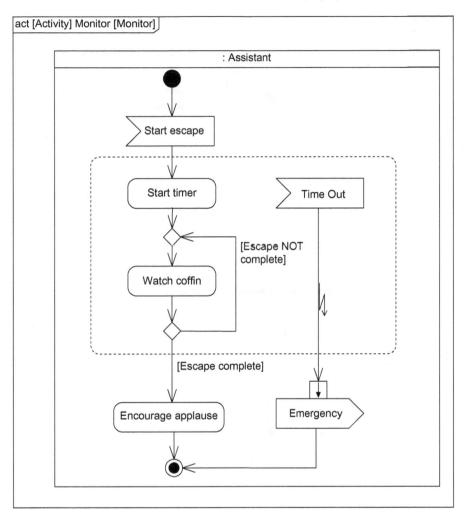

Figure B.30 Example of activity diagram

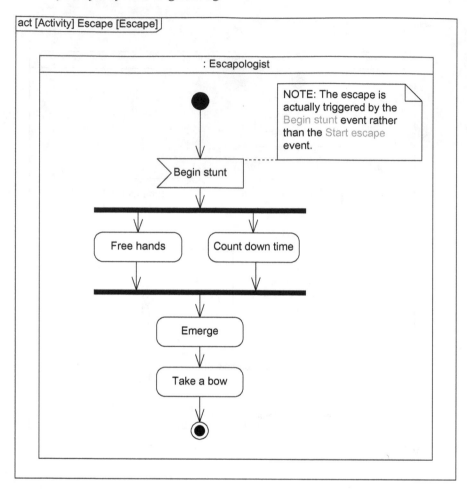

Figure B.31   Example of activity diagram

B.3.4 Use case diagrams

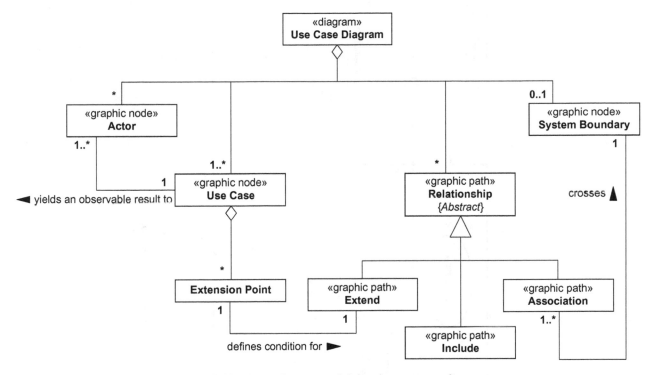

Figure B.32 Partial meta-model for the use case diagram

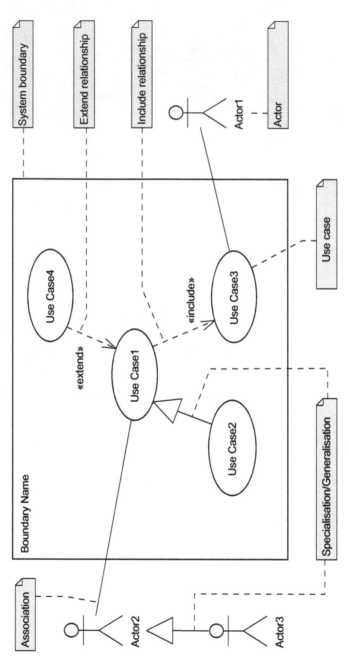

Figure B.33   Use case diagram notation

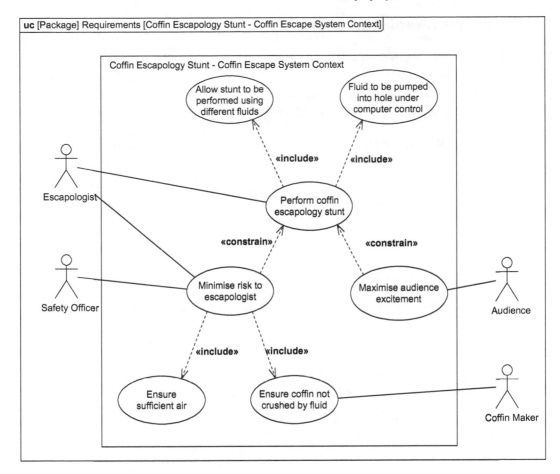

Figure B.34 Example of use case diagram (Product Context)

B.4   Cross-cutting concepts

This section contains diagrams for the following *cross-cutting concepts* that can be applied to any diagram:

- *Allocations* (Figures B.35–B.38)
- *Auxiliary constructs* (Figures B.39–B.41)

B.4.1   Allocations

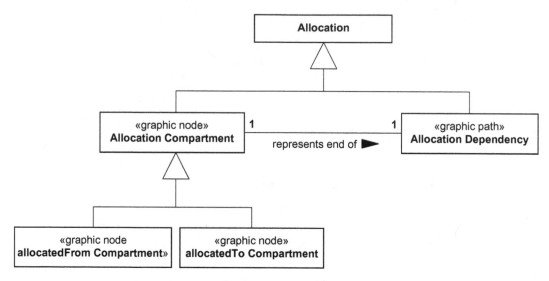

Figure B.35   Partial meta-model for allocations

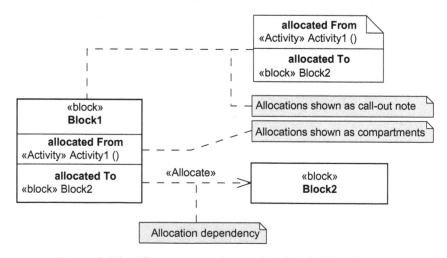

Figure B.36   Allocation notation on block definition diagram

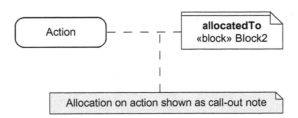

Figure B.37   Allocation notation on activity diagram

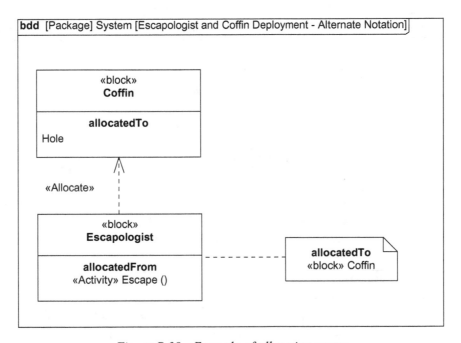

Figure B.38   Example of allocation usage

B.4.2   Auxiliary constructs

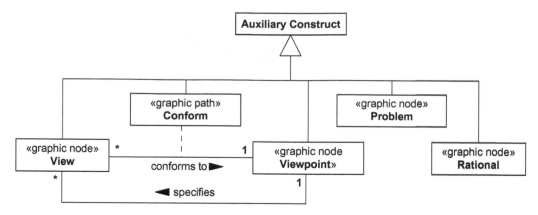

Figure B.39   Partial meta-model for auxiliary constructs

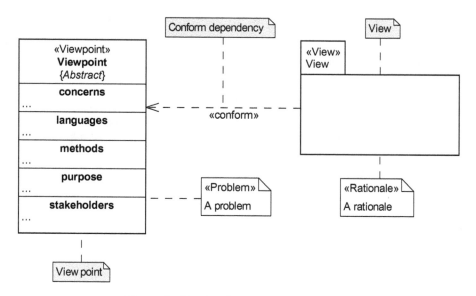

Figure B.40   Auxiliary construct notation

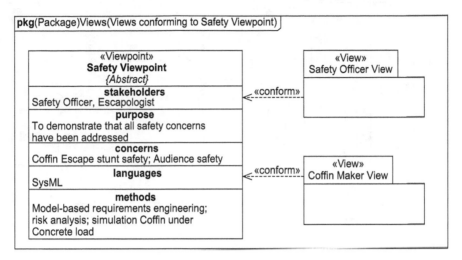

Figure B.41   Examples of auxiliary constructs

B.5   Relationships between diagrams

SysML consists of nine diagrams that are used to capture and model different aspects of a System. Figure B.42 illustrates the main relationships between the diagrams (with the exception of the *package diagram*).

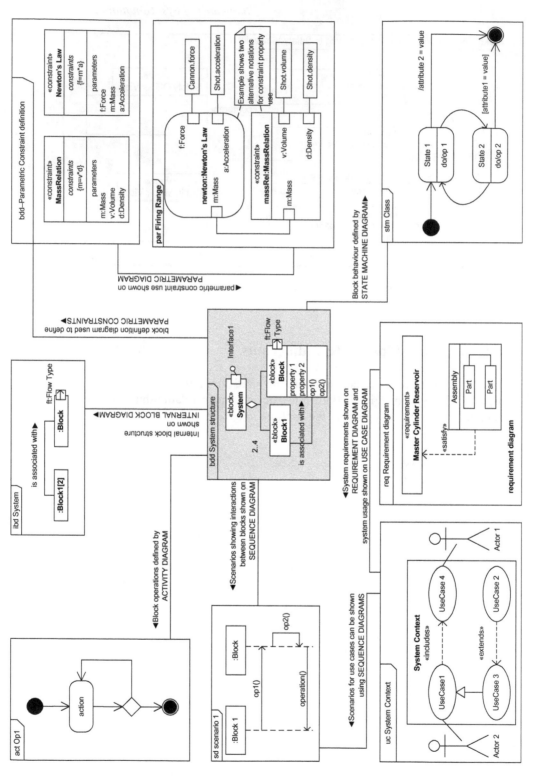

Figure B.42   Relationships between SysML diagrams

Appendix C

Summary of diagramming guidelines

Concern for man and his fate must always form the chief interest of all technical endeavours. Never forget this in the midst of your diagrams and equations.

Albert Einstein (1879–1955)

C.1 Introduction

This appendix summarises the diagramming guidelines described in Chapter 6. No new information is added; indeed the descriptive text for each diagram is condensed in this appendix and the reader is directed to Chapter 6 for the full text.

C.2 Naming conventions

This section defines general naming guidelines that should be followed when producing SysML diagrams.

When modelling Standards etc. or producing models for customers, any naming conventions described in the Standard or used by the customer should be followed.

C.2.1 Structural diagrams

Figure C.1 illustrates the naming conventions to be followed when producing SysML *structural diagrams*.

The case of the text used in all elements indicates the convention to be adopted for that element. For example, an *association* should be named all in lower case whereas a *property* should be named in sentence case (i.e. initial word starts with a capital letter, all others with a lower case letter).

C.2.2 Behavioural diagrams

Figure C.2 illustrates the naming conventions to be followed when producing SysML *behavioural diagrams*.

The case of the text used in all elements indicates the convention to be adopted for that element. For example, a *message* should be named all in lower case whereas a *use case* should be named in sentence case (i.e. initial word starts with a capital letter, all others with a lower case letter).

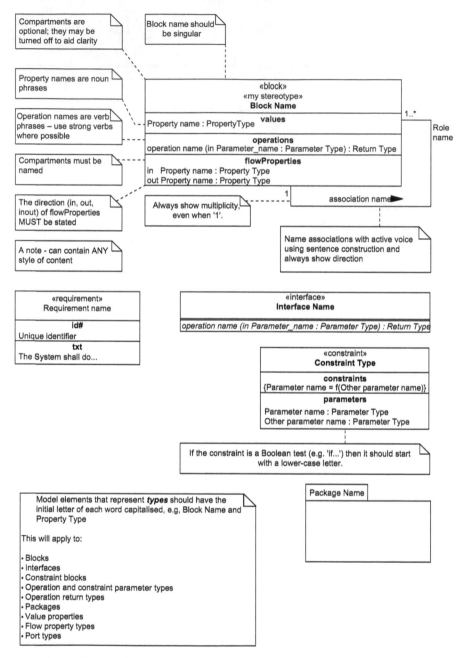

Figure C.1   Naming conventions – structural diagrams

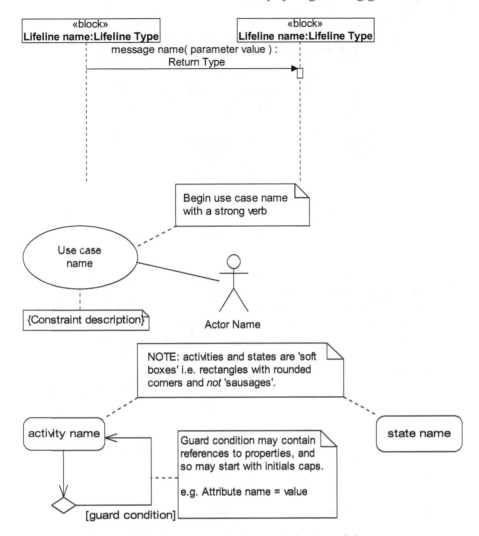

Figure C.2   Naming conventions – behavioural diagrams

C.2.3   Stereotypes

Figure C.3 illustrates the naming conventions to be followed when using *stereotypes*.

C.3   Diagram frame labels

This section defines guidelines to be followed when labelling diagrams.

All SysML diagrams must have a diagram frame that contains the name of the diagram. Each diagram should be named in the following fashion:

<**frame tag**> [model element type] <model element name> [diagram name]

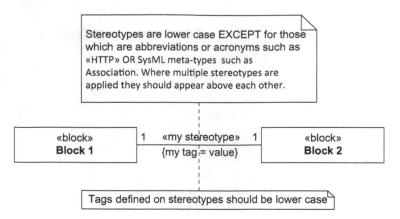

Figure C.3   Naming conventions – stereotypes

Each part is separated by a space and the *frame tag* is bolded. The *model element type* and *diagram name* parts of the name are in brackets. The *frame tag* and *model element name* are mandatory.

The abbreviations shown in Table C.1 should be used to indicate the type of diagram – known in SysML as the *frame tag*. If using a tool that automatically adds a *diagram frame* and that does not allow the *frame tags* to be changed, then the tag names used by the tool will be used.

The following shows the *model element type* associated with the different diagram kinds:

- activity diagram – activity
- block definition diagram – block, package, or constraint block
- internal block diagram – block or constraint block
- package diagram – package or model
- parametric diagram – block or constraint block
- requirement diagram – package or requirement

Table C.1   Diagram frame labels

Diagram type	Frame tag
Activity diagram	act
Block definition diagram	bdd
Internal block diagram	ibd
Package diagram	pkg
Parametric diagram	par
Requirement diagram	req
State machine diagram	stm
Sequence diagram	sd
Use case diagram	uc

- sequence diagram – interaction
- state machine diagram – state machine
- use case diagram – package

The *model element type* indicates the *namespace* for the elements contained on the diagram.

The *model element name* identifies which model element type the diagram is describing.

The *diagram name* is used to give the diagram a unique name. This is particularly important when different diagrams of the same type are drawn for the same model element. The diagram name would differentiate between these diagrams since they would have the same diagram kind, model element type and model element name.

For example, an Ontology View has been defined as part of an Architectural Framework meta-model. It has been given the abbreviation ONT and has the *stereotype* «ontology view» associated with it. The diagram is a usage of a SysML *block definition diagram*. An Ontology View is created in a *package* called MBSE Ontology and is intended to show a simplified Ontology. The *diagram frame* for this diagram would look like Figure C.4.

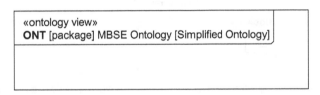

Figure C.4   Example of diagram frame showing user-defined view abbreviation replacing frame tag

In a tool that doesn't allow replacement of *frame tags*, then the *diagram frame* would look like Figure C.5.

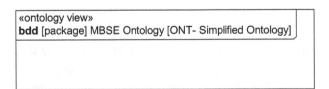

Figure C.5   Example of diagram frame showing user-defined view abbreviation added to diagram name

C.4   Additional guidelines

This section contains additional guidelines that apply to particular diagram types.

C.4.1   *Block and internal block diagrams – showing interfaces*

This section defines guidelines to be followed when producing *block definition diagrams* and *internal block diagrams* that show *interfaces* (Figure C.6).

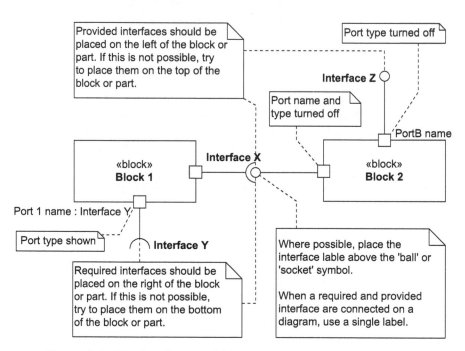

Figure C.6   Block and internal block diagrams – showing interfaces

C.4.2   *Block and internal block diagrams – showing item flows*

This section defines guidelines to be followed when producing *block definition diagrams* and *internal block diagrams* that show *item flows* (Figure C.7).

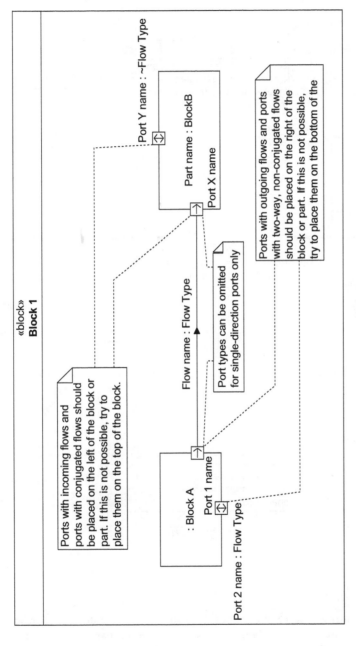

Figure C.7   Block and internal block diagrams – showing item flows

C.4.3 Activity diagrams

This section defines guidelines to be followed when producing *activity diagrams* (Figure C.8).

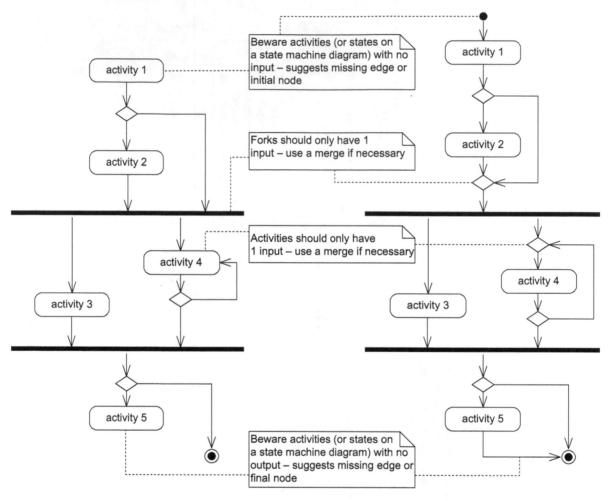

Figure C.8   Activity diagrams

C.4.4 Use of colour

The use of colour can be used to add extra information to a diagram or to make diagrams clearer. However, colour should not be used without careful consideration. As a general rule, all diagram elements should be drawn with black text on a white background.

Where colour is used, then the diagram must include a key that explains the colour scheme and thought should be given to its choice and purpose. For example:

- How well will the colour reproduce when printed in black and white or greyscale?
- Are any fonts or other symbols that lie on top of the colour readable?
- Will the chosen colours be problematic to those who are colour-blind?
- What meaning is attributed to the colours used?
- Have such meanings been made clear in a key?

In addition, some tools allow diagrams to be produced that have 3D effects, gradient fills, shadows and curved lines that can be applied to diagram elements. These should *not* be used, and should be turned off in the tool's options.

C.4.5   Tool settings

Other common diagramming settings that need to be considered include the display of *navigability arrowheads* and *role names* on *associations*, whether whole-part *relationships* should default to *composition* or *aggregation*, whether *association names* should be displayed by default, whether *compositions, aggregations* and *generalisation relationships* should be displayed in a tree layout, what colours should be used for diagram elements such as *blocks, requirements, and use cases*.

A SysML tool should allow such settings to be changed once for a model and not force the modeller to change the settings for every diagram. Even more desirable is the ability to define these settings for all models created with the tool. This allows standard settings to be rolled-out across an entire organisation. Unfortunately, not all tools allow changes to default settings to be made.

C.5   Model structure

When creating a SysML model it is important, in order to aid navigability and ease of use, that the model is well structured. However, it is impossible here to define a structure that is suitable for all projects; any structure adopted must be set up so as to meet the needs of the project for which the model is being created. The authors have created models that have been structured in many different ways. Some examples of structuring adopted by the authors on projects include by:

- Life Cycle Stage
- Engineering process or activity
- System and subsystem
  - Structure
  - Behaviour
- Team
- Architecture framework
- Modelling framework

Sometimes model structure is a combination of these. For example, a model might first be structured by Life Cycle Stage, then within each Stage further structured by System. Figure C.9 shows part of a model of a Standard (ISO15288:2008 – see [ISO15288:2008] and the Process model in Appendix E) that is structured according to the seven views Process modelling Framework described in Chapter 7. Note the use of additional *packages* to contain aspects of the model such as styles (symbol colours etc.), *stereotypes* and scripts (the tool in which this model was produced allows the user to enhance functionality through user-defined scripts).

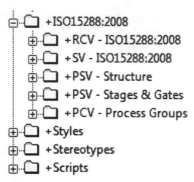

Figure C.9   Example of model structured by modelling Framework Views

Another example is given in Figure C.10. Here, the model is structured largely into a structural and behavioural split influenced by engineering activity. For example, the 'Coffin Escape Schematic', 'Requirements', 'Stakeholders' and 'Scenarios' *packages* contain the parts of the model concerned with Requirements, whereas the 'System', 'Constraints', 'Processes' and 'Units and Types' packages contain the parts of the model concerned with design, defining System structure and behaviour.

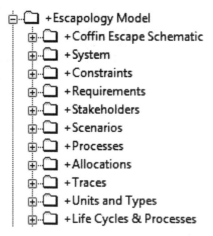

Figure C.10   Example of model structured largely by engineering activity and structural and behavioural split

Some SysML tools have a very useful facility that allows the model to be navigated both by the *package* structure (as in Figures C.9 and C.10) and by model Perspective and View. The two diagrams in Figures C.11 and C.12 illustrate this. These examples are taken from the Martian invasion case study model, discussed in Chapter 13.

The model structure shown in Figure C.11 is structured in a similar way to the model shown in Figure C.10, showing a structure based on a structural and behavioural split influenced by engineering activity.

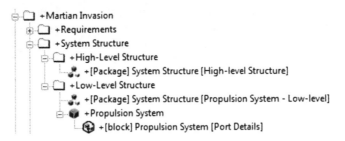

Figure C.11   Model structure – viewed by package

As discussed in Chapter 13, the model has been constructed using an Architectural Framework that defines a number of Perspectives and Viewpoints (see Chapter 10 for a discussion of Viewpoints, Views and Perspectives). The model consists of a number of Views that conform to the Viewpoints (which are simply the definition of Views). Irrespective of the model structure defined by the user, the tool allows the model to be navigated by the Perspectives and Views defined by the Framework. An example is shown in Figure C.12, which shows the *packages* containing the Views that make up the System Perspective. The root package shows the Perspective and the sub-Packages correspond to each View in that Perspective (not all Views are shown). The View *packages* show all the model diagrams that conform to that View, no matter where in the *package* structure shown in Figure C.11 they reside. The Perspective and View structure is defined by and enforced by the tool; the user is not allowed to change this structure in any way.

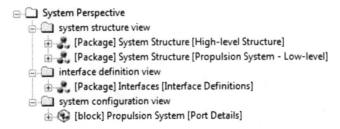

Figure C.12   Model structure – viewed by Perspective and View

Note that the *package* names for the View *packages* are lower case, which contradicts the naming convention described in section C.2.1. This is because the tool used requires the use of *stereotypes* to name Views in a way that makes them browsable as shown in Figure C.12; so the *package* labelled system structure view is displaying the all diagrams stereotyped «system structure view» and similarly for the others. The naming convention can thus be seen to be consistent with the guidelines for naming *stereotypes* given in section C.2.3.

Finally, many SysML tools will suggest a predefined model structure when a new model is created in the tool. While such structures may be of use in suggesting a starting point for the way the model is organised, they are rarely of much use beyond that. The model will be much easier to navigate if time is taken to define the structure that makes sense to the users of the model. The structure is up to you, but should be covered in your engineering Processes or modelling style guides.

Appendix D

Using SysML concepts in UML

I did never know so full a voice issue from so empty a heart: but the saying is true 'The empty vessel makes the greatest sound'.

William Shakespeare (1564–1616), Henry V – ACT IV, SCENE IV

D.1 Introduction

SysML includes some useful notation and concepts not found in UML, in particular *required* and *provided features*, *flow properties* and parametric *constraint blocks*. The diagrams omitted from SysML (*timing* and *deployment*) may prove problematic for systems engineers wishing to fully model a System, particularly those working with software engineers who may be modelling with the UML and therefore using the omitted diagrams.

One solution for systems engineers is to use UML rather than SysML, but to *add* SysML constructs to UML. This appendix illustrates how this may be done.

D.2 Features

SysML allows for *properties* and *operations* to be marked as *required*, *provided* or *required and provided*. Adding this to UML is achieved by defining three *stereotypes* (Figure D.1).

An example of these in use is shown in Figure D.2.

D.3 Full and proxy ports

SysML allows for *ports* to be marked as *full* or *proxy*. Adding this to UML is achieved by defining two *stereotypes* (Figure D.3).

An example of these in use is shown in Figure D.4.

D.4 Flow properties and ports that use them

In order to model the SysML concept of *flow properties* a new *stereotype* is needed, along with an associated *tag* that uses an *enumerated* type. This is seen in Figure D.5.

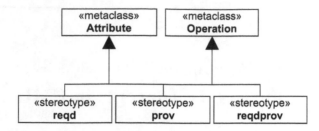

Figure D.1   *Stereotypes to add required, provided, etc., features to UML*

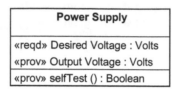

Figure D.2   *UML class showing use of provided and required features*

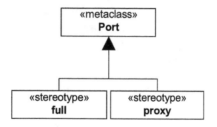

Figure D.3   *Stereotypes to add full and proxy ports to UML*

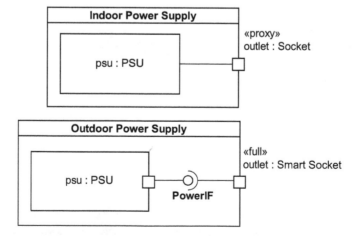

Figure D.4   *UML class showing use of full and proxy ports*

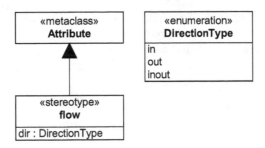

Figure D.5 *Stereotypes to add flow properties to UML*

A comparison of a *class* using this *stereotype* and the corresponding SysML *block* is shown in Figure D.6.

Figure D.6 *A comparison of flow properties in SysML (a) and UML (b)*

Although SysML no longer explicitly includes the idea of a *flow port* (this concept was dropped in SysML version 1.3, the version that this book is based on) it does allow for *ports* that are typed by *blocks* containing *flow properties* to be represented differently (see, for example, Figure B.5). In UML such *ports* could be indicated using a «flow» *stereotype* along with a *tag* to indicate the *direction* of the *flow*. These are defined as shown in Figure D.7.

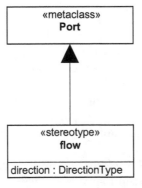

Figure D.7 *UML stereotype definition for identification of ports with flow properties*

Note that the diagram in Figure D.7 makes use of the 'DirectionType' defined in Figure D.5. Also, the notion of a *port* being *conjugated* is found in UML as well as SysML, so it does not have to be redefined.

A comparison of UML diagram using this *stereotype* and the corresponding SysML diagram is shown in Figure D.8.

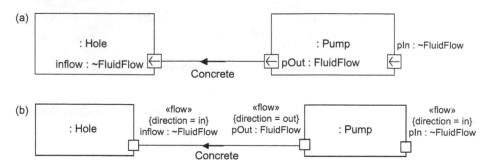

Figure D.8   A comparison of ports with flow properties in SysML (a) and UML (b)

UML does allow alternative images to be associated with *stereotypes*, with stereotyped elements displayed using the alternative image rather than the textual stereotype notation. The various *flow port stereotype* definitions could be defined with alternative images in order to make the UML diagram much more similar to the SysML, but care is always needed when defining new graphical symbols as their use may make reading a diagram difficult for those not familiar with the new symbols. A standard UML element with a *stereotype* makes it clear to the reader that the basic UML notation has been extended.

Where SysML has *item flows*, these are based directly on UML's *information flows*, which can, therefore, be used in UML to represent *item flows*. This has been done in Figure D.8.

D.5   Parametric constraints

SysML has the concepts of parametric *constraint blocks*. These are defined on a SysML *block definition diagram* and used on a *parametric diagram*. Examples are shown in Figures D.9 and D.10.

Again, UML can be extended through *stereotypes* to include these concepts. Figure D.11 shows an example of the definition of the needed *stereotypes*. Again, this diagram needs to be accompanied by text and constraints describing the use of the *stereotypes*.

Figure D.12 shows a UML *class diagram* defining two parametric constraints using the *stereotypes* defined in Figure D.11. Note the use of an additional 'constraints' *compartment* on these *classes*. UML allows for any number of additional named *compartments* to be added to a *class*.

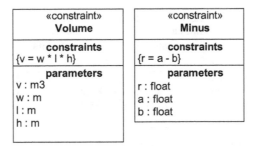

Figure D.9   *SysML parametric constraint block definition*

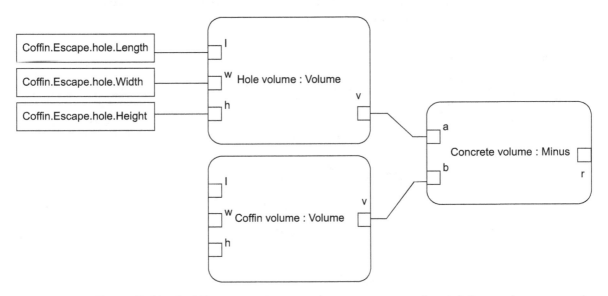

Figure D.10   *SysML parametric constraint property usage (partial diagram)*

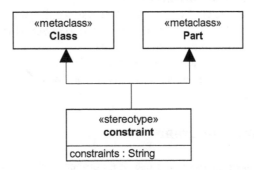

Figure D.11   *UML stereotype definitions for parametrics*

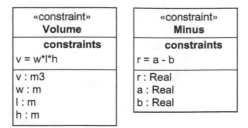

Figure D.12   UML parametric definitions

Figure D.13 shows the use of UML *parts* and the *stereotype* from Figure D.11 to describe the usage of parametric *constraint blocks*.

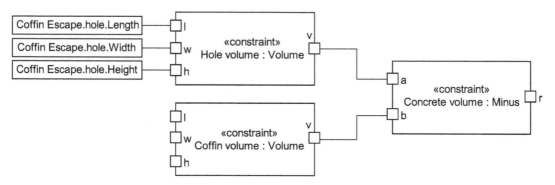

*Figure D.13   UML diagram showing use of parametric constraints
(partial diagram)*

D.6   Activity diagrams

SysML introduced some small notational additions to *activity diagrams* that allow rates and probabilities to be added to *activity edges*, and the concepts of buffering or no overwrite to be added to *object nodes*.

All of these concepts can be added to UML using either the existing constraints notation (for probabilities and defined rates) or *stereotypes* (for discrete and continuous rates and for the *object node* notations).

The *stereotypes* needed are shown in Figure D.14.

UML diagrams produced using these *stereotypes* will look very similar to their SysML counterparts.

D.7   Requirement diagrams

SysML *requirement diagrams* make use of a number of stereotyped *dependencies*, together with stereotyped *blocks* and the *nesting relationship*. The required *stereotypes* are shown in Figure D.15.

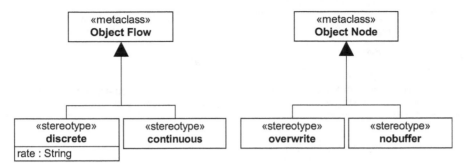

Figure D.14   Activity diagram stereotypes

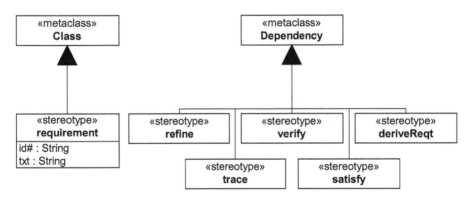

Figure D.15   Requirement diagram stereotypes

By stereotyping *dependencies* and *classes*, and using *composition* to replace *nesting*, *requirement diagrams* can easily be drawn in UML. Note that the *nesting relationship* is part of the UML, but is usually used to show structures of *nested packages*. The meaning of the *nesting relationship* in its use on SysML *requirement diagrams* is one of *composition* to show that a *requirement* is composed of a number of sub-*requirements*. For this reason the *composition relationship*, rather than the *nesting relationship*, is recommended. In fact, earlier versions of the SysML specification used the *composition relationship* rather than the *nesting relationship*.

An example of a UML *class diagram* used as a *requirements diagram* is shown in Figure D.16.

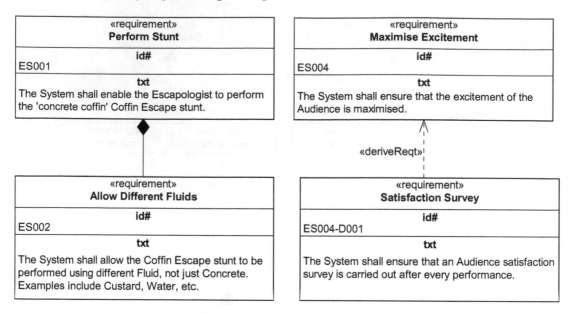

Figure D.16   UML class diagram used to model requirements

The definition of the «testCase» *stereotype* is left as an exercise for the reader.

Appendix E

Process model for ISO15288:2008

I have my standards. They're low, but I have them.

Bette Midler

E.1 Introduction

This Appendix summarises what is perhaps the most widely-used systems engineering Standard in the world: ISO/IEC 15288:2008 Systems and software engineering – System Life Cycle Processes [1].

The Appendix presents information on ISO15288:2008 using the "seven views" approach to Process modelling that is discussed in Chapter 3.1, five out of the seven possible Views are presented; no Information Views or Process Behaviour Views are given as the Standard is written at a level which does not allow these Views to be abstracted and modelled.

The Views are given without commentary and are intended to be used as a reference in conjunction with a reading of the Standard. As an aid to understanding the content of ISO15288:2008, the reader is also directed to the INCOSE Systems Engineering Handbook [2].

E.2 Requirement context view

RCV [package] RCV - ISO 15288 [Standard Context]

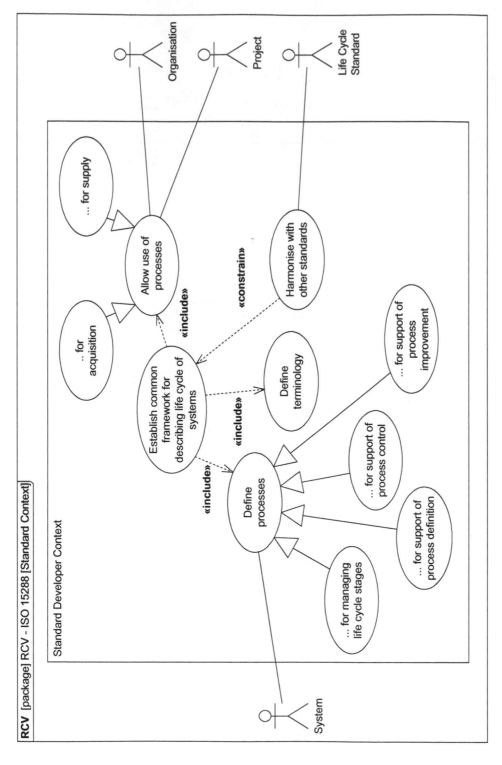

Figure E.1 Requirement context view

E.3   Stakeholder view

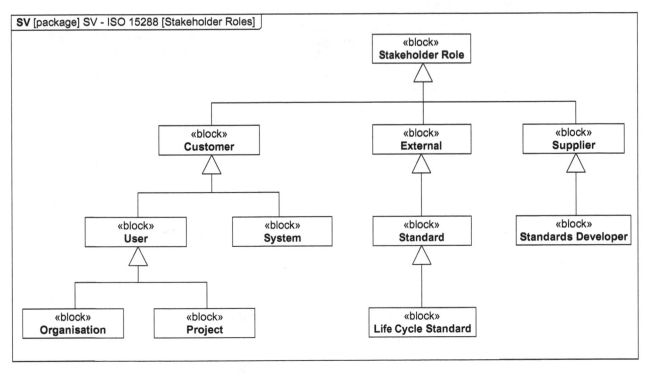

Figure E.2   Stakeholder view

E.4   Process structure view

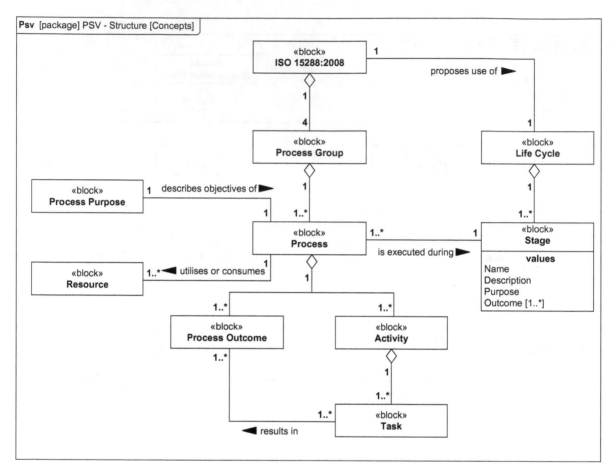

Figure E.3   Process structure view

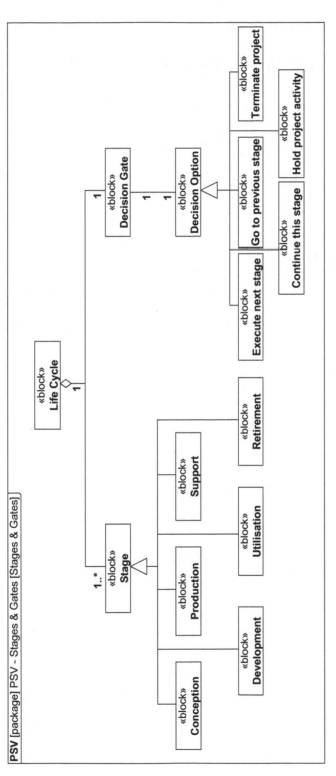

Figure E.4　Process structure view – 'stages' and 'decision options'

E.5   Process content view

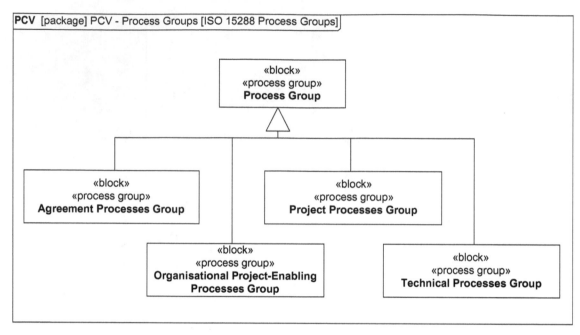

Figure E.5   Process content view – 'process groups'

E.5.1   Process content view – agreement processes group

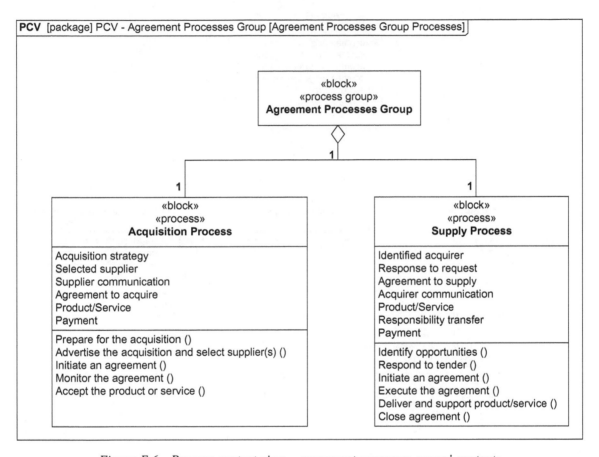

Figure E.6   Process content view – agreement processes group' contents

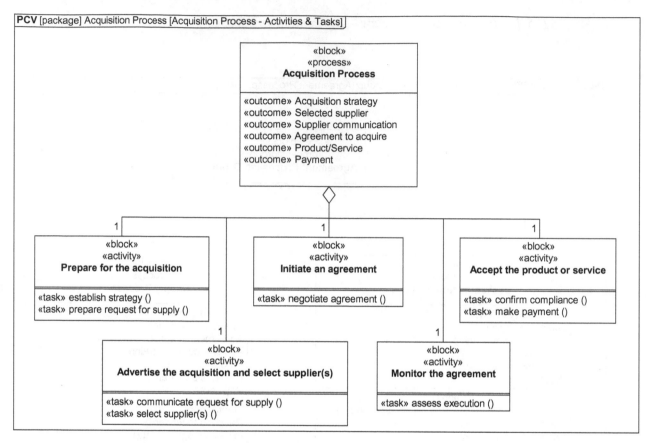

Figure E.7   Process content view – 'acquisition process' – activities and tasks

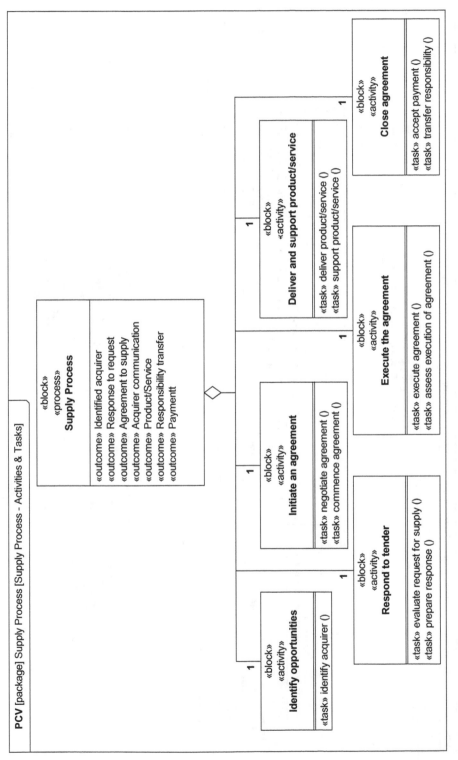

Figure E.8   Process content view – 'supply process' – activities and tasks

E.5.2 Process content view – organisational project-enabling processes group

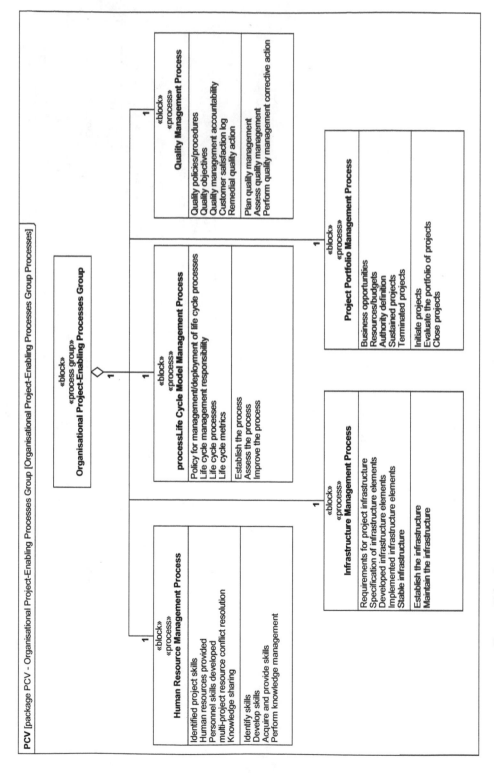

Figure E.9 Process content view – 'organisational project-enabling processes group' contents

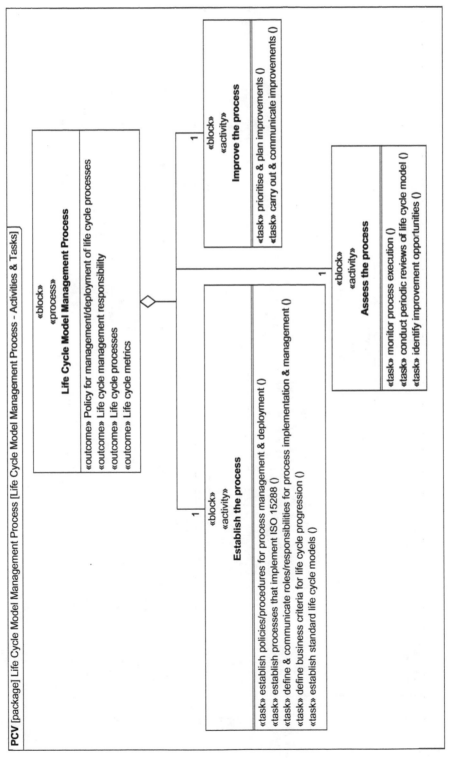

Figure E.10   Process content view – 'life cycle model management process' – activities and tasks

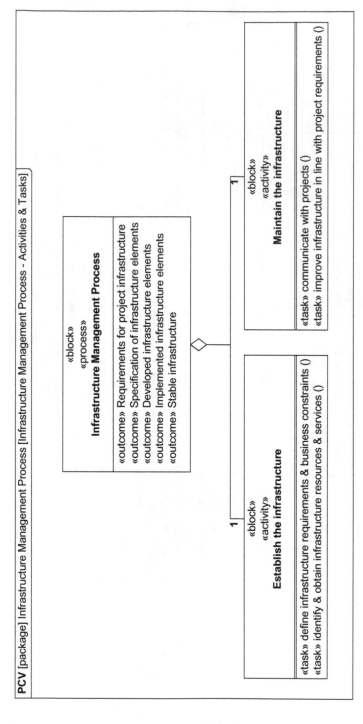

Figure E.11   Process content view – 'infrastructure management process' – activities and tasks

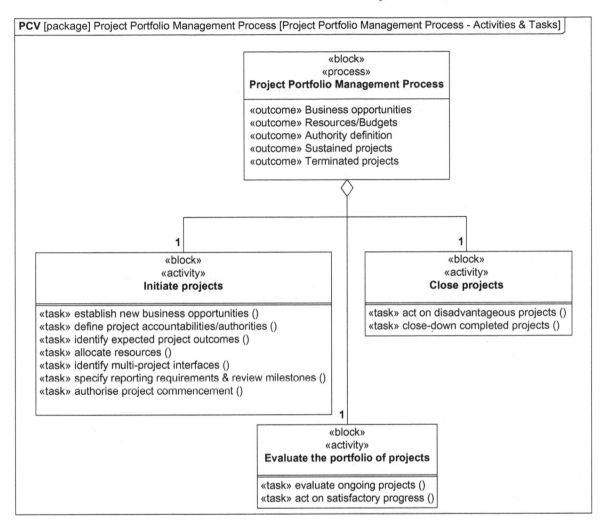

Figure E.12   Process content view – 'project portfolio management process' –
activities and tasks

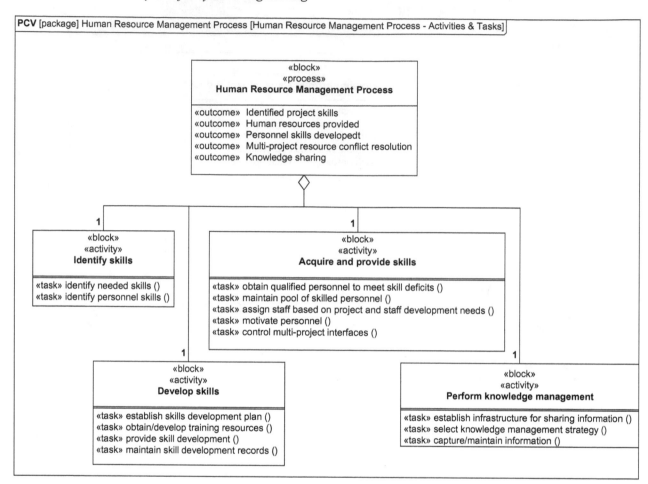

Figure E.13   Process content view – 'human resource management process' – activities and tasks

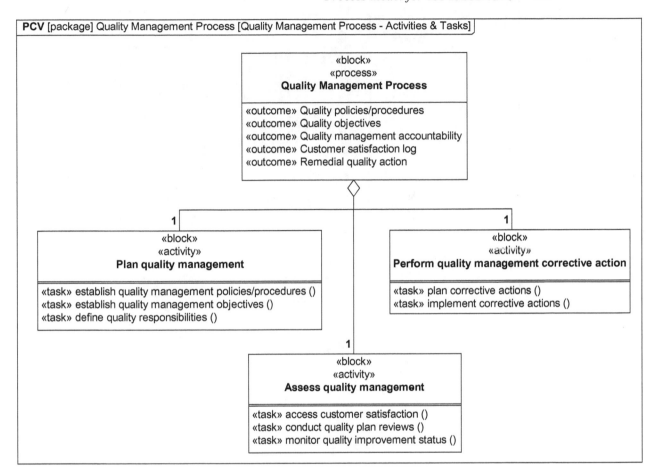

Figure E.14   Process content view – 'quality management process' –
activities and tasks

E.5.3 *Process content view – project processes group*

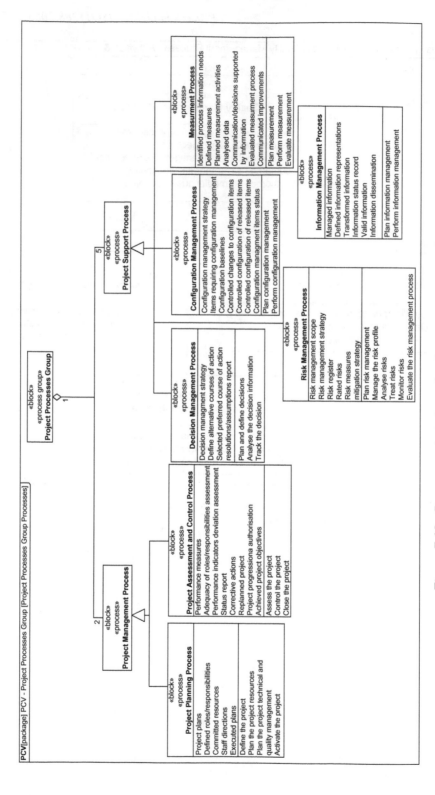

Figure E.15 *Process content view – 'project processes group' contents*

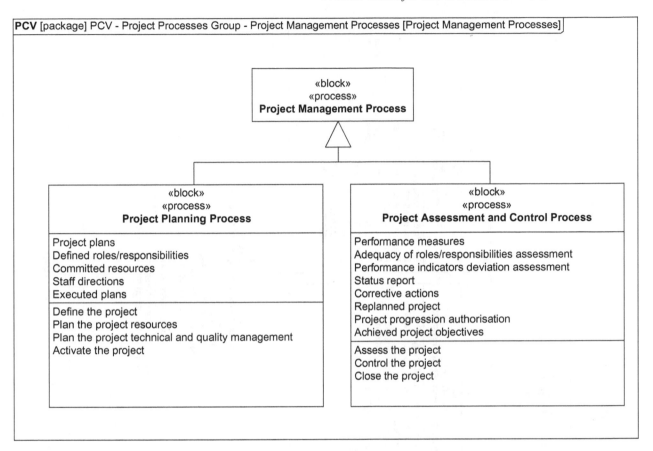

Figure E.16   Process content view – 'project processes group' – 'management'

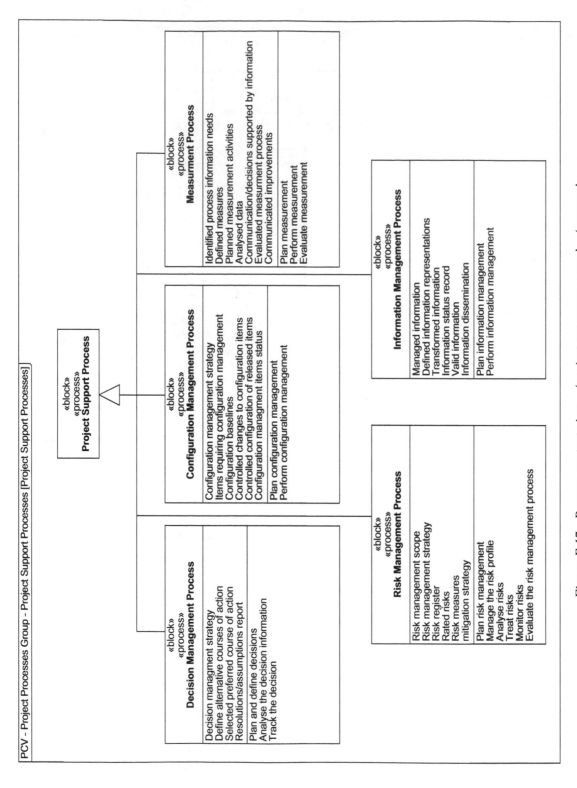

«block»
«process»
Project Support Process

«block»
«process»
Decision Management Process

Decision managment strategy
Define alternative courses of action
Selected preferred course of action
Resolutions/assumptions report

Plan and define decisions
Analyse the decision information
Track the decision

«block»
«process»
Configuration Management Process

Configuration management strategy
Items requiring configuration management
Configuration baselines
Controlled changes to configuration items
Controlled configuration of released items
Configuration managment items status

Plan configuration management
Perform configuration management

«block»
«process»
Measurment Process

Identified process information needs
Defined measures
Planned measurement activities
Analysed data
Communication/decisions supported by information
Evaluated measurement process
Communicated improvements

Plan measurement
Perform measurement
Evaluate measurement

«block»
«process»
Risk Management Process

Risk management scope
Risk management strategy
Risk register
Rated risks
Risk measures
mitigation strategy

Plan risk management
Manage the risk profile
Analyse risks
Treat risks
Monitor risks
Evaluate the risk management process

«block»
«process»
Information Management Process

Managed information
Defined information representations
Transformed information
Information status record
Valid information
Information dissemination

Plan information management
Perform information management

Figure E.17   Process content view – 'project processes group' – 'support'

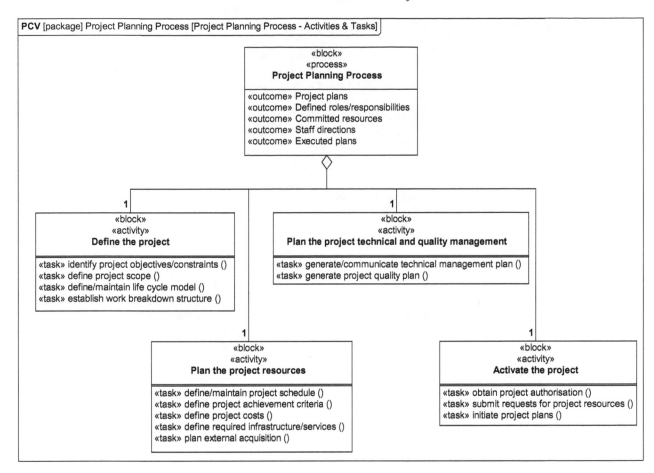

Figure E.18   Process content view – 'project planning process' – activities and tasks

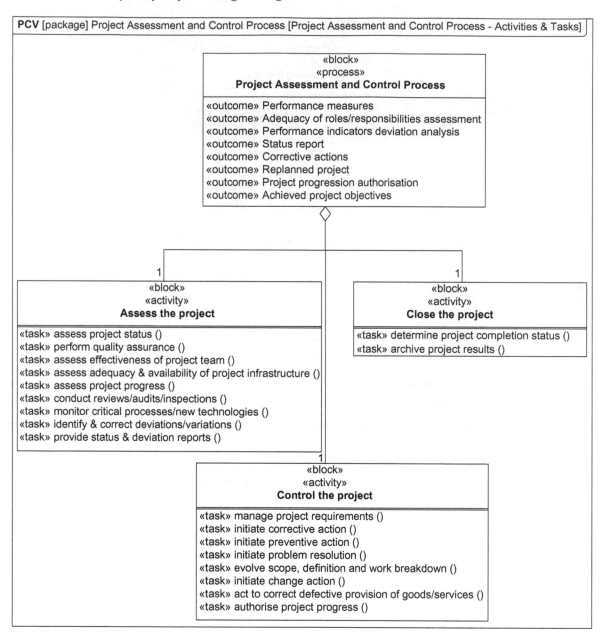

*Figure E.19   Process content view – 'project assessment and control
process' – activities and tasks*

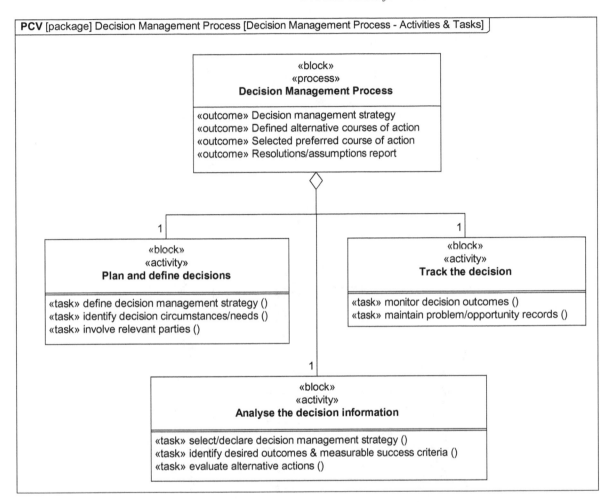

Figure E.20   Process content view – 'decision management process' – activities and tasks

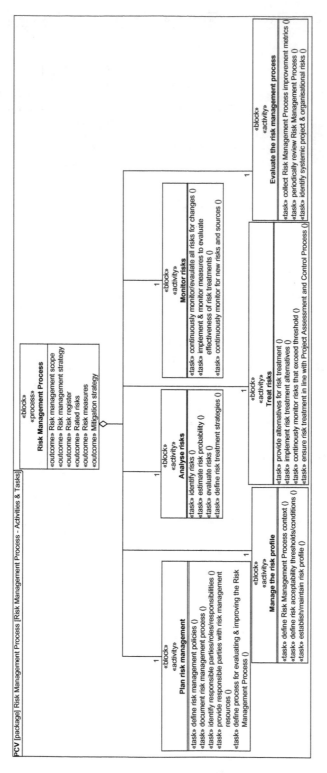

Figure E.21 Process content view – 'risk management process' – activities and tasks

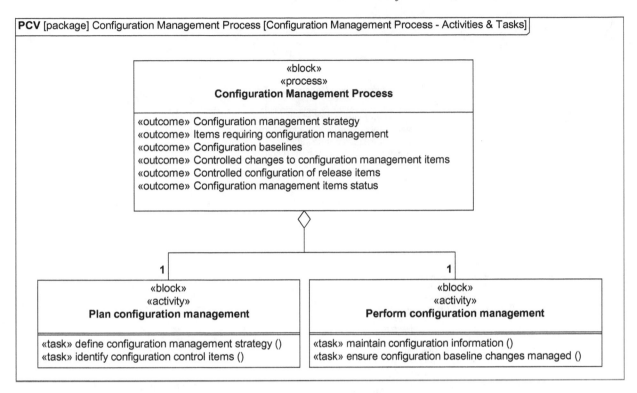

Figure E.22 Process content view – 'configuration management process' – activities and tasks

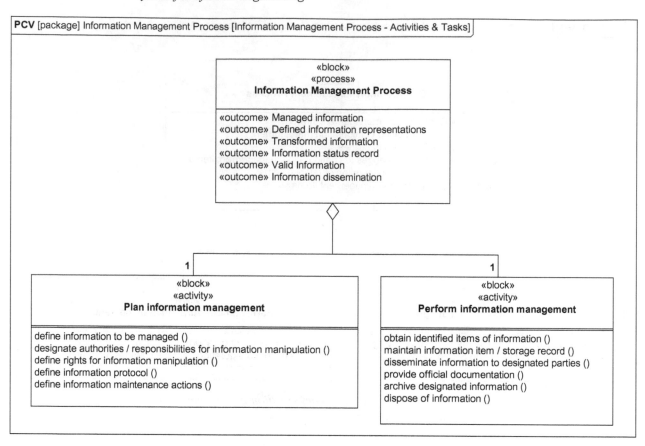

Figure E.23   Process content view – 'information management process' – activities and tasks

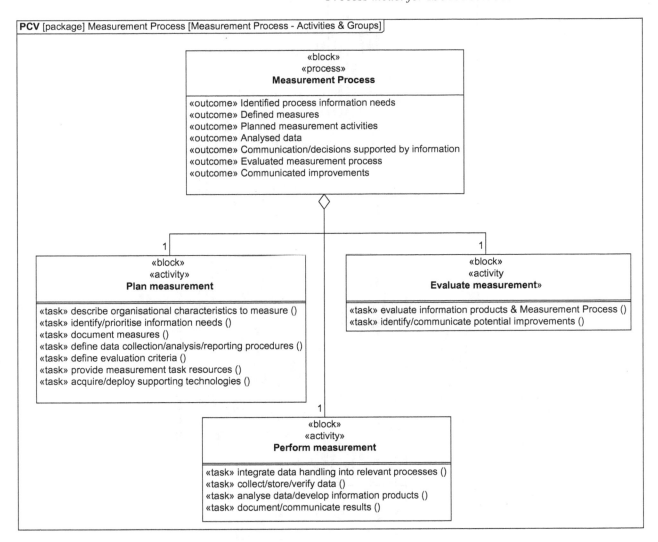

Figure E.24   Process content view – 'measurement process' –
activities and groups

E.5.4 Process content view – technical processes group

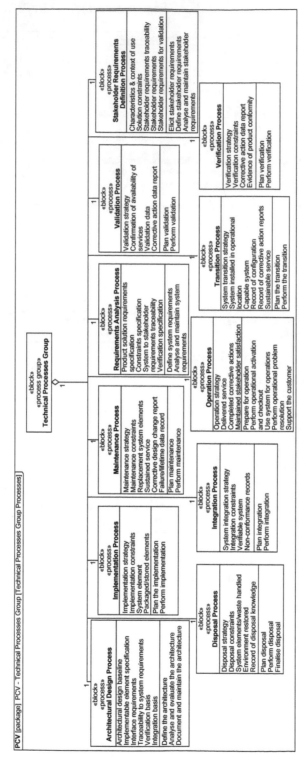

Figure E.25   Process content view – 'technical processes group' contents

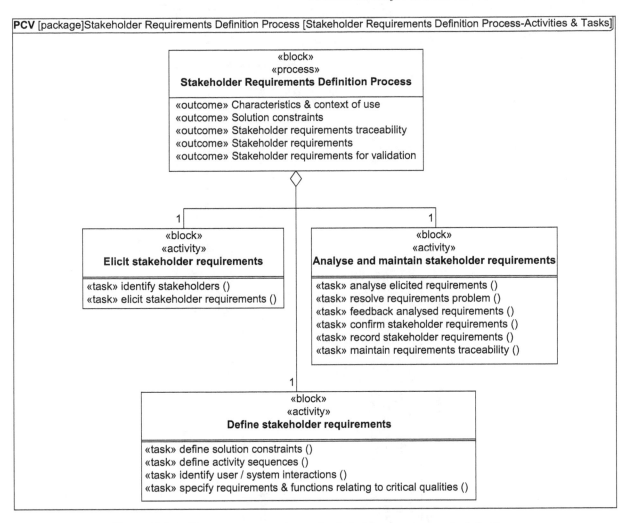

PCV [package]Stakeholder Requirements Definition Process [Stakeholder Requirements Definition Process-Activities & Tasks]

«block»
«process»
Stakeholder Requirements Definition Process

«outcome» Characteristics & context of use
«outcome» Solution constraints
«outcome» Stakeholder requirements traceability
«outcome» Stakeholder requirements
«outcome» Stakeholder requirements for validation

1

«block»
«activity»
Elicit stakeholder requirements

«task» identify stakeholders ()
«task» elicit stakeholder requirements ()

1

«block»
«activity»
Analyse and maintain stakeholder requirements

«task» analyse elicited requirements ()
«task» resolve requirements problem ()
«task» feedback analysed requirements ()
«task» confirm stakeholder requirements ()
«task» record stakeholder requirements ()
«task» maintain requirements traceability ()

1

«block»
«activity»
Define stakeholder requirements

«task» define solution constraints ()
«task» define activity sequences ()
«task» identify user / system interactions ()
«task» specify requirements & functions relating to critical qualities ()

*Figure E.26   Process content view – 'stakeholder requirements definition
process' – activities and tasks*

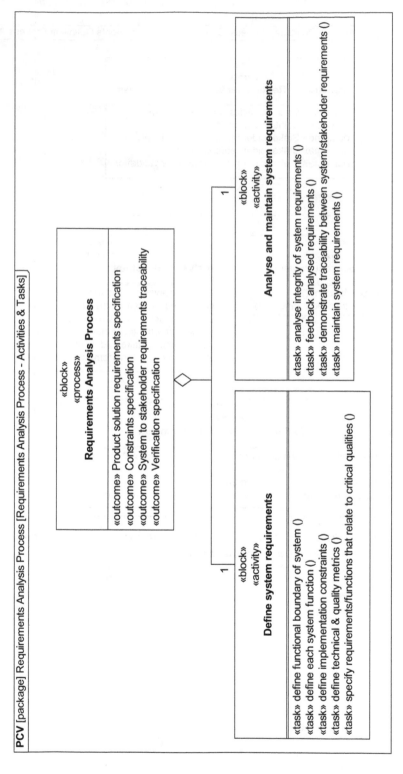

Figure E.27   Process content view – 'requirements analysis process' – activities and tasks

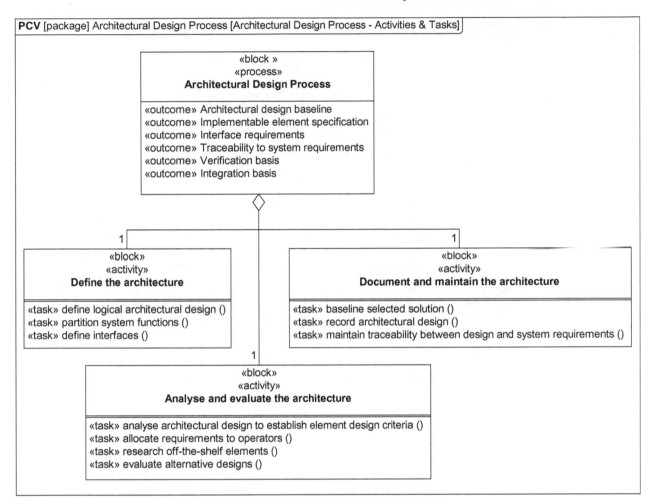

Figure E.28   Process content view – 'architectural design process' –
activities and tasks

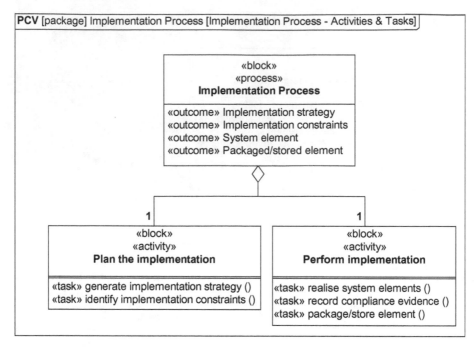

*Figure E.29   Process content view – 'implementation process' –
activities and tasks*

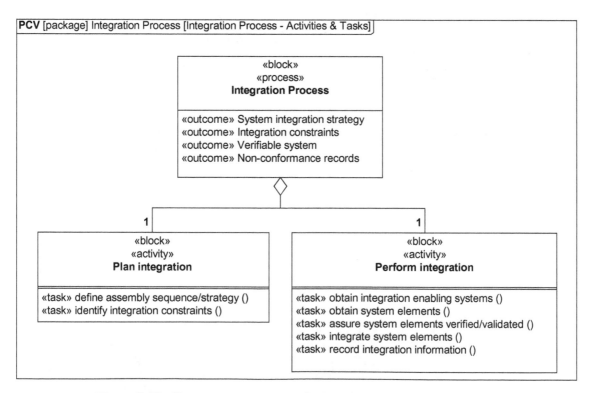

*Figure E.30   Process content view – 'integration process' –
activities and tasks*

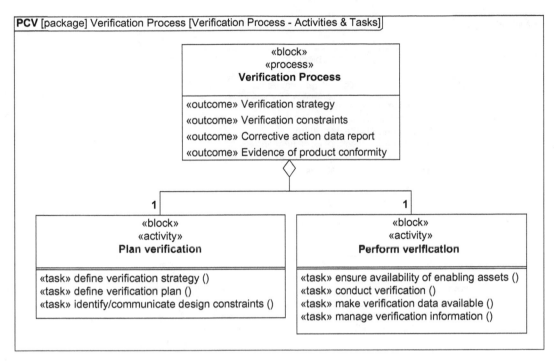

Figure E.31   Process content view – 'verification process' –
activities and tasks

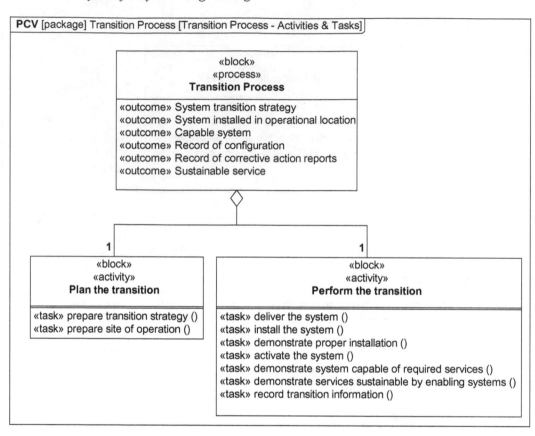

Figure E.32   Process content view – 'transition process' – activities and tasks

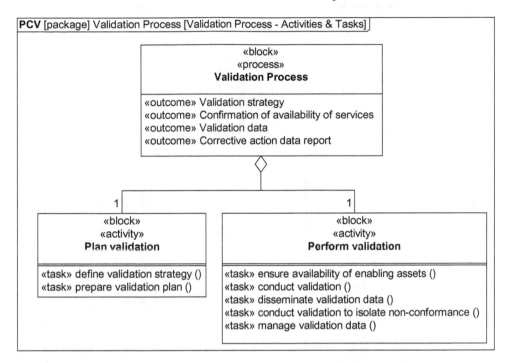

Figure E.33   Process content view – 'validation process' – activities and tasks

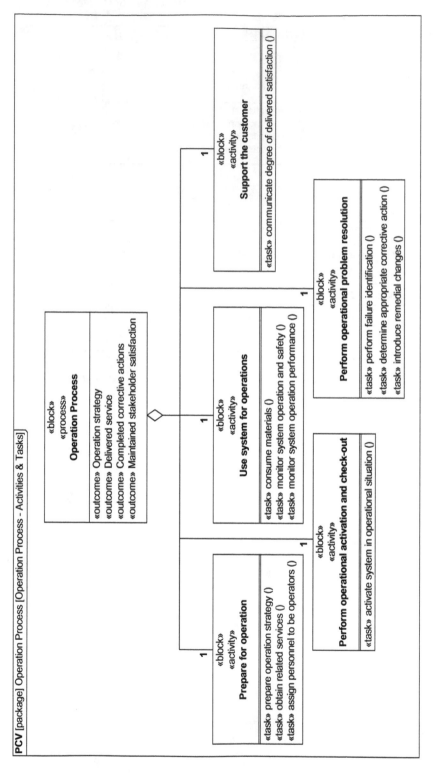

Figure E.34 Process content view – 'operation process' – activities and tasks

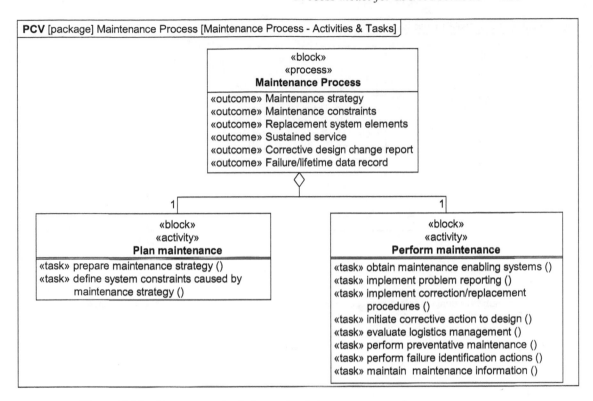

Figure E.35   Process content view – 'maintenance process' –
activities and tasks

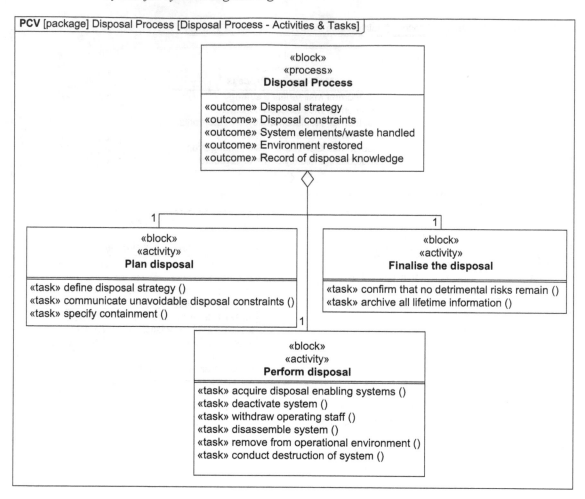

Figure E.36   Process content view – 'disposal process' – activities and tasks

References

1. ISO/IEC. 'ISO/IEC 15288:2008 Systems and software engineering – System Life Cycle Processes'. 2nd edn. International Organisation for Standardisation; 2008
2. INCOSE. *Systems Engineering Handbook – A Guide for System Life Cycle Processes and Activities*. Version 3.2.2, INCOSE; 2011

Example MBSE processes

Here's a stick and a gun and you do it.
But wait 'til I'm outta the room'.

Lenny Bruce

F.1 Introduction

This appendix contains some example of MBSE processes that have been referred to in the main text. Each process is defined using the "seven views" approach that was described in Chapter 7.

The MBSE processes that are describe cover the following areas:

– ACRE Process.
– SoSACRE Process.
– Competency assessment Process.
– Tool assessmentProcess.
– Process mapping Process.
– STUMPI Process.
– Architecture Process.

The description for each View is kept to a minimum as all Processes are described in more detail elsewhere in this book.

The Process Structure Views for each Process have been omitted as they are all subsets of the MBSE Ontology that has been used throughout this book.

The Stakeholder View for each Process is presented but each one is a subset of the overall Stakeholder View that is shown in Figure F.1.

– 'Configuration Manager'. This Stakeholder Role is responsible for ensuring that the model and all the other System Artefacts are correctly controlled, managed and configured. This will require a basic understanding of modelling, as it is the model itself as well as the Artefacts that are generated from it that will be held under configuration control. These Artefacts may take on many different forms, such as models, documents, hardware and software.
– 'Assessment Manager'. This Stakeholder Role describes the Stakeholder Role of the Person who is responsible for defining, setting up and managing Competency assessments.

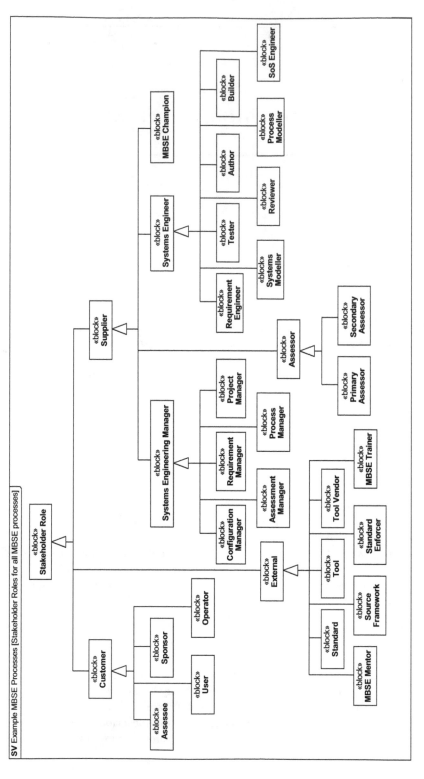

Figure F.1   Stakeholder view for all MBSE processes

- 'Requirement Manager'. This Stakeholder Role will require good management skills and also an understanding of the Requirements engineering activities that are being used on Projects. The manager need not be an expert in this field but certainly needs to understand the fundamental of the work being carried out. This may seem quite obvious but, in real life, it is worryingly common to find managers who understand very little of what they are managing.
- 'Process Manager'. This Stakeholder Role is responsible for the definition, creation and consistency of Processes. This will involve understanding the need for the Processes and, where necessary, setting up Processes, for example.
- 'Project Manager'. This Stakeholder Role describes the Stakeholder Role of the Person who will be in charge of the Project as a whole. Note that this Stakeholder Role requires, quite obviously, good management skills, but will also require that they have a basic understanding of any areas that they will be managing. For example, if the Project Manager is overseeing a Project where an Architecture is being generated, then it is essential that the Person playing this Stakeholder Role has an understanding of what Architecture is.
- 'Primary Assessor'. This is the Stakeholder Role of the Person who will be leading the Competency assessment and, therefore, will require very good inter-personal skills in order to make the assessment flow in a comfortable and consistent fashion. The Primary Assessor must also have a very good working knowledge of all of the Competencies that are being assessed. This is for very pragmatic reasons as anyone who is leading the assessments needs to be able to make judgement calls about whether the Assessee truly understands the subject matter and their interpretation of it.
- 'Secondary Assessor'. This Stakeholder Role is a support Stakeholder Role associated with the Primary Assessor. A basic knowledge of the Competencies being assessed is required, although not to the level of the 'Primary Assessor'. Good communication skills are also required for this Stakeholder Role, especially good writing skills.
- 'Requirement Engineer'. The area of Requirements engineering is one that is fundamental to systems engineering and, hence, MBSE. The Stakeholder Role here has an emphasis on understanding the modelling of Requirements and, therefore, will include required Competencies that relate to Context modelling, Use Cases, Scenarios, validation and traceability. Unlike a traditional Requirements engineering Stakeholder Role, there is a strong need for modelling skills as well as understanding the fundamentals of Requirements engineering.
- 'Systems Modeller'. This Stakeholder Role covers a multitude of activities and will, in reality, usually be split into a number of sub-types. Areas of expertise that must be covered here include understanding interfaces, specification, design, testing and traceability This is perhaps the most loosely defined of all the Stakeholder Roles here as the scope is so large. Having said this, however, it should be pointed out that the 'Systems Modeller' requires very strong modelling skills and these skills may be applied to any of the aforementioned activities. Therefore, it is possible for the 'Systems Modeller' to require a high level of Competence in almost any area, depending on the nature of the work.

- 'Tester'. This Stakeholder Role is primarily involved with the verification and validation activities that are applied throughout the Life Cycle. Again, the Competencies necessary for this Stakeholder Role may differ depending on the type of testing activities required.
- 'Reviewer'. This Stakeholder Role is essential for all aspects of MBSE. Interestingly, there are two main variations on this Stakeholder Role (not shown on the diagram) that cover "mechanical reviews" and "human reviews". A mechanical review is a straightforward verification review that does not require any real human input but simply executes a pre-defined rule. Examples of these include SysML syntactical checks and checks based on a Process. These mechanical reviews tend to be quantitative in that they can be measured in terms of numbers or values and, very importantly, they may be automated. This is essential for MBSE as it is one of the benefits that was discussed in Chapter 1 of this book. The human reviews require reasoning and will tend to be qualitative and are typically very difficult, if not impossible, to automate using a tool. The 'Reviewer' Stakeholder Role will require a good understanding of any area in which they are involved with reviewing.
- 'Author'. This Stakeholder Role is concerning with taking models and turning them into beautiful text. Caution needs to be exercised, however, as the vast majority of the text generated by the author will form part of the model; therefore, good modelling skills will be necessary for this Stakeholder Role.
- 'Process modeller'. Having a well-defined Process is crucial when defining any approach to work and, in keeping with the MBSE philosophy, this Stakeholder Role requires good modelling skills as well as an understanding of Process concepts and the business. The Stakeholder Role of the 'Process Modeller' will also require a good understanding of any areas in which the Processes will be either defined or applied; therefore, it is possible for the 'Process Modeller' to require a large number of Competencies.
- 'Builder'. This Stakeholder Role is concerned with taking the model and turning it into a real System. This will include building System Elements, integrating them into the System itself, installation and so on. Of course, this is another Stakeholder Role that on real Projects may be broken down into a set of lower-level Stakeholder Roles with different skillsets and, hence, different Competency Scopes.
- 'SoS Engineer'. The Stakeholder Role of the 'SoS Engineer' is one that may be used in conjunction with any of the other systems engineering Stakeholder Roles in order to elevate it to the level of Systems of Systems. Key skills here will include integration, understanding of Requirements and verification and validation.
- 'MBSE Champion'. This Stakeholder Role is essential when it comes to implementing MBSE into a business. The 'MBSE Champion' needs to have strong modelling skills but need not be an expert. The 'MBSE Champion' must be visible in the business, have good communication skills and be able to address any MBSE-related queries that arise. The key word here is "address"

as it is not the Stakeholder Role of the MBSE Champion to solve all the problems. In many instances, it may be that the MBSE Champion can solve issues, in which case all is well and good. The MBSE Champion, however, does need to know who the appropriate Stakeholder Roles are who can solve any problem. For example, if a tool-related issue arises, then the MBSE Champion may not have the specific expertise to solve the problem outright. On the other hand, they must be able to understand the nature of the problem and then relate this to an expert who can solve it. The Stakeholder Role of MBSE Champion, therefore, will often be one of a go-to person for all things MBSE-related. The effective use of an MBSE Champion is also one way to ensure that the MBSE knowledge and experience within a business is captured, controlled and used so that the same mistakes are not always repeated.

- 'MBSE Mentor'. The MBSE Mentor must be an expert in the field of MBSE or the specific area of MBSE as necessary. The MBSE Mentor, unlike the 'MBSE Trainer' must build up an excellent working relationship with the business. This will involve getting to know and understand the nature of the business, getting to know and understand specific issues and getting involved with Projects. Indeed, the MBSE Mentor should be a valuable member of any Project team where they are contributing to a Project. This does not mean that they need to work full-time on the Project, but they must be known to the team and able to be called upon by the team or the MBSE Champion at any point. Continuity is key to a good MBSE Mentor, so it should not be the case that every time there is an issue that a different person turns up as the MBSE Mentor. Continuity is essential for a good working relationship.

- 'MBSE trainer'. The MBSE trainer must be an established and recognised expert in the field of MBSE. They must possess excellent theoretical knowledge of the subject and also have practical experience of applying MBSE on real Projects. Unlike the 'MBSE Mentor', the MBSE trainer does not need an in-depth understanding of the business nor necessarily need to form an on-going relationship with the business.

All of these descriptions apply to the Stakeholder View presented for each Process.

F.2 The 'approach to model-based requirements engineering – ACRE' process

F.2.1 ACRE – requirements context view (RCV)

The diagram in Figure F.2 shows that the basic Need for the ACRE Context is to define an approach for requirements engineering ('Define requirements engineering approach'). There are two main constraints in this Use Case, which are:

- The approach that is defined must be model-based ('Must be model-based'). This is clearly because this is part of the larger MBSE effort described in this book.

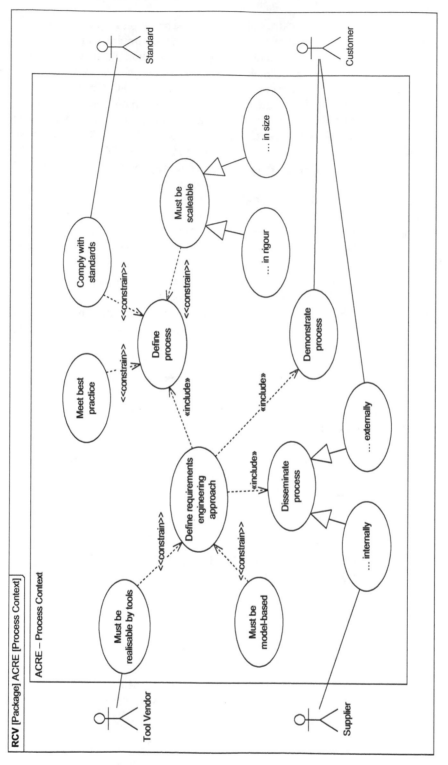

Figure F.2   ACRE – requirements context view (RCV)

– The approach must be realisable by any appropriate tools ('Must be realisable by tools'). This means that not only must it be possible to realise the approach in tools, but that the approach should be flexible enough to allow realisation in different tools from different Tool Vendors.

There are three main inclusions that make up the main Use Case.

There is an obvious need to actually define the Process ('Define process') as the Process will form the heart of the definition of any approach. This is constrained in three ways:

– The Processes that are defined must comply with Standards ('Comply with standards'). This compliance refers to anything that may be thought of as a Standard, for example an international standard, an industry standard and an in-house standard.
– The Processes that are defined must comply with best practice models ('Meet best practice'). This is very similar to the previous point but has a wide scope and will include methodologies, legislation and proprietary models.
– The Processes that are defined must be scaleable ('Must be scaleable') in two ways. The Processes must be scaleable in terms of the size of the Project ('...in size') so that the Processes may be applied to very short Projects of just a few days, right up to long-term Projects of many years. The Processes must be scaleable in terms of the levels of rigour of the Project or System ('...in rigour') so that it may be applied to non-critical systems, mission critical systems and anywhere in between.

Part of the definition of the approach also includes the ability to demonstrate the Process to a Customer ('Demonstrate process'). This is vital in terms of inspiring the Customer and also facilitates audits and assessments significantly.

The Process must also be disseminated so that people are aware of it and how it is to be used ('Disseminate process'). This must be done both internally to the business ('...internally') and externally to the Customer ('...externally').

F.2.2   ACRE – process content view (PCV)

The diagram in Figure F.3 shows the Process Content View for the ACRE Process. Note that there is only a single Process here, named the 'ACRE Process'.

The *properties* on the *block* represent the Process Artefacts, as usual, and it can be seen that these are all typed to either elements from the MBSE Ontology (such as 'Need') that make up Views or the actual Views from the ACRE Framework.

The *operations* on the *block* represent the Process Activities, which may be described briefly as:

– 'assemble source information', where the Source Element Views are created.
– 'elicit requirements', where the Needs are elicited from the Source Elements in the form of the Requirement Description View.
– 'identify context definitions', where the Context Definition Views are identified from Needs.

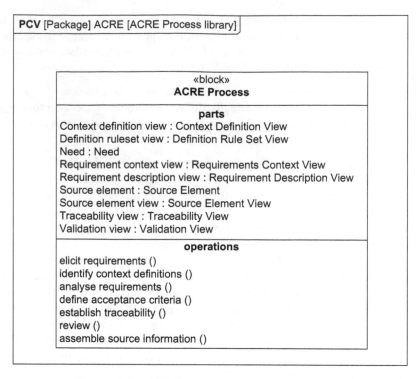

Figure F.3   ACRE – process content view (PCV)

- 'analyse requirements', where the Requirement Context Views are created, based on the Context Definition Views and based on the requirement Description View.
- 'define acceptance criteria', where the Validation Views are created based on the Use Cases that were identified as part of the Requirement Context views.
- 'establish traceability', where the Traceability Views are created.
- 'review', where all the ACRE Views are reviewed.

The PCV for ACRE comprises this single Process.

F.2.3 ACRE – stakeholder view (SV)

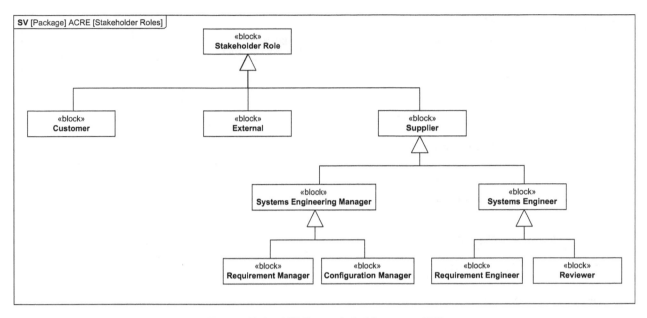

Figure F.4   ACRE – stakeholder view (SV)

F.2.4 ACRE – information view (IV)

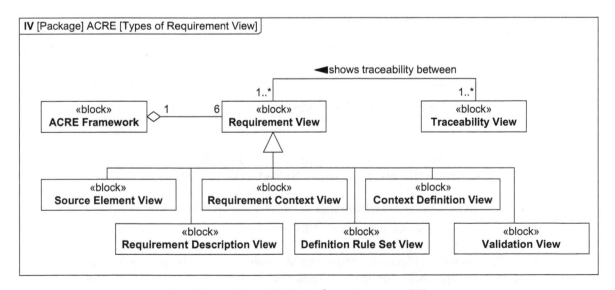

Figure F.5   ACRE – information view (IV)

F.2.5   ACRE – process behaviour view (PBV)

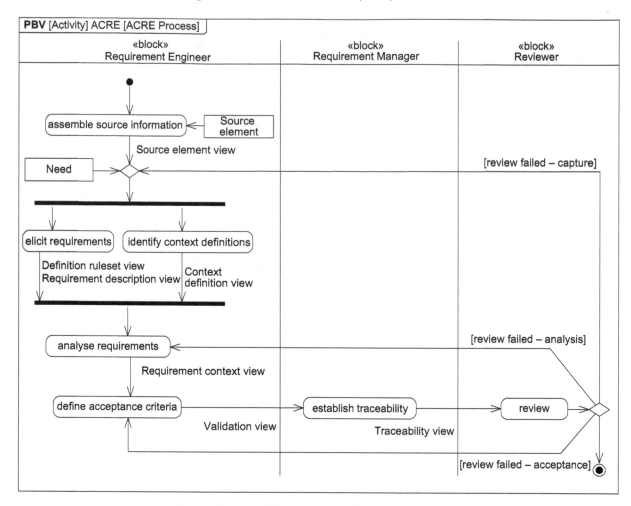

Figure F.6   ACRE – process behaviour view (PBV)

F.3   The 'system of systems approach to model-based requirements engineering – SoSACRE' process

F.3.1   SoSACRE – requirements context view (RCV)

The basic Needs for expanding the ACRE Process for Systems of Systems are shown in the following Context.

The diagram in Figure F.7 shows that the main Use Case is to 'Provide SoS requirements approach' that must be applicable to different types of Systems of

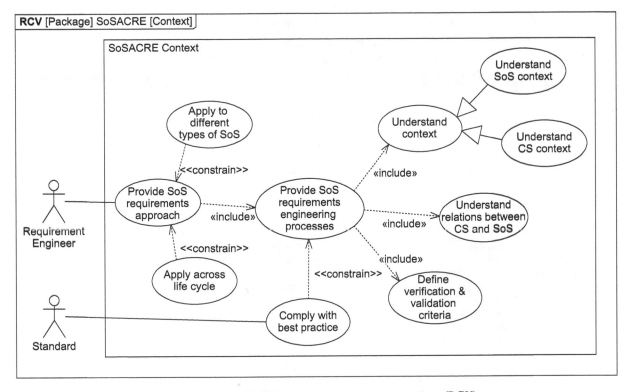

Figure F.7 SoSACRE – requirements context view (RCV)

Systems (the constraint 'Apply to different types of SoS') and also across the whole Life Cycle (the constraint 'Apply across life cycle').

There is one main Use Case that helps to realise this, which is to 'Provide SoS requirement engineering processes'. This may at first appear a little odd as there is only a single include relationship shown here, but this leaves room for future expansion, for example to define Processes for Requirements management. This has three main inclusions, which are:

- 'Understand context', which applies to both the System of Systems level ('Understand SoS context') and the Constituent System level ('Understand CS context').
- 'Understand relations between CS and SoS', which provides the understanding of the interfaces and interactions between the Constituent Systems and their System of Systems.
- 'Define verification & validation criteria', which ensures that the System of System both works and satisfies its original Needs.

All of this is constrained by the need to meet current best practice ('Comply with best practice').

F.3.2   *SoSACRE – process content view (PCV)*

The set of Processes that are defined for the SoSACRE approach is shown in the following Process Content View.

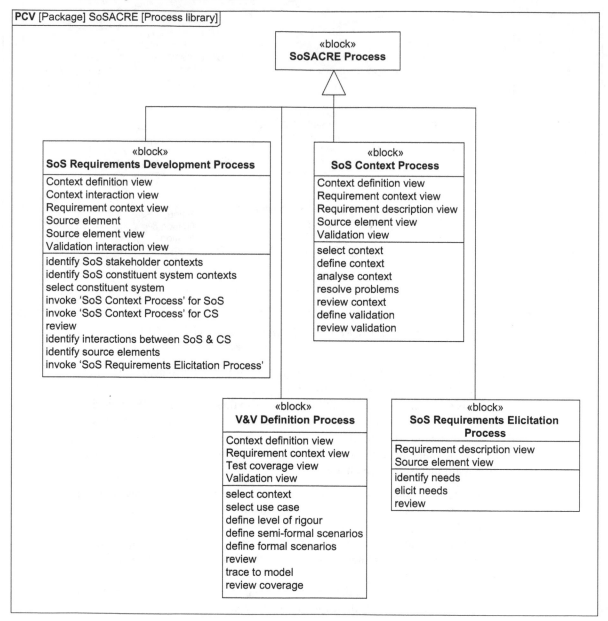

Figure F.8   SoSACRE – process content view (PCV)

The diagram in Figure F.8 shows that there are four types of 'SoSACRE Process', which are described as follows:

- 'SoS Requirements Development Process', which is the overarching Process that interacts with the other Processes. The main aim of this Process is to identify the Stakeholder Roles and Constituents Systems and then invoke the Context Process for both the System of Systems and its associated Constituent Systems. The Process then identifies the interactions between the System of Systems and its Constituent Systems.
- 'SoS Context Process', which defines the Context for either the System of Systems or a Constituent System, depending on which point it is invoked from the SoS Requirements Development Process.
- 'V&V Definition Process', which defines a number of Scenarios, both Formal Scenarios and Semi-formal Scenarios, that are then used to demonstrate that the original Use Cases can be validated.
- 'SoS Requirements Elicitation Process', which identifies the basic Needs for the System of Systems.

F.3.3 SoSACRE – stakeholder view (SV)

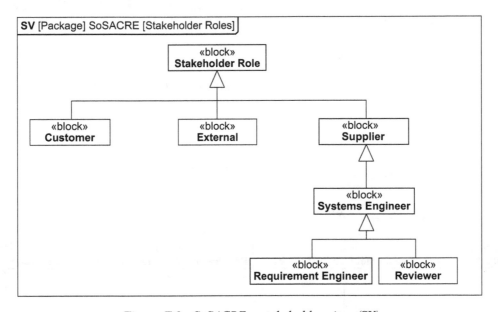

Figure F.9   SoSACRE – stakeholder view (SV)

F.3.4   SoSACRE – information view (IV)

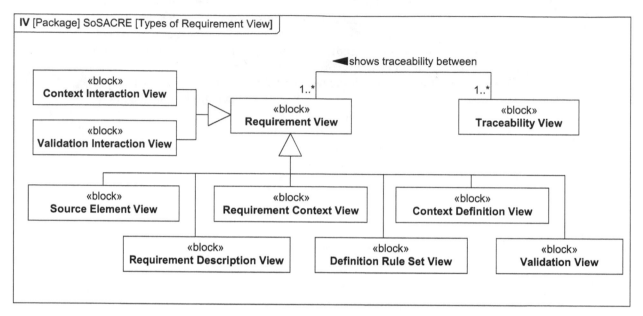

Figure F.10   *SoSACRE – information view (IV) for all views*

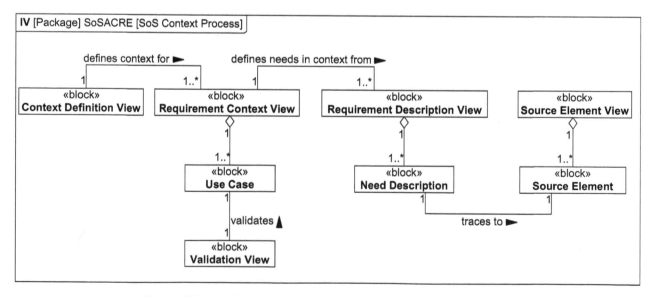

Figure F.11   *SoSACRE – information view (IV) for context process*

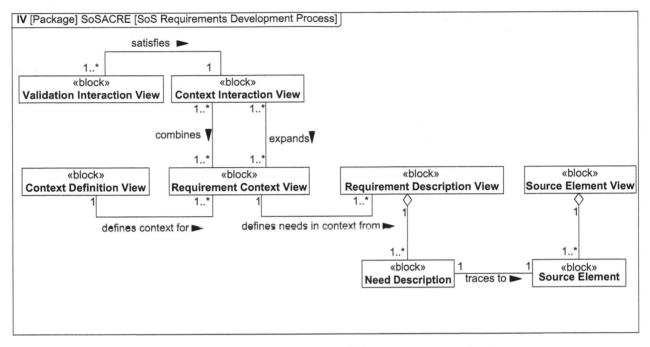

Figure F.12 SoSACRE – information view (IV) for requirements development process

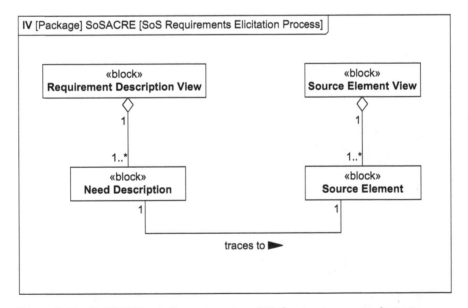

Figure F.13 SoSACRE – information view (IV) for requirements elicitation process

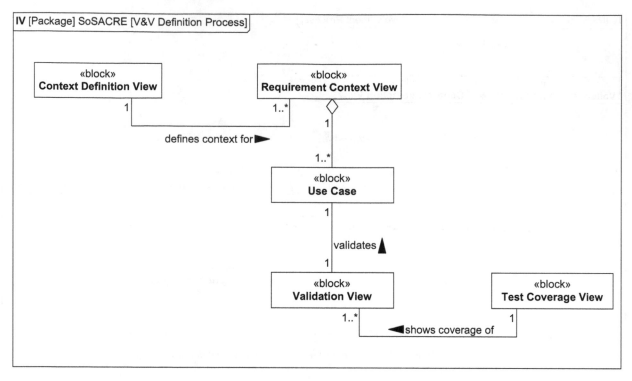

Figure F.14   SoSACRE – information view (IV) for V&V definition process

F.3.5   SoSACRE – process behaviour view (PBV)

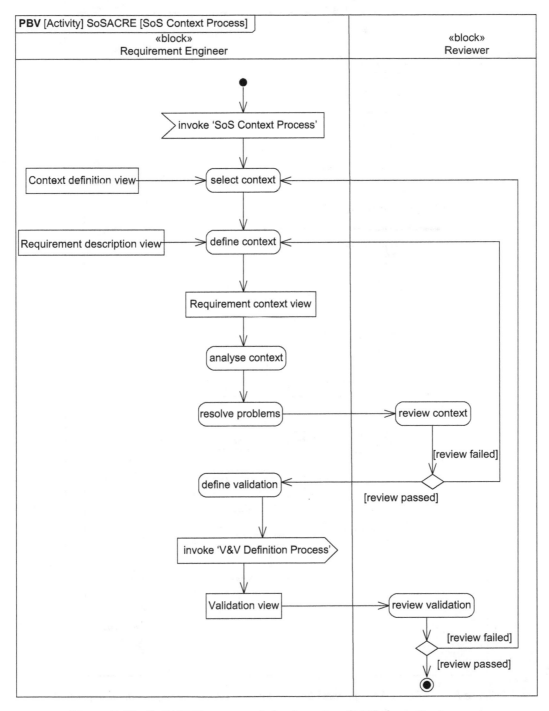

Figure F.15   SoSACRE – process behaviour view (PBV) for context process

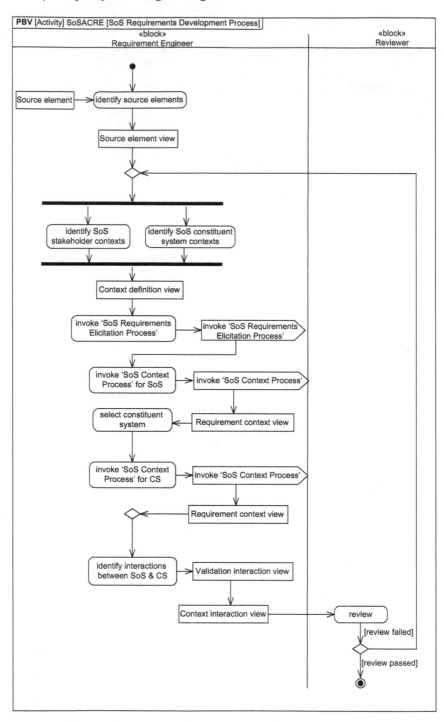

*Figure F.16   SoSACRE – process behaviour view (PBV) for requirement definition
process*

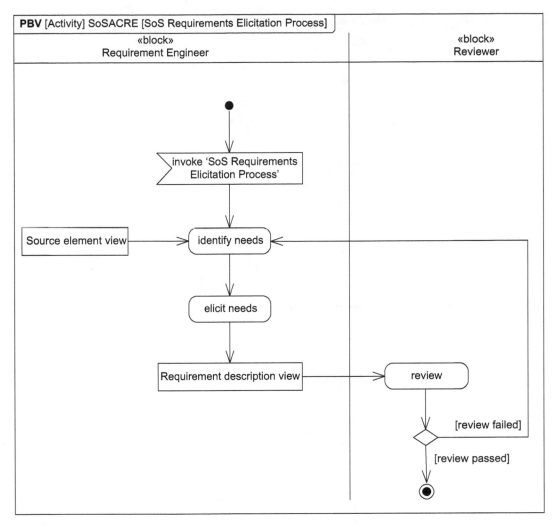

Figure F.17   SoSACRE – process behaviour view (PBV) for requirement elicitation process

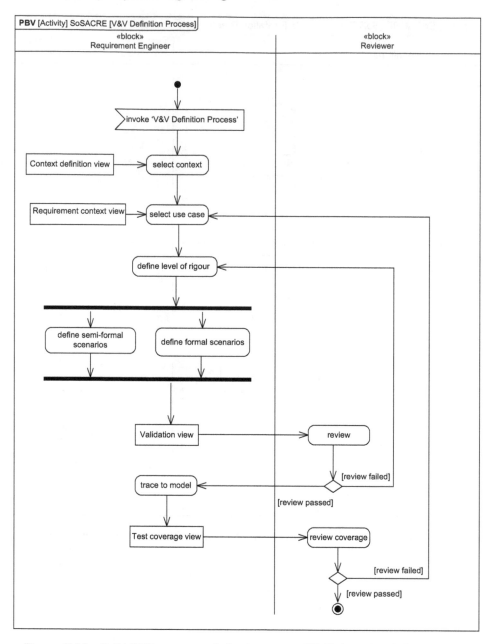

Figure F.18   SoSACRE – process behaviour view (PBV) for V&V definition process

F.4   The 'universal competency assessment model – UCAM' process for competency assessment

F.4.1   *UCAM – requirements context view (RCV)*

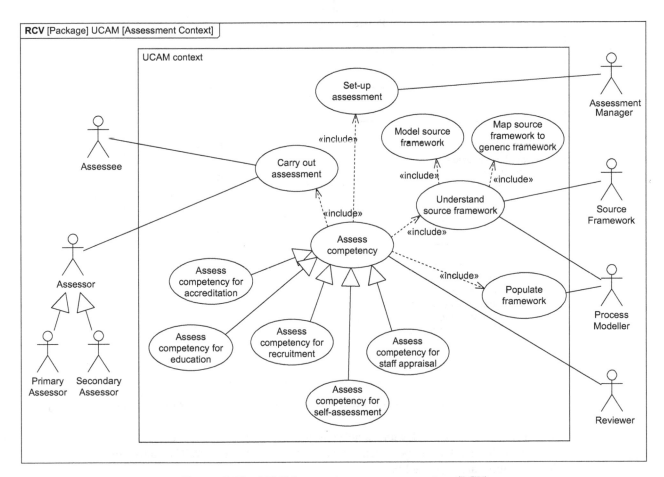

Figure F.19   UCAM – requirements context view (RCV)

F.4.2   UCAM – process content view (PCV)

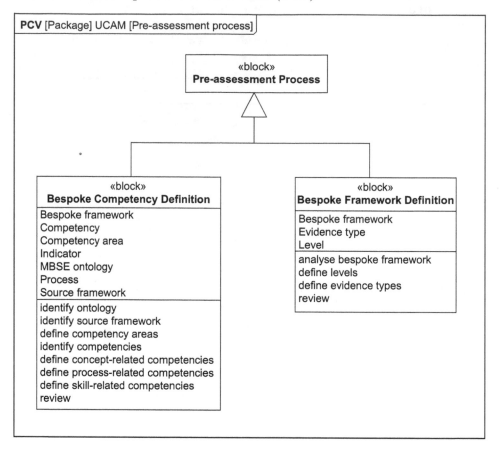

Figure F.20   UCAM – process content view (PCV) for pre-assessment processes

This Process is concerned with identifying and defining the Competency Areas, Competencies and Indicators associated with a bespoke Framework. The Activities in the Process are described below.

The Activities for the 'Bespoke Competency Definition' Process are described as follows:

- **The 'identify ontology' Activity.** This Activity is relatively straightforward and consists of identifying the Ontology that will underlie the bespoke Framework. In this example, this will be the MBSE Ontology.
- **The 'identify source framework' Activity.** The main aim of this Activity is to identify any source Competency Frameworks that may be used as an input to creating the bespoke Competency Framework. An example of this would be the INCOSE Competencies Framework that has been used elsewhere in this book.
- **The 'identify competencies' Activity.** The MBSE Competency Framework that was introduced previously in this chapter has a number of Competency Areas that have been defined that allow the individual Competencies to be classified into groups.

- **The 'define concept-related competencies' Activity.** This competency area is based on the MBSE Ontology and is defined in order to determine if the assessee holds sufficient knowledge concerning the key concepts that make up the Ontology. For example, consider the 'Systems Concepts' competency which forms part of the 'MBSE Concepts Competency Area', and then determine which areas of the ontology apply. In the MBSE Ontology, the following concepts, shown as a subset of the MBSE Ontology, were identified as being relevant. Each of the Ontology Elements shown here has been identified as relevant to the Systems Concepts Competency. The very fact that they exist on the MBSE Ontology means that they must be important concepts that must be understood by any Person who holds a Stakeholder Role that requires this Competency. The Indicators in the Competency, therefore, should identify areas that the assessee must understand.
- The **'define process-related competencies' Activity.** The competencies that exist in the Life Cycle Process Competency Area are, again, quite straightforward to define, as the information concerning the Processes is already part of the MBSE model. The information for the general Processes will relate both to the Ontology and the need for that particular Process.
- **The 'define skill-related competencies' Activity.** When defining skill-related Competencies, the Process model within the MBSE model is used as the main source. This is true for both Technical and Soft Skill areas but, as was stated previously, this book is focussing mainly on the Technical Skills, although examples of Soft Kill-related Competencies are provided in Appendix G.
- **The 'review' Activity.** Finally, the partial 'Bespoke Framework' that has been generated so far is reviewed and is then used as the main input to the next Process – the 'Bespoke Competency Framework Definition' Process.

The Activities for the 'Bespoke Framework Definition' Process are described as follows:

- **The 'analyse bespoke framework' Activity.** The main aim of this Activity is to take the partial Bespoke Framework from the previous Process and to consider the different Competencies and their associated Indicators that will form a basis of the Levels and Evidence Types.
- **The 'define levels' Activity.** The main aim of this Activity is to define one or more Level that each Competency may be held at. These may be based directly on one of the source Frameworks, such as the INCOSE Competencies Framework, or may be created specifically for the Bespoke Framework, as defined in the MBSE Competency Framework that is used in this book.
- **The 'define evidence types' Activity.** For each Level that was defined in the previous Activity, it is now necessary to identify and define a number of acceptable Evidence Types. These Evidence Types will be entirely dependent on the Organisation and the way that they work. For example, Evidence Types that are suitable for a large multi-national Organisation will not necessarily be the same as those defined for a small company with just a few employees.
- **The 'review' Activity.** Finally, the Now-complete Bespoke Framework is now reviewed.

The following Process Content View shows the core UCAM Processes.

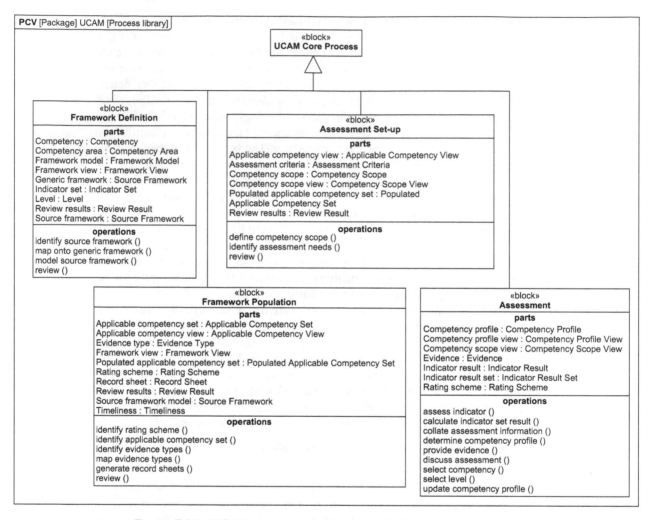

Figure F.21   UCAM – process content view (PCV) for core processes

The Core Processes for UCAM are described as follows:

- 'Framework Definition', which identifies and models one or more source Framework and maps this onto the generic Framework. This is carried out once per source Framework.
- 'Framework Population', where the Rating Scheme, Record Sheets and other information necessary for using the Framework are defined. This is carried out once per Framework.
- 'Assessment Set-up', where the set of Assessments is set up in terms of identifying the Needs, setting up the Artefacts and so on. This is carried out once per set of Assessments.
- 'Assessment', where the actual Assessments themselves are executed and the Competency Profiles are created. This is carried out once per Assessee.

F.4.3 UCAM – stakeholder view (SV)

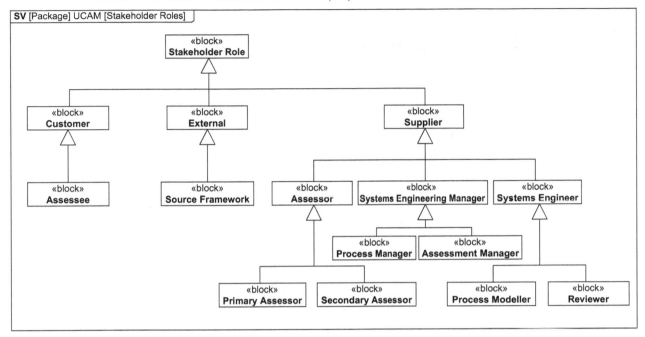

Figure F.22 UCAM – stakeholder view (SV)

F.4.4 UCAM – information view (IV)

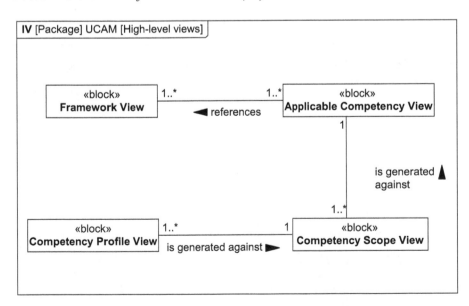

Figure F.23 UCAM – information views (IV)

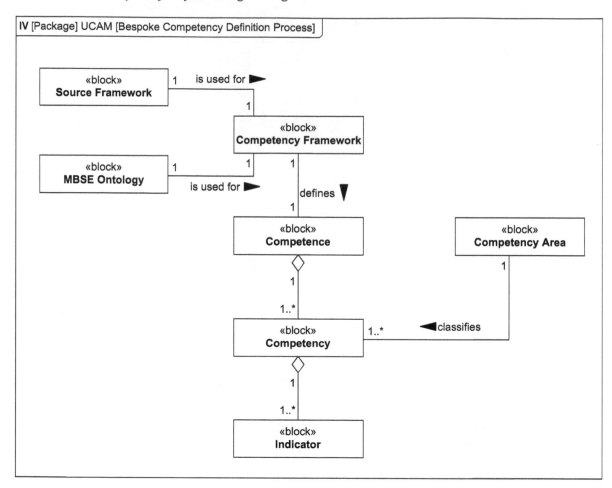

Figure F.24   UCAM – information view (IV) for bespoke competency definition process

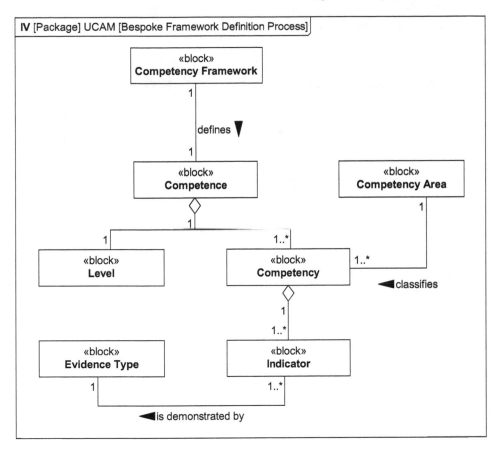

Figure F.25 UCAM – information view (IV) for bespoke framework definition process

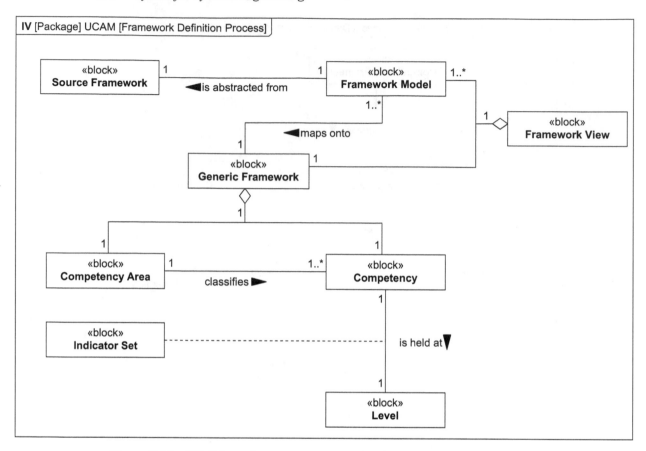

Figure F.26   UCAM – information view (IV) for framework definition process

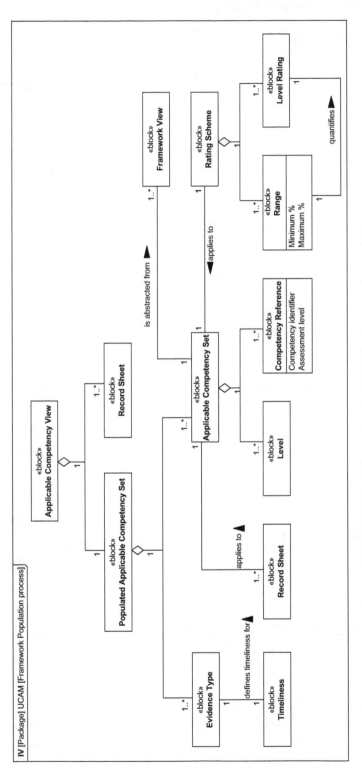

Figure F.27 UCAM – information view (IV) for framework population process

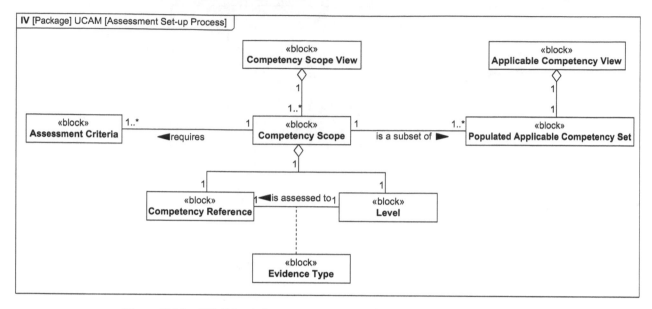

Figure F.28   UCAM – information view (IV) for assessment set-up process

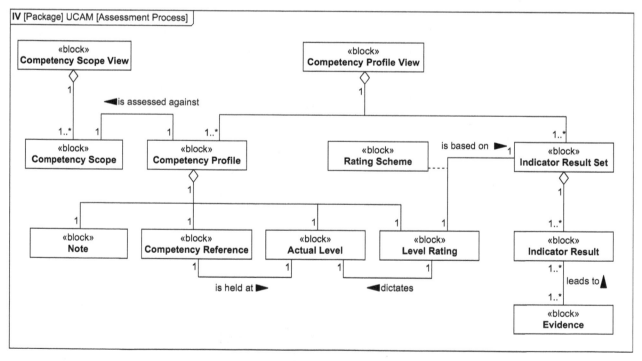

Figure F.29   UCAM – information view (IV) for assessment process

F.4.5   UCAM – process behaviour view (PBV)

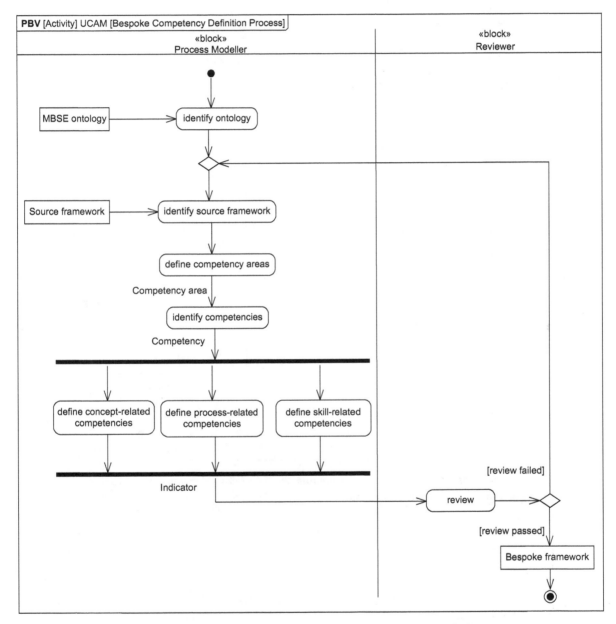

Figure F.30   *UCAM – process behaviour view (PBV) for bespoke competency definition process*

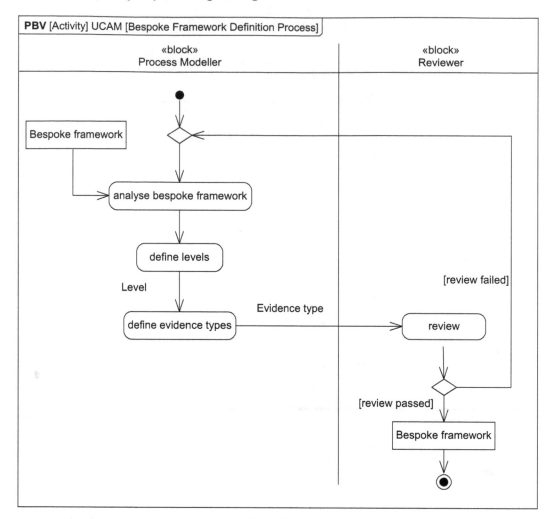

*Figure F.31   UCAM – process behaviour view (PBV) for bespoke framework
definition process*

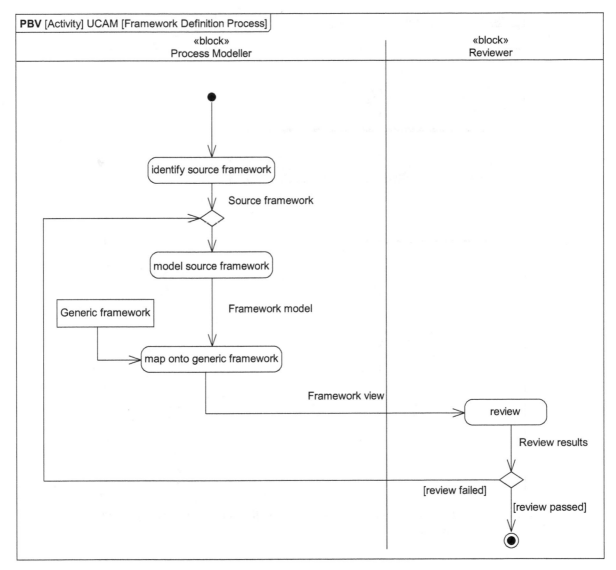

*Figure F.32   UCAM – process behaviour view (PBV) for framework definition
          process*

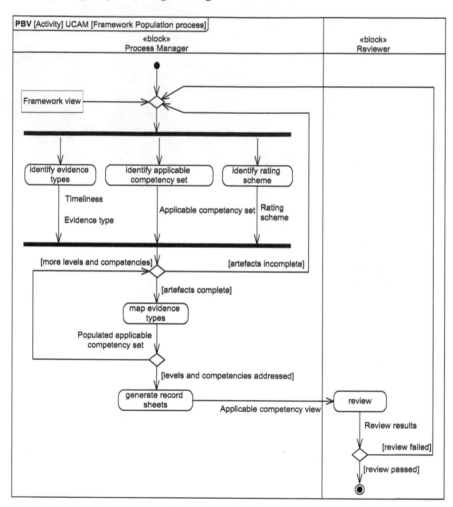

Figure F.33   UCAM – process behaviour view (PBV) for framework population
process

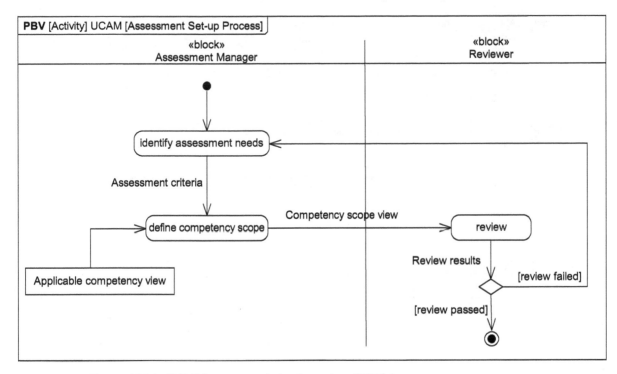

Figure F.34   UCAM – process behaviour view (PBV) for assessment set-up process

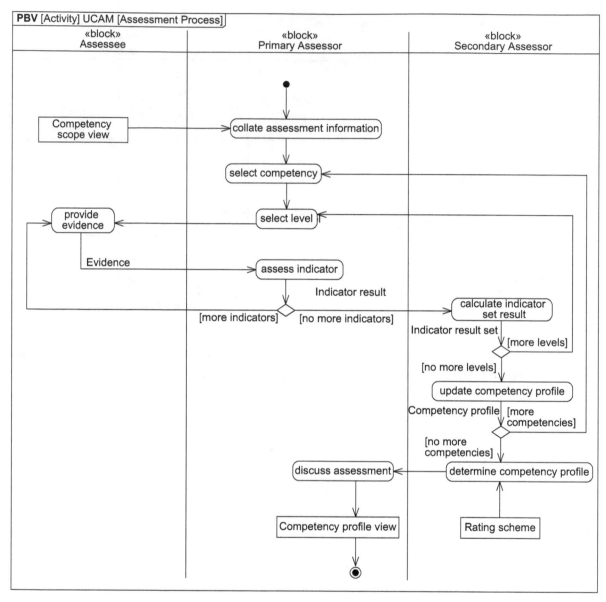

Figure F.35   UCAM – process behaviour view (PBV) for assessment process

F.4.6 Process instance view (PIV) for UCAM

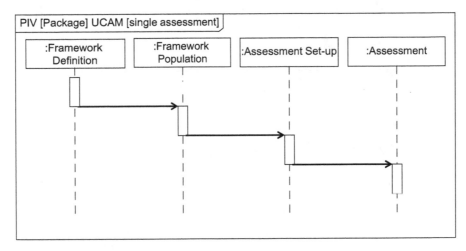

Figure F.36 UCAM – process instance view (PIV) for single assessment

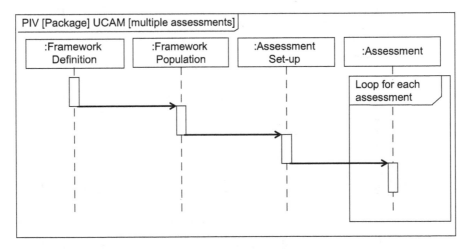

Figure F.37 UCAM – process instance view (PIV) for multiple assessments

F.5 The 'model-based tool evaluation – MonTE' process

F.5.1 MonTE – requirements context view (RCV)

In order to realise the full benefits of model-based system engineering, "sharp" tools are essential ('Provide tools'). There are four main issues that will be discussed in this section:

– Considering the types of Tools available ('Identify tool'). Before any sort of Tool selection may be performed, it is important to identify the types of Tools

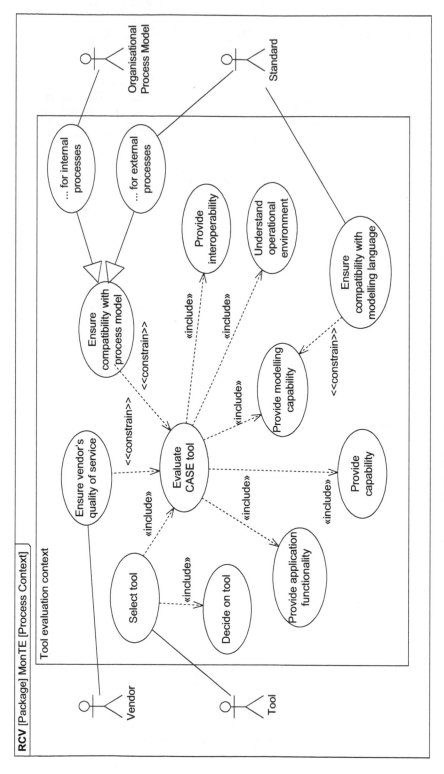

Figure F.38 MonTE – requirements context view (RCV)

that may be applicable to model-based systems engineering whether these are individual Tools ('...for individual tool') or Tool chains ('...for tool chains').

- Understanding the need for the Tool ('Understand need for tool'). This includes considering how the Tools will be used ('Understand use') and what the major constraints on its use will be ('Understand constraints').
- Using Tools with existing processes ('Ensure compatibility with process'). This involves looking at which main Views in the Process each Tool will be used for, as well as how the Tools will be used in conjunction with one another.
- Considering Tool selection ('Select tool'). When the Tools have been identified and their usage is understood, it is important to carry out a Tool selection exercise that will look at various aspects of each Tool, measure them and then use the results as a basis for deciding between Tools.

F.5.2   MonTE – process content view (PCV)

The following Process Content View shows the Process library for the MonTE Process set.

The diagram in Figure F.39 shows the Processes that make up the MonTE Process set. These Processes are described as follows:

- **'Ideal Tool Requirement Capture'.** The main aim of this Process is to capture the basic Needs of the ideal Tool. Essentially, this Process is concerned with carrying out a requirements engineering activity concerning the Tool needs and producing a model of what the ideal Tool should look like. The information presented previously in this chapter should be used as a guide for considering your needs for a tool and to understand how the Tool will be used with its relevant Processes. The 'Ideal Tool Evaluation' process will typically only need to be executed once for each Tool selection exercise.
- **'Evaluation Tool Capture'.** The main aim of this Process is to take each candidate Tool and to produce a model that captures the Tool and its features, constraints and operation. This is then used to compare back to the model for the ideal Tool that was created in the previous Process.
- **'Tool Analysis' – 'Tool Verification'.** The main aim of this Process is to compare the ideal Tool model with the model for a candidate Tool.
- **'Tool Analysis' – 'Tool Validation'.** The main aim of this Process is to assess whether the candidate Tool satisfies the Needs for the Ideal tool.
- **'Result Definition'.** The main aim of this Process is to take the outputs of the two 'Tool Analysis' Processes and to present them in some form of report that may then be used as an input to the decision-making Process (not shown here).

The basic way that these Processes work can be seen by considering the main Artefacts of the Processes in the form of the Information View (IV).

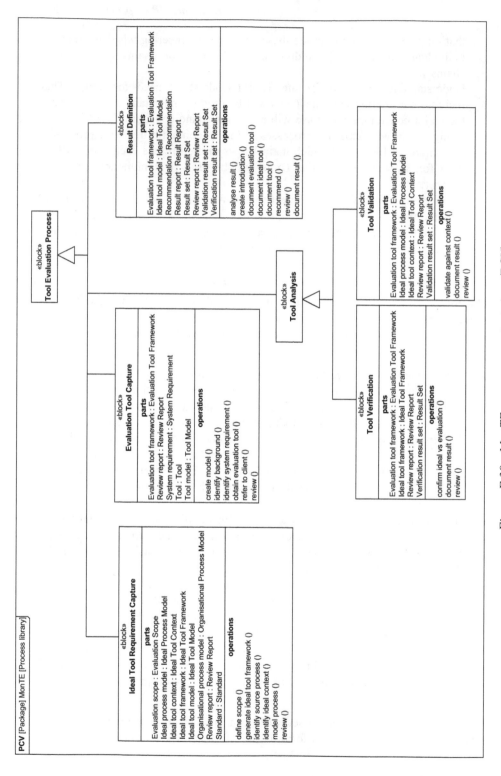

Figure F.39 MonTE – process content view (PCV)

F.5.3   MonTE – stakeholder view (SV)

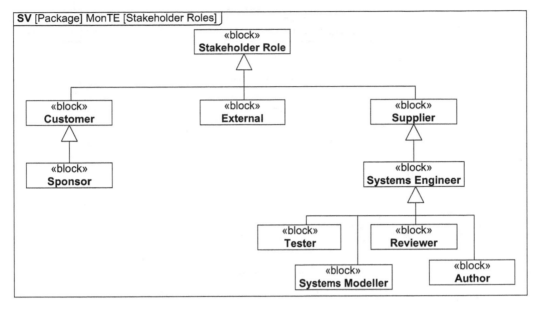

Figure F.40   MonTE – stakeholder view (SV)

F.5.4   Information view (IV) for MonTE

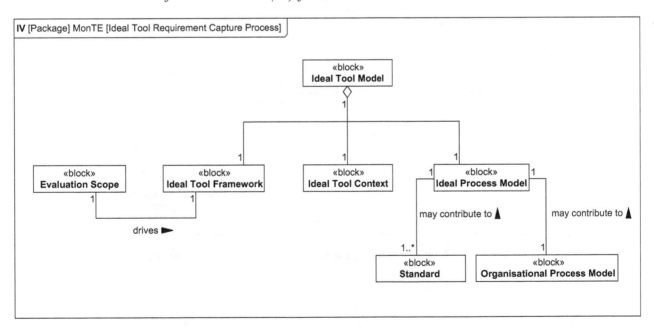

Figure F.41   MonTE – information view (IV) for ideal tool requirement capture process

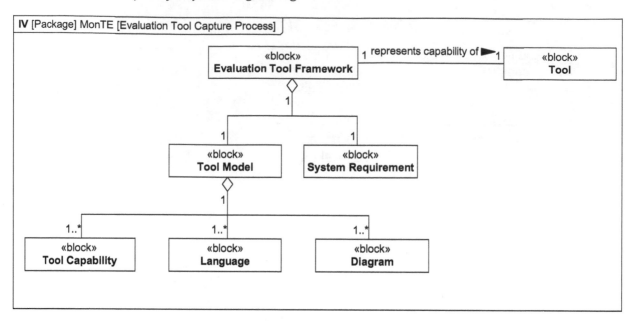

Figure F.42   MonTE – information view (IV) for evaluation tool capture process

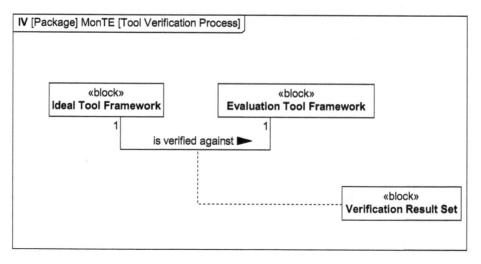

Figure F.43   MonTE – information view (IV) for tool verification process

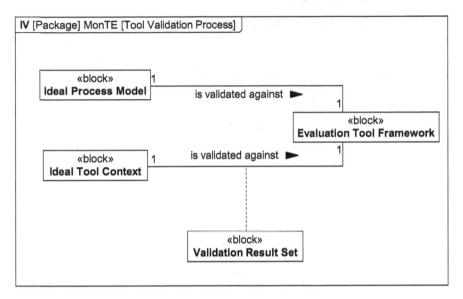

Figure F.44   MonTE – information view (IV) for tool validation process

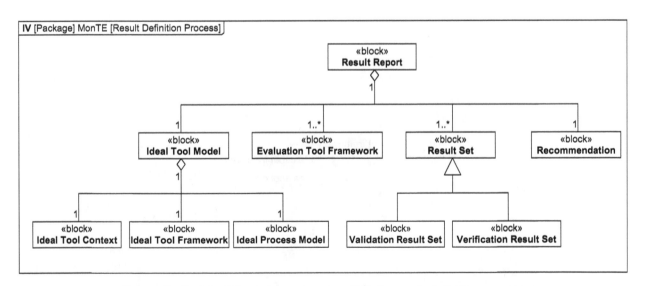

Figure F.45   MonTE – information view (IV) for result definition process

F.5.5   Process behaviour views (PBV) for MonTE

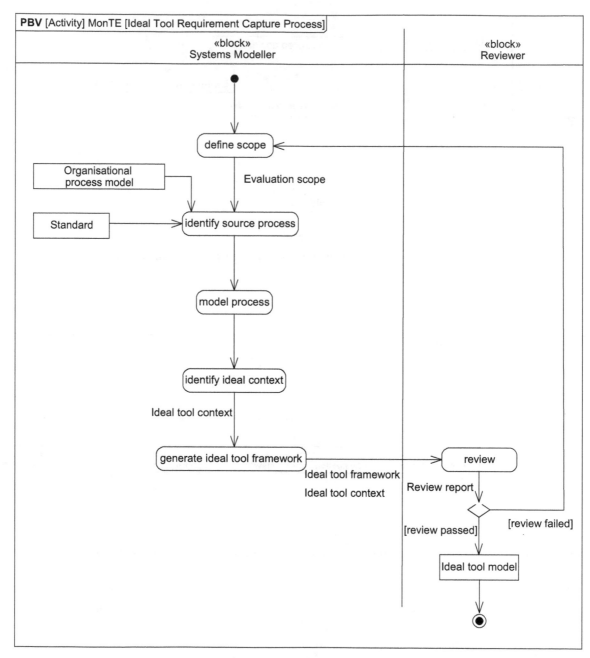

*Figure F.46   MonTE – process behaviour view (PBV) for ideal tool
requirement capture process*

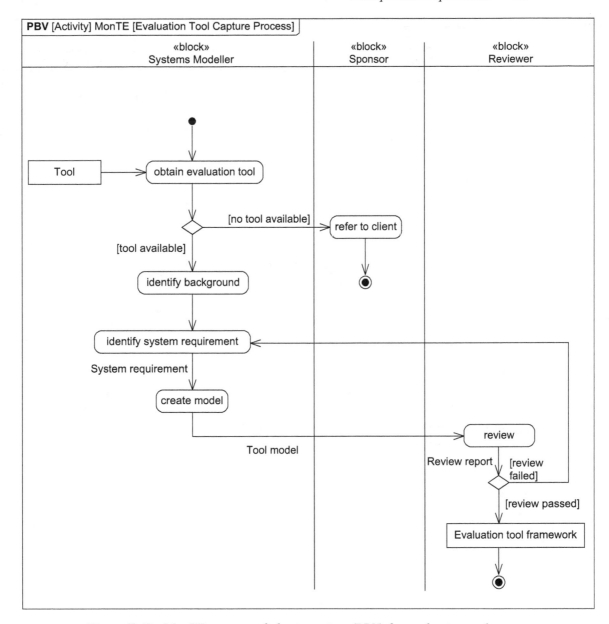

Figure F.47   MonTE – process behaviour view (PBV) for evaluation tool capture process

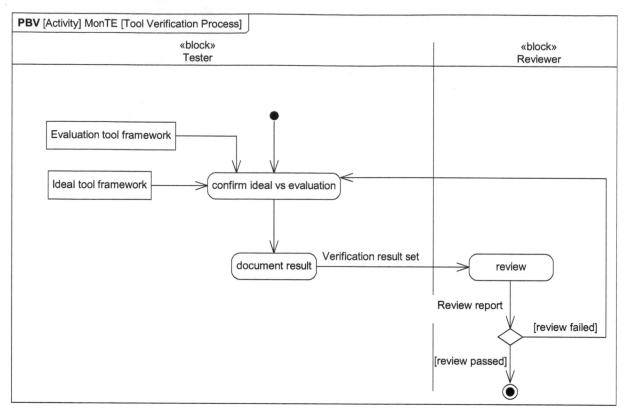

Figure F.48   MonTE – process behaviour view (PBV) for tool verification process

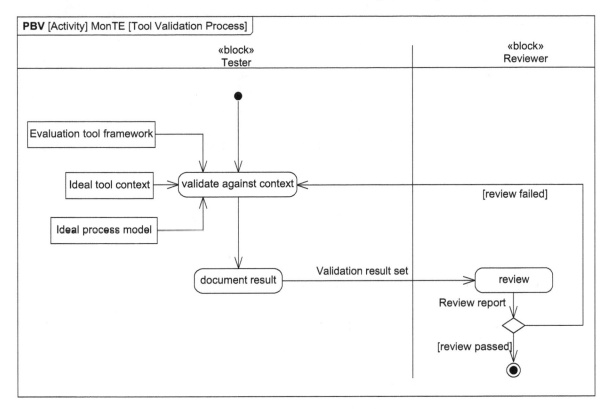

Figure F.49   MonTE – process behaviour view (PBV) for tool validation process

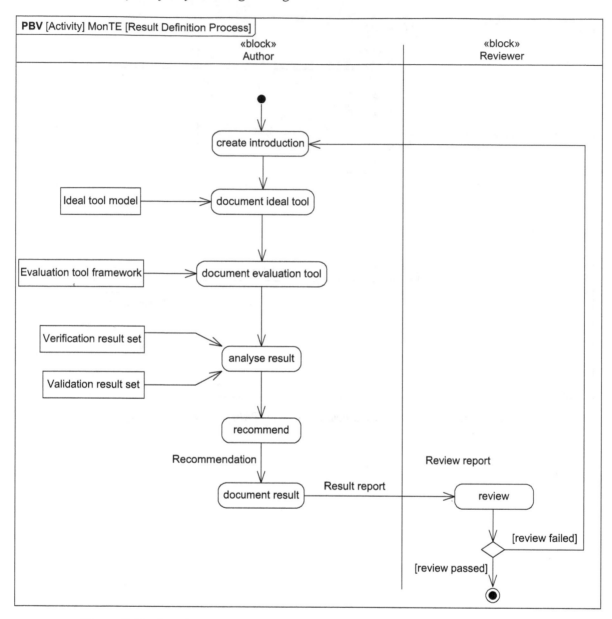

*Figure F.50   MonTE – process behaviour view (PBV) for result definition
process*

F.5.6 MonTE – process instance view (PIV)

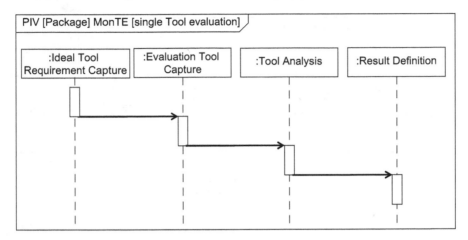

Figure F.51 MonTE – process instance view (PIV) for single tool evaluation

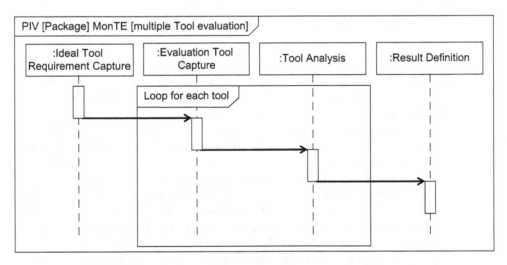

Figure F.52 MonTE – process instance view (PIV) for multiple tool evaluation

F.6 The 'process mapping process (PoMP)' process

This section introduces a simple process for process mapping. This process is, of course, defined using the "seven views" approach.

F.6.1 PoMP – requirements context view (RCV)

The first view that will be considered here will be the requirements that will look at why we are defining the process mapping process in the first place. This is realised in the use case diagram below.

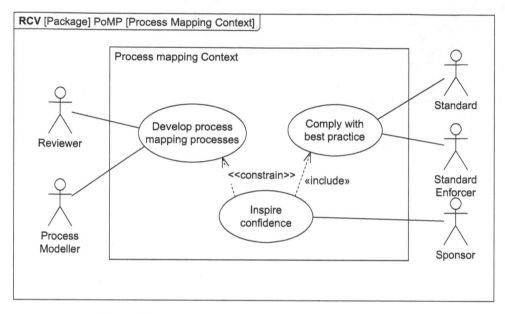

Figure F.53   PoMP – requirements context view (RCV)

The diagram in Figure F.53 shows a simple Requirements Context View for a mapping process. At the moment, this is modelled at a high level of abstraction and will be described in more detail subsequently in this section. Note that the main requirement is stated quite simply as 'develop process mapping process' which has three actors associated with it – the 'Process engineer' which represents the person or group of people who will be developing the process, the 'Source process' that represents the model to be mapped against and, finally, the 'Reviewer'. There is one single constraint on this requirement, which is to 'inspire confidence' and is related to the 'Sponsor' and the 'Standard enforcer'. In this case, the exercise is being carried out at the request of sponsors who require some confidence that their processes map onto the relevant standards. The standards enforcer is involved as any mapping that is produced, and any compliance issues will need to be approved by the appropriate authority.

F.6.2   PoMP – process content view (PCV)

The Process Content View, for the process mapping application, consists initially of three processes as shown in Figure F.54.

The diagram in Figure F.54 shows the Process Content View that identifies the processes that have been created along with their relevant artefacts (represented by attributes) and activities (represented by operations). These are the three processes that will be executed in order to meet the requirements from Figure F.1.

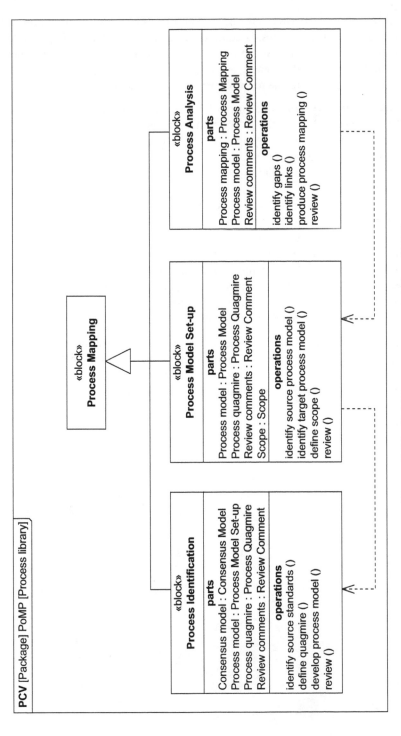

Figure F.54   PoMP – process content view (PCV)

In this case, three processes have been identified as being necessary to meet the requirements. All of these processes could have been shown as a single process but consider the number of attributes and operations for that single class and imagine how the complexity would increase.

The three processes that have been identified are described as follows:

—   **'Process identification'.** The aim of this process is to identify all the relevant source processes that are applicable to the mapping exercise. One of the main outputs here is the 'Process quagmire' which is a variation of the information view and is realised by a class diagram where each class represents a different source process. In the situation where only a single source standard is being used, this quagmire is quite simple (more or a puddle than a quagmire), however, as soon as more than one source process is used, the complexity increases and the quagmire becomes deeper and deeper.

—   **'PM set-up'.** The main aim of this process is to define the scope of the assessment or audit (which processes in the target process will be evaluated) and then to identify the relevant parts of each source process.

—   **'Process analysis'.** The aim of this process is to actually perform the mapping between the source processes and the target process. This involves looking for both links between them as well as gaps.

In terms of the way that these processes are executed, they are quite 'tightly coupled'. This means that the relationships between the processes are actually dependencies and, hence, does not allow for much freedom in terms of variation of execution. This can be seen on the diagram with the dependency relationships between the processes.

F.6.3   PoMP – stakeholder view (SV)

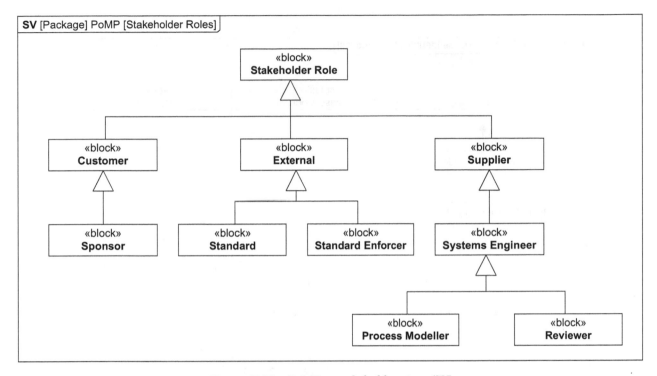

Figure F.55   PoMP – stakeholder view (SV)

F.6.4   PoMP – process instance view (PIV)

PoMP – Process Instance View (PIV)

PIV [Package] PoMP[regular scenario]

:Process Identification

:PM Set-up

:Process Analysis

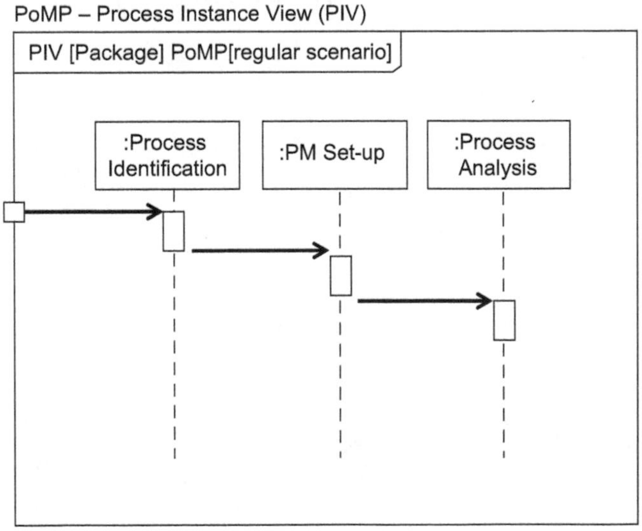

Figure F.56   PoMP – process instance view (PIV)

F.6.4   PoMP – process behaviour view (PBV)

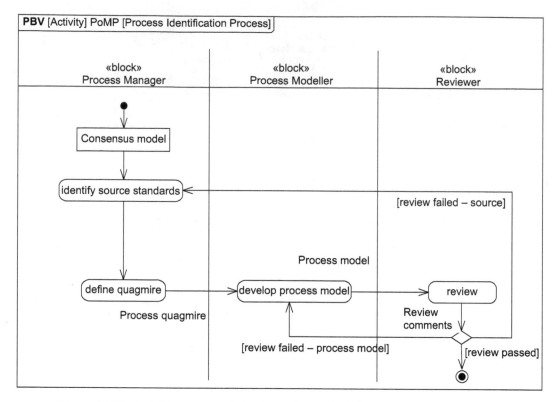

Figure F.57   PoMP – process behaviour view (PBV) for 'process identification'

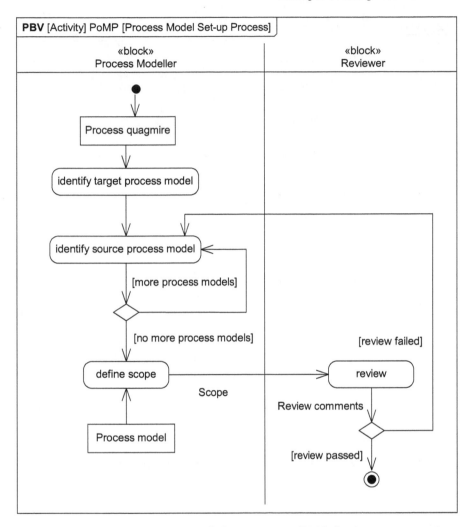

Figure F.58   PoMP – process behaviour view (PBV) for 'process set-up'

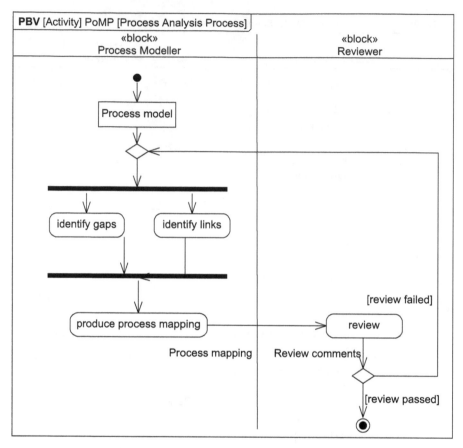

Figure F.59   PoMP – process behaviour view (PBV) for 'process analysis'

F.6.5 PoMP – information view (IV)

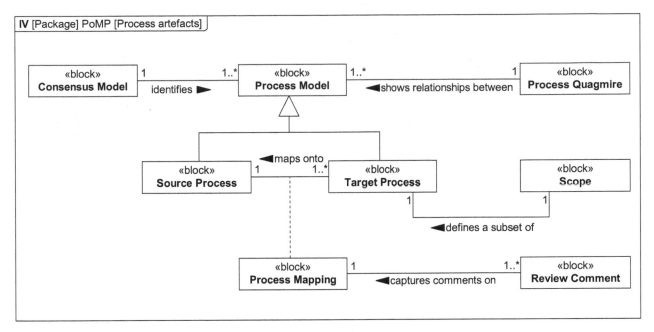

Figure F.60 PoMP – information view (IV)

F.7 The 'students managing project intelligently – STUMPI' process for generic life cycle activity teaching and training

F.7.1 STUMPI – requirements context view (RCV)

The diagram in Figure F.61 shows the 'Requirement Context View' for the STUMPI Process. The main aim of the STUMPI Context is to allow a set of Processes for systems engineering development to be defined ('Define development processes') which can be used for both engineering ('Define engineering processes') and management ('Define management processes') processes. This definition of Processes must allow the user to:

– Define Activities ('Define activities') that allow the Process to be executed.
– Define Artefacts ('Define artefacts') that will allow the inputs and outputs for the Process to be specified.
– Define Stakeholder Roles ('Define Stakeholder Roles') that will allow the Stakeholder Roles for the Process to be identified and defined.

The main constraints on the process definition are to:

– Ensure that the approach can be taught, learned and adopted quickly ('Ensure ease of use').

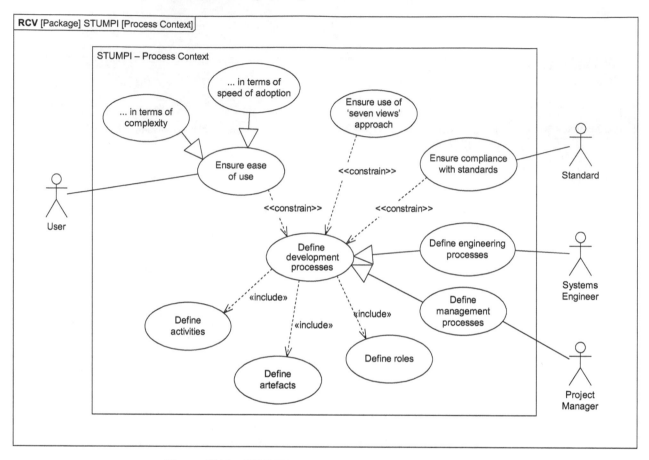

Figure F.61   STUMPI – requirements context view (RCV)

- Ensure that the approach complies with best practice ('Ensure compliance with standards').
- Ensure that the approach promotes the "seven views" approach ('Ensure use of "seven views" approach').

This Process Context View provides the basis against which the resultant Processes may be validated.

F.7.2   STUMPI – process content view (PCV)

The diagram in Figure F.62 shows the two basic Process Groups that make up the STUMPI Process set.

The diagram in Figure F.63 shows the core STUMPI Processes for the Engineering Group.

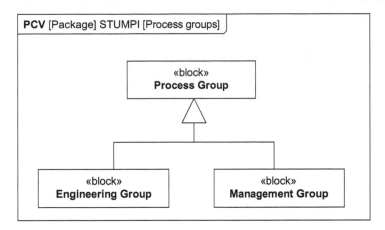

Figure F.62   STUMPI – process content view (PCV) showing process groups

The core STUMPI Engineering Processes are described as follows:

- 'Stakeholder Requirements', where the basic Needs for the System are identified by looking at various Contexts.
- 'Analysis', where the basic problem behind the System is understood.
- 'Design', where the solution for the System is defined.
- 'Implementation', where the System is constructed.
- 'Verification and Validation', where the system is tested.

The diagram in Figure F.64 shows the core STUMPI Processes for the Engineering Group.

The core STUMPI Management Processes are described as follows:

- **'Project Planning'**, where the Project Schedule is defined according to the Life Cycle and its associated Processes.
- **'Project Monitoring'**, where the progress of the Project is monitored against the Project Schedule.
- **'Project Collation'**, where all the Project Artefacts are collected together and controlled.

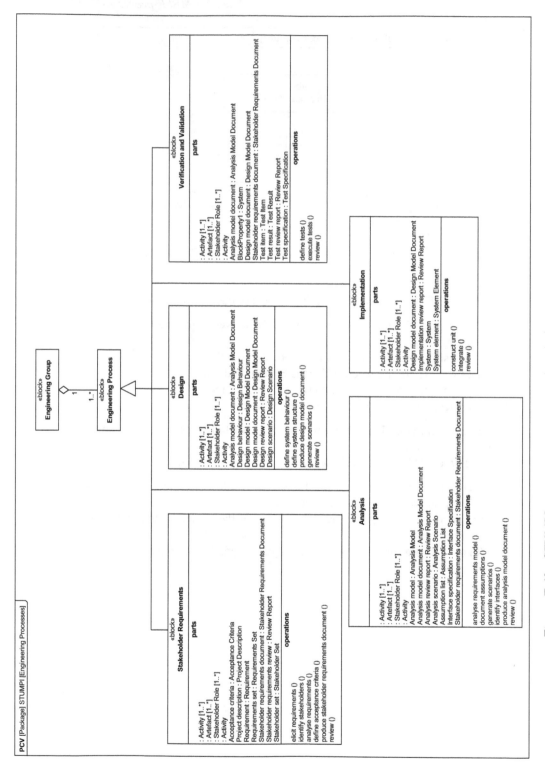

Figure F.63   STUMPI – process content view (PCV) showing engineering group processes

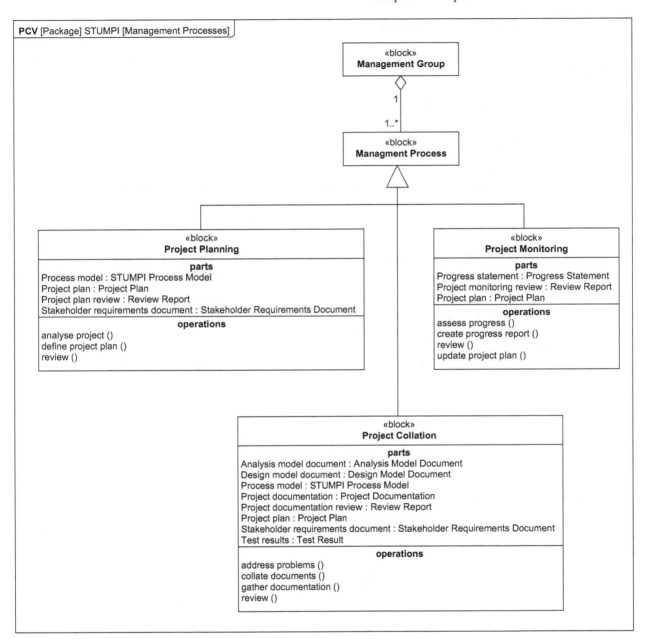

Figure F.64   STUMPI – process content view (PCV) showing management group processes

F.7.3   STUMPI – stakeholder view (SV)

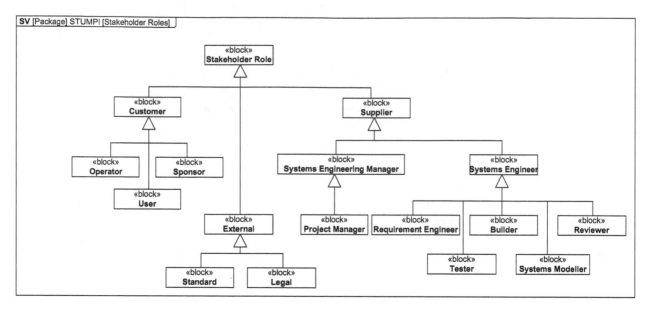

Figure F.65   STUMPI – stakeholder view (SV)

F.7.4   Information views (IV) for STUMPI

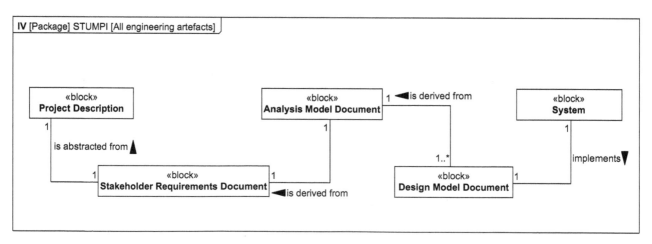

Figure F.66   STUMPI – information view (IV) for all engineering artefacts

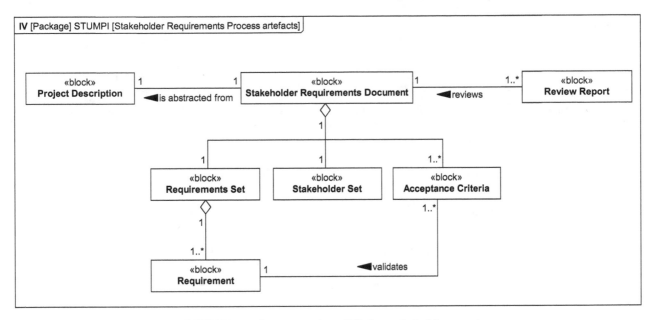

Figure F.67   STUMPI – information view (IV) for stakeholder requirement process artefacts

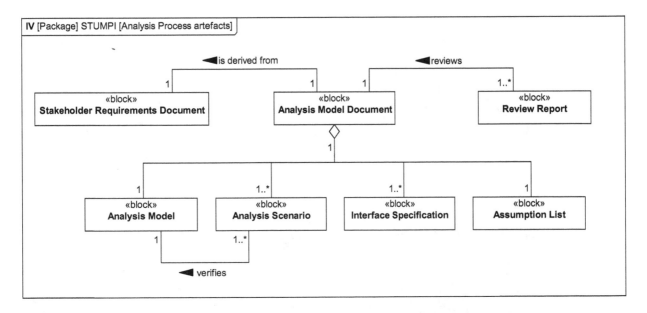

Figure F.68   STUMPI – information view (IV) for analysis process artefacts

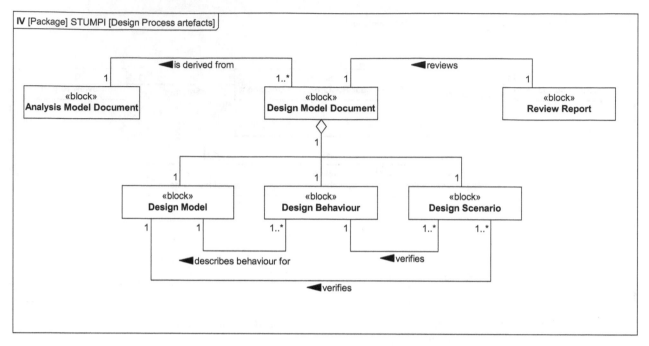

Figure F.69   STUMPI – information view (IV) for design process artefacts

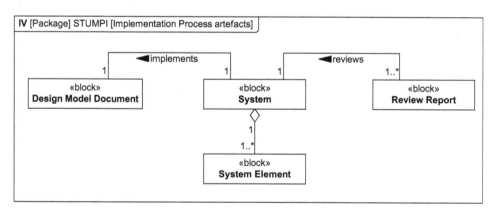

Figure F.70   STUMPI – information view (IV) for implementation process
artefacts

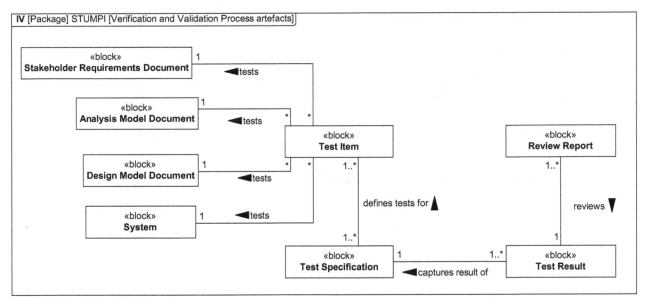

*Figure F.71   STUMPI – information view (IV) for verification and validation
process artefacts*

F.7.5   STUMPI – process behaviour view (PBV)

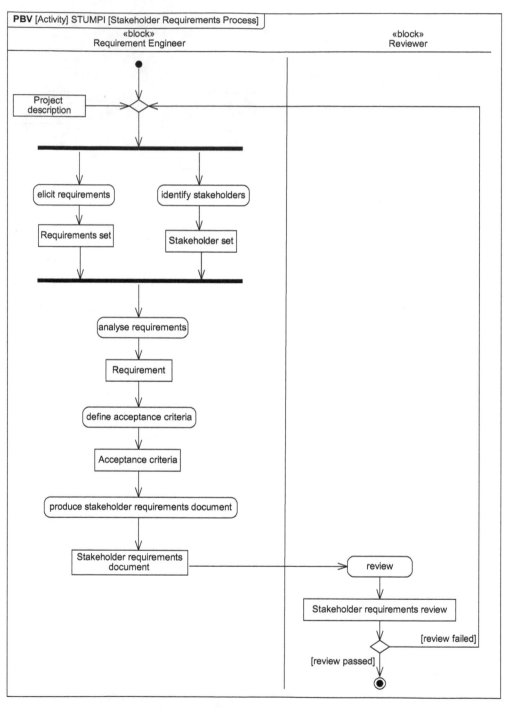

*Figure F.72   STUMPI – process behaviour view (PBV) for stakeholder
requirements process*

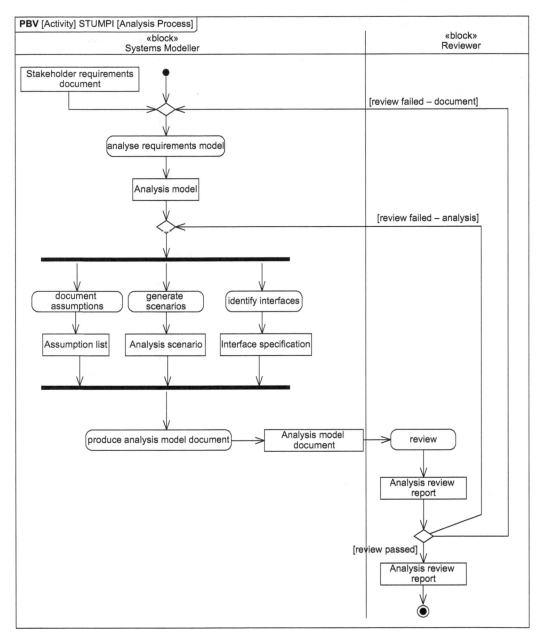

Figure F.73   STUMPI – process behaviour view (PBV) for analysis process

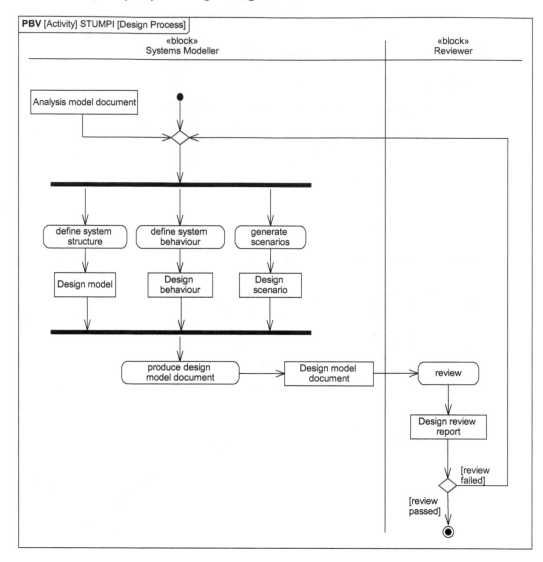

Figure F.74   STUMPI – process behaviour view (PBV) for design process

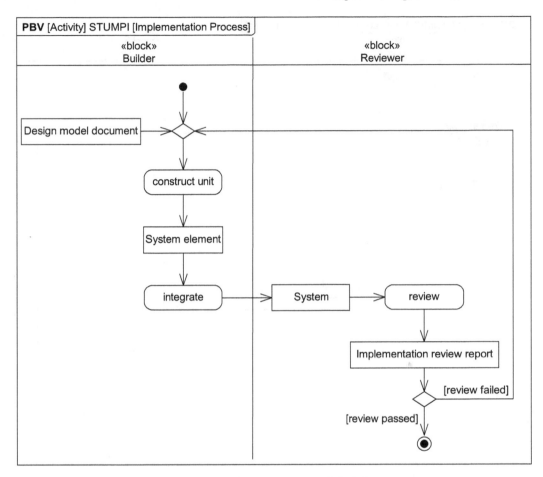

Figure F.75   STUMPI – process behaviour view (PBV) for implementation process

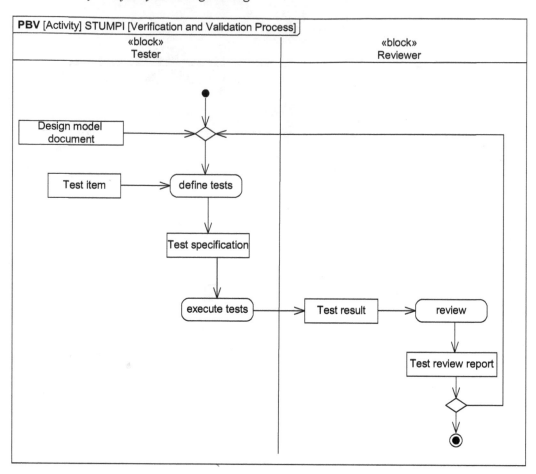

*Figure F.76   STUMPI – process behaviour view (PBV) for verification and
validation process*

F.7.6   Process instance view (PIV) for STUMPI

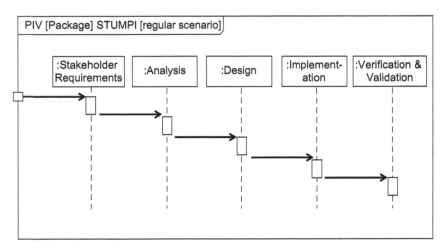

Figure F.77   STUMPI – process instance view (PIV) for regular scenario

F.8   The 'architecture definition and construction (ArchDeCon)' process

F.8.1   ArchDeCon – requirements context view (RCV)

The basic Needs for the ArchDeCon Processes are shown in the following Context.

The diagram in Figure F.78 shows the overall Context that describes the Use Cases for Architectures and Architectural Frameworks.

The main Use Case is concerned with defining an approach to modelling Architectures and Architectural Frameworks ('Define approach to modelling architectures & architectural frameworks'). This has two main inclusions:

- Any approach must support the definition of Architectures ('Support definition of architectures'). Such support must allow Architectures to be defined that model both the structural aspects ('...for structure') and the behavioural aspects ('...for behaviour') of the System being represented by the Architecture. When defining an Architecture, it is essential that an established architectural design process is followed ('Follow architectural design process') and that any Architecture conforms to a defined Architectural Framework ('Conform to architectural framework'). Too often Architectures are produced seemingly simply for the sake of producing an Architecture. For this reason it is essential that the Needs of the Customer are understood ('Understand needs for architecture') so that the Architecture is produced for a defined purpose and so that it can be validated.

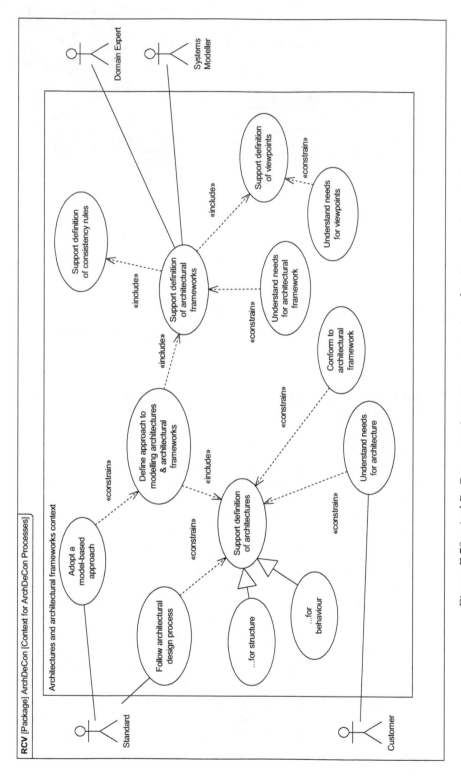

Figure F.78   ArchDeCon – requirements context view showing generic context

- Any approach must support the definition of architectural frameworks ('Support definition of architectural frameworks'). Any Architectural Frameworks should be defined in terms of a number of Viewpoints ('Support definition of viewpoints') and should have Rules defined to ensure consistency ('Support definition of consistency rules'). Just as with an Architecture, it is essential that the reasons why the Architectural Framework is being created are understood ('Understand needs for architectural framework'). Similarly, the Needs for each Viewpoint defined as part of an Architectural Framework must also be understood ('Understand needs for viewpoints').

Whatever the approach to modelling Architectures and Architectural Frameworks, it should be a model-based one ('Adopt a model-based approach'), using all the techniques described in this book.

The Context presented in Figure F.78 covers Architectures and Architectural Frameworks in general and is the guiding Context for this chapter. However, when it comes to the definition of an approach to the creation of Architectural Frameworks, then we can define a more focussed Context. This has been done, and is shown in Figure F.79.

The diagram in Figure F.79 shows the Context for the definition of an approach for the definition of Architectural Frameworks. The main Use Case that must be fulfilled is to 'Define an architectural framework for creating architectural frameworks', constrained by 'Comply with best practice' such as Architectural Framework Standards (e.g. ISO42010). In order to 'Define an architectural framework for creating architectural frameworks' it is necessary to:

- 'Allow needs that the AF is to address to be captured'. When defining an Architectural Framework, it is important that the Needs that the Architectural Framework is to address can be captured in order to ensure that the Architectural Framework is fit for purpose.
- 'Support definition of ontology for AF domain'. When defining an Architectural Framework, it is essential that the concepts, and the relationships between them, are defined for the domain in which the Architectural Framework is to be used. This is the Ontology that forms the foundational basis of the definition of the Architectural Framework's Viewpoints. Such an Ontology ensures the consistency of the Architectural Framework. The Architectural Framework must support such a definition of an Ontology.
- 'Support identification of required viewpoints'. The Viewpoints that make up the Architectural Framework need to be identified. As well as supporting such an identification, the Architectural Framework must also 'Support identification of relationships between viewpoints' and 'Support identification of grouping of viewpoints into perspectives'.
- 'Support definition of viewpoint needs'. In order to define the Viewpoints that make up an Architectural Framework, it is essential that the Needs of each Viewpoint be clearly understood in order to ensure each Viewpoint is fit for purpose and that the Viewpoints defined meet the overall Needs for the Architectural Framework.

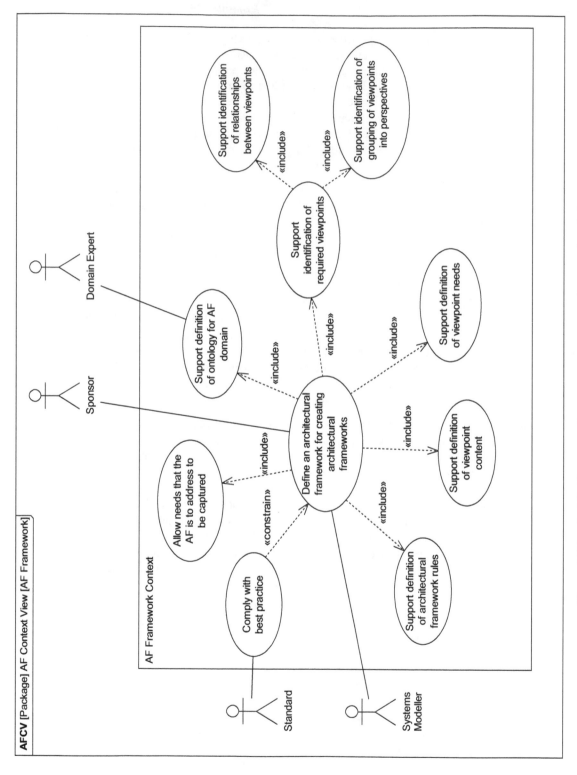

Figure F.79   ArchDeCon – requirements context view showing detailed context

- 'Support definition of viewpoint content'. An Architectural Framework is essentially a number of Viewpoints that conform to an Ontology. Therefore, when defining an Architectural Framework it is essential that each Viewpoint can be defined in a consistent fashion that ensures its conformance to the Ontology.
- 'Support definition of architectural framework rules'. When defining an Architectural Framework, it is often necessary to constrain aspects of the Architectural Framework through the definition of a number of constraining Rules. It is therefore essential that a Framework for the definition of an AF supports the definition of such Rules.

F.8.2   ArchDeCon – process content view (PCV)

The ArchDeCon Processes may be summarised as follows:

- 'AF Definition Process'. The aim of this Process is to understand the underlying need for the AF. It uses the other three ArchDeCon Processes to identify Architectural Framework Concerns for the Architectural Framework and put them into Context, define an Ontology and define Viewpoints, Perspectives and Rules.
- 'Ontology Definition Process'. The aim of this Process is to identify and define the main concepts and terms used for the AF in the form of an Ontology.
- 'Viewpoint Definition Process'. The aim of this Process is to identify and define the key Viewpoints and to classify them into Perspectives. It also defines any Rules that constrain the Viewpoints and Architectural Framework.
- 'Context Process'. The aim of this Process is to create a Context that can be used to create either an 'AF Context View' or a 'Viewpoint Context View'.

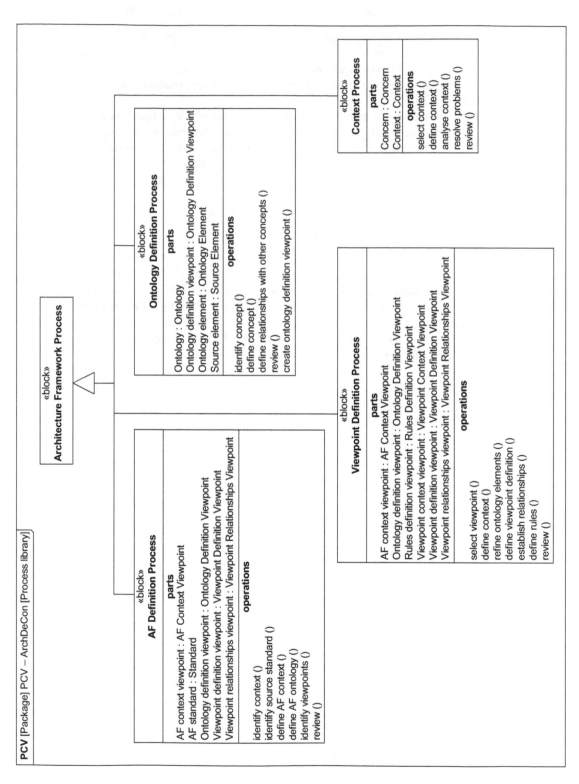

Figure F.80   ArchDeCon – process content view (PCV)

PCV [Package] PCV – ArchDeCon [Process library]

«block»
Architecture Framework Process

«block»
AF Definition Process

parts

AF context viewpoint : AF Context Viewpoint
AF standard : Standard
Ontology definition viewpoint : Ontology Definition Viewpoint
Viewpoint definition viewpoint : Viewpoint Definition Viewpoint
Viewpoint relationships viewpoint : Viewpoint Relationships Viewpoint

operations

identify context ()
identify source standard ()
define AF context ()
define AF ontology ()
identify viewpoints ()
review ()

«block»
Ontology Definition Process

parts

Ontology : Ontology
Ontology definition viewpoint : Ontology Definition Viewpoint
Ontology element : Ontology Element
Source element : Source Element

operations

identify concept ()
define concept ()
define relationships with other concepts ()
review ()
create ontology definition viewpoint ()

«block»
Context Process

parts

Concern : Concern
Context : Context

operations

select context ()
define context ()
analyse context ()
resolve problems ()
review ()

«block»
Viewpoint Definition Process

parts

AF context viewpoint : AF Context Viewpoint
Ontology definition viewpoint : Ontology Definition Viewpoint
Rules definition viewpoint : Rules Definition Viewpoint
Viewpoint context viewpoint : Viewpoint Context Viewpoint
Viewpoint definition viewpoint : Viewpoint Definition Viewpoint
Viewpoint relationships viewpoint : Viewpoint Relationships Viewpoint

operations

select viewpoint ()
define context ()
refine ontology elements ()
define viewpoint definition ()
establish relationships ()
define rules ()
review ()

F.8.3   *ArchDeCon – stakeholder view (SV)*

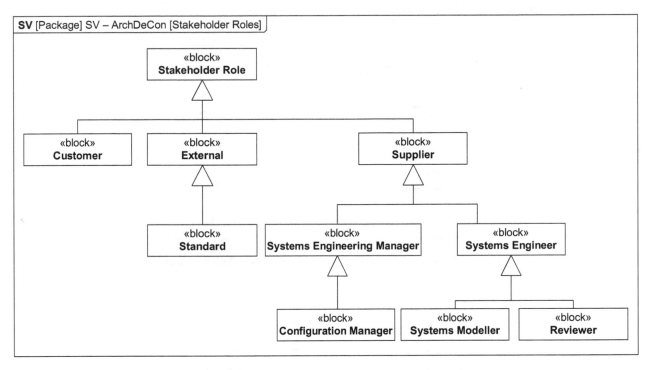

Figure F.81   ArchDeCon – stakeholder view (SV)

F.8.4   *ArchDeCon – information view (IV)*

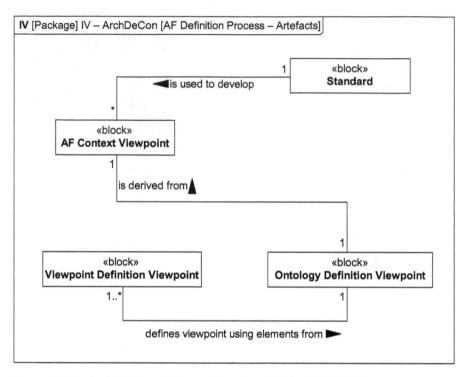

Figure F.82   ArchDeCon – information view (IV) for AF definition process
artefacts

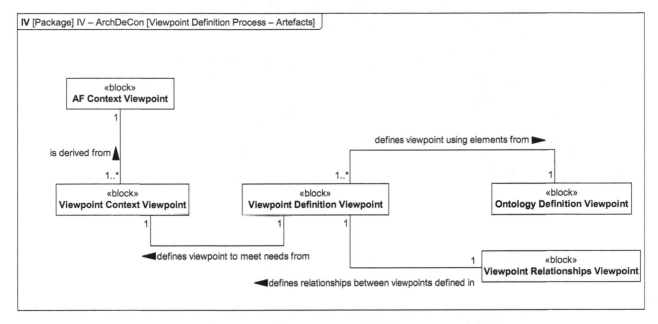

Figure F.83   ArchDeCon – information view (IV) for viewpoint definition process artefacts

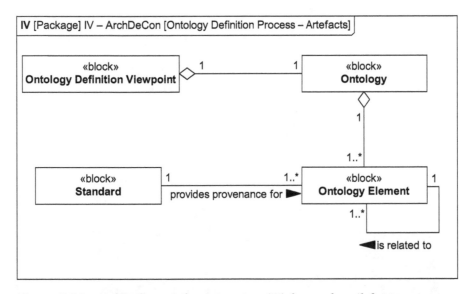

Figure F.84   ArchDeCon – information view (IV) for ontology definition process artefacts

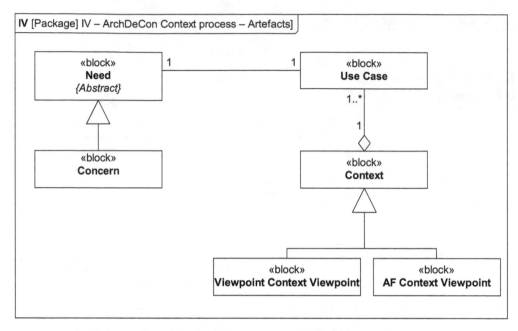

Figure F.85   ArchDeCon – information view (IV) for context process artefacts

F.8.5 *ArchDeCon – process behaviour view (PBV)*

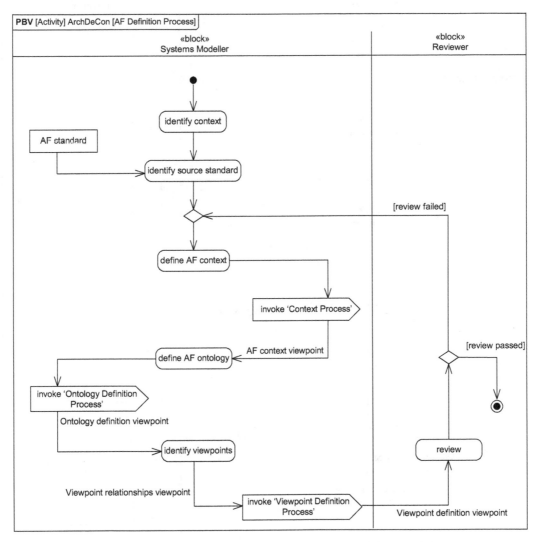

Figure F.86 *ArchDeCon – process behaviour view (PBV) for AF definition process*

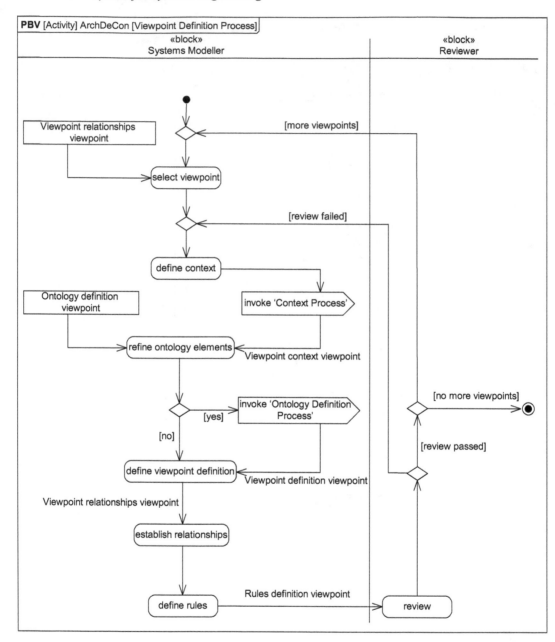

Figure F.87   ArchDeCon – process behaviour view (PBV) for viewpoint definition process

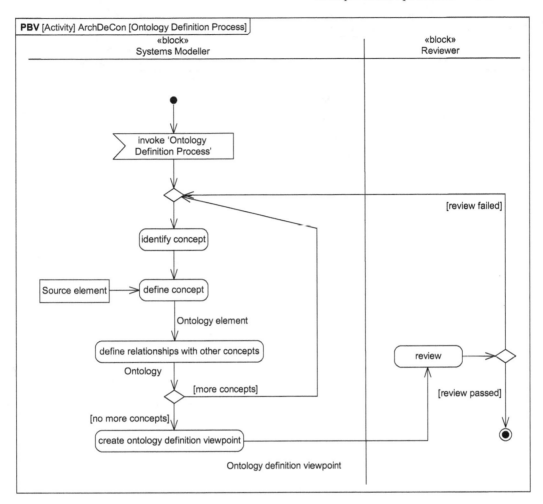

Figure F.88   ArchDeCon – process behaviour view (PBV) for ontology
definition process

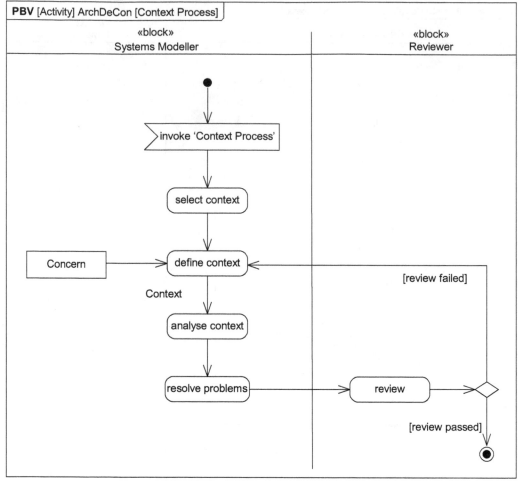

Figure F.89   ArchDeCon – process behaviour view (PBV) for context process

Competency Framework

'Some people spend their lives always trusting to luck,
Some people based their lives on a questionable *love*'

Julian Cope

G.1 Introduction

This appendix describes the MBSE Competency Framework that can be used as a basis for carrying out assessments as described in Chapter 14. This appendix also defines a number of Competency Scopes for the Stakeholder Roles identified as being important for the realisation of MBSE in an Organisation.

The diagram in Figure G.1 shows a recap of the key concepts associated with Competence taken from the MBSE Ontology that has been used throughout this book. An example Competency Framework, the MBSE Competency Framework will now be described that is based and, therefore, is consistent with the MBSE Ontology. It should be stressed that the Competency Framework provided here is for guidance only and is not intended to be definitive for all MBSE activities in all Organisations. The Competency Framework presented here is based on real work and has been applied in industry.

G.2 MBSE competency framework – levels

The MBSE Ontology identifies four Levels of Competence at which individual Competencies may be held. These are summarised in the following table.

The diagram in Table G.1 shows the set of Indicators for each Level in the form of a summary table. These are described in more detail below.

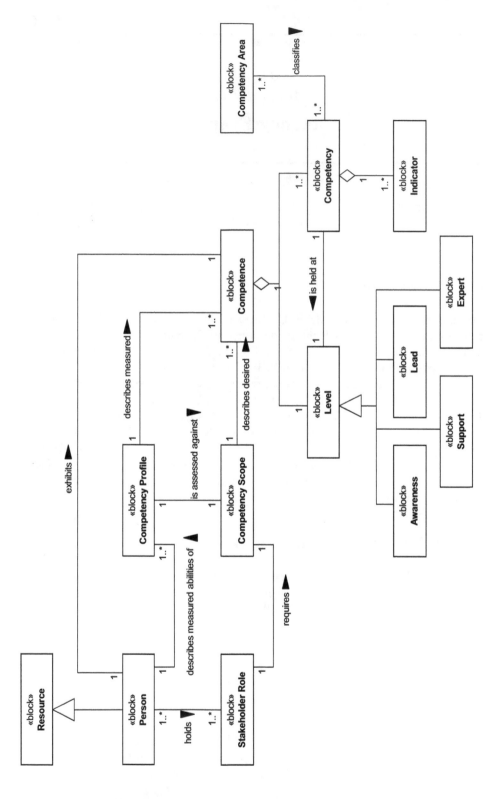

Figure G.1 Subset of the MBSE ontology focused on competence

Table G.1   Summary of indicators for each level

Level	Description	Indicators
Level 1 – Awareness	'speak knowledgeably about a particular aspect of the Competency. The main aim is for the assessee to demonstrate that they understand each Indicator	Unique for each 'Competency'
	fully, and back this up with examples – either theoretical or real-life'.	
Level 2 – Support	'reflect the ability to implement the concepts that were discussed at Level 1 for this Competency'	Has achieved Level 1, 'Awareness', for this Competency
		Has implemented the concepts discussed at Level 1
		Has been trained in some way
		Has supported other people in the implementation of work Activities that use the Indicators in Level 1
		Has created Artefacts related to the Competency as characterised by the Indicators for Level 1
		Has controlled Artefacts (applied version control, etc.) related to the Competency as characterised by the Indicators for Level 1
		Has had Artefacts reviewed and has been able to address any issues that have arisen as a result of the review
		Can identify best practice in the Competencies, such as Standards, books, methodologies, etc.
Level 3 – Lead	'reflect the ability to be able to lead the Activity that was described at Level 1 and implemented at Level 2'	Has achieved Level 2, support
		Has led Activity at a Project level
		Has managed Level 2 Activity (version control, release, setting work, assessing review responses, etc.)
		Has formally reviewed Artefacts
		Has experience facing clients
		Has some formal affiliation to a professional body, such as associate or full membership
Level 4 – Expert	'reflect the ability to be a true, recognised expert in the field that is described by this Competency'	Has achieved Level 3, Lead
		Holds formal Chartered status from a recognised professional body
		Has published in the field
		Has external recognition
		Has led Activity at the strategic or Programme level
		Has mentored Level 2 and Level 3 staff
		Has contributed to best practice
		Is currently active in recognised professional bodies

G.2.1   Level 1 – awareness

This Level identifies a number of Indicators that are required to be understood and that will be used as the basis for assessment of all the other Levels. These Indicators are specific to the Competency at Level 1, whereas at higher Levels, the Indicators are the same across *all* Competencies.

The main aim of this Level is for the assessee to demonstrate that they possess the ability to *'speak knowledgeably about a particular aspect of the Competency. The main aim is for the assessee to demonstrate that they understand each Indicator fully, and back this up with examples – either theoretical or real-life'*.

For example, to obtain 'Level 1 – Awareness', in the 'Modelling' Competency, the assessee must demonstrate that they: understand the need for modelling (first Indicator), can provide an appropriate definition of modelling (second Indicator), and so on for all the Indicators.

By understanding all the concepts in this book, then Level 1 can be easily achieved.

G.2.2   Level 2 – support

The indicators defined at 'Level 2 – Support' are the same across all of the Competencies, whereas the ones at 'Level 1 – Awareness' are different for each Competency.

The main goal of this Level is for the assessee to demonstrate that they can *'reflect the ability to implement the concepts that were discussed at Level 1 for this Competency'*. In this example, the Indicators that are defined apply to the Indicators that were identified in Level 1. These Indicators are defined as follows:

– *Has achieved 'Level 1 – Awareness', for this Competency.* Therefore, for the 'Modelling Competency' the assessee must have met the criteria – they are able to demonstrate their knowledge – for the Indicators specified.
– *Has implemented the concepts discussed at Level 1.* Therefore, for the 'Modelling Competency' the assessee must have actually worked on a Project where they have been able to: understand the need for modelling (first Indicator), provide an appropriate definition of modelling (second Indicator), and so on for all the Indicators.
– *Has been trained in some way.* This is usually by a course or in some cases by on-the-job experience, in the areas described by the Indicators at level 1. Therefore, for the 'Modelling Competency' the assessee must have actually been trained to: understand the need for modelling (first Indicator), provide an appropriate definition of modelling (second Indicator) and so on for all the Indicators.
– *Has supported other people in the implementation of work activities that use the Indicators in Level 1.* Therefore, for the 'Modelling Competency' the assessee must have supported people on a Project where they have been able

to: understand the need for modelling (first Indicator), provide an appropriate definition of modelling (second Indicator), and so on for all the Indicators. Examples of this on real Projects include contributing to creation and generation of Artefacts, and participation in workshops.

- *Has created Artefacts related to the Competency as characterised by the Indicators for Level 1*. Therefore, for the 'Modelling Competency' the assessee must have produced, or contributed to the production of Artefacts that demonstrate that they can: understand the need for modelling (first Indicator), provide an appropriate definition of modelling (second Indicator), and so on for all the Indicators.
- *Has controlled Artefacts (applied version control, etc.) related to the Competency as characterised by the Indicators for Level 1*. Therefore, for the 'Modelling Competency' the assessee must have applied version control to Artefacts that they have produced that demonstrate that they can: understand the need for modelling (first Indicator), provide an appropriate definition of modelling (second Indicator), and so on for all the Indicators.
- *Has had Artefacts reviewed and has been able to address any issues that have arisen as a result of the review*. Therefore, for the 'Modelling Competency' the assessee must have actually worked had their Artefacts reviewed by others where they can demonstrate that they: understand the need for modelling (first Indicator), provide an appropriate definition of modelling (second Indicator) and so on for all the Indicators.
- *Can identify best practice in the Competencies, such as Standards, books, and methodologies*. Therefore, for the 'Modelling Competency' the assessee must be able to reference best practice, techniques, approaches, Standards, etc. that demonstrates that they can: understand the need for modelling (first Indicator), provide an appropriate definition of modelling (second Indicator), and so on for all the Indicators.

This list of Level 2 Indicators is then applied to all Competencies in the Competency assessment in exactly the same way. Therefore, when assessing against level two using this approach, there are never "new" indicators that are introduced, just the same ones applied to all the Competencies.

G.2.3   Level 3 – lead

The Indicators defined at 'Level 3 – Lead' are the same across all of the Competencies, whereas the ones at 'Level 1 – Awareness' are different for each Competency.

The aim of this Level is for the assessee to demonstrate that they can *'reflect the ability to be able to lead the activity that was described at Level 1 and implemented at Level 2'*.

In the same way that generic Indicators are defined at Level 2 that apply to all Competencies, the same is done for Level 3. These Indicators are described as follows:

- *Has achieved 'Level 2 – Support'*. The assessee must have achieved Level 2 and, therefore, Level 1 (which was one of the Level 2 indicators).

– *Has led activity at a Project level.* Therefore, for the 'Modelling Competency' the assessee must be able to demonstrate that they have led a team or group of people where they have been able to: understand the need for modelling (first Indicator), provide an appropriate definition of modelling (second Indicator), and so on for all the Indicators. Typically, the group that was led by the assessee would be made up of primarily Level-2 people in the relevant Competencies.

– *Has supervised Level-2 activity.* Therefore, for the 'Modelling Competency' the assessee must have supervised people who are at Level 2, where they can: understand the need for modelling (first Indicator), provide an appropriate definition of modelling (second Indicator), and so on for all the Indicators. This supervision may be management supervision in the same group or may also include mentoring of Level-2 people, perhaps from other groups in the Organisation.

– *Has managed Level-2 activity (version control, release, setting work, assessing review responses, etc.).* Therefore, for the 'Modelling Competency' the assessee must be able to demonstrate that they have been involved with assessing work, setting work, etc. where they can: understand the need for modelling (first Indicator), provide an appropriate definition of modelling (second Indicator), and so on for all the Indicators. Again, notice how the level of responsibility is increasing – at Level 2 the assessee was required to have their work set and managed, at Level 3 the assessee sits on the other side of the table and performs the setting of the work.

– *Has formally reviewed Artefacts.* Therefore, for the 'Modelling Competency' the assessee must be able to demonstrate that they have reviewed Artefacts on real Projects where they: understand the need for modelling (first Indicator), provide an appropriate definition of modelling (second Indicator), and so on for all the Indicators. Yet again, the Level-3 assessee is now sat across the table from the Level-2 person and is performing the reviews.

– *Has experience facing clients.* Therefore, for the 'Modelling Competency' the assessee must be able to demonstrate that they can represent the Organisation where they can: understand the need for modelling (first Indicator), provide an appropriate definition of modelling (second Indicator), and so on for all the Indicators. This is the first Indicator that reflects an outgoing image to the outside world, where the Organisation's reputation may be at stake.

– *Has some formal affiliation to a professional body, such as associate or full membership.* Therefore, for the 'Modelling Competency' the assessee must be able to demonstrate that they have found the relevant professional body that relates to modelling and that shows that they can: understand the need for modelling (first Indicator), provide an appropriate definition of modelling (second Indicator), and so on for all the Indicators.

Again, these Level-3 Indicators, like the Level-2 Indicators, are applied to all the Competencies in the Competency Scope. Therefore, when assessing against Level three using this approach, there are never "new" indicators that are introduced, just the same ones applied to all the Competencies.

G.2.4   Level 4 – expert

The Indicators defined at 'Level 4 – Expert' are the same across all of the Competencies, whereas the ones at 'Level 1 – Awareness' are different for each Competency.

The aim of Level 4 is for the assessee to demonstrate that they can *'reflect the ability to be a true, recognised expert in the field that is described by this Competency'*. The Indicators for Level 3 are as follows:

- *Has achieved 'Level 3–Lead'*. This is similar to the criteria of both Level 2 and Level 3, each of which requires attainment of the previous Level for qualification.
- *Holds formal Chartered status from a recognised professional body*. Therefore, for the 'Modelling Competency' the assessee must be able to demonstrate that they have found the relevant professional body that relates to modelling and that shows that they can: understand the need for modelling (first Indicator), provide an appropriate definition of modelling (second Indicator), and so on for all the Indicators. The assessee must hold the Chartered status qualification or equivalent.
- *Has published in the field*. This includes books, first or second author on paper, first author on published public presentations. Therefore, for the 'Modelling Competency' the assessee must be able to demonstrate that they have published work that shows that they can: understand the need for modelling (first Indicator), provide an appropriate definition of modelling (second Indicator), and so on for all the Indicators. Due to the size of the Organisation, this will again mean publications in the public domain whereas for a large organisation, internal publications may, or may not, be considered.
- *Has external recognition*. This includes speaking at public events, invited presentations, awards, and panels. This is similar to the previous Indicator but this time relates to oral communication, rather than written. Therefore, for the 'Modelling Competency' the assessee must be able to demonstrate that they have presented papers, spoken at events, etc. that show that they can: understand the need for modelling (first Indicator), provide an appropriate definition of modelling (second Indicator), and so on for all the Indicators.
- *Has led activity at the strategic or Programme level*. Therefore, for the 'Modelling Competency' the assessee must be able to demonstrate that they defined Process, policy, etc. that relates to modelling and that shows that they can: understand the need for modelling (first Indicator), provide an appropriate definition of modelling (second Indicator), and so on for all the Indicators. At the expert Level, the assessee must be seen to be driving the relevant disciplines forward both within and without the Organisation.
- *Has mentored Level 2 and Level 3 staff*. Therefore, for the 'Modelling Competency' the assessee must be able to demonstrate that they have mentored staff in relation to modelling and that shows that they can: understand the need for modelling (first Indicator), provide an appropriate definition of modelling (second Indicator), and so on for all the Indicators. Notice again that the level of responsibility is increasing all the time and that the mentoring for this Indicator applies to all Levels below.

- *Has contributed to best practice*. This includes development of recognised methods, methodologies, and tools. Therefore, for the 'Modelling Competency' the assessee must be able to demonstrate that they have contributed to the knowledge pool and that shows that they can: understand the need for modelling (first Indicator), provide an appropriate definition of modelling (second Indicator), and so on for all the Indicators.
- *Is currently active in recognised professional bodies*. Therefore, for the 'Modelling Competency' the assessee must be able to demonstrate that they have found the relevant professional body that relates to modelling and that they are actively involved in activities that show that they can: understand the need for modelling (first Indicator), provide an appropriate definition of modelling (second Indicator), and so on for all the Indicators.

These Indicators apply to all the Indicators identified at Level 1. Therefore, when assessing against Level four using this approach, there are never "new" indicators that are introduced, just the same ones applied to all the Competencies.

G.3   Evidence types

An essential part of the MBSE Competency Framework is to define the Evidence Types that will be used to assess each of the Indicators that make up the Competency. Each of the four Levels, therefore, has its own Evidence Types defined, as follows:

G.3.1   Level 1 – awareness

The main goal of 'Level 1 – Awareness' is to: '*speak knowledgeably about a particular aspect of the Competency. The main aim is for the assessee to demonstrate that they understand each Indicator fully, and back this up with examples – either theoretical or real-life*'.

With this is mind the following Evidence Types were defined:

- *Tacit knowledge*. This means that the assessee can talk knowledgably about the selected Competency. It is important that the assessee can demonstrate that they truly understand the key concepts and is not just repeating something verbatim from a book or the Internet. This is an essential Evidence Type in that the Level cannot be achieved without this being demonstrated. It was decided that there would be an indefinite Timeliness set for this Evidence Type, providing of course that the assessee can answer questions successfully.
- *Informal training course*. This means that the assessee may have attended some form of training course of workshop related to the Competency. This is an optional Evidence Type and is, therefore, not essential to gain this Competency Level. It was decided to attach a Timeliness of two years to this Evidence Type. Therefore, for any course to be considered, it needs to have been attended in the last two years.

This Level was deemed to be the minimum acceptable Level for all Competencies in the Applicable Competency Set for all employees for this Organisation.

G.3.2 Level 2 – support

The main goal of this Level is for the assessee to demonstrate that they can '*reflect the ability to implement the concepts that were discussed at Level 1 for this Competency*'.

With this in mind, the following Evidence Types are defined:

- *Formal training course.* This means that the assessee must have some training in the relevant area. The training course itself must be formally recognised by the company as being of sufficient quality to be deemed appropriate to gain the Level. For example, a course from an accredited institution, a course provided by a professional body (with associated Continued Professional Development, or equivalent, points), a course that has been specifically mapped to a relevant Competency Framework or a course that is recognised as contributing to professional qualification. This training must have taken place in the last five years.
- *Activity – Artefact.* The assessee must be able to demonstrate that they have been involved with work activity in this area. The evidence that will be accepted is proof that they have been involved in creating an Artefact by being a documented contributor. This must have taken place in the last two years.
- *Activity – sworn statement.* Activity on a Project may also be demonstrated by having a formal statement from a Level 3 or Level 4 Person to state that they have contributed to a Project and met the requirements of Level 2. This must have taken place in the last two years.
- *Activity – formal review.* It is also possible to demonstrate activity by having work formally reviewed. In this organisation, all work is formally reviewed by Level 3 or level 4 personnel before it can be released. There is a formal process for this in the Organisation, therefore review Artefacts are deemed as acceptable proof. This must have taken place in the last two years.

This Level was deemed to be the minimum level for any staff to hold if they were to be involved with relevant work activities in this area.

G.3.3 Level 3 – lead

The aim of this Level is for the assessee to demonstrate that they can '*reflect the ability to be able to lead the activity that was described at Level 1 and implemented at level 2*'.

With this in mind, the following Evidence Types are defined:

- *Educational qualification.* In order to achieve this Level, it is necessary to hold a minimum qualification of a Master's degree in a related discipline. There is no time limit on when this qualification was held.
- *Lead activity.* The assessee must have led activity on a Project which can be demonstrated by being the lead author of a relevant Project Artefact. This must have taken place in the last year.
- *Reviewer.* The assessee must have been a reviewer for an Artefact on a Project. This must have taken place in the last year.

This Level was deemed to be the minimum Level for any staff to hold if they are to hold the job title of, or call themselves, a consultant.

G.3.4　Level 4 – expert

The aim of Level 4 is for the assessee to demonstrate that they can '*reflect the ability to be a true, recognised expert in the field that is described by this Competency*'.

With this in mind, the following Evidence Types are defined:

– *Professional qualification.* The assessee must have achieved formal Chartered status or higher. Nothing short of full, government-recognised Chartered or Fellow-status will count, and the awarding body must be an official government-recognised professional body.
– *Publications.* The assessee must have published work in a recognised format. This includes writing books and peer-reviewed papers. Non-peer-reviewed papers, such as some conferences and (definitely) white papers will not be recognised.
– *Public speaking.* The assessee must have spoken publically on behalf of the Organisation. This includes conference presentations, invited talks, seminars, and so on.
– *Activity definition.* The assessee must have been directly responsible for the definition of company policy, Process or approach.

This Level was deemed to be the minimum Level for any staff to hold if they are to formally represent the Organisation in this area.

G.4　MBSE competency framework – competency areas

The MBSE Ontology describes a Competency Area as a classification of one or more Competency. These Competency Areas will typically be arranged into a classification taxonomy, as shown below.

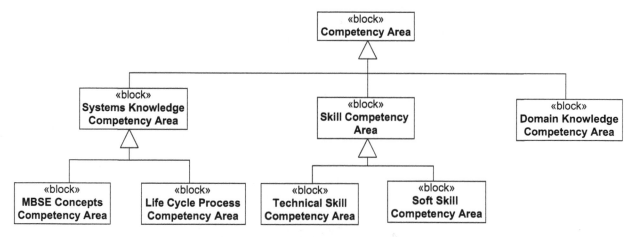

Figure G.2　Taxonomy for 'competency area' types

The different types of 'Competency Area' are shown here in the form of a classification hierarchy. When describing these Competency Areas, it is important to try to relate each one to other concepts in the MBSE Ontology or the Organisation which will make the individual Competencies easier to define. These Competency Areas are:

– *The 'MBSE Concepts Competency Area'*. This Competency Area is based directly on the MBSE Ontology. The individual Competencies will, therefore, relate to the MBSE Ontology concepts which means that it is possible to ensure coverage of all important areas of MBSE that were introduced in Chapter 3 and that have been used throughout this book.

– *The 'Life Cycle Process Competency Area'*. This Competency Area applies to the Life Cycle Processes that are used within an Organisation are based directly on the Processes from the Process model for the Organisation. These will be based on the wider MBSE model.

– *The 'Technical Skill Competency Area'*. This Competency Area applies to specific techniques that are necessary to carry out the MBSE activities in the Organisation, such as ACRE and "seven views". that have been described in Part 3 of this book. These will be based primarily on the MBSE Processes.

– *The 'Soft Skill Competency Area'*. This is a Competency Area that is often be covered by in-house human-resource Processes and Framework rather than stem from technical areas.

– *'Domain Knowledge Competency Area'*. This Competency Area is directly related to the field in which the Organisation operates and will usually be an in-house Framework that maps onto some industry-specific source.

The MBSE Ontology shows that one or more 'Competency Area' classifies one or more 'Competency', each of which is made up of one or more 'Indicator'. The competencies along with their associated indicators will now be described in the following sections.

G.5   MBSE competency area – MBSE concepts

The following diagram shows the competencies that have been defined for the 'MBSE Concepts Competency Area'.

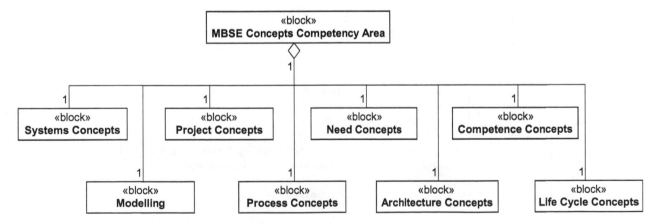

Figure G.3   MBSE competencies – 'MBSE concepts competency area'

The following table describes the competencies and their associated indicators for the 'MBSE Concepts Competency Area'.

Table G.2   Competency and indicator descriptions for the 'MBSE concepts competency area'

Competency	Description	Indicators
Modelling	This Competency relates to generic modelling.	- Understands the need for modelling - Can provide an appropriate definition of modelling - Understands the concept of abstraction - Understands the concept of connection to reality - Understands the concept of different approaches to modelling - Understands the concept of consistency - Can define what a view is - Understands the difference between modelling and drawing pictures - Understands structural modelling - Understands behavioural modelling
Systems Concepts	This Competency relates to the concept of a System and the related concepts that are necessary to demonstrate understanding of this concept.	- Understands the concept of a System Understands the concept of a System Context and its relationship to a System - Understands the concepts of System of Interest and Enabling System and the relationships between them - Understands the concepts of System of Systems and Constituent Systems and the relationships between them - Understands that there are different classifications of System of Systems - Understands the concepts of System Element and its relationship to Constituent System - Understands that a System is realised by one or more Product - Understands the concepts of a Product and a Service and the relationship between them
Project Concepts	This Competency relates to the concept of a Project and the related concepts that are necessary to demonstrate understanding of this concept.	- Understands the concepts of Project and Programme and the relationships between them - Understands the concept of Project Context and the relationship to a Project - Understands the relationship between Project and System - Understands the relationship between Life Cycle and Project - Understands the concepts of Organisation and Organisational Unit and the relationships between them - Understands the relationship between Organisational Unit and Project - Understands the concept of Organisational Context and Organisational Unit

Process Concepts	This Competency relates to the concept of a Process and the related concepts that are necessary to demonstrate understanding of this concept.	- Understands the concept of a Process - Understands the concept of a Process Execution Group and its relationship to Process - Understands the relationship between Process and Service - Understands the concepts of: Artefact, Activity and Stakeholder Role and their relationship to Process - Understands the relationship between Stakeholder Role and Activity - Understands the relationship between Stakeholder Role and System - Understands the relationship between Artefact and Activity - Understands the concept of Resource and its relationship to Activity
Need Concepts	This Competency relates to the concept of a Need and the related concepts that are necessary to demonstrate understanding of this concept	- Understands the concept of a Need - Understands the concepts of the different types of Need: Requirement, Capability, Goal and Concern - Understands the relationship between these types of Need - Understands the concept of a Need Description and its relationship to Need - Understands the concept of a Source Element and its relationship to Need - Understands the concept of a Rule and its relationship to Need - Understands the concepts of Use Case and Context and their relationship to Need - Understands the concepts of the different types of Context, such as: System Context, Stakeholder Context, Project Context and Organisational Context - Understands the concept of a Scenario and to relationship to Use Case - Understands the concepts of the different types of Scenario: Formal Scenario and Semi-formal Scenario
Architecture Concepts	This Competency relates to the concept of a Architecture and the related concepts that are necessary to demonstrate understanding of this concept.	- Understands the concept of Architecture - Understands the relationship between Architecture and System - Understands the concepts of Perspective and View, their relationships to each other and to Architecture - Understands the concept of Architectural Framework and its relationship to Architecture - Understands the concepts of Ontology and Viewpoint and their relationship to Architecture

(Continues)

Table G.2   (Continued)

		- Understands the relationship between Ontology and Viewpoint - Understands the relationship between View and Viewpoint
Competence Concepts	This Competency relates to the concept of a Competence and the related concepts that are necessary to demonstrate understanding of this concept.	- Understands the concept of Competence - Understands the concepts of Competency and 'Level' and their relationship to Competence and each other - Understands the concepts of the different types of Level: Awareness, Support, Lead and Expert - Understands the concepts of Indicator and Competency Area and their relationship to Competency - Understands the concepts of Stakeholder Role and Competency Scope, the relationship between them and how these relate to Competence - Understands the concepts of Person and Competency Profile, the relationship between them and how these relate to Competence - Understands the relationship between Person and Stakeholder Role - Understands the relationship between Competency Scope and Competency Profile - Understands the concept of Resource and how it relates to Person
Life Cycle Concepts	This Competency relates to the concept of a Life Cycle and the related concepts that are necessary to demonstrate understanding of this concept.	- Understands the concept of Life Cycle and Life Cycle Model and the relationship between them - Understands the concept of Stage and its relationship to Life Cycle - Understands the concept of Gate and its relationship to Stage - Understands the concept of Process Execution Group and its relationship to Stage - Understands the concept of System and its relationship to Life Cycle - Understands the concept of Project and its relationship to Life Cycle - Understands the concept of Life Cycle Interaction and its relationship to Life Cycle - Understands the concept of Life Cycle Interface Point and its relationship to Life Cycle Model - Understands the concept of Life Cycle Interaction and its relationship to Life Cycle Interface Point

These competencies and indicator may now be used as a basis for a Competency assessment exercise.

G.6   MBSE competency area – life cycle process

The following diagram shows the competencies that have been defined for the 'Life Cycle Process Competency Area'.

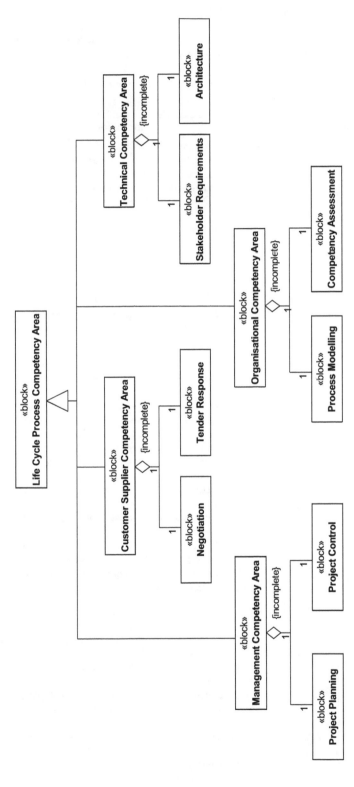

Figure G.4 MBSE competencies – 'life cycle process competency area'

The following table describes the competencies and their associated indicators for the 'Life Cycle Process Competency Area'.

Table G.3   Competency and indicator descriptions for the 'life cycle process competency area'

Competency	Description	Indicators
Process Modelling	This Competency reflects the ability to model Processes	- Holds the 'Process Concepts' Competency - Understands that each Process or set of Processes must be driven by its own Context - Understands how Stakeholder Roles have a relationship with Processes in terms of involvement and responsibility - Understands the drivers behind Process modelling (complexity, communication, lack of understanding) - Understands the importance of the Ontology - Is aware of different approaches or techniques to Process modelling - Is aware of the importance of Views - Understands how a good Process model may be used (assessment, audits, Process improvement, etc.)
Competency Assessment	This Competency reflects the understanding of assessing Competency	- Holds the 'Competence Concepts' Competency - Understands Competency assessment must be driven by its own Context - Understands the specific drivers behind why someone may wish to perform a Competency assessment - Can define Competency - Understands the difference between Capability and Competency - Understands the concept of Competency groups or areas - Understands what Indicators are and how they are used in Competency Assessment - Understands what a Competency Level is and how it is used in Competency Assessment - Can provide examples of how the output of an assessment may be used
Project Planning	This Competency reflects the understanding of planning projects	- Holds the 'Project Concepts' Competency - Holds the 'Process Modelling' Competency - Understands the need for good Project management - Understands the Project management-related concepts from the MBSE Ontology - Understands the relationship between Project management concepts and Life Cycles and Life Cycle Models - Understands the relationship between Project management concepts and Processes and Process Execution Groups

		- Is able to allocate time to Life Cycle and Process behaviours to create the Project Schedule - Understands the difference between the ideal schedule, planned schedule and actual schedule - Understands that a schedule may be related to and even dependent on other schedules
Project Control	This Competency reflects the understanding of controlling projects	- Holds the 'Project Concepts' Competency - Holds the Project Management Competency - Understands how the time elapsed on Project relates to the schedule - Is able to predict deadlines based on the Life cycle and Process behaviours - Can identify dependencies with other Projects and their schedules - Can identify potential conflicts within the schedule - Is able to define corrective actions - Is able to report accurately on the progress and status of the Project against the schedule
Tender Response	This Competency reflects the understanding of responding to tenders	- Holds the 'Stakeholder Requirements' Competency - Holds the 'Project Management' Competency - Is able to model the needs of a tender - Is able to define different candidate Scenarios - Is able to relate the Requirements model to Processes that enable Capability on the business - Understands the core business activities of the Organisation, such as Processes, Capabilities and Goals - Is able to identify key Stakeholder Roles from the business model required to satisfy the Needs of the tender - Is able to relate Competencies to identified Stakeholder Roles
Negotiation	This Competency reflects the understanding of negotiation	- Holds the 'Communication' Competency - Understands the Stakeholder Roles held by the people involved in the negotiation - Understands the basic Competencies required for the Stakeholder Roles of the people involved in the negotiation - Understands the model that represents the Needs of the subject of the negotiation - Can identify points of flexibility within this model - Has clear Goals for the negotiation - Has exit activities defined

(Continues)

Table G.3   (Continued)

Stakeholder Requirements	This Competency reflects the understanding of Stakeholder Requirements	- Holds the 'Need Concepts' Competency - Understands the concepts relating to Needs on the MBSE Ontology - Understands the difference between defining a Need and understanding a Need - Is able to define Contexts based on different drivers - Is able to identify and resolve conflicts between Needs - Is able to establish traceability to and from Needs - Is able to validate Use Cases using Scenarios
Architecture	This Competency reflects the understanding of Architecture	- Holds the 'Architecture Concepts' Competency - Understands how Architecture relates to Systems - Is able to identify and select an appropriate Architectural Framework - Is able to define an Architectural framework where necessary - Is able to realise Views based on defined Viewpoints - Is able to demonstrate consistency between Views using the Ontology - Is able to establish traceability with the Views

These competencies and indicator may now be used as a basis for a Competency assessment exercise.

G.7   MBSE competency area – technical skill

The following diagram shows the competencies that have been defined for the 'Technical Skill Competency Area'.

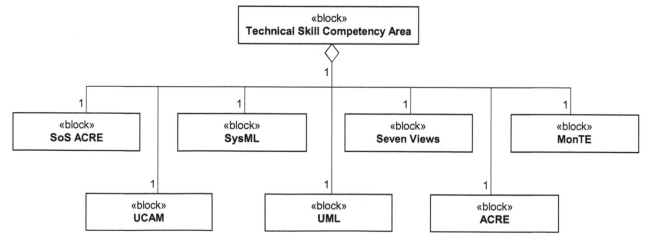

Figure G.5   MBSE competencies – 'technical skill competency area'

The following table describes the competencies and their associated indicators for the 'Technical Skill Competency Area'.

Table G.4   Competency and indicator descriptions for the 'technical skill competency area'

Competency	Description	Indicators
UML	This Competency reflects the ability to use the Unified Modelling Language (UML).	- Must hold the 'Modelling' Competency - Is familiar with the background to UML - Is familiar with the ownership of UML - Can name the six structural diagrams - Can name the seven behavioural diagrams - Understands the use of each of the structural diagrams - Understands the use of each of the behavioural diagrams - Understands the relationships between the diagrams - Understands the language extension mechanisms - Can explain what the UML meta-model is
SysML	This Competency reflects the ability to use the Systems Modelling Language.	- Must hold the 'Modelling' Competency - Is familiar with the background to SysML - Is familiar with the ownership of SysML - Can name the five structural diagrams - Can name the four behavioural diagrams - Understands the use of each of the structural diagrams - Understands the use of each of the behavioural diagrams - Understands the relationships between the diagrams - Understands the language extension mechanisms
Seven Views	This Competency reflects the ability to use the "seven views" approach to process modelling.	- Must hold the 'Process Modelling' Competency - Must understand the MBSE Ontology - Is able to realise Views using defined Viewpoints - Is able to demonstrate consistency relationships between the Views - Must understand how each View may be used for different purposes - Must appreciate different tools and techniques that can be used to realise the Views - Is able to tailor the Views - Understands how the "seven views" relate to the wider Enterprise Architecture
UCAM	This Competency reflects the ability to use the UCAM Competency assessment model processes.	- Must hold the 'Competency Assessment' Competency - Must understand the key concepts in UKSPEC - Must be familiar with at least one other external framework (e.g. INCOSE, SFIA, etc.) - Must understand the MBSE Ontology

Table G.4   (Continued)

		- Is able to demonstrate consistency between Views - Must understand how each View may be used for different purposes depending on the Context - Must appreciate different tools and techniques that can be used to realise the Views - Is able to tailor the Views - Must be able to suggest uses for Competency output
ACRE	This Competency relates specifically to the ACRE Process.	- Must hold the 'Modelling' Competency - Must hold the 'SysML Modelling' Competency - Understands the concepts and terms used in the ACRE ontology - Is able to realise Views using defined Viewpoints - Is able to demonstrate consistency relationships between the Views - Must understand how each View may be used for different purposes - Must appreciate different tools and techniques that can be used to realise the Views - Is able to tailor the Views - Is able to use ACRE with other Processes
MonTE	This Competency relates specifically to the MonTE process.	- Must hold the 'Modelling' Competency - Must hold the 'SysML' Competency - Understands the need for tool evaluation in general - Understands the specific needs for the tool evaluation exercise - Must understand the MBSE Ontology - Is able to realise Views using defined Viewpoints - Is able to demonstrate consistency relationships between the Views - Must understand how each View may be used for different purposes - Must appreciate different tools and techniques that can be used to realise the Views - Is able to tailor the Views - Understands the required capabilities for an ideal tool - Understands how the tool will be used in industry - Understands Processes within the business that will make use of the tool
SoSACRE	This Competency relates specifically to the SoSACRE process.	- Must hold the 'ACRE' Competency - Understands the concepts relating to systems of systems from the MBSE ontology - Understands the difference between SoSACRE and ACRE

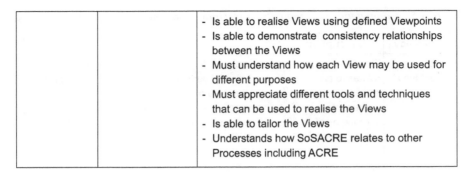

		- Is able to realise Views using defined Viewpoints - Is able to demonstrate consistency relationships between the Views - Must understand how each View may be used for different purposes - Must appreciate different tools and techniques that can be used to realise the Views - Is able to tailor the Views - Understands how SoSACRE relates to other Processes including ACRE

These competencies and indicator may now be used as a basis for a Competency assessment exercise.

G.8   MBSE competency area – soft skill

The following diagram shows the competencies that have been defined for the 'Soft Skill Competency Area'.

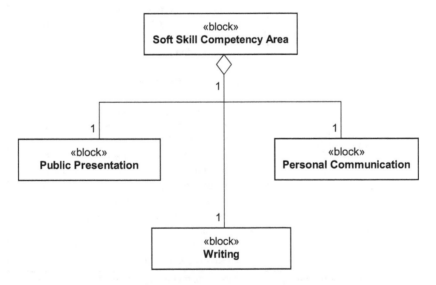

Figure G.6   MBSE competencies – 'Soft Skill'

The following table describes the competencies and their associated indicators for the 'Soft Skill Competency Area'.

Table G.5   Competency and indicator descriptions for the 'soft skill competency area'

Competency	Description	Indicators
Public Presentation	This Competency relates to an individual's ability to present information to one or more people	- Understands the need to know the expectations of the potential audience, such as: who the audience are, the type of presentation (conference, lecturing, meeting, one-on-one) and the subject - Understands the need for good presentation material, such as slides, personal notes, etc. and that the material - Understands what constitutes good presentation material, in that it must be: well-structured, graphically well-presented and configuration-controlled - Understands what constitutes good support material, in that it must be: well-structured, graphically well-presented and configuration-controlled - Understands the need for adequate support resources, such as projectors, microphones, pointers and flip charts - Understands the need to tailor the presentation for different audiences, in terms of the presentation material, support Material and the way that the material is pitched - Understands the need to practise and rehearse the presentation to check the content, timing and presentational ability - Understands the need to articulate ideas in a simple fashion, in terms of the language, assumptions about knowledge and slide clutter - Understands the need to speak clearly and speak to the audience and to: greet people, face audience, manage expectations, speak clearly and draw conclusions - Understands that appearance is important and will vary depending on the audience and that it must be congruent with the type of presentation and the audience expectations - Understands the need to address questions before and after presentation, to check the presenter's understanding of question and the questioner's understanding of answer
Writing	This Competency relates to an individual's ability to present information through writing	- Understands that all written Artefacts must be spell-checked and proof-read - Understands that all written artefacts must grammar-checked - All Artefacts must have a good structure, for example having a distinct beginning, middle and end and be written according to a plan or model

		- All Artefacts must be appropriately and correctly referenced where appropriate. The level of referencing will depend on the type of Artefact, for example academic papers will require more rigour than informal presentations - Artefacts should use diagrams and tables in order to improve communication with audience. However, these should be used only where there is a purpose and not gratuitously - It is essential to understand needs of audience and to address these needs in the Artefact - All Artefacts must be controlled, for example by effective use of configuration control and versioning
Personal Communication		- When communicating, it is important to put people at ease, to establish trust and be non-threatening - It is important to keeping to point of the presentation or topic of discussion - It is essential not to "beyond speak" (BS) and talk beyond your own knowledge or experience without stating so - It is essential that the communication is two-way, therefore listening to the comments, observations and feedback from the audience is crucial - It is important to understand that there are different types of questions and to answer accordingly, for example. Open questions that promote discussion, closed questions that require a specific answer and so on - It is important to focus on salient points - It is important to control the presentation, which may include knowing when to stop and move on from a specific point, or to say "no" to the audience - It is essential to recap using summaries and conclusions at the end of the presentation or discussion - It is essential to obtaining consensus where possible or, where not, to obtain consensus on what the differing points of view are - It is important to discuss the way forward and talk about where to go next

These competencies and indicator may now be used as a basis for a Competency assessment exercise.

G.9 Competency scopes

The stakeholder view for a subset of the MBSE activities described in this book is shown below. Due to scope limitations in this book, the emphasis here is on the 'Supplier' roles and some of the 'External' roles, therefore none of the 'Customer' roles are shown and many of the 'External' roles are missing.

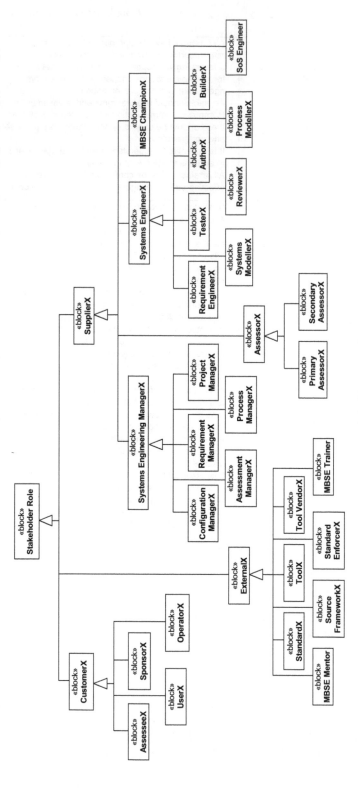

Figure G.7 Stakeholder view for MBSE roles

Each of the stakeholder roles shown here has two Competency scopes defined – one generic scope based on the INCOSE Systems Engineering Competencies Framework and one bespoke scope based on the MBSE Competency Framework. A short discussion is then provided that justifies the shape of each scope.

G.10 Generic scopes

The following diagrams show the generic scope that will be used as a basis for all the Competency scopes that use the INCOSE Competencies Framework.

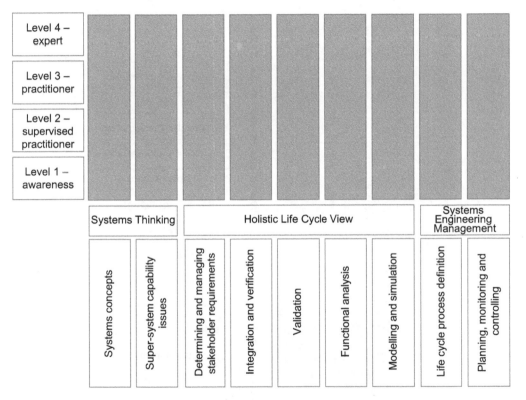

Figure G.8   Generic competency scope based on the INCOSE competencies framework

The diagram in Figure G.8 identifies the competencies and their associated levels for a generic Competency scope. Note that not all of the competencies from the INCOSE Systems Engineering Competencies Framework are shown here.

The diagram in Figure G.9 identifies the competencies and their associated levels for a Competency scope based on the MBSE Competency Framework that is

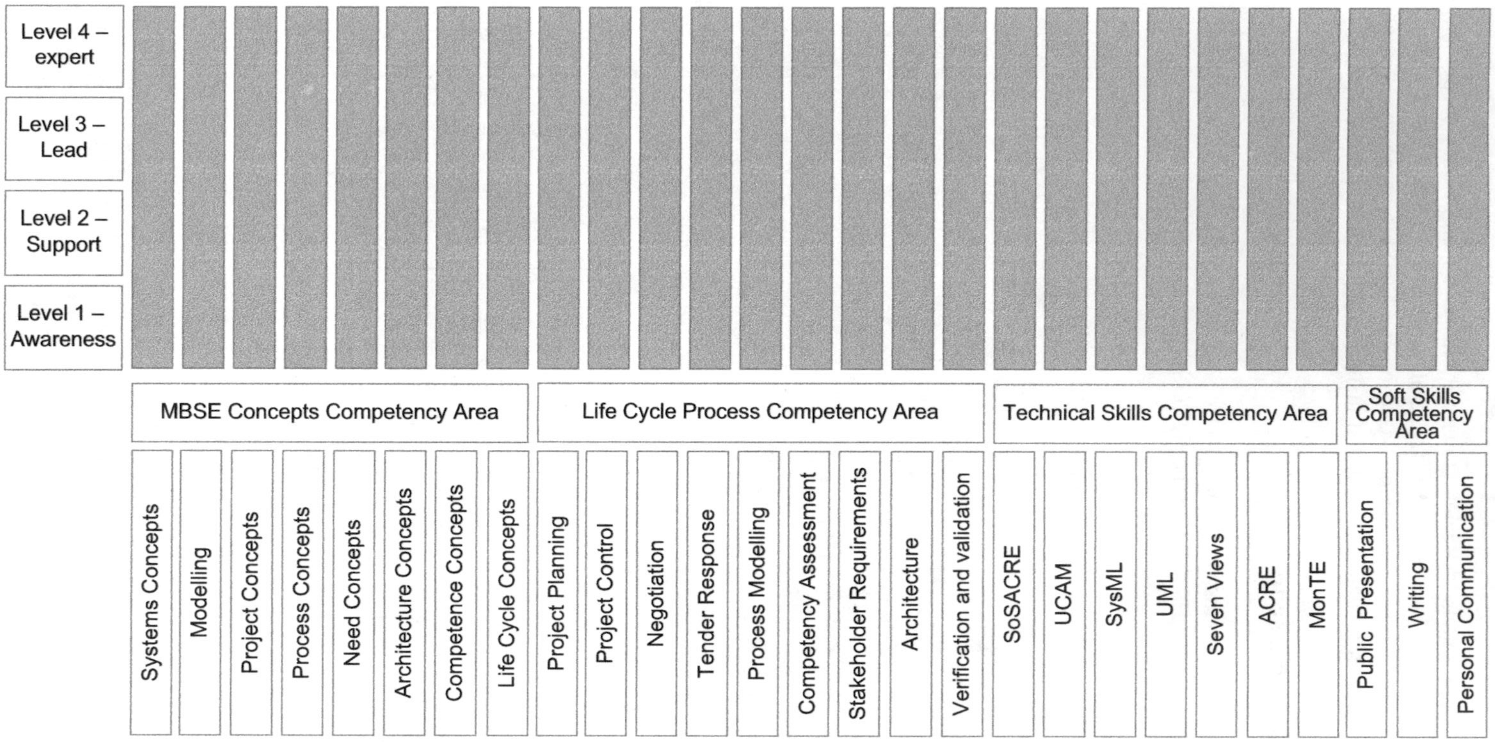

Figure G.9   Generic competency scope based on the MBSE competency framework

defined in this book. Note that all of the competencies that have been described in this appendix have been used to construct the scope. In reality, this would be narrowed down using the concept of the 'Applicable Competency Set'; see Chapter 14 and Annex F for more details.

G.11 Competency scope – 'configuration manager'

The following two diagrams show the Competency scopes for the 'Configuration Manager' role.

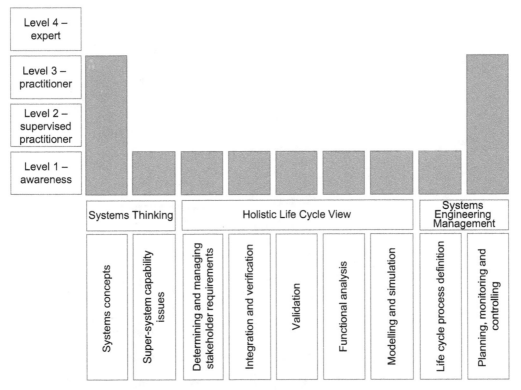

Figure G.10 Competency scope for 'configuration manager' based on the INCOSE competencies framework

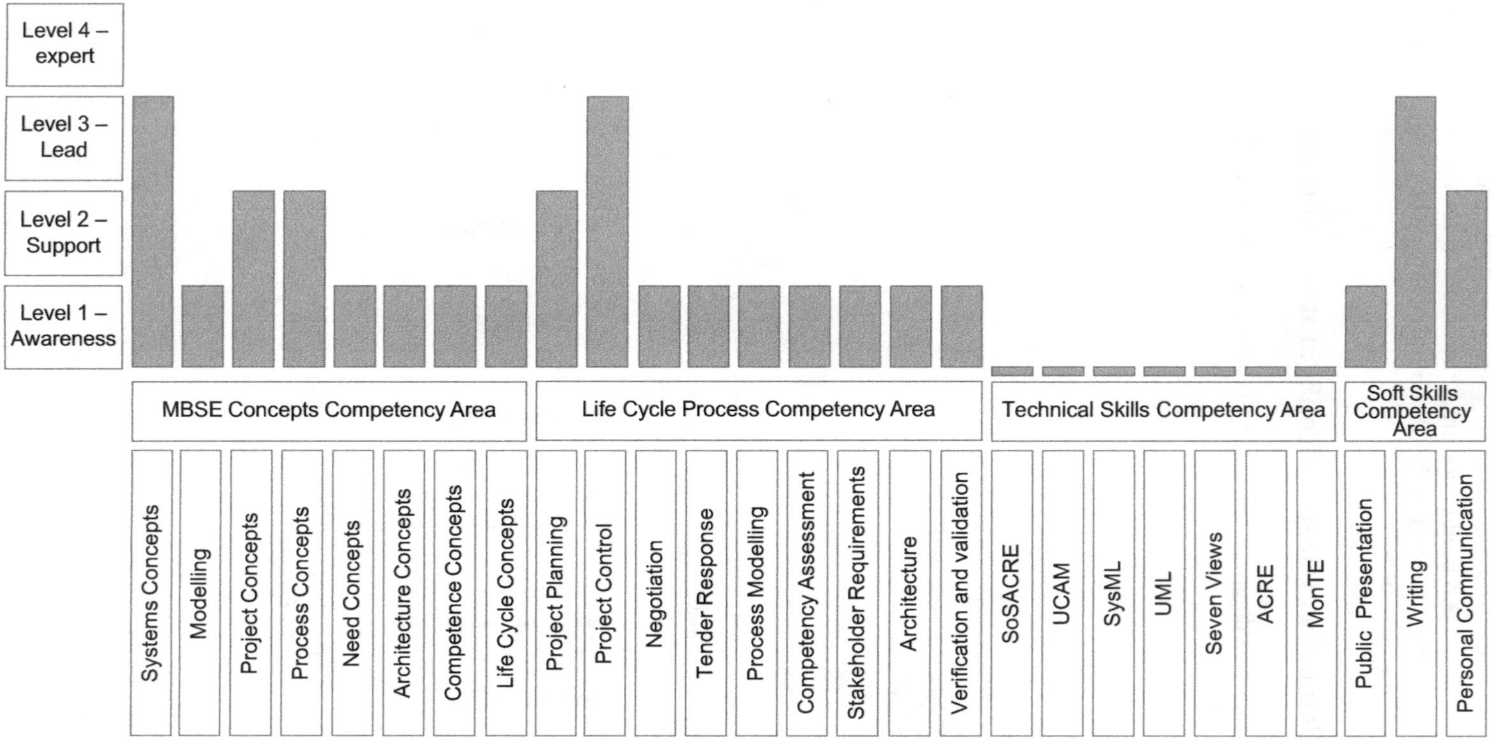

Figure G.11 Competency scope for 'configuration manager' based on the MBSE competency framework

This Stakeholder Role is responsible for ensuring that the model and all the other System Artefacts are correctly controlled, managed and configured. This will require a basic understanding of modelling, as it is the model itself as well as the Artefacts that are generated from it that will be held under configuration control. These Artefacts may take on many different forms, such as models, documents, hardware, and software.

G.12 Competency scope – 'assessment manager'

The following two diagrams show the Competency scopes for the 'Assessment Manager' role.

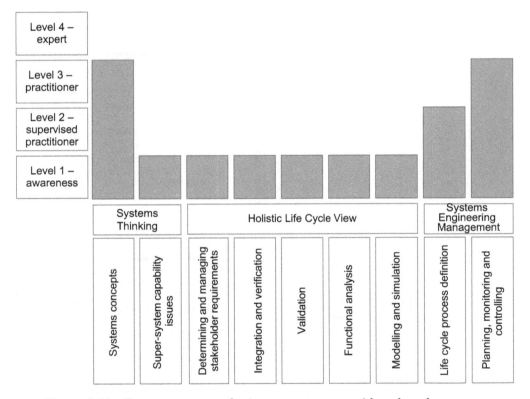

Figure G.12 Competency scope for 'assessment manager' based on the INCOSE competencies framework

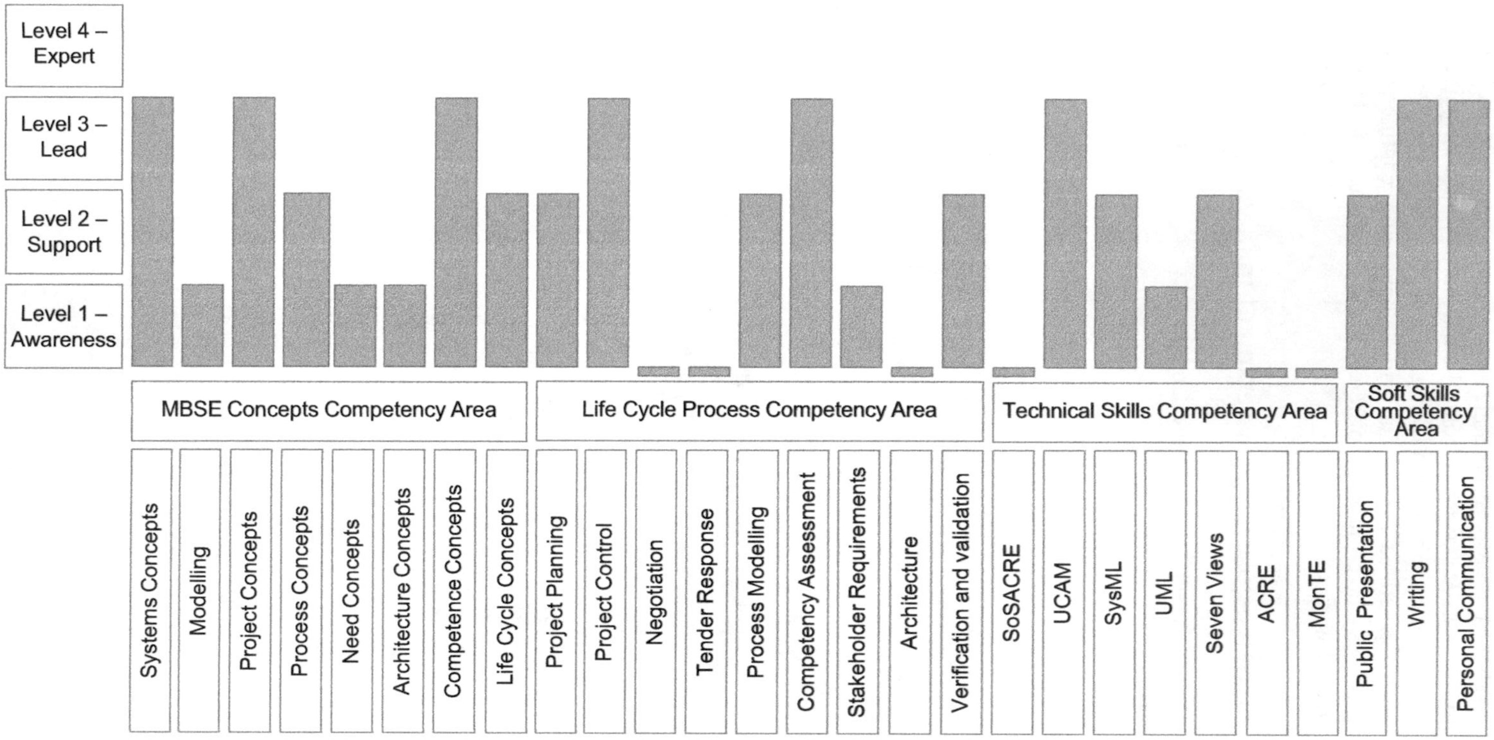

Figure G.13   Competency scope for 'assessment manager' based on the MBSE competency framework

This Stakeholder Role describes the Stakeholder Role of the Person who is responsible for defining, setting up and managing Competency assessments.

G.13   Competency scope – 'requirement manager'

The following two diagrams show the Competency scopes for the 'Requirement Manager' role.

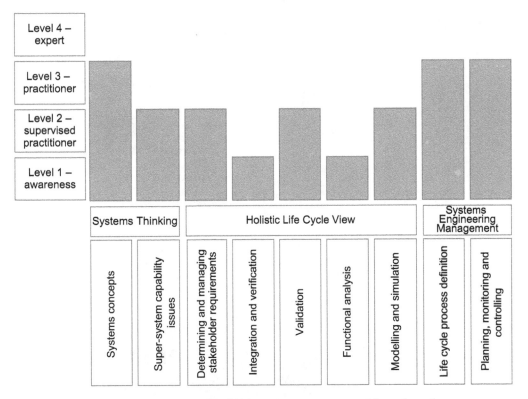

Figure G.14   Competency scope for 'requirement manager' based on the INCOSE competencies framework

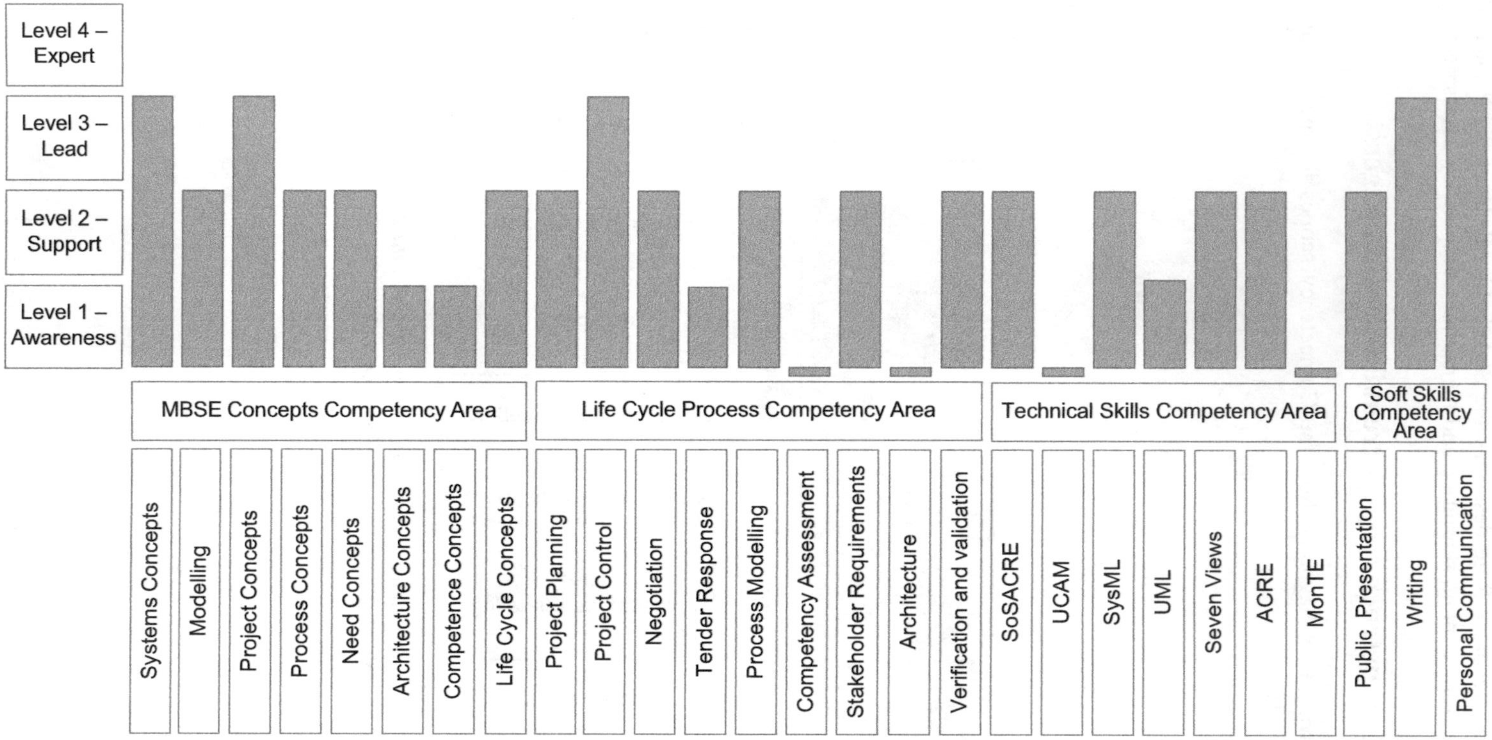

Figure G.15 Competency scope for 'requirement manager' based on the MBSE competency framework

This Stakeholder Role will require good management skills but also an understanding of the Requirements engineering activities that are being used on Projects. The manager need not be an expert in this field but certainly needs to understand the fundamental of the work being carried out. This may seem quite obvious but, in real life, it is worryingly common to find managers who understand very little of what they are managing.

G.14   Competency scope – 'process manager'

The following two diagrams show the Competency scopes for the 'Process Manager' role.

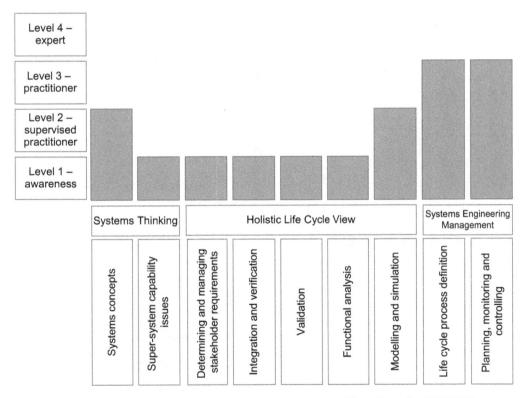

Figure G.16   Competency scope for 'process manager' based on the INCOSE competencies framework

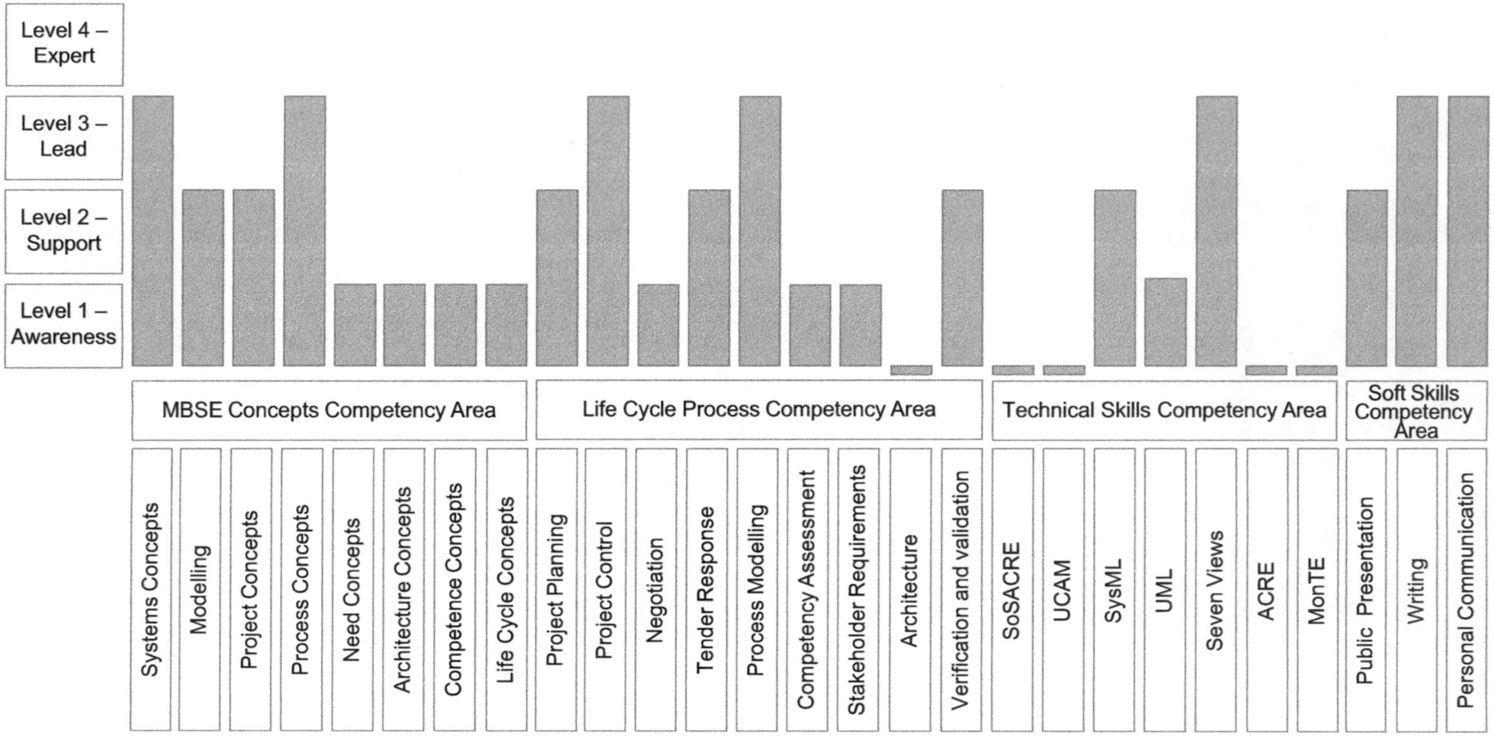

Figure G.17   Competency scope for 'process manager' based on the MBSE competency framework

This Stakeholder Role is responsible for the definition, creation and consistency of Processes. This will involve understanding the need for the Processes and, where necessary, setting up Processes, for example.

G.15   Competency scope – 'project manager'

The following two diagrams show the Competency scopes for the 'Project Manager' role.

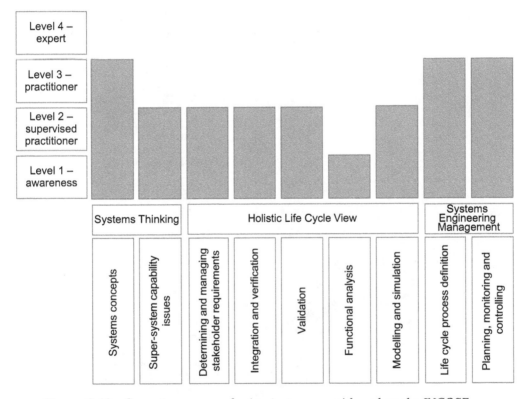

Figure G.18   Competency scope for 'project manager' based on the INCOSE competencies framework

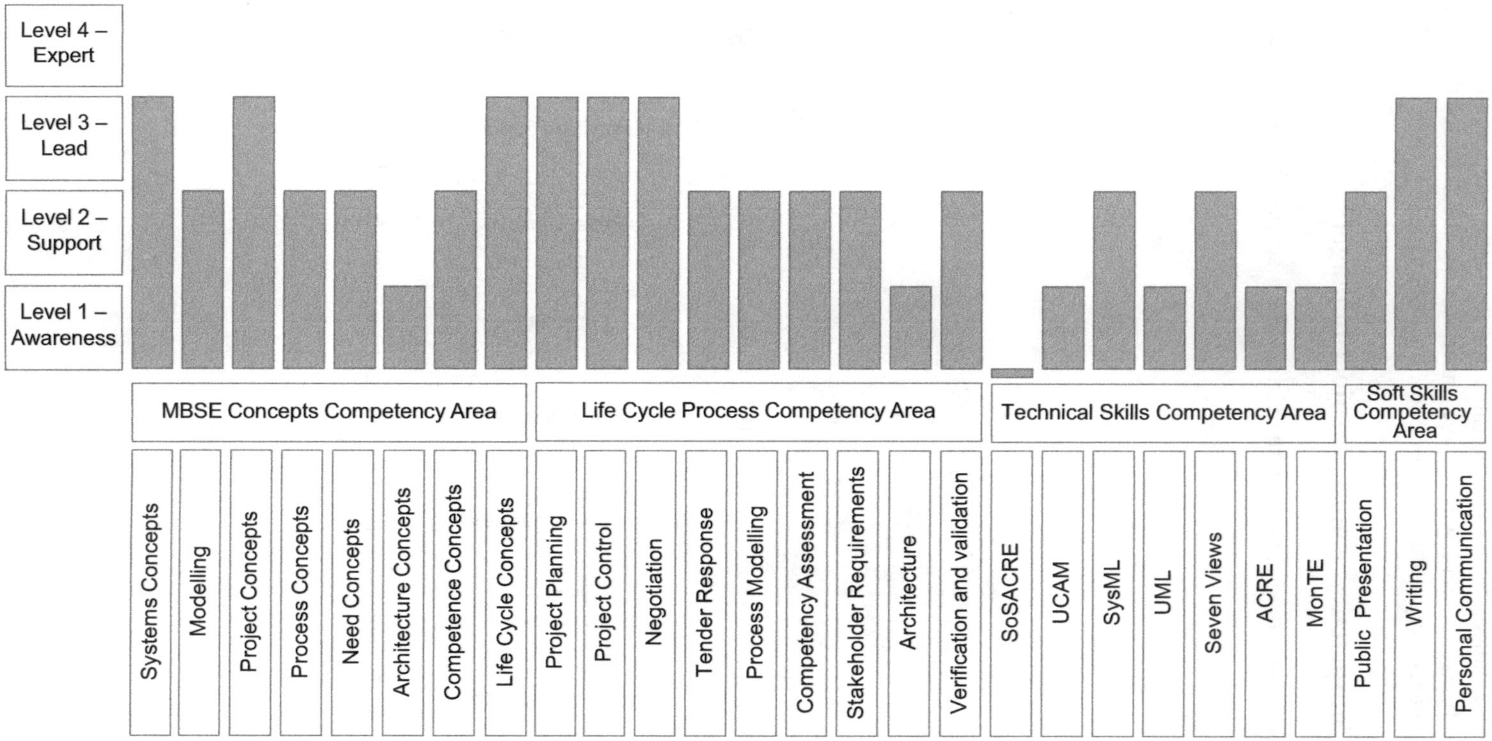

Figure G.19 Competency scope for 'project manager' based on the MBSE competency framework

This Stakeholder Role describes the Stakeholder Role of the Person who will be in charge of the Project as a whole. Note that this Stakeholder Role requires, quite obviously, good management skills, but will also require that they have a basic understanding of any areas that they will be managing. For example, if the Project Manager is overseeing a Project where an Architecture is being generated, then it is essential that the Person playing this Stakeholder Role has an understanding of what Architecture is.

G.16   Competency scope – 'primary assessor'

The following two diagrams show the Competency scopes for the 'Primary Assessor' role.

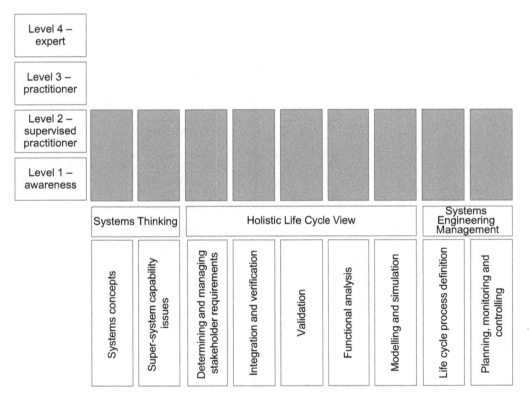

Figure G.20   Competency scope for 'primary assessor' based on the INCOSE competencies framework

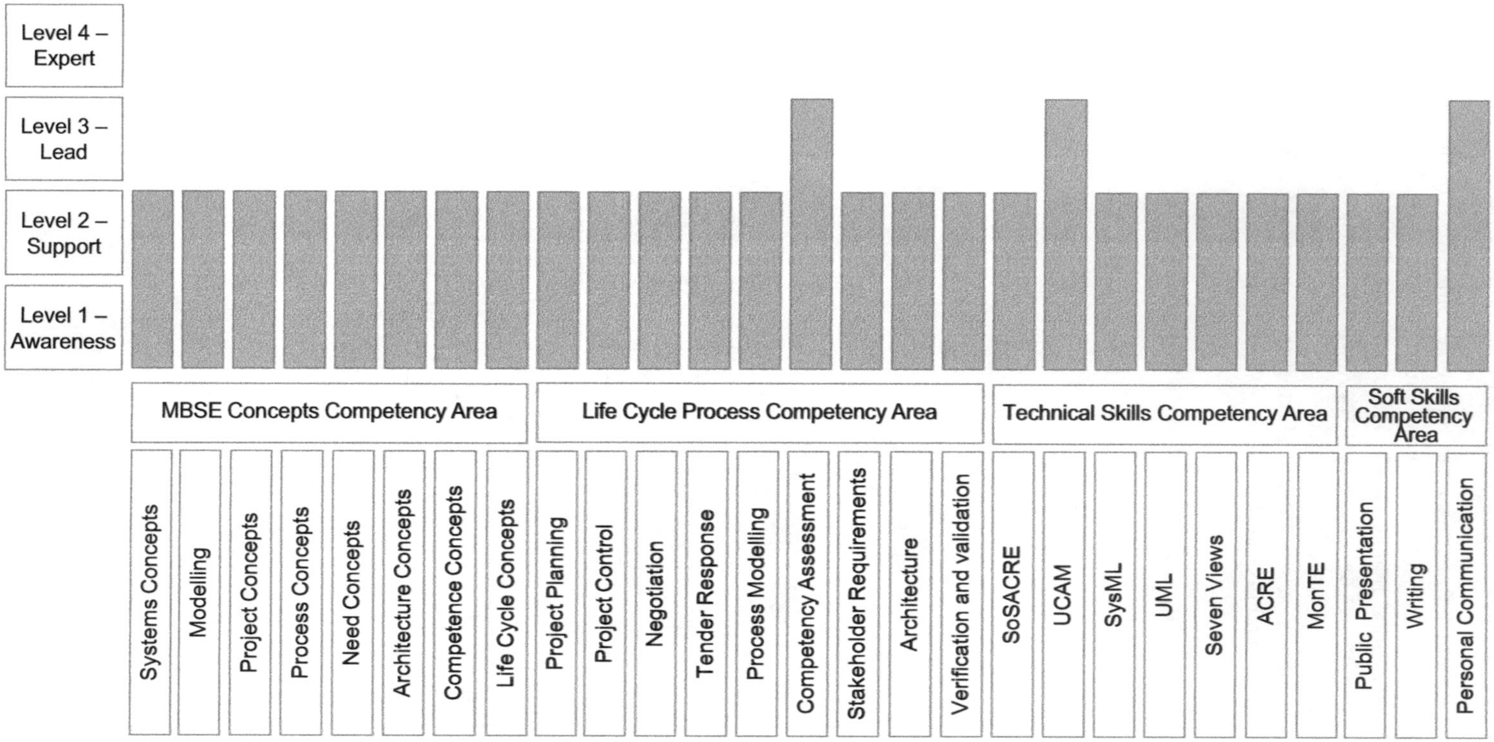

Figure G.21 Competency scope for 'primary assessor' based on the MBSE competency framework

This is the Stakeholder Role of the Person who will be leading the Competency assessment and, therefore will require very good interpersonal skills in order to make the assessment flow in a comfortable and consistent fashion. The Primary Assessor must also have a very good working knowledge of all of the Competencies that are being assessed. This is for very pragmatic reasons as anyone who is leading the assessments needs to be able to make judgement calls about whether the Assessee truly understands the subject matter and their interpretation of it.

G.17   Competency scope – 'secondary assessor'

The following two diagrams show the Competency scopes for the 'Secondary Assessor' role.

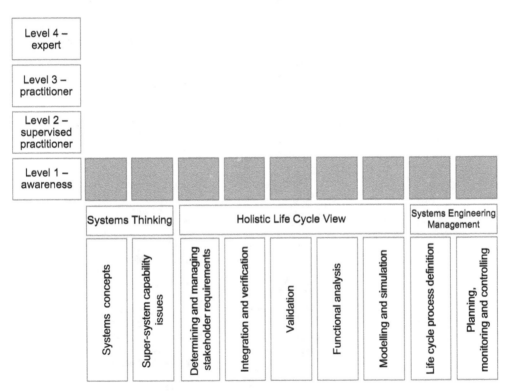

Figure G.22   Competency scope for 'secondary assessor' based on the INCOSE competencies framework

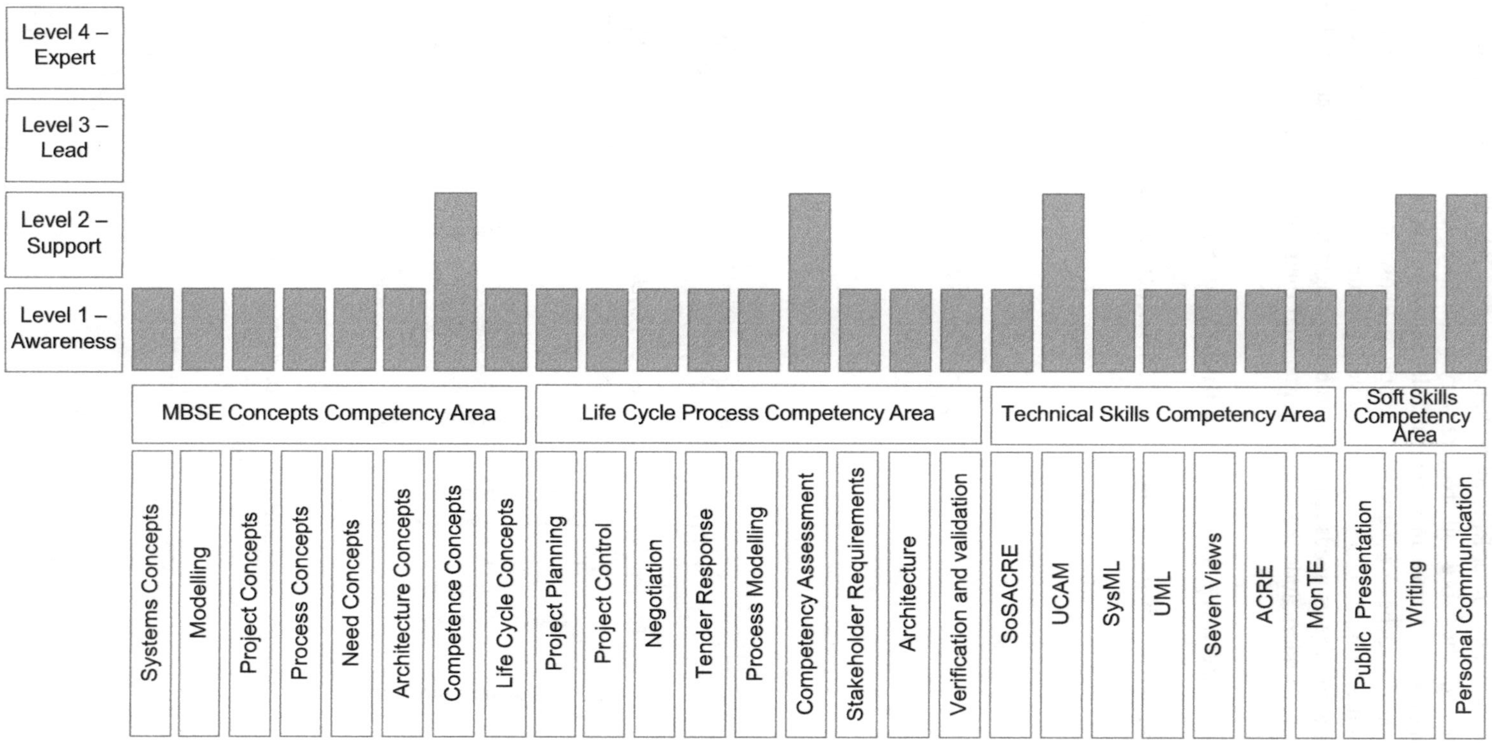

Figure G.23   Competency scope for 'secondary assessor' based on the MBSE competency framework

This Stakeholder Role is a support Stakeholder Role associated with the Primary Assessor. A basic knowledge of the Competencies being assessed is required, although not to the level of the 'Primary Assessor'. Good communication skills are also required for this Stakeholder Role, especially good writing skills.

G.18   Competency scope – 'requirement engineer'

The following two diagrams show the Competency scopes for the 'Requirement Engineer' role.

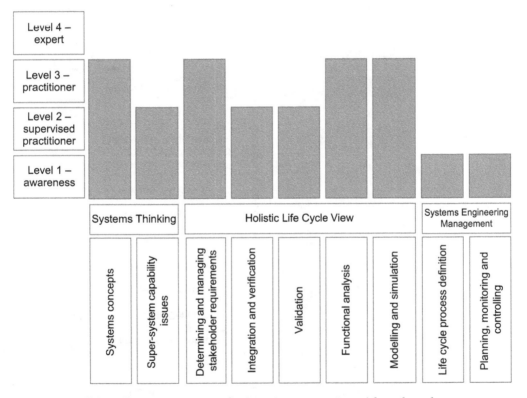

Figure G.24   Competency scope for 'requirement engineer' based on the
INCOSE competencies framework

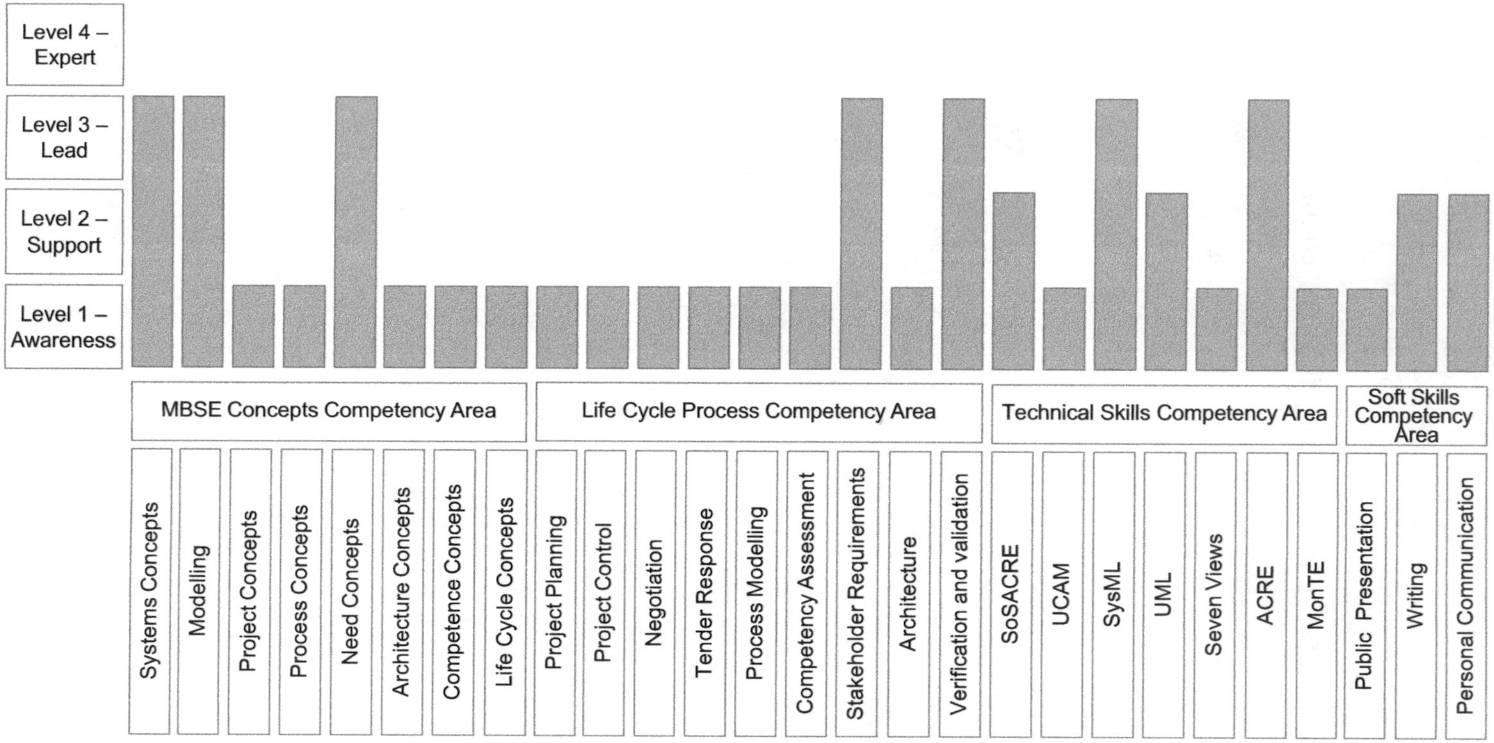

Figure G.25 Competency scope for 'requirement engineer' based on the MBSE competency framework

The area of Requirements engineering is one that is fundamental to systems engineering and, hence, MBSE. The Stakeholder Role here has an emphasis on the understanding the modelling of Requirements and, therefore, will include require Competencies that relate to Context modelling, Use Cases, Scenarios, validation and traceability. Unlike a traditional Requirements engineering Stakeholder Role, there is a strong need for modelling skills as well as understanding the fundamentals of Requirements engineering.

G.19   Competency scope – 'systems modeller'

The following two diagrams show the Competency scopes for the 'Systems Modeller' role.

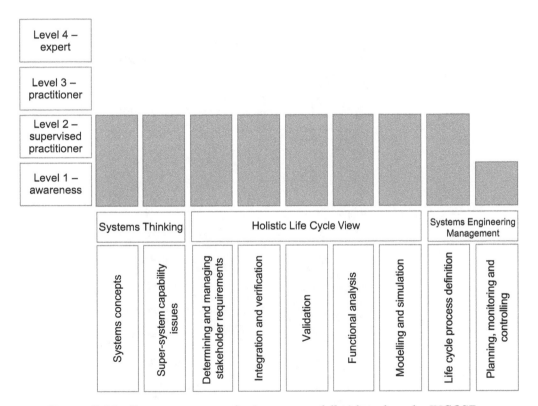

Figure G.26   Competency scope for 'systems modeller' based on the INCOSE competencies framework

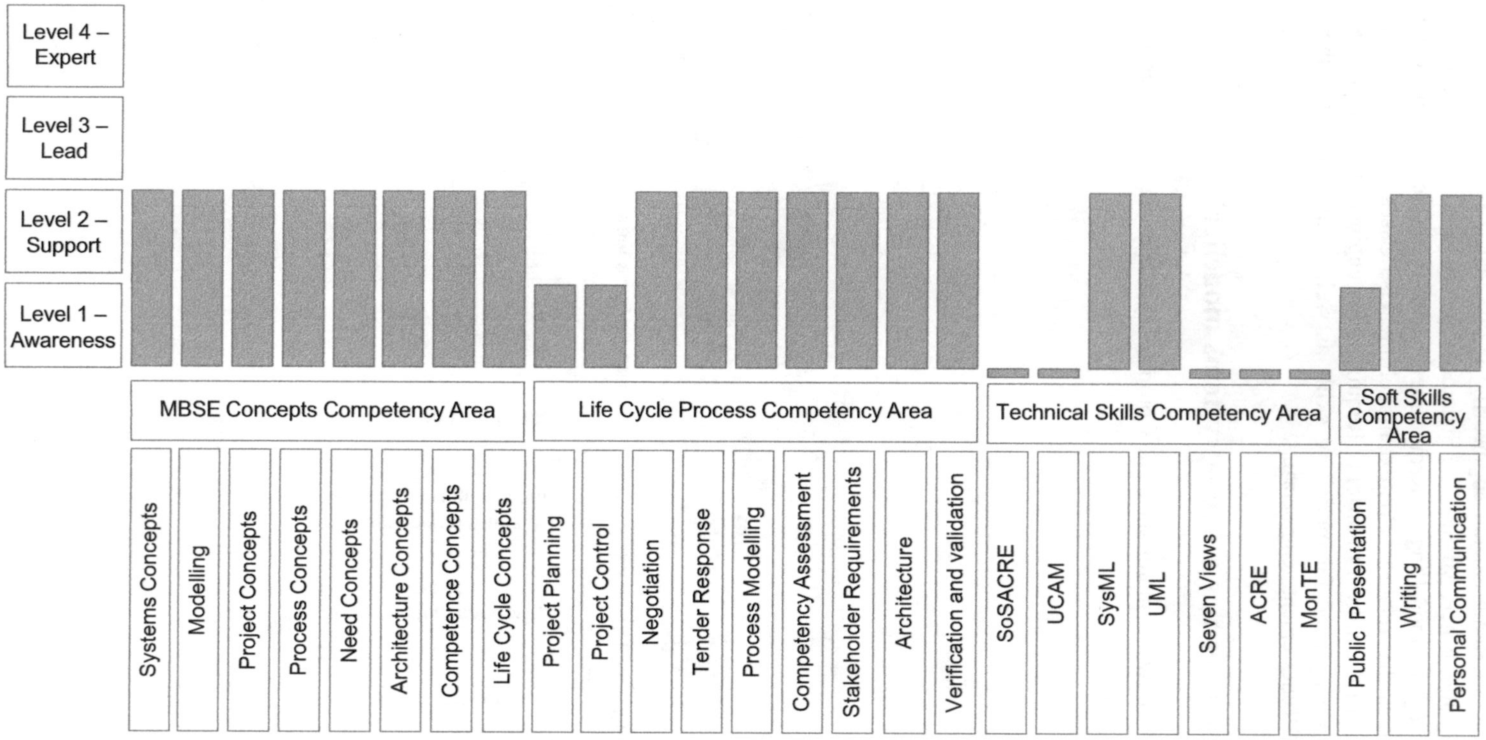

Figure G.27 Competency scope for 'systems modeller' based on the MBSE competency framework

This Stakeholder Role covers a multitude of activities and will, in reality, usually be split into a number of sub-types. Areas of expertise that must be covered here include understanding interfaces, specification, design, testing, and traceability. this is perhaps the most looselydefined of all the Stakeholder Roles here as the scope is so large. Having said this, however, it should be pointed out that the 'Systems Modeller' requires very strong modelling skills and these skills may be applied to any of the aforementioned activities. Therefore, it is possible for the 'Systems Modeller' to require a high level of Competence in almost any area, depending on the nature of the work.

G.20   Competency scope – 'tester'

The following two diagrams show the Competency scopes for the 'Tester' role.

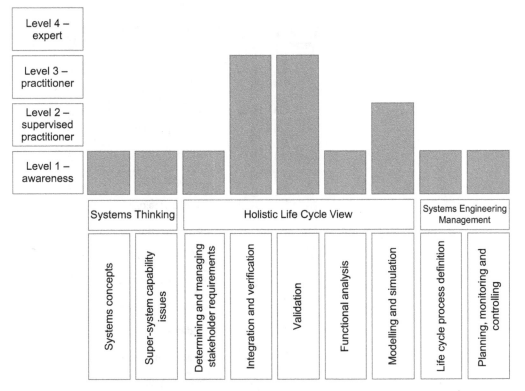

Figure G.28   Competency scope for 'tester' based on the INCOSE competencies framework

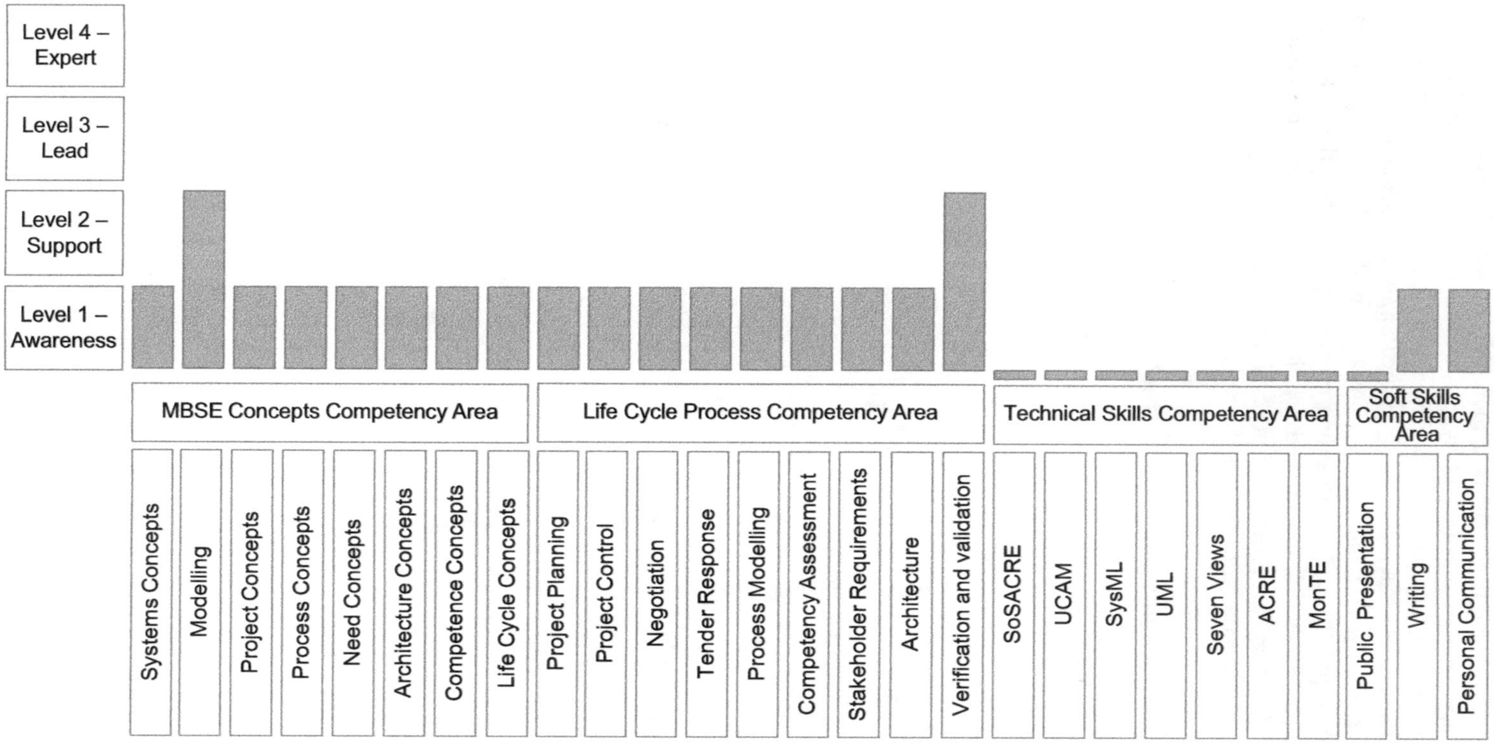

Levels

- Level 4 – Expert
- Level 3 – Lead
- Level 2 – Support
- Level 1 – Awareness

MBSE Concepts Competency Area
- Systems Concepts
- Modelling
- Project Concepts
- Process Concepts
- Need Concepts
- Architecture Concepts
- Competence Concepts
- Life Cycle Concepts

Life Cycle Process Competency Area
- Project Planning
- Project Control
- Negotiation
- Tender Response
- Process Modelling
- Competency Assessment
- Stakeholder Requirements
- Architecture
- Verification and validation

Technical Skills Competency Area
- SoSACRE
- UCAM
- SysML
- UML
- Seven Views
- ACRE
- MonTE

Soft Skills Competency Area
- Public Presentation
- Writing
- Personal Communication

Figure G.29 Competency scope for 'tester' based on the MBSE competency framework

This Stakeholder Role is primarily involved with the verification and validation activities that are applied throughout the Life Cycle. Again, the Competencies necessary for this Stakeholder Role may differ depending on the type of testing activities required.

G.21   Competency scope – 'reviewer'

The following two diagrams show the Competency scopes for the 'Reviewer' role.

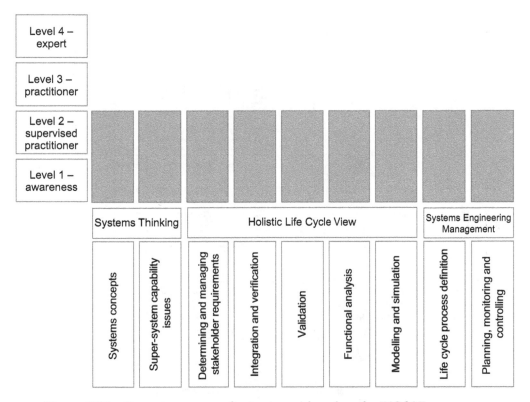

Figure G.30   Competency scope for 'reviewer' based on the INCOSE competencies framework

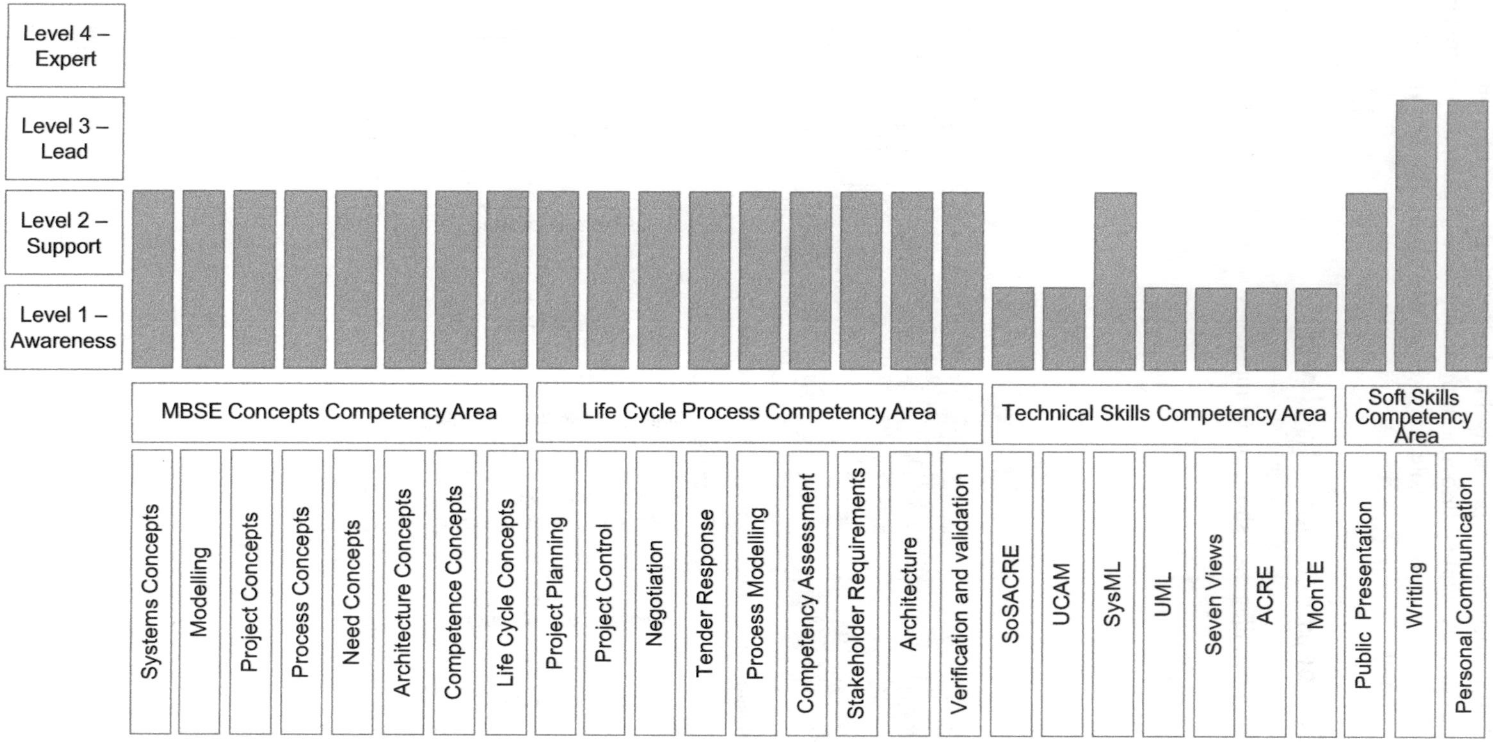

Figure G.31 Competency scope for 'reviewer' based on the MBSE competency framework

This Stakeholder Role is essential for all aspects of MBSE. Interestingly, there are two main variations on this Stakeholder Role (not shown on the diagram) that cover "mechanical reviews" and "human reviews". A mechanical review is a straightforward verification review that does not require any real human input but simply executes a pre-defined rule. Examples of these include SysML syntactical checks and checks based on a Process. These mechanical reviews tend to be quantitative in that they can be measured in terms of numbers or values and, very importantly, they may be automated. This is essential for MBSE as it is one of the benefits that were discussed in Chapter 1 of this book. The human reviews require reasoning and will tend to be qualitative and are typically very difficult, if not impossible to automate using a tool. The 'Reviewer' Stakeholder Role will require a good understanding of any area in which they are involved with reviewing.

G.22   Competency scope – 'author'

The following two diagrams show the Competency scopes for the 'Author' role.

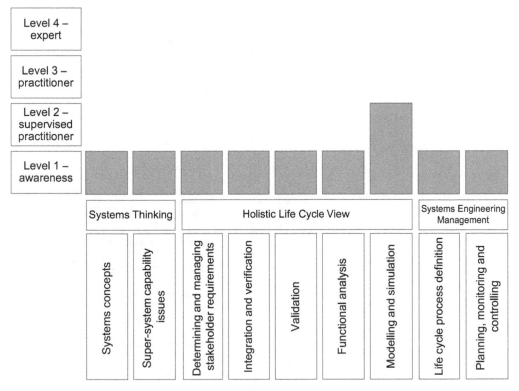

Figure G.32   Competency scope for 'author' based on the INCOSE competencies framework

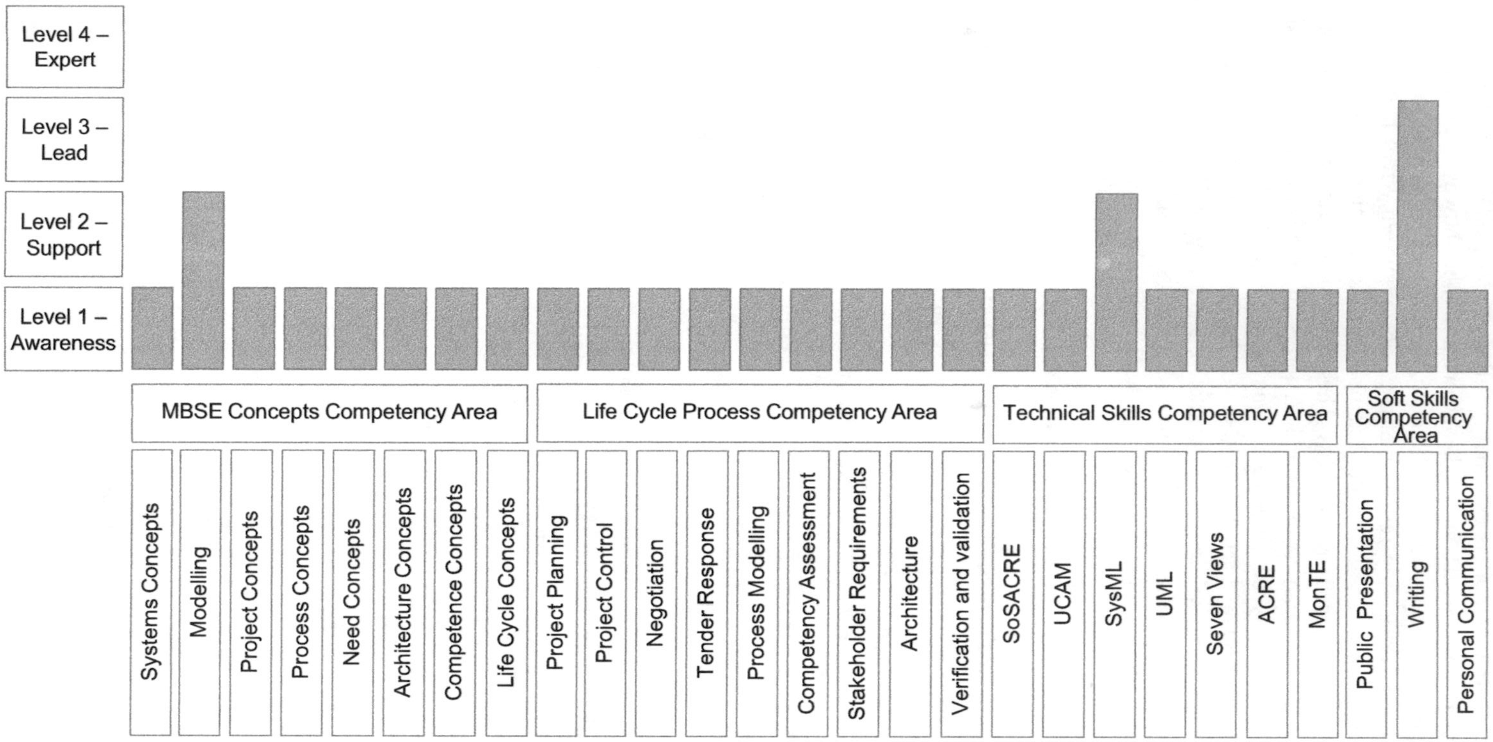

Figure G.33 *Competency scope for 'author' based on the MBSE competency framework*

This Stakeholder Role is concerned with taking models and turning them into beautiful text. Caution needs to be exercised however, as the vast majority of the text generated by the author will form part of the model, therefore, good modelling skills will be necessary for this Stakeholder Role.

G.23 Competency scope – 'process modeller'

The following two diagrams show the Competency scopes for the 'Process Modeller' role.

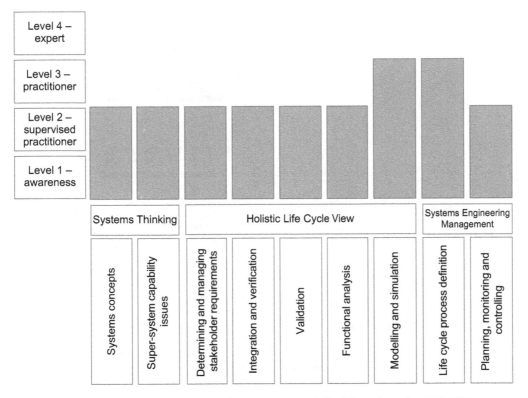

Figure G.34 Competency scope for 'process modeller' based on the INCOSE competencies framework

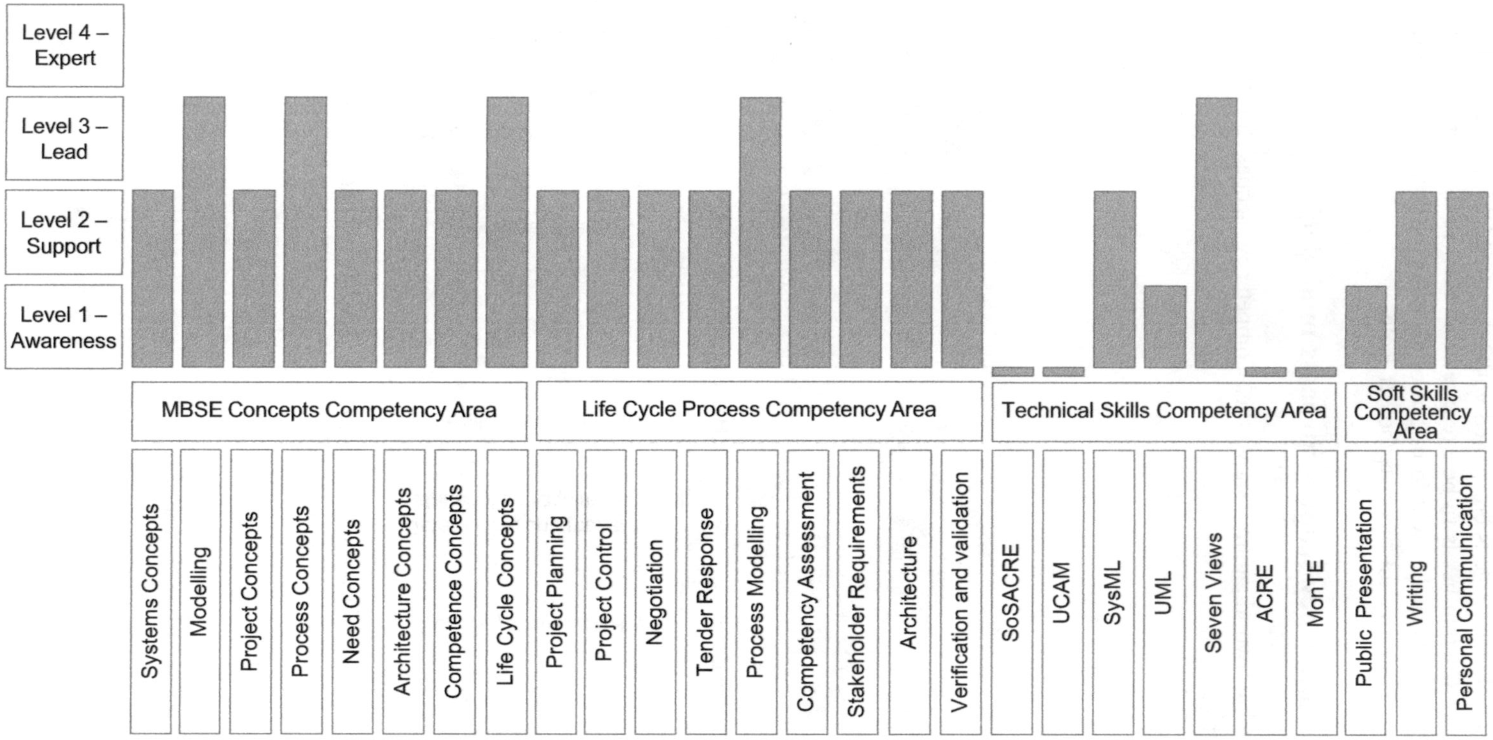

Figure G.35 Competency scope for 'process modeller' based on the MBSE competency framework

Having a well-defined Process is crucial when defining any approach to work and, in-keeping with the MBSE philosophy, this Stakeholder Role requires good modelling skills as well as an understanding of Process concepts and the business. The Stakeholder Role of the 'Process Modeller' will also require a good understanding of any areas in which the Processes will be either defined or applied, therefore, it is possible for the 'Process Modeller' to require a large number of Competencies.

G.24   Competency scope – 'builder'

The following two diagrams show the Competency scopes for the 'Builder' role.

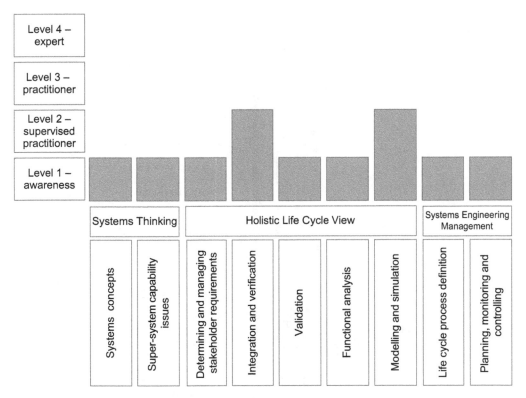

Figure G.36   Competency scope for 'builder' based on the INCOSE competencies framework

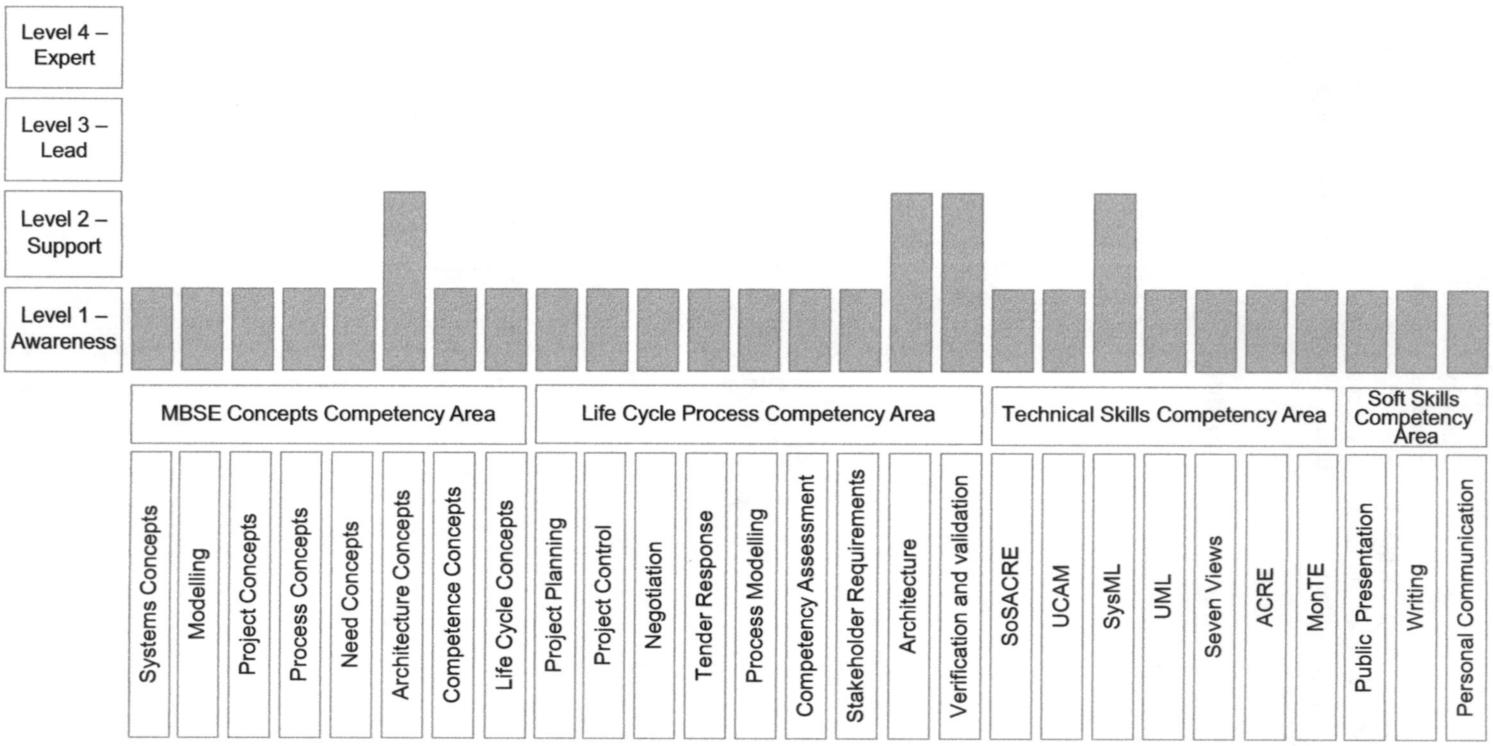

Figure G.37 Competency scope for 'builder' based on the MBSE competency framework

This Stakeholder Role is concerned with taking the model and turning it into a real System. This will include building System Elements, integrating them into the System itself, installation, and so on. Of course, this is another Stakeholder Role that on real Projects may be broken down into a set of lower-level Stakeholder Roles with different skillsets and, hence, different Competency Scopes.

G.25 Competency scope – 'SoS engineer'

The following two diagrams show the Competency scopes for the 'SoS Engineer' role.

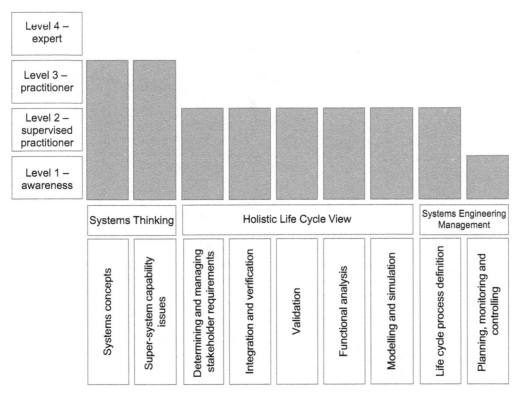

Figure G.38 Competency scope for 'SoS engineer' based on the INCOSE competencies framework

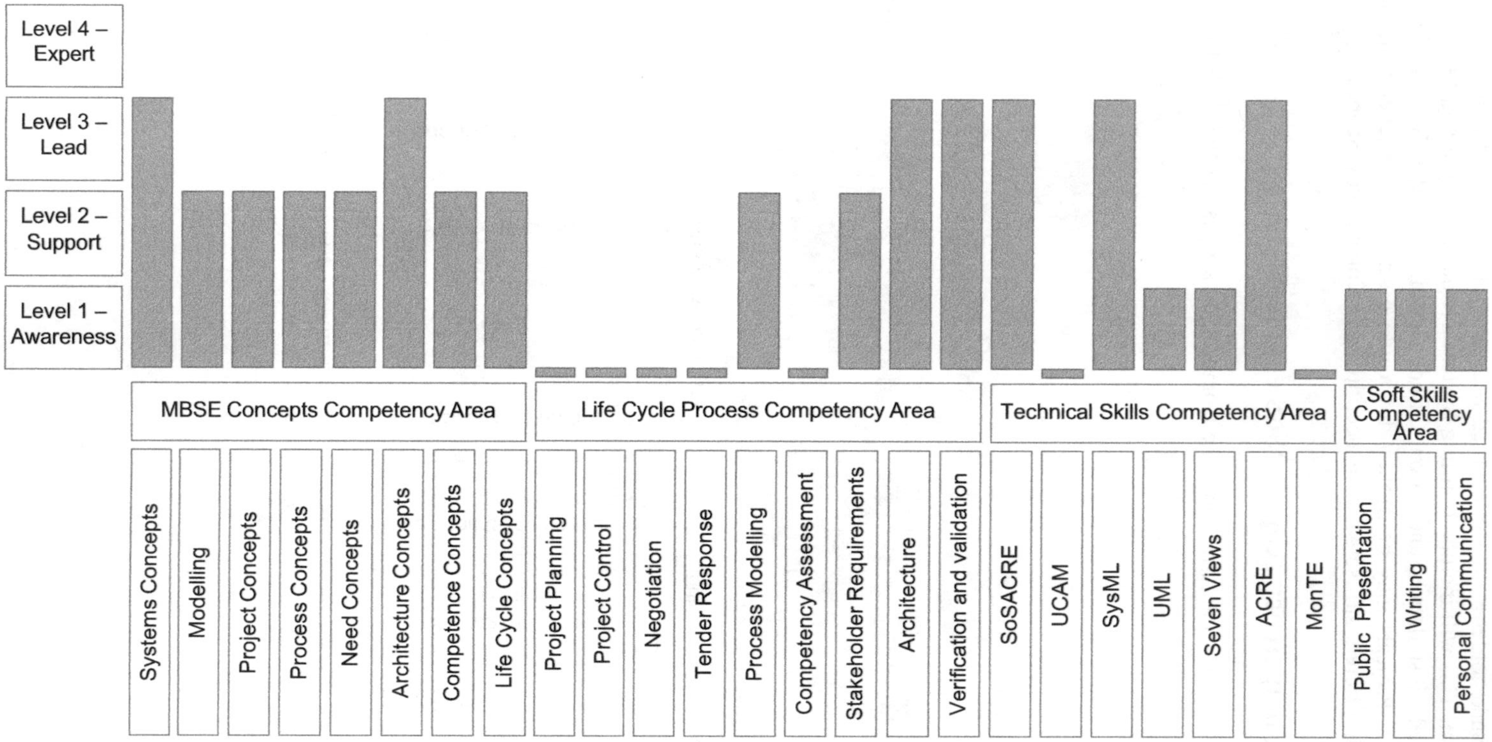

Figure G.39 Competency scope for 'SoS engineer' based on the MBSE competency framework

The Stakeholder Role of the 'SoS Engineer' is one that may be used in conjunction with any of the other systems engineering Stakeholder Roles in order to elevate it to the level of Systems of Systems. Key skills here will include integration, understanding of Requirements and verification and validation.

G.26 Competency scope – 'MBSE champion'

The following two diagrams show the Competency scopes for the 'MBSE Champion' role.

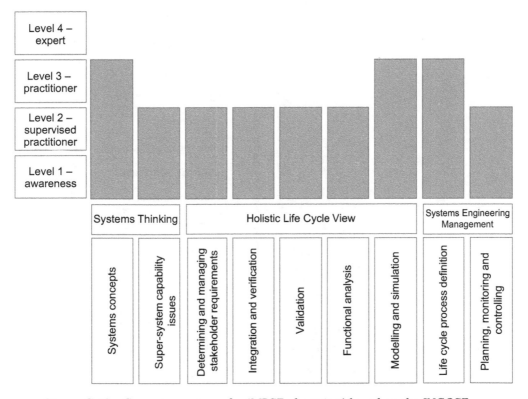

Figure G.40 Competency scope for 'MBSE champion' based on the INCOSE competencies framework

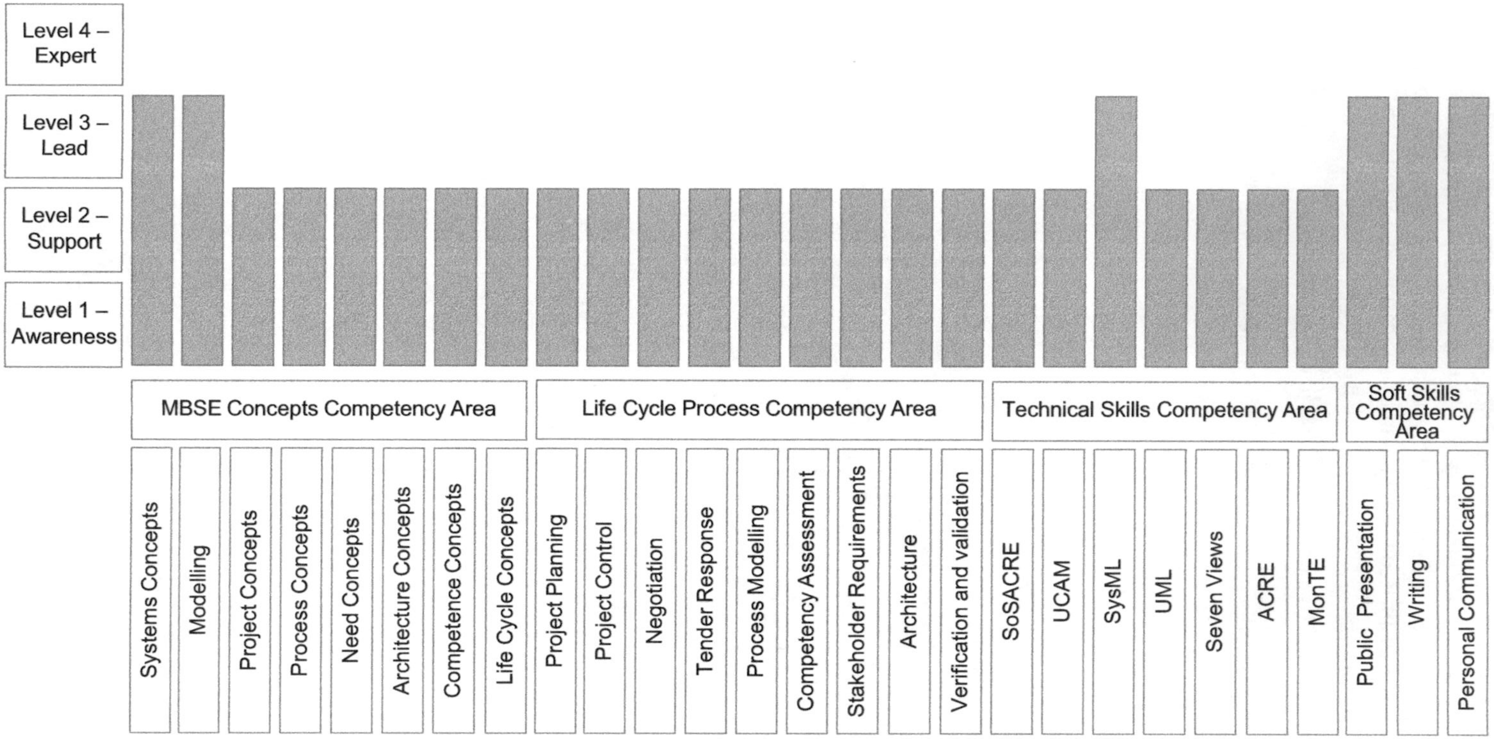

Figure G.41   Competency scope for 'MBSE champion' based on the MBSE competency framework

This Stakeholder Role is essential when it comes to implementing MBSE into a business. The 'MBSE Champion' needs to have strong modelling skills but need not be an expert. The 'MBSE Champion' must be visible in the business, have good communication skills and be able to address any MBSE-related queries that arise. The key word here is "address" as it is not the Stakeholder Role of the MBSE Champion to solve all the problems. In many instances, it may be that the MBSE Champion can solve issues, in which case all is well and good. The MBSE Champion, however, does need to know who the appropriate Stakeholder Roles are who can solve any problem. For example, if a tool-related issue arises, then the MBSE Champion may not have the specific expertise to solve the problem outright. On the other hand, they must be able to understand the nature of the problem and then relate this to an expert who can solve it. The Stakeholder Role of MBSE Champion, therefore, will often be one of a go-to person for all things MBSE-related. The effective use of and MBSE Champion is also one way to ensure that the MBSE knowledge and experience within a business is captured, controlled and used so that the same mistakes are not always repeated.

G.27   Competency scope – 'MBSE mentor'

The following two diagrams show the Competency scopes for the 'MBSE Mentor' role.

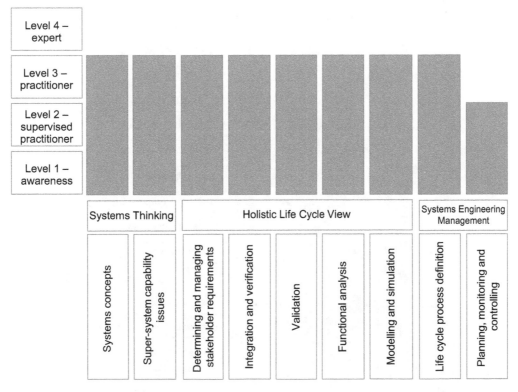

Figure G.42   Competency scope for 'MBSE mentor' based on the INCOSE competencies framework

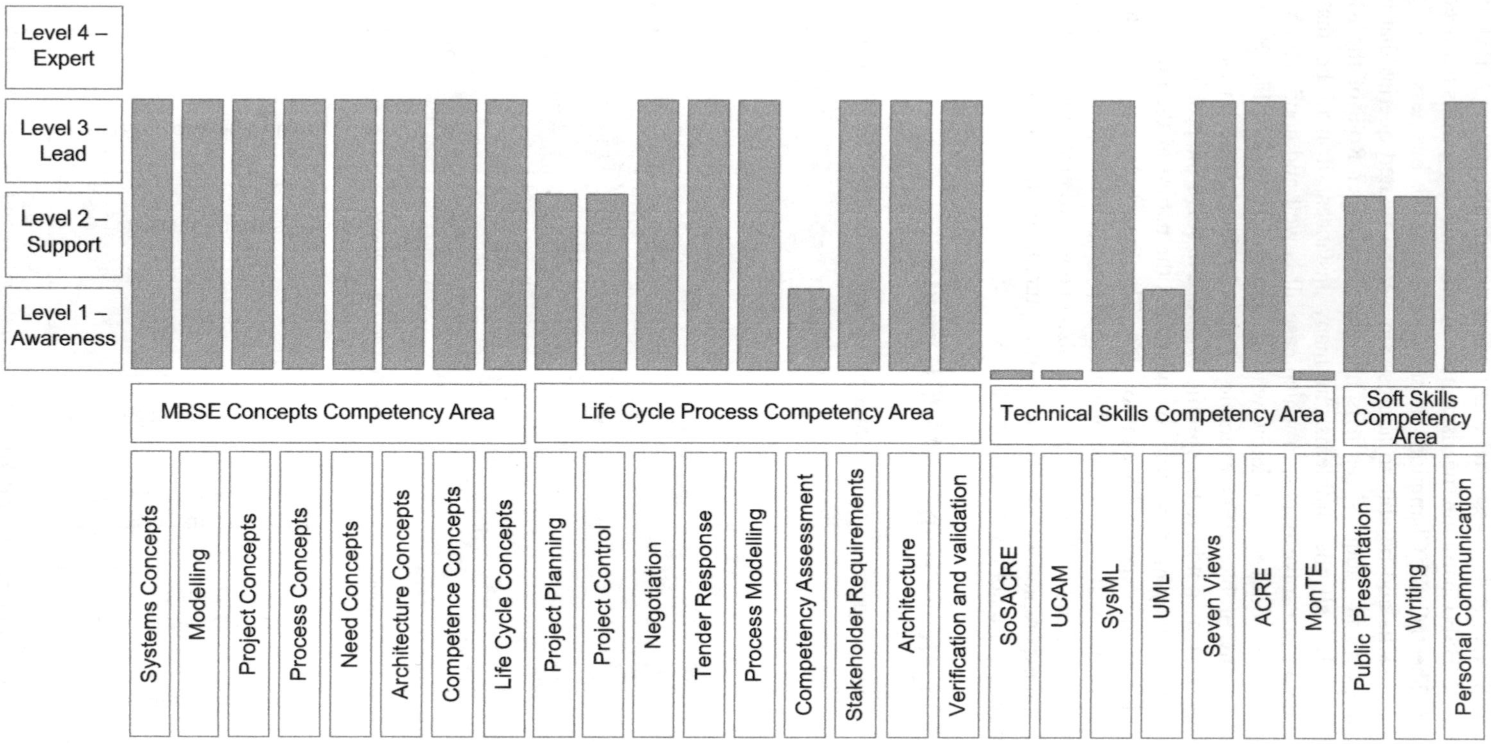

Figure G.43   Competency scope for 'MBSE mentor' based on the MBSE competency framework

The MBSE Mentor must be an expert in the field of MBSE or the specific area of MBSE as necessary. The MBSE Mentor, unlike the 'MBSE Trainer' must build up an excellent working relationship with the business. This will involve getting to know and understand the nature of the business, getting to know and understand specific issues and getting involved with Projects. Indeed, the MBSE Mentor should be a valuable member of any Project team where they are contributing to a Project. This does not mean that they need to work full-time on the Project, but they must be known to the team and able to be called upon by the team or the MBSE Champion at any point. Continuity is key to a good MBSE Mentor, so it should not be the case that every time there is an issue that a different person turns up as the MBSE Mentor. Continuity is essential for a good working relationship.

G.28 Competency scope – 'MBSE traincr'

The following two diagrams show the Competency scopes for the 'MBSE Trainer' role.

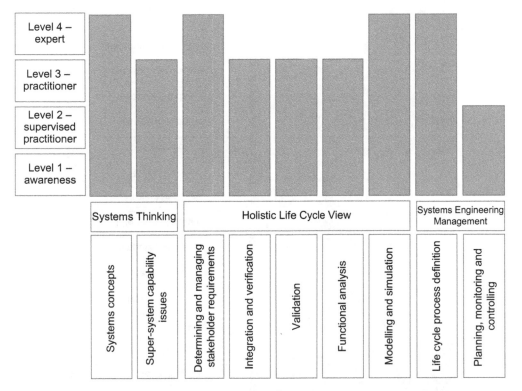

Figure G.44 Competency scope for 'MBSE trainer' based on the INCOSE competencies framework

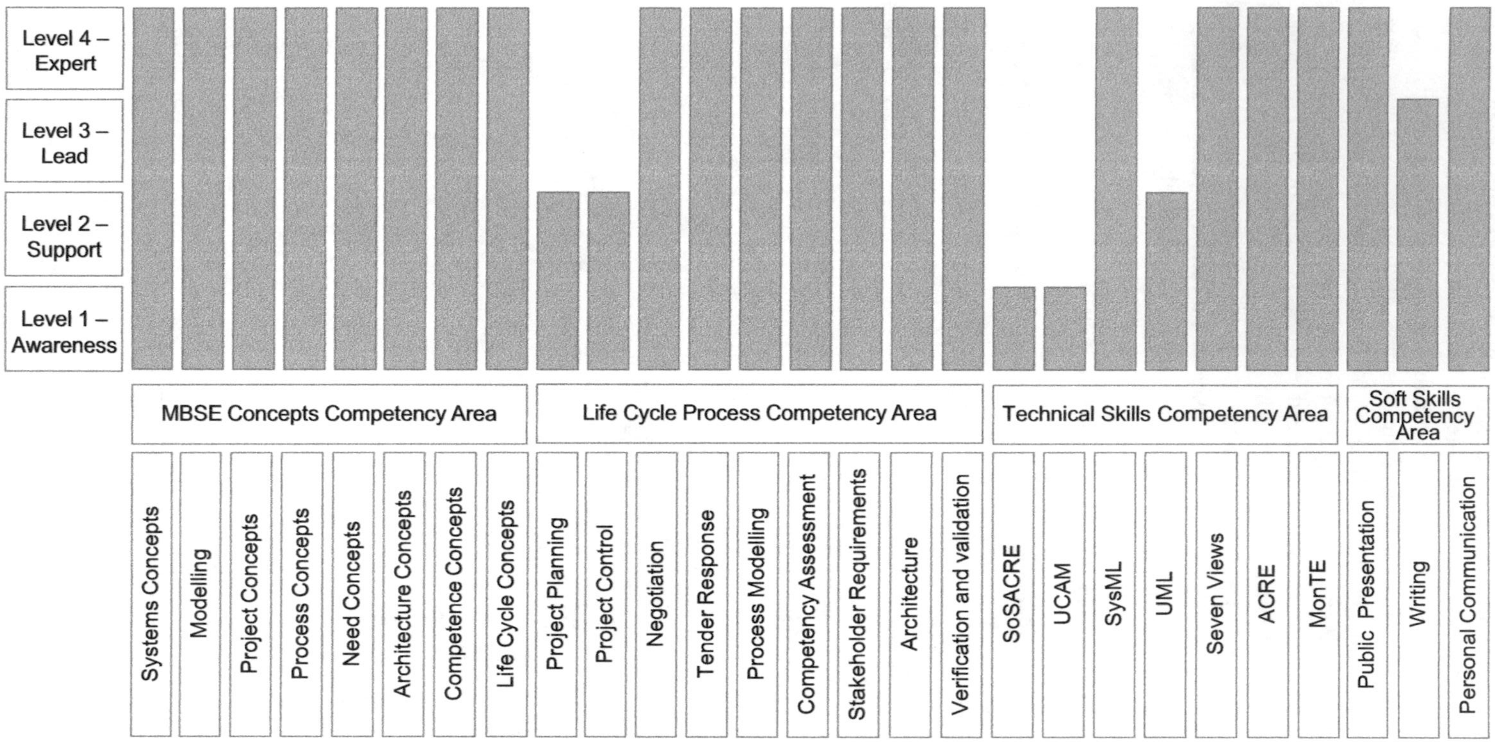

Figure G.45   Competency scope for 'MBSE trainer' based on the INCOSE competencies framework

The MBSE Trainer must be an established and recognised expert in the field of MBSE. They must possess excellent theoretical knowledge of the subject and also have practical experience of applying MBSE on real Projects. Unlike the 'MBSE Mentor', the MBSE trainer does not need an in-depth understanding of the business nor necessarily need to form an ongoing relationship with the business.

Appendix H

The MBSE memory palace

Strange days indeed – most peculiar mama!

John Lennon, 'Nobody told me (there'd be days like these)'

H.1   Introduction to the memory palace

A memory palace is a mnemonic device that has been used for thousands of years as an aid to remembering large amounts of information [1,2]. The memory palace uses a series of points, or loci, that make up a pathway or route that is well known to you. At each point a set of unusual images is constructed that make up a memorable, if somewhat peculiar story.

Generally speaking, the more ludicrous, bizarre and downright obscene these images are than the more memorable the whole memory palace will be.

The following section provides a simple memory palace that may be used to remember all (almost all) of the concepts that make up the MBSE Ontology that is used throughout this book.

H.2   Strange days

Strange days indeed! I lead a very full an interesting life, but there are some days when even I can't explain what on earth is happening to me. Consider this morning, for example. . . .

I was rudely awakened this morning by an intense feeling of discomfort – I was tossing and turning and felt like I hadn't slept a wink. When I looked down, I realised the reason for my discomfort – my bed had been transformed into a massive hard-backed book. And not just any book, oh no, this was an academic text titled *The Art of Confidence Trickery and Subterfuge*. I had a bad feeling that this book would feature in everything that I did today.

Undeterred by this, I tucked the whole book under my arm (no mean feat) and headed out onto the landing only to find the Pillsbury Dough Boy massaging his own stomach.

I ignored the overly-large pastry-based interloper, but at the doorway to the bathroom, my entrance was blocked by a very stressed-looking Peter Piper who was nervously pretending to comb his hair.

I took my book and headed down the staircase only to find (can this day get any weirder?) an extreme unicyclist taking his life into his own hands by cycling up and down the bannister.

From the foot of the stairs and into the kitchen, I was somewhat surprised to see Archie Gemmell, the famous Scottish footballer from the 1970s, drinking down an archaic medicine, or tincture.

I decided to leave the kitchen, grab a snack from the cupboard and have breakfast on the move. I opened the cupboard only to find the Jolly Green Giant who, for reasons best known to his own giant self, was offering me a can of processed peas as a nutritious breakfast alternative.

I fled the house, via the back door, only to find the annoying opera-singing guy from a series of car insurance adverts shouting loudly in my back garden, projecting his voice across the land.

I raced past the fake opera singer opened the back gate, only to trip over a giant toilet flushing mechanism – who put that cistern there?

This was all too much for me, so I took my book from under my arm, opened it up and considered my strange day so far –the Pilbury Dough Boy, Peter Piper pretending to comb his hair, the death-defying unicyclist, Archie Gemmell, the Jolly Green Giant, the annoying opera singer and a toilet cistern? Could I possibly make sense of all this?

Strangely enough, each of these odd occurrences was related to my book – my context.

The book stated that the Pilbury Dough Boy was just trying to kneed himself, and then went on to describe that his kneaded dough came from some elephant sauce, that was strictly controlled by the king, who ruled Pilbury land. Did he always massage with his hands? No, sometimes he used a suit case which he realised came from a scene featuring Super Mario from a video game. It was all on my context.

The book also had something to say about Peter Piper. This was Peter's third attempt at comb pretence having failed at comb pretence A and B, he hoped to succeed with comb pretence C by using a spirit level in place of a comb. He then gave up on his comb pretence and produced a picture of a silhouette of a person. He then used this profile to scoop up some discarded baked goods, steak rolls, I believe.

The death-defying unicyclist, the book went on to say, was only practising on the bannister as his dream was to appear on the big stage. He was putting into action a plan where he would cycle around the stage wearing a selection of evening wear, swimwear and casual clothing, while leaping over a farmer's gate. He was literally putting his life on the line as if the gate leap failed, then he may well end up be decapitated in a bizarre gate-related execution.

Despite what I was reading in the book, I was getting concerned about Archie Gemmel's behaviour. I could see him peering through my kitchen's Perspex window, getting a good view of the dead elephant that was in the back garden. I could see nothing, due to the elaborate window frame, but Archie made the frame work for him and pointed at the view of the dead elephant, while muttering a eulogy under his breath.

The Jolly Green Giant, meanwhile, was still offering me the processed peas. He recommended me to serve them with baked goods, steak rolls again I think, as this was what Salvador Dali used before creating his surreal artwork. I was not sure about this arty fact, but was assured that I could improve my own art-related activities by applying more sauce to the baked goods.

Inspired by my artistic snack, I progressed to read more about the annoying opera singer who was still projecting forth his favourite aria in an impromptu performance. I say impromptu as it was not described in the programme, but this could be due to the poor organisation of the eunuchs who wrote the programme.

The final chapter concerned of the whole problem with the toilet cistern. This was perhaps the finest cistern in the whole constituency –indeed some may say a cistern of cisterns. I noticed that the elephant problem had yet to go away as the cistern was full to brim with cistern elements. Did I then see a knight in shining armour whose breast plate was emblazoned with a 20th century student comic book? Probably not, I would imagine that Sir Viz was a product of my over-active cistern.

Most peculiar, mama.

H.3   Strange days revisited

Did the previous section make any sense? Probably not (if it did, you should be worried).

Can you remember any of it? Probably.

Each of the key strange occurrences relates directly to a concept from the MBSE Ontology. Therefore, revisiting the first few paragraphs (note that the use of italics and bold font is not the same here as described in Chapter 2):

I was rudely awakened this morning by an intense feeling of discomfort – I was tossing and turning and felt like I hadn't slept a wink. When I look down, I realised the reason for my discomfort – my bed had been trans-formed into a massive hard-backed book. And not just any book, oh no, this was an academic text entitled 'the art of confidence trickery and subterfuge'. **[Context]** *I had a bad feeling that this book would feature in everything that I did today.*

Undeterred by this, I tucked the whole book under my arm (no mean feat) and headed out onto the landing only to find the Pillsbury Dough Boy massaging **[Need]** *his own stomach.*

I ignored the overly-large pastry-based interloper, but at the doorway to the bathroom, my entrance was blocked by a very stressed-looking Peter Piper who was nervously pretending to comb his hair. **[Competence]**

I took my book and headed down the stair case only to find (can this day get any weirder?) an extreme uni-cyclist taking his life into his own hands by cycling up and down the bannister. **[Life Cycle]**

From the foot of the stairs and into the kitchen, I was somewhat sur-prised to see Archie Gemmell, the famous Scottish footballer from the 1970's, drinking down an archaic medicine, or tincture. **[Architecture]**

I decided to leave the kitchen, grab a snack from the cupboard and have breakfast on the move. I opened the cupboard only the find the Jolly Green Giant who, for reasons best known to his own giant self, was offering me a can of processed peas as a nutritious breakfast alternative. ***[Process]***

I fled the house, via the back door, only to find the annoying opera-singing guy from a series of car insurance adverts shouting loudly in my back garden, projecting his voice across the land. ***[Project]***

I raced past the fake opera singer opened the back gate, only to trip over a giant toilet flushing mechanism – who put that cistern there? ***[System]***

With this in mind, re-read the previous section and try to spot the key MBSE concepts.

H.4   Summary

This brief, final appendix has provided a simple memory palace for remembering the MBSE Ontology. The use of memory palaces, although quite strange, has been proven over millennia and should not be dismissed out of hand.

Feel free to change the story provided here to fit your own mind and memory. This memory palace description has been cleaned up and toned down for the purposes of publication.

References

1.   'How to develop a super powerful memory', by Harry Lorraine, Frederick Fell Publishing 1958, reprinted 1996
2.   'A question of memory', by David Berglas and Guy Lyon Playfair, Jonathon Cape Ltd, 1988

Index

Note: Page numbers followed by '*f*' and '*t*' refer to figures and tables, respectively.

Printed in the USA
CPSIA information can be obtained
at www.ICGtesting.com
JSHW051410221024
72173JS00006B/1337